Client/Server

UNLEASHED

Neil Jenkins, et al

SAMS
PUBLISHING

201 West 103rd Street
Indianapolis, IN 46290

For Stephanie—I loved a lifetime's worth. Neil Jenkins.

Copyright © 1996 by Sams Publishing

International Standard Book Number: 0-672-30726-x

Library of Congress Catalog Card Number: 95-74784

99 98 97 96   4 3 2 1

Interpretation of the printing code: the rightmost double-digit number is the year of the book's printing; the rightmost single-digit, the number of the book's printing. For example, a printing code of 96-1 shows that the first printing of the book occurred in 1996.

Composed in AGaramond and MCPdigital by Macmillan Computer Publishing

Printed in the United States of America

Publisher and President	*Richard K. Swadley*
Publishing Team Leader	*Rosemarie Graham*
Managing Editor	*Cindy Morrow*
Director of Marketing	*John Pierce*
Assistant Marketing Managers	*Kristina Perry*
	Rachel Wolfe

Acquisitions Editor
Rosemarie Graham

Development Editor
Todd Bumbalough

Software Development Specialist
John Warriner

Production Editor
Heather Stith

Copy Editor
Anne Owen

Indexer
Cheryl Dietsch

Technical Reviewer
Jeff Shockley

Editorial Coordinator
Bill Whitmer

Technical Edit Coordinator
Lorraine Schaffer

Resource Coordinator
Deborah Frisby

Editorial Assistants
Carol Ackerman
Andi Richter
Rhonda Tinch-Mize

Cover Designer
Tim Amrhein

Book Designer
Gary Adair

Copy Writer
Peter Fuller

Production Team Supervisor
Brad Chinn

Production
Michael Brumitt
Susan Knose
Ayanna Lacey
Erich J. Richter
Mark Walchle

Overview

Part IV Intranets

Contents

Part II   Building the Blueprint

Acknowledgments

I would like to thank the following people for their help and support in the creation of this book. It would not have been possible without their help, support, and guidance.

I would like to thank John Enck for very kindly allowing me to use his work for sections of the middleware chapter (Chapter 11).

Thanks to Chris Weiss and Sam Marwaha, both of Arthur D. Little; they started a spark that became this book.

Gawaine Mellors of ComputerLand continually provided me with various pieces of hardware and software information. Tricia Reed of RCI Inc. critiqued my work and helped put it together better. Joe Chiappetta provided support on the tuning and performance optimization sections. Andy Greig came to the rescue with additional Apple information. Kevin Keys at RCI Europe Ltd. provided the sense and sensibility in some of the views expressed and also helped me to understand that others were out there having problems too!

Thank you also in no small measure to the staff at AL Solutions, Alan Herbage, Jagjivan Ram, Andrew Stewart, and Sian McDermott for putting up with all the arguments, discussions, and views.

The development team of Rosemarie Graham, Todd Bumbalough, and Heather Stith helped me enormously to get the book done and reasonably on time too. Thanks to Jay Wilbur and the team at iD for Quake, a game that shows even client/server can be fun and gave me the opportunity to let off some steam!

Thanks also to you, the reader, for purchasing this book, I hope you enjoy it as much as I did creating it.

Finally, personal thanks to my wife who has supported, cajoled, and pushed me right through to the end, always helping and keeping the coffee hot.

-Neil Jenkins

About the Authors

Neil Jenkins is a full-time PC consultant specializing in client/server systems, local area networking and wide area networking. Neil has worked extensively in the USA and Europe. He has designed, developed, project-managed, and implemented client/server systems and netwoks in Europe, Latin America, and North America. He is currently a freelance consultant working for AL Solutions Ltd., providing technical consultancy to clients on client/server, systems management, information systems staregy, research and development, local area netowking, wide area networking, and PC support. Neil is the author of *Understanding Local Area Network, 5th Editon* by Sams Publishing. Neil lives in Stony Stratford, England, UK with his wife and three children. He can be reached at 100265.1327@compuserve.com.

ADVANCED INFORMATION SYSTEMS, Inc. Michael Richards is the CEO of Advanced Information Systems (AIS), Inc. AIS is a professional software development and consulting firm that offers a range of products and services and specializes in Oracle development. A primary objective of AIS is to provide technical solutions in the form of management consulting, project staffing, independent consultants, and training services.

AIS offers a popular approach to client/server development called Rapid Application Foundation (RAF). RAF is a set of predeveloped code libraries coupled with skills transfer. RAF is offered as a one- or two-week training system that is tailored to develop an in-house application system. AIS clients receive a well-crafted client/server system that takes advantage of today's premier development systems, including Oracle and Visual Basic. Oracle and other tools can be purchased at a discount from AIS. You can reach AIS at (800) 327-9725.

Tim Evans, author of Que Publishing's *10 Minute Guide to HTML* and *10 Minute Guide to Netscape for X Window*, is a UNIX system administration and network security consultant. Employed by Teratec Development Corporation, his full-time contract assignment for the past four years has been at the DuPont Company's Experimental Station in Wilmington, Delaware, home of the company's Central Research and Development Department. He pioneered development of DuPont's own Web, known as DuPont-Wide Web, or DW2, which is widely used within the company for information sharing via its worldwide network. Previously, Tim worked for the U.S. Social Security Administration in various staff jobs for more than 20 years. In 1991, before the Internet got hot, he brought that government agency onto the Internet. At both DuPont and the SSA, he provided support for large numbers of UNIX users, running UNIX on a variety of computer systems, ranging from PCs to workstations to minicomputers. You can reach Tim via Internet e-mail at tkevans@tkevans.com.

Ellen Gottesdiener is president of EBG Consulting, a Carmel, Indiana–based facilitation, consulting, and training firm specializing in helping organizations create usable business and technical models for information systems. She is a JAD facilitator and a technical trainer in the areas of client/server, object technologies, and business re-engineering. She is a certified Enterprise Technology Institute, International (ETI) learning facilitator.

Prior to founding EBG, Ellen maintained, developed, and managed IS projects for CIGNA Corporation. She has over 17 years experience in information and business systems definition, development, and maintenance. Ellen has presented numerous workshops and seminars at local and national IS conferences. Articles by Ellen on JAD, RAD, IS retraining, client/server methodologies, and business and technical modeling have appeared in IS trade journals. She may be reached via e-mail at 73201.3153@compuserve.com.

Paul Hipsley is president and CEO of HIP Solutions, Inc., and Director of HIP Solutions, Australia Pty. Ltd. Paul has written for Sams before on the book *Developing Client/Server Applications with Oracle Developer/2000.* He is also a speaker and trainer concerning Oracle topics, including Oracle CDE tools, third-party integration, and the Oracle7 database. He has more than 15 years experience as a computer professional with expertise in project management, Oracle CASE methodology, analysis, relational database design, client/server applications development, and product integration. You can reach Paul at 74557.2053@compuserve.com.

Lee Huang is a principal with 4Front Technologies, a New York consulting firm that specializes in client/server system development and business process re-engineering. He has worked as a project manager and technology strategist for companies such as Pepsi-Cola, Andersen Consulting, and Philip Morris. He has conducted seminars and classes around the country on how to successfully implement client/server technology, business process re-engineering initiatives, and workflow systems. He has also written several articles on topics such as client/server project management for various computer industry publications. You can reach Lee at 72772.1247@compuserve.com.

Vinay Nadig is the founder and president of Disha Strategic Solutions, an information technology consulting firm based in Richardson, Texas. He is involved in helping clients chart out technology strategies to improve their competitive edge. During a career in information technology spanning the last decade, he has helped companies define client/server architectures, re-engineer business processes, and implement cutting-edge methodologies in IT management. Currently he is involved in implementing business information strategies that show his clients how to architect their data, processes, and applications. His specialties include designing client/server and Internet networks based on Windows NT Server, Microsoft BackOffice, and RDBMSs to solve customer management needs. Additionally, he has developed implementation models for Enterprise Architecture Planning (EAP), process analysis, and groupware.

As a complement to technology architecture plans, Vinay is also involved in designing new IS organizations to fit today's client/server challenges. With the help of Disha's proprietary KFA (Key Factor Analysis), he is helping clients redesign their IS departments to meet business goals and objectives. Vinay holds a bachelor's degree in mechanical engineering and an MBA emphasizing IS management.

Charles Wood is a Systems Engineer at Analytical Technologies. He graduated with bachelor's degrees in computer science and finance from Ball State University in 1986, and is a Certified PowerBuilder Developer (CPD). Along with developing software in PowerBuilder, C++, COBOL, and QuickBasic, Charles has taught C and C++ at Indiana Vocational Technical College. He is currently pursuing his MBA at Butler University (when he can find the time). He lives in Indianapolis with his wife, Lyn, and his two daughters, Kelly and Kailyn.

Tell Us What You Think!

As a reader, you are the most important critic and commentator of our books. We value your opinion and want to know what we're doing right, what we could do better, what areas you'd like to see us publish in, and any other words of wisdom you're willing to pass our way. You can help us make strong books that meet your needs and give you the computer guidance you require.

Do you have access to CompuServe or the World Wide Web? Then check out our CompuServe forum by typing **GO SAMS** at any prompt. If you prefer the World Wide Web, check out our site at http://www.mcp.com.

> **NOTE**
>
> If you have a technical question about this book, call the technical support line at (800) 571-5840, ext. 3668.

As the team leader of the group that created this book, I welcome your comments. You can fax, e-mail, or write me directly to let me know what you did or didn't like about this book—as well as what we can do to make our books stronger. Here's the information:

FAX: (317)581-4669

E-mail: enterprise_mgr@sams.mcp.com

Mail: Rosemarie Graham
           Comments Department
           Sams Publishing
           201 W. 103rd Street
           Indianapolis, IN 46290

Introduction

I tried to think of the most inspiring sentence I could to set the scene for this book and for you as you begin to develop client/server systems. However, the only words that kept springing to mind were: **Don't do it!**

Many vendors and software houses will tell you that client/server is easy to move to and implement. Many of the same companies will tell you that client/server can be implemented with little or no impact to your current systems or business processes. Finally, most companies will tell you that all this can be achieved with Product Hunky-Dory 2000 from Ripemoff Associates—"Client/server without the pain."

These things are not true. More so perhaps than any computing environment prior to it, client/server requires a great deal of planning, assessment, and skill to be achieved successfully. It changes your computing systems (for the better), yet often makes you look long and hard at what you already have and what you are doing with it. Above all, for client/server to be truly successful (and in turn, for you to be successful also), you have to look at the business processes and systems that are being created to fulfill your business needs. If you apply client/server to a business process that everyone knows is ineffective, then you can only expect to automate what is already broken, and you will fail.

Client/server is rarely built with any one tool or product. This is because by its nature, client/server is distributed and modular and operates on a number of platforms. These may be tough words, but this book is about aiding you in building great client/server systems and assisting you in avoiding the many pitfalls that spring up along the way.

Client/Server promises scalable architectures, distributed data, and business transactions at the desktop and, in theory at least, presents the ultimate computing environment for most managers. Yet client/server is fraught with difficulty. Recommended tools are few and far between when compared to the wealth of tools associated with online transaction programming (OLTP). The tools that are available are nowhere near as mature or robust as their OLTP counterparts. Development has typically been on one machine (normally a minicomputer or mainframe computer), and most programmers do not relish the new experiences of PC development. In addition, the newness of the client/server products creates a certain amount of resistance by IS departments to adopt them. These departments fear the lack of management capabilities, robustness, and proof within a large-volume environment.

Even more important than the previous issues, an organization's reluctance to change creates a distinct lack of creativity, something that is essential in the development of beneficial client/server systems. The development of client server systems is further hampered by the reluctance to change the way people work; departments feel that it is easier to automate what is already there rather than construct new systems alongside new working methods.

But some businesses are changing and evolving. The companies that begin to embrace client/ server development in a structured fashion will gain competitive advantage and obtain business benefit, both tangible and intangible, for their investment. This return on investment, coupled with improved workflow in the developed systems, graphical, user-friendly screens, and the ability to provide accurate single-source information, will seriously improve a company's profitability and viability. By using techniques developed and outlined in this book, companies can begin to develop client/server systems that deliver real benefit rather than the typical examples of maximum investment with little return or mission-critical system rewrites that fail with maximum risk.

For you, client/server presents a significant challenge. You will need to acquire or improve skills, overcome both business and technical obstacles, and focus on using the technology to enable business improvement/re-engineering rather than letting the technology drive the business. You will need to do things better and faster. This book aids you in building applications that model the business structure. These new applications are more likely to support new business changes and larger numbers of users than the previous legacy systems you may have been involved in. These applications need to be scalable, yet flexible enough to support multiple environments and GUI platforms.

This book is aimed at giving you a thorough understanding of client/server systems. It covers all aspects of developing a client/server system, be they technical, business, or political. It does not pull any punches. I set out to write this book so that when you experience difficulties you can overcome them with the help and advice of all those other managers and developers who have felt the same pain. If this book helps you in these areas, then, for me, it will have been a success.

Above all, have fun building these systems; fun improves creativity, develops high performance teams, builds morale, and is probably the best motivator there is.

Go to it.

Neil Jenkins

PART

IN THIS PART

Introducing Client/Server

Information: The Driving Force

1

by Lee Huang

IN THIS CHAPTER

How many times have we seen Captain Kirk of the Starship *Enterprise* face a life-or-death situation? I recall one *Star Trek* adventure where the *Enterprise* was battling an enemy ship. The *Enterprise* was in peril because her phasers were unable to penetrate their opposition's protective shield. "Computer, give me information on their shield's weak spots," ordered Captain Kirk. The computer searched through its enormous database and immediately discovered the coordinates of a weak area. The enemy ship was destroyed within seconds. Captain Kirk emerged victorious once again, not because he was braver or stronger, but because his computer system *contained the information that he needed and quickly provided it to him.*

Have you ever thought of information access as being a strategic weapon in your company's arsenal to succeed in today's competitive business environment? If not, you should. In today's business world, companies are facing new challenges daily. With globalization, the world is quickly evolving into an electronic village where companies from around the world are competing with each other in the same marketplace. New start-up companies with less overhead and bureaucracy are able to provide superior customer service and can deliver new products faster than their larger, but slower, competitors. More and more sales and delivery forces are equipped with state-of-the-art hand-held computers to make them more responsive to customer requests. Companies that used to be staunch adversaries are now becoming allies to defeat common opposition.

What must you do to triumph in this competitive climate? As companies struggle with this question, they are discovering that one key component to their solution is information access. Companies and their employees must have easy access to accurate and reliable information in order to support their decision-making and to identify new opportunities.

How were sales affected at the New York City locations when competitors opened up new stores within a quarter of a mile of ours? Of our 10 million customers, how many placed more than 10 orders during the past two years? Complex questions such as these are being asked every day. People need the right answers immediately in order to make the right decisions. They cannot afford to make the wrong decisions because millions of dollars and customer satisfaction may be at stake.

Only companies that can successfully capture accurate information and then easily access it when they need it will continue to prosper and maintain an advantage over the competition. As the importance of information increases and the demand for it becomes a top priority, companies are taking steps to provide it. Companies are actively reviewing their informational requirements as well as re-engineering their business processes. They are also identifying new methods of acquiring information, providing powerful analysis tools, and selecting efficient methods to share this information within the organization. To accomplish these goals, companies have turned to client/server technology. This chapter explains what client/server is, what its advantages are, and what issues are involved in implementing it.

Why the Move to Client/Server?

The move to client/server has marked a major development in the evolution of the PC. This development was brought about by the recognition that companies had lavished vast sums of money on purchasing PCs in order to provide their users with desktop processing. Processing which, in theory, reduced the processing load on a central computer (normally a mainframe) and thus saved the company money. The mainstream use of PCs and LANs has typically been to provide the users with normal office working functions such as file sharing and printing. In order to capitalize on the expenditure on PCs, companies have needed to use the PC for more than just office functions.

This need for better use of PCs in turn led to the idea of splitting up business applications so that some of the processing was done locally on the client and some remotely on the server. Taking this view further meant that companies could begin to move away from a centralized computer system (normally based around a mainframe) and could rely on a networked system of clients and servers to run their business. The ultimate goal became the removal of the corporate mainframe from the company and a vast savings in turn. This process of moving away from a centralized computer system to a network is often referred to as downsizing. The promise from vendors of robust, fast, distributed client/server systems means that many companies have begun to move along the client/server route for application development.

Client/server computing has become a major technology in the business environment today. Yet it is still very much in its infancy when compared to the 20 years or so of development that has been lavished on the mainframe infrastructure. Currently few tools are robust enough to provide the same level of performance and reliability as a centralized computer system. However, companies' business strategies are also changing so rapidly that a centralized system cannot be developed or modified to meet the business needs quickly enough. This is the main area where the implementation of a good client/server system can seriously improve a company's business systems. By having many servers providing distinct business functions, adding new functions to the overall system is relatively easy. This advantage is best illustrated by a sample company.

Suppose The Widget Company has problems meeting the demand of a particular customer because the stock item the customer wants is out of stock and unavailable for several weeks. The Widget Company's computer department has electronically implemented a gateway into a secondary supplier of these parts through a client/server system. When a salesperson requests this particular stock item, the application running on the salesperson's PC (the client) finds out that the item is out of stock from the main supplier and automatically connects to the second supplier through the gateway. The salesperson doesn't need to know that supplies are coming from this second source. The customer receives his parts as normal, and when the main supplier has the item in stock again, the client program automatically detects this fact and once again uses this main supplier. Now consider that The Widget Company wants to offer the best price from either supplier; by slightly modifying the client program, both servers can be accessed at the same time, and the lowest price can be retrieved and offered to the customer.

Client/Server Technology: Your Business Solution

According to recent studies, 85 percent of Fortune 1000 companies are using client/server technology to deliver business solutions. Some have already implemented sophisticated client/server systems and are reaping the rewards. Others are actively involved in the development process and are eagerly anticipating the benefits that the completed system will provide. Client/server technology, including the sales of software and hardware products along with professional services, has evolved into a billion-dollar industry. This heavy financial investment and resource allocation to implementing client/server systems shows a clear commitment from companies to this technology.

Large corporations are not the only companies transitioning to client/server. Midsize and smaller companies are also making the move to client/server. As new client/server products and tools appear on the market almost daily, competition among vendors is increasing dramatically. This competition has lead to price reductions as well as a realization that midsize and smaller companies can reap the same benefits from client/server as a larger company can. Therefore, many new marketing campaigns and products are focused directly on the needs of midsize and smaller companies. Client/server systems can be implemented by any company regardless of its size.

Client/server technology provides a company with a strategic direction and competitive advantage. This technology enables companies to develop powerful, yet flexible, systems of all types to solve specific business needs. You can develop a client/server system that supports a small department with only three users or a mission-critical, enterprise-level system that supports thousands of users across the country, even the world. On-line transaction processing systems, executive information systems, as well as decision support systems can be designed. A client/server system can provide remote access capabilities, which enable people working in the field to access information as if they were physically in the office. Users can transparently access information from a variety of different data sources regardless of the source's physical location. The user no longer needs to know where the data is coming from. In addition, client/server systems can share information with other software applications, such as word processors and spreadsheets, and also be integrated with more advanced technologies such as document imaging. Companies are developing client/server systems to solve a variety of different business needs.

For example, one consulting firm turned to client/server technology to solve an internal problem when management realized that it was unable to accurately track client account information. Client account reports were generated from a mainframe system at headquarters and then distributed by hard copies to partners in regional offices. By the time people received the reports for review, however, the information was already outdated. In addition, reports were often lost in interoffice mail. A client/server system was developed to replace this manual and inefficient process. The client/server system transfers information from the mainframe to database servers located at regional offices on a daily basis. Partners can then use the user-friendly front-end application, which contains powerful analysis tools, to review and analyze their client account information on-line at any time, 24 hours a day.

What Is Client/Server?

Client/server is the technology that companies are depending on to transport them into the 21st century. But what exactly is so magical about this term client/server? It's the technical term that even CEOs and CFOs are familiar with, the term that captures trade show headlines, the term that all new products must have on their sales brochures, and the term that every systems professionals wants to have on their resume. Even some end-user communities are demanding client/server systems, saying "I don't care what the system is, just make sure it's client/server!"

Client/server is an architecture in which a system's functionality and its processing are divided between the client PC (the front end) and a database server (the back end). System functionality, such as programming logic, business rules, and data management, is segregated between the client and the server machines. The appropriate segregation of system functionality between the front end and the back end differs with each system and depends on the importance that the system designer places on such factors as fast performance, business rules enforcement, application maintainability, and security.

The end user uses the front-end application to request information from a database server. The database server receives these requests, processes them, and sends the results back to the client to be displayed. The system's processing to handle these tasks of database access and information presentation is also segregated between the client and the server. The processors in both machines are utilized in tandem to quickly satisfy user requests.

Although a logical and a physical separation exists between the client and the server, a client/server system coordinates the work of both these components and efficiently uses each one's available resources to complete assigned tasks. Client machines communicate with the server across a local-area or wide-area network. In addition, a complete client/server system may involve more than one server. Each server available on the client/server system may handle a specific function.

The Client Side

The only part of a client/server system that most end users ever see is the client side. The client side consists of the front-end application and the computer that an end user uses to access information from the database. Most client/server applications have a graphical user interface (GUI). A GUI front end provides a user-friendly, point-and-click interface that is more intuitive to use than a character-based system. A GUI contains visual controls, such as push buttons and drop-down listboxes, and can also display graphical images. GUI applications are usually designed according to certain industry standards. By following these standards, your client/ server applications will have a standard look and feel that translates into a reduced learning curve.

Behind the graphical interface is complex event-driven programming that determines what the application will do in response to the user's actions. Behind every event, such as a button click, is some programming that invokes an action. This action may be to send a request to the database, validate data entry, display information, perform calculations, or open another screen. To ensure that the front-end application can accomplish all these different tasks quickly and efficiently, the client machine must meet certain hardware requirements regarding processor speed and memory.

The Server Side

If you think of a client/server system as a sports car, the GUI front-end application would be its flashy exterior and plush interior. The GUI gives a smooth ride and hides all the grinding and churning of the powerful engine that's underneath the hood. The database server is that hard-working engine.

The server, or back end, consists of a database management system (DBMS) and the computer that it runs on. The DBMS stores information in databases and enables multiple clients to access it simultaneously. Front-end applications can read, update, insert and delete data from the database through structured query language (SQL), an industry standard for relational database access. To ensure fast performance, a DBMS may support advanced features such as stored procedures and triggers. The DBMS also performs numerous functions to maintain the database, including ensuring data integrity, managing locking, handling transaction processing, enforcing business rules, and supporting indexes. To handle all of these tasks and responsibilities efficiently, the physical server is usually a high-end, dedicated machine. It should also be scalable so that it can support an increased number of users as well as larger volumes of data in the future.

The Network

The third component of a client/server system is the network. Client computers communicate with the server through the network. The network plays a major role in determining the performance of a client/server system because it controls how fast client requests are carried to the server and how fast results are brought back to the client. In developing a client/server system, one of the goals of the developer is to efficiently segregate processing between the client and the server in order to minimize network traffic. When a client/server system is implemented, the network architecture should be optimized to ensure that it can properly support the increased traffic that will be generated.

Benefits of Client/Server

A properly designed client/server system provides a company and its employees with numerous benefits. Such a system enables people to do their jobs better by allowing them to focus their time and energies on acquiring new accounts, closing deals, and working with customers, rather than on administrative tasks. It provides instant access to information for decision-making, facilitates communication, and reduces time, effort, and cost for accomplishing tasks. The following sections outline the major benefits of client/server.

Improved Information Access

A well-designed client/server system provides users with easy access to all the information that they need to get their jobs done. With a few mouse button clicks, the user-friendly front-end application displays information that the user requests. This information may reside in different databases or even on physically separate servers, but the intricacies of data access are hidden from the user. The client/server system also contains powerful features that enable the users to further analyze this retrieved information. Therefore, they can manipulate this information to answer "what-if" questions. Because all this information access and functionality is provided from a single system, users no longer need to log into several different systems or depend on other people to get their answers.

Increased Productivity

A client/server system increases its users' productivity by providing them with the tools to complete their tasks faster and more easily. For example, a powerful data-entry screen with graphical controls and programming logic to support business rules enables users to enter information more quickly and with fewer errors and omissions. It automatically validates information, performs calculations, and reduces duplicate data entry. Client/server systems can be integrated with other technologies such as e-mail, document imaging, and groupware to lead to additional productivity gains.

Automated Business Processes

A client/server system can automate a company's business processes and be a workflow solution by eliminating a great deal of manual labor and enabling processes to be completed sooner with fewer errors. For example, a company's current business process of completing a purchase order is completely manual. It involves searching through a cabinet to find a purchase order form, filling it out, performing all the calculations with a calculator, determining who should approve it, and then sending it to that person through interoffice mail. A client/server system can automate this process and accomplish it in a fraction of the time. An electronic version of the purchase order can be designed in the front-end application and be available on-line. Using the GUI, a user quickly enters the information, and the system automatically performs all the calculations. Then the form is automatically routed across the network to the appropriate person (based on a business rule) for approval. The approver immediately receives the purchase order in their electronic in-box for review and does not have to wait for it to arrive through interoffice mail.

Powerful Reporting Capabilities

Because the information in a client/server system is stored in a relational database, the information can be easily queried for reporting purposes. Programmers can, of course, quickly create new reports by using SQL. However, client/server systems can provide features that enable end users to create their own reports and customize existing ones without having to learn SQL. With these capabilities, users can generate reports much faster than in the past and are no longer completely dependent on IS to provide reports. Those people who used to take a hard copy report and then retype all the information into a spreadsheet so that they could generate reports save a tremendous amount of time by using the client/server system.

Improved Customer Service

A company can improve its customer service by providing faster answers and minimizing the number of times that a customer has to contact the company. A client/server system enables customer service representatives to service their customers better, and one key reason is its ability to provide information from different data sources. A bank, for example, may have several physically separate databases. Each of these databases stores a specific type of customer account information, such as savings, mortgage, and student loan. Currently, a customer who has all three types of accounts with this bank and needs information on all them has to call three different numbers, which is very inconvenient. A client/server system can be designed to provide a customer service representative with access to information from all three databases. Therefore, the customer only needs to call one number. Customers are looking for this type of convenience.

Rapid Application Development

Most client/server development tools enable programmers to create applications by taking advantage of object-oriented programming techniques and developing application modules. By reusing objects and code that have already been written for existing systems, new client/server systems can be developed much faster. GUI design tools provide drag-and-drop facilities that allow programmers to quickly create visual screens without having to program the underlying code. Client/server applications can also be easily modified in case a change, such as a new business rule, is necessary. In addition, client/server tools can be used to quickly create system prototypes that enable the developer to demonstrate the system to users and get immediate feedback. (Please see the next section, "Ignore the Myths," for additional information on this topic).

Cost Reductions and Savings

A client/server system reduces costs in a number of ways, some of which are easier to quantify than others. Many companies have replaced their mainframe systems with client/server and saved millions of dollars in annual maintenance costs. Others have benefitted from the on-line information access and significantly reduced their paper-associated costs including its purchase, storage, and distribution. This on-line information also enables people to quickly identify marketing campaigns and sales strategies that are failing and then cancel them before wasting any more money. Because people can accomplish their tasks faster, they save time and effort, which also translates into a financial savings. Also, as employees are empowered and able to do more, the number of employees can be reduced, if that is a company goal.

Increased Revenue

A client/server system does not generate revenue itself. However, by providing easy access to crucial information along with data analysis tools, it can play a significant role in contributing to increasing revenue by enabling people to identify opportunities and to make the right decisions. The following are some examples of how a client/server system contributes to increased revenue:

- Enables a new product to be developed faster so that it hits the market sooner
- Enables a company to spot sales opportunities faster
- Identifies which marketing campaigns work well and should be used again
- Identifies what types of products and features a particular customer base wants
- Identifies sales trends that you can use to your advantage

Quick Response to the Changing Marketplace

Businesses are changing rapidly. The marketplace is now more competitive than ever and will continue to be more and more so. Companies are faced with the challenge of keeping their business up-to-date, and they must do business efficiently in order to remain in the marketplace.

The computer systems that were developed in the 1980s tended to be based around a centralized computer system. LANs were connected to this system, yet little or no real business processing was done on the LANs or the PCs. Any change to the business was made on the centralized system. If a new product was to be sold or a new accounting system was to be implemented, it was normally placed on the main computer. As time went on and more and more systems were placed on the centralized computer, the costs of running this machine rose. The time to change this system if a new business function was needed also increased. Over time, this situation has become so bad that it is not uncommon to hear of systems taking in excess of three years to develop and implement when the product needs to be ready for the marketplace in six months. Clearly companies cannot continue to take so long to get systems and product to market in today's fierce business environment.

Successful client/server systems break up a company's major business areas into several distinct units, which can be considered stand-alone although they are integrated. If these systems are correctly developed, they can deliver enhancements and new products to market faster than a centralized system can. The reasons for this are as follows:

- The business area is smaller and therefore can be changed more quickly.

- The changes in a client/server system do not normally affect as many users as changes to a centralized system do.

- Smaller systems can be prototyped quickly with a lot of user input, which leads to a faster development time.

- A network operating system can support many different types of servers. Implementing a new function on a specific server can be faster than trying to implement a new product on a mainframe or midrange system.

Ignore the Myths

Just as it is important to understand the benefits of client/server systems, it is likewise important to recognize the myths that have become associated with them. A sophisticated client/server system does not instantly appear once the shrink wrap is ripped off, the box opened, and the software installed. Unfortunately, many marketing campaigns and sales brochures make it seem as though developing a client/server system is that easy. Developing and implementing a successful client/server system is a challenging undertaking that requires a tremendous amount of hard work and comes at a price. The two biggest myths surrounding client/server development are that robust client/server systems can be developed overnight and that implementing a client/server system is inexpensive. Too often senior management believes these myths. It is imperative that everyone be able to differentiate reality from myth at the start of the development effort. People should be excited about client/server but also have realistic expectations.

"Client/Server Systems Can Be Developed Overnight"

Many advertisements state that you can develop a client/server system within a few days or even a few hours. This type of statement is misleading at best. You can certainly develop a client/server system that has a few screens with minimal functionality in a very short period of time. But if you need to develop a robust system that supports 50 concurrent users, provides subsecond response, supports business rules, has reusable objects, and ensures data integrity, you cannot accomplish this task overnight.

Designing, developing, and implementing a client/server system requires the completion of an enormous number of tasks, all of which take time. The functionality of the system must be determined by interviewing end users and reviewing specifications. The front-end application's graphical user interface must be carefully designed so that it is user-friendly. Using object-oriented development techniques to create objects that can be reused in future projects requires planning. Identifying the best method to segregate processing between the client and the server requires analysis. A data model must be designed, the database created, and data loaded. The full life cycle of a sophisticated client/server system takes time to complete. But if the first client/server system is developed correctly, then future development efforts can be accomplished much faster by reusing available objects and code.

"Moving to Client/Server Technology Is Inexpensive"

Some people are also under the false impression that moving to client/server technology is an inexpensive effort. In reality, developing your first client/server system and building the infrastructure requires a financial investment that is not insignificant. New software, including development tools, the DBMS, testing tools, and data modeling products, needs to be purchased. New hardware, including servers and client machines, needs to be purchased, and existing hardware needs to be upgraded. The development staff must be sent to client/server training courses, and consultants must be brought on board. In addition, a support structure must be put in place.

Moving to Client/Server

Companies are introducing client/server systems into their organizations from two general directions. Some companies are downsizing to client/server and replacing their mainframes. Others are upsizing to client/server and replacing their file server-based database systems. Other companies have decided to integrate client/server technology with their legacy systems, rather than replace them. Whether companies downsize or upsize to client/server systems, they will encounter a tremendous amount of change, both technical and cultural.

Downsizing

Most system downsizing initiatives focus on the replacement of mainframe systems with a more flexible and cost-effective technical platform. Companies are actively examining the roles that their mainframes will play in their future. Many that are downsizing have decided that the mainframe did a great job during its time but that client/server systems should replace it. The three main issues that have led to this decision are as follows:

- The mainframe's inability to support ad hoc queries
- Inability to quickly modify mainframe programs
- The high maintenance and support costs for keeping a mainframe running

Many people refer to information as a corporate asset. That asset is useless if people cannot access it. As the demand for quick answers, fast decision-making, and ad hoc queries increases, companies are realizing that the mainframe's inability to provide needed information is costing them missed business opportunities and lost customers. In addition, existing mainframe applications simply cannot be modified fast enough to respond to changes in the business environment, such as new tax laws or new governmental regulations. The support of these inflexible programs and the high maintenance expenses of the mainframe itself costs some firms millions of dollars annually.

Not Replacing, But Integrating

Other companies that have mainframes are not eliminating them in favor of client/server systems. Instead, they are integrating the two technologies and taking advantage of both their strengths.

These organizations want to continue to leverage their investments in mainframe applications, databases, hardware, infrastructure, and operational procedures. However, they also realize that certain processes are better handled by a client/server system. Therefore, these companies decide on a project-by-project basis which environment to develop the application in, according to internal criteria. For example, systems that are batch processes and do not require user interaction may be written for the mainframe, and systems that require a great deal of end-user interaction are developed on client/server. Sometimes the two technologies are so tightly integrated that the mainframe acts as the database server in the client/server system.

Upsizing

Many smaller to midsize firms that have their mission-critical database applications residing on file servers are upsizing to client/server. These companies have encountered limitations with their current systems as they have grown in size and their processing requirements have changed. They are turning to client/server because their current systems are incapable of supporting the increased requests, managing the larger number of concurrent users, handling the increased volumes of data, and providing acceptable performance. In addition, these companies are placing more emphasis on data integrity, security, information sharing, reliability, and scalability. Because their existing systems do not adequately provide all these features, they are upsizing to client/server, which will.

Many larger companies that are downsizing their mainframe are also simultaneously upsizing their file server-based database applications. These downsizing and upsizing efforts must be coordinated to ensure that there is no redundancy of work and that the client/server applications are interoperable and able to share information.

Adjusting to Client/Server Changes

Designing, developing, and implementing a successful client/server system requires increased end-user involvement, introduces new roles and responsibilities, and necessitates the development of many new skills.

In the past, the Information Systems (IS) department often developed new systems without any end-user input. Times have changed though. As end users have become more computer-savvy, they expect to be, and should be, actively involved in the development process. IS and end users must work together as a team to get the job done. IS has to improve their communication skills and to gain a better understanding of how the business works. In addition, the IS staff must, of course, acquire the new technical skills required to build the client/server system.

Client/server changes the way that the company runs the business, which affects how people do their jobs. Because client/server systems are so powerful and flexible, their development is often conducted in conjunction with business re-engineering initiatives. Companies are analyzing their internal and external workflow and determining methods of streamlining their business processes. Client/server systems are enabling much of this re-engineering to become a reality because they can automate business processes. This re-engineering translates into people having to learn new ways of doing their jobs in addition to the new computer system. With all of this change that people throughout the company must adjust to, change management must be properly handled for the client/server system to be successful.

Client/Server Models

Client/server systems can be classified based on the way in which the systems have been built. The most widely accepted range of classifications has come from the Gartner Group, a market research firm in Stamford, Connecticut (see Figure 1.1). Although your system will differ slightly in terms of design, these models give you a good idea of how client/server systems can be built.

These models are not, however, mutually exclusive, and most good systems will use several of these styles to be effective and efficient. Over time, client/server systems may move models as the applications are replaced or enhanced. These models demonstrate that a full definition of a client/server system is a system in which a client issues requests and receives work done by one or *more* servers. The more servers statement is important because the client may need to access several distinctly separate network systems or hosts. The following sections describe each of the five basic models.

In its simplest form, client/server identifies a system whereby a client issues a request to a second machine called the *server* asking that a piece of work is done. The client is typically a personal computer attached to a LAN, and the server is usually a host machine such as a PC file server, UNIX file server, or midrange/mainframe.

FIGURE 1.1.

Five basic client/sever models.

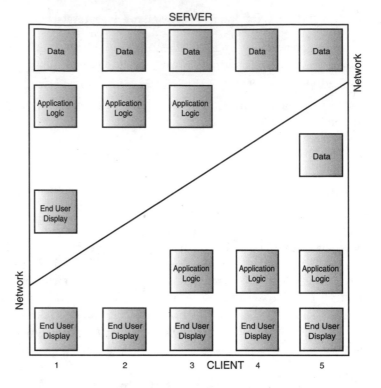

The job requests can include a variety of tasks, including, for example:

- Return all records from the customer file database where name of Customer = Holly
- Store this file in a specific file server data directory
- Attach to CompuServe and retrieve these items
- Upload this data packet to the corporate mainframe

To enhance this definition you should also consider the additional requirements that a business normally has.

Model 1: Distributed Presentation

Distributed presentation means that both the client and the server machines format the display presented to the end user. The client machine intercepts display output from the server intended for a display device and reroutes the output through its own processes before presenting it to the user.

As Figure 1.2 shows, the easiest model is to provide terminal emulation on the client alongside other applications. This approach is very easy to implement using products such as WallData's Rumba or Attachmate but provides no real business benefit other than to begin a migration to client/server. Sometimes a company may use a more advanced form of terminal emulation whereby they hide the emulation screen and copy some of its contents, normally key fields, onto a Visual Basic or Borland Delphi screen. This copying is often referred to as *screen scraping*. Screen scraping enables a company to hide its mainframe and midrange screens and present them under a PC interface such as Windows or OS/2. The major benefit of screen scraping is that it allows a system to migrate from an old mainframe-based system to a new client/server system in small incremental steps.

FIGURE 1.2.

Distributed presentation: terminal emulation and screen scraping.

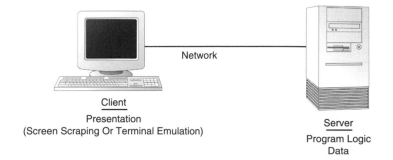

Network

Client
Presentation
(Screen Scraping Or Terminal Emulation)

Server
Program Logic
Data

Model 2: Remote Presentation

It may be necessary to move some of the application's program logic to the PC from the host computer. The second model, as shown in Figure 1.3, allows for some business/program logic as well as the presentation to reside on the PC. This model is particularly useful when moving from a dumb terminal environment to a PC-LAN environment. The logic can be of any type; however, validation of fields, such as ensuring that states and zip codes are valid, are ideal types of logic.

FIGURE 1.3.

Business or program logic on the PC.

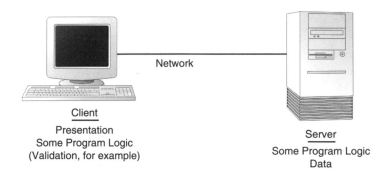

Network

Client
Presentation
Some Program Logic
(Validation, for example)

Server
Some Program Logic
Data

The difference in this model is that the host does not format the data with the remote presentation model. The client and server processes communicate through more advanced protocols, such as IBM's Advanced Peer-To Peer Communications (APPC). The server sends a raw data stream to the client. The client formats the data and presents it to the end user. All the core system application logic still resides on the server; some validation logic may be moved or duplicated on the client.

Model 3: Distributed Logic

A distributed logic client/server application splits the logic of the application between the client and server processes. Typically, an event-driven GUI application on the client controls the application flow, and logic on the server centrally executes the business and database rules. The client and server processes can communicate using a variety of middleware tools, including APPC, Remote Procedure Calls (RPC), or data queues.

Differentiating between the remote presentation and distributed logic models isn't always easy. For example, if a remote presentation application performs some calculations with the data it receives, does it therefore become a distributed logic application? This overlap between the models can sometimes make the models confusing. Figure 1.4 shows the distributed logic client/server model.

FIGURE 1.4.

The distributed logic client/ server model.

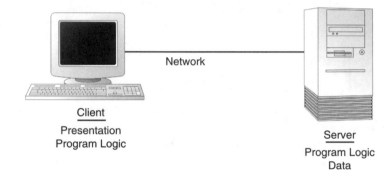

Model 4: Remote Data

With the remote data model, the client handles all the application logic and end-user presentation, and the server provides only the data. Clients typically use remote SQL or Open Database Connectivity (ODBC) to access the data stored on the server. Applications built in this way are currently the most common in use today. Figure 1.5 shows this model.

FIGURE 1.5.

In the remote data model, all the application logic resides on the PC.

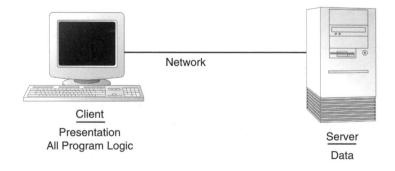

Model 5: Distributed Data

Finally, the distributed data model uses data distributed across multiple networked systems. Data sources may be distributed between the client and the server or multiple servers. The distributed data model requires an advanced data management scheme to enforce data concurrency, security, and integrity across multiple platforms. As you would expect, this model is the most difficult client/server model to use. It is complex and requires a great deal of planning and decision-making to use effectively. Figure 1.6 shows this model.

FIGURE 1.6.

The distributed data model.

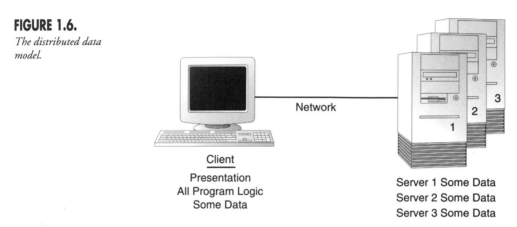

Client
Presentation
All Program Logic
Some Data

Network

3
2
1

Server 1 Some Data
Server 2 Some Data
Server 3 Some Data

Summary

Client/server technology is taking a hold in corporations because it is able to provide a strategic direction and a competitive advantage. Well-designed client/server systems provide users with easy access to accurate and meaningful information on a timely basis. These user-friendly systems increase productivity, automate business processes, enable enhanced reporting, and provide flexible application development environments. Developing and implementing client/server systems to realize all of these benefits, though, comes only after a great deal of hard work and investment, despite what marketing hype portrays. Whether a company is downsizing from a mainframe, integrating client/server with mainframe systems, or upsizing, there is a learning curve, and there are financial investments to be made. However, as many companies are finding out, client/server technology is worth the effort because it is delivering business solutions that enable companies to succeed in today's increasingly competitive business environment.

Planning for Client/Server

2

by Lee Huang

Proper planning and preparation is critical to the success of any client/server project. Before the first line of code is written or the first screen designed, a number of technical and nontechnical issues must be addressed, and a number of tasks must be completed. It is essential that the project's management team clearly recognizes all the challenges that they face upon starting a client/server project. Some of these challenges include defining project scope, gaining corporate support for the project, learning business processes, putting together a talented project team, and building a solid technical infrastructure for the new system. The ability to properly handle these matters will determine the ultimate success or failure of the client/server system.

Upon starting a client/server project, most companies are aware that they will encounter many technical challenges and that they will need to spend time and energy handling them. They realize that they will have to learn new design strategies, programming skills, and optimization techniques that are critical to the development of a robust and flexible client/server system. Unfortunately, many companies lose sight of the fact that the nontechnical issues are just as crucial in determining whether the client/server project is a success or failure. These nontechnical issues, which include gaining end-user support and handling change management, are often overlooked or not properly handled. As you go forward with your client/server project, it is imperative that you have detailed plans for handling all these issues, technical and nontechnical, and are able to execute them properly. This chapter discusses these issues and the challenges that you will encounter as you prepare to develop and implement your client/server system.

Defining the Project's Scope

Every client/server project must have a clearly defined scope. The scope identifies the business objectives of the client/server system and describes what the end-users will be able to accomplish by using it. Clearly stating the scope ensures that everyone will have the same expectations for the final system. After the scope is agreed to by all involved parties (management, end user community, and the IS department, for example), it should be formally documented and copies distributed.

The scope of a client/server project is usually defined by either a business problem that must be resolved or a new process that can improve the business by providing capabilities that are not currently available. Imagine a situation where sales representatives have to log into three different systems to get the information that they need to support the decisions they make. This is an inefficient use of the sales representatives' time. The scope of the project may be to develop a client/server system that enables the sales representatives to log into a single system that provides access to all the data that they need and even provides additional graphing capabilities.

The scope of a client/server system is often determined by representatives from the IS (Information Systems) department and the business divisions working together. The business side of the company understands the business processes, and IS knows how technology can improve it. Client/server systems that are built solely by the IS division for the business areas often fail, so you should avoid this type of approach.

It is important to ensure that the scope of your project is realistic. You do not want to be too ambitious and attempt to develop a system that is more complex and sophisticated than you are capable of handling. If you are new to client/server technology, try to limit the scope of your project. Because there are a myriad of new things to learn and obstacles to be encountered, you need to give yourself the time and opportunity to become familiar with the technology, the methodologies, and the techniques required to develop a successful client/server system. You need to learn how to walk before you can run. Sometimes you may also have to crawl first!

Even if you are experienced in developing client/server systems, it is still wise to carefully examine your project's scope. You need to ensure that the scope is manageable and that you have the skills and resources necessary to get the job done properly and successfully. Many companies that have undertaken projects of tremendous scope that involved the development of a single massive mission-critical system or several client/server systems (such as accounting, finance, marketing) at once have failed. They started work on the project only to discover that the scope was too enormous and that they did not have the necessary skills and experience to develop the systems. In addition, they realized that they had underestimated the complexity of coordinating all the development efforts and the difficulties of integrating all the systems.

Determining Whether Similar Projects Exist

As you define the scope of your client/server project, you also need to determine whether any other group in your company is engaging on another project that is the same or similar to yours. Although this step may seem obvious, it is sometimes overlooked. Other times, it is simply not pursued with great vigor because discovering similar projects is frequently a difficult task, especially at large companies. IS is decentralized at many large companies, and there is often a lack of communication between different IS organizations. As a result, compiling a complete listing of all projects that are taking place within a company's various offices and departments is difficult, if not impossible. Regardless, it is worth putting effort into ensuring that there are no similar projects to yours because you definitely do not want to duplicate work that is already being conducted elsewhere. If multiple projects with the same goals and objectives are undertaken, senior management should question the reasons behind such duplication.

If a similar project exists, there may be opportunities to combine resources and work on the development effort together, or perhaps one group is better equipped to complete the project themselves. If a similar project is linked by business practices to your new development project, the business process may have to be looked at within both projects. By combining this part of the development, you can save time and streamline the process. In addition, similar projects may be able to share development costs.

It is also important to identify any projects similar in scope to yours that have been attempted in the past and failed. There are several reasons for understanding the history of such projects.

First, you want to learn from the other project's mistakes and not repeat them. For example, were there technical problems or personnel problems that led to its failure? Second, you need to clearly differentiate your project team from the one that failed. You do not want the original team's failure to reflect on your team. You also need to determine whether the end users and management have already participated in several rounds of meetings and are tired of discussing the details of this project. If they are, then you need to take immediate steps to ensure their active participation as your project commences.

Getting Management's Approval

For your project to be successful, you must get management's approval as well as its firm support and commitment. Management needs to do more than simply give the OK to go ahead with the project; it needs to support the project in the following three ways:

- **Provide adequate financial support**

  The company must be willing to invest money in properly financing the development effort. This money will be used to pay for such items as software, hardware, salaries, and training.

- **Grant the project team appropriate authority**

  The project team must be authorized and empowered to make the decisions that are necessary to expeditiously develop the system and carry out the project plan. They must not have to constantly turn to management to approve their requests. Responsibility without authority is inefficient and leads to project failure.

- **Allow end users to participate in the client/server project**

  Management must allow members from the end-user community to take time away from their regular responsibilities to actively participate in the development effort throughout its full life cycle. The end users should be involved in various activities, such as gathering requirements and testing the system.

However, getting this support for your client/server project is often difficult and may turn into a project itself. You must convince management that the scope and objectives of your project are worth investing time, money, and resources in. Getting management's approval is not something that you accomplish in a day. First, you must determine who in the management structure has the authority to approve the project and grant all the necessary support. Depending on each organization, the decision maker(s) that has the ultimate say as to whether the project goes forward may be an individual such as a CIO or perhaps a group such as a technology planning committee. You must also identify those individuals who do not have the authority to approve the project but do have the clout to either arbitrarily stop a project if they disapprove it or have the ability to influence a decision maker. You must identify all these players because any one of them can potentially keep your project from getting started if he or she opposes it. Because a client/server system often involves people and processes from multiple departments, you may need to get approval from many different senior people in different departments.

Once you have identified the decision makers, you must convince them that the project is worthwhile and persuade them to support it. To accomplish this feat, you must hone your sales skills. Getting management to buy into a client/server system is often difficult because management may not understand its benefits, may want to keep the status quo, or may not want to spend the money. To allay these concerns, you must be prepared to discuss the benefits of the project in terms that managers understand and can relate to. Describe your client/server system as being a business solution, not just a technical solution. You do not want to talk about just the technical benefits of client/server because many of the managers will not care. Management will not agree to develop the client/server system because it is a great new technology that provides many "gee-whiz" features. They will approve the project and invest money, time, and resources only if it can solve business problems, add value to the company, and provide an acceptable return on the investment.

You must focus on the business benefits that the system provides and how the change will improve the business environment by improving customer service or getting products to the marketplace faster. By recognizing what is important to the decision makers, you can successfully sell the project to them and get their approval and support. For example, I remember one senior executive who was environmentally conscious and wanted the company to promote that image. One of the major factors that convinced him to approve the client/server system was its ability to dramatically reduce the amount of paper used for hard-copy reports because all the information would be online.

Deliverable Dates and Scope Creep

After you have successfully convinced management to support your project and started planning for the system, you need to protect yourself against two phenomenons. The first involves the project's deliverable date. This milestone date should be determined by the project team only after careful assessment of how long it will take to complete everything. Unfortunately, management often dictates a deliverable date that is impossible to meet. For example, management may request that the system be implemented within two months when it will require at least six months to implement. This situation then leads to the existence of two deliverable dates. The first date is the realistic (unofficial) deliverable date that is determined by the project team and is based on how long it will take to complete the work. The other date is the public (official) deliverable date that is presented to the company and may be based on political influences or picked out of the air by someone in management who does not understand client/server technology.

These two deliverable dates are rarely the same. If they differ significantly, a major problem exists because the pressure of the unrealistic date will lead to low morale and finger pointing as target dates are missed. Your vision of a delivering a quality system on time will turn into a nightmare. Therefore, if management starts to make outrageous demands for getting the system implemented sooner, you must immediately discuss with management why its deliverable date is impossible to meet. The options are to either meet that date but remove a lot of the system's functionality or go with the realistic deliverable date. This situation is not easy to handle, but it must be addressed as early in the process as possible.

After you have finalized the project's scope, you also want to avoid a phenomenon called *scope creep*. Scope creep occurs when people start requesting that new features and capabilities be added to the system after the scope has already been agreed upon. Managers may innocently ask for more functionality, but they do not understand the ramifications of their requests and the additional work that filling such requests may require. With scope creep, people generally expect you to increase the functionality of the system but complete the project with the same resources and time frame as the original scope. The response to scope creep is to clearly state that any increase in functionality or expectations will require a re-evaluation of the project's scope and that new timelines and resource requirements will probably result. You must be prepared to handle scope creep and to understand its impact on your project.

Building Excitement in the End-User Community

You must design and execute a solid strategy to build excitement among the end-user community for the client/server system. It is necessary to gain the support of the system's end users because they play an integral role in the development process. Without working closely with them, there is no assurance that the final system will meet their needs and expectations. Because you will be working with them throughout the project life cycle, it is important to develop a positive relationship where they see the project as a priority and want to stay actively involved. (Remember though, by approving the project, management has already determined that end users *will* spend time working on it. However, it is always better if the end users *want* to work with you rather than *have* to work with you.)

The end users participate in the following activities:

- Interview sessions to gather requirements and perform functional analysis
- Reviewing and providing feedback concerning design specifications
- Prototyping
- Answering your questions
- System testing
- Training sessions

Unfortunately, convincing some end users to actively participate and to get involved may be very difficult to do in certain situations. Users often cannot focus on the development of the future systems that will take away some of the work they do today! Some people may feel that their participation in the project is more work for them and takes time away from their regular responsibilities. Others may still harbor some distrust or fear of IS because IS traditionally has not involved end users in the development process and has appeared unapproachable.

To overcome these objections, you need to clearly emphasize why the system is important to them and how it will benefit them in their ability to perform their jobs. The end users need to understand that the system is being built for them, that it is their system, and thus that they have a vested interest in its success. The users must realize that only their active participation and enthusiasm will ensure that the final product meets their needs.

To build excitement among the end users and to keep them actively involved, take the following steps:

■ **Conduct demos on a regular basis.**

End users will appreciate you taking the time to provide them with demonstrations of the system as it is being developed. In addition, when they see that you have incorporated their suggestions into the system, they will realize that they are indeed contributing to the system and will be appreciative and continue to be involved.

■ **Highlight end-user contributions.**

When you discuss the project or give demonstrations, highlight the contributions that end users have made. Everyone enjoys receiving credit for their ideas, but such highlights also demonstrate to other end users, who may be more reluctant to assist, that their suggestions will also be considered.

■ **Be responsive to end-user questions.**

Spend time with end users answering their questions, and they will do the same for you when you have questions for them. Make sure that you speak to them in normal English and don't overwhelm them with technical jargon.

■ **Designate an end-user liaison to be on the project team.**

The end-user liaison is a member of the project team who performs many roles. From the end-users' perspective, this individual ensures that their best interests are being protected as the project continues. (Additional information on the role of the end-user liaison is discussed in the section "Roles and Responsibilities.")

■ **Conduct periodic status meetings with end-user representatives.**

Periodic status meetings with end-user representatives to keep them apprised of the project's status are helpful. These representatives can then disseminate the information to the rest of the end-user community.

■ **Send back summaries after interviews.**

After you have interviewed end users in order to gather requirements for the system, send back a written summary of what was discussed at the meeting. This summary shows the end users that you recorded their input and also provides them a feedback mechanism to ensure that the information you recorded is accurate.

Handling Opposition to Client/Server

As you go through the process of gaining support from management and the end-user community for client/server technology and your client/server project, you will encounter some individuals who oppose client/server, and others who would prefer that your project fail. You must identify these individuals and be prepared to handle their opposition.

As discussed previously, many people from different areas throughout the company play a role in determining the ultimate success or failure of the client/server system. Each person has an agenda as well as an opinion concerning the impact of client/server technology. They will ask themselves questions such as "Is client/server the direction that the company should take?," "What does client/server mean for my career?," and "Is it in my best interest for this client/server project to succeed?" The answer for some people is that it is in their own best interest to oppose client/server. Some will voice their opposition openly. These people are easier to handle because you are directly faced with their arguments and you can respond accordingly. For example, they may clearly state their conviction that client/server technology is not the right direction for the company to take and that the company should continue to rely on mainframe systems. Others, however, will hide their opposition and take surreptitious actions against the acceptance of client/server and your project. The dreaded corridor conversations begin to belittle your project.

The following are some not-so-obvious reasons that people may have for either opposing client/server in general or your client/server project in particular:

- Many people see client/server as a threat to their jobs. Companies that plan to downsize and replace their mainframe systems with client/server systems may find themselves with a staff of mainframe developers who are worried that their jobs are in jeopardy.

- A senior member in IS may not understand client/server technology and does not want to admit his ignorance. He may be fearful that people will realize how little he knows about client/server so he may attempt to block its acceptance.

- Client/server projects are often high-profile projects that get a lot of attention because they have high expectations and involve new technology. Some individuals who are working on less recognized projects may feel left out and even jealous.

- A previous client/server team may have failed in its attempt to implement a client/server system, and members of that team may not want your client/server project to succeed where they failed.

Although these situations are unpleasant to discuss, you need to be aware of their existence because your client/server project may depend on your successful handling of this type of opposition. Many projects have failed when these situations were not identified and resolved and these opponents were able to take actions that either stopped the project or caused it to fail. There is no single answer for properly handling these situations because each has its own unique circumstances and pressures. Some situations may dictate that you confront the individual with the problem, and others may require taking the issue to a higher authority. You need to assess the political climate and who has what authority, and then use some business savvy in selecting the best course of action.

Building a Winning Project Team

Once you have gotten the green light for your project from management, you must put together a client/server project team that possesses the skills, experience, and talent necessary to deliver a quality system on time and within budget. The project team is responsible for designing, developing, and implementing the client/server system as well as keeping the company updated about the project's progress and maintaining end-user participation. Building a winning team is a major challenge because client/server requires many new skills (such as GUI design and object-oriented development) and methodologies (such as GUI testing). To put together a successful team, you need to first understand what technical expertise and business knowledge your team requires, and then acquire individuals who have those skills. You need to identify what skills your company has in-house that are available to you and where you are going to get the skills that you don't currently have. If this project is your company's first client/server system, you do not have the all the necessary skills internally. If the project is a large-scale client/server project, you will probably not have enough available in-house people. Many companies build a successful client/server project through a combination of internal IS staff working with consultants.

Roles and Responsibilities

Every client/server team, regardless of the size of the project, has similar roles to be filled and responsibilities to be accepted. You will see different titles for these roles, but the responsibilities will be generally the same. Regardless of the title that you use, roles such as the following must be clearly defined for the project team:

- The project manager is responsible for ensuring the overall success of the project, overseeing all development efforts, ensuring that deadlines are met and that deliverables (such as applications and documentation) meet expectations, conducting status meetings, and reporting progress to management and the end-user community.

- The business analyst determines functional requirements for the system by interviewing end users to determine their needs and requirements. This person develops functional design specifications including business process maps and business rules.

- The technical architect is responsible for the design of the client/server architecture and ensuring that all the components are properly defined and implemented.

- The front-end application designer designs the user interface of the front-end application by following GUI design standards and ensuring that the interface is intuitive to use.

- The front-end application programmer does the programming for the front-end application.

- The common objects programmer determines what objects (such as an application login screen) can be shared by other front-end application programmers and programs them.

- The database administrator is responsible for maintaining the database and the database server and ensuring that they can be used by the developers. This person ensures that the server is physically tuned for optimal performance and that all database entities (such as tables and indexes) are properly created and available.

- The data modeler is responsible for creating the data model to support the client/server system. This person ensures that the data will be efficiently stored and easily accessible by the system.

- The database programmer is responsible for writing stored procedures and triggers and ensuring that all SQL code is efficient. This person ensures that the front-end application can quickly access the data that it needs from the database.

- The end-user liaison is a member from the end-user community who has a keen interest in technology. This individual assists in building excitement among the end users because of his understanding of their expectations. He also shares his knowledge of the business with the business analyst.

- The network specialist addresses all network issues that can affect the system, such as protocol issues, network traffic, and packet sizes. This person ensures that the network is up and running and that its architecture can support the client/server system.

- Software/hardware support representatives are responsible for ensuring that the computers used by the project team are correctly configured and working properly. For example, if additional memory must be added to a computer, a hardware support representative would install it.

- Testers are responsible for testing the system to ensure that it meets functional requirements and is stable enough to be used in production. During testing, these people log bug reports and ensure that these bugs are properly fixed in subsequent versions of the system.

- The standards coordinator is responsible for defining standards (such as programming standards) to be followed by the development team and ensuring compliance with those standards.

- The documentor is responsible for creating end-user documentation on how to use the client/server system as well as technical documentation for the programmers to use.

- The trainer is responsible for developing training material and conducting training classes for the end-user community on how to use the client/server system.

The size and scope of the client/server project determines how many people will be required to fill each of these roles. For example, if you have a large-scale project with a multimillion dollar budget that involves implementing a very complex mission-critical client/server system, you may need several individuals to fill one role. For example, this type of project may require many front-end application programmers working together to get the job done. Conversely, if your system has a smaller scope, a single individual may hold multiple responsibilities. For example, one person may be responsible for all the front-end application design and programming.

In addition, not all of these people are full-time team members. Some individuals, such as those doing the training and documentation, only need to be available during certain phases of the project. Others, such as those who provide hardware and software support, need to be available upon request.

Reskilling

For a company to build an internal IS staff that has the necessary skills to complete the client/server project, the company must invest in reskilling its staff. This process usually starts by sending employees to training courses on how to program with a specific front-end development tool or to work with a relational database management system. By attending these courses, the employees learn the fundamentals of client/server development.

However, it is important to realize that simply attending a few client/server courses does not mean that the employees will return to the office and be able to immediately design a sophisticated client/server system that supports a hundred users. New client/server developers must be given the opportunity to build and hone their skills. They need time to learn efficient programming techniques and all the nuances of the different client/server tools before they become truly proficient. For example, there are many different ways for a programmer to program the retrieval of data from the database and display it on a screen. An experienced developer knows which is the best method to use because it will provide sub-second response, employ reusable code, and minimize network traffic. A recent graduate from a training course will not realize all the different methods that are available to her and may select the method that provides the worst performance.

The best way for new client/server developers to continue improving their skills is to work closely with more experienced developers who may be other staff members or outside consultants. In this way, the new developers can quickly learn the proper techniques and have their questions answered. The company should also hold frequent code reviews for new programmers to ensure that they are utilizing proper programming techniques. Holding internal technical training sessions is also very helpful. Perhaps once a week for an hour, have a resident expert, a speaker from the outside, or someone who just attended a training course discuss a particular client/server topic. In addition, having a knowledge base system that serves as a central repository of technical information that people can refer to will benefit everyone. If you don't currently have this type of system available, it is good practice for a new developer to build this application.

Working with Consultants

Unless your internal IS staff is experienced in all facets of developing client/server systems, you should hire consultants to assist you with the project. Companies that are embarking on their first client/server systems definitely should have consultants work with them to successfully handle all the technical and implementation issues. Consultants provide the technical expertise necessary to develop a robust system faster and their experience will enable you to avoid many of the problems that you would otherwise fall prey to if you worked on the project alone. In addition, by working closely with consultants, you will quickly learn from them.

The following are some general qualifications you should look for in potential client/server consultants:

- Has client/server programming and development expertise
- Has full life-cycle experience in developing client/server systems
- Emphasizes business process analysis
- Able to align technology with business goals
- Able to discuss issues clearly with management and end users
- Focuses on properly handling change management issues
- Provides mentoring services on client/server technology to full-time staff

When selecting a consulting firm, you need to be objective in your evaluation process. Some companies make the mistake of selecting consultants who have provided them with solutions on other platforms (such as mainframe, midrange, and desktop) without carefully considering whether these consultants are the best ones to develop their client/server system. These companies' perspective is that they can save time by shortening the evaluation process and perhaps get a better price on the project because they already have a relationship with the consulting firm. However, if the consulting firm is not experienced in client/server, the consultants will be learning client/server on your company's time, and your company will be the recipients of their mistakes. I know one company that was happy with a consulting firm that provided its midrange application. This company turned to the same firm, which had no client/server experience, to develop a client/server system. The system was a disaster because the consultants simply took all the limitations of a mainframe application and moved it to a client/server system without utilizing any of the advantages of client/server.

Team Dynamics

Once the people have been selected for the project team, the team must work efficiently and effectively together. The project manager must act as a coach and create an atmosphere where full-time staff and consultants work as an integrated team. Because the client/server team will be comprised of people from different departments and companies, many people will be working together for the first time. There are so many components to developing a successful client/server system that no one person knows everything. Everyone must be encouraged to speak up and to contribute their ideas and knowledge. Sometimes the quietest person has the best solutions to a problem.

Procedures must be established that determine how individuals in different roles will interact with each other. Accountability for accomplishing various tasks must also be defined. Only when these guidelines are firmly understood by everyone will the team members be able to work efficiently together. For example, front-end application programmers and the database administrator will need to work very closely. If a front-end application programmer needs to have a table created on the database, he must follow a procedure for sending a request to the database administrator, who in turn is responsible for creating it within a certain time period. Such procedures and accountabilities prevent situations where people start blaming each other for delays.

Technical Planning

As you begin work on your client/server project, your team must first make decisions on many technical issues. By properly addressing these issues, you can ensure that your development process will be smooth, the system will meet expectations, and your company will be able to efficiently use client/server. The following sections explain the important technical issues that you need to consider.

Scalability

As you plan for your client/server system, you must ensure that it will be scalable. *Scalability* refers to a system's capability to support more users, manage greater volumes of data, and handle increased workload. A client/server system must be able to handle increased access and greater demands without requiring many modifications. The ability to scale well is absolutely crucial because your client/server system will inevitably need to support more users and a greater workload than is originally planned.

For example, the following situations will lead to the increased utilization of your client/server system:

- As your company grows, more employees may need to access the client/server system. For example, more telephone sales representatives will need to use an order entry system as the number of orders increases.

- After the client/server system has been implemented, end users will ask if it can be expanded to provide additional functionality and new features.

- People from other departments will want to access some of the data that you have captured for their own purposes. This access will lead to increased workload.

- You will be asked to integrate the client/server system with another system. These systems will then be sharing resources such as the database server.

■ The volume of data stored on the database will increase daily.

■ People will want to create new reports, and ad hoc reporting will increase.

If your system is not scalable, you may end up rewriting code or purchasing more powerful software and hardware when one of these situations arises. For example, if you attempt to have 50 people simultaneously access a system that was only designed to support 25 concurrent users, the system may grind to a halt. To remedy the situation may require that you purchase a more powerful relational database that can better handle the increased usage. At this point, you will basically need to initiate another project to convert the client/server system to a new database. It is better to anticipate the growth and select software and hardware products that enable you to develop a client/server system that scales well and is powerful enough to support increased demands in the future.

Multiplatform Support

Because most companies have a heterogeneous environment, your client/server system will likely have to support multiple platforms, especially if different departments will use your system. For example, your client/server system may have to be used by a finance department that uses PCs, an advertising department that uses Macintoshes, and an engineering department that supports UNIX. Certain client/server products can support multiple platforms, and others cannot. You need to ensure that your client/server solution can support different platforms if necessary.

Selecting Client/Server Development Tools

A variety of different software products, including the front-end application development tool and the database management system, must be selected in order to develop the client/server system. Obviously, the technical capabilities and features that the product possesses must be thoroughly evaluated and compared to other competitive products. However, several other factors must be considered as well. As a general rule, be cautious of products that are in Version 1.0 because they may not be as robust as other products that have been on the market longer. You also need to ensure that enough people in your area know how to use the product for you to hire as full-time employees or consultants. You should also examine the stability and strategic direction of the product's vendor. With the number of mergers and acquisitions that are taking place within the software industry, you want to ensure that the product will continue to survive and be supported.

Avoiding Over-Dependence on Vendors

Review your development schedule if it is overly dependent on the delivery of a new product or bug fix from a vendor. Relying on a vendor's future delivery of a product and having it in your project's critical path is very risky. Product deliveries are often late, and there is no guarantee that the promised fixes will be available in a maintenance release. Of course, it is not always possible to avoid this dependence, but you should have a contingency plan in the event that the product is delayed for several months. One strategy is to be a beta site for the product so that you can see how well development is going and if the features that you need are in the product.

The Development Environment

Ideally, the members of the development team will work in a development environment that is dedicated entirely to them and completely under their control so that they do not adversely impact productions systems that are being used and vice versa. Unfortunately, this kind of environment is not always possible due to financial considerations and resource constraints. At the minimum though, the development team must have its own database server. The team must not do client/server development on a production machine that end users are using to do their jobs. The development team will be constantly reconfiguring, fine-tuning, optimizing, testing, and downing the database server, and all of these tasks will affect a production system by either degrading performance or making it completely unavailable to end users. Having a dedicated network for development is also beneficial. With a dedicated network, your development effort will not be affected by other network traffic or network maintenance that takes place. In addition, you can test different network configurations without affecting anyone else.

Developing Reusable Code

Developing reusable code that can be shared should be a principle of the development team. By intelligently designing your client/server system, much of the code, objects, and functions can be reused by other programmers on the current project as well as on future projects. By using object-oriented development techniques and modular methods, such as inheritance, on the front-end application and stored procedures on the database side, development time can be significantly reduced and application maintenance can be made easier. In addition, reusing common objects in the front-end application will provide your systems with a consistent look and feel. Users will already be familiar with these standard interfaces when new systems are rolled out, so training time will be reduced.

Reusing Code from Other Client/Server Systems

By reviewing other client/server systems that are being used at your company, you should be able to find some code, objects, or database entities that you can reuse in your system. Anything that you reuse will save you time because you do not need to spend time creating it yourself. For example, if another system has a data-entry screen that captures customer information such as their name and address, and you need a similar screen in your system, you should reuse it. One of the main benefits of client/server technology is the ability to reuse existing code, and you should take full advantage of this benefit.

Data Transfer Issues

If your client/server system will be getting its data from other sources, you must carefully examine these data sources and define plans for obtaining data from them. If you are downsizing off of a mainframe, you need to take the existing information off of the mainframe, convert it into a format that the client/server system can read, and then import it. This example is a one-time data conversion effort. However, if your client/server system will receive daily downloads from another system, you need to ensure that these download processes work properly and can be completed within a certain time period. While planning for these data transfers, you need to consider many of the obstacles that you will encounter, which include data translation issues involving different data types and field lengths, reserved words and characters, massive volumes of data, and customized programs that may need to be written to handle the actual translation and transfer. Proper planning for these data transfer issues will ensure that all the data within the client/server system is accurate and complete.

Security

Two types of security must be considered for your client/server system. The first type of security measure is designed into the system itself and ensures that only authorized people have the ability to access the system, use specific functionality, and view certain information. Security measures can be implemented based on such qualifications as people's positions or their departments and then enforced through the use of login IDs, passwords, and encryption. These security measures guarantee that confidential or restricted information will not be compromised.

The other type of security that is frequently overlooked is in regards to the physical database server. Because the database server in a client/server system is usually not physically large and does not cost as much as a mainframe, people often overlook the importance of properly securing it. Too often, the database server resides in a room that is not locked and is easily accessible. This situation is a problem because anyone can walk into the room and turn it off, accidentally pull out the power plug, or even steal it. The database server should be in a secure area that only authorized personnel can enter. Companies should implement the same security measures and precautions that they do for their mainframes.

Reviewing Network Architecture

The network architecture must be reviewed to ensure that it is capable of supporting the client/server system. The client/server system may lead to additional network traffic as well as more users, and the network must be able to handle this increased load and continue to provide acceptable performance for all services. The network architecture and topology should be reviewed and may need to be optimized to meet the new demands. If the client/server system needs access to information on other systems, such as a mainframe, gateway products may also need to be implemented. If there are remote users or wide area access, dial-up facilities and leased lines may need to be considered.

Remote Access

If your client/server system will be used by employees, such as sales representatives, who are not in the office, you need to make special preparations to support them. The client/server system must be specially designed to support remote access by taking into consideration what information the employees need, the volume of data that has to transferred, and the time sensitivity of the data. In addition, a robust remote access strategy and network infrastructure must be in place to support the most efficient and cost-effective access method, which may be remote node or remote control. Only by taking remote access requirements into consideration early in the planning process can you ensure that remote users will have easy access and fast response time when they use the client/server system from the field.

Testing

The thorough testing of all components of a client/server system is crucial to its success, and it requires tremendous planning and preparation. Testing a client/server application with its graphical user interface, stored procedures, and middleware is more complex than testing a character-based procedural application. Testing a client/server application requires learning new testing tools specially designed for GUI applications and a new methodology. You need to plan for testing because it cannot be done in a few weeks just prior to the completion of the project. If you do not properly test your application, your credibility, as well as the support for the move to client/server technology, will be jeopardized. Testing a client/server system requires coordination and scheduling because people from different departments must be involved. The technical infrastructure for supporting testing must be put in place, which involves granting testers access to required files and ensuring that their machines meet configuration requirements. In addition, there must be *accurate* volumes of *meaningful* test data along with test scripts available in order to properly test all the functionality of the system and to ensure that the system's performance is acceptable.

Powerful Hardware Is Not a Panacea

Some production client/server systems suffer from poor performance even though the performance problems were already identified during the development process. Unfortunately, they were not properly handled because of a common, but erroneous belief that more powerful hardware will solve all performance problems. You must not fall into this trap. If demonstrations of your client/server system are slow, you may hear the statement, "Don't worry about the application's poor performance because we can get a bigger server later to solve the problem." This type of statement should lead to two immediate concerns.

The first is that the project team may not have enough experience designing and developing client/server systems. Poor performance of a client/server system is often caused by poor application design, not hardware limitations. The developers on the project may not have the expertise working with the new development tools, segregating processing between client PCs and the database server, and minimizing network traffic. The second concern stems from the fact that individuals on your team will blindly rely on hardware to solve performance problems. More powerful hardware will not automatically compensate for a poorly designed application's performance problems. There are definitely situations, such as those involving tremendous volumes of data, where a more powerful server will yield significant performance improvement. However, you should always first review your application's design and data model rather then gaining a false sense of security by believing that bigger hardware is a guaranteed panacea.

Standards

You need to identify what standards your development project will adhere to. If this project is your company's first client/server project, you must establish standards. Otherwise, there may already be existing standards at your company to follow. There are many types of standards and specific reasons for abiding by them:

- **Software standards**

  Many companies standardize on specific software products such as development tools, databases, and operating systems. The client/server tools that you select should conform to these standards if it is appropriate. After all, you don't want to develop a system using products that cannot operate with other systems. By using standard products, you can use the company's existing skills. In addition, you may not need to buy additional software because the company already has it.

- **Industry standards**

  Selecting only development tools that support certain industry standards such as Open Database Connectivity (ODBC) ensures that you follow a strategic direction and that your client/server systems can be properly integrated because they meet certain standards and requirements. It is imperative, though, that you continue to stay educated on new industry standards that are being developed, as well as existing standards that are evolving.

- **Programming standards**

  Programming standards regarding GUI design, naming conventions, and programming techniques are important so that other programmers who need to support or modify the code can quickly read and understand it. Adhering to programming standards also makes the code easier to reuse in the future.

Remember that standards are not absolute, however. Always use your judgment in following them. For example, if the client/server database management system that your company selected to be its standard hits a performance wall with 25 concurrent users, you need to select another database product and establish a new standard when you develop a system that supports 100 concurrent users. Another situation where you will not follow established guidelines may involve GUI design. If you are designing a client/server system that will be used on a small pen-based computer by delivery people, the application's graphical user interface must have extra large buttons and text in order for the users to read it on such a small screen.

Technical Support Programs

Your developers must have ready access to technical support. Purchasing a technical support program from your client/server tools vendors is an absolute necessity in getting your client/server system developed quickly. Developers should not spend hours and days searching for answers to problems that can be immediately answered by a technical support representative. The developers' time is better utilized designing and programming. Sometimes management does not see the benefit of spending thousands of dollars for a support contract. One response is to translate the time spent by developers tracking down answers into dollars based on their hourly rate. Another method is to state that investing $5,000 in a support contract is similar to hiring a full-time employee who is a specialist and always available. Other good sources for technical support assistance are online services, such as CompuServe and the Internet, as well as local user groups. In addition, you should purchase multiple sets of technical manuals for the development team. Sharing a single set of manuals among several people is inconvenient and can lead to wasted time.

System Support Staff

Although the system's completion may be a few months or even a few years away, plans for having a support staff that handles end-user questions and problems must be in place far in advance of the first day that the system goes into production. You want to ensure that the support staff has an adequate number of people so that they are not overwhelmed by calls and the end users don't start getting busy signals. The support staff must be properly trained in both the functionality of the system as well as how to do client/server technical troubleshooting in order to provide quick and accurate answers. If the system will be used by many people at several different locations, then it may be necessary to have more than one support team, especially when the company first starts using the system.

Summary

Companies of all shapes and sizes are moving to client/server technology. Most people are aware of the benefits that can be gained from client/server, but they often are not aware of all the up-front planning that is required. A tremendous amount of planning must be completed in preparation for the transition to and implementation of client/server. After these up-front issues are properly addressed, you are on your way to successfully developing and implementing client/server systems.

Business Process Re-engineering

3

by Lee Huang

Many companies are undertaking business process re-engineering (BPR) initiatives in order to reinvent themselves and to work more efficiently and effectively in today's competitive business environment. Succeeding at BPR requires gaining a thorough understanding of existing business processes, applying re-engineering techniques to improve them, and implementing new technology to facilitate the improvements. The recommended changes produced from a business process re-engineering effort are usually dependent on taking advantage of new technology, such as client/server, which has the power and flexibility to support the new business requirements. BPR efforts are often conducted in conjunction with client/server projects because BPR's deliverables are the functional requirements for a new client/server system. Many companies are combining their business process re-engineering initiatives with their client/server development projects to provide a true business solution in an efficient manner. This chapter presents a step-by-step approach to successfully conducting business process re-engineering. It discusses how to build a team, conduct user interviews, and re-engineer business processes. Successful completion of BPR can lead to a smoother development and implementation of your client/server system.

What Is Business Process Re-engineering?

A *business process* describes a collection of tasks that must be completed in a specific sequence in order to accomplish an overall goal. Individuals, often in different departments and locations, who are involved with a particular business process work together in a coordinated effort to accomplish tasks that contribute to the completion of common goals. Everyone is expected to complete his or her work accurately and efficiently so that the overall goals and objectives are accomplished in a timely manner. Every business process has an input, which starts the process, as well as an output, which is an action or product that results after the process is completed.

Business process re-engineering is the thorough evaluation of a company's existing business processes, followed by the dramatic changing of them for optimization and streamlining purposes. By scrutinizing an existing business process, redundant and inefficient tasks and procedures that slow down or hinder its completion can be discovered, and other areas for improvement can be identified. The objective of re-engineering is to then eliminate these shortcomings and drawbacks by radically changing the process so that new and improved methods for accomplishing the goals in a more efficient and effective manner can be implemented. Successful re-engineering is based on the philosophy that every task and procedure must be examined and may be potentially changed; nothing is beyond modification. Unproductive tasks are eliminated, organizational barriers, and layers of bureaucracy that cause delays and lack of accountability are removed, lengthy approval processes are shortened, bottlenecks are removed, and users are empowered with new tools and access to information in order to do their jobs faster and better.

The main themes of BPR are customers, competition, and speed of change. Figure 3.1 shows what the business process re-engineering of a company can provide. As you can see, the results are comprehensive and valuable.

FIGURE 3.1.

What business process re-engineering provides. (Used with permission of Alan Herbage, AL Solutions Ltd.)

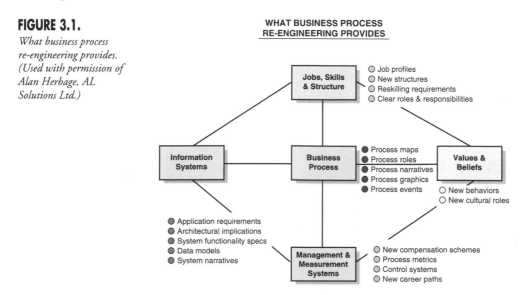

Integrating BPR and Client/Server Efforts

The successful implementation of re-engineered business processes often relies on the design and development of a new system that provides the capabilities to support these improved processes. In many cases, the functional requirements for a new client/server system are the results and recommendations produced from the business process re-engineering initiative. By aligning technology with business requirements, a client/server system can bring your re-engineered business processes off of the drawing board and into your work environment. Client/server technology is often selected as the technical solution because of its power, flexibility, and ability to be integrated with other technologies, such as image processing. In addition, a client/server system can be easily modified to handle any future changes that may be made to business processes. It makes these new re-engineered business processes possible by automating tasks, enabling immediate information access and sharing, eliminating repetitive tasks, providing process monitoring tools, and facilitating workflow. As a company commences on its joint business process re-engineering and client/server projects, it needs to decide how to conduct these efforts and to staff them.

Separate Teams

Some companies prefer to look at the business process re-engineering and the client/server initiatives as two individual projects that are related to each other and have some overlapping activities. In doing so, they organize two separate teams. One team focuses on conducting the business process re-engineering effort by examining processes and streamlining them. Then the other team takes those findings and concentrates on developing the client/server system. The two groups only work together to turn over the re-engineering team's deliverables to the development team. The re-engineering team discusses and reviews its findings and requirements with the client/server team because its deliverables, such as business process maps and business rules, serve as functional specifications for the new system.

One Core Team

Other companies look at business process re-engineering and client/server development as different components of a single project. Such companies form a core team of individuals who work on both the business process re-engineering and the client/server development. Specialists are brought on board to perform specific tasks, but this core group of individuals actively participates in both the re-engineering and the technical sides of the combined project. Of course, putting together this type of core team is a major challenge because it is not easy to find individuals who possess the skills to handle both re-engineering and client/server development responsibilities. However, having a core group that is involved throughout both projects rather than having separate teams has many benefits:

■ **Fewer repetitive activities**

Individuals working on business processing re-engineering and client/server development encounter many of the same tasks and face similar issues. For example, the fear of change that both re-engineering and client/server bring is a common issue. A single core team of individuals who understand the impact that business changes have on the employees can address the issue once instead of having separate teams do it on multiple occasions. In addition, this way you can ensure that the answers that are given are consistent.

■ **Established relationships with management and end users**

If a single core group is handling the business re-engineering and client/server effort, then relationships with members from management and the end-user community only need to be built once. An enduring relationship is better than constantly having different teams of people come in and introduce themselves, start from scratch, and ask many of the same questions. Developing and maintaining a relationship takes time and is very important, because the better you know management and the end users, the more support you will get and the faster that your questions will be answered. In addition, such relationships allow for continuity as you progress through the project's life cycle.

■ **No time required for turn over**

With a single team, the activity for the formal turnover of the re-engineering deliverables to the client/server development team is eliminated. Therefore, development can start that much sooner because this core group already understands what needs to be done. Work on the client/server system can probably start even sooner because some technical tasks can be started before all the re-engineering is completed. Parts of the client/server system's infrastructure can be developed in parallel with the business process re-engineering effort because the same people oversee both pieces. Any changes can be immediately identified and handled. Of course, there will still need to be knowledge transfer and specification reviews with some of the technical specialists who join the team for development, but the total time that is required for this process is significantly reduced.

■ **Fewer questions and faster issue resolution**

With a single core team, the development process progresses more quickly because there are fewer questions concerning the business requirements, and the questions that are asked are answered much more quickly. There are fewer questions because the same people who re-engineered the processes are assisting in designing the system.

In addition, many questions can probably be answered immediately by someone on the team, which saves the time spent trying to contact others for answers. For example, if a question is raised as to why a process was redesigned in a certain way, the question can be immediately answered because the person who did the re-engineering is still on the team, which eliminates any misunderstandings or misinterpretations. For questions that cannot be answered, the individuals from the core team will know which end user to ask because they conducted the interviews. This setup removes the dependency, which exists with having separate teams, of having to find a person on the re-engineering team and have that person be the middleman. With separate teams, anyone on the development team with a question would have to spend time tracking down someone on the re-engineering team and then waiting for an answer. Internal politics and contention between teams is removed, and a more focused and productive team emerges.

As more companies start integrating their business process re-engineering and client/server initiatives, they are turning to individuals who possess both re-engineering and client/server skills. Client/server specialists should gain an understanding of business process re-engineering, learn its techniques, and be able to combine these new skills with their client/server talents. Client/server developers are taking on more and more responsibilities, and a better understanding of the business and its associated processes is one of the new requirements. With this combination of business and technical skills, client/server developers will be able to provide true business solutions.

Handling Concerns of BPR

As previously discussed, you may encounter some resistance when you discuss client/server technology. You will also face some of the same challenges when conducting a business process re-engineering effort and interviewing various people. Some of their concerns for business process re-engineering and client/server will be very similar, such as the fear of the change that these projects bring to how they accomplish their jobs on a daily basis and what this change does to their careers. Many individuals have been doing the same routine for many years, and they do not know what they want to change. Resistance is to be expected and the best solution is to be ready for their concerns and to reply to them properly during the interviews and meetings.

The following table lists some of the common concerns voiced by people towards business re-engineering and client/server and some recommended responses to properly handle them.

Concern	Response
I will lose my job due to the re-engineered business processes and new technology.	This is a very real concern that individuals should have in certain cases. The best way to handle this delicate situation is to discuss with senior management and human resources the best approach to handling it. Every situation is different. One perspective is that if the company does not streamline and automate, it will be overwhelmed by the competition and everyone will lose his or her job.
I will lose control over my work environment.	A client/server system along with new business processes gives you more control over your work environment. New tools are available to get the job done easier and information that you need is available at your fingertips. You become more self-sufficient and are empowered to make decisions.

I designed the current process and want it to stay.	State that the current process that the person developed is obviously very successful because it has been used for so many years and has enabled the company to accomplish so much. However, now with the newer technology and the change in how business is done, some changes are a natural course.
I have been doing the same thing for many years and do not want to change.	Explain the benefits of the client/server system and explain how it will improve the way that the job is done. Give examples of how many currently manual tasks that take hours can now be accomplished in a few minutes. Just as the business environment has changed, a company must also change and improve its methods in order to remain competitive.
Sharing information with others will mean the loss of my own importance.	By sharing information with others, you will all be able to accomplish your goals more quickly and efficiently. Everyone will share in the rewards for this improvement. In addition, others will be sharing information with you, so that you will also have access to more information. This additional information will enable you to make quicker and better-informed decisions.
I am afraid of computers.	This issue must be addressed early in the process. Users must receive proper training so that they become familiar with using a computer. For those that have gone through the training but are still intimidated, some hand-holding is helpful.

Using Existing Process Documentation

As you embark upon your business process re-engineering effort, you will probably find some existing documentation describing the business process that you will be analyzing. This documentation may consist of general descriptions or diagrams of the existing processes and its information flow. Reading this existing documentation is helpful in order to gain a preliminary understanding of the process and perhaps an understanding of its history. With this basic understanding, you can ask intelligent questions when you meet with the individuals involved in the process. Remember though, the existing documentation should not be a substitute for any research, interviews, or analysis that must be conducted. Your goal is to question everything, including all the existing documentation. You should not rely solely on the existing documentation because one of the following conditions is likely to exist:

- The documentation is old, and the process has changed.
- The documentation does not contain the detail that the re-engineering effort requires.
- The documentation was created from an incorrect perspective. (For example, the documentation may have been written from a manager's perspective who believed that a business process was being completed in a certain way. In reality, though, that process is being accomplished in a totally different manner.)
- People who contributed to the documentation have left the company so the information cannot be validated.
- The documentation is inaccurate or incorrect.

Conducting Interviews

Upon starting your analysis of the current business process that you will be re-engineering, you will conduct interviews (meetings) with the individuals who are involved in the business process. The goal of these initial interviews is to gain an understanding of each person's responsibilities and their role in completing the business process. After you have met with each person, you will know what each person does and have a detailed understanding of the entire business process as it is currently accomplished along with recommendations for improving it.

Scheduling Interviews

Scheduling interviews with each person in a timely manner is often difficult because everyone has a very busy schedule. In addition, because each meeting will probably last a few hours, the people you are interviewing must be able to set aside a major part of the day for you. Because you will be meeting with people from different departments, you need to understand what their commitments are so that those commitments do not adversely affect your own project schedule. When scheduling interviews with end users for functional requirements gathering, you need to take into account the following events that may limit their availability:

- Conferences
- Month end
- Quarter end
- Year end
- Budgeting period
- Departmental meetings
- Vacation
- Training sessions
- Tax season
- Holidays

The ability to schedule interviews and then to conduct them as planned has a major impact on the project plan and its timeline. This situation is one where management's support is crucial. Management must clearly state that active participation in the interview process is a high priority. Management should require that each person spends time doing it and should provide coverage for people's regular responsibilities while they're being interviewed.

Running an Interview

Conducting a successful interview requires strategy and up-front planning because you need to acquire information, ask probing questions, and still make the interviewee feel comfortable and at ease. You will need to ask a number of questions in order to gain an understanding of their role and responsibilities, how they do their job, and the decision-making process they use to handle certain situations. Anything you can do to make the interviewee comfortable and interested in participating in the interview is very helpful. Try to make the interviewees realize that the client/server system and re-engineering effort are being conducted to help make their jobs easier so that they look forward to contributing to its development. The following are some important points to remember when conducting an interview:

- Find out the interviewee's position on re-engineering and a new system before the meeting so that you can allay any concerns that the interviewee may have at the beginning of the meeting.
- Know what the interviewee does prior to meeting with him or her in order to show that you prepared for the meeting.
- Speak in business terms that the interviewee understands, not technical jargon.
- Be sensitive to people that may be tired of these requirements gathering interviews because they have done so many for other projects.

- Have a dedicated note taker or tape recorder to capture information.

- Be aware of comments from the interviewee that reveal resistance toward the new initiatives.

- The requirements gathering process is an iterative process so let the interviewee know that you will probably have further questions to ask him or her in the future that may require additional meetings.

- After the meeting, write a summary of the interview and send a copy back to the interviewees so they can verify accuracy. This step also provides feedback to them that shows that you listened to what they said.

Asking the Right Questions

Successful interviewing plays a crucial role in the outcome of your re-engineering effort and the development of the client/server system. You have to ask the right questions to get accurate and complete information that you need to properly re-engineer the process and to subsequently design the client/server system. The interviewee may overlook information that you need to know, forget about exception processing, and assume that you know things that you don't. You need to continue to ask insightful questions and probe deeply on unclear points. Also, remember that different people have different agendas so some may purposely attempt to keep information from you. You may want to ask the following list of questions during an interview in order to fully understand the existing business process:

- What specific tasks are your responsibility in completing the business process?
- Why do you complete your tasks in the way that you do?
- How do you know when to start performing your tasks?
- What steps are performed to complete each task?
- What information and tools do you have to have access to in order to complete your tasks?
- What do you do if information or tools that you need are unavailable?
- Do you have to contact other people for information to complete your tasks?
- Are you dependent on information from specific reports to complete your tasks?
- What business rules do you follow to support your decision-making?
- Which of your tasks are manual and slow down the entire business process?
- How long does each task take to complete?
- How long should each task take to complete?
- Which tasks require the most time?
- Which of your tasks are time-sensitive?
- What bottlenecks exist as you complete your tasks?
- What is the cost (such as lost time or wasted money) of these bottlenecks?

■ How do you remove the bottlenecks?

■ How do you monitor the status of your progress?

■ What events interrupt the business process?

■ What do you do if a problem arises during the business process?

■ Are there any measures that monitor how well your tasks were completed?

■ What departments or other processes are dependent on the completion of your tasks?

■ How do you notify others that your tasks have been completed?

■ How is the completed work transferred to other people that need access?

■ Is there too much paperwork, such as forms and memos, to fill out?

■ Are there too many people involved in the approval process?

■ How could you save time and reduce costs in accomplishing your tasks and completing this business process?

■ What computer systems and software programs do you use to complete your tasks?

■ What information and functions do these systems provide you with?

■ Is the information that these systems provide to you accurate?

■ What are the strong points of the system?

■ What are the weak points of the system?

■ Do you have to use too many different systems?

■ Do the different systems all provide consistent information?

■ How often are the systems unavailable to you due to problems?

■ Who do you call if you encounter problems with the system, and how long does it take to resolve them?

Business Process Mapping

Business process mapping is an activity that depicts a business process in a diagram format called a business process map. A *business process map* is similar to a flow diagram and is a visual depiction of a business process. It is a road map that describes what tasks are completed, their relationships to other tasks, how information flows throughout the process, and the steps for decision-making. It shows task dependencies, conditional paths, and whether tasks take place sequentially or in parallel. Inputs that initiate the process and each task as well as their outputs are identified.

An accurate and detailed business process map is very important to a re-engineering effort because it clearly represents the entire business process. This document is used to explain and review the process with other people and also serves as a functional flow diagram for the client/server development team. Start developing the business process map after the first interview by depicting what the interviewee does and their role in the business process. Then add to the business process map after each interview. After all the interviews have been completed, you will have a complete map for the current business process.

Re-engineering the Current Business Process

By carefully analyzing the business process maps and thoroughly evaluating all your findings from your interviews, you can identify those areas that should be changed and improved. Then, by assessing the various steps of the current business process and how people do their work, you can determine new methods for completing the tasks, eliminating areas of inefficiency, and selecting new technology that will streamline and optimize the business process. After a re-engineered business process has been designed, a new business process map detailing the new process should be developed so that you can easily compare the complexity and inefficiencies of the current process with the new improved one.

Identifying Areas for Re-engineering

As you examine the business process maps and evaluate how individuals perform their tasks, the following are some situations that can be re-engineered:

- Individuals constantly performing repetitive tasks
- Duplicate data entry
- Manual tasks, such as having to bring paper forms to other people's offices
- A lot of time spent waiting for information (such as reports) to be received from other sources
- Excessive dependence on others to provide information or complete a task before you can complete yours
- Delays in the process where people are waiting and not being productive
- Excessive number of memos or forms to fill out
- Manual routing of paper forms
- Excessive meetings
- Long approval processes that involve multiple people
- Excessive travel between locations
- Excessive administrative tasks
- Lack of process management facilities

Indications That a Business Process Should Be Re-engineered

Business processes that undergo re-engineering usually have at least one of the following qualities:

- The business process takes too long to complete.
- The business process is too complicated and frustrates the employees.
- Individuals involved in the business process do not have access to information that they need on a timely basis to complete their responsibilities.
- Customers complain about the business process.
- The business process does not accomplish what it is intended to accomplish.
- The business process costs too much to complete.
- The competition performs the same business process better than you.
- Management cannot monitor the status of the business process.
- Too many organizational barriers, such as bureaucracy and administrative tasks, exist.
- The process was successful in the past, but its success in the future cannot be guaranteed.
- No one knows why the business process is completed in a certain way.

Suggestions for Re-engineering

After you have identified areas in the business process that should be improved, the following are some suggestions for re-engineering them.

- Combine several tasks into one.
- Eliminate unnecessary tasks.
- Replace a task with another task that can accomplish the same objective faster and more accurately.
- Have a single person complete a series of tasks instead of a group.
- Determine what new technology enables a process to be completed more efficiently and accurately.
- Identify someone who may be better suited to perform a particular task.
- Identify methods for providing required information more quickly and easily.
- Implement a new approval process that does not get delayed if a person is slow in making a decision.
- Accomplish more tasks in parallel rather than sequentially.

Business Process Re-engineering Software

There are a variety of different software products you can use to assist you with your business process re-engineering efforts. These products provide a wide range of different features ranging from basic flow charting to advanced ones that provide process modeling and process simulation. Basic graphics and flow charting software make it easy to develop and maintain professional business process maps that reflect the business processes and operational activities. More powerful business process modeling software provides advanced diagramming facilities, process modeling tools, graphical decomposition of activities, and cost measurement facilities. The sophisticated products even have simulations that show how much better a re-engineered business process is from the original and what the benefits and gains of re-engineering are. One of the more popular products that is on the market today is Process Charter from Scitor Corporation.

Summary

Many companies are undergoing business process re-engineering initiatives to improve efficiency and productivity. Conducting a BPR initiative is a very challenging task that requires sales skills (getting management and end-user support), people skills (alleviating concerns), and technical skills (interviewing, mapping business processes, and the re-engineering itself). In many cases, a client/server system is developed to implement the new business processes. Client/server technology often enables the new business processes to get off of the drawing board and become reality. Because of this connection, many companies are integrating their BPR and client/server efforts.

Client/Server Components

4

by Neil Jenkins

When you build client/server systems, you need to consider the components that will make up your completed system. A client/server system typically consists of a number of clients, a number of servers, and a connecting network made up of LANs and WANs. This chapter covers the main components that make up client/server systems in the marketplace today. This chapter is by no means an exhaustive list either! Rather than present a complete list of features in each component, this chapter focuses on the value each component gives to client/server systems. Most companies do not have the luxury of being able to build their client/server systems from scratch, but the systems outlined in this chapter have a very large number of connectivity capabilities, making them suitable for use in almost any existing environment. This chapter is split into the three main components for client/server systems:

- Clients
- Servers
- Networks

Clients

The following sections introduce those operating systems that run at the user's desktop. These systems form the client in a client/server system. In terms of number of installed systems, the Microsoft Windows range of products is the most widely used.

Microsoft Windows 3.x, Windows 95, and Windows NT

For client operating systems, Microsoft currently dominates the market with its Windows 3.1, Windows for Workgroups, and Windows 95 products. It faces some competition from the likes of Apple, IBM, and various desktop implementations of UNIX, but Windows is clearly the dominant force on the desktop and will be for some time to come. Building on the success of Windows 3.1 and Windows 95, Microsoft has also begun to capture a large share of the server operating system market. The strategy Microsoft is adopting to achieve this goal is to extend the original Windows operating system along an evolutionary path, which will make Windows available to the desktop, midrange, and high-end servers.

Windows 3.1 is a host-based windowing system that runs on Intel 386-based PCs and above and is a graphical extension to DOS. DOS was designed to run a single program at a time and had limited support for graphical output. Windows enables multiple programs to run concurrently and supports sophisticated high-level graphics. Like other GUIs, it provides a graphical user interface with a consistent look and feel that enables user interfaces that are consistent across different applications to be created. In contrast, DOS requires that each application provides its own user interface. Windows 3.1, Windows 3.11, and Windows for Workgroups have been superseded by Windows 95.

Microsoft's Windows 95 gives improved use of 32-bit processing and network support and is less resource-hungry than Windows NT. Windows 95 is the upgrade from Windows 3.x, yet it does not have DOS as the underlying operating system, although it can run DOS applications. Windows 95 provides full 32-bit support with pre-emptive multitasking, OLE 2.0 support, and multithreading. Realistically, Windows 95 requires an Intel 486-based PC with 8 MB of RAM to run. Figure 4.1 shows the Windows 95 desktop environment.

FIGURE 4.1.

A sample Windows 95 desktop.

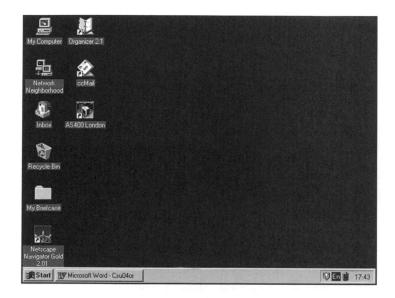

Microsoft's server strategy is based on Windows NT, which is a 32-bit, Windows-compatible, multitasking operating system and is portable across Intel- and RISC-based hardware. Currently, two versions are available: the Workstation Edition and the Server Edition. The Workstation Edition is intended to cater to the workstation and can be considered as a client operating system, although the system requirements are considerably higher than that of both Windows 3.x and Windows 95 in terms of minimum processor and memory requirements. The Server Edition is essentially a network operating system and is specifically covered later in the chapter. With the Server operating system, Microsoft may pose a threat to both NetWare and UNIX at the server level. Because Windows NT can run at both client and server levels, you gain benefit in consistency; however, you do incur a greater hardware requirement at the client.

The next few paragraphs outline some of the Windows products' features that are beneficial to the development of client/server systems.

OLE

With the launch of Windows 3.1, Microsoft included improved performance and reliability in the product. Other innovations included the use of TrueType scalable font technology, improved support for existing MS-DOS applications within the Windows environment, support for multimedia, and support for object linking and embedding (OLE). With the release of OLE 2.0, OLE technology has emerged as one of the cornerstones of Microsoft's move to an object-oriented architecture, as it provides the infrastructure elements that future releases of Windows will build on to provide a native object storage system and distributed system features. OLE 2.0 is implemented as a set of dynamic link libraries (DLLs) for Windows 3.x, Windows 95, and Windows NT.

OLE creates an environment in which applications can share data seamlessly. All data can be thought of as objects; for example, a spreadsheet chart, a paragraph of text, or a graphic image can all be thought of as objects. All these objects can be shared between applications using OLE. OLE is implemented in Windows as an "open" standard so that developers can give their applications OLE capabilities. The standard includes guidelines for how the user interface should operate so that procedures for using OLE will be similar from one application to the next.

In the early days of computing, if you wanted to produce a document that contained a mixture of text and graphics from different applications, the only thing to do was to print out the required source documents, and then merge them using good old-fashioned scissors and glue. The advent of electronic cutting and pasting improved this situation. To create a document under Windows using this method, data is electronically cut or copied from one application and stored on the Clipboard. The Clipboard is an area of memory for storing clipped data. From the Clipboard, the cut data is then pasted to the target document.

The disadvantage of this method is that if the data source that has been cut and pasted changes, the whole process has to be repeated in order to have the most up-to-date information in the final document. The next advance in data sharing under Windows was dynamic data exchange (DDE). DDE works by creating a link between two files, a report in a word processor and a chart in a spreadsheet, for example. Suppose you pasted a cell from the spreadsheet into the word processor document. With DDE, when the original spreadsheet file is changed, this change is automatically passed through to the cell in the word-processor document, eliminating the need to manually keep the two synchronized.

The main drawback of DDE is that the receiving document needs to be able to understand the data it gets from the sending application. Also, DDE sends only the data, so any formatting information is lost. The format of the data is the responsibility of the receiving application. Another limitation is that DDE does not provide a way to run the application that originally created the pasted data.

OLE has overcome these problems. OLE is an advance on DDE because it enables data from different applications to be integrated, regardless of different data formats. It also enables different forms of data to be integrated, such as text, graphics, sound, and even video.

Additionally, OLE enables you to instantly call up the application that created the information by clicking the embedded object in the document.

OLE comes with its own terminology, which it is beneficial to know. There are three main terms used in OLE. The *OLE object* is any object that can be linked or embedded in a client document, such as a cell from a spreadsheet or an image from a graphics program. An *OLE server* is an application that provides support for some kind of OLE object. For example, a graphics application would be a server application for a picture that was embedded in a word-processor document. The *OLE client* is the class of application that receives, stores, and presents objects created by the server application. Using the same example of a spreadsheet application and a word processor, the client is the word processor. In OLE 2.0, the client is redefined as a container, and inserted objects can be activated in place. For example, when a spreadsheet object is activated within a word-processor document, the menu items and frame controls of the word processor become those of the spreadsheet. Effectively, the word processor becomes a spreadsheet program while the contained spreadsheet has the focus.

Embedding

Embedding is something that OLE makes possible. You can think of embedding as an extension of the idea of electronic cutting and pasting. However, two main differences exist between cutting and pasting and embedding. With embedding, the client does not need to understand or be able to process the data in the object that is being embedded. For example, the object may contain an image of the data for the client to display or an icon that marks an object's place in a document, such as for sound recordings or a video clip.

The second difference is that when the user double-clicks the image or icon, the server application is automatically started. Normally, the server application will be used to edit the object. But note that with an embedded object, the original data file is not updated, only the image in the client is updated. After quitting the server application, the user is automatically returned to the client document.

Linking

Linking is another important capability that OLE provides. Linking is similar to DDE, except that with OLE, two applications with incompatible data types can be linked. When a link is set up between an object in a client document and a server application, the object operates in the same way as an embedded object as far as the user is concerned. The only difference is that when the user double-clicks an object, the original data file (not a copy, as in embedding) is loaded into the server application to be edited.

After editing, any changes to the server data file are reflected in the client document. If the server object is linked into any other client documents, the changes will be automatically seen in those documents as well. This facility has many uses, but its real importance is that it enables users to choose the best application for creating different parts of a compound document.

(A *compound document* is a file that contains multiple embedded objects, such as tables, graphs, and so on.) It also ensures that users stay synchronized with the latest data.

The client and server applications communicate with OLE dynamic link libraries, the two-way conversations being facilitated by DDE. The only restrictions to using OLE is that the client and server applications, along with the OLE libraries, must be on the same machine. However, the data (the linked objects themselves, such as graphics files) could reside anywhere on a network. For example, keeping source files on a file server and linking into them from several documents is a good way of ensuring that users in different locations have the most current data and provides the benefit of storing data only on the one file server rather than multiple client machines.

COM

Underlying OLE 2.0 is Microsoft's Component Object Model (COM), which specifies how OLE objects should interact by defining the general interface mechanisms that all objects should use when communicating with each other. An object interface is a set of functions, called methods, which together implement a particular object service. COM also defines certain specific interfaces, such as the drag-and-drop interface, that ensure that objects developed by different vendors will work seamlessly together when using such features. Using COM, objects communicate by calling each other's interface methods. A collection of methods that implement a particular object's services are made available to other objects through an interface table. The interface table holds a pointer to each available interface method, so developers are free to develop the code behind the interfaces using any language that is able to call functions using pointers, such as C, C++, and Pascal.

COM defines a structured storage interface, which describes how objects are saved on disk. In OLE 2.0, this interface is implemented as a hierarchical storage system that is layered on top of resident MS-DOS, Windows NT, or Macintosh file systems. Structured storage is designed for dealing with compound documents. It keeps track of where objects are in the document and provides a framework for storing details about each object. The main omission from Microsoft's COM is that it does not support inheritance. Inheritance is a fundamental feature of any object-oriented system and enables specialized objects to be derived from more general objects. Microsoft maintains that there are hidden pitfalls to implementing inheritance that are best solved by using Microsoft's notion of aggregation. With aggregation, developers must explicitly build a list of pointers to a derived object. This approach allows developers to build in controls that prevent objects from inheriting features in a dangerous way; however, this approach also imposes a degree of restriction on the developer.

ActiveX

Microsoft's Internet strategy is aimed at providing the enabling technologies, called ActiveX Technologies, to make active Internet applications a reality. ActiveX Technologies include client technologies, server technologies, tools, and applications and embrace all popular Internet standards, languages, and platforms. ActiveX is a set of open technologies that moves the Internet beyond static documents to provide users with a more active, exciting, and useful experience. Bridging both Sun Microsystems' Java technology and Microsoft's industry standard object technology (OLE), ActiveX gives users and developers a platform for applications on the Internet while preserving their investments in applications, tools, and source code.

For users, ActiveX Technologies will make the Internet easy to learn and use. The computing interface and the Internet interface will be more unified, removing the distinction between local and network resources such as files. The search tools and navigation structures will be the same. The Help resources will be integrated, so users will have a single way to obtain assistance whether that content resides on their local machines or on the network. Microsoft is integrating this technology into new versions of Windows 95 and Windows NT.For developers and content creators, the ActiveX Technologies strategy lets developers leverage and integrate their varied investments in tools, training, and source code to add value to the Internet. Microsoft will support the developers' choice of programming languages and tools, including Microsoft Visual Basic, Visual C++, Internet Studio, FrontPage, Java, or third-party tools. Because ActiveX Technologies are language- and vendor-independent, developers can take full advantage of their existing investments of time, money, and work as they move to the Internet. They can leverage their experience with the Windows operating system, ActiveX Controls (formerly called OLE Controls), Office applications, and other Microsoft technologies, as well as a range of third-party Windows development tools, including Borland Delphi, PowerBuilder, and Symantec C++.

For content providers, Microsoft will facilitate the migration to a new business model. Providers have offered free content to establish their presence on the Internet, but as the market matures, they'll have a commercially viable way to distribute active information and consumer services. Microsoft will offer ways to measure usage and record financial transactions, as well as new ways to support the unprecedented performance and scalability demands that will be placed on information servers.

Because Microsoft believes that corporate Intranet applications also will be tremendously popular, it is making business use of the Internet a key strategic focus. For example, it is integrating Web protocols into its popular Windows NT Server through its Internet Information Server product. It is enhancing Microsoft Office so that Office tools serve as both Web creation tools and Web browser enhancements.

X Window

The X Window system (X) is a vendor- and hardware-independent, network-based windowing system. It was developed at MIT and has become the de facto industry standard for window-based applications in the UNIX environment.

The X Window system provides a graphic display system based on a set of hierarchical, resizeable windows. One of the primary design goals of the X Window system was to specify a mechanism, not a policy, for creating user interfaces, so X does not provide a specific user interface, but instead supports a varied set of tools that are used to build user interfaces. It also can support different styles and policies. Another major design goal of X Window was portability.

There were four fundamental design goals in developing the X Window system:

- The system had to be able to be implemented on a variety of displays.
- Applications display had to be device-independent.
- System operation had to be transparent to the network.
- The system had to be an extensible system.

The first three of these goals help to distinguish X from many other windowing systems, such as the Macintosh window system or Microsoft Windows.

The structure of X is based on client/server models except that the terminology is reversed, which makes it somewhat confusing to understand. The part of X that manages windows and user input is referred to as the X server and is completely independent from the applications that create windows and display information in them. The X server resides on the machine that provides the user with an access point via keyboard or mouse, and it is a server in the sense that it provides a windowing service to applications that may be elsewhere in the network. What is referred to as the X client is the application itself, which will be linked into library code that defines the user interface.

The X client and X server communicate by means of the X protocol, which is a communications protocol defined within X. This protocol can have one of four formats and allows for communication between multiple clients and servers. It can operate over any reliable duplex byte stream interprocess communication mechanism. The X protocol is asynchronous, which means that requests are not normally acknowledged. This speeds up response time over a network. However, direct client-to-client communication is not supported under X. All client-to-client communication is routed through a server. This separation of the X client and X server means that a user can initiate applications on several different computer systems in a network, and those applications can simultaneously open windows on a display at the user's terminal or workstation. Using an X-based window manager, the user can move windows, resize windows, and shrink windows to icons. In addition, X supports cut-and-paste operations, scroll bars, pull-down windows, pull-right windows, and pop-up windows.

The basic X Window system released by MIT includes the following components:

- **X server software** The X server software resides on the machine that provides the user access point and handles video output and input from the user through devices such as a keyboard and a mouse.

- **X library (Xlib)**   The X library is a well-defined set of portable interfaces to the X protocol for clients. It contains all of the lowest level program interfaces to the X Window system.

- **X intrinsics toolkit (Xt)**   The Xt library is a library of C routines on which other toolkits can be built. The interface to this library is standardized by the X Consortium as part of the X Window system. The intrinsics define routines that a developer can use to create and manipulate interface objects.

- **Athena widget set**   The Athena widget set is provided as a part of the X distribution. A widget set is a collection of program objects that provides commonly used interface functions. All widgets conform to a particular look and feel. Several different widget sets are available from different vendors.

- **Display manager (xdm)**   The display manager is responsible for managing the user access point.

- **Window manager (uwm and twm)**   A window manager is usually an X client, running on any host machine on the network. The window manager enables windows to be moved and resized. It is possible to use X without a window manager, but all windows will remain static. Some window managers are not X clients, but run on the X server, which significantly reduces network traffic.

- **Terminal emulator (xterm)**   The terminal emulator, xterm, provides a terminal within a window. Clearly this is a common need and hence a vital function. Xterm emulates a VT102 and a Tektronix terminal.

- **Elementary applications**   Some of the applications that come with the basic X distribution include the kind of applets that come with MS-Windows. They may include a digital alarm clock, a calculator, a screen editor, and xeyes, a pair of eyes that watch the cursor as it moves around the screen.

Most manufacturers add their own enhancements to these basic facilities. The most popular of these enhancements is the OSF/Motif extension, which has become the dominant standard under UNIX.

OSF/Motif

The Open Systems Foundation (OSF) was formed in 1988 by a small group of companies, including IBM, Digital, and HP. One of the goals of OSF was to define the look and feel for a graphical user interface. That GUI is now known as Motif and, until recently, was in direct competition with Open Look, which was promoted by UNIX International and its members, including Sun and AT&T. However, Open Look is no longer being promoted as a rival to Motif.

The usual components of Motif are as follows:

- **The Motif X Toolkit**   The MotifX Toolkit constitutes the Application Programmer's Interface and is currently implemented as a single C library.

- **The Motif Window Manager (mwm)**   The Motif Window Manager adds the look and feel of the Motif environment. A major advantage of the mwm is that it has a look and feel that is very similar to Microsoft Windows. This makes it easier for users to transfer skills from using Microsoft Windows to Motif, and vice versa.

- **The Motif User Interface Language (UIL)**   The UIL is a prototyping language that has its roots in the Digital Windows widget set XUI. It is not available on all Motif-based systems, but it enables developers to prototype the user interface. The User Interface Language is an interpreted language that looks like C. The Motif Toolkit includes functions for accessing UIL data and widgets from a Motif C program.

Note that it is possible to turn a PC into an X terminal by installing the appropriate software, although the PC will need to be at least a 386 with an Ethernet card, VGA, and mouse. Quarterdeck's DESQview/X provides this capability under MS-DOS. Any comparison between X Window and PC environments, such as Microsoft Windows or the Apple Mac, quickly reveals that they are quite distinct. X Window is oriented towards multiuser systems and networks, whereas Microsoft Windows and the Mac are essentially single-user environments with no inherent networking capability.

IBM OS/2

IBM's main client operating system is OS/2. By the mid 1980s, DOS was beginning to show its limitations. With the introduction of more sophisticated hardware and the demands of more complex applications, MS-DOS was limited by its 16-bit architecture and lack of support for multitasking. About this time, Microsoft and IBM teamed up to jointly develop what they saw as the next generation of desktop operating system. Initially, the new operating system was called DOS 5.0 internally by Microsoft, but it later was renamed OS/2. It would support 32-bit addressing and pre-emptive multitasking, which would enable it to fully exploit the new 32-bit Intel chips, such as the 80386 and upwards.

One of the major advantages of OS/2 over DOS was the introduction of its host-based GUI, Presentation Manager (PM), which, not surprisingly, also resembled Program Manager, the Microsoft Windows GUI. OS/2 was expected to fill the gap between DOS and larger operating systems such as UNIX. IBM and Microsoft expected DOS users to instantly switch to OS/2, but many users opted to stay with DOS, to switch to Microsoft Windows, or to change to UNIX instead.

With the downfall of the early versions of OS/2 came the demise of the close working relationship between Microsoft and IBM. In 1992, IBM, without the help of Microsoft, relaunched OS/2 with improved support for running DOS and added support for running Windows applications. However, these added features had come at a price: they were added using Microsoft Windows code licensed from Microsoft. So for every copy of OS/2 sold, IBM had to pay a royalty to Microsoft, and inevitably this cost was passed on to the customer. With the release of a later version of OS/2 called *OS/2 Special Edition for Windows* or simply *OS/2 for Windows*, IBM got around this problem.

The latest version of OS/2, OS/2 Warp, contains no Microsoft code, so no royalty needs to be paid. The price is around half of that for the original version of OS/2. The main drawback, however, is that IBM will need to update its OS/2 every time Microsoft releases a new version of Windows. At present, it is uncertain if IBM will be able to provide native support for Windows 95 into OS/2.

OS/2 has had a reputation for stability and performance, yet it has largely been relegated to a niche role by Microsoft Windows. It has seen the greatest acceptance by corporate sites looking for a stable 32-bit client, often as a front end to an IBM mainframe or AS/400 in a client/server setup. OS/2 has also seen limited acceptance as a server-based operating system in conjunction with IBM's LAN Server and Warp Server products, although this combination has not posed a serious threat to either NT Server, UNIX, or NetWare, which are the dominant midrange server operating software products.

IBM's SOM

IBM's SOM is based on the concepts of object orientation (OO). The general principle behind all object-oriented systems is the same. Objects are formed from the combination of an amount of data and a number of the related functions, called methods, that interact with the data. Each object presents the outside world with an interface through which its data can be accessed. The interface is a means of executing the object's internal methods, and it is not possible to get at an object's internal data except by using the interface, which is its internal functions. Object-oriented systems operate by objects sending messages to each other. Sending a message consists of one object calling another object's method and possibly passing one or more parameters in the process. Object-oriented systems also support a number of other features, such as inheritance and polymorphism. The things that objects are capable of doing are defined by an object model, which ensures consistency of interaction between objects.

The creation of objects by combining data and methods is called *encapsulation* and is the means by which object-oriented systems can hide complexity. Developers do not need to know how an object works; they just need to know what services its methods will provide and how to send a message to it. Encapsulation is common to all object models; however, its implementation varies between vendors.

IBM's SOM defines a generic behavior for objects, which overcomes a number of problems often encountered when trying to make objects based on different implementations communicate with each other. The four main problems are as follows:

- Objects are created from templates, called *classes*, which are arranged hierarchically. However, you can combine classes only if they are programmed in the same dialect of object-oriented development language. For example, you cannot mix-and-match classes developed using versions of SmallTalk from different vendors, such as Digitalk and ParcPlace Systems.

- The mechanisms for handling persistence, storing objects, and combining classes varies greatly between different object languages. When a class definition is amended or updated, there is no automatic method for propagating these changes to applications that were compiled using the old class versions. All such applications must be recompiled or manually updated.

- Generally class libraries are delivered in source code format, rather than binary, so they have to be compiled and linked into user applications.

SOM solves each of these problems. SOM is language-independent and even permits objects to be defined in a non–object-oriented language such as C or COBOL. SOM implements a common set of methods for handling persistence. SOM dynamically binds applications to object code in the repository at run time, which means that all applications that use SOM objects automatically use the most up-to-date versions. Finally, SOM supports objects supplied in executable form. A recent extension to SOM, DSOM, adds location transparency so that users do not need to be aware of which computer an object resides on in order to make use of it. DSOM achieves this transparency by using a full implementation of the OMG's CORBA specification.

Apple

Apple makes the Macintosh range of desktop computers (Macs). Macs have a reputation for being of a high quality and easy to use, but also of being more expensive than PCs. The reputation for ease of use is due to the System 7 operating system, which presents the user with a graphical user interface. Until recently, the choice of running either Windows or Macintosh software has been based on the choice of hardware platform because Mac software is not compatible with PCs and vice versa.

However, Apple launched a challenge to the Intel/Microsoft domination of the desktop with the release of its Power Macintosh, or PowerPC desktop computer. It is based on a RISC (Reduced Instruction Set Chip) processor developed by IBM. Along with Apple, IBM and Motorola have developed PowerPC technology. Perhaps the best examples of this technology are IBM's PowerPC-based RS/6000 range. The PowerMac is able to run Mac software and native PowerPC software with a performance comparable to Intel's Pentium-based PCs. The PowerMac also provides support for DOS and Windows applications through Insignia's SoftWindows emulation package. Performance for Microsoft Windows applications is unfortunately comparable to that of a low-end 486 PC.

The main problem with this technology is that the entry-level PowerMacs do not include the emulation software and require 16 MB of RAM. By the time users have paid for SoftWindows and the extra RAM, the price of a PowerMac is around that of an entry-level, Pentium-based machine. This fact may put off many PC users who are choosing between a Pentium and a PowerMac, particularly because there is a shortage of native PowerPC software, and Mac software is significantly more expensive than PC software.

PowerOpen Association

Apple, in conjunction with IBM, Motorola, Bull, and others, has formed the PowerOpen Association, whose aim is to agree on an open operating environment for the new breed of PowerPCs. The PowerOpen's environment is based on IBM's AIX (UNIX) operating system and provides developers with a standard ABI (application binary interface) for developing applications. This environment will be hardware-, operating system-, and GUI-independent and will provide an API (application programming interface) that will include support for X Window, Motif, AIX, and Mac applications. This environment could provide a platform that could potentially unite the Mac and OSF communities. Through the use of SoftWindows, the PowerPC could provide a platform that will support DOS/Windows or Mac clients and UNIX-based servers.

The Universal Client

Recently Apple announced its plans to turn the PowerMac into the "Universal Client." To achieve this goal, Apple is enhancing the current System 7.x operating system to make better use of RISC technology and integrating it with OpenDoc and a new series of Open Transport protocols. Apple Open Transport is a modern networking and communications subsystem for the Mac OS. Open Transport is based on industry standards and brings a new level of networking connectivity, control, and interoperability to Mac OS systems while preserving and enhancing the hallmark of the Macintosh and Mac OS—built-in support for easy-to-use networking. OpenDoc provides a means to co-ordinate distributed applications and to manage compound documents, which are made up from a variety of different data types. Open Transport will provide a single API for programmers to write their applications to and will support all the major communications protocols.

The upgrade of the Apple operating system will proceed in three stages. The first step was the release of System 7.5, which included support for multithreading and various other new features. However, support for pre-emptive multitasking and memory protection is not included. These features will be added to later releases. The next release after System 7.5 is Mac OS V8.0, codenamed Copland, and is due for release in 1997. V8.0 will include the addition of a microkernel, memory protection, a new I/O architecture, and support for OpenDoc. The final phase of roll out for the "Universal Client" is expected in late 1996. This release will include pre-emptive multitasking, a hardware abstraction layer, and possibly a new CPU.

OpenDoc

OpenDoc is a rival technology to Microsoft's OLE 2.0. It is an object-oriented, compound-document architecture designed to provide cross-platform support. Although OpenDoc owes much of its technology to Apple, it is being jointly developed by the members of the Component Integration Laboratories (CIL), whose members include Apple, IBM, Novell, Oracle, Sun, WordPerfect, and Xerox. The OpenDoc architecture considers a document to be made up of a number of smaller units, or parts, which are dynamically bound to form the overall compound document.

Parts are the fundamental building blocks in OpenDoc. Each part holds its own unique data that is displayed in the document, such as text, spreadsheet cells, graphics, and so on. This unique data is the part's intrinsic content. But parts also can contain other parts, and every compound document has a single root part into which all the other parts are embedded. New applications will be able to be assembled by mixing and matching parts and then plugging them all together. Parts editors will be used to display and manipulate a particular kind of content and may also serve as components of the compound document as well. The three core technologies to OpenDoc are Apple's Bento storage mechanism, a scripting language based on Apple's Open Script architecture, and IBM's SOM.

Bento is a portable object storage library and format that allows OpenDoc to store and exchange compound documents and multimedia. Documents stored in Bento are platform-independent and can be accessed independently of the application that creates them. A library for reading and writing Bento is available in source code form from Apple. The library is highly efficient, platform-independent, and very portable. Bento is in use on many platforms, including Microsoft Windows, Macintosh, OS/2, and various flavors of UNIX. Bento storage provides each part with its own data stream area within a document file, which stores data relating specifically to the part. References between streams enable parts to be integrated into a single document. Each object is also given a unique ID that is used to track the object if it is moved between systems. You can track multiple versions of objects and store incremental changes that are made rather than storing a whole new version of a document. This significantly reduces the amount of disk space that is required to keep track of multiple revisions of documents.

The basic object model underlying OpenDoc is IBM's SOM, which provides a standard binary object interface and calling mechanism for distributed objects. Because SOM is language-neutral, it enables parts to be created in a variety of languages to communicate with no additional effort on the part of the programmer. This language neutrality contrasts with Microsoft's OLE 2.0, which is biased towards C++.

OpenDoc's scripting is used for creating compound documents and implements a set of standard verbs that are intended to be as general as possible. This is so that the same verb can be used in different contexts. For example, a verb that means "move to the next item," could mean "move to the start of the next paragraph" in a text document, whereas in a spreadsheet it might mean, "move to the next cell."

Although the current OpenDoc technology is lagging behind OLE 2.0, the use of parts and IBM's SOM are likely to provide a standard for compound documents that is easier to use and more flexible than Microsoft's OLE 2.0. Another reason why this technology may prove successful is that the CIL intends to make OpenDoc compatible with other compound document architectures, including Microsoft's OLE 2.0.

Servers

This section outlines the various hardware components that can act as servers in a client/server system. Remember that a complete system may consist of any number of servers and include different makes.

PC-Based Servers

Trusting your company's valuable business data to a PC server is not a step you should take lightly. You need to carefully choose a system with proven reliability, integrity, and performance. You need to make sure that each system offers expansion and upgrade options as your demands increase; your server must be able to grow with your business. PC-based file servers are available from a wide range of vendor companies including IBM, Hewlett Packard, and Compaq.

Regardless of vendor, the key requirement for PC-based servers is server dependability. You need to ensure that your server of choice offers high availability and data integrity, including hot-swappable drives, offline backup processors, remote paging and alert capabilities, redundant power supplies, and both internal and external network management capabilities. Some of the main features required for reliable client/server systems include error checking and correcting (ECC) memory and RAID disk subsystems to give real protection against data loss. Hot-pluggable hard drives are becoming a necessity also; in the event of a disk crash, the drive can be removed and replaced without turning off the file server.

Support staff should be able to access critical file server information instantly and be able to diagnose problems or areas of concern and remedy them quickly. Newer file server products such as Compaq's Proliant range can notify staff of potential problems before they become critical.

In line with the much higher requirements for processing power and storage capabilities, the PC servers are continually increasing the capacities they can support and provide. Support for four Pentium Pro multiprocessors is now available from the likes of HP (in the NetServer range) and ALR, and disk capacity is approaching the areas more commonly occupied by midrange systems.

You should ensure that the PC-based servers you are considering can run the database and systems management tools that you require in your client/server system, and, as with all the hardware discussed in this book, you should try to find people willing to demonstrate the servers working live.

UNIX Servers

UNIX-based servers are available from many hardware vendors; the most popular machines are the RS/6000 range from IBM, the HP-UX range from Hewlett Packard, and the DEC Alpha range from Digital. These machines, like PC systems, can be scaled up from individual workstations through to enterprise-level servers. These machines are typically used at the client level for today's numeric-intensive and graphic applications. These client systems range from entry-level clients to advanced, high-performance, 3D-graphics workstations. They can benefit users in the following types of environments:

- Computer-aided design (CAD)
- Electronic design automation (EDA)
- Statistical analysis
- Geographical information systems (GIS)
- Scientific visualization
- Technical publishing
- General business

UNIX servers are also ideally suited for both the commercial and numeric-intensive computing environments at the server level. They offer a wide range of performance options that allow an application to scale from single-processor systems to SMPs or to the massively parallel SP.

They support an extensive range of connectivity, storage, and media options. These systems offer systems management and integrated high availability features to implement mission-critical business applications. At the moment, the main growth areas for UNIX-based servers are in the areas of network-based applications such as Web servers, groupware such as Lotus Notes, transaction processing, and database serving.

UNIX servers can act as very large-scale servers. For example, IBM's RS/6000 SP is an open parallel computer based on IBM's proven AIX and RISC technologies and provides outstanding price/performance while running a large number of RS/6000 applications. The SP has the flexibility to function as an application server or data server or to run combinations of interactive, batch, serial, and parallel jobs concurrently. A comprehensive suite of system management functions allows you to administer and operate the system from a single control workstation. In addition, the system has been designed for reliability and availability through redundancy of critical components, nondisruptive maintenance, and support of advanced, high-availability software. The SP is an ideal computing platform for solving large, complex client/server business problems.

IBM AS/400

IBM manufactures one of the most successful midrange computer systems. This system is called the AS/400 and has superseded IBM's older midrange computer, the System 3x range. The AS/400 is based on bringing together the core components of a computer system and integrating them into the operating system of the AS/400.

In the IBM AS/400 operating system, advanced database capabilities in the form of DB/400 and key system management functions are already built into the machine and come supplied as standard. This integrated function helps make the AS/400 Advanced Series easy to install and maintain and makes it easy for users to access the information and applications they need to become more productive. When compared to systems that offer similar function, the total cost of AS/400 Advanced Series ownership can be much less. There are several reasons for this lower cost. First, key system functions are built-in and tested to work together. This integration provides you with a relational database management system, security system, network management system, communications, performance monitoring, and other facilities at no additional cost. Second, integrated functions reduce programming costs, so you won't have to pay outside vendors or take time away from your own developers as with traditional systems. Third, simpler operation helps users become more productive more quickly.

The AS/400 Advanced Series has one of the largest commercial application portfolios in the industry—more than 25,000 in all. The portfolio includes a very wide range of application types, ranging from groupware to database marketing to home pages on the Internet. Perhaps the AS/400's biggest strength is that it can adapt as technologies change without changing the way your business or your applications work.

New technologies are providing new challenges and opportunities in the way you can run your businesses. The AS/400 Advanced Series is continuing to deliver the new tools and technologies that will help you bring these technologies to your business solutions and build your competitive edge. As a result, the AS/400 has become one of IBM's most successful products.

The AS/400 has an open approach to communications, and products are available to link the AS/400 into even the most complex networked systems. The AS/400 Advanced Series can interact with other computing environments, including UNIX, AIX, Windows NT, and Windows 95, and many of the applications being written for them.

Particularly worth noting is the AS/400's suitability as a data warehouse. Data warehousing is the ability to leverage your organization's investment in data by making it more accessible to more users. The AS/400 Advanced Series incorporates special design features that make it ideal for data warehousing applications. These features include DB2 symmetric multiprocessor processing (SMP) and deliver outstanding performance and enormous file capacity.

Year after year, the performance range of AS/400 Advanced Series has increased while its integrated hardware, software, and system design have been preserved. The result is that investments in applications, data, and user skills have been protected. IBM has stressed that this will continue to be the case in the future as AS/400 Advanced Series performance increases even more. Because the same operating system that runs an AS/400 Advanced Series supporting two users also runs high-end models that support several thousand users, applications don't need to change when the machines do.

For example, take a look at Table 4.1, which compares one of the smallest AS/400s to one of the largest, and you get an idea of the scalability of the AS/400.

Table 4.1. Comparison of two models of AS/400 to show scalability.

AS/400 Advanced Series Model 200	*AS/400 Advanced System Model 530*
Main storage: 8 MB to 128 MB	Main storage: 512 MB to 4096 MB
Disk storage: 1.03 GB to 23.6 GB	Disk storage: 1.96 GB to 520.09 GB
Local attachment of workstations	Local attachment of workstations
Twinaxial: 0-280	Twinaxial: 0-7000
ASCII: 0-126	ASCII: 0-3150
LocalTalk: 0-217	LocalTalk: 0-5425
Communications lines: 1-20	Communications lines: 1-200
LAN adapters: 0-2	LAN adapters: 0-16
Optical libraries: 0-4	Optical libraries: 0-22

From integrated, centralized systems to open, distributed environments, the AS/400 Advanced Series offers a range of systems to meet today's client/server computing needs.

The Mainframe

Many people thought the advent of client/server computing would effectively kill the mainframe environment as companies began to downsize their computer systems to smaller, more economical systems. This, however, has not been the case. In fact, there has been something of a resurgence in the popularity of the mainframe in the last two years as companies have realized that the mainframe makes a good, large data server in a client/server system. This resurgence has been helped by the immediate emphasis of many mainframe vendors on the suitability of the mainframe as a server machine and the subsequent launch of software and connectivity products that fulfill the needs of customers needing more open connectivity.

Although the focus of most client/server systems is on smaller PC and midrange-based systems, the mainframe is very much a part of the picture. The mainframes available today from companies such as IBM, Amdahl, and Hitachi Data Systems (HDS) are getting faster and faster and smaller and smaller. The scalability of the smaller mainframes allows them to encroach on the higher ends of the midrange market and gives you more of a choice for your high-end servers. Similarly, the midrange market is encroaching on the high-end PC file server market.

Network Operating Systems for Client/Server

Novell is the world's leading supplier of network operating systems and has dominated the PC LAN market ever since it came into existence. In the same way that Microsoft owns the desktop market, Novell owns the server market. Although UNIX is the dominant operating system on high-end servers, Novell's NetWare is the network operating system of choice for application servers. However, Novell is not without competition in the server market. Three other major competitive products include Microsoft's NT Server, IBM's Warp Server, and Banyan's VINES.

NOVELL, UNIX, AND WINDOWS NT

Most server products compete with NetWare rather than UNIX, which until the release of Windows NT Server has remained unchallenged on the high-end server. Windows NT from Microsoft represents a serious challenge to Novell. This is because it is positioned to potentially fulfill three different roles, that of the desktop operating system, network operating system, and server operating system. In the process, Microsoft threatens to unite the desktop and server with a single operating system. This will be at the expense of Novell's NetWare and its UNIX share of the market. In this light, it seems likely that the imminence of Windows NT is probably what prompted Novell to acquire USL. Novell clearly needed a way to compete with Windows NT on the server. Playing a central role in the development of UNIX will enable it to do just that.

To strengthen its central role in UNIX development, Novell has introduced a number of products that provide a link between the desktop and UNIX. For example, Novell's UnixWare combines the UNIX and NetWare products and comes in separate client and server editions: the Personal Edition and the Application Server version. UnixWare provides PC users with GUI access to UNIX and supports multiple sessions of Windows and DOS under UNIX on a 386 or above processor. The system requirements compare very favorably with NT. The client requires 8 MB of RAM, and the server requires 12 MB. Microsoft is still working hard to cram the next version of NT into 12 MB; the current version of NT requires at least 16 MB. Novell's LAN Workplace provides GUI access to UNIX systems and other network resources using the TCP/IP protocol, without the need for NetWare.

Novell NetWare

Novell's approach to serving the LAN user is unique in that it has chosen to concentrate its efforts on producing software that will run on other vendors' network hardware. NetWare runs on virtually any IBM or compatible and supports all major LAN vendors' hardware, including the Apple Macintosh. Novell's philosophy is to make itself a de facto industry standard by dominating the marketplace. For example, if a major corporation insists on purchasing IBM's Token Ring network, then Novell is happy to supply compatible NetWare to enhance the Token Ring's performance.

Topology

NetWare can run on a number of different topologies. Depending on the hardware you select, NetWare can run on a network configured as a star, a string of stars, a token ring, and even a bus topology. Running NetWare on 3Com's Ethernet bus hardware, for example, results in a bus topology. When running on ARCnet hardware, NetWare functions efficiently in a token bus environment. Northern Telecom and other PBX manufacturers offer their customers NetWare, utilizing the star topology of a PBX, and Proteon runs NetWare on hardware organized as a string of stars.

NetWare and the Concept of a File Server

NetWare is designed for true network file server support. To understand this approach, you need to know how a file server functions under Novell's software. In effect, the file server software forms a shell around the operating system and is able to intercept commands from application programs before they can reach the operating system's command processor. The workstation user is not aware of this phenomenon. The user simply asks for a data file or a program without worrying about where either is located.

To understand this interaction between the file server and the individual workstations, look at what happens when a workstation issues a request for a particular file. The network interface to the network file server (the *network shell*) resides in each workstation. It is responsible for intercepting network commands from an application program. The interface shell can run on DOS, Windows, OS/2, Macintosh, Windows NT, and Windows 95.

When an application program requests a specific file, the shell must first determine whether the request is for a local file (residing on the workstation's own disk drives) or a network request for information located on a file server. If the information is located on the workstation's own drives, the request is passed back to the command processor, where it is handled as a normal I/O operation. As a particular file is located and loaded into the workstation's CPU for processing, the user notices the red light on the disk drive go on.

What if the requested file is located on a file server? In this case, the request translator issues a read request to the file server, which locates the file and transmits it to the workstation in the form of a *reply packet*. The packet is received by a *reply translator*, which converts this information into a form the local workstation can handle. The command processor then provides the application program with this data. The workstation is completely unaware of the internal mechanics of this operation. The network file server is so fast that local and network responses appear to be equally fast except in cases of unusually heavy network traffic.

NetWare Routers and Gateways to Other Networks

NetWare makes it possible for networks to communicate with other networks, as well as with mainframe computers. The following sections explain how.

Routers and Router Software

A router connects networks using different hardware. One network, for example, might use ARCnet's interface cards and cabling while another network uses IBM's Token Ring interface cards and cabling. NetWare provides router software, which permits these two networks to share information.

The software can reside on a dedicated workstation, but it is now also built into the NetWare operating system and thus is another process for the file server to handle. In order to handle routing internally, there must be at least two available expansion slots, one for each network interface card for each respective network. The router remains invisible to users whether it is running on a dedicated PC workstation or as a process within the NetWare file server.

Novell offers multiprotocol routing software that runs on NetWare LANs. This software routes several different protocols, including UNIX's TCP/IP and Apple's AppleTalk, so that users on these different networks can communicate with NetWare LAN users. This software allows you to build mixed computing environments for your client/server system.

SNA Gateway for Micro-Mainframe Communications

Novell offers gateway software and hardware for its NetWare LANs that enable network users to communicate with IBM mainframes. Novell's NetWare for SAA in conjunction with its NetWare 3270 LAN workstation for SAA enables multiple gateways on the same network, so you can send mainframe print jobs to LAN printers, view the current status of the gateway, and pool LU sessions. In addition, the NetWare for SAA product can connect to IBM AS/400 systems. With the newer client/server AS/400 systems, there is no need for NetWare for SAA. Client Access/400 can be used to connect Windows 3.x and Windows 95 clients.

Using this type of device can immediately allow you to integrate your mainframe screens alongside your new client/server systems. It can also improve workflow in that users do not have to have multiple screens on their desks!

NetWare Connect

Novell also offers NetWare Connect. This software product allows users to dial into a server or LAN. LAN users using LAN-based communications packages can also use it to dial out. In this way, Novell can support remote access to client/server systems as well as remote node and remote control connectivity.

System Fault-Tolerant NetWare

Any company that relies completely upon computers for information processing is fearful of a system failure. Novell has developed system fault-tolerant NetWare to overcome this potential disaster. There are three different levels of system fault tolerance, depending on the degree of protection required. What makes Novell's approach so unusual is that while it has provided the software tools for hardware duplication (to prevent downtime), the user may purchase off-the-shelf hardware in order to realize significant cost savings.

Level I NetWare protects against partial destruction of the file server by providing redundant directory structures. For each network volume, the file server maintains extra copies of file allocation tables and directory entries on different disk cylinders. If a directory sector fails, the file server shifts immediately to the redundant directory. The user, not inconvenienced, is unaware of this automatic procedure.

When a Level I system is powered up, it performs a complete self-consistency check on each redundant directory and file allocation table. It performs a read-after-write verification after each network disk write to ensure that data written to the file server is re-readable. Level I software's hot-fix feature checks a sector before trying to write data to it. If a disk area is bad, the disk drive controller writes its data to a special hot fix area. The hot fix feature then adds the bad blocks to the bad block table, so there is no possibility of losing data by writing it to these bad blocks in the future.

Level II software includes the protection offered by Level I, plus a number of additional features. At this level, Novell offers two options to protect the LAN against the total failure of the file server. The first option is *mirrored drives*, which means supporting two duplicate hard disk drives with a single hard disk controller. Every time the file server performs a disk write function, it mirrors this image on its duplicate hard disk. It also verifies both hard disk drives to ensure complete accuracy. If the hard disk fails, the system switches to the mirrored drive and continues operations with no inconvenience to users.

The second option under Level II is *duplexed drives*, in which virtually all the hardware is duplicated, including the disk controller and interface. If a disk controller or disk drive fails, the system switches automatically to the duplexed alternative and records this switch in a log. The performance of a duplexed system is far superior to that of a single system because of *split seeks*. If a certain file is requested, the system checks to see which disk system can respond more quickly. If two requests occur simultaneously, each drive handles one of the disk reads. This technique greatly enhances the file server's performance.

Level II also includes a Novell feature known as the *transaction tracking system (TTS)*, which is designed to ensure the data integrity of multiuser databases. The system views each change in a database as a transaction that is either complete or incomplete. If a user is in the middle of a database transaction when the system fails, the TTS rolls the database back to the point just before the transaction began. This action is known as *automatic rollback*. A second procedure performed by the TTS is roll-forward recovery; the system keeps a complete log of all transactions to ensure that everything can be recovered in the event of a complete system failure.

Level III software incorporates all features from Level II and adds a duplicate file server connected by a high-speed bus. If a file server fails, the second file server immediately assumes control over network operations. This is by far the best, most resilient system to have for client/server; however, it is also the most costly.

Novell, NetWare, and the Future

Novell believes the computer industry is now well into a second stage of LAN connectivity, in which LANs are connected to mainframe and midrange computers by gateways or by direct interfaces. Over the past several years, Novell has planned an architecture to be consistent with a future characterized by increased connectivity, seamless flow of information between large and small computers, and multivendor compatibility. Novell's plan, known as their Universal Networking Architecture (UNA), is to move toward a network architecture that will encompass any platform.

The major emphasis today in many large corporations is still on the mainframe or host computer. The LAN user is concerned with accessing mainframe applications and not with direct peer-to-peer communications between a microcomputer program and a mainframe program. Such concepts as peer-to-peer communication, ease of use, and transparency for end users will characterize the next (or third) stage of LAN connectivity.

Novell sees this third stage as a time in which, for example, an individual database record can be updated with information from various programs running on different-sized computers using different protocols and operating systems. All these differences will be resolved by NetWare in a manner that is transparent to the end user.

One piece of evidence that Novell is very serious about its UNA is its inclusion of MHS in every package of NetWare. Licensed from Action Technology, MHS provides CCITT X.400 electronic mail standards. These standards are the key to making electronic mail programs that run on different computers able to provide a universal envelope. The destination LAN's electronic mail program can open and decode this envelope.

NetWare and the Use of Heterogeneous File Servers

Novell has been developing file server software that enables a variety of different types of computers to serve as file servers under NetWare. A DEC VAX computer, for example, can do so with NetWare VMS. The VAX's file server capabilities are transparent to the end user, who still sees DOS files in their familiar format. NetWare for the Macintosh now permits an IBM DOS-based machine to serve as a file server for an AppleTalk network. NetWare translates the native AppleTalk commands from Macintosh workstations into its own Network Core Protocol, processes the commands, and then translates its own commands back into the AppleTalk protocol that the Apple workstations understand. This entire process is transparent to Apple users and PC users alike.

In December 1988, Novell announced its NetWare server strategy would include support for Network File Systems (NFS) and IBM's Server Message Block (SMB) protocols. Novell also indicated it would support Microsoft LAN Manager clients with the NetBEUI/DLC protocol. Novell's long-range NetWare server strategy, however, is to provide a broad platform capable of supporting several different kinds of file servers, including those running under UNIX, VMS, and OS/2. Connectivity to the Internet and support of the Java development language also are being added to NetWare.

Novell differentiates between *native-mode* and *host-mode* file servers. Native-mode file servers are designed for a specific hardware platform (a dedicated NetWare Intel 80486-based file server, for example) and so are inherently more efficient. Host-mode servers, on the other hand, run on top of an operating system such as UNIX or OS/2 (which also supports such services as file and print functions). There is a considerable movement in the computer industry toward server-based database applications that use such host-based server platforms as OS/2, Windows NT, and UNIX. Novell has indicated that it will support both its own native-mode server and those host-mode servers that support database applications.

NetWare for UNIX

Novell has licensed version 3.12 of NetWare to a number of vendors including Data General, IBM, and HP. These vendors ported NetWare to run on their own UNIX environments. This product was known as Portable NetWare and is now known as NetWare for UNIX. All the standard DOS and NetWare commands can be used with it.

Novell is planning a version of Portable NetWare that is processor-independent. Processor Independent NetWare (PIN), as it will be known, will operate on a variety of different processor-based machines. This way, NetWare can harness the strengths of the individual chip types such as Intel, RISC, mainframe, and so on.

Novell is working with several traditional minicomputer vendors including Hewlett Packard, Digital Equipment Corporation (DEC), and Sun Microsystems to develop native NetWare versions that will run on RISC chip-based systems—powerful machines based on the HP-PA chip, DEC's Alpha chip, and Sun's SPARC chip. The advantage for users of running native NetWare (in contrast to Portable NetWare) on a RISC-based computer is that the network operating system's performance will be optimized for that particular computer.

NetWare's Movement Toward Protocol Transparency

A virtually universal NetWare platform would provide support for multiple protocols, and Novell has been moving toward this vision. Such a platform would enable a user to have transparent access to a number of computing resources. These resources might include multiple server/client protocols and various subnet protocols.

Novell views the future as a time when the microcomputer will be at the center of computing and not a mere appendage to mainframe computers. To make this dream come true, however, the artificial barriers separating computing resources must be eliminated.

The various protocol differences create incompatibilities for UNIX-based minicomputers, DEC computers running VMS, SNA-based IBM mainframe computers, and other computing resources (such as Sun workstations running NFS protocol). Novell envisions a time when its software will help break down the barriers that make communication difficult among these different platforms.

Novell's Open Data Link Interface

Open Data Interface (ODI) software offers an interface between LAN adapter cards and different protocols. The Open Data Link Interface serves as a Novell response to Microsoft's Network Device Interface Specification (NDIS). ODI can handle as many as 32 transport protocols and 16 different adapters simultaneously. A single network is able to support multiple protocols and different types of adapter cards.

Instead of leaving the network manager to grapple with the multiprotocol issue, ODI makes the entire matter transparent to users. In effect, ODI acts as a standard network interface so that vendors need only develop network software with one generic driver. ODI provides the necessary translations required, as well as the appropriate network drivers.

ODI is composed of a link support layer that contains two programming interfaces: Multiple Link Interface (MLI) for LAN adapter device drivers and Multiple Protocol Interface (MPI) for LAN protocols. The link support layer coordinates the sending and receiving of packets by sorting the packets it receives into the correct protocol stack, which can consist of as many as 32 queues for such disparate protocols as IPX/SPX, TCP/IP, OSI, and AppleTalk.

Among the many vendors who welcomed Novell's ODI announcement in early 1989 were Apple, Compaq, and Western Digital Corporation. Sytek Corporation also indicated support for ODI by incorporating it into its Multiple Protocol Architecture and LocalNet Integrated Network Connectivity products. Sytek will develop drivers for baseband and broadband network adapter cards that use Novell's Multiple Link Interface. Novell indicated it would provide ODI-compliant drivers for its own LAN adapters, as well as for those offered by IBM and 3Com Corporation. ODI is consistent with Novell's philosophy of offering a universal platform for different network operating systems.

NetWare 4.x

NetWare 4.x is Novell's network operating system designed for enterprise computing. It can accommodate up to 1,000 users on a single server. Netware 4.x is based on the 32-bit architecture of the Intel 386 through Pentium processor range. Version 4.x is similar to the previous Novell 3.12 operating system, yet several significant improvements have been made. The major feature of 4.x is Netware Directory Services (NDS). NDS is an enterprise-wide service linking file servers and network resources, such as printers, together into a hierarchical, object-oriented directory. NDS is based on the CCITT's X.500 directory linking standard. It is a globally distributed database that provides a single point of login and is built to allow easy partitioning and replication to all servers.

Designed primarily for large networks, NetWare 4.x enables a network manager to manage dozens of file servers from a single console. It also offers enhanced remote communications. The software uses Novell's Packet Burst and Large Interpret Packet protocols, which are designed to permit larger packets to be transmitted, and cuts back on the number of acknowledgments needed to be sent to ensure that transmissions are received accurately.

Another major feature found in NetWare 4.x is a set of specifications Novell jointly developed with Kodak. Among the services provided are the ability to receive, transmit, and store images over the network. Security also has been greatly increased under NetWare 4.x. A network manager can restrict use of various network resources to authorized users. These rights define file privileges such as read, write, and delete. The network manager can also define the actions a user or program are allowed to perform. NetWare 4.x also adds powerful auditing functions. The network manager can audit collections of network containers, which are collections of network objects, server hard-disk volumes, and the events that occur with these objects. He can assign separate auditors by using different auditor passwords.

Still another significant security feature implemented in NetWare 4.x is packet authentication. The network operating system now attaches a unique, randomly generated signature to each packet generated by a workstation or server. This approach prevents intruders from capturing packets and forging a user's session identification to gain access privileges.

NetWare 4.x can take advantage of the Intel Pentium processor. It does this by using the Pentium's multithreading capabilities that allow two 32-bit instructions to process at the same time. Depending on the file server's load, this feature can improve performance by 35 percent.

Novell has stated that it will no longer develop or enhance NetWare 3.12 and that companies should transition to NetWare 4.x. For more detailed reading on Novell's NetWare 3.12 and 4.1, I recommend that you read *NetWare Unleashed* by Rick Sant'Angelo, from Sams Publishing.

UnixWare

Novell's intention to be the strategic partner of major corporations with enterprise-wide LANs has led it to add a UNIX-based product to its networking portfolio. UnixWare is a network operating system that adds native NetWare's SPX/IPX protocol to UNIX's System V release 4 (SVR4.2). It includes support for X Window as well as the ability to mount NetWare volumes.

A graphics-oriented desktop manager interface is found on both the personal UnixWare and unlimited-user server version, the Application Server. The GUI can be configured to look like the industry standard Motif OpenLook or HP Openview interfaces. UnixWare is ideal for companies that are already running NetWare over LANs as well as UNIX. It makes it possible to view and access both NetWare and UNIX files from the graphical user interface.

Windows NT Server

Microsoft supplies a file server network operating system called Windows NT Server. The NT Server software runs on top of Microsoft's 32-bit operating system, Windows NT. Microsoft's Windows NT is a very powerful, true 32-bit network operating system that is available in client and server versions. Among NT's key features are pre-emptive multitasking, multithreaded processes, portability, and support for symmetric multiprocessor processing (SMP).

Pre-emptive multitasking permits simultaneous foreground and background multitasking. Windows NT, rather than specific programs, determines when one program should be interrupted and another program executed. Multithreaded processes refers to the threads under NT that function as execution agents. Multiple threads of execution within a single process means that threads allow a process to execute different parts of a program on different processors simultaneously.

Windows NT uses the NT File System (NTFS). This file system supports file names up to 256 characters. It also permits transaction tracking. Transition tracking means that if the system crashes, NT rolls data back to its previous state just before the system crash.

Windows NT data links include support for the IEEE 802.2 specifications (Token Ring and Ethernet), the Synchronous Data Link Control (SDLC) protocol, the X.25/QLLC protocols, and the Distributed Function Terminal (DFT) specification.

Windows NT's Architecture

Microsoft designed Windows NT to be modular and portable. It is composed of a kernel as well as several different subsystems. Subsystems are available for applications running OS/2- and POSIX-compliant programs. A Virtual DOS machine (VDM) runs MS-DOS and 16-bit Windows applications.

The kernel is responsible for NT's basic operations. It allocates and synchronizes multiple processors as well as handling interrupts and error exceptions. An NT Executive manages the interface between the kernel and various subsystems. An I/O Manager handles device-independent input/output requests. The Hardware Abstraction Layer (HAL) is system-specific. It translates the NT Executive's commands into a form that can be understood by the hardware found in the physical platform running NT. By isolating hardware-specific NT commands into the HAL, Microsoft has created an architecture that makes it easy to port this network operating system to other platforms. For enhanced portability, virtually all of NT, with the exception of the HAL, is written in the C programming language.

Performance Features of Windows NT

Windows NT is a true 32-bit network operating system. Applications can execute multiple commands simultaneously. Windows NT also supports systems with multiple processors and provides the ability to perform symmetric multiprocessor processing (SMP), which means several processors can divide the work equally. A company needing exceptional performance can purchase a super server with several microprocessors, and NT will be able to take advantage of all this processing power. SMP allows system and applications requirements to be evenly distributed across all available processors, thus making everything perform much faster.

NT includes peer-to-peer networking software so that NT users can share files and applications with other users running NT or Windows for Workgroups. Another major performance advantage of NT is its method of accessing memory. It uses a flat memory model that, unlike a paged memory approach, enables applications to access up to 2 GB of RAM. Now application programmers can write larger applications.

The performance possible under NT comes at a price. The program requires at least an Intel-based 486 DX machine with at least 12 MB of RAM and 100 MB of secondary storage. Microsoft also has agreements with several companies, including Digital Equipment Corporation and MIPS Computer Systems to provide NT on a number of hardware platforms. These latest generations of microprocessors currently include Intel and RISC systems, such as the MIPS R4000 and Digital Alpha AXP.

Security Under NT

Windows NT requires users to enter a password each time they start the operating system regardless of whether they're connected to a server. Another security feature of NT is the User Manager. This program ensures that passwords adhere to corporate policy. The User Manager also permits each NT machine to be configured for the number of users, with all users given their own privilege level. You also can create groups and give everyone in a group the same privileges.

Another key security feature is the Event Viewer. This program enables network managers to view a log of all network errors and violations, including the time, date, and type of violation, as well as where the event occurred and the name of the user involved. Each time NT is started, a password is required.

NT is certifiable at U.S. government C2-level for secure environments. Microsoft has indicated that it will offer enhancements in the future that will raise NT's security level and make it even more appealing to government agencies.

Running NT with Other Network Operating Systems

Windows NT Server provides built-in file-sharing and print-sharing capabilities for workgroup computing and an open network system interface that includes built-in support for IPX/SPX, TCP/IP, NetBEUI, and other transports. NT Server is compatible with existing networks such as VINES, NetWare, UNIX, LAN Manager 2.x, and Windows 95.

Windows NT features application program interfaces (APIs) that permit network operating systems (NOS) vendors to write client software for their products to run with this product. Windows NT supports Simple Network Management Protocol (SNMP) so server activities can be managed by any SNMP network management program.

NT supports Macintosh clients, treating them as equal citizens on the network. It supports AppleTalk File Protocol v 2.1 and has full AFP security built-in. PC-created files appear with the correct Macintosh icons and resource information; Macintosh users can double-click these files to start up the right application. Macintosh users can access NT Server as they would any AppleShare server. NT's printing subsystem can handle all Macintosh PostScript print jobs on NT-based printers and send PC-originated print jobs to AppleTalk-connected printers.

Connecting NT to the Rest of the World

Windows NT comes with a service known as Remote Access Server. This service enables DOS, Windows, and NT clients to dial into an NT network, log in, and work as if they were LAN-connected, only slower. This service can handle up to 256 connections, and it uses NT's basic security scheme, including Data Encryption Standard (DES)-encrypted passwords and optional call-back. For remote communications, Windows NT also supports the X.25 protocol and Integrated Services Digital Network (ISDN). Security can be set up so that dial-in users have access to the entire LAN or just the server they dial in to.

SNA Server

The SNA Server for NT service provides connectivity to IBM mainframes through 3270, advanced program-to-program communications (APPC), NetView, and the IBM AS/400. SNA Server uses a client/server architecture to distribute the communications processing, and each PC uses standard LAN protocols to connect to the SNA Server.

Systems Management Server

The Systems Management Server allows you to centrally manage hardware and software on your LAN. You can manage PCs as assets and distribute new software and patches to them from this server. The Management Server also allows you to conduct network protocol analysis and to troubleshoot individual PCs. Because of these features, the Management Server is a very valuable tool in an NT client/server enterprise network.

Internet Information Server

Microsoft's Internet Information Server (IIS) is a Web server integrated into Windows NT Server. As such, it provides the NT platform with a host of Web applications. With the Internet Information Server, you can quickly install all the services required for the Internet and Intranets (World Wide Web, FTP, Gopher, and so on) through a graphical setup.

The IIS provides an Internet Service Manager application that simplifies operational issues by displaying all options in a graphical menu, helping you to find all IIS servers on your network and allowing you to manage remote servers over the Internet. It also optimizes site management and analysis by logging a rich collection of information directly to SQL Server for further analysis. The IIS contains a Performance Monitor to measure all Internet events in real time, and then review them for comparison and analysis for optimal capacity planning of the server. SNMP is included for reporting to a management console, if required.

IIS brings the power of Windows NT Server directory services to the Internet by providing the option of requiring user IDs and passwords to access privileged areas of your Web site. Use of Windows NT Server access control lists and users security manager delivers a sound way to safely share information with specific users or groups of users over the Internet or on your own network. Built-in Secure Sockets Layer support keeps secure communications private by encrypting the conversation between IIS and all browsers that support SSL, including Netscape Navigator, Microsoft Internet Explorer, and others. In addition, IIS extends the capabilities of the Microsoft BackOffice family of products over the Internet. The integration with BackOffice and the solutions offered for it provide some of the easiest ways to use the Web to deliver commercial solutions to your Internet customers and users.

OS/2 Warp Server

IBM's Warp Server started as a derivative of Microsoft's LAN Manager (it was originally called LAN Server), but it has differentiated itself significantly from that product. Perhaps the major improvement found in Warp Server is enhanced communications links to IBM midrange and mainframe computers. This section examines some of this network operating system's major features and explores reasons why some readers might find this program desirable for their local area networks.

Warp Server is a network operating system that runs under OS/2. This file server software provides what IBM terms "requester/server relationships" (and what the rest of the industry refers to as client/server relationships). A *requester* is a network workstation that allows users to access shared resources as well as the processing power of a server. A requester has either OS/2 LAN Requester or DOS LAN Requester installed. A DOS application running in DOS compatibility mode at an OS/2 LAN Requester workstation can access printer and disk resources on an OS/2 Warp Server.

Regardless of the term used, the software, when running under a truly multitasking operating system, enables distributed databases on a LAN to become a reality. Users need only request a particular record, and the actual processing takes place elsewhere on the network. IBM offers several products that enhance the feature set of both OS/2 and Warp Server. The Communications Manager product provides advanced peer-to-peer communications for OS/2. The DB2/2 Database Manager product provides distributed database technology that can span from PC file servers right up to corporate mainframes.

Warp Server offers enhanced database access functions because of the availability of the optional Distributed Database Connections Services/2 (DDCS/2), a component of IBM's Systems Applications Architecture. This feature permits connections between host databases and the databases on remote network client stations.

The concept of a *domain* is very important on a Warp Server network. A group of workstations and one or more servers comprise a domain. A user who is given a user ID for the domain can log on to the domain from a requester workstation and access the domain resources. The network administrator designates one network server within each domain as the domain controller; the domain controller manages that domain and coordinates communication between servers and requesters. Warp Server requires that a minimum of one domain be created and that a server act as a domain controller. A further server can be designated the backup domain controller.

One very valuable feature of Warp Server (known as location independence) enables the network administrator to treat a group of network servers as a single server. In such a case, users can access files on any server without being required to know which server the information resides on.

Unlike other network operating systems, Warp Server utilizes OS/2's power to track network activity and issue alerts. Its graphics-oriented user interface is consistent with IBM's Systems Application Architecture (SAA), the company's long-range plan for providing a uniform interface across its product line. Another SAA goal is to provide transparent movement of information across IBM's range of computers. Warp Server is preferable to other network operating systems for customers who have a heavy investment in IBM mainframe equipment. It offers enhanced micro-mainframe communications with its Communications Manager and enhanced access to mainframe databases with its DB2/2 and DDCS/2 range.

Security Under Warp Server

User Profile Management (UPM) enables network administrators to require validation for a user ID and password at logon time. Warp Server's access control system provides additional security by providing a set of permissions that allow a network administrator to grant users various levels of access to shared resources.

Network administrators also can grant various operator privileges for areas such as Accounts Operator, Print Operator, Comm Operator, and Server Operator. These operators have the following privileges:

■ A user with Accounts Operator privileges can manage users and groups within a domain. This user has the privileges to add, modify, or delete users and groups.

■ Users with Print Operator privileges can manage print queues and print jobs. They can create, modify, or delete printers or queue servers within a domain. They also can share print queues and manage remote jobs on shared queues. These management tasks can be performed from the command line or by using Print Manager.

■ Users with Comm Operator privileges can manage serial devices. These users can share serial devices and manage shared serial devices as well.

■ Users with Server Operator privileges can manage aliases and other shared resources. They can view network status within a domain. They also can create, modify, or delete aliases or other shared resources. An *alias* is a nickname for a resource. These nicknames are created because they are much easier to remember and use than the more official *netname* for a resource.

IBM LAN Server/400

IBM has another product similar to Warp Server called LAN Server/400. What is interesting about this product is that it is a file server running on an adapter card that fits into IBM's Midrange AS400 computer. This means that a company can consolidate its main computer (AS400) with its file servers. The card is referred to as the File Server I/O Processor or FSIOP for short. The benefit of using this approach includes the potential availability of the disk drives on the AS400 (up to 128 gigabytes per FSIOP).

The LAN Server/400 FSIOP can run IBM Warp Server and Novell NetWare 4.1 and also act as a Lotus Notes Server. It provides AS/400-based companies with an interesting option for running their client/server systems as it offers a very high level of robustness and integration between the business server (the AS/400) and the network operating system.

Banyan VINES

Designed for large enterprise-wide networks, VINES offers a preview of the next stage of network connectivity. Its transparent bridges and global directory (StreetTalk) make it a leader in internetwork connectivity.

> **NOTE**
>
> Banyan's software technology is a group of integrated services delivered consistently across multiple networks throughout an enterprise network.

Banyan Systems' VIrtual NEtworking System (VINES, previously an acronym and now a trademark) is a network operating system based on a heavily modified version of UNIX. VINES places a premium on internetwork connectivity, security, and transparent operations. VINES supports a wide variety of hardware platforms, including IBM's Token Ring, SMC ARCnet, Interlan Ethernet, 3Com's EtherLink and EtherLink Plus, and Proteon's ProNET-10. It requires a dedicated file server.

All VINES services, including naming, file, printer, and mail, execute as UNIX processes. These services can be stopped and started from the server without disrupting other services. Although computer industry experts have long extolled the multitasking and multiuser capabilities of UNIX, they have pointed out that its wide acceptance by the general public would be hindered by its lack of a user-friendly interface. VINES version 6.0 provides support for clients running DOS, Windows, Windows 95, OS/2, Macintosh, and a variety of UNIX clients. A VINES 6.0 server can communicate with clients supporting the following protocols: VINES/IP, IPX, IP, AppleTalk, and NetBIOS.

StreetTalk

> **NOTE**
>
> The key to VINES' internetwork connectivity is its distributed database, StreetTalk, which provides a global directory for network communications.

StreetTalk is VINES' distributed database, which serves as its resource-naming service. Resources can represent users, services (such as printers, file volumes, or gateways), and even lists. The StreetTalk name structure is threefold, with each part separated by the @ symbol.

```
object@group@organization
```

As an example, Alan Williams, an account executive in PolyTex General's Western regional office, might have a StreetTalk name such as the following:

```
ALANWILLIAMS@SALES@WESTERN
```

With StreetTalk and VINES, a user does not need to know pathways or the location of users (or other resources). If Alan needs to send a message to Greg Guntle working in the Southwestern regional office, he needs only to know Greg Guntle's name. StreetTalk takes care of the mechanics of finding Guntle's node address and routing the material to him accurately.

StreetTalk Management

Banyan added several new management features with its StreetTalk III version. Network managers can rename users and move groups across a network. This approach is vastly superior to the former method of deleting users and lists, and then re-entering them with new names and profiles.

A StreetTalk Directory Assistance (STDA) feature functions as a replicated, advanced, easy-to-use, fast StreetTalk name lookup service comparable to an automated white and yellow pages directory. Users can search lists, printers, file services, and other services or nicknames by name, description, attributes, or patterns.

Banyan Systems has taken several VINES system-level services, including StreetTalk, and incorporated them in its Enterprise Network Services for NetWare (ENS). This product enables Novell NetWare LANs to enjoy the single-login directory services enjoyed by VINES users. Because many companies have several LANs running different network operating systems, ENS offers network managers with LANs running both VINES and NetWare to manage these LANs using VINES' superior system services.

Security Under VINES

VINES provides several different layers of security. A network administrator can require a password for login to the network. He or she can also specify the hours and days permitted for a particular user to log in to the network. VINES version 3.0 and later contains security software known as VANGuard.

VANGuard lets the administrator limit the number of simultaneous logins, set specific locations from which users must log in, and require users to change their logins at specified intervals. In addition, users' access can be restricted to a specific file server.

Under VINES, each user, service, and communications link has an access rights list (ARL), which specifies the users who are authorized to use it. The network administrator can establish the access rights to a file volume, but individual files cannot be restricted.

VINES Gateways to Other Networks

The major strength of VINES is in its ability to provide transparent access to network resources, regardless of where they are or what protocol they happen to be using. Banyan's TCP/IP routing software enables a PC user to access TCP/IP resources whether they reside on a local network or a wide area network without worrying about these physical details.

As an example, VINES mail can be sent to SMTP mail users using the SMTP Mail Gateway option. VINES mail addresses are automatically converted into the standard SMTP format (user@host@domain) or UUCP-style address (host!host!host!user). The VINES' TCP/IP program encapsulates TCP/IP packets within VINES packets for travel across a VINES network.

A server equipped with the TCP/IP routing option strips the VINES headers and sends the packets to an attached TCP/IP host or gateway.

Emulating an IBM 3274/6 cluster controller, the VINES 3270/SNA option supports up to 96 concurrent sessions per server with up to 32 sessions supported by a single communications link. The software permits up to four concurrent host sessions and one DOS session per PC. In addition to providing 3278/79 terminal emulation, the software permits host print jobs to be performed on local PC printers, file transfers, and APIs so that users can build DOS-based applications to communicate with SNA host applications.

Banyan also offers a VINES SNA Communications Server. This software includes 3270 terminal emulation features, NetView support, and up to 254 concurrent sessions. This server offers access to IBM Advanced Program-to-Program Communications (APPC) at both the desktop and server. This allows client/server applications to interact at the desktop, server, and host.

VINES and Symmetric Multiprocessor Processing (SMP)

A number of super file servers have been developed that use multiple processors. Multiple processors use either symmetric multiprocessor processing (SMP) or asymmetric multiprocessor processing (AMP). Under SMP, work is divided among processors on the basis of volume of work with each processor receiving an equal share. Under AMP, work is divided on the basis of job type. VINES (4.0 and later) offers support for SMP on servers such as Compaq's dual-processor SystemPro and AT&T's four-processor StarServer E.

The VINES Applications Toolkit

The Banyan VINES Applications Toolkit is an advanced UNIX System V development environment for VINES, providing C language APIs for X.25, TCP/IP, and serial interfaces to support network communications. Several other features are noteworthy:

- The Toolkit provides access to VINES Socket Communications protocols, enabling developers to write media-transparent applications.
- A UNIX/DOS bridge file service enables DOS-based programs to share and interchange source code with the UNIX environment.
- A network compiler implements remote procedure calls, which generate the code required for application-to-application communications.

VINES Network Management

Banyan offers network management software that provides LAN and LAN-interface statistics, as well as detailed information on servers, disk activity, and overall network performance. Designed as a network diagnostic tool, this software provides network administrators with information on file server cache size, percentage of cache hits, the number of times the file system was unavailable, and such vital signs of overall network performance as total messages sent and received, number of messages dropped, and the average amount of swapping. In addition, network administrators can view activities across multiple servers simultaneously.

Banyan offers the VINES Assistant for enhanced network management functions. This software enables a network manager to modify global network configurations, automate maintenance tasks, and monitor server capacity. The VINES Assistant also can perform historical performance analysis. Network managers can graphically view and analyze historical performance metrics as well as closely monitor server resources and performance.

VINES now supports IBM's NetView, enabling an IBM host running NetView to monitor a VINES network. VINES also supports the Simple Network Management Protocol (SNMP), which provides the hooks necessary to link with SNMP-based network management systems.

The Future for VINES

Banyan has a number of plans for VINES to run on additional platforms. The company plans to add UNIX and Windows NT client support, enhance VINES' e-mail capabilities, and provide new system-level services. It has already developed a Santa Cruz Operation UNIX version of VINES and has indicated development of software that will enable VINES users to exchange files with NetWare users. One system-level service that could make VINES more interesting to managers of enterprise-wide networks is the ability to support large image and sound files.

In order for VINES to remain attractive to companies with enterprise-wide networks, the product's ability to facilitate communications with other communications platforms will be improved, according to Banyan Systems. The company intends to enhance its Intelligent Messaging system to act as a server platform for messaging-enabled applications such as workflow management. Intelligent Messaging will support Vendor Independent Messaging (VIM), Novell's Message Handling System (MHS), Microsoft Corporation's mail application programming interface (MAPI), and Apple's Open Collaborative Environment (OCE).

Banyan Systems also will add support of the CCITT X.400 and Simple Mail Transfer Protocol (SMTP) e-mail standards directly into its Intelligent Messaging system.

Summary

The components required to build your client/server systems will normally be dictated to a certain extent by the technology that already exists within your company. As a result, your connectivity and component needs may narrow to a few required devices. However, you may have noticed that each component discussed in this chapter can integrate via communications protocols with each other. This makes deciding which the servers and clients to use so much more difficult.

At the end of the day, therefore, the decision should be based on the business needs regarding the software that you develop to fulfill business requirements. The remainder of this book focuses on how to deliver client/server systems and how to take advantage of the technologies outlined in this chapter.

PART

II

IN THIS PART

Building the Blueprint

Considerations for Migrating to Client/Server

5

by Neil Jenkins

Moving to client/server is a big move. The client/server environment can give significant advantage to those developing in it, yet can also cause a lot of problems if it is not planned and implemented well. For every well-built client/server system, there are as many, if not more, equally monumental disasters that have either failed to deliver the business benefits that were expected or had to be completely scrapped for some reason.

This chapter focuses on the things you need to think about if you are about to embark on the journey of building a client/server system. Migrating to client/server systems forces an organization to take a good look at the systems that it already has in place. Throughout this chapter, I will refer to an organization's current systems as its *legacy* systems. I refer to them in this way to help you distinguish the difference between legacy and new client/server. The move to client/server can be done for a number of reasons. This fundamental change is being brought about by the way that companies are beginning to use their computers and Information Systems (IS) to leverage competitive advantage. The advent of new techniques such as business process re-engineering, rightsizing, and downsizing have caused the IS divisions to focus on building better systems for the business. As the business has begun to change, so have the Information Systems. It's fair to say that the start of personal computing, workgroup computing, and client/server will be viewed in years to come as causing the same revolutionary effect on IS as the use of Online Transaction Processing did to the batch environment.

The problem now, however, comes from the confusion and chaos that reigns in the current client/server marketplace. The client/server environment itself is made up of many fundamental components—the client, the servers, the network—and can be of any number of permutations. These components are typically from different vendors, and interoperability is a major issue. Deciding which environment to be in, how to build it, and perhaps, above all, how to deliver the competitive advantage has become the major dilemma for client/server systems builders in the late 1990s. In addition, confusion reigns in the vendor arena as future enhancements and the support of older systems come into question. Future enhancement plans are not normally forthcoming or known, and support for older systems is typically withdrawn shortly after the newest versions come to the marketplace.

It is not all doom and gloom, however. The client/server computing models define the way successful organizations will use technology for the next decade. It is the result of the downsizing and re-engineering activities within business that has brought about the move from mainframe and midrange computing to the desktop/local area network environment. The use of effective client/server tools, new development environments, and graphical user interfaces (GUIs) will allow the business to work far better with their information than they have done in the past. Effective use of data warehousing and information accessibility via ad hoc queries will allow the users to shrug off their continual reliance on IS personnel for the supply of data, reports, and the like. The freedom brought about will still have to be properly controlled, managed, and further developed; however, I believe that the role of IS has now irrevocably changed. Your Information Systems staff must begin to develop an understanding of client/server, its possible architectures, concepts, requirements, and support needs. The staff must be in a position to offer this understanding to the user community so that your business continues to develop its solutions. Failure to do so will result in an IS department that forever maintains the current legacy systems and a business that will, in time, go nowhere.

When developing or planning for client/server, you must take into account certain considerations, which cover three main areas. In the remainder of this chapter, I will cover these areas in detail. The areas are:

- The business impact of client/server
- The hardware impact of client/server
- The software impact of client/server

The Business Impact of Client/Server

A client/server system is made up of business requirements. There should be some defined or analyzed beneficial reason for moving to client/server. This reason normally exists because a company takes the view that it can build a competitive advantage by moving to client/server. Where possible, companies are taking every advantage to reduce costs, improve quality and quantity of product, and provide better service. The successful companies of the late '90s have realized that they need to be market driven, competitive, and demonstrate added value that sets them apart as an organization.

The industry has come a long way since client/server systems started. Many developers and systems managers understand the problems that have faced users since the early days of IS implementation, and the end users are starting to understand both the technology and, more importantly, the types of business problems client/server implementations will help them solve. This is a step removed from the situation that existed only two years ago, when all manner of surveys showed that end users neither understood the term "client/server" nor trusted suppliers to advise them on the best way to go—although many of them intended to implement some type of client/server solution. Be aware that client/server is often sold to the user environment as a cost-cutting exercise; this is a danger because it invariably does not reduce cost as much as companies expect. The business gains are more valuable. A lot of early adopters of client/server were disillusioned because the systems did not live up to the hype.

When costs weren't necessarily decreased and the solution of a focused business problem, such as reducing time to market, had not been specifically identified, the potential for end-user dissatisfaction was very high. Scant regard had been paid to the volumes of applications that users had implemented on mainframes, and these mainframes suddenly appeared to be ostracized from the client/server world. Worse still, IS departments were expected to remove or downsize from these machines, which normally ran the core business. Now companies have realized that the main benefits from client/server solutions can best be attained by a focus on some other key areas.

Your business development should be based around devolving information and data in the fastest way to those who need to make use of it. The IS division of old was often seen as an obstacle to this goal.

How Do You Migrate Legacy Data and Applications?

There is a problem. You do not have a clean slate to work from. Unfortunately, your company has to run a current system that in many ways confines and constrains what you can do with your client/server development. You face a difficult decision: whether to migrate the systems you have to a client/server model or base or to begin a new rewrite of those systems. Each answer has both advantages and disadvantages. These topics will be covered in more detail in Chapter 19, "Developing Mission-Critical Applications."

Should You Migrate or Should You Rewrite/Re-engineer?

It is always possible in some way to move (slowly) your existing legacy systems to the new client/server environment. The question you must ask is whether it is financially viable to do so. Do you move what you've got by evolving it, or do you start again by rewriting the new? If you rewrite, should you in turn re-engineer the way the work is done or the way the process is handled in order to get further improvement? This last point is a particularly important topic to understand relating to process analysis and Total Quality Management.

What About Rehost/Rebuild?

If you can simply move the system onto a smaller, better box by "rehosting" it, you may also have the opportunity to rebuild parts of it or store it in a different way. In moving the systems, do you rebuild them in a different fashion such as putting them onto multiple servers instead of just one?

The Costs of Client/Server

Client/server is not a case of something for nothing. Client/server has added a significant level of complexity to development because developers must now develop two systems instead of one. You must develop a front-end system and any number of back-end systems. In addition, the front-end itself, although presenting a seamless interface to the user, may itself be made up of a number of systems. You must figure out how to let the systems talk to each other easily, and without a big sacrifice in response time, and—a key point—you must maintain both the front-end and the back-end system as your operation changes and grows.

You have added a level of expense, as well, because you will need to purchase very fast workstations. Essentially, you have to run a graphical user interface (GUI) and then layer the front-end database on top of that! To support those two layers of CPU drain, you must buy the fastest server and workstations that you can possibly afford, with as much Random Access

Memory (RAM) as you can afford. Although faster equipment is a definite advantage, the architecture and design of the system is a far more critical factor. The best equipment and a poorly designed system can run slower than an average server and an efficiently designed system!

Because you have the expense of two development efforts instead of one, and because you need very fast workstations that can run two operating systems instead of one, you can expect client/server setups to be more expensive than a typical file server—perhaps two to three times more—but not nearly as expensive as mainframe.

R&D Is Essential

Within most commercial organizations, there is a reluctance to spend company money on research and development (R&D). Research and development is normally viewed as a waste of money; it often does not relate to a specific current business activity and thus is viewed with skepticism. It is not normally viewed as providing a return on investment.

This could not, however, be further from the truth. Now more than ever before, time, money, and effort should be spent on proactive research and development within a systems organization. The reasons for this are numerous, yet perhaps the biggest driver is the rate of change within the information technology industry. Currently processor chips, hard disk storage systems, CD-ROM drives, and RAM modules are rapidly increasing in size and speed every 18 months, and this trend is sure to continue well into the next century. With this rate of change comes the incredible power available within the client machine and the server machines. R&D, therefore, must become the manager between this rate of change and the business developments. The R&D activities should provide the vision for the use of new technology within the business. Obviously, R&D must be planned, budgeted, and justified; yet if a company is serious about developing new computer systems based on new technologies, it must be proactive with research and development. After all, the client/server systems you develop over the next few months will soon become your constraining legacy systems in a few years' time. They, too, will need to be replaced by more functionally rich, technically advanced systems born out of R&D activities and the changes in the industry. Client/server is not just a project with a beginning and an end; it is an ongoing process.

What Is the Risk and the Payback?

Pick up any computer industry magazine, and you will find it littered with tales of woe of client/server systems gone bad. A worrisome trend also to be aware of is the competitive nature of client/server vendors pointing out the failures of their competitor's products. The reality in these situations is that it is rare for a product to fail (after all, if you looked long enough, you would find equally as many successes and failures of any particular product). It is the planning, timeliness, development, and implementation that makes a client/server system win or lose.

There are essentially three lines of thought that a company follows when developing client/server. The first is that client/server is such a high risk that they decide to develop their first set of systems using business areas that return little or no financial payback. Areas typically include accounts and payroll. The end result becomes a large cost implementation for zero return; client/server is branded a failure. Even if there are some efficiency improvements, the returns are nowhere near as good as major improvements in the key business streams.

Far worse, however, is the company with the short-sighted view that they have to dive onto the client/server bandwagon for all their systems and embark on a complete computer system redesign and rebuild in a month. They decide to redevelop their mission-critical applications in client/server without anywhere near adequate knowledge of the environment. Result? Massive development cost, massive deployment, and massive risk. The system is implemented and fails almost immediately, leaving the organization with major systems problems and inexperience on how to fix this predicament. Many tool vendors are keen to point out their competitors failures at this level. Be shrewd and ask them theirs, also, because they have to have them! Another thing to realize when talking to vendors is that the company is only as good as the salesman you are talking to. One person makes you believe that the system will solve all your problems. Another might give you information about possible system incompatibilities.

The final line is to pick an application that provides the luxury of delivering business benefit and yet is not mission-critical as your first development application. This gives you the ability to learn, plan, develop, and deliver much more effectively. Development costs are reasonable and normally pale against the business return. The reasoning behind my recommendation for this approach is that client/server takes time to learn and experience. The more you do it, the better you become.

The Global Problem

Without a doubt, the hardest client/server systems to get right are those developed to be implemented across the globe. I am not talking about the application on the client residing only in one location, but the client application running in different geographic locations around the world. Figure 5.1 shows an example of this with the client application being based in North America, South America, and Eastern Europe.

FIGURE 5.1.
*A client/server system
geographically spread.*

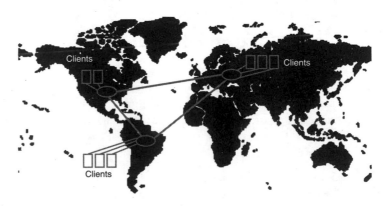

The global environment adds additional complexity for the developers in that there are additional issues to consider:

- **Language Differences** (American English, International English, Spanish, French, German)—Do you provide the application in multiple languages or are all users expected to understand your native tongue?

- **Support**—Who now supports the application at the desktop? Local teams have to be trained and helped.

- **Time Differences**—Supporting an application across the other side of the globe is very difficult when there may be a 12-hour time difference.

- **Requirements**—The business rules for each of these countries may have certain different nuances that lead to the application having some country-specific business logic within it.

- **Configuration Differences**—Different countries code pages in the operating system to support their character sets, keyboards, and language. (Mercifully, the mouse is the same around the globe!) These differences also have to be planned for in user and system testing.

- **Piloting and Implementing**—Both require staff to visit the sites and to implement to some degree; this requires additional planning, management, and resources.

- **Political Impact**—Do they really want it? If not, you will find that once implemented, the system will fail due to a lack of ownership, support, and "perceived" technical understanding. You must make sure that the business environment and possibly the IS department in the respective countries are supporting you 110 percent.

- **Version Control**—Once implemented, who maintains the code and stores the code? Can the countries make their own changes? Experience shows that there is no easy answer to this one. Central control results in inadequate local business functionality; distributed control results in a key system that rapidly gets so out of control and unsynchronized that no one area or team understands how the constituent parts are made up.

- **Currency**—Any new global client/server system has to deal with multiple currencies such as the dollar, pound, franc, and peseta.

User involvement from the countries about to use the newly developed systems seriously improves the quality of the system. Users can highlight the issues outlined in the preceding section and also take on the responsibility of ensuring that they are in the final system. If you can, try to relocate them to the development site for a short period so that they are giving you full-time attention during the design and development process.

Make sure that you fully understand the technical environment within the respective companies around the globe so that you can plan any necessary hardware and network changes well in advance of actual implementation.

Involving resources from the IS departments in the countries also benefits the development. If there are differences of opinion on the technical infrastructure or development tools to be used, try to resolve these prior to implementation. This is somewhat strange advice, but problems in countries after implementation are normally blamed on the tool rather than other factors. Ensuring buy-in at the IS department is one of the biggest problems in developing distributed, global client/server systems.

Local system testing is not indicative of the results that can be expected in a regional office. WAN (Wide Area Network) connections are considerably slower than LAN (Local Area Network) links; therefore, plan into your project response-time testing in the distant locations so that the networks can be improved and the application changed if required.

The Hardware Impact of Client/Server

The hardware in a client/server environment is considerably different than that in a mainframe environment or even that in a standard LAN-based file server environment. The hardware is often viewed as having to allow more flexibility, to be more adaptable, and to be just as reliable as your current mainframe system, as well as being *significantly* cheaper.

In the traditional mainframe or midrange environment, as shown in Figure 5.2, the terminals have no intelligence. All calculations and other processing actions take place at the host machine. These processing actions would typically include searches, sorts, calculations, data validation, data security, reads, writes, and deletes.

FIGURE 5.2.

A typical, traditional mainframe environment.

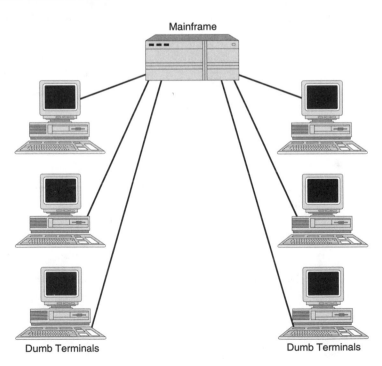

This means that the mainframe in a mainframe environment must be a very powerful and very expensive machine. Also, because every additional user-interface feature consumes expensive processing time, the user interface in a mainframe environment must necessarily be kept very simple and primitive in order to avoid overtaxing the machine. As a result, mainframe screens are character-based and are not known for being user-friendly. When was the last time you saw a character screen that looked really great?

A mainframe operation has the additional disadvantage that the central machine is very expensive to acquire, to program, and to maintain. Very rarely does an operation have an on-site backup machine; therefore, if the central machine is down, the entire operation is down until the central machine is repaired. This situation is particularly difficult when running a global system that may spread across many different geographic time zones.

Mainframe systems do have some distinct advantages: they tend to have very sophisticated security systems, and they tend to be very robust. Generally, system crashes of mainframe systems are infrequent, and because of the data recovery features of mainframe systems, rarely do crashes result in lost data. Mainframe and midrange systems can also store very large volumes of data and support many thousands of concurrent users.

Consider the local area network environment shown in Figure 5.3. In a file server environment, the server merely stores all the data and directs the data to the workstations and makes sure that there are no collisions (two workstations modifying the same record at the same time).

FIGURE 5.3.

A typical local area network (LAN) environment.

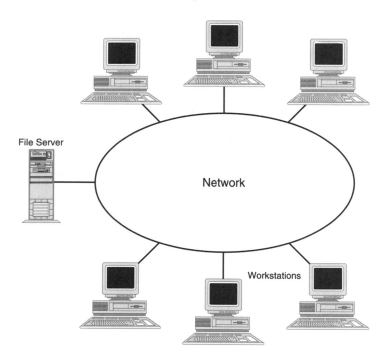

All calculation and processing takes place at the workstations: searches, sorts, calculations, data validation, and data security. Before a workstation can do its job, it must request the data from the server. These requests generate a great deal of conversation between the server and workstations. For example, consider a simple two-level sort of 10,000 records. For the workstation to do this sort, the file server must send each record across the network. If every record contains 50 fields, the file server sends all 50 fields, even though the workstation needs only two fields for the sort.

These back-and-forth requests for data generate a great deal of traffic over the LAN, meaning that the network must be very fast in order to maintain acceptable response time. Even under the best of conditions, the response time will be good, not great, because of the tremendous amount of network traffic that an active file server-based database generates. Therefore, the very architecture of the LAN creates a response-time problem. Adding to the problem is the fact that most organizations that are moving toward LAN technology are also moving toward user-friendly graphical user interfaces (GUIs), which are characterized by the Macintosh, OS/2, and Microsoft Windows interfaces. This GUI technology, with all its screen graphics, is very "hungry" for processing power. It requires so many CPU cycles to support the screen objects and the user-friendliness that it can make the entire workstation appear sluggish.

Although it may be relatively slow because of the network traffic and the graphics, the LAN/GUI idea has caught on because of four very desirable qualities:

>A LAN with GUI clients is not expensive.

>LAN with GUI clients is flexible and scalable.

>LAN with GUI clients is easily replaced.

>LAN file server development with GUI is quick, flexible, and relatively inexpensive.

A LAN with GUI Clients Is Not Expensive

The LAN environment with suitable client workstations interacting with the file server is not expensive relative to the larger midrange and mainframe environments in terms of support, physical hardware, and maintenance. It does not require a fabulously expensive central computer. A Macintosh PowerMac or an Intel Pentium with 32 MB of RAM and a fast hard disk will handle most situations. At today's market prices, this type of machine represents an investment of less than $3,500.

LAN with GUI Clients Is Flexible and Scaleable

Because the machinery is less expensive, a company has maximum flexibility in choosing a server and workstations. Whether the need is for a two-person office or for a 20-person branch operation, file server technology can be adapted to the need. Such is not the case with a mainframe system. A minicomputer system such as a small AS/400 may be ideally suited for a medium-sized branch, but it just cannot compete in the small areas.

LAN with GUI Clients Is Easily Replaced

Because the file server is in roughly the same price range as the workstations, a breakdown of the server will not put an operation out of business for any longer than it could take to convert one of the workstations to the server and to install the backup copies of the database. This makes for a highly flexible operation with minimal downtime due to equipment failure. This technique is effective for smaller environments.

LAN File Server Development with GUI is Quick, Flexible, and Relatively Inexpensive

Traditionally, mainframe and minicomputer systems development projects have been slow, inflexible, and expensive. Long development times cost a lot of money. In today's world, business conditions change so rapidly that a long-term mainframe project may be out-of-date by the time it is completed. Even if it is not outdated, a mainframe development project is very expensive compared to the cost of microcomputer development. In microcomputer development, even the mistakes are far less costly. In real dollars, a mainframe project that goes 25 percent over budget can be a much bigger disaster than a microcomputer project that goes 100 percent over budget.

File server technology, when combined with GUI technology, has cut development time from years to months; it has cut prototyping time from months to weeks—sometimes even days. This has made it possible to develop solutions so quickly that the business needs can be met and the system delivered within the required time frame. A product needed in three months can be realistically delivered within the three months time frame. How often are systems developed currently that when finished, because of delays and so on, have missed the time to market and are no longer effective?

The Problems of the LAN

When deciding on your computer systems for your client/server development, bear in mind the two main issues surrounding file server, LAN, and GUI systems. The main issues here are *data integrity* and *response time*.

Because of its relative youth, the LAN environment for database work is nowhere near as stable as that experienced on the minicomputer and mainframe computer environments. The microcomputer operating systems and microcomputer databases are not as robust as minicomputer and mainframe systems. System crashes are more frequent and data loss is more possible. This raises some concern about using file server and LAN technology to store mission-critical data.

One fact that contributes to the data integrity problem is that individual users who make casual mistakes can have a much greater impact than a person with the same level of security access could have on a mainframe system. For example, in a LAN environment, if a user at one workstation ignores the rules and loads a floppy disk that has not been sanitized for viruses, that one user action could cause the entire system to come crashing down.

The preceding example does not happen often, but it does happen frequently enough to warrant some concern about the robustness of microcomputer databases and to warrant some extra caution when administering those databases.

Response time is the number two user-interface issue of file server databases, behind the aforementioned data integrity. Aside from the database not running reliably, lack of speed has historically been the number-one user complaint. The color and graphics of GUI are pleasant changes, but users do not like to sit and wait while the machine "thinks" (it's at this point they sometimes hit the Reset switch thinking the machine has crashed!). When users push a button or type a series of characters, they want "instant" response.

Users are accustomed to very fast (often subsecond) response time from their legacy applications. Like it or not, response time is a very big issue. If you want to effectively downsize by moving the GUI/file server technology into more and more mission-critical applications, you will have to deal with the response time issue. This issue gets interesting when applied to client/server. This is because it may not be possible to improve the response time of any one particular transaction, but it may be possible to improve the overall process significantly. Ask yourself the question: Is it better for the user to go through 20 mainframe screens each taking one second or one client/server system screen taking five seconds? The "perceived" response time of the client/server system is slower, yet the overall process is some 15 seconds faster! User education and training can circumvent a lot of the perception problems.

Client/Server Technology

I've covered the main considerations of both the LAN environment and the host computer systems. The real benefit in client/server development comes from using the strengths of both of these systems to the extent that they become one integrated client/server system. Taking advantage of the flexibility and low cost of the workstation/LAN environment and the reliability, integrity, and multiuser capabilities of the minicomputer and mainframe environments, you can begin to build great client/server systems. You must endeavor to get the best from both of these environments:

- The response time and data integrity of mainframe character-based systems
- The speed of development, flexibility, and cost savings of PC/LAN/file server GUI-based systems

The systems you build should achieve this balance by intelligently dividing the processing work between the front end (the clients) and the back end (the servers). The back end handles all the global data manipulation tasks: searching, sorting, storing, and security. The front end handles all the local user interface tasks: screen management, local calculations, and query-building.

Client/Server: An Example

Here is one example of intelligently splitting the work done by the client and a server. When a client workstation requests data from the server, the server sends back only the data needed to satisfy the query. If the workstation is displaying six fields on the screen in a repeating list, the server sends back only those six fields for each record, not the entire 50 fields that may be contained in the actual record on the server. When the user double-clicks to modify a particular record, the server sends all 50 fields for that one record. The workstation makes the modifications and then sends the updated record back to the server for storage. The result of splitting the work will be a system that is fast, secure, reliable, easy-to-use, and inexpensive.

The Software Impact of Client/Server

The biggest difficulties you will experience when starting client/server development will undoubtedly be with the software you choose, use, and implement. This is because the development of client/server systems requires an extra amount of effort in the design and building of the architecture that traditionally has not been the responsibility of the application development team.

You have already seen that a client/server system is made up of a number of parts, as shown in Figure 5.4. Each of the pieces in the puzzle was normally handled by one section of an IS department. Within a client/server system, these pieces are now inexorably linked. This situation creates a number of issues and considerations that have to be overcome.

FIGURE 5.4.

Parts of the client/server puzzle.

The Client/Server Puzzle - All The Pieces

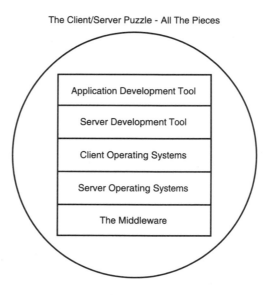

The Tools Are Linked

You should realize that the tools needed to build a client/server environment are linked. This is different than developing on a single machine system, such as COBOL on a mainframe. In the client/server world, you have to have a tool that can be used for client development and server development. Don't forget that you also may need a tool for access between the two. This tool is often called *middleware* or the glue that connects the client to the servers. Because you have now added potentially two further tools to your application development kit bag, the complexity of the system has increased. Be aware also that the tools used on the client machine need to be as robust and scalable as the tools you used in your previous legacy systems (typically minicomputer or mainframe).

The first generation of client/server development tools that have appeared over the past few years basically offered no more than graphical rapid application development (RAD) on PCs. Using these tools focused you on what you see on the screen rather than on the complexity of the application underneath (this is why tools such as PowerBuilder, Visual Basic, and Delphi are often referred to as "gloss"). These early tools forced the user into the world of middleware and often created problems with scalabilty. They tightly integrate user interface code with application logic, requiring that all the logic reside on the client. If that logic involves data access, the scalability that would be provided by moving that logic to the server becomes almost impossible. This integration also forces all data to be moved across the network between client and server, resulting in potential difficulties with the network and response time.

Newer tools, the so-called second generation of client/server application tools, are now beginning to appear. These tools are beginning to ease the increased levels of complexity and seriously improve the productivity of the programmer on the user interface, application logic, data management, and server integration. These tools also include sophisticated services to handle the development process, which typically involves teams of developers. Also, the tools' deployment capabilities accommodate a range of cross-platform enablers at the interface, middleware, and networking levels. Tools at this level include Progress and Magic.

It is very difficult to move company-wide development from the mainframe to client/server because you may not have the same tools and capabilities that were an integral part of host development. These tools have recently begun to appear on the market, yet they are still in their early days when compared to the development suites that are available in the mainframe or midrange environments.

In addition to these changes, you have to consider how you are going to build your component parts of the client/server system. You will have to cross-skill your developers if your systems are to be effective. I firmly believe that the role of the programmer is changing. A programmer of the future will be employed for his or her ability to develop and program rather than for the languages he or she knows. This is because the client/server world is building developers that have to know both server and client environments if they are to be effective. Programmers will need to focus more on logic and concepts rather that the syntax of programming languages. In the ever-evolving client/server environment, tools surface and become obsolete very rapidly.

Networking and the Operating Systems

A programmer once said that he had developed on an AS/400 an application that had buried within its code the "mother of all arrays." This array required a lot of programming logic, disk I/O, and CPU utilization. This programmer then began to develop client/server systems, and not one of them worked. There is a particular reason for this, and that reason should be a consideration of yours when developing client/server systems and staffing your development teams. The reason is that application development departments are normally based on one machine. In most sites, this machine is the corporate mainframe. As you move to client/server, you will undoubtedly need to shift these resources across to client/server development. A few of these resources will begin the new task of client development. You will probably find that this approach does not work. The code that will be developed will be like those arrays: slow, cumbersome, and ineffective. This is because development on the client is very different than development on the server platform. Development on mainframe or midrange machines is not normally hindered by the lack of random access memory in the machine or the speed of disk I/O. Yet on the client, these things become vital. You should therefore get your client development team trained on the more physical aspects of the client environment. This will aid them in the development process. Client systems should also be modular in design such that an application is made up of a number of parts that are loaded and unloaded when necessary. This design speeds up operation and improves the application.

Understanding the network environment is another valuable lesson that needs to be taught. The development teams are often used to the data that they are accessing being on the same machine. This is no longer the case with client/server. It *may* be on the same machine, but it is more than likely on another local computer on the LAN or may even be in another country via the Wide Area Network (WAN). Data location also gets even more complex if the application has to interact with multiple servers, each providing pieces of the overall application data. The network provides the means to access this data, and the programmers should be aware of the additional considerations involved. This knowledge is particularly relevant to developing systems with great response time.

The Software Tools Are Rapidly Changing

The software tools for the development of client/server systems are rapidly changing. It is currently one of the major growth areas. You are now faced with the unenviable position of moving to client/server; you study the products available and realize that a great one will be along in three months, then another, then another. You end up never starting. The tools you pick today to develop your client/server system will not necessarily be the tools you end up developing with for the future. Therefore, do not spend forever picking a tool; any tool with the right developers (such as ones who have tried and succeeded, tried and failed, and learned from their mistakes) will work for your system.

When selecting tools for large-scale application development, you need to consider their development capabilities, deployment capabilities, and the flexibility of the tool to adapt to changes over time. For example, development tools used to build company-wide applications must support complexities across the user interface, logic, and data components of the application. In terms of deployment, the tools must be able to handle the issues presented by multiple computing platforms, ever increasing numbers of users, and multiple databases.

The tools must also provide flexibility over time. Products, services, and business units continually evolve; development and deployment environments must mirror and support these changes. Today's departmental application may evolve into an enterprise-wide application tomorrow. One large department may be divided into two business units and become geographically split, possibly internationally. Second generation client/server development environments are designed to handle such changes.

How Big Is the Application?

There are many common elements to application development. There are numerous business tasks and requirements, each of which dictates that programmers may select different approaches and implement them using different tools.

A company that typically has small, self-contained projects that are delivered to small numbers of users would require a tool environment that could be developed in quickly, and each project could be considered a "throwaway." In another company, an individual department might need to access key corporate data through a flexible GUI. In both instances, a RAD approach with first-generation development tools would be suitable to get the job done quickly and efficiently. In these situations, a high-end tool would be overkill.

Even in the context of scenarios such as these, developers should proceed with caution. Many applications are originally approached as "departmental" only to become required for longer than planned, implemented across multiple departments (even across the globe), sometimes even becoming critical to the enterprise. It is a good idea to examine the enterprise implications of an application, even if at first it seems to be one easily handled by first-generation tools. I cannot stress this point enough. This problem frequently occurs in the development of client/server applications.

Most companies, however, require sophisticated and widely used applications. These applications handle complex parts of a company's business and need to be designed for longevity, reliability, and serious business benefit. The problem is you never know how much more complex the business will become over time. Many business issues could drive significant changes in the infrastructure: a move into new channels, a merger or an acquisition, or even the forming of new partnerships. The company may double or triple if business expands, or the organizational structure itself may be in flux due to rightsizing initiatives.

An organization may be in the process of distributing responsibility for different aspects of the business to business units around the globe. To further complicate things, the company may, at a later point, decide to return to a more centralized management structure. In this case, an organization should combine extensive planning with second-generation client/server technology to develop the types of applications to meet its changing needs.

Considerations for the Software Tools

A client/server development environment must address the three components present in any application: user interface, application and business logic, and data management and data access.

User Interface

The presentation services, or *user interface*, is the portion of an application that manages the way the user interfaces with the application. Although developers spend a lot of time on this portion, it typically represents only 12 percent to 50 percent of the total development effort for that application. Unfortunately, this element is usually what makes or breaks the application to most users.

The most critical aspect of user interface development is to ensure that the visual components of the development process are separable from logic and data. When developing the user interface, you should ensure that the interface has the following properties:

- Has reusable user interface objects, modules that can be used in other programs
- Can be used for cross-platform development, for example, Windows and OS/2 if required
- Uses the various client/server models to meet the business needs
- Capable of internationalization, can support multiple languages, currencies, and typefaces if required

User Interface Objects

Most tools today offer good graphical development environments. But in selecting a tool, developers must not confuse graphical development environments with object orientation. Being able to create code or an object by using a graphical tool does not mean that that code or object can be reused in another application or in another setting without recoding. An object-oriented development environment allows programmers to take advantage of predesigned object components that have been built by commercial developers or other internal developers. The big benefit to you is that reusable user interface objects offer the capability to set standards across an organization, ensuring consistency and a common look and feel across applications; this results in improved productivity for end users. Applications take on the same "look and feel" across the organization.

Reusable user interface components will greatly enhance programmer productivity because they have already been debugged, tested, and documented. Examples of reusable commercial products are predefined application templates designed to shortcut key aspects of complex development and custom controls designed for the Windows environment. Reusable objects are available for most client/server development tools, including Visual C++, Delphi, Progress, and Visual Basic.

Cross-Platform Support

It may not be possible to develop your application for one particular operating system and user interface. You may find that you have to develop for X Window, Windows, and OS/2. These add complexity to the development environment and obviously dictate a development language that supports all your required systems. Choosing a tool that offers cross-platform support will help you deal with this complexity.

The Client/Server Models

In reality, businesses are driven by both events and procedures. Yet the truth is that most popular development tools are implemented assuming only a procedural model of development. This follows the "first this, then this, then this" mentality. As organizations begin defining business events in addition to business procedures, it becomes increasingly important for a development tool to be able to easily handle both event-driven and procedural programming models. The user interface tools must allow the varied use of the client/server models to achieve the business goal; if a tool locks you into a particular model, don't use it. The best systems make good use of each of the five different client/server models mentioned in Chapter 1, "Information: The Driving Force."

Internationalization

As more corporations expand beyond their local borders, they must provide applications with screens, reports, and messages in native languages. Tools that allow developers to develop a single version of an application that handles multiple languages can dramatically impact the effectiveness and timing of global applications. Applications developed with these tools should be able to simultaneously "understand" different languages and character sets input by different users.

Application and Business Logic

Business logic is the heart of client/server application development and represents the main work effort for application developers in a project. When evaluating tools for development, you should consider the following in terms of application logic capabilities:

- Modularity to handle complexity
- Role of transactions
- Object orientation
- Ease of integration with other technologies
- Database and platform independence
- Capability to provide batch processing

Modularity

A development tool should not have to combine user interface logic with business logic, especially if scalability is an issue. Also, just because an application was designed with a client/server tool does not mean it was designed to handle increasing degrees of complexity. Scalability comes from well-thought-out and well-structured techniques. The development tool and developers you choose should foster the modular development of business logic, producing objects that are reusable and applications that can easily handle increasing complexity. Do not expect the tool to do all this for you; good developers can make this happen for most good tools.

Role of Transactions

The first series of client/server systems were typically used to develop either decision support applications or applications involving simple transactions or light transaction loads. Tools such as PowerBuilder and Visual Basic flourished in these environments. Large-scale applications bring not only increased transaction complexity but also the requirement for increased transaction loads. Tools such as Progress are much better suited to these applications.

Object Orientation

Object orientation in second-generation client/server environments helps mask the complexity of the underlying enterprise infrastructure; it also provides the benefit of reuse, significantly increasing developer and programmer productivity.

Companies building large-scale applications are finding they can design reusable libraries for use by large development teams. These reusable libraries capture important complex business logic, reducing the chance that developers will introduce logic errors. Reuse can also dramatically speed up the development process, especially when a large-scale, complex application is being designed. These objects can be used in whatever application is required. The programmer sends a set of parameters (data) to the object, the business logic is applied to this data, and the results are returned to the calling program.

Integration with Other Technologies

Businesses are no longer stand-alone. It is inevitable that systems are now also becoming networked. Your applications at some point will need to "talk" to other systems. Not in a "Terminator 2: Skynet" malignant fashion, but more from an ability-to-exchange-information point of view. Your systems will need input and output capabilities to do this. Systems must be able to interact with other applications and data. Furthermore, the development tool used to create these systems should provide this capability without forcing the developer to drop into C or some other low-level language. Examples might include Electronic Data Interchange (EDI) links to your customers and banks, built-in electronic mail (e-mail) to the Internet, and automatic data extraction from a supplier's database.

Database and Platform Independence

Pilot or departmental applications often need to deal with only one database or platform. But large-scale applications must often be able to seamlessly access multiple, and possibly heterogeneous, databases as well as be able to run across multiple operating systems. For example, corporate-wide client/server applications often need to access and update legacy data as well as newer heterogeneous data sources across the enterprise. This data is found on a variety of flat files, hierarchical mainframe systems, and relational databases running on many hardware platforms.

Therefore, when selecting client/server tools, it is important to evaluate their capabilities in these areas. A client/server tool must allow the programmer to develop a single set of logic that will work across multiple databases and/or operating system platforms. Figure 5.5 shows how a potential client/server system might have to link with a variety of new and existing databases across both LANs and a WAN.

FIGURE 5.5.

The potential database accesses required for a client/server system.

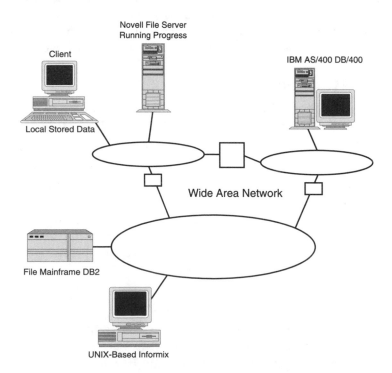

The client machine might need to access data simultaneously from the local Novell NetWare file server running the Progress database, local data on the client itself in Microsoft Access, a local IBM AS/400 running DB/400 on another internal LAN, an IBM mainframe running DB2 across a WAN link, and a Hewlett Packard UNIX processor running Informix across a WAN link.

Role of Batch Processing

I expect you thought that client/server would kill off batch processing! Well, that's not the case. Even in an event-driven client/server world, there are requirements for batch reporting and processing. For example, large statistical consolidation reports should be run offline. A second-generation client/server tool should be able to handle batch processing and should also let a developer address this part of the application using the same skill set required to build all the other parts of the application.

Data Management and Data Access

In terms of data management, the development of large-scale applications dictates the need for a consistent repository for data definitions and business rules. This repository should be seamlessly integrated into the development tool to ensure maximum developer productivity. The considerations are quite simple on this; make sure that the development tool you choose provides such a repository.

Further, as part of the overall modular architecture of client/server as shown in the five models, data should be separate from application logic and business rules. This is a big shift from traditional programming methods and will cause your programmers the biggest grief. This separation allows data to change without affecting the integrity of the application. In addition, with a good technical infrastructure, the data can be moved from platform to platform with no modification or minimal modification to the client application. When data is integrated with business logic, the entire application must be changed and modified each time a data element changes. This is where the major maintenance costs come in. Separation of data from application logic provides a faster way to maintain and change applications.

Summary

Client/server development and migration takes time to learn. You are not born with it. It is like learning to ride a bike. First you wobble a lot and fall off, and then you get more stable and don't fall off as much. In time, you are riding like the best.

Client/server is the same; each development project is different. As such, the considerations to be made are also unique to each project. In time, as you face and overcome more and more client/server challenges, you will gain the experience to identify early on the problems that might trip you up or cause the project to falter. Successful client/server is about overcoming these obstacles and delivering the business benefit.

Steps for Migrating to Client/Server

6

by Neil Jenkins

You have seen from the previous chapter that building client/server systems requires a good deal of thought at the initial stages in order to overcome the variety of difficulties that often arise. When you consider moving to client/server, create a sound project plan that identifies the main activities that need to be done. This plan also provides a framework for solving the issues that have been identified in Chapter 5, "Considerations for Migrating to Client/Server."

This chapter lays out the foundation of project management for client/server and helps you plan and identify the various steps that will help build good client/server systems.

Client/Server Factors for Success

Many factors contribute to the success of a client/server development project. Good use of project management and a methodology are two of the most essential ingredients. They increase the likelihood of achieving the planned project goals and also promote a working environment where the morale is high and the concentration is intense. This environment is critical today where technology for client/server is so fluid, and the need for isolating the developer from the specific technologies is so significant.

Project Management

Client/server project management does not differ that much from traditional development planning, but it does contain a number of nuances that distinguish it from a normal development process. These nuances are as follows:

- A complete plan including technical and hardware-based work
- Early user involvement throughout the project life cycle (analysis and prototyping)
- Extended system and user testing activities
- A structured implementation plan and project review
- Team building and staff morale activities (optional!)
- A next project enhancement review
- Proof of concept activities including both hardware and software research, development, and testing

Furthermore, the structure of a client/server development project is somewhat different to that of a traditional single system development project. New activities are in the project plan, including workflow design (see Chapter 15, "Workflow"), prototyping, and legacy system integration (see Chapter 19, "Developing Mission-Critical Applications"). When these tasks are added to a project plan, the duration of the project plan is likely to increase.

Commonly, a client/server application development plan is supposed to be completed faster than a traditional system. An organization's first client/server development project, however, does not follow this rule. In fact, the project normally takes longer than everyone thinks or plans that it will. Organizations and project planners usually do not take into consideration the extra time required to get over the learning curve of new systems, tools, and technologies as well as then having to apply these new things to a business process that is being built from scratch or redesigned. Invariably, a first client/server system project will overrun its planned duration by at least 30 percent. Such a project normally runs over budget as well, although this amount is harder to track because the costs are normally intangible, such as learning time, unproductive time due to the lack of knowledge, and the time spent holding meetings that do not resolve anything (have you been to those also?). As it is wrong to assume a person with a toolbox full of mechanics tools is capable of repairing your Porsche, so it is also wrong to assume that the right client/server tools will make a good developer. Figure 6.1 shows how the first project built using client/server relates to normal projects.

FIGURE 6.1.

The first client/server project will take more time than a normal development project.

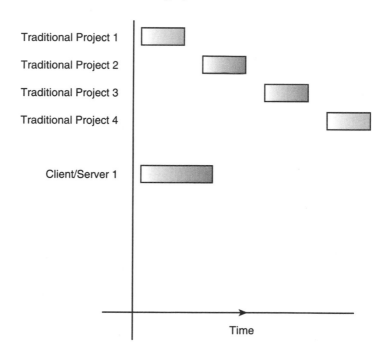

The only way to overcome this time consumption is to spend more time up front planning and determining the scope of the project, perhaps spending time also training staff members before they move onto the development project. As your development experience and that of your development staff improves, the project duration will reduce, as long as you keep the same number of staff. Figure 6.2 shows how you can expect development time to decrease as your client/server development experience grows. This figure obviously assumes that you are moving to a client/server toolset that you will use for a number of projects. If you continually change toolsets after each project, you will find your development becomes very complicated. Your IS staff will need to become learn-on-the-fly developers!

FIGURE 6.2.

This graph shows how development time is reduced as experience with client/server increases.

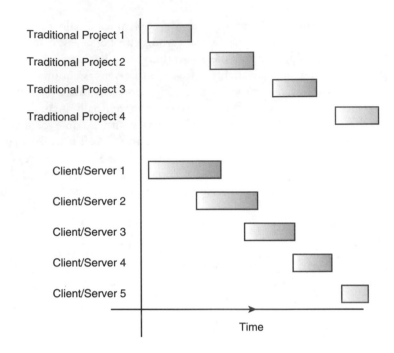

Training has a big effect on these development times as does experience, therefore one of the key steps is to plan any additional time for training into your project life cycle. You should consider the previous experiences and training the development team has had.

The Methodology

It has been said that a good methodology can make good development can make a good system; the opposite is also true. A bad methodology and indeed a bad project plan often causes a project to go sour. The purpose of a methodology is to give you, the project planner, the toolkit to get the job done, tools that ease your workload, and tools that help you get to where you are going. A methodology should span the entire life cycle of the project and assist with all aspects, not just the application development, but also the analysis, prototyping, and implementation.

Plenty of good books on project development methodologies are available, and indeed many of the major IS vendors, such as Ernst & Young, IBM, and Arthur Anderson, will gladly sell you their own. There are, however, few methodologies with a bias towards client/server systems design, development, and implementation. Those that are available fail to cover the main models of client/server and concentrate on the use of only one model. Your ability is needed to spearhead the development and the use of multiple models and to plan this system effectively.

A Sample Plan

The following list details the steps necessary to move to client/server. This list is by no means exhaustive but will give you a good head start in your planning. The sections that follow describe each of the steps.

Initial Planning	Conduct initial systems planning
	Gather requirements
	Identify current processes
	Identify current systems
	Analyze applications and data
	Prepare and implement the plan
Initialize Project	Get business signoff
	Identify development in long-range plan
	Initiate project
	Staff project
	Begin training
	Continually refine the plan
Define Architecture	Gather data
	Expand data to next level
	Conceptualize system
	Prototype
	Develop workflow scenarios
	Develop proposed architecture
	Select new technologies
	Research and develop new technologies
Analysis	Develop logical data model
	Define general systems design
	Locate data
	Prepare external system design
Design	Verify prototype
	Verify workflow
	Build detailed design
	Design system and user test plans
	Design data conversion methods

Development	Build development environment
	Code and test units and modules
	Test the system
	Revalidate workflow
	Redevelop based on workflow
Rollout Planning	Conduct site surveys
	Acquire software and hardware
	Plan site implementation
	Install and test hardware
Testing	Conduct user testing
	Conduct stress testing
	Conduct pilot rollout
	Conduct pilot review
Implementation	Develop backout plan
	Develop support, maintenance, and upgrade procedures
	Train users
	Conduct controlled rollout
	Convert data
	Provide support
	Scale up
Post-Implementation	Review support
	Review the project
	Plan for the next stage

Initial Planning

The purpose of the initial planning step is to develop a thorough understanding of the current environment. This step is all the work a project manager does to get the project off the ground. It is made up of six parts outlined in the following sections. Each part focuses on a main section of work to be completed prior to starting the main project.

Initial Systems Planning

The initial systems plan has to contain the initial business and systems plan as well as the initial scope documentation of the project and a description of what is to be delivered. Items covered include draft budgets, team members skill sets, and time frames. These documents form the start of detailed planning and will be subject to much change over the life cycle of the project. Remember that project planning is a tool to help you deliver the system, not a means to get it done. If the plan has to change, change it; don't try to hit the time frames and deadlines if you know that they cannot be done. It is better that the system is done late and right than wrong and on time!

Gather Requirements

Requirements gathering at this early stage forms the basis of detailed analysis and clarifies the project from both a user and a systems standpoint. The requirements begin to flesh out the scope and identify areas where the project may expand (a phenomenon known as *scope creep*). These areas are where users, and possibly the systems department, will increase the deliverable requirements (normally without any consideration for increasing the staffing numbers or time frame). At this stage, requirements are determined by analyzing current needs.

Identify Current Processes

An understanding of the current processes can provide valuable insight into the use and/or abuse of the current system and help identify areas that can be improved by modifying the processes. As outlined in Chapter 3, "Business Process Re-engineering," modifying the processes some-times can bring more benefit that modifying the systems. In order to achieve the maximum benefit, be prepared at this stage to identify the improvements to be made to both systems and processes. At this point in the process, your users start to play a key role in the development of the project. Use them to show you the current processes.

Identify Current Systems

Spend some time in the project analyzing the current system from both a hardware and a software viewpoint. At this early stage, you can begin to build a picture of what the newly designed system might look like and the levels of investment, if any, that need to be implemented through out the project life cycle. This investment will probably be in the form of new computers, software packages, and tools to deliver the system. This task presents you with what can be considered your initial system architecture.

Analyze Applications and Data

By looking at the applications and the data that makes up these applications, you can begin to plan the future data structures and interfaces that are to make up your new system. Considerations at this stage include the databases that are to be used and any required interaction with legacy systems. If the latter is required, areas such as data access and middleware to those legacy systems may need to be reviewed.

Prepare and Implement Plan

Now that you have a firmer grasp on the project that is to be undertaken, take the time to review and replan. The analysis work done so far is likely to have identified needed changes to the scope and to the technical environment that will affect the work to be done. Changes of this nature can be resolved in a number of ways. Consider changing time frames, changing staffing numbers, or possibly (and increasing more popular) outsourcing areas of work. There is no perfect way to handle such development changes. One solution will work well for you on one project, and a different one will work on the next project. Experience with other client/server projects helps you to know what solution is best.

Initialize Project

Initializing the project deals with turning the preparatory work completed in the initial planning step into an agreed-upon project that moves forward. This section of the plan creates the commitment and staffing required to achieve the end goal, the successful delivery of the project. Pay special attention to the following sections; these sections can be some of the most difficult due to their challenging nature. At this point in the process, you will see just how committed the organization is to completing the project.

Get Business Signoff

Obtain business approval and user signoff that this project is to go ahead, and then start the project. Running projects is difficult if you do not have user and IS department backing; projects will often fail without such backing. In all circumstances, developing a system will be an uphill struggle for you if you do not have user signoff. Without end-user signoff, the users will not accept the system with open arms and it will fail. A well-defined and well-developed project is useless if no one uses it.

Identify Development in Long-Range Plan

Make sure that the project fits within your company's medium- to long-range plan. If the project exists solely in order to bring a product to market, the project should still be part of the wider scope of the company. Obtaining commitment and support for a project that is not part of the company's wider scope is difficult because the project is not seen as critical.

Initiate the Project

Publish the scope and the plans; begin to staff the project and to gather momentum. Launch the project, and say that it is started!

Staff the Project

Staff your project with the resources needed to complete the project in a timely fashion. When you develop a client/server system, this step is where your problems will really start. If you are developing a true client/server system, you will require resources from a number of departments within the IS department. These resources can be either part-time or full-time on your project depending on your needs. There are inevitably advantages and disadvantages to both types of involvement.

Full-Time Involvement

Full-time involvement enables you to build a team that is effectively a client/server development unit to develop the project. The full-time staff members (with your leadership) can begin to cross-train and become multiskilled. They can focus their effort on the business need without continually being interrupted for other things. As a result, they are normally more productive.

Complications arise when you are not effectively allowed to choose your team members from other departments; managers of these other areas may see this project as an opportunity to pass onto you those staff who are not particularly good. To overcome this problem, identify the staff who you think would work well in the team-based environment that you are creating. You will have to convince their managers of the benefits of adding these staff to the development team. This is often difficult because it requires the managers to shift their thinking from functional teams to the development team that you will be creating. If you are not successful in convincing the managers, you may need to seek support from the senior management teams in order to get approval. Individuals who have difficulty working in a group will soon cause you management problems that can be easily avoided. I have seen whole project teams turn against a loner and seriously reduce work effort. The team will be faced with considerable challenge in the project development itself without having to face the challenge of working well together.

You as the project manager will have to spend an amount of your time leading and managing staff in this environment that you have had no time to learn about and work with. Be firm and fair. Do not relinquish management of your team members to their previous managers; in my experience, this method causes more problems than it solves. Do not allow meetings to turn into "bitch" sessions. Although a certain amount of complaining can be productive and can pinpoint problems with the current system, it can also sidetrack your progress and deter your focus.

Elite?

The project team that you create to develop client/server will be viewed by those left maintaining the systems as somewhat elite. This is one of the most difficult problems for managers trying to determine team structures and the best way to get the job done. There is always a certain amount of jealousy towards individuals working on what are perceived as the better projects.

The staff rarely consider the client/server system to be just another development project. You can handle this opinion in one of two ways:

- Identify the client/server team as an elite group that should be watched, developed, and nurtured because it represents the new way of working that will be necessary as you progress into the client/server arena

- Deny that the client/server team is elite, and overcome this opinion with effective continual communication from the project team to the other staff

Whichever option you choose will to a certain extent determine how you interact with the rest of the department.

Part-Time Staff

Part-time staff can be brought into the project when needed; this option can often be useful for your key technical personnel and your key users. These people are often working on many other projects and the time that they can effectively contribute to your project is limited. Also, the role that they play on the project may not warrant full-time involvement. A technical staff member may only be required to solve an awkward technical issue, for example. You do not have to spend any great deal of time managing them, and they do not form part of your team, so, in effect, you can have a smaller full-time team, which will work better for you. Small teams work better because they communicate and interact better.

Part-time staff often fail to grasp the complete picture of the development, however. Any direction given to them as to how to complete their assigned tasks must be concise, accurate, and well-discussed. Part-time staff can also be difficult to communicate with as they may be juggling any number of projects. You will need to manage this situation to get necessary information. Be aware also that because part-time staff members do not report directly to you, you will also have the added burden of dealing with their managers for scheduling and resource management issues, which adds an extra level of complication.

Begin Training

Identify the key areas where training is required and incorporate this training into the project plan. Avoid compromising this training for any reason as doing so will result in much greater difficulties for you later in the project life cycle. Where possible, identify the aims and objectives of the training with all staff members before they attend so that they can get the most from the classes. In addition, they may then ask pertinent questions of the class tutors that may assist the development effort to some degree. Most tutors will also provide some telephone assistance to students for a period after courses, which can provide additional help with problems that occur.

Training should also be supported once the individual has returned from the class by ensuring that the trained staff are put to the tasks almost immediately. Producing production systems in C++ is rather difficult if you haven't used the tool for three months since you were trained on it. Reviews of completed work and discussions of tool problems lead to information sharing within the team and help nurture technical understanding and should be encouraged.

Continually Refine Plan

The plan you originally created was not cast in stone. Good project management is about using tools and your abilities and experience effectively. Therefore, as development and project activity gets underway, refine the plan or schedule as events and tasks occur. Continual planning in this way can significantly improve your responsiveness to scheduling and planning problems. If an early task is not going to be completed on time, you can determine the effect that it will have on the plan and replan for this eventuality. It is, after all, better to see the iceberg on the horizon and aim to avoid it rather than hitting it. If a task is not part of your critical path (those tasks that must be completed on time to meet the schedule), it may be acceptable to delay it for a time. If a task is a critical one, you may be able to add staff to get it done. Or you may realize that the task is going to be late and that other tasks later in the project need to be replanned as a result. Either way, these routes are far more acceptable than blindly stumbling through the project!

Define Architecture

Client/server development places a heavy burden on the architecture definition phase. The lack of experience in building client/server solutions, combined with the new paradigm experienced by the user community, leads to a considerable amount of prototyping of applications. The prototyping will cause you to rethink your architecture. Such a step is reasonable and appropriate with today's technology. The tools for prototyping the client/server platform are powerful enough that prototyping is frequently faster in determining user requirements than traditional modeling techniques were (and it's more fun).

Gather Data

Analysis of the existing area or business process to be redefined will lead to an understanding of what is to take place with the new systems. This information should help to identify the structure of both hardware and software that will need to be implemented. At this stage in the development, you should clearly understand the technology to be implemented from a hardware perspective and the required high-level data structures.

Expand Data to Next Level

After you have gathered the data for the business area, spend time analyzing the next level of detail of the architecture. This task should solidify your understanding and also give additional information that can be used in the prototyping phase. Expanding the data available is also part of the workflow design phase.

Conceptualize System

Begin to conceptually design what the finished system will look like. You can do this task from a technical infrastructure and hardware viewpoint, a user front-end viewpoint (via prototyping), and from a software viewpoint. This conceptual design provides a useful means to provide the whole team with the vision of what the completed system is to contain. This vision is much easier to visualize and explain when presented in a pictorial format.

Visualizing the infrastructure can, at this early stage, identify the changes and enhancements that are to be made to the existing systems. User visualization and prototyping are discussed in more detail in Chapter 15.

Visualizing the data structures and schematics helps the development team identify the key relationships between the business information within the data structures. These relationships really affect the final structures of the databases, tables, and indexes that are to make up the systems, and they help you in making the choice of which models to use within the overall application. At this point in the project, visualizing the product or system provides an excellent point of reference for the next development stages.

Prototype

Set a quick realistic time frame for the development of the prototype with continual user involvement. The prototype should be used as a proof of concept tool to identify whether the system can be built in the way designed and outlined by the analysis work before detailed development gets under way. Be prepared to call a stop point in the prototype development. The prototype time frame often begins to increase as more and more gets added to the prototype that is not required at this stage.

Develop Workflow Scenarios

Designing workflow is covered in detail in Chapter 15. The benefit of identifying multiple ways of building your system it that the user community can decide which scenario works best for its business needs. Also, the ability to have multiple scenarios shows good varied application of both new design techniques and the different client/server models. Multiple scenarios aid discussion on what will work for the user base. Discussing the advantages and disadvantages of a workflow system is very difficult if you have nothing to compare it to.

Develop Proposed Architecture

Once the prototype has been finalized, the base architecture has been defined, and the data structures have been laid out, you can move on to developing the new proposed architecture both at a hardware and software level. The architecture can be planned, and where possible, begin to be implemented as a parallel task to the development of the system. If, for example, you are moving from Intel 486 processor-based PCs running Windows for Workgroups to Intel Pentium-based machines running Windows 95 as part of your infrastructure, you can carry out this task without affecting the rest of your project. It is often wise to get as many tasks as possible successfully completed prior to the implementation of the new system rather than making them an additional activity as part of the implementation phase.

Select New Technologies

If your development project is based on the use of some new technologies for the organization, you should ideally select and test these technologies as early as possible within the project life cycle. Doing development of this nature is very risky. You do not, after all, want to go on to do further development work if something were fundamentally wrong with the technologies you based earlier development on. Furthermore, it is not very sensible to begin development of a core business system with a new development language that hasn't been proven in the field, regardless of what the language vendor tells you. This is a recipe for disaster. The worst case scenario for you here is that you may have to seriously replan the project because a technology is not living up to the requirements you are placing on it or that the vendor has told you it can meet.

My advice is to be prepared to drop technologies and research new ones if necessary rather than to continue development with concerns about the underlying technologies. You may be fortunate in that problems may not arise within this project, but experience has shown that if an infrastructure of a development tool is not satisfactory, at some point in the future of the development of IS systems these problems will arise, and the cost of resolution at that point is significantly higher than if the problem were identified now. Many of the failures of particular products within the client/server environment can be attributed to not stopping the project when these issues came to light at this stage.

Research and Develop New Technologies

Any technology that is new to the company should be thoroughly researched before being used as part of your new client/server environment. The risks of trying to implement a new technology without adequate training, understanding, and knowledge of it are too high and will result in costly failures. Know what is required of a technology product, test it in a laboratory environment, and put it through its paces in real-world tests that give you the information you want rather than what a magazine review or a salesperson passes on to you. Only then can you effectively be sure of its success within your project.

Sometimes the product or new technology that you want to use will still be in a Beta state. The immediate reaction to this situation is that products in the final stages of development are still prone to bugs and errors as well as some missing functionality. There is, however, an argument that says the adoption of such a new product can lead to a competitive advantage for your organization and system. Again, the answer is to approach with caution, and test the product thoroughly in your environment to ensure that is both stable and robust to the extent that you require before pursuing it as a major component of your architecture. You should also ask the vendor to show you a site that has the technology you are considering in production. This site can give you an honest, actual scenario instead of the standard sales pitch.

If a piece of technology fails your requirements at this stage, you have a number of options open to you. You might search for a product that has similar functionality and may be able to provide you with what you need. This solution often works when selecting middleware products because there are so many of them on the market today. Alternatively, you may decide that you need to redesign the system in some way. Suppose that you expected to store some client data within a local database on the client. If this database failed to be robust enough, you might consider housing the databases on a server elsewhere on the network, such as an IBM AS/400.

Finally, you might decide that this technology is not ready yet for integration into your organization as it does not provide you with the stability that you need in order to implement the system effectively. This is the worst case because you now have to determine what you will do with this component of the project. The best thing to do is try to identify other solutions, be they via the use of workflow, other tools, or a different client/server model, that enable you to achieve the goal without the piece of technology you were relying on. Invariably, you may need to make the decision that this piece may need to be dropped and the application redesigned as a result. This decision is difficult, yet, as stated earlier, is better than continuing to develop the system only to fail later on. It is often questionable whether from a managerial viewpoint it is wise to admit complications and failure early on, yet I think that in the risky business of client/server development you will be far better off identifying and working to resolve issues early. Have the courage to identify them, and don't expect it to be a failure on your part, as it normally is not.

Consider the 15-person client/server development project that decides to use a new application development language to develop a client/server system. In the very early stages of development, it becomes clear to all involved that the tool is not stable, it is slow to work with, and it cannot handle the complexity of the data structures required within the new business application. The project manager has these issues highlighted to him yet continues development nonetheless. Eventually, the team realizes that they are not moving forward as fast as they would like and the delivery date of the implemented system is moved from November to August of the following year. The technology continues to create problems, and the system slowly takes shape. However, the system continues to crash, have slow response times, and not attain the performance levels that the users expect. August comes and goes; by December, the Systems

Vice President cancels the project 18 months after conception and at a cost in excess of two million dollars. Don't fall into this trap. In the client/server world, you cannot trust the technology as you could in the centralized systems environment. With client/server, you must trust your ability and your team's ability to correctly apply the technology.

Analysis

The analysis step deals with bringing together the data gathered in earlier steps and putting together the constituent parts to build the new client/server system. This step is very important because it lays the foundation for the entire project. If you are new to client/server systems, plan additional time into the following stages in order to review and review again. Doing so will build your experience and also reduce difficulties in the later steps.

Develop a Logical Data Model

Developing a logical data model puts the business application into perspective. Drawing a logical data model electronically (or even on paper!) will help you visualize the relationships of the main data types within the application. Such a model is easier to understand than trying to work with physical database relationships. The various inputs and outputs to the process should also be included so that the entire process is modeled. From this logical data model, the physical databases can be developed and tested. The logical model is often easier to understand and should be documented. The logical data model is also used to determine the locations of the physical databases once the application is complete. It can also be used to determine to a certain extent the models that can be used within the final system.

Define General Systems Design

The overall system can now be defined. The design of the system includes the hardware, operating systems, and physical locations of both client machines and server machines. It also includes the software breakdown of what processes and pieces of the applications reside on the clients and the various servers (if you have more than one).

The systems design finishes off the jigsaw puzzle of the system. This design makes it possible for everyone to see the constituent parts, the makeup of the application, the equipment used, and how the completed systems will interact. All that is left now is to build it!

Locate Data

Locating the data is often considered one of the difficult aspects of client/server development. Yet following some simple guidelines and using the client/server models can help you with these decisions. Data has to have a variety of attributes when used in a client/server system. These attributes often determine the locations that you place the data in the system infrastructure. The attributes are typically the following:

- Rate of change
- Accessibility
- Number of users
- Temporary or permanent condition
- Relationships with other data

The Rate of Change attribute measures how fast and how often the data changes. Data that changes on an almost real-time basis should be placed on high-volume, transaction-based databases that are typically on a midrange or mainframe computer. Data that changes infrequently may be moved to less costly platforms, such as PC file server databases.

The Accessibility attribute measures how readily available the data is to all those who need it. If the data is to be made available to a large number of users around the world who must access the data at the same time and with fast response, you should place the data in a centralized location. The data that is needed by only the small local workgroup, however, may be placed a small UNIX server at the local office.

The Number of Users attribute is self-explanatory. As the number of users increases, the requirements of the server machine also increase. The diversification of global client/server systems can also begin to dictate the type and number of servers as the number of countries accessing the data increases. At the opposite end of the spectrum, data that is to be accessed by the user only can be located either on the client machine or the user's private data area on a network. The main advantage to using client-based databases is the reduction of resource requirements in order to store on a database server, but client-based databases do not yet have the robustness of server systems.

The Temporary or Permanent attribute determines where the data should be stored. Data that is created on a temporary basis for the user, perhaps while they are logged onto a client/server system, can be created on the client machine. Data that the company needs to store (in other words, permanent data) should be housed on a server machine on the network.

The Relationships with Other Data attribute indicates how this piece of data relates to other pieces of corporate data. If this piece of data is highly linked, such as a master customer file, it should be located on a easily accessible, high-volume server, which is normally the main production computer for an organization. If the data is predominantly stand-alone or its links are relatively inconsequential, then it can be placed on file server systems. Determining data relationships identifies the data that makes up the enterprise-level data model. This data is intrinsic to the smooth operation of the company. Moving enterprise-level data to smaller platforms, such as PC LANs, can be a disaster as the updating and management of this data is normally spread across the entire organization. As a result, downsizing this data results in lack of access and lack of consideration for the entire business process, culminating in failure of the project.

Prepare External System Design

Most modern client/server systems also need to connect to systems outside of the organization. Client/server systems may need to be able to receive electronic file transfers, handle EDI transactions, or connect to services on the Internet. An external systems design forms part of the overall system design and documents and diagrams how the connection to outside systems takes place. Special mention is made of the external system design in this section because this design requires additional planning and activities. These activities include meeting and reviewing requirements with the providers of these external systems.

Most organizations that can provide you with interfaces to their systems can also develop client/server systems, and you may be able to gain valuable information and advice from these contacts. More than likely, however, the external systems providers only provide you with information through their existing interfaces. In most organizations, these interfaces tend to be older technologies than those you would ideally like to integrate into your new system. Therefore, additional design work must be done to figure out how these technologies are to interface with your new client/server system at hardware, software, and network levels.

Design

The design step takes the analysis work and the logical models discussed earlier in this chapter and combines them to begin the actual development of the system. In addition, prototyping is used to create a working model of the finished system. Although the prototype is only used as a visual tool for discussion purposes, it is highly effective. As your experience grows, you will be able to develop prototypes that can also become the basis of the actual system to the point where there is a lot of code reuse. The design step involves some other ongoing tasks as well. You begin to develop the plans for converting any existing data and to develop the system and user testing plans.

Verify Prototype

Verifying the prototype is covered in detail in Chapter 15. Suffice to say that in light of the detailed work done so far, the prototype should be reviewed again in order to ascertain that the principles, workflow, and design still fit the new system.

Verify Workflow

Verifying workflow is covered in more detail in Chapter 15. Design considerations, external interfaces, and infrastructure may all demand changes to the workflow. Where possible, the workflow should be based on the user requirements. Sometimes circumstances that arise because of the constraints of the aforementioned systems components make this impossible.

Build Detailed Design

In a large system, the design may be built in two parts: a preliminary detailed design and the actual detailed design. A preliminary design is helpful when you have a project team made up of smaller teams or outside companies that are doing pieces of work for you. Normally, however, you can go directly to the actual detailed design.

The detailed design contains all the documented analysis of the new system. This documentation includes the requirements, data structures, file layouts, hardware and software standards, interface guidelines, external systems information, and any other information you think is necessary to build the system.

Design System and User Test Plans

At this stage, begin to consider and plan what testing is to be done, by whom, and when. Testing a client/server system is considerably different than testing traditional centralized systems, and additional care must be taken to get it right. Due to the added complexities of developing client/server systems, the actual testing is also more complex than testing a centralized system. As a result, you should plan more time for both system and user testing. Also, think about how you are going to do user testing. Are you going to run a small test environment first, or are you going to have only key users test the application? Whatever you decide, you must begin to plan these activities now so that the testing can be done on schedule.

Design Data Conversion Methods

If you're moving from an existing legacy system to a new client/server system, some data will need to be converted. The data conversion routines or methods should be designed and tested prior to implementation. This step may seem obvious, but there have been many instances of data conversion taking place without testing, resulting in inaccurate data. Although the main data conversion will most likely be done at implementation, designing the data conversion methods now ensures that there is a well-defined method for converting the data and that the conversion is completely accurate.

Development

The development step is where the application or applications are programmed and created. Each piece of the application is also tested to see whether it performs its required function. It is not possible at this stage, however, to test the entire application. The development of the application will raise issues with regard to the suitability of previous workflow designs. At this point, you have the opportunity to revalidate the workflow. Take advantage of this opportunity; it is the final time to make programming modifications before the application is implemented.

Build Development Environment

If you are developing a system using tools that are new to you, you will need to build a development environment for your developers to use. A development environment contains both the software and access to the hardware that is required to develop your client/server system. Ideally, you should use tools that allow application code that is being developed to be locked to the developer writing that code. This feature prevents multiple copies of programs and units from being changed at the same time. In addition, take particular care when developing the data models and the data dictionaries. If your RDBMS can secure access to the data structures you are developing, take advantage of this feature. You don't want two people or more modifying the database structures at the same time. If your system does not provide these version control facilities, you must provide a manual or partially automated method of maintaining your development code so that it is kept secure.

Code and Test Units and Modules

Coding and testing units and modules form the guts of the project. During this stage, the application programmers sit down and generate the real code for the system in whatever language you have chosen to use. The best approach for developing the total application is to break up the application development work into a series of modules small enough to be handled by individual developers. Assign each developer his or her modules and begin the development. Each module should be coded and tested as far as possible. Groups of modules that are intended to work together will need to be tested together once those groups, also called units, are completed. Switching to a mentality of testing the constituent parts of the application as soon as possible after development eases the development team's burden during the testing phases. Testing the parts also highlights the common small problems that occur.

Program documentation (the bane of programmers' lives) should also be written at this stage. Documentation within most modern application development systems can be placed with the source code such that subsequent programmers can understand the notes the original programmer wrote. The beginning of each source file for both the client programs and the server programs should contain a text list of modifications, updates, and revisions made to the file so that there is effectively an audit history for the source with dates and the names of those who worked on the program. Insist that the major blocks of code within the source file are documented with explanations of the key areas. Do not, however, go overboard and document every line. Another key piece of documentation is a brief explanation of the function of all procedures. These explanations may seem evident to the developer now, but later they may not. In time, other programmers will need to change, enhance, or modify the code. Having this list will prove invaluable when it comes to future enhancements. As the completed modules come together, you will be ready to move to the next phase of system testing.

Test the System

System testing within the client/server environment is not just about finding bugs or program logic errors. During system testing, you should also consider the flow of the system. Does the system feel right when it's used? Only you, your developers, and your user base can determine what works for your organization. Minor modifications to the system at this stage can improve its success when it's implemented.

Create a list of all areas that have problems and spend time with the development team prioritizing this list. In this way, you can build a comprehensive guide to the redevelopment activities that are needed to move forward.

A good way of forcing the issues out into the open is to use other programmers and IS staff as the test users. Something within the personality of IS staff members allows them to be quite brutal when critiquing others' work! The effort from these people shouldn't be great, perhaps one hour per staff member, but the resulting list of problems, likes, and dislikes will be worth the time investment. Be aware that many of the comments are likely to deal with minor changes, such as "This font is two pixels too large," "I prefer red rather than pink," and so on. These changes should obviously be put at the bottom of the priority list and left to the user base to advise you on at the later user testing stage. If there is an overwhelming response on any one particular visual attribute, then let common sense prevail and change it, but don't spend many days resolving these details.

Revalidate Workflow

As you system test, response from those testing will include statements like "This menu option is really needed," or "Why do I have to do so many mouse clicks when a speed button or hot key would work much better?" These comments question the workflow of the system. The *workflow* is the set of steps taken in the application to complete the business process.

Workflow, as discussed later in Chapter 15, can make or break a client/server system. After the system testing is completed, get together a small team of key users and ask them to use the system and concentrate specifically on the workflow. You are looking for the effectiveness of the system when used by the people who will probably manipulate this technology on a daily basis. As a result, they can find the areas that could be improved early in the process. Your goal modeling and event response modeling will be tested during this process for their accuracy and relevance. If they are slightly off the mark, you can make the changes now to correct the differences. If any changes are made, you should test the system again and pay particular attention to the area that was changed.

Redevelop Based on Workflow

You may be shaking in your boots at this stage; redeveloping an application in part at this stage has not normally been done in the traditional predictive environment of so many legacy systems. However, because the client/server environment requires much more in terms of the freedom for the users to respond to the events of the customers they are servicing, you must pay particular attention to the workflow. The majority of this redevelopment work will focus on changing the way applications respond to user input, the menu environment that the user works with, the logical flow of the information through the system, and the way in which the user interacts with that information. Because the business and application logic is already complete, this stage does not take very long.

Rollout Planning

Rollout planning deals with the planning of the physical implementations of the system you have developed. Because client/server applications are spread across many different platforms, the physical implementation tasks are more complex than that of a single-platform system such as an AS/400 with dumb terminal access. In addition, the rollout work can be done alongside the development effort rather than having to take place after the development work is completed.

Site Surveys

During the development phase, you can begin some of the parallel rollout activities if you have resources available. The client/server system that you are going to implement will need to be in one or more locations. These locations could be a local department, the complete company, another company, or any combination of these in any number of geographic regions. As a result, a significant amount of planning is required to do the physical installation. If you are going to create a site implementation plan for each location, you need to get an understanding of the complexity of the site. In all implementation situations, you should do a site survey.

A site survey entails visiting (or getting a team member to visit) the locations that are receiving the system. While at the site, you need to document and understand the environment by finding out the following information:

- The location of all hardware to be used, both existing and new
- The location of any communications and server equipment
- The physical cabling infrastructure within the building or location
- The level of experience of the user base with regard to the particular products being implemented
- The support systems (both software and hardware) that can be provided
- The equipment and cabling that may need to be purchased prior to implementation

Once created, a site survey document could be used by any individual to move forward with the site implementation plan. The level of complexity of a site survey is seriously increased when the site is located in another country, as the language barriers immediately become apparent. Also, the local regulations may be considerably different to what you have experienced before.

Software and Hardware Acquisition

From a site survey comes the list of hardware, software, and networking components that are required for the client/server implementation. This equipment should be ordered well within the time frame necessary to implement it. Be aware that hardware, software, and network availability can vary wildly from country to country. Experience shows that it is normally always better to get the products you need from within the country where you are implementing the system.

Suppose you needed a particular router connected to your WAN link. By shipping the router from your country, you might invalidate the warranty and have a router in a country where no one locally could support the hardware. If the router failed due to hardware problems, you might have an office down for an unacceptable period of time.

Some software companies also impose restrictions on what countries their products can be used in. These restrictions in turn can create licensing problems for you. Bear this fact in mind when deciding where and how to purchase your software. In addition, if you are dependent on connectivity software, such as emulation software, you may find that the appropriate character codes to support that country's language will need to be loaded on your servers as well as the client machines.

Planning Site Implementation

Planning a site implementation can be compared to a military operation. You want to know exactly what to do when and in what order. Plan for contingency time and float time for when things go wrong. A basic site implementation plan contains time for the cabling installations, server installations and setup, client installations and setup, protection device and software installations (for example, UPS and virus scanners), connectivity testing, user training, and documentation.

Installing and Testing Hardware

Follow the site plan, and install and test the equipment. From a staff development viewpoint, you should try to have at least two people do a client/server installation. A skilled person can handle the implementation and be mirrored by a less experienced person. Actual implementations are one of the best ways to develop and train your less-skilled staff. You obviously cannot rely on your very inexperienced staff to handle the complete installation.

From a team dynamics viewpoint, it is also beneficial for two staff or more to handle the installation. When things go wrong, two pairs of hands are available to resolve the complications. Handling implementation difficulties on your own can be very difficult and time-consuming. Obviously, the reverse is also true; do not use staff on site installations unless they are required. Too many people can be counter-productive.

Testing

Testing is extremely important in all computer systems development, especially client/server systems. Allowing the testing to be carried out entirely by your development staff is not enough. Testing needs to be taken to the users and into the jungle where the application will be used! This section discusses user testing and stress testing in some detail. Both types of testing are required in order for the testing process to be successful. A highly technically capable application will fail if it doesn't meet the users' needs, and a user-friendly workflow system will fail if it is technically unreliable.

User Testing

The testing phase of a client/server plan is perhaps the most crucial time of the project. It is the time when the user base begins to experience the system that you and they have developed over the previous months.

User testing should be structured in two ways. The first part of the tests should be on based on dummy data where possible and should begin to identify how the system works to the users testing it. This testing should follow a set pattern or routine developed by the users so that they can quickly develop their understanding and knowledge before fully testing the system. The second part of the testing should not follow any routine, and the users should use the system in the way they have been taught but without further supervision. This part represents the real-world working environment much more accurately.

Like system testing, you are identifying additional bugs and problems with the system that will need to be fixed prior to implementation. Make particular note again of any workflow issues that arise from this particular testing and decide whether the workflow is going to be modified. When requests arise for visual changes, such as colors, fonts, and graphics, determine whether these requests are fairly unanimous. Only address those requests that are unanimous. The user testing environment should last no more than two weeks ideally. The length of time required to complete the changes that are necessary as a result of this testing will depend on the nature of the changes.

Stress Testing

Stress testing is very difficult to do on a client/server system. Organizations implementing client/server projects are faced with a tremendous number of decisions. These decisions have an impact on how effective and efficient the overall implementation will be. In the past, most decision makers have used information from vendors, personal experience, gut feelings, industry benchmarks, and references to help them differentiate products and vendors. These information sources did not always represent their particular company's computing environment, and, as a result, force-fit extrapolations of accessible data were made to allow comparisons.

End-user testing requirements now go far beyond industry benchmarks for the client/server environment. The application must be tested in a number of areas for it to be considered stress tested successfully. The main areas of testing that need to take place are compatibility testing of the products that are integrated together for large numbers of users, operating system performance testing for large workloads at both the client machine and the server machines, and scalability testing.

Compatibility testing is an extremely important part of any development effort. Compatibility testing of new software applications is often a time-consuming, laborious, and expensive process whose importance is sometimes overlooked. However, as anyone who has been through the process knows, thorough effort spent in this portion of the implementation can pay off handsomely later in the form of more satisfied end users and lower support costs. Compatibility ensures that the system components interact properly and correctly without error for the total number of users required for the final environment.

Operating system performance at both the client and the server machines is an area that has considerable interest from end users, but it is difficult to test. The world of open systems has brought the potential of implementing a specific application or middleware layer on many different kinds of operating systems that all use the same hardware architecture underneath.

Scalability testing represents the third area of interest for both IS departments and computer vendors. Scalability testing ensures that your system performs equally as well running 100 gigabytes of data as it does when it runs 1 gigabyte. Scalability tests are often not performed. Companies then find themselves with the dilemma that the system they had developed that worked fine for the 20 users locally attached to it grinds to a halt when they add the other 80 users that need the system.

Especially in the area of open systems, people are anxious for information on how different components in a client/server environment will scale. SMP (symmetric multiprocessing) versus MPP (massively parallel processing) scaling has been the subject of considerable debate within the industry, and companies who are implementing large-scale client/server projects need good information on the scaling characteristics of both of these architectures in order to make informed decisions for their projects.

In addition, the database's ability to scale is another area that requires significant investigation. Many companies have found that databases and applications that behave well in a 10-gigabyte environment do not necessarily exhibit the same "good behavior" in a 100-gigabyte environment. Similarly, operating system scaling is also a factor. The operating system must be able to handle additional processors, tasks, and users efficiently. A good example of this kind of desire for information is Windows NT Server. There is considerable interest in the industry in determining how far Windows NT scales efficiently and on what architecture(s) (Intel, Mips, PowerPC, Alpha, and so on). Also, applications that are developed in one environment need to run efficiently and effectively in larger, more complex environments. Scaling has become a tremendous issue as end users embark on large projects, like data warehousing, on nonmainframe architectures.

Pilot Rollout

The day has finally arrived. It is now time to roll out the application in a production environment through a small controlled pilot project. This project is aimed at reviewing the application and the attributes of the application within the live production data environment. A pilot project should be made up of a number of users of varying ability with the existing systems. These users are then trained properly on the new system, as you would in a full rollout, and then the system goes live for a set period of time, and you monitor the results. In particular, monitor the technical aspects of the system in terms of response time at the client and stability of the applications, the network, the clients, and the servers. Log the errors when they arise.

From a business viewpoint, study the users' responses to the system: the ease with which they pick up and use the system, the time it takes them to feel comfortable with the system (this helps refine training plans), and the level of satisfaction they feel. You can gauge these responses by asking the users to rate the main functions of the system on a scale of 1 to 5 (1 being the lowest, 5 the highest) and averaging the responses.

You should also consider the viability of contacting those people or customers that are on the receiving end of the new business system to determine whether they felt that the service was improved and where in particular they noticed improvements. Once the time frame for the pilot is over, gather all the feedback documentation together and hold the pilot review.

Pilot Review

The pilot review stage is geared toward identifying both the successes and the concerns with the pilot project and therefore the overall application. As a result of a pilot review, you may decide to rollout the application, delay the rollout until some minor changes have been made, or in the worst cases, you might have to go back to the drawing board and restart. If you choose the last option is the case, you probably did not do enough detailed design and development work earlier on or your analysis was flawed.

Implementation

The final stretch is within sight. Implementation deals with the delivery of the system to the user base. You should also consider the worst and develop a backout plan should your implementation go wrong at some stage. Training should be given in a controlled manner prior to the implementation so that your users can begin to work with the new system almost immediately.

Develop Backout Plan

Assuming that the pilot project is successful, you should move straight into system rollout. However, before you rollout to large numbers of users, make sure that you develop a backout plan if you can. If everything goes really wrong on implementation, it can sometimes be better to return the users to the previous state. Suppose a router is shipped to another country (bad move in the first place), gets there, and appears to be working fine. You arrive to install the system that is LAN-based and needs to talk through the router to your IBM AS/400 acting as a database server in the United States. Clearly, if the router fails and cannot be quickly replaced and fixed, a backout plan might indicate the use of a multiplexor and controller to return the users back to their AS/400 legacy systems. You also may want to consider having a contingency plan for the pilot test.

Develop Support, Maintenance, and Upgrade Procedures

In order to do a successful implementation, you must back up the implementation with your support, maintenance, and upgrade procedures. Developing a set of structured procedures is the key to delivery of a good system and its continued enhancement and support. The support procedures should be documented either on paper or on electronic format and should be readily available to all the support staff and those staff in other countries who may provide the support functions locally.

Train Users

You have redesigned the business process, and you have designed a new application vastly different from the legacy systems that your user base is used to. As a result, significant time needs to be spent training the user base how to use this new system. Bear in mind that there may also be some simple issues that will arise. The legacy systems that use dumb terminals showing screens of green on black are somehow quietly reassuring compared to the vibrant colors of a GUI. Such simple differences cause some users to fear the new technology; some may even question their ability to use the new system. These problems should be overcome with a good training plan.

Do not assume that because you are implementing PCs into the department to receive the system that everyone there is an expert. Also, do not expect the users to have time to RTM (Read The Manual). These assumptions do not work. Plan the training to cover the users' actual needs rather than their perceived needs from IS (these needs are normally considerably different). Spend time training on what a PC is, where the on/off switches are, how to move the mouse (yes, even this basic), and how not to just switch it off if an error occurs. In most organizations I have worked for, lack of training accounts for a possible 60 percent of the support calls to the help desk. Never lose patience with users. Your attitude toward them can sometimes sway their opinion of the system. As I said earlier, an excellent client/server application is no better than any other application if no one uses it.

Training on the application will depend on the nature of the application, but in most applications that service some sort of customer, consider using role-play. Role-play helps get the users comfortable with system by asking them to work as if they were on the live production line. After users have gone through five to six role-play examples, you will find them eager to begin providing real service.

With one customer service-based system, I used role-play to overcome the users' fear that the client/server system was not providing them with the data that they needed when answering a member's telephone call. I actually telephoned them as a member and then did the role-play over the phone. Inventive ways to train will bring down your training time, encourage and motivate the staff, and result in a successful system.

Conduct a Controlled Rollout

A controlled client/server system rollout is again planned like a military operation. The implementation plan is used to implement equipment, software, networks, training, and support at exactly the time the business needs them. The biggest consideration at this stage is how to do the implementation. This decision is based on both the nature of the business and the nature of the application.

You may decide to do a "big bang" approach and implement all the users at the same time. This approach is risky because a mistake anywhere in the process will leave large numbers of users with problems. However, this approach may be the only way to deliver the product for business reasons. If it is, make sure that you spend extra time on the stress testing because you will not have time to hold up implementation to correct stress problems without facing further complications.

Perhaps a better route is to do a phased implementation over a fixed period of time. For example, you may decide to implement a new customer sales system for 120 users over a three-month period by implementing some 40 systems each month, which breaks down into four weeks of 10 users per week. Assuming a one-week training time, you could train the users and then allow them to run the new system almost immediately. If at any point stress problems begin to occur, you can freeze the rollout until the problems are resolved without significantly affecting the whole business area.

Convert Data

The biggest driver towards a big bang approach is if the new client/server system needs access to a new database that everyone uses. For example, Chiappetta Hotels Incorporated runs an internal inventory management system that holds their hotel memberships and the inventory of all their hotels across the country. The inventory is real-time and is accessed by all employees. Suppose they moved into a different business area selling different products and needed to modify this core inventory system that all employees access. The data would need to be converted to the new type, and all systems would need to be upgraded immediately. This kind of core business change causes the biggest concerns for IS management in developing systems and is also obviously the biggest risk. I would recommend that you do not try a development project of this nature until you have some experience of smaller, less risky client/server projects under your belt.

Provide Support

The moment the first live system has been implemented, you will begin to get support calls. You will probably get a peak number of calls within the first month of implementation, and then the calls will reduce to a lower number. Try to capture as much information early on from these support calls as they may identify problems, training issues, or usability improvements that can be made. Do not just resolve the problem; try also to fix the cause so that the problem doesn't happen again.

Scaling Up

With scalability testing, you will have determined how the system might be increased in size and how the system can be scaled up. If the project is successful, you will find that the user base will be demanding increased numbers of users across all your offices within a short space of time. If this happens, pat yourself on the back; you did a good job!

Scaling up should be planned exactly as the initial implementation stages were, including all the same activities. If scaling up also involves implementations in other countries, remember the notes on site surveys presented earlier in the chapter.

Post-Implementation

The normal perspective on projects is that once implementation is complete, the project is finished. This is not the case. If you spend time developing a post-implementation strategy, you can improve your users' acceptance of the project. You can take the time to review, improve, and modify the support structure the users receive.

From a personal perspective as well as an IS perspective, you should also review the project in its entirety. This is an excellent learning period for all involved as to the success of the project. Finally, you can begin to ask, "Where does the application go from here?" and plan the future enhancements.

Support Review

After the project is complete, the implementation has been done, and the users are trained and no longer bothering you, spend some time reviewing the support environment. Track the support calls that come in, look at upgrade requests that have been placed, and determine how well the system is functioning.

Such a review helps you and your team identify better ways of providing support and tackling those issues that regularly occur and may need to be resolved. A support review should only take one day, but it may identify further areas of improvement that will bring benefit to the user areas.

Project Review

A project review can be both a celebration and a post-mortem. This step gives you time to review and reflect on the development that has taken place. You should be blunt and honest with the project teams involved; review the good and bad times in the project. Discussing the issues and how they were resolved, how the team ran, how the time frames were met or missed, or how far the budget was over will give you valuable insight into how to handle the next project even better.

From a learning viewpoint, this review is most important. It allows you to take time to analyze the project and consider those areas that worked well, and those areas that did not. Identifying those areas that didn't work can help you to improve on subsequent projects. Feedback from colleagues and project team members must be taken into consideration also.

Next Stage Planning

You spent a great deal of time, effort, and possibly money developing this client/server system for your organization. Yet where does the system go from here? To prevent this system from turning into your new corporate legacy system, spend time planning the next enhancements to it and identifying whether they are possible to do within the business area. In this way, you can upgrade your client/server systems with a phased approach that delivers further business benefit with each iteration and does not allow the application to stand still.

As your ability increases, you will find that there are areas within each of the previous applications that you built that could be improved. By analyzing these potential improvements, you may decide that the business benefit of such changes makes it justifiable to do them.

Summary

The steps involved in moving to client/server are similar to those involved in a traditional development environment with some additional key tasks. At the beginning of any client/server development projects, consider the following key questions:

> What needs to be in place for this project to work?
>
> What steps have to done before, during, and after the project?
>
> Who needs to be involved?
>
> Are you going to pilot the application?
>
> Who are the members of pilot group going to be?
>
> What are the success measurements for the pilot team?
>
> What changes can ease the move?
>
> Does a new architecture need to be in place before the move to the new system?
>
> What will the impact be on the existing technology and networks?

These questions will prepare you for many of the difficulties and opportunities ahead. If you know your business well, you can be successful; knowing your systems well will also make you successful. Ask yourself, what are my key deliverables and where am I going? Both answers are needed to change. Always be realistic when planning; remember planning is as much about you dealing with people and working with their issues, workload, and constraints as it is with using planning tools and plotting Gantt charts. Throughout the development of your project, consider your plans to be changeable, not cast in stone.

Database Management Systems

7

by Advanced Information Systems (AIS)

IN THIS CHAPTER

Database management systems (DBMS) were created to provide a shared data storage mechanism for both users and programs. The essential tasks of a DBMS are to provide a means of defining data to the system, storing data on physical devices, and allowing users to access and change the stored data. Beyond these central functions, a DBMS must also provide security from unauthorized access, recovery in the event of a system failure, concurrency so that multiple users can access the database at the same time, and integrity checking so that data in different parts of the database remains logically consistent. Quickly implementing these DBMS principles into a client/server system is a challenge that has been successfully addressed by a number of vendors over the past decade.

Relational Database Management Systems

Relational Database Management Systems (RDBMS) grew out of a body of theory first advanced by E.F. Codd at IBM in 1969. Codd's relational model established a formal system for data storage that separates the internal representation of data from its logical representation and access. In the early '80s, the first databases based upon the relational model appeared on the market to challenge the dominant hierarchical and network database models, which were previously represented by IIMS and IDMS respectively. By the late '80s, RDBMSs had prevailed over these older technologies and began to play an integral role in the emerging client/server paradigm.

RDBMSs have now become so ubiquitous in the client/server arena that people often re-flexively think of relational databases when they hear the term *server.* The RDBMS market today is becoming increasingly a commodity market, with vendors beginning to converge on features and price. What is becoming more important is the level of service, off-the-shelf solutions, and supporting tools that database and third-party vendors supply.

Today, RDBMSs represent one of the largest and fastest growing market segments in the software industry with overall sales exceeding $7 billion in 1994. Indeed, the key players in this market represent the largest software giants in the world, including Microsoft, IBM, Oracle, Computer Associates, and Sybase. Oracle is the undisputed RDBMS market leader, holding down 56 percent of the global RDBMS market. Sybase and Informix each control about 12 percent of the UNIX market. Computer Associates Ingres has shrunk to less than 5 percent of that market, and Microsoft's SQL Server and IBM's OS/2 continue to grow in the Windows NT and OS/2 markets.

The power of RDBMSs lies in their ability to hide the details of data storage and retrieval from the database user. In hiding these details, RDBMS vendors have also lowered the technical hurdles for a broad community of database users. Not only is a relational database more accessible to application developers, who can concentrate more of their efforts on application code, but also to business end users, who can now choose from a growing array of visual tools to formulate questions and retrieve data from the database. This widening user domain has been largely due to the acceptance of Structured Query Language (SQL) as the mother tongue of all RDBMSs.

RDBMS Architectures

RDBMS architectures have a number of characteristics that differentiate them from other data storage models. The most important difference is in the separation of the physical view of the data, the underlying way each vendor stores and manipulates data, from the logical view of the data, the way the user perceives and accesses data. In a relational database, all data is logically stored in tables, which users perceive as collections of rows and columns, similar to spreadsheets.

The task of the logical database designer then is to organize the data within the business environment into a set of interrelated tables without regard for the specific data structures a RDBMS uses internally. Likewise, database users do not need to concern themselves with the low-level tasks of defining data structures in memory or writing code to access data on disk. Instead, a database user only needs to learn a few relatively simple SQL commands and leave the data manipulation and access routines to the RDBMS.

Another defining attribute of a RDBMS is the system catalog, which is a set of tables that hold information about the RDBMS itself. System catalogs typically hold information about tables, indexes, physical disk allocations, users, permissions, data types, and so on. System catalogs themselves can be queried just like any user-defined table to get information about the database. When database objects are created, changed, and deleted, the system catalog tables are also automatically updated.

Lacking logical pointers that order or link data together, RDBMSs must often conduct an exhaustive search on disk to locate a particular value or set of values. This kind of search is called a *table scan*, and it can take a while to complete. Fortunately, RDBMSs have a built-in mechanism called an index that provides a faster alternative to table scans. An index is a separate data structure from the table and stores only the sorted values of a given column (or collection of columns) and their physical addresses. An index can significantly reduce the number of I/Os required to find a particular row of data. Instead of reading the data on disk directly, the RDBMS first looks up the value in an index, finds the physical locations of the value, and then goes after the data on disk.

Another important attribute of a RDBMS architecture is the notion of integrity constraints. Tables are related by keys. A *key* is some column or combination of columns that uniquely identifies each table. A unique key in one table can exist as a nonunique column in another table. For instance, in an Employees table, an employee may be uniquely identified by her Social Security number. This Social Security number occurs multiple times in the Payroll table, where a row is inserted for each payroll check issued. A RDBMS must supply some mechanism for keeping these tables in synch so that when an employee is deleted from the Employee table the

Payroll table does not end up with orphan rows that do not match any employee. An integrity constraint is a built-in rule that is automatically invoked to maintain database integrity. These rules are defined by the database designer and thereby lessen the burden of database integrity maintenance for programmers.

Another critical part of the RDBMS architecture, which is also transparent to users, is the optimizer. The *optimizer* is an expert system that determines the most efficient sequence for the database to follow in processing any given query. The optimizer evaluates all reasonable data access paths, taking into consideration table sizes, indexes, and common keys. The shortest access path, called the *plan*, is selected and executed. Databases like Sybase and Oracle, which support stored procedures, store and reuse the plan associated with the stored procedure. DB2, on the other hand, generates the plan from embedded SQL during program compilation.

RDBMS Pros and Cons

As RDBMSs have matured over the past 15 years, their ability to handle issues related to transaction control, concurrent users, database recovery, and query optimization have also greatly improved. Concurrently, RDBMS application development has been greatly augmented by a whole new generation of visual programming tools that greatly simplify the task of database integration. These architectural improvements have encouraged users to build ever larger and more complex database applications.

The following sections explain in greater detail some of the chief advantages of current RDBMS technology over other data storage and retrieval systems. The last section deals with the disadvantages of RDBMS.

Database Design

Relational databases allow designers to closely map database objects to real-world entities— leading to shorter design phases and more intuitively obvious models. Logical relational database design also lends itself to more objective standards of accuracy than nonrelational designs. Various database design issues are also well-understood (such as the trade-off between performance and data redundancy) and can be readily identified and quantified, thereby simplifying the relational design solution.

Database Programming

The advent of SQL as the RDBMS query language standard has greatly simplified the data access operations that have to be written into database applications. As a result, the sheer amount of application code that once had to be written to access and process external data sources has been dramatically reduced. In particular, SQL coders no longer have to concern themselves with opening, processing, and closing files; they can just concentrate on the sorting, grouping, and filtering of query results. Due to the nonprocedural nature of SQL, RDBMS data access and manipulation is far more flexible, economical, accurate, and less prone to error than the complex systems of yesterday. Today's RDBMS do, however, provide for procedural extensions to SQL with Oracle PL/SQL (Procedural Language Extension/Structured Query Language) and Sybase Transact SQL.

RDBMSs also allow for a high level of concurrent access among a large community of users with varying transaction, decision support, and batch processing requirements. Furthermore, today's RDBMSs manage concurrency, transaction consistency, and data integrity with much less application intervention than what is required for nonrelational databases.

Performance

In the mid-'80s, most RDBMSs required a continual regimen of tuning and pruning to satisfy the seeming voracious demands of online transaction processing (OLTP) environments. However, performance has improved steadily over the past decade to the point that all of the leading UNIX RDBMSs have by now comfortably outpaced the demands placed upon them by most OLTP applications. And although RDBMSs still generally require more I/Os than nonrelational databases, this overhead is being masked by advances in optimizer engineering, physical storage organization, and parallelization of RDBMS routines.

Another advantage of RDBMSs is that application performance can often be improved without changing the application itself (although application tuning should not be ignored when considering performance issues). This separation of database maintenance from application development allows database administrators to tune and supplement physical resources as required with no impact on application source code.

Intelligence

RDBMS vendors are building increasing intelligence into their database servers using a variety of integrity constraints, monitors, and procedural repositories. Integrity constraints not only help to enforce referential integrity, but they have been extended to help ensure the validity of database values through the use of rules, defaults, and triggered events. These constraints reduce the window of vulnerability for accidental integrity violations leading to data inconsistency. Most database servers also have utilities that will check for database inconsistencies—both logical and physical.

Monitors are being increasingly incorporated into RDBMS architectures to help databases adjust to the varying demands placed upon them. These monitors are often tied into expert system modules that automatically balance loads, invoke recovery operations, and trigger events when certain resource thresholds are exceeded. These activities reduce the amount of direct operational intervention and improve overall database integrity and reliability.

Finally, servers are increasingly functioning as repositories not only for standard database objects, such as tables and indexes, but also for database objects that contain program and business logic. These program objects, called *stored procedures*, allow database developers to create common data access routines that are precompiled and can be shared by multiple applications. These routines help to reduce database traffic and offload processing overhead from the client to the server (which may or may not be desirable, depending on the overall database application architecture). RDBMSs are also beginning to serve as a repository for business entities, rules, and processes that can be used to represent policies, workflows, and business function definitions.

Openness

RDBMS applications are becoming increasingly scalable and open due to the separation of the physical database implementation and the physical database's capability to grow without affecting the application itself. Most RDBMSs support a variety of platform environments, making relational databases among the most open software categories on the market today.

The SQL standard has also enforced a degree of logical consistency and openness among the various vendor offerings that has lead to greater application portability and interoperability. Furthermore, with the widespread use of ODBC drivers from Microsoft, RDBMSs have achieved a new level of openness by enabling back-end databases to be interchanged with minimal program modification.

Distribution

Because RDBMSs hide the physical data access operations from the application, the user does not need to know the location or source of the RDBMS's data to use the data. Once slow and impractical, these design objectives are getting a new boost from advances in distributed database engineering, including database replication, triggers, remote stored procedures, and gateways. These advances are already being used to support global architectures in finance, brokerage, and manufacturing. These advances also help provide fault tolerance. For instance, if a production system should fail, users can be switched to a replicated standby database, a setup which guarantees the around-the-clock availability of the data.

The Downside

For all of their much-heralded merits, relational databases are not perfect and are ill-suited for certain kinds of tasks. One inherent weakness is their lack of support for complex data, including objects, multidimensional tables, and hierarchies. In particular, RDBMSs do not interface well to object-oriented programs written in languages like C++ and Smalltalk, which internally reference complex objects. These types of applications are often better served by Object Database Management Systems (ODBMS), which can mirror complex application objects in their storage and access routines. Most of the RDBMS vendors, however, have plans in place to provide greater object support in their upcoming releases.

Related to this problem is the limited support for media and text. Most RDBMSs allow various media data, such as audio, graphics, and video to be stuck into a generalized data type called a BLOB, which is shorthand for binary large objects. Similarly, text data is usually stored in a generic text data type. Although BLOBs and text data types allow nontraditional data to be stored and accessed, they cannot be easily manipulated or filtered based upon any intrinsic information content.

Another disadvantage of RDBMSs is that they can be much slower than some of the competing database technologies, particularly when they have not been properly optimized for performance. RDBMSs pay an inherent performance penalty for their flexibility and ease of use. For instance, a hierarchical database like IMS can get to the data very fast but can't easily perform an ad hoc query. An RDBMS may require more I/O to get the same data, but it can dynamically retrieve any combination of data from any number of related tables based on any number of conditions.

Finally, although SQL is far easier to use than writing custom data access routines in a programming language like C, it is by no means meant for everyone. Some MIS shops made the early mistake of trying to train every casual database user in SQL. This strategy can quickly alienate business users and bog down a database with poorly written SQL. Fortunately, this problem is being partially addressed by a number of visual query products that help users to graphically frame questions and browse the results.

Object Database Management Systems

Object database management systems (ODBMS) are a natural outgrowth of the object-oriented trend in software development. This class of data-management products is closely coupled to object-oriented programming languages and allows developers to store and access complex data structures, known as *objects*. ODBMS applications typically involve unconventional data like diagrams, images, and time-series data that does not easily fit into a row-and-column relational model.

The main strength of the object approach lies in its ability to more closely represent real-world entities and store these as objects in the database. Objects not only contain data, but can also store programmatic logic that describes an object's behavior. The promise of the object-oriented approach is that reusable plug-and-play software modules will eventually automate and drastically streamline application development. Until recently, interest in ODBMS technology was limited to a small audience of object-oriented enthusiasts and academics. Now, however, ODBMSs are beginning to establish a foothold in traditional MIS environments as the object-oriented paradigm continues to win converts and gain wider acceptance.

Databases were designed to allow data to be stored and retrieved. Relational database management systems (RDBMSs), as discussed earlier, solve the data management problem by storing data in its most basic form inside simple two-dimensional structures called tables. However, with the advent of object-oriented programming, data structures inside of programs have become increasingly complex and are organized according to object-oriented principles that do not easily translate into a relational format.

ODBMSs differ from relational database management systems in both the way data is stored and the way it is accessed. In an ODBMS, data objects can be built up from a number of component data elements and can represent complicated relationships using object-oriented concepts such as encapsulation, inheritance, polymorphism, class hierarchies, and user-defined data types. RDBMSs, on the other hand, store data at the most atomic level and leave it up to the developer to reassemble the pieces of data together into meaningful objects using SQL.

In an ODBMS, data relationships are built-in and data access is more predetermined. Rather than storing explicit relationships among data elements, RDBMSs store only the data itself in independent tables and use SQL join statements to build dynamic relationships by accessing data residing in different tables.

Another basic tenet of object-oriented design is the ability to encapsulate procedures, called *methods*, with objects. Although some RDBMSs do provide stored procedures, a simple mechanism for encapsulating procedures with tables, these procedures do not meet the requirements of true object-oriented design.

By storing data as objects, ODBMSs reduce the translation layer between how data is represented inside a program and how it is represented inside the database. This reduction can dramatically simplify the data access routines for an object-oriented application developer and speed up performance. It does, however, complicate the task of database maintenance because the database frequently needs to be restructured to accommodate new data associations.

ODBMS client/server processing is built around either a object server or a page server architecture. The object server architecture splits processing between the client and the server in a more cooperative manner than that found in a page server architecture. Using a page server architecture, the ODBMS defers most database processing responsibilities to the client through the application programming interface. The server is reduced to a file server status, managing storage and passing requested data to the client a page at a time.

In an object server architecture, the client is typically responsible for manipulating objects locally, coordinating transactions, and managing the programming language interface to the object. The ODBMS server still takes on many of the traditional roles played by their RDBMS cousins, namely, query optimization, persistent storage management, checking out objects to clients, concurrency management, and enforcing integrity constraints. Object servers vary in the way they store and execute methods. Some ODBMSs are more active, storing and executing methods on the server side, similar to stored procedures in an RDBMS. Others store methods in libraries, which the application processes execute, on the client side.

ODBMS technology still lacks the maturity of the RDBMS market in handling many bread-and-butter data management issues such as locking, automatic rollback, database recovery, and security. Most of the contenders in this market are relatively new and small, with less than 200 employees, and are no match for the titans of the RDBMS world, such as Oracle, IBM, and Microsoft. With sales of about $85 million in 1994, the ODBMS technology still represents less than 4 percent of the overall database market. Industry analysts expect this market share to grow to over 10 percent over the next two years and pass the $1 billion sales mark by the end of 1998.

Product Category Overview

The preceding section looked at some of the ways ODBMSs differ from the more established RDBMS technology. Within the ODBMS world, products can be placed along a spectrum as to how well they can co-exist with the relational model. The following sections are an overview of the three major subcategories that ODBMS products fall into: pure object-oriented, object wrappers, and object-relational.

Object-Oriented

A purely object-oriented ODBMS offers all of the facilities found in a conventional database system such as a data model, concurrent access, transaction management, and a query language. In addition, these systems offer features that are unique to an object-oriented environment including data abstraction, encapsulation, inheritance, and user-defined data types. ODBMSs typically assign permanent identifiers to objects, called Object IDs, to pre-establish joins among tables and enhance performance. Objects are stored in object libraries and are reusable.

Pure object-oriented ODBMS also generally rely on languages such as C++ or Smalltalk for application development and lack a standard query language such as SQL. These types of ODBMSs are most appropriate for projects requiring complex data modeling and distributed data management where the object paradigm is well-understood. Examples of pure ODBMSs are GemStone, Ontos, ObjectStore, and Versant.

Object Wrappers

An object wrapper is not a true database, but rather a layer of software that sits between an object-oriented application program and a non-ODBMS database. The object wrapper simplifies data access by breaking down complex objects into smaller data elements that the database can handle. When a program requests an object from the database, the object wrapper automatically reassembles and delivers the object.

Object wrappers improve programmer productivity by making the object-to-database translation transparent to the developer. However, they do little to address the inability of RDBMSs to efficiently model complex data and do not provide the performance gains that other ODBMS products can offer in accessing complex objects. Examples of object wrappers include Odapter from Hewlett Packard, Enterprise Objects Framework from NeXT Computer, and Persistence from Persistence Software.

Object-Relational

The idea behind this type of ODBMS is to marry the best features of relational and object-oriented databases. Sometimes referred to as hybrid databases, these object-relational database management systems (ORDBMS) allow developers to model their data as objects, yet still access data relationally using SQL-like queries. Like pure ODBMSs, ORDBMSs use unique object identifiers and allow objects to be reused. In addition, ORDBMSs also take advantage of the table metaphor to structure data storage and access. ORDBMSs have made great strides in recent years and tend to be stronger in the area of data management than pure ODBMSs. Examples of ORDMBSs are Informix/Illustra, UniSQL, and Matisse.

Many of the top relational vendors are also beginning to extend their existing databases to embrace object-oriented concepts such as user-defined data types, data encapsulation, and support for BLOBs. IBM, Oracle, Sybase, and Ingres have all announced object-oriented support for future releases of their database architectures. Currently, the ANSI SQL3 Committee is developing standards to support these RDBMS extensions. IBM is also using the ObjectStore ODBMS for its next-generation application development framework.

On the other side of the fence, the trend now is also for purely ODBMS vendors to "relationalize" their databases by incorporating SQL interfaces into their object architectures. Examples of this development include SQL++ from Objectivity and ObjectSQL from Ontos.

ODBMS Standards

In the last few years, ODBMS vendors have become increasingly responsive to standards presented by the Object Database Management Group (ODMG), a standards committee representing most of the ODBMS vendors. The ODMG has been working to standardize ODBMS interfaces in order to help the technology gain broader acceptance—in much the same way that SQL helped to legitimize relational technology. In 1994, the ODMG published their work for establishing a common database interface standard called ODMG-93. The ODMG is currently preparing a major revision of that standard, which will be entitled ODMG-95.

The ODMG standard presents a common object model and defines the syntax for defining objects independent of any specific object-oriented language. The ODMG is also developing standards for C++ and Smalltalk bindings and an object query language (OQL) that's based on a superset of SQL. This OQL will allow developers to frame queries using both an object programming language and a SQL-like language.

Concurrent with the ODMG standards is the current effort by the ANSI SQL3 Committee to bring the object model into the SQL fold. However, some ODBMS proponents are concerned that the SQL3 standard will not adequately account for the underlying structural differences of the object model. Work is also underway to bring together the ODMG object query language and SQL3.

ODBMS Pros and Cons

Learning from the past, ODBMS vendors have inherited many of the best features from the older relational, hierarchical, and network database models. This eclectic borrowing has given them an architectural edge over some of these older database technologies.

Performance

ODBMSs often outperform relational systems by a significant margin. This performance is due to their use of built-in pointers to establish data relationships and pre-assemble complex objects. The trade-off is in the inability of ODBMSs to create new relationships within the data on the fly.

Complex Data Modeling

ODBMSs are best suited for application environments with complex data modeling requirements. ODBMSs often allow database designers to develop real-world models that encapsulate behavior as well as data. The key to complex data modeling lies in the ability of the ODBMS to establish new abstract data types from primitive data types and to pass these on through inheritance. RDBMSs, by contrast, provide a much less efficient data modeling technique through the use of views. Because views get built at query time, they can lead to serious performance degradation.

Scalability/Portability

Most ODBMSs scale from PC platforms up to large, multiprocessor (MP) UNIX systems. And with their advanced indexing and partitioning methods, some ODBMS offerings can allow databases to grow with little adverse impact on performance.

Because ODBMSs are typically tied into portable host languages like C++, vendors have been able to realize a high degree of interoperability among hardware platforms. This type of portability allows developers to build robust architectures that flexibly distribute processing and storage tasks within a client/server environment. This flexibility also means programmers can develop applications on PC platforms and deploy them on midrange production platforms.

Weaknesses

One serious shortcoming of ODBMSs is their dependence upon object-oriented host languages such as C++. RDBMSs, by contrast, have tended to separate their database engines from the host languages that access them.

The learning curve for a language like C++ is a steep one, and few organizations can spare the time and expense to train their existing staff in these esoteric languages. On the other hand,

RDBMSs, with their more extensive client/server interface support, give MIS shops the opportunity to leverage existing skills and focus training on easier-to-use 4GL and visual programming languages, such as Visual Basic.

Some ODBMS vendors, Objectivity and UniSQL, for example, are beginning to offer database engines with multiple language interfaces.

Summary

In this chapter, you learned the differences between relational and object database management systems.

Relational databases use a nonprocedural language called SQL to access data, allow designers to closely map database objects to real-world entities, are becoming increasingly scalable and open, and are theoretically capable of distributing both data and processing across multiple servers at disparate locations.

Object databases are a natural outgrowth of the object-oriented trend in software development. They can outperform relational systems significantly, help model complex data, and scale from PC platforms up to large MP UNIX systems. The three subcategories of ODBMS are pure object-oriented, object wrappers, and object-relational.

Data Warehousing

8

by Neil Jenkins

In this chapter, you learn about the main areas of effective data warehousing. You will be able to answer the following questions:

- What is data warehousing?
- Why do companies use data warehousing?
- What is client/server data warehousing?
- How can I avoid data problems?
- How can I manage all my data effectively?

Understanding Data Warehousing

The term *data warehousing* describes the practice of storing company data in a secondary location, which is typically away from existing production systems. The location would be one from which the information can be proactively reported and queried against. The data is likely to be snapshots of live production data. The data entering the data warehouse comes from the operational environment in almost every case. The data warehouse is always a physically separate store of data transformed from the application data found in the production environment. Even though the data warehouse may be physically separate from the application data, they can both be on the same computer.

Data warehousing has become one of the main types of computer systems for organizations in the 1990s. A data warehouse provides information processing by providing a solid platform of integrated, historical data from which to do analysis.

Normally an organization's main business systems are not highly integrated. A data warehouse provides the facility for integration in this kind of business environment. A well-built data warehouse organizes and stores the data needed for providing information and analytical processing over a long historical time perspective. The ultimate goal of data warehousing is the creation of a single logical view of data that may reside in many different, separate physical databases. This view provides developers and business users with a single working model of the enterprise's data, something which is absent in virtually every organization.

The data warehouse is optimized for analysis of large volumes of data rather than the speed of performance of individual transactions. For example, a customer servicing application has its data optimized to provide fast access to that individual customer and that customer's orders. This application can quickly give you the answer to the query, "Show me Andy Stewart's Customer record and all his purchases this month." A data warehouse application for this customer servicing organization will be optimized for providing information on many customers and their many orders. For example, the data warehouse application can quickly give you the answer to the query, "Show me all customers who have purchased product X in the last six months."

Data is extracted periodically from the core business databases and placed into secondary databases to form an organization's information repository. People in the organization then use the information repository as a pool of information to test and report against. A variety of tools, such as those in the following list, can be used to access this pool:

- Custom-built applications
- Executive Information Systems (EIS)
- Decision support systems
- Simple reporting tools and report builders

Users can view the information in a number of ways, the most popular being through graphical analysis and reporting tools, such as Cognos' Powerplay. Tools like Powerplay can present textual information, such as the number of customers purchasing products X, Y, and Z, as a graph, bar chart, or pie chart. With a simple mouse button click or keystroke, the information can then be viewed in a different way, such as product X sales by month by geographic region.

As you can see, data warehousing is a fundamental approach that can be used to meet an organization's reporting, querying, and statistical analysis needs. A data warehouse might be set up like the one shown in Figure 8.1.

FIGURE 8.1.

A sample data warehouse environment.

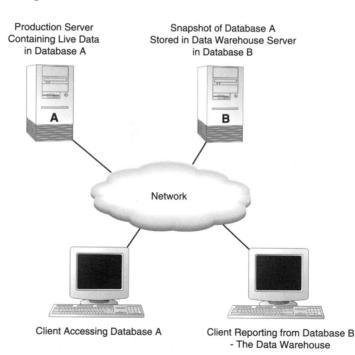

Components of the Data Warehouse

Most organizational data warehouses consist of three main types of data:

- Mainframe or midrange production data held in hierarchical and network DBMS (An estimated 75 percent of corporate data is held in these types of DBMS, such as IMS and DB2/400.)

- Departmental data held in proprietary file systems (such as VSAM, RMS) and RDBMS (such as Informix, Oracle)

- Private data held on workstations and private servers

The data warehouse itself is enabled through middleware technologies. Alliances between middleware technology providers and hardware suppliers have created a new market for data warehouse technologies. Chapter 11, "Understanding Middleware," discusses middleware in more detail.

Updating a Data Warehouse

A data warehouse or the databases within a data warehouse are updated regularly. For most companies, the most frequently used databases are updated daily (typically in an overnight batch run or file transfer). A database containing the customer detail records might be updated daily, for example. Other databases that do not change frequently may be updated weekly or sometimes even monthly. For example, a database containing information on available product types might be updated weekly, but a database containing airport codes might only need to be updated monthly.

Handling Reports and Statistical Analysis

Reporting and statistical analysis do not have to be done in real time. Reports and statistics can be processed based on data that is 24 hours or more out of date. Reports and statistical analysis that analyze trends such as the sales of product A this year compared to sales of product A this time last year require information to be stored and calculated by length of time. A one-day difference in the information that is not completely current normally does not make any significant difference to the result or trend. To take advantage of this fact, organizations have begun to set up data warehouses on hardware other than that which runs their core business functions or on an existing processor but with a lower running priority. The reasons for setting up separate data warehouses are numerous, as explained in the following sections.

Best Use of Available Computers

Data warehousing allows reporting and statistical work to be moved away from an organization's main computer. As a result, the core business or production applications on the main computer can use the extra available processing power on the main computer to run faster. Computer A running 60 production users and 15 data analyzers will operate faster if the data analyzers are moved across to another machine, for example.

When running on the same computer, the reporting and analysis functions of a data warehouse can be restricted in the processor time usage they receive in comparison to that received by the production business applications, such as an interactive legacy system.

Removal of Database-Intensive Work

Reporting and data analysis work is often database-intensive. Data warehouse selections can read and write hundreds of thousands of records and contain complex database joins. A production application deals with the same complex joins, but it is normally only active against a small number of records during each transaction.

Modular Environment and Protection

If a data warehouse system crashes, core business systems residing on other computers or networks can continue to operate. By positioning your company systems on different machines, you can minimize the negative effect that any one machine has when it malfunctions. In addition, the data warehouse can be placed on a smaller and typically less expensive computer than the main production server. For example, an IBM AS/400 site might place their data warehouse on a large PC file server.

The Benefits of Data Warehousing

Because of the way a data warehouse can handle reports and analysis, a business can derive business benefit from data warehousing. The benefits come in a number of ways:

- Improved reporting and selection tools.
- Large reductions in the amount of printouts because reports can be viewed and analyzed online through graphical views on client workstations.
- Removal of reporting cycles because users can now create reports any time they need them.
- Ability to set thresholds. Suppose that a client computer always shows a map of Europe when it is switched on. By using a data warehouse, you can configure the computer to color red any region that shows a shortfall of more than five percent in sales earned to date against the budget.
- Ability to summarize data at a high level and then break down information into its core components by using *drill down* techniques.

Drilling Down

In a drill down technique, a computer application shows information at a summary level. When a user clicks or otherwise activates that information, it shows a screen that demonstrates how that information is derived. Each key press or mouse click breaks down the information into more and more detail.

Suppose that the Managing Director of Patricia Reed Associates wanted to look up some information on the company's European customers. Figure 8.2 shows how the high-level data warehouse might appear.

FIGURE 8.2.

An example of the summary level for a data warehouse.

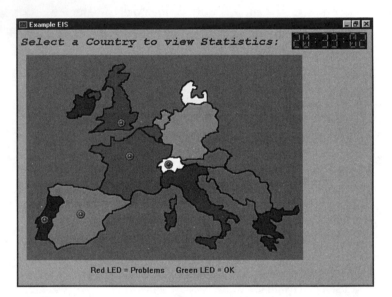

Drilling down into the information reveals that the total of 500,000 European customers is made up of 100,000 Northern European customers, 200,000 Western European customers, 50,000 Southern European customers, and 150,000 Eastern European customers (see Figure 8.3).

Drilling down further into the Southern European data reveals figures of 40,000 and 10,000 customers for Portugal and Spain respectively. Figure 8.4 shows this lowest level of detail held in the data warehouse system. Note that it presents the information in a different format more pertinent to the information it displays.

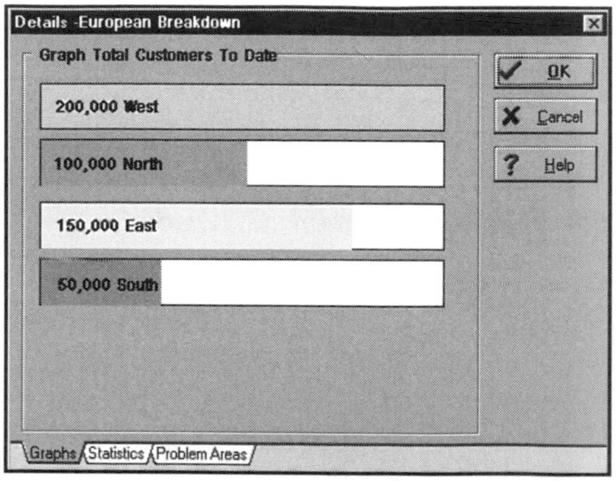

FIGURE 8.3.

Drilling down to the next level of information.

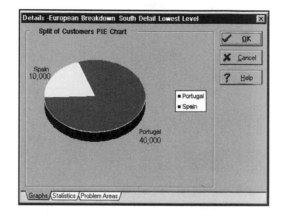

FIGURE 8.4.

The final level of available information.

Exception Reporting

Exception reporting allows you to see only the information that is out of the ordinary that you may want to act upon. How many times have you received large reports only to use less than 10 percent of the information they contained? Invariably, you scan a printed report to pick out the good points or the bad points of the information that it is presenting. These points can be considered exceptions to the norm and can be reported on. For example, you could do a report that shows only the salespeople who exceeded their sales targets by 10 percent so that you can commend and support your company's outstanding salespeople. To find out which salespeople need help and encouragement, you could also include the salespeople who missed their sales targets by 15 percent.

Figure 8.5 shows how this report might appear. In this example, you are not considering those who have an average performance; you are looking at only those who fall either side of the exception levels your organization has set (in this case, -15 percent and +10 percent).

Therefore, you want your exception reports to list only figures outside of this range. The below target report could be used to coach and encourage better performance while the above target report could be used to recognize and reward achievement. Data warehousing tools allow you to analyze the data that you require so you see only what you need to. Newer data warehousing tools can also provide you with ready-made reports and graphs on the exception thresholds that you set; these tools only produce the reports once these thresholds are met.

FIGURE 8.5.

Exception reporting example.

Exception Report Example -15% and +10%				
Name	Jan	Feb	Mar	Average
Andrew Stewart	10	12	14	12
William Tuck	-20	-15	-16	-17
Frank Ortiz	-22	-20	-15	-19
Robert Cavinato	10	10	14	11
Christine Jenkins	15	16	17	16
Total	-1	1	3	1
Sales Target by Month - Exception Report				

Data Warehousing in a Client/Server Environment

Client/server systems can be utilized in the development of data warehouses. Because the client has an amount of intelligence in a client/server environment, the data warehouse system can be built in a number of ways. Depending on your information needs, one or more of the client/server scenarios described in the following sections will fit your organization.

Client Presentation/Server Selection

In the client presentation/server selection scenario, the data warehouse server uses its processing time to perform the data selection and format the result set as shown in Figure 8.6. The server then sends the results set back to the individual user, typically as a data file to be used in popular data manipulation tools such as Excel or Lotus 1-2-3.

The selection or analysis is typically created on the server through a server-based tool, such as Query/400 on the IBM AS/400. Query/400 is a feature-rich yet reasonably easy-to-use database query and selection tool.

FIGURE 8.6.

Client presentation/server selection scenario.

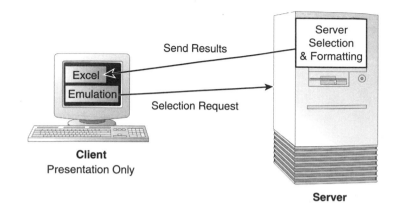

FIGURE 8.6 labels:
Send Results
Selection Request
Server Selection & Formatting
Excel
Emulation
Client
Presentation Only
Server

Client Presentation and Selection/Server Processing

In the client presentation and selection/server processing scenario, the client machine processes a selection criteria through a front-end tool such as Cognos' Powerplay. The selection is then passed to the server to be processed. Processing time on the server is used to create the results set that is then sent back to the client and presented in the original tool. The client handles formatting and presentation. Figure 8.7 shows an example of this scenario.

FIGURE 8.7.

Client presentation and selection/server processing.

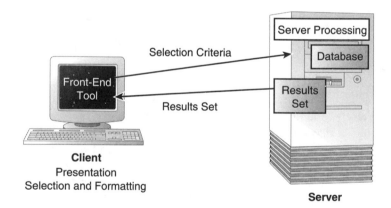

FIGURE 8.7 labels:
Selection Criteria
Results Set
Server Processing
Database
Results Set
Front-End Tool
Client
Presentation
Selection and Formatting
Server

You can use this scenario to create effective business applications that can hide the underlying tools and application logic from the user. Users can generate their selections with simple key presses (or mouse clicks in the GUI world). This example shows how data warehousing can be effective as a readily usable tool in any organization without involving hours of programming and development from the IS departments.

Client Presentation, Selection, and Processing

In the client presentation, selection, and processing scenario, the client issues a selection request to the server. The server generates a result set and sends it back to the client. The client then runs further application logic on the results set that has been received (see Figure 8.8). This logic may be further partitioning or subsetting of the data or more complex mathematical analysis that would otherwise tie up the processing time of the data server.

FIGURE 8.8.

The client presentation, selection, and processing scenario.

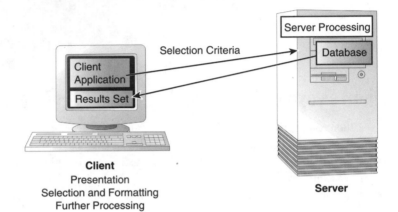

Selection Criteria

Client
Application

Results Set

Server Processing

Database

Client
Presentation
Selection and Formatting
Further Processing

Server

The Right Tools and the Right Training

When organizations begin to develop whole departments around data warehousing, they often make two fundamental mistakes. First, they do not provide anywhere near the correct level of skilled staff or training for unskilled staff in these departments. Do you trust the figures currently coming out of your statistics or management information areas? If not, then the likelihood is that the staff are inadequately skilled to interpret, diagnose, or create the information. All too often organizations ask for statistics and give the job to someone who doesn't understand sums, counts, averages, medians, and means! You need a good information analyst who understands the business and its values instead of the person who just knows the latest version of Excel.

Which tools to use is the second area of concern. How much data duplication goes on today in your environment? How many reports are printed out and then at some stage rekeyed into a spreadsheet in order to print out (again!) the same numbers in a better presentation or a smarter graph! How much better could reports be if employees had tools that presented the data in the format they wanted without them having to rekey, retype, and reprint? (How often does the individual who rekeys the information compare both sets line by line to ensure they are correct?) How much faster and accurate would reports be if the information were online? How much more beneficial would reports be to the business if the information were always up-to-date? You need tools that can effectively deliver all these features to your benefit, with online graphical views, accurate reporting, and no more rekeying.

Do you have any users who are PC powerhouses? These users have to play with every function of every tool and try to conceive a business use for it to prove their own worth. Avoid putting these people on your data warehouse team. The majority of data warehouse systems can be effectively reported from using tools such as Excel. Yet Excel and products like it contain such a wealth of tools that they could be overkill for your requirements. Develop a good feel of what you want before you pick the tools to use. Remember that the underlying data has to be correct if the tool is going to work for you. Tools such as Excel can hide the inaccuracy of data in the warehouse if used incorrectly.

Try where possible to eliminate manual calculations from information within tools. It is a sad day when you as the systems manager attend a meeting where all the attendees are using data from your data warehouse, but not one report matches another because each attendee has calculated totals and averages differently. The "Spreadsheet Manipulator" often attacks by twisting numbers in this way. A number of users will find their data does not match that of the attendees as if some phantom had altered the figures! At least if everyone reports the same figures the figures will be the same even if they are incorrect!

The Problems of Data Warehousing

Data warehousing, like most computer systems, has its limitations that can cause problems to an organization. The data warehouse must be readily accessible and available to users needing to provide a business function. Yet organizations often consider data warehousing to be a function of Information Systems. What occurs today is the creation of end-user computing or business support departments within the IS organization. These departments typically spend most of their time creating and running individual reports, mail shots, and print runs for the user base. Obviously in an environment where overhead needs to be reduced, the use of expensive IS staff in this way is not beneficial.

The best thing to do in all cases is to train the user community to handle these tasks themselves by using the correct tools. You can therefore delegate and diversify the requirements and production of the reports and selections to those areas that also fully understand the resultant data and reports being produced. IS should not be involved in generating and interpreting data in the data warehouse; IS should be concerned only with the timely and reliable delivery of the information to the user base.

There are cultural challenges when a data warehouse is implemented. The IS department will be providing new kinds of services, and data previously 'owned' by user divisions now has to be widely available. Prototyping and user ownership have important roles to play in winning commitment to the fundamental changes in data ownership that creating a data warehouse involves. Furthermore, users' expectations will be significantly raised by their new facilities, which will result in pressure for data as close as possible to real-time to be available from the warehouse.

From an organization's perspective, the data warehouse is a potential security risk. For example, a user accessing the warehouse may be able to collect and use company data in a fraudulent way. Ensuring that the data warehouse is protected by strict security access measures and restricted functionality levels will help prevent the misuse of this data.

Data in the data warehouse needs to be accurate; it does, however, come from data in the production systems. Over time, a company's databases may become inaccurate due to changes made to them by the core workforce. Inaccuracies in an organization's databases can lead to financial loss, reduced customer satisfaction, and other areas of bad business. The data warehouse is somewhat of a double-edged sword with regards to these problems. Firstly, because analysis of the warehouse deals with potentially thousands of records, inconsistencies and inaccuracies will appear a lot quicker than if one user of the production system were to go through each piece of data. Secondly, to your benefit, once a problem has been identified, your data warehouse and data tools can identify all the problem areas and which records are inaccurate. Ensuring data accuracy is an ongoing activity, not just a small, short clean-up project. Referential integrity can help keep the data clean and accurate. Data accuracy should be high on both the Systems department's and User department's agendas.

Financial Loss

Financial loss can come as a result of a data warehouse in a number of ways. Users incorrectly keying in or calculating financial activity can affect financial loss. Consider also mail shots from a marketing data warehouse. In Europe, you can get reduced postal costs if your mail is sorted in postcode order (similar to the USA zip code) and if each piece of mail has an accurate post code. This reduction is because the postal service does not have to subsequently sort your mail. By using analysis tools on your postcode and zip code information, you can accurately identify the incorrect postcodes and zip codes, and then you can purchase software from the mail companies that can correct your data. This increases your data accuracy and gives you the reduced postal costs.

Reduced Customer Satisfaction

Perhaps the biggest issue in many organizations today is continually trying to improve customer satisfaction. A satisfied customer will invariably return for more business. If your name happens to be Mrs. Sian McDermott, it is infuriating for your mail to come through to Mr. Shiny MacDiddymouse. How soon will you as the customer respond to such a marketing piece? If other information is sent to you that is inaccurate, how likely are you to respond? In an era where it costs 10 times more to get a new customer than it does to retain an existing customer, businesses should be placing significant effort into ensuring that the data in production systems and data warehouses is accurate. By collecting information about customers in data warehouses and doing target mailings rather than the traditional blanket mailings of old, a company can reduce its advertising costs and increase the return on its investment.

Other Problem Areas

Inaccuracies in data can lead to reporting problems like those described earlier; data may be incorrectly grouped together leading to inaccurate figures. If data is incorrect on addresses used for mailshots from a data warehouse, the mail may not get through. Consider also that your systems may not cater to multilanguage character sets as used in some of the European countries. The layout of an American customer's address pulled from your warehouse will look different than that of a Greek or Dutch customer. Inaccurate mailing addresses can result in returned or lost products. Companies usually have to absorb these costs. You need to make sure that the data warehouse and any front-end tools are set up to handle these differences appropriately.

The Information Process

The success of an organization's data warehouse depends on the quality, integrity, and reliability of the data within it. To increase the chances for a data warehouse to succeed, companies should develop an information process. An *information process* deals with the management of corporate information, including its accuracy, relevance to the business, accessibility by the user base, timeliness, and consistency of definition.

Data has to be accurate if it is to be valuable to a corporation. Relevant data means that the data contained within the data warehouse is meaningful to the organization; each piece of data held is useful and is held for a purpose. Identifying relevant data within an organization can be a challenge in itself. Yet typically the senior executives can give you 80 percent of the requirements for relevant data. These requirements tend to be the key figures that they use to determine the status of the company from a financial, operational, and managerial perspective.

Data accessibility at the correct levels is an important point as well. How often are users restrained from getting to the right information at the right time? Data in an organization and in a data warehouse has to be accessible if it is to be really useful. Data timeliness is also an important issue. Timeliness is concerned with the rate of change of data within the warehouse. Companies need to decide how often the data needs to be updated in order to meet organizational needs.

Finally, data consistency is often considered the most problematic area of the information process. Definitions of data can ensure consistency. Data inconsistency is the result of users placing different meanings and interpretations on data. For example, Julia from Accounts arrives at a meeting stating that the company has 100,000 customers. Naomi from Operations also arrives with her report stating that there are 107,000 customers. There is obviously an inconsistency here. While investigating this inconsistency, you might find that the Accounts department measures customers as paying customers, and Operations measures customers as those who have paid for products and those who have just inquired about products. Neither report is strictly incorrect; the different definitions of customer caused the inconsistency. This problem also surfaces when developing applications. Therefore, spending time defining what the corporate data is and how it is measured can seriously improve your information process and the quality of your data warehouse.

Looking after data, its integrity, and also its quality has often been viewed as the responsibility of the Information Systems department. This view is gradually changing, however, and the emphasis is now moving to a team of individuals working on the management of the corporate information pool, be it production systems or data warehouse. Sure, IS continues to handle the storage, backup, recovery and technical facets of the information, but this new breed of department begins to develop the knowledge and skill base for maintaining the quality of the data.

The Information Process department's role is to look after the corporate data and know how the data is created, maintained, and perhaps deleted from the business systems. It documents the detailed data definitions and determines and provides new ones where applicable. Instead of the IS department, it becomes the central focus for the provision of information within an organization.

Decision Support Systems and EIS

Decision support systems (DSS) provide the information required for senior management to make effective decisions based on information gathered from both internal and external data sources (such as an internal data warehouse and an electronic feed from the stock exchange). Decision support systems correlate data using a variety of tools. They can be used to set measurements and thresholds on levels of the business. The technology is therefore both useful and powerful when combined with the data warehouse environment.

DSS now have access to improved connectivity in the form of middleware, improved presentation through standardized interfaces and automated data management products. With a good data warehouse environment in place and the improved usability of GUI tools, business users are now seeing the benefit of these technologies.

EIS stands for Executive Information System. An EIS tool has to be an easy and powerful access tool to the data sources within a data warehouse. It should be available to everyone that needs access, not just the executives as the name suggests. EIS and DSS tools are sometimes also referred to as data mining tools.

EIS originally started as a handful of traditional query tools that offered improved productivity, but in practice tended to increase the user's clerical-type activity. EIS ended up just improving (slightly) the information process that was already broken. EIS allowed users to believe they were getting business benefit from systems, yet they only became more efficient at automating what needed to be changed.

In the new client/server environment, business information needs from an EIS are much clearer than they were previously. The user requirements for the EIS are now clear-cut. They are as follows:

- Comprehensive, readily available data
- Simple user interface, GUI
- Customizable tools
- Portability of data to other platforms
- Justifiable cost

The EIS is evolving as both a computer suite in its own right and as a DSS. The newer EIS tools coming to the marketplace will be much more intelligent than those of today. They will begin to assist the users in evaluating their problems and analyzing their data. The EIS will begin to guide the user rather than requiring the user to understand a great deal of the fundamental ways the EIS works.

An EIS must give online analytical processing that is flexible and gives multidimensional views of data. An EIS user needs to be able not just to drill down into data, but to specify conditions or criteria that the EIS should apply to the data warehouse. The user should be notified when a change in the data means that his or her criteria have been met such that he or she can act on the result. This capability allows the user to be much more proactive rather than reactive. If you can see the problem on the horizon, you can avoid it after all. If a sales problem begins to appear in June, at least you have time to correct before December when the final figures and targets are in.

Summary

Data warehousing has to meet the demands of process-oriented, re-engineered business. At the same time, a data warehouse and its implementation can play a part in facilitating the re-engineering of the business processes in which knowledge-based workers, including executives, are involved.

The effective use of good EIS and DSS tools can realign the broken keel of an organization and set it on the right path. The data warehouse provides the information repository so key in today's business. But always be aware that the data warehouse is only as good as the data within it.

Networking

9

by Vinay Nadig

The concept of *networking* as it is known today began in the early 1980s. With the emergence of the PC and popular desktop productivity tools in the early to mid-80s, end users depended upon their PCs for decision support. But usually a company's mission-critical applications as well as data were stored on mainframes or minicomputers. "Connectivity" was established by terminal emulation (3270, and so on) and serial file transfer methods. As PCs and PC software became more sophisticated, LANs proliferated from the mid- to late '80s for their file serving and resource-sharing capabilities. Still, traditional MIS organizations viewed LANs as "minor league." Most, if not all, of a company's mission-critical applications ran on centralized mainframe or minicomputer platforms.

With the acceptance of client/server computing as a technology platform for mission-critical applications, the network assumes enormous importance. Networks, whether local area or wide area, provide the basic plumbing for client/server applications. The network is probably the single most important component of distributed, mission-critical client/server applications. All too often, networks are designed without considering a number of new variables that client/server introduces. As a client/server designer, you cannot ignore networks when you design new applications. After an overview of network basics, I discuss the various factors affecting client/server network design in this chapter. If you are already familiar with the basics of networking, you may want to skip directly to the end of this chapter.

The Basics

Understanding the basic components of networks provides a good foundation for designing client/server infrastructure. Basically, networks need to facilitate "device-to-device" communication. The International Organization for Standardization (ISO) proposed a model of communications known as the *Open System Interconnection (OSI)* model. Although there are other models (IEEE, XNS, SNA, and so on), the OSI model is a good building block for understanding the more recent network design issues.

The OSI Model

The OSI model or framework consists of seven distinct layers. Each layer describes communication functions for specific parts of the network. See Figure 9.1 for the OSI model.

- **Layer 1: Physical layer.** The lowest layer in the OSI model deals with the transmission of signals across a physical medium that connects communications devices. This medium may be wire (coaxial cable, fiber, copper, and so on) or wireless (microwave, satellite, and so on).

- **Layer 2: Data Link layer.** This layer deals with the transmission of data between devices over the physical media. Ethernet, Token Ring, FDDI, and so on operate on this layer. Data link layers provide unique identifiers for each physical device.

FIGURE 9.1.

The OSI model.

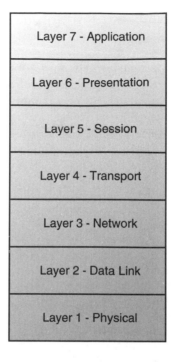

Layer 7 - Application

Layer 6 - Presentation

Layer 5 - Session

Layer 4 - Transport

Layer 3 - Network

Layer 2 - Data Link

Layer 1 - Physical

■ **Layer 3: Network layer.** This layer deals with the transmission of data between devices on different networks. This is unlike the physical and data link layers, which deal with devices within a network. Network layers introduce the concept of network addresses to facilitate internetworking device traffic.

■ **Layer 4: Transport layer.** This layer deals with the management of the data into packets and streams. This layer, along with the session, presentation, and application layers, deals with end-to-end communication, from data stream origination to data stream destination, for example.

■ **Layer 5: Session layer.** This layer deals with the establishment of a valid "session" or instance between a client (*data stream origination*) and a server (*data stream destination*). In three-tier client/server architectures, the role of the server and the client are sometimes reversed.

■ **Layer 6: Presentation layer.** This layer deals with the software and hardware that control the devices that users interact with. From a practical perspective, this could be the user desktop environment like Windows, OS/2, System 7, and so on.

■ **Layer 7: Application layer.** This layer manages user interaction with the network. This is the layer that the user sees. It may be the interface that generates the data packet (an SQL query, for example).

Protocols

The OSI model provides a conceptual framework for designing networks. Vendors have applied this model and come up with products, or more specifically, *protocol suites* or just *protocols*. Protocols are a set of specifications and software controls that manage all or some of the seven layers of the OSI model. Many of the widely used "protocols" today, TCP/IP, for example, are actually sets of protocols. TCP/IP is made up of four component protocols: IP (Internet Protocol), TCP (Transmission Control Protocol), UDP (User Datagram Protocol), and ARP (Address Resolution Protocol). Purely from a technical perspective, these types of protocols are *protocol suites*. Generally, protocols and protocol suites are used interchangeably.

In some protocols, the model is not strictly adhered to, but the end result is the same (for example, device-to-device communication). Client/server application project leaders, architects, and developers must understand the protocols available, what they mean, and how they differ in features and capabilities.

TCP/IP

TCP/IP (Transaction Control Protocol/Internet Protocol) is fast becoming the de facto industry standard for client/server applications. Originally sponsored by the government, TCP/IP has grown to be the protocol of choice for multivendor, heterogeneous platform systems integration. TCP/IP is the default protocol in UNIX systems. Because high-volume, transaction-oriented client/server applications usually run (or have done so, until now) on UNIX-based database platforms, TCP/IP has gathered momentum in the client/server battlefield.

Essentially, TCP/IP follows the OSI model but compresses the seven-layer model into four layers. Essentially, the four layers that TCP/IP follows are the application, transport, network, and the physical layers.

XNS

XNS (Xerox Network Services Internet Transport Protocol) follows a five-layer model and was developed by the Xerox Corporation. This protocol was primarily used to connect Ethernet devices. For this discussion, interest in this protocol is limited to its proprietary derivatives, one of which is Novell's *Internet Packet Exchange Protocol (IPX)*.

IPX

IPX (Internet Packet Exchange Protocol) is the default protocol in Novell's NetWare networks. Considering that NetWare is still a dominant force in the network operating system market, IPX is a major player in client/server. Novell defines IPX as a "service" that permits applications to send and receive information in the form of messages across a network. IPX follows the five-layer XNS model. It can be found in a large percentage of PC or workstation-based

LANs. IPX provides value-added services such as the *Service Advertising Protocol (SAP)*. SAP enables IPX servers to broadcast their identities and hence their services across the network. In the NetWare environment, database services can only run as *NLMs (NetWare Loadable Modules)*, and these services are broadcast using SAP. Because of the model it follows, IPX is a very "chatty" protocol, meaning that it generates a lot of network traffic. Novell has worked on this and provided less chatty versions in the current versions of NetWare. With version 4.1, Novell has beefed up NLM reliability and wants to position NetWare as a viable application server in a client/server environment.

AppleTalk

AppleTalk is Apple Computer, Inc.'s protocol to connect Macintosh computers and other network devices. It follows the OSI model closely. Phase 2 of AppleTalk provides the connectivity protocol for Macintosh computers and other non-Apple technologies like Ethernet, Token Ring, and so on.

DECnet

DECnet is Digital Equipment Corporation's proprietary slant on the OSI model. It mirrors the OSI model and provides the protocol suite that is followed in most VAX shops. Although Digital has maintained support for DECnet, its future looks uncertain. For traditional VAX shops, DECnet was a necessity. With many VAX shops migrating to Alphas and other so-called "open" platforms, other protocol suites are now available. DECnet may play a decreasing role in the client/server field as the market confusion begins to clear.

SNA (Systems Network Architecture)

SNA is IBM's proprietary networking architecture. SNA was originally proposed to provide remote access to large mainframe computers. SNA is also seven-layered although it does not exactly fit the OSI model. This architecture is important for client/server designers. A number of mission-critical applications on IBM mainframes will be converted to client/server applications. Mainframes may play a role in the new architecture as data storage devices or even servers; therefore, SNA will continue to play a part. Issues like SNA gateways from PC-LAN–based networks to mainframes for data access will affect network design.

LAN Protocols

While not protocols in the strictest sense, ARCnet, Ethernet, and Token Ring are frequently referred to as *networking protocols*. A basic understanding of these protocols is necessary because most, if not all, existing LANs use one of them.

ARCnet

ARCnet, designed in the '70s, has a fairly large installed base. It follows a star-wired topology. Because of its low throughput of 2.5 Mbps, vendors do not provide products following this protocol any more.

Ethernet

Ethernet continues to be the most popular LAN protocol. It can be installed using any kind of wiring, in a star or bus topology. (Note that Ethernet can be installed in a physical star but not a logical star.) Ethernet has a maximum throughput of 100 Mbps. There is a large volume of vendor products and support for this technology. Basically, Ethernet handles network traffic problems using a protocol called *Carrier Sense Multiple Access with Collision Detection (CSMA/ CD)*. Using this protocol, each node on a Ethernet network checks to make sure that the network is not carrying traffic from other nodes before sending any messages. In the event of collision (or messages from nodes being sent simultaneously), Ethernet adapters detect the collisions and delay transmissions in an effort to reduce collisions.

Token Ring

The most expensive of the networking protocols is *Token Ring*. Invented by IBM, it operates at a maximum throughput of 16 Mbps. Token Ring networks avoid collisions by circulating a "token" or a packet of data around the LAN. This token must reach a node before it can send messages. After the token comes back to its originator, it is purged, and a new token is generated and circulated. This is called *token passing*.

Cables, Topologies, and Your Network

Cables, wires, and wireless media constitute an important part of your networks. Special attention must be given to this piece of the networking puzzle. Client/server applications stress network bandwidth considerably. Cabling a network properly is one of the essential building blocks of high-bandwidth networks. Although cabling can be a science in itself, I will discuss some of the more frequently used types in this chapter. *Topologies* refer to the arrangement of computers and other network devices in a network. That is, are devices connected serially one after the other through the cable, or are they connected to a central point, which then distributes cable out in different directions for other devices to get connected? *Star* and *bus* are two topologies that client/server architects should understand.

Coaxial Cabling—the 10 Base 2 Scheme

Coaxial cable is similar to that used in TV cables but differs slightly in some of its electrical characteristics. Usually, networks cabled with coaxial cables follow the *10 Base 2 scheme*, wherein devices are connected together in a "bus" or linear topology, as shown in Figure 9.2. If a device fails in this serial arrangement, all devices behind this device in the network also fail. The disadvantages of using such a scheme to support mission-critical applications are obvious. This system of cabling is hardly used anymore. Cabling schemes have evolved to more reliable levels.

FIGURE 9.2.
Bus topology.

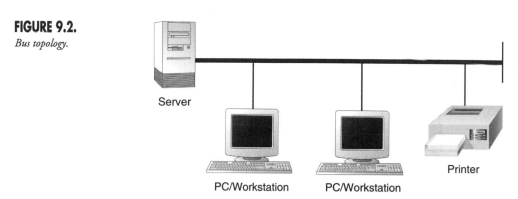

Server

PC/Workstation   PC/Workstation   Printer

Unshielded Twisted Pair (UTP) Cabling—the 10 Base T Scheme

UTP cables are a higher grade of telephone wire. There are five categories or grades of UTP: Category 1 to Category 5. Most existing buildings are usually cabled using Category 3. However, Category 5 is a higher grade rated for voice, data, and video and should be the de facto standard for all new Ethernet cabling projects. Ethernet networks cabled using UTP follow the *10 Base T scheme*, wherein devices are connected together in a "star" topology. Basically, computers and other devices are connected to multiport hubs, and these hubs are connected to servers, as shown in Figure 9.3. Ethernet switches may also be used to segment networks.

Fast Ethernet

10 Mbps Ethernet is proving no longer to be sufficient as users demand more bandwidth for their applications. As client/server applications incorporate video, sound, and large graphic files, network bandwidth becomes the bottleneck. The first alternative to designers is *fast* or *100 Mbps Ethernet (100 Base T)*; it is simply Ethernet at 100 Mbps. Fast Ethernet involves using 100 Mbps network interface cards in PCs, workstations, and servers. 100 Mbps hubs and switches are also a necessity. The attraction of 100 Mbps networking is that you can run it on existing UTP cabling. It will also run on Category 3 and Category 5, so recabling your premises will not be a necessity. You can evolve your network backbone first to 100 Mbps and migrate users gradually without upsetting existing operations.

FIGURE 9.3.
Star topology.

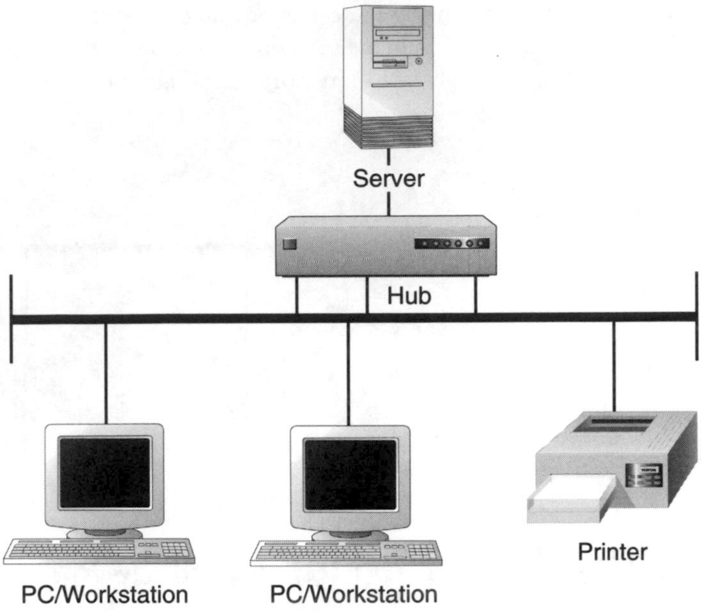

FDDI (Fiber Distributed Data Interface)

Basically, *FDDI* networks use fiber-optic cables instead of copper wires. FDDI networks are also rated at 100 Mbps. Fiber-optic cables have some inherent electrical advantages over copper cables. You can use fiber for distances up to 1 kilometer (between devices without a concentrator), compared to the 100 meters when you use Category 3 or 5. However, using FDDI networks means that you have to recable entire buildings and campuses. This is expensive, although organizations have chosen to use fiber for network backbones. Most organizations do not use fiber to their users' desktops. The cost per node or seat for FDDI is expensive, especially compared to fast Ethernet. The rash of new products being introduced in the fast Ethernet or 100 Base T arena makes it hard to justify FDDI to every desktop.

CDDI (Copper Distributed Data Interface)

CDDI networks are rated at 100 Mbps and can run over Category 5 UTP cables. CDDI is an alternative to FDDI networks. One of the main benefits is that it can run over existing UTP Category 5 cabling. In many instances, this will prevent recabling. Building CDDI networks also involves using CDDI network interface cards and CDDI hubs and switches. Although cost per seat is not as high as FDDI, it is still more expensive than 100 Base T networks. Still, CDDI is a viable alternative for 100 Mbps networking.

ATM (Asynchronous Transfer Mode)

ATM is heralded as the answer to the network bandwidth crunch. Able to run on Category 5 UTP and fiber cables, theoretically it can go from 51 Mbps to 2 Gbps. The reality on LANs today is more in the range of 25 Mbps to 155 Mbps. ATM will play a significant role in network design for client/server applications needing huge bandwidths. Desktop video, high-volume document imaging, and interactive TV are some applications. In the short term, look for ATM to replace your existing network backbone (connecting file servers, application servers, communication servers, and so on). ATM is a new way of networking. Unlike Ethernet, it is not a shared protocol. ATM dedicates pipelines for data to flow between point to point. This in effect facilitates "dedicated" sessions between client and server over a network.

Internetworking or Linking Your LANs Over a Wide Area

So far, the discussion has centered on networking over a local area: for example, inside a building and in a campus at most. This is mainly because of cabling length considerations and partly due to the protocols used. But your business needs its employees, customers, suppliers, partners, and so on to be linked over a wide geographic area as well. *Internetworking* or *wide area networks* refers to networking computers and LANs over wider geographical areas. The focus here is to link data and applications from disparate LANs. Essentially, WANs consist of two components: internetworking devices present at each LAN site and a method of carrying data from one site to another. Bridges and routers are examples of internetworking devices. They pass messages from one LAN to another based on certain header information and routing criteria. The method of carrying data from one site to another usually refers to leased lines, ISDN, Frame Relay, and so on, provided by the telecom companies. These physical media and protocols actually pass the data between sites. The following discussion looks at some of the important components that client/server designers should understand.

Repeaters

Repeaters provide the most inexpensive way to connect LANs. A repeater takes the signal (data/message) on a length of cable and regenerates it, preventing signal loss (*attenuation*). Repeaters are a simple way to increase the maximum transmission distance that your cables are rated for. However, repeaters do not play a role in WANs. They are more a factor in linking LANs in the same building, maybe between two departments/workgroups, and so on. Repeaters are not very "intelligent." They generate unnecessary network traffic. With the advent of more "intelligent" devices, repeaters are not such a great factor in network design.

Bridges

Using bridges is a more efficient method of connecting networks than using repeaters. Figure 9.4 illustrates a WAN that connects two sites with bridges.

FIGURE 9.4.

Bridges being used in a WAN.

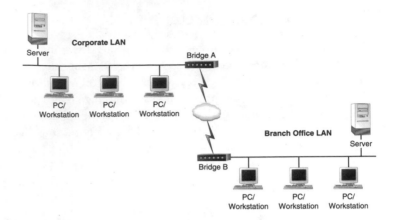

When a node on the corporate LAN sends messages (data), eventually the data packets arrive at Bridge A. Bridge A looks at the sender or source and the receiver or destination information. It then looks up a table (that it maintains and constantly updates). If the receiver is a member of this table (for example, local node of the corporate LAN), Bridge A puts the data packet in a local bin (for example, the LAN carries the data to the local recipient). If the receiver is not a member of this table (for example, an external recipient—in this case, a node on the branch office LAN), Bridge A puts the data packet in an outgoing bin. These data packets are then transmitted by whatever WAN method (leased lines, dial-up, Frame Relay, ISDN, and so on) you have in place to the remote LAN. At the branch office, Bridge B simply turns around and repeats the same process. Bridges provide reliable and fast internetworking between LANs.

Routers

Routers provide intelligent connection services between LANs. Essentially, routers are similar to bridges in that each LAN in a WAN needs at least one router. However, unlike bridges, network devices are aware of routers in the network. A router can read data packets addressed to it and determine the level of urgency with which it needs to pass them on. A router can fragment large data packets into smaller ones if it thinks that would be more efficient. Routers maintain sophisticated "routing tables" and update them dynamically across a WAN. Routers are also intelligent enough to find the best route (for example, the least costly) between source and destination in a WAN, thereby decreasing telecommunication charges. Because of the intelligence involved, routers have more overhead than bridges.

Gateways

Gateways provide the highest degree of intelligence in connecting devices. Gateways usually operate at the software level. Suppose that you need a connection between a database on SQL Server residing on a Windows NT Server and a DB/2 database residing on a mainframe. You use a gateway to achieve this. Therefore, a gateway is essentially a translator. It translates between different protocols. In this example, the translation may be between IPX and SNA using an SNA gateway. Gateways provide more than mere connection; they provide a method of communication between devices. Gateways are invaluable when you have heterogeneous application/data platforms. They allow your applications to talk to each other. Gateways typically are difficult to configure and maintain. If you have a number of platforms and you decide to use gateways for each of them, you will end up with too many gateways. Gateways will be a part of your architecture, but use them with caution. Figure 9.5 illustrates how gateways play a part in internetwork design.

FIGURE 9.5.

Bridges, routers, and gateways.

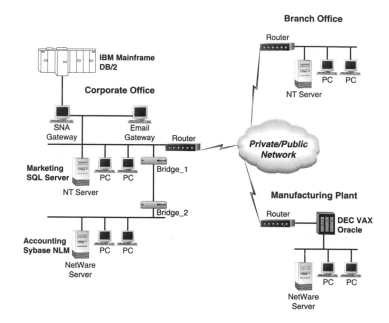

WAN Protocols

Telecom providers and vendors are introducing products and services at a dizzying rate in the area of *WAN protocols*. It is important for you to have an understanding of certain WAN protocols and how they could help and/or hinder your client/server application over a wide area network.

X.25

X.25 is a low-speed packet-switching technology used in transaction processing environments such as order entry. Because of its extensive use of error correction and data recovery, speeds beyond 56 Kbps are difficult to achieve. This makes it almost a nonplayer in today's bandwidth-hungry client/server application demands. But if you need strong error checking and are transferring only electronic mail and small files, X.25 is still a viable choice. AT&T offers a service called AT&T Mail, which is based on X.25 networks. Sprint's Sprintmail is also based mostly on an X.25 network.

Frame Relay

Frame Relay is an evolution of existing X.25 *packet-switching* networks. What this means is that it breaks data streams into packets with addresses and contents. Frame Relay uses "frames" of data instead of packets. Error correction and data recovery are not performed during transmission, thereby greatly increasing speed. Because it uses statistical multiplexing, Frame Relay utilizes bandwidth efficiently and reduces long-distance transmission costs. Because of its high speed and bandwidth usage, Frame Relay offers a practical solution to client/server designers for linking LANs for CAD/CAM, imaging, and SQL-based decision-support applications.

SMDS (Switched Multimegabit Data Service)

SMDS operates at speeds ranging from 56 Kbps to 34 Mbps. It is a connectionless WAN service. This means that you are not limited to the number of partners in a WAN. This is different from Frame Relay, which emulates *leased lines*, meaning that every site on the Frame Relay WAN has to subscribe to the service. But SMDS is limited to metropolitan area networks, reducing its impact on true enterprise-wide networks. It is intended as a universal service but has yet to see widespread commercial use.

ATM (Asynchronous Transfer Mode)

ATM is heralded as the answer to most LAN-WAN bandwidth issues. However, client/server designers have to decide whether they want their networks to evolve into ATM or build networks on whatever ATM devices and services are available now. While most of the trade press is concentrating on how ATM can be integrated at the desktop/LAN level, ATM is becoming a functioning alternative at the WAN level. For high-bandwidth-consuming video applications with voice and data bundled over it, ATM may provide the best solution. Right now, although ATM's costs may prohibit you from proceeding with implementation, it should play a part in your network design.

SONET (Synchronous Optical Network)

SONET operates on fiber-optic cables and can achieve blinding speeds of up to 2.5 Gbps. Long-distance carriers have to deploy the fiber first before SONET becomes a practical reality nationwide. But in the world of parallel databases, super computers, and gigabytes of video and graphical data, SONET will definitely play a role.

ISDN (Integrated Services Digital Network)

ISDN services and products are big players in the remote LAN access market, and to a certain extent in the videoconferencing markets. Basically, you should consider ISDN as a way to extend your LAN to remote and mobile users. ISDN is not necessarily marketed by the vendors for building WANs. For a *Basic Rate Interface (BRI)* connection, you get two 64 Kbps channels for data and one 16 Kbps channel for voice or call-setup information. If your client/server application has a number of users scattered in small or home offices, consider ISDN as a method to link them occasionally to your servers.

Putting It All Together

Having gained an understanding of network issues, the challenge for you as a client/server architect is to design networks that provide fast, efficient, and seamless transfer of data for your applications. Unfortunately, there is no magic equation that you can plug some numbers into and come up with a network design. Capacity planning is still at its infancy in the LAN and WAN arenas. However, there are a number of known issues that affect network design when you are building a client/server application. You can address them, and together with your network designers (in-house technical staff, or system integrators), you can design optimum networks.

Client/Server Factors Affecting Network Design

Although there are a number of issues that are purely technical in network design (like tuning network performance, deploying network management methods, and so on), you can still address certain high-level issues during the planning stage. Because the network is "the computer" or "the application" in client/server architectures, it is difficult to separate application design from network design. I will present a framework here that you can use to plan for networks in client/server applications.

Client/Server Framework for Network Design

The basis of this framework is that "application factors" and "strategic factors" drive your network design. Let me clarify what that means: As you start to build new systems, business requirements drive application specifications. As you start your data modeling, systems specifications, and so on, you should begin to specify "application factors" also. These factors will directly affect the design of your networks. From another angle, you must consider factors like cost, MIS skill sets, and so on. You have to consider these factors in designing each component of your network, for example, cabling, WAN links, protocols, and so on. Figure 9.6 shows an illustration of this framework.

FIGURE 9.6.

Client/server framework for network design.

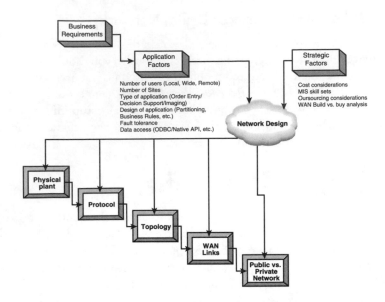

Before delving into the analysis, you must understand the features and benefits of the various products and specifications available in each network component (for example, physical plant, protocol, and so on). You may depend on your own skill sets or hire outside expertise to help you in this. Basically, you must come up with a grid of features for each network component. For example, you would analyze where UTP 5, FDDI, ATM, and so on would be most appropriate under the physical plant component. You would repeat this exercise for each of the components. At the end of this process, you will have a pretty good picture of where things fit.

The application factors that affect network design most are the following:

- **Number of users.** When you are designing your network, plan for the number of users. This analysis must include how many users connect over a local area network, how many connect over a wide area network, and how many would be "casual" or "occasional" users. Suppose that the number of users of your client/server application will be 25, all over an Ethernet LAN. If you use the design framework discussed earlier, you would concern yourself with the physical plant, protocol, and topology. WAN links would not matter because your application would be localized. On the other hand, if your application is going to span the enterprise and be accessed by hundreds of users scattered all over the globe, you would use all the steps in the framework. How you decide which protocol to choose, which topology to choose, and so on will depend on your expertise, industry standards, application compatibility, and outside resources available to you. Some examples would include: If your application is based on a UNIX-based database, the protocol of choice would be TCP/IP because it would seamlessly integrate into the database and operating system. If you are heavily tied into IBM, deciding on a Token Ring topology may be prudent. And depending upon the bandwidth your application needs, your physical plant may be UTP 5 for normal bandwidth needs to FDDI and ATM for larger bandwidth needs. This is where you would use the features and benefits analysis discussed earlier in the section "Client/Server Framework for Network Design."

- **Number of sites.** The number of sites your application will span affects wide area network links, protocols, and the decision to build or buy a WAN. Will dial-up lines suffice for the WAN? What kind of internetworking devices (bridges, routers, and so on) will be used? If you require more bandwidth than dial-up lines, will you choose X.25 leased lines or Frame Relay? How does ISDN play a role in your WAN? For simple file transfers under 1 MB, not requiring frequent updates, you may choose to use dial-up lines to connect your remote sites. If your application is designed in such a way that databases synchronize, real-time updates are a necessity, and network availability is important, you must consider leased lines (at 56 Kbps, T-1, or T-3 speeds), ATM, and other faster methods. Also, a large number of sites may affect your decision to build your own private network. If you decide that network management and reliability issues are best left to a service provider, you may simply choose to outsource the whole network.

- **Type of application.** Mainframe-based computing is optimized for online and batch transaction processing. Network design typically tries to follow these time-honored methods. But the essence of client/server computing is decision support and heterogeneous data access—typically embodied by ad hoc queries and sudden bursts of traffic on the network. So the type of application (whether it is order-entry, workflow-imaging, or an executive information system) affects network design heavily. In a LAN, if you have identified that a group of your application's users mostly perform ad hoc queries, you may consider using Ethernet switches to provide dedicated 10 or 100 Mbps pipes to these users. If video and imaging files play an important role, ATM on the LAN and ISDN on the WAN may have to be considered. If you know that a certain site is only going to access this application to send nightly updates, even dial-up lines may suffice. My point is that the type of application you deploy weighs heavily on network design.

- **Design of application.** This is a double-edged sword. Frequently, when client/server applications do not deliver on performance, everyone ends up pointing fingers at each other. The application designers say that the network is not optimized, and the network designers say that the application is poorly designed. But the fact is that it is becoming difficult to separate these two issues at the design stage.

Suppose that your application has a business rule that loans above $100,000 require an extended credit check. So when a loan request above $100,000 is entered into the application, a verification process is initiated and the results are brought back to the user before allowing him or her to continue. Simple stuff. But there are a number of ways you can implement this rule. You could build the code at the client level, where your client hardware processes the code, with SQL queries flying back and forth through the network for data access. You could implement stored procedures or triggers at the database level so that all processing is done on the server, reducing network traffic. Or you can implement a "Business Rules" server in a third tier in the client/server architecture that processes all business rules. Whichever way you handle it, the network is involved in some way or fashion, and you must consider the impact.

- **Fault tolerance.** How mission-critical is your application? If you are establishing fault tolerance at each level (by adding servers, by establishing intelligent routers, and so on), your network is affected. You may consider ATM or CDDI for your LAN backbones to connect your fault-tolerant servers. If your application is spread over a wide area, there are many points that a telecommunications link could fail. You must consider sophisticated routing technology, which can identify an alternate route for your information. And you may want to make the network itself fault-tolerant by establishing backup links.

- **Data access.** How, where, and what data you access in your application affects your network. If your application requires data to be dumped from a mainframe database, gateways play an important role. Gateways bring translation overhead with them. This may result in slower performance for your users. Therefore, you must find ways to increase performance, by tuning the network or by switching technology. Even in a nonmainframe world, heterogeneous database access brings issues like ODBC and native database APIs to the foreground. Using ODBC is simple and reliable, but it may not be fast enough for certain applications. Native database APIs may be a better solution if you are a single database shop. You must consider the constraints on network performance when choosing your preferred methods of data access.

Summary

Client/server applications affect network design considerably. The emergence of products and services such as ATM, fast Ethernet, and ISDN provide client/server designers with an array of choices. As client/server designers, you should understand the various components of a network: the physical plant, protocols, topologies, and WAN technologies. A number of application factors affect network design. These factors include number of users, number of sites, type of application, design of application, and method of data access. With an understanding of network components and these application factors, you will be able to plan for reliable networks to support your client/server applications.

System and Network Management

10

by Neil Jenkins

Perhaps the most complex challenge presented to companies moving to or creating new client/ server systems is how to effectively manage the new environment. Invariably, these companies are finding this challenge far more difficult and complicated than they had originally thought. This complexity is a result of new technologies that are implemented or infrastructures that are developed that may cross many different vendors and products. Many organizations end up using different platforms and products to deliver their client/server systems. Companies that had traditionally only operated on one or possibly two platforms are now faced with managing a distributed network of client/server systems possibly on four or five platforms that are all interconnected. This distribution of processing and data is where the greatest difficulty occurs.

Systems managers are forced to organize their support environment around these complex parameters. The increased size and complexity of the installed systems increases the number of resources that need to be supported. In turn, this increase raises the costs to the company of supporting the installed base and begins to negate the benefits of moving to client/server systems. Also, because staff in today's marketplace tend to specialize in one or two specific subjects, the systems manager is forced to employ more staff than is perhaps required in order to cover all the areas of the installed base. Unanticipated costs such as these can lead to quick disillusionment with the client/server computing model.

Other difficulties occur if organizations believe a client/server system is pretty much the same as any other distributed or centralized computing environment, and thus can be maintained by existing staff with existing tools. This scenario often leads to worse problems because the organization is inadequately staffed to manage such a complex environment. System problems take longer to resolve, and often only the symptom is fixed, not the underlying cause. Management tools also play a large part in the effective management of a client/server system, and it is wrong to assume that a toolset designed to manage a single platform or topology will also effectively manage a distributed client/server environment.

Systems management involves managing both people and projects. It addresses the processes, procedures, people, and automated tools that are used within a systems division. As you begin to plan and build a client/server system, you must begin also to define what your systems and network management approaches will be. Defining these approaches will help you ease into the task of managing this new environment and avoid many of the pitfalls that can occur. The systems management approach should cover the following areas:

- The systems processes—what needs to be done and what is required to do it
- The systems procedures—how it's done
- The systems people—who does it
- The systems tools—what is used to do it

In addition, systems management covers the main practical, technical areas of the installed client/server system:

- Configuration management
- Fault management

- Security
- Performance
- Network management
- Accounting management

Systems Processes

In a traditional computing environment, there are only one or two main platforms to work on. An organization might have a PC LAN platform and a mainframe platform, for example. The systems department is normally split into smaller departments to support such an environment. This division often leads to network staff and applications staff becoming dedicated to one platform. When a LAN upgrade is required, the PC network team handles it with little or no involvement with the mainframe team because the upgrade doesn't affect that team.

The environment for a client/server system is considerably different. In the client/server environment, the applications and data may span many different platforms. When a systems change is required, it is likely to affect several areas in a traditional systems department. The department has not experienced this kind of situation before, and problems arise because staff members are very protective of their own environment (which is, after all, human nature). To minimize the disruption, the systems processes that span multiple platforms and must be identified.

The systems processes begin to take shape along logical (rather than technical) divisions. Figure 10.1 shows a new systems organization that can be used to develop client/server systems.

FIGURE 10.1.

A client/server systems organization.

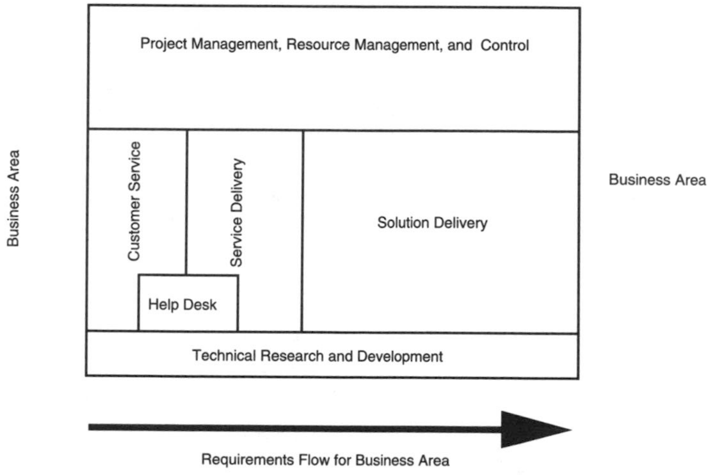

As you can see from Figure 10.1, the organization is not based around skills or particular platforms. The organization is based around the main processes that need to be achieved based on the requirements of the business area.

The Customer Service Process

All good systems departments maintain that the business areas that they service are their customers. When an organization is developing client/server systems, understanding and developing systems that match the requirements of the requesting business area can become increasingly difficult. To do the customer service process, key business analysts and application developers must work effectively with the business areas to determine what systems need to be built. These staff develop the first draft specifications and outlines of a system. In doing so, the staff in this process use resources from the management process and may need to use resources from the technical research process. These two processes are discussed later in the chapter.

In addition to the development of the requirements, this process also contains the help desk function. This function includes the main fault reporting, error recording, and first line of support. By placing these tasks in this process, your organization can proactively manage and react upon major areas of concern. For example, if a department is experiencing major difficulties in its call center application (perhaps the incoming calls are taking too long), the help desk staff and customer service staff may recommend workflow improvements to the call center management. This process is not concerned with platform, networks, or location of data. These areas are handled by the other processes.

The Service Delivery Process

The service delivery process manages the technical environment in operation within the company. Most of the routine systems management activities are handled on a regular basis within this organizational unit. These activities may include the following:

- Procurement, installation, and configuration of new equipment
- Backup and restoration of data to PCs, LANs, UNIX servers, mainframes, and midrange computers
- Performance tuning and capacity planning
- Disaster recovery planning and testing
- Inventory management of software and hardware
- Network management

In addition to these activities, this process also handles support changes to the production client/server applications. These changes may include writing fixes, tracing and fixing programming errors, and making minor application improvements. By having an area focus on the process of service delivery, you can continuously maintain and improve the existing systems.

Traditionally, this process may have been handled by many functionally different departments, such as PC systems, networking, mainframe operations, and programming. This traditional structure results in departments focusing only on their small piece of the client/server puzzle, whereas the new process outlined in this section covers the wider picture.

The people who handle this process cover all the platforms within the organization. As a result, these staff become multiskilled across platforms (which is essential to supporting a client/server environment well). New products and tools can be developed for this process by the technical research and development team. The service delivery team can also request that the technical research team look into products from outside vendors that will improve the service to the company. The service delivery team should not perform this task themselves because they need to concentrate on maintaining the smooth running of the existing systems. This division of tasks prevents the common problem of operations departments taking time out of their normal day to research a new product. What usually occurs is that the research takes far too long or, somewhat worse, results in an ill-chosen product or wasted time when not enough time was spent on proper research.

The Solution Delivery Process

The solution delivery process concentrates on the development of new products and/or business systems for the company. It uses the draft specifications from the customer service team, major input from the business area, project management steering and guidance from the management process, and the involvement of both the service delivery and technical research teams. This process should be handled in small controlled project teams that are empowered and focused on getting the business solution completed. It would be easy to assume that this process is the traditional application development department, yet this process involves so much more than that.

A Business Focus and Business Input

Application development teams tend to focus wholeheartedly on the delivery of programmed systems using one tool. As you have seen in other chapters, this focus is not the best approach when developing client/server systems as the technology stands today. The solution delivery process has to develop business awareness and the ability to focus on the business problem first, and the tools second. Being skilled in using a certain tool is not as important as being able to understand the business. Tools always change over time, but a competent business analyst can use his/her skill on many different projects and business problems.

If possible, business input should come from full-time members of the business area. Having assigned business users allows development to proceed quickly and efficiently without the need to continually arrange user review meetings to generate input. Most companies, however, are loathe to make this level of commitment as these business users are normally too vital in their regular positions to be freed up to handle these projects. This issue is a continual struggle for the client/server developer because the future system needs a lot of user input to cover the multitude of business requirements. Good personnel management is the only way of getting good user involvement, and if the business area cannot free up resources, then investigate other ways of staffing the team, such as splitting the load over other key users. One thing is certain; the project will fail if there is not continual user involvement throughout its life cycle.

Project Planning

Project planning is essential when developing client/server systems and forms a key part of the overall systems management strategy. You can generate plans quickly and efficiently using a variety of planning tools, including Microsoft Project and Project Workbench.

It is not necessary to plan to the extreme, including every little detail. Plans become difficult to maintain and track when this is done. Don't plan down to the smallest detail; for example, you can waste a lot of time worrying about what a Gantt chart says when working on the task can cure the problem. Planning should never be used to such an extent that it replaces common sense and experience.

Likewise, a project methodology, where a team uses a well-documented and promoted tool to aid development, can assist in the development or can detract if it is followed religiously and other more intangible pointers along the way, such as experience or the views of the team members, are ignored.

Support from the Other Processes

The solution delivery team calls on support from the service delivery and technical research teams during development. The service team can help integrate the new system and plan the support structures and procedures to ensure that its installation and continued operation can be a success. The technical research team contains the technical gurus and designers of the technical environment that are normally called upon to supply the key technical ability and knowledge about the platforms and systems being used. The people who assist the solution delivery team in these ways do not need to be full-time; they can be added to the development team when needed.

The Management Process

The management process normally consists of one or two senior systems managers that handle the control-oriented aspects of the department. This process handles the following tasks:

- Resource management
- Staff planning
- Budgeting and financial control
- Senior management
- Director representation
- Business area liaison

In addition, staff experienced in project management and change management may work within this process to support the other processes.

The Technical Research and Development Process

This technical research and development process handles the further development of technology within an organization. This process should be handled by the technical strategists, network architects, and platform specialists. These staff members are focused on improving and developing the internal systems. The positions can be handled by one person or several depending on the capabilities of the staff that you have and the size of the workload.

Requests from the other processes for new technical tools, systems, and products should come to this area to be researched. This team works with the service delivery team to implement new systems. The technical research team is also the keeper of the standards. It develops the configuration standards and systems management standards that the service delivery team implements.

Putting all the technical specialists on one team allows the team members to become multiskilled far quicker than if they were organized in a traditional structure that separates specialists according to their area of expertise.

Systems Procedures

As outlined in the preceding section, the processes involved in developing and organizing to be effective in client/server systems are very different from those in the traditional single system environment. The best methods of maintaining client/server systems involve spending time developing the procedures that should be followed by the systems staff to look after the installed base. Having procedures protects an organization from the myriad of potential problems that can develop within client/server applications.

You can develop many different kinds of procedures; however, you should start with these main procedures:

- Configuration management procedures
- Fault management procedures
- Security procedures
- Performance procedures
- Network management procedures
- Accounting management procedures

Configuration Management Procedures

Configuration management procedures should include software standards for the operating systems, network operating systems, protocols, packages, tools, applications, and utilities used within the company. The standards should include detailed configuration guides, parameter settings, support numbers, and step-by-step installation notes. These standards should be applicable to both purchased products and internally developed products. The combination of comprehensive software guides and systems that are all configured to conform to certain standards reduces support costs.

These procedures should also include hardware standards for all the physical computer systems in the company, including portables, desktop computers, file servers, mainframes, and midrange computers such as DEC or IBM AS/400. These standards should include detailed configuration guides for the systems. Such a guide for a file server, for example, would include processor type, storage mediums, amount of memory installed, and descriptions of its network cards and their configurations.

The network is often a forgotten component of any client/server system, yet in many respects it is the most important component because it is very difficult to do any form of client/server without the network. Therefore, it also should have configuration procedures and documented standards for the many devices on the network, both wide area and local area. Of particular interest are the standards for the protocols to be used on the network.

Fault Management Procedures

Fault management procedures are fairly self-explanatory. All these procedures deal with the management and resolution of errors that occur within the client/server environment. The procedures must cover basic support, ranging from what to do when a user computer has stopped, through when a local area network has crashed, and up to when the entire wide area network has failed. Each level of problem may have a different procedure to fix it. Although it often feels like it should be, panic is not a procedure!

The procedures should be documented in a logical, rational, well-thought-out manner and, where possible, should be tested and continually reviewed. As in all procedures, the service delivery team is responsible for following and testing these procedures.

Security Procedures

A distributed client/server system that makes a company's data and business information available across public and private networks is vulnerable to theft and damage, either accidental or deliberate. You should have security and backup procedures in place to protect the integrity of this data. Security procedures may include time-bound methods of changing user passwords, password rules (such as no passwords less than five characters), and company employment policies that give some protections against viruses. In the ever-growing world of interconnected networks and the Internet, sound security procedures become more and more important. Chapter 23, "Securing a Client/Server System," covers security in more detail.

Performance Procedures

Users are becoming increasingly more dependent on client/server systems to be more productive in their jobs and roles. Performance monitoring and capacity planning are important to prevent sluggish response times to user needs. Performance procedures include the optimizing of database servers, the management of subsystems, disk storage, and memory on midrange machines, and structured query language (SQL) utilization on mainframes. Each of these areas can have significant impact on the computer in question. Having documented standards allows the service delivery team to effectively manage these computers in order to provide the best service to the business.

Network Management Procedures

Network management becomes more complex in a distributed client/server environment. Procedures help people monitor the network, know what to do when failure occurs, and report what occurs on the network.

Due to the continual interaction between a client machine's application and the servers that it interacts with, network traffic invariably increases. Do not consider developing and implementing a client/server system without also considering (and possibly developing) enhancements to your network or seriously learning about the effects any new network might have on existing ones. For example, LANs operating in a networking mode (that is, really only sharing files and printers) can typically have far more users per LAN than a client/server LAN.

If the overall traffic of one client/server user has increased relative to a file- and print-sharing user, all clients have increased traffic to the server or servers. Therefore, there is more network traffic on a network with an unchanged bandwidth. If the bandwidth was under-utilized, then this change is not usually a problem. If the bandwidth is close to full utilization, response time problems occur. These problems can be resolved by either reducing the number of users per LAN or increasing the bandwidth by moving to faster network topologies.

Accounting Management Procedures

Accounting management procedures show the correct ways of managing costs associated with the client/server systems. Usage of server time and storage capacity can be monitored, and if the organization operates a charge-back system where IS resources are cost charged back to user departments, the costs can be monitored and charged.

Systems People

Most companies are unprepared for the impact of client/server computing on the systems team. As a result, most companies do not understand the changes that must occur to their systems management activities. This impact occurs for a variety of reasons. Perhaps the biggest reason is that client/server technology does not fit well into a systems organization based on a hierarchical structure. The best way to reduce this impact is to restructure the systems organization as a process-driven organization as outlined previously in the chapter. Some staff will find it very difficult to change to fit into this structure. Managers will have to take a long hard look at whether these staff members can be helped in this transition or whether they may have to move out of the organization. This decision is always difficult, but the difficulty caused by keeping on staff who cannot or, worse, will not adopt new working practices is far greater.

Information technology is treated as an expense rather than an asset, and staff are not correctly educated in this new environment. It is vital to allow staff to experiment with new tools and new techniques in order for them to understand concepts that will be quite foreign to them. Failure to provide time to experiment will result in a lack of knowledge transfer, which will lead to increased time frames, poor morale, and bad product.

It is wise to pilot concepts and design techniques such that staff can get a feel for the differences above and beyond their previous working environment. Client/server should be viewed as much more of a challenge, and this challenge in turn breeds motivation, better time frames in the long term, and good business systems.

Departmental structures within organizations are getting flatter in the late 1990s, which means there are fewer managers. But managers are not leaving organizations, they are becoming hybrids. They are aligning their technical skills with their management and people skills. These kinds of staff members can be very effective at managing and helping to develop client/server systems.

When restructuring your organization to meet the needs of managing your client/server environment, consider each staff member within your current resource pool as unique. Assess how these staff members will fit into your process-driven team and how they will aid you in delivering first-class client/server systems. Your first and perhaps natural choice for them may not be the best place in the long term. Bear in mind that you want staff to cross-train and develop skills in many areas. Above all, remember that your systems can only be as good as the staff that develop and run them.

Systems Tools

Within the client/server environment, there is a burgeoning marketplace for systems management and network management tools. This chapter covers several of the main tools. At present, no one tool is going to give you a completely integrated view of your client/server environment. As time passes, products will begin to appear that meet large portions of your needs. In the meantime, it is best to develop your processes and procedures on the tools that best fit your environment and get those areas correct so that as the tools improve you can make a natural transition to them and be effective from the first day of implementation. Choosing tools that support and integrate with other tools will bring an advantage, yet the rate of change is so fast at present that the advantage may be short-lived. Each tool should have a complete set of standards and an operating policy, as explained in the "Configuration Management Procedures" section.

The Main Practical Areas

Systems management also deals with the more practical aspects of client/server development. The six main areas are configuration management, fault management, security, performance, network management, and accounting management.

Configuration Management

Establishing a good support environment for desktop and server software and hardware is a key strategic issue for any systems department wanting success from its client/server applications. Organizations normally allow some configuration of client workstations by the users of those workstations. Maintaining configuration control in the client/server environment is almost impossible using manual means due to the complexity and diversity of the applications and platforms. Automated approaches need to become an essential part of your systems management process.

The potential problem is that there are many devices with complex client/server applications, most of which are changing continuously. Every client workstation has a different configuration from every other client, identifying it as unique within the total network. Each of these devices requires management. The complex software on every desktop that is born out of the application development from client/server models must attach, interact, and coexist with the relevant server pieces of the system. The growing use of notebooks, portables, laptops, and other mobile computing equipment that only occasionally connect to the network makes support and configuration control issues even worse. Diversity of this kind can lead to a large increase in support costs if the environment is not managed effectively.

Studies now show that it can cost over twice as much to support a client/server environment as it does to support a similarly sized environment with terminals accessing centralized hosts. Of course, these studies do not figure in the value of the additional business function and flexibility that client/server systems provide.

Configuration management consists of keeping track of what devices are attached to a network and maintaining this information in a database for quick retrieval. The database can contain valuable information about the device, including the type of hardware attached and the type of software installed. This type of information is often produced by an automated network inventory program; the information such a program can retrieve and store about each workstation or device can include the following:

- The amount of RAM installed in the workstation
- The microprocessor installed (Intel 80386, Intel 80486, Pentium, PowerPC, and so on)

- The coprocessor (if any) installed
- The type of network interface card installed
- The type of video interface card installed (VGA, SVGA, and so on)
- The operating system and its version
- The application programs and their version numbers
- The network operating system running on the machine and its version number
- The serial number and any warranty information

By using this database to keep vital information on all workstations, interface boards, printers, and other devices, the systems manager is able to organize systems resources more efficiently. When a client/server system is built using many different platforms, it becomes very important to maintain a central inventory of equipment and configurations of the devices out on the network. This inventory is particularly of value when the devices may be geographically distributed across the world. When implementing a client/server system, this inventory can be queried against to determine numbers of devices and other information.

An advantage of maintaining a network inventory in a database is that a manager can create network configuration reports for planning purposes. How many workstations, for example, are still using Intel 80386SX microprocessors? These machines will not be able to take advantage of Microsoft's Windows NT. How many machines only have four megabytes of RAM installed? These machines will have to be upgraded to at least eight megabytes of RAM to take full advantage of Windows 95 software running a developed client/server application. A client/server manager might also be interested in learning how many workstations are still running MS-DOS 6.22. What would it cost to upgrade these workstations to Windows 95, in order to provide them with the new applications?

Another important function of inventory software is to provide the information needed to solve network problems. In many companies with large local area networks, a network user who is having trouble running a particular program can call a network help desk and request help. The help desk specialist can use information provided by the network inventory software (in the configuration database) to examine the user's hardware and software configuration. The specialist might determine (for example) that a RAM shortage is causing the user's machine to lock up when a graphic file is loaded into a client/server application. Troubleshooting client/server systems is covered in more detail in Chapter 21, "Supporting Client/Server."

Another user might be having a problem with a certain program because of its incompatibility with the version of TCP/IP running on the workstation. The network inventory program can help the supervisor isolate this problem.

LAN configuration programs can also provide a network manager with information about the status of all network devices, including bridges and routers. Some programs provide this information in a graphical format. (For example, the network supervisor's screen might show a device displayed in red to indicate that it is either turned off or malfunctioning.)

Configuration management is vitally important when implementing client/server systems. A multiplatform system takes considerably more configuration that a single-platform environment. At any one time, a client workstation might be interacting with a host legacy mainframe application, a local IBM AS/400 midrange computer, a file server storing security and file settings, a database server housing local graphical data, and an external supplier computer connected over the wide area network. Such an environment would require not only a configuration section for each computer being attached to but also the correct configuration settings so that all the connectivity methods work correctly together in a robust, stable environment. Figure 10.2 shows how these configurations might be set up.

FIGURE 10.2.

An example of multiple configuration settings on a client workstation.

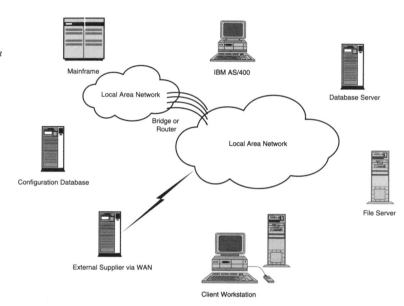

Having a configuration database can substantially improve support and help standardize and maintain configurations much more effectively.

Fault Management

Fault management is the systems management function concerned with documenting and reporting hardware and software errors. An example of a hardware error is a failed personal computer on the network; a sample software error is a database update failure. A systems manager may need to know how many bad packets are being produced, how many times packets must be retransmitted on an Ethernet network, whether a workstation is transmitting a beacon signal on a Token Ring network, and so on. Each error needs to be collected and monitored so that the resilience of a client/server system can be maintained. Automating this collection and monitoring adds value to any installed client/server system. Errors can be trapped and acted upon quickly, minimizing problems for end users.

As an example, *The Frye Utilities for Networks* includes the NetWare Early Warning System, an example of how a client/server manager can use specialized software for fault management. A client/server manager might set the program's thresholds so that it issues an alert under the following conditions:

- The file server does not respond to a user request to read from a database stored there.
- The file server's utilization reaches a certain percentage of capacity.
- Packets are discarded because they have crossed over 16 routers.
- A printer is off-line.

The program can be instructed to notify the manager in a number of different ways. One method would be to display a 25-line message on the manager's monitor. A second method might be to transmit an electronic mail message automatically. If an electronic mail program with a notify feature (such as cc:Mail or Novell Groupwise) is installed on the network, the manager hears a beep and sees a message on-screen indicating that an e-mail message has just been received.

If a Hayes-compatible modem is available to the network, the Frye Utilities NetWare Early Warning System program can be instructed to transmit a pager message (for people who are rarely in their offices). The program can also be instructed to send a fax, but perhaps its most unusual option (assuming the proper hardware is installed) is to provide incoming voice notification and outgoing voice notification.

With these options installed, a network manager can call the LAN and receive a voice update concerning error conditions. The outgoing voice notification option enables the program to call a number and send a voice message. (Imagine the reaction of a network manager who receives a call at home at 3 A.M. from the LAN and hears a digitized voice describe network error conditions telling him that his client/server database has failed!)

Fault management is a very useful way of preventing problems on networks because you can use it to track and resolve many easily avoided repetitive problems after they have begun to occur. In this way, fault management takes network administration from a reactive role to a proactive one.

Performance Management

One of the most difficult tasks when using client/server systems is ensuring that the system has efficient performance and that its service is not deteriorating. Client/server performance management can be divided into client performance, server performance, and network performance. Each area is intrinsically linked with the others in so far as overall performance gains can be achieved by increasing the performance of any one component; significant improvement can obviously be gained by improving all three. Performance management should also be applied to both the local and wide area networks. Network performance is covered in the "Network Management" section later in this chapter.

Client Performance Management

Client performance very much depends on the type of client workstation that is required for the client/server system. Typically, client workstations will run one of the following operating systems in a distributed system: OS/2, Windows 3.x, Windows NT, Windows 95, Apple System 7.x, or UNIX. In all the operating systems, increases in the amount workstation RAM or upgrades in processor chip type and speed will improve performance. Depending on the type of application being developed, however, other factors can deliver performance improvements as well. These improvements can include faster graphics cards, better network interface cards, changing the BUS type on IBM PC compatible systems to PCI, or changing any local storage devices, such as hard disks, to faster ones.

Server Performance Management

Server performance management is a considerable task in itself. The server in many respects is more complex than the client portion of the system. Because the server often has to deal with multiple user access concurrently, its design and implementation must be well-thought-out, well-designed, well-documented, and well-implemented. If you are creating your first client/server system, do not expect to get server configuration correct the first time. Try wherever possible to communicate with other companies and individuals who may have created a similar environment to the one you are creating. Be prepared to learn from your mistakes and do not be afraid to rectify them.

Servers across all platforms tend to operate in a similar way and the techniques for managing their performance are also similar. Performance management of servers can be broken down into the following four main areas that need attention:

- CPU utilization
- Disk cache and disk storage capacities
- RAM
- Communications subsystems, including LAN and WAN adapters

Each area needs to be monitored primarily for trends. An increasing usage trend over time will eventually hit a threshold level that will cause difficulties. Overburdening in any of these areas will cause the machine to slow down and may even cause the machine to fail (the word *crash* sounds so much more spectacular).

Use the server operating system tools and additional tools that you see fit to manage and measure each of these areas. You should set threshold limits for each of these areas and have warning alerts distributed when these thresholds are passed. Try to resolve problem situations proactively; for example, do not wait for a 95-percent utilized CPU to hit 100 percent.

The second major area of server performance concerns the actual server application section of the client/server system. This section is often a Relational Database Management System (RDBMS) of some type. Special care must be taken in optimizing this RDBMS to meet your application needs. To optimize database server performance, you must identify the areas that will yield the largest performance increases over the widest variety of situations and focus your research on these areas. The biggest benefit in database server performance is gained by ensuring that your system has good database design, index design, and query design. Problems in any one of these areas will have a negative impact on server performance.

The best way to determine the optimum running of your database engine is to use the variety of information tools available to you. These tools include the database vendor and supplier, the server vendor and supplier, the server operating system vendor, external consultants and third-party specialists, online research tools such as the Internet and CompuServe, and the wealth of books available. As you develop client/server systems, your server systems will improve considerably as your in-house experience also grows.

Security Management

Another major system management function is security. A system manager must keep a network secure from unauthorized access, as well as from invasion by computer viruses. Protecting a network from unauthorized users means limiting the access of a company's own network users, as well as eliminating network access by noncompany employees. A company's own network users should be restricted to the applications that they need to do their job and no more. In a client/server environment, security must encompass access at the client side, access to any server devices, and also access to any other systems that may be outside of the company, including online services such as the Internet. Additional levels of security for database server access should, where required, also be implemented.

Limiting a Company's Own Network Users

A network manager should use features found in most network operating systems (such as NetWare) and database management systems to limit access by network users to the company's most important devices, servers, databases, directories, and files. Where possible, the manager should use the techniques of server authentication to provide additional levels of security. In Microsoft's Windows 95, server authentication forces a user signing on at a client to be verified against a Novell NetWare user ID or a Windows NT Server user ID. If the authentication fails, the user is unable to access even the local client.

The network should require passwords for users when they log into a network and into a specific server. This function can be automated as part of your client/server system, or you can allow the user to input this information. Bearing in mind that the client/server system may access multiple servers, determine the best methods of signing on to servers. Otherwise, the poor user may be faced with many user ID and password logins.

Some additional ways you can enhance password protection when users log into the network are the following:

- Prevent users from placing their passwords in configuration files for automatic login by making it company policy that this is not allowed. (Batch files can be viewed by unauthorized users.)

- Require the user's password to have a certain number of characters.

- Require the user to change a password at intervals (such as every 30 or 60 days).

- Prevent users from using the same password twice.

- Have a company policy that forces user passwords to contain random combinations of letters. (Passwords that represent the names of spouses, children, or pets are often too easy for outsiders to guess.)

- Prevent users from logging into the network from several different workstations concurrently.

- Restrict users from logging into the network during certain hours and even during certain days of the week (Saturdays, Sundays, and so on).

- Use a network operating system (such as NetWare) that encrypts passwords so that sophisticated users cannot examine the password file and learn users' passwords.

- Prevent users from writing their passwords on scraps of paper and taping these notes to their computers or monitors because they are afraid they will forget them!

- Discourage users from logging into the network and then leaving their workstations unattended for extended periods of time. Unauthorized users can do enormous network damage if they take advantage of this situation.

- Make sure network managers are notified whenever an employee is terminated or voluntarily leaves a company so that this person's network account can be disabled or eliminated.

- Assign temporary users a network account with an expiration date and with very limited access to sensitive network files and client/server applications.

- Prohibit network users from giving their passwords to other users.

Preventing Unauthorized Users from Dialing into a LAN

Network security becomes even more difficult to maintain when users are permitted to log in from remote sites. Intruder detection provides one level of protection. This protection can be enhanced by limiting the number of unsuccessful login attempts before locking the user's account. After three (or perhaps five) unsuccessful login attempts, users might be required to contact the network manager to reset the account. This measure prevents unauthorized users from dialing in repeatedly and using a random password generator to try to break into a network.

Another effective way to prevent unauthorized users from logging into a LAN from a remote site is to use a call-back modem that receives a call, requires a password, and then calls the user back after a random number of seconds. The call-back modem is programmed with a table containing a list of authorized users, their passwords, and their phone numbers.

Protecting a Network from Computer Viruses

Viruses are self-replicating bits of computer code that hide in computer programs (and often in RAM). They attach themselves to other programs and accompany them when they are copied to other disks or onto a network. Once activated, these viruses can disrupt the programs to which they are attached. When they hide in RAM, viruses attach themselves to more and more programs as each one is executed. Imagine a database update program destroying your database file, or a network virus bringing down your system in the middle of a key customer transaction!

A virus is particularly disruptive on a network; it can spread rapidly through a network's various directories and subdirectories, potentially damaging data. The solution for many network managers is to install preventive software that checks for viruses before other software is executed, usually detecting a virus before it can do any damage. Many programs also destroy the virus once it is detected.

Central Point's Anti-Virus software serves as an example of how many of these programs function. It checks for viruses by verifying files' checksums and checking for other file irregularities. A terminate-and-stay-resident (TSR) program loads into memory and checks programs before they are executed. It notifies the user when a virus has been detected, names it, and then destroys it. The program is capable of removing viruses from infected files, boot sectors, and partition tables without having to delete these files.

On many networks, only the LAN manager can load files onto the network. Often the network manager will test a program on a local workstation and scan it for viruses before adding the program to the network. Users are normally prohibited from uploading files and programs directly from bulletin boards onto the network.

Active virus protection must play a part in your final installed client/server system. Protect against viruses on the clients, the networks, and each individual server. This protection can get costly when your environment spans many machines, but the costs incurred in the loss of key corporate data due to virus damage is often far higher.

Network Management

Because of the complex network technologies that will exist in your client/server environment in both the WAN and LAN sections, you must be prepared to adapt to unforeseen network events that may occur. Regretfully, systems do fail. You may be used to failures of single machines or small networks, and it can be quite daunting for a large-scale client/server system to turn belly up and stop. The overall design of the client/server systems you build and implement will be more complex than those systems you may use today. They will also be built using more varied devices than you may use currently. To maintain system integrity and to protect against downtime, you must begin to look at structured ways of measuring network performance and to be able to analyze just what traffic occurs on the networks.

The complexity of the new components, be they applications, users, or hardware technologies, necessitates some sort of tools that allow you to view your network in a controlled manner to determine potential errors, bottlenecks, and likely failure points. By looking at the network in this way, you can begin to configure and run the network at its best level. It is very likely that in the delivery of your client/server system, you need to use considerably more protocols than you previously used. For example, you may have been running an IBM AS/400 environment whose protocol was primarily SNA. When you diversified into client/server, you may have found that you added IPX/SPX, Netbios, and TCP/IP to the protocols running across your networks. The protocols are the vehicle that carries the data packets between the clients and servers within your new environment. The only way to fine-tune and optimize this environment is to take a good look at these protocols and examine their flow around the network.

Investing in a good network protocol analyzer and placing it in the hands of a knowledgeable person will seriously improve your ability to resolve complex and often critical network problems. Network efficiency needs to be monitored by the network supervisor who examines network traffic statistics. By examining printer usage statistics, for example, the supervisor might determine that certain log reports need to be spooled and printed after peak hours. As another example, heavy usage of certain accounting programs may place a premium on file server access, which can slow the entire network. The supervisor might decide to add a separate file server for an accounting department in order to speed up the rest of the network. By being proactive in network performance management, the network manager or supervisor can maintain good service levels for the end user community.

Several companies, including Network General, Hewlett-Packard, Spider Systems, and Novell, offer network analyzers. Network General's Watchdog serves as an example of software (and hardware) that a network manager can use to ensure that a network performs efficiently. The workstation into which this software is loaded includes a network interface card that allows the workstation to capture real-time network data. The Watchdog provides detailed statistical information about network traffic patterns. This information can be displayed graphically so that the network manager can view which workstations are generating the most traffic. Microsoft provides a system monitoring program with Windows NT.

The Watchdog can report which workstations are generating packets with the most errors (a sign that the workstation might have a defective network interface card). The network manager can also monitor the traffic between a file server and a print server or between two workstations to examine potential bottlenecks that might be causing network traffic congestion.

It is good practice to gather information about network traffic at all times, even when the network is running smoothly. By gathering network traffic statistics when the network is performing efficiently, a benchmark can be used to discover why a network suddenly begins to operate sluggishly. The Watchdog also has a cable test function that enables the network manager to check a network segment to see whether there is a cabling problem. Microtest's Compass has similar features and functionality. Chapter 22, "Performance Tuning and Optimization," covers the use of the network protocol analyzer in more detail.

Accounting Management

Accounting management is the network function associated with allocating network costs to users and their departments. A network operating system such as NetWare provides the built-in capability to perform this task. Under NetWare, a network manager can keep accurate track of when specific individuals use specific network resources (file servers, hard disks, or printers). Users can then be charged for using a print server, a file server, and even a gateway.

Users can be charged for how many blocks of information they read from a file server and how many blocks they write to a file server. Network managers can even vary the charge rates for connections so that they are less expensive for users who log into the network during off hours. A network manager can set charge rates for service requests so that users who want to print during prime time will pay considerably more than users who are willing to print during the late afternoon or evening.

Summary

When moving to the new world of client/server systems, it is all too easy to forget the areas of systems management that I have outlined in this chapter. To a certain degree, users take these practices for granted in a well-run, single-system environment. Therefore, you should plan systems management into your client/server development or migration strategy at a very early stage and begin to research the additional skills, tools, practices, and procedures that you may have to have in place.

Bear in mind that you may have to change your organizational structure to effectively support this new environment, and that this restructuring will cause your staff some pain but will give you a better operating environment than before.

Wherever possible, use the features and facilities of your core systems to provide the basis of your systems management approach, as these will improve your environment. And finally, do not expect to get it right the first time around. If you do, I applaud you, but learn from the mistakes and begin to gather the experience that this environment can offer. You will find it considerably more challenging and enjoyable than your older systems.

Understanding Middleware

by Neil Jenkins

11

During the development of client/server systems, there is a need to hide the complexities of interaction between the client machine and the server machine. This need has led to the development of a suite of products that provide this functionality. These products have been named *middleware*. Middleware has become a catchall term for a range of different software technologies designed to provide connectivity in mixed computer environments. Unfortunately, due to the many different ways in which client/server systems can be built, middleware is now used to describe everything from a basic structured query language (SQL) connection used in a database environment to a full-blown transaction processing system like IBM's CICS.

This chapter uses the following definition of middleware: Off-the-shelf connectivity software that supports distributed processing at run time and is used by developers to build distributed software. This software provides high-level communications protocols to allow either whole applications or processes within applications to span a network.

With the advent of local area networks and interconnected PCs, more and more companies focused on interconnecting their databases and host systems. In the early days, this interconnection was handled by simple gateways. Yet these gateways could not provide the interaction that was and still is required at the client level. Companies realized that software was required to sit between these PCs and host systems, to sit in the middle so to speak. Middleware was born. This software needed to contain the features and functionality that would make it as secure and as robust as the host systems of the time. This area is still the major development focus for middleware today. Although client software (particularly middleware) has not been noted, so far, for its distributed excellence, this fact is changing. Client software's strength has always been ease of use and installation. As a result, middleware has become a major requirement in successful client/server systems providing working distributed processing.

As the information systems world increases in complexity, the need for generic middleware solutions to enable interoperability of systems and portability of applications becomes increasingly more important. Information systems are evolving from the world where simplicity in the connection services was sufficient to one where transparency of connection, ease of management, portability of business function and logic, and rapid development and rapid deployment of distributed function to enable modular applications are the requirements to support the business.

The Database Connectivity Challenge

The challenge of client/server systems is database connectivity. Database connectivity involves the ability to access multiple, heterogeneous data sources from within a single application running on the client. A second challenge is flexibility; the application should be able to directly access data from a variety of data sources without modification to the application. For example, an application could access data from Foxpro in a stand-alone, small office environment and from SQL Server or Oracle in a larger, networked environment. These challenges are day-today occurrences for programmers of off-the-shelf applications and for corporate developers attempting to provide solutions to end users or to migrate data to new platforms. These challenges grow exponentially for developers and support staff as the number of data sources grows and the complexity of the completed applications increases.

Data Source Differences

Database problems become apparent in the differences among the programming interfaces, DBMS protocols, DBMS languages, and network protocols of unrelated data sources. Even when data sources are restricted to relational DBMSs that use SQL, significant differences in SQL syntax and semantics have to be resolved.

The primary differences in the implementation of each of these components are the following:

- **Programming interface**. Each DBMS supplier provides its own proprietary programming interface. The method of accessing a relational DBMS may be through embedded SQL or an API.

- **DBMS protocol**. Each DBMS supplier uses proprietary data formats and methods of communication between the application and the DBMS. For example, there are many different ways to delineate the end of one row of data and beginning of the next.

- **DBMS language**. SQL has become the language of choice for relational DBMSs, but many differences still exist among SQL implementations. For example, one difference is the use of DECODE in Oracle.

- **Networking protocols.** Many diverse LAN and WAN protocols exist in networks today. DBMSs and applications must coexist in these diverse environments. For example, SQL Server may use DECnet on a VAX, TCP/IP on UNIX, and Netbeui or SPX/IPX on a PC!

To access various database environments, an application developer would have to learn to use each DBMS supplier's programming interface, employ each DBMS supplier's SQL, and ensure that the proper programming interface, network, and DBMS software were installed on the client system. This complexity makes broad database connectivity unfeasible for most developers and users today. If the number of supported DBMSs increases, the complexity increases severely.

Approaches to Database Connectivity

DBMS suppliers and third-party companies have attempted to address the problem of database connectivity in a number of ways. The main approaches have included using gateways, a common programming interface, and a common protocol.

The Gateway Approach

In the gateway approach, application programmers use one supplier's programming interface, SQL grammar, and DBMS protocol. A gateway causes a target DBMS to appear to the application as a copy of the selected DBMS. The gateway translates and forwards requests to the target DBMS and receives results from it. For example, applications that access SQL Server can also access DB2 data through the Micro Decisionware DB2 Gateway. This product allows a DB2 DBMS to appear to a Windows-based application as a SQL Server DBMS. Any application using a gateway would need a different gateway for each type of DBMS it needs to access, such as DEC Rdb, Informix, Ingres, and Oracle.

The gateway approach is limited by structural and architectural differences among DBMSs, such as differences in catalogs and SQL implementations and the usual need for one gateway for each target DBMS. Gateways are a valid approach to database connectivity and are essential in certain environments, but they are typically not a broad, long-term solution.

The Common Interface Approach

In the common interface approach, a single programming interface is provided to the programmer. It is possible to provide some standardization in a database application development environment or user interface even when the underlying interfaces are different for each DBMS. This standardization is the result of creating a standard API, macro language, or set of user tools for accessing data and translating requests for, and results from, each target DBMS. A common interface is usually implemented by writing a driver for each target DBMS. Microsoft's ODBC follows this approach. Figure 11.1 shows how this interface fits architecturally within the client system.

FIGURE 11.1.

The common interface approach.

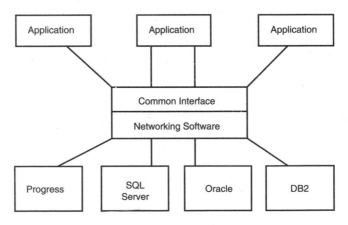

Applications accessing heterogeneous data sources concurrently via a common interface approach

The Common Protocol Approach

The DBMS protocol, SQL grammar, and networking protocols are common to all DBMSs, so the application can use the same protocol and SQL grammar to communicate with all DBMSs. Examples are remote data access (RDA) and distributed relational database architecture (DRDA). RDA is an emerging standard from SAG, but it is not available today. DRDA is IBM's alternative DBMS protocol. Common protocols can ultimately work very effectively in conjunction with a common interface.

Common interfaces, protocols, and gateways may be combined. A common protocol and interface provides a standard API for developers as well as a single protocol for communication with all databases. A common gateway and interface provides a standard API for developers and allows the gateway to provide functionality, such as translation and connectivity to wide area networks, that would otherwise need to be implemented on each client station, but a common gateway or protocol still requires a common interface to hide complexities from developers.

A Basic View of Middleware

Figure 11.2 shows the basic view of how a client workstation interacts with a database server through a network.

FIGURE 11.2.

A simplistic view of a client/server system.

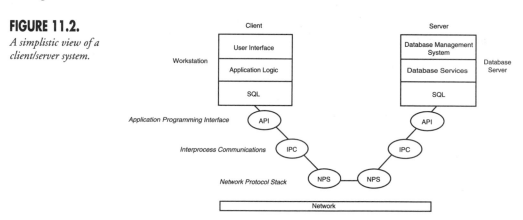

When an application at the client end requires data from the server, a transaction is sent from the application logic via SQL to the network. This transaction is passed through an application programming interface, an interprocess communications protocol, and a network protocol stack to the server. The application programming interface and the interprocess communications portions of the process can be made up of middleware.

Figure 11.3 shows where middleware sits in the client/server system. On the left side of the diagram, a business application is communicating to middleware that is then communicating to a business server on the right side of the diagram. These systems are physically separate and may be located anywhere.

FIGURE 11.3.

The position of middleware in a client/server system.

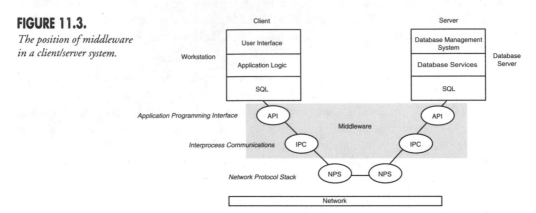

In some cases, the middleware can also provide the database language vocabulary as well. Examples of this type of middleware include Rumba Database Access and ODBC products from Microsoft.

High-Level Middleware Communications Types

Middleware products, at a high level, use one of three communications types:

- Synchronous transaction-oriented communications
- Asynchronous batch-oriented communications or message-oriented middleware (MOM)
- Application-to-server communications

Synchronous Transaction-Oriented Communications

Middleware that uses synchronous transaction-oriented communications involves back and forth exchanges of information between two or more programs. For example, a PC running ODBC retrieves host system-based information requested by the PC application. The synchronized aspect of this communications style demands that every program perform its task correctly; otherwise, the transaction will not be completed.

Products of this type include the following:

- Products that provide APIs that allow PC programs to communicate with an AS/400 using APPC fit in this type because APPC is synchronous transaction-oriented.

- Products that support TCP/IP sockets so that PC programs can communicate with other sockets-based systems are synchronous transaction-oriented as well. This approach is similar to the APPC approach for the AS/400. Applications that support Winsocks for Microsoft Windows work in this way.

- Products that provide APIs, high-level language APIs (HLLAPIs), or extended HLLAPIs (EHLLAPIs) that let PC programs communicate with mainframe and midrange programs through an intermediate terminal emulation program are included in the synchronous transaction-oriented group. This kind of product is the origin of the "screen scrape" programs. By using this technology, your application program communicates with a terminal emulation program package through APIs to sign on to the host computer, and then interact with the host application as if the PC program were a display session user. Examples of these packages include Rumba Office from Walldata, products from Netsoft such as Netsoft Elite, and the Attachmate series.

- Microsoft Windows-oriented communications products that support the Windows Dynamic Data Exchange (DDE) or Object Linking and Embedding (OLE) facilities to create links between host-based information (typically again accessed through Windows-based terminal emulation sessions) and native Windows programs are also synchronous transaction-oriented products. With DDE and OLE, you can create a hot link between information on a host application screen (through terminal emulation software) and a spreadsheet handled by a native Windows application (such as Excel or Lotus 1-2-3). Note that both applications involved in DDE or OLE conversation must support the DDE or OLE formats. Both Rumba and Netsoft support these formats for the AS/400.

Asynchronous Batch-Oriented Communications

In the asynchronous batch-oriented communications type, messages are sent either one at a time or in batches with no expectation of an immediate response (or sometimes of any response at all). For example, a server database update program uses a data queue facility to send subsets of updated records to PC programs that then update the local client-based database. Or a PC program uses a file transfer API to send sales order records to an AS/400 program as they're entered. This method is commonly called *message-oriented middleware* and is covered in more detail in a later section of this chapter.

Application-to-Server Communications

Middleware can also link a business application with a generalized server program that typically resides on another system. A database server, an image server, a video server, and other general-purpose servers can communicate with an application program through a middleware solution.

Products in the server-oriented middleware range include the following:

■ Products that conform to the Windows-based ODBC specification are server-oriented middleware. Under this specification, vendors provide an ODBC driver that, on one side, provides a consistent set of SQL-oriented access routines for use by Windows programs and, on the other side, manages access to the vendor's remote database. ODBC is covered in more detail in a later section of this chapter.

■ Vendor-specific remote access products and a handful of generic SQL-based remote access solutions, which offer alternatives to remote database access through ODBC, are also categorized under server-oriented middleware. Oracle's Oracle Transparent Gateway range is an example of an SQL-based remote access product.

■ On the edge of the server-oriented middleware market is the transaction-processing workhorse CICS. CICS is available for OS/2, mainframes, and AS/400.

The Main Types of Middleware

Several main types of middleware can be used to build client/server systems. The following sections cover these well-known types:

DCE (distributed computing environment)

MOM (message-oriented middleware)

Transaction-processing monitors

ODBC

DCE

The facilities outlined in this section as part of DCE have become available in many other products in some shape or form. DCE is an combined integrated set of services that supports the development of distributed applications, including client/server. DCE is operating system- and network-independent, providing compatibility with users' existing environments. Figure 11.4 shows DCE's layered approach.

The architecture of DCE is a layered model that integrates a set of technologies, which are described in more detail in the following sections. The architecture is layered bottom-up from the operating system to the highest-level applications. Security and management are essential to all layers of the environment. To applications, the environment appears as a single logical system rather than a collection of different services. Distributed services provide tools for software developers to create the end-user services needed for distributed computing. These distributed services include the following:

- Remote procedure call and presentation services
- Naming or directory services
- Time service
- Security service
- Threads service
- Distributed file services
- PC integration service
- Management service

FIGURE 11.4.

The distributed computing environment.

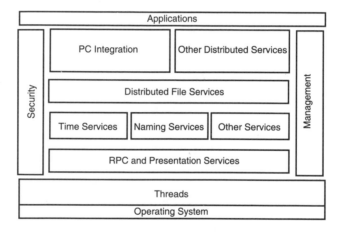

Remote Procedure Call (RPC)

The Remote Procedure Call (RPC) capability is based on a simple premise: make individual procedures in an application run on a computer somewhere else within the network. A distributed application, running as a process on one computer, makes procedure calls that execute on another computer. Within the application, such program calls appear to be standard local procedure calls, but these calls activate subprocedures that interact with an RPC run-time library to carry out the necessary steps to execute the call on the remote computer. RPC manages the network communications needed to support these calls, even the details such as network protocols. This means that distributed applications need little or no network-specific code, making development of such applications relatively easy. In this way, RPC distributes application execution. RPC extends a local procedure call by supporting direct calls to procedures on remote systems, enabling programmers to develop distributed applications as easily as traditional, single-system programs. RPC presentation services mask the differences between data representations on different machines, allowing programs to work across multiple, mixed systems.

RPC is used to allow applications to be processed in part on other servers, which leaves the client workstation free to do other tasks. RPC allows clients to interact with multiple servers and allows servers to handle multiple clients simultaneously. RPC allows clients to identify and locate servers by name. RPC applications, integrated with the directory services, are insulated from the details of the service. This characteristic will allow them to take advantage of future enhancements.

Naming Services

The distributed directory service provides a single naming model throughout DCE. This model allows users to identify by name resources such as servers, files, disks, or print queues and to gain access to these resources without needing to know where they are located on a network. As a result, users can continue referring to a resource by one name even when a characteristic of the resource, such as its network address, changes.

The distributed directory service seamlessly integrates the X.500 naming system with a replicated local naming system. Developers can move transparently from environments supporting full ISO functionality to those supporting only the local naming service component. The service allows the transparent integration of other services, such as distributed file services, into the directory service. The global portion of the directory service offers full X.500 functionality through the X/Open Directory Service API and through a standard management interface.

The directory service allows users or administrators to create multiple copies of critical data, assuring availability in spite of communication and hardware failures. It also provides a sophisticated update mechanism that ensures consistency. Changes to names or their attributes are automatically propagated to all replicas. In addition, replication allows names to be replicated near the people who use them, providing better performance.

The directory service is fully integrated with the security service, which provides secure communications. Sophisticated access control provides protection for entries. The directory service can accommodate large networks as easily as small ones. The ability to easily add servers, directories, and directory levels makes painless growth possible.

Time Service

A time service synchronizes all system clocks of a distributed environment so that executing applications can depend on equivalent clocking among processes. Consider that many machines operating in many time zones may provide processes as part of a single application solution. It's essential that they all agree on the time in order to manage scheduled events and time-sequenced events.

The distributed time service is a software-based service that synchronizes each computer to a widely recognized time standard. This service provides precise, fault-tolerant clock synchronization for systems in both local area networks and wide area networks. Time service software is integrated with the RPC, directory, and security services. DCE uses a modified version of DEC's Time Synchronization Service.

Threads Service

Developers want to exploit the computing power that is available throughout the distributed environment. The threads service provides portable facilities that support concurrent programming, which allows an application to perform many actions simultaneously. While one thread executes a remote procedure call, another thread can process user input. The threads service includes operations to create and control multiple threads of execution in a single process and to synchronize access to global data within an application. Because a server process using threads can handle many clients at the same time, the threads service is well-suited to dealing with multiple clients in client/server-based applications. A number of DCE components, including RPC, security, directory, and time services, use the threads service.

Security Service

In most conventional timesharing systems, the operating system authenticates the identity of users and authorizes access to resources. In a distributed computing environment where activities span multiple hosts with multiple operating systems, however, authentication and authorization require an independent security service that can be trusted by many hosts. DCE provides such a service. The DCE security service component is well-integrated within the fundamental distributed service and data-sharing components. It provides the network with three conventional services: authentication, authorization, and user account management. These facilities are made available through a secure means of communication that ensures both integrity and privacy. The security service incorporates an authentication service based on the Kerberos system from MIT's Project Athena. Kerberos is a trusted service that prevents fraudulent requests by validating the identity of a user or service.

After users are authenticated, they receive authorization to use resources such as files. The authorization facility gives applications the tools they need to determine whether a user should have access to resources. It also provides a simple and consistent way to manage access control information.

Every computer system requires a mechanism for managing user account information. The User Registry solves the traditional problems of user account control in distributed, multivendor networks by providing a single, scalable system for consolidating and managing user information. The User Registry ensures the use of unique user names and passwords across the distributed network of systems and services, ensures the accuracy and consistency of this information at all sites, and provides security for updates and changes. It maintains a single, logical database of user account information, including user and group naming information, login account information, and general system properties and policies. It is well-integrated with Kerberos to provide an integrated, secure, reliable user account management system.

MOM

MOM is a class of middleware that operates on the principles of message passing and/or message queuing. MOM is characterized by a peer-to-peer distributed computing model supporting both synchronous and asynchronous interactions between distributed computing processes. MOM generally provides high-level services, multiprotocol support, and other systems management services. These services create an infrastructure to support highly reliable, scalable, and performance-oriented client/server systems in mixed environments.

MOM is perhaps the most visible and currently the clearest example of middleware. One of the key attributes of middleware is that it should provide seamless integration between different environments. MOM uses the concept of a message to separate processes so that they can operate independently and often simultaneously. For example, a workstation can send a request for data, which requires collection and collation from multiple sources, while continuing with other processing.

This form of so-called asynchronous processing allows MOM to provide a rich level of connectivity in many types of business systems. MOM can handle everything from a simple message to download some data from a database server to an advanced client/server system with built-in workflow. In general terms, MOM works by defining, storing, and forwarding the messages. When a client issues a request for a service such as a database search, it does not talk directly to that service; it talks to the middleware. Talking to the middleware usually involves placing the message on a queue where it will be picked up by the appropriate service when the service is available. Some MOM products use a polling method to pick up messages instead, but the principle is the same; the messaging middleware acts as a buffer between the client and the server. More strictly speaking, middleware is the requester on the client and the service on the server; as with MOM itself, there can be many instances of both requesters and services on a single client or server. MOM insulates both the client and server applications from the complexities of network communications.

MOM ensures that messages get to their destinations and receive a response. The queuing mechanism can be very flexible, either offering a first in, first out scheme or one that allows priorities to be assigned to a message. The use of queues means that MOM software can be very flexible. Like other forms of middleware, it can accommodate straightforward one-to-one communications and many-to-one communications. Message passing and message queuing have been around for many years as the basis for Online Transaction Processing (OLTP) systems. The MOM software can also include system management functions such as network integrity and disaster recovery.

You can think of MOM as being similar to electronic mail systems such as Lotus cc:Mail. Although MOM uses similar mechanisms and can indeed provide the foundation for electronic mail, a key difference exists between MOM and electronic mail systems. Electronic mail passes messages from one person to another, whereas MOM passes messages back and forth between software processes.

MOM differs from database middleware in that database middleware vendors' expertise and products focus on providing their customers with the integration of data residing in multiple databases throughout the customers enterprise. Their solutions normally require a communications component for managing and supporting sessions between the front-end client and one or more back-end database servers. Their designs are normally specific to accommodate the distribution and integration of their own DBMS on multiple platforms. Products from MOM companies who specialize in this environment provide users with a general-purpose solution that can be more readily used for any-to-any environments, including SQL to SQL and SQL to non-SQL (IMS, for example), and for non-DBMS data files. MOM products provide direct process-to-process communications and are not just restricted to accessing data.

The Advantages of Using MOM

In many modern client/server applications, there are clear advantages to using MOM. It provides a relatively simple application programming interface (API), making it easy for programmers to develop the necessary skills. The API is portable, so MOM programs can be moved to new platforms easily without changing the application code. The flexibility of the API also extends to legacy applications so that distributed computing can be introduced gradually without incurring a massive reprogramming exercise. MOM is a good tool to use as you begin your initial client/server development.

MOM is also a valid middleware technology on a system that uses object-oriented technology. Objects, by their very definition, interact with one another by using messages. Message passing and message queuing allow objects to exchange data and can even pass objects without sharing control. Therefore, message-oriented middleware can be a natural technology to complement and support object technology.

Problems with MOM

The main problem with MOM is that its function is restricted to message passing. In other words, it does not include facilities to convert data formats. If, as in many systems, data is to be transferred from mainframes to PCs, the data conversion from EBCDIC to ASCII formats must be handled elsewhere. The MOM software only provides the transport and delivery mechanisms for messages; it is not concerned with the content. As a result, the application must take responsibility for creating and decoding messages. This additional responsibility increases the application's complexity.

MOM's simplicity also can slow performance because messages are usually processed from a queue one at a time. The problem can be solved by running multiple versions of the message-processing software, although this approach is not ideal. This particular problem means that MOM is not usually suitable for applications that require real-time communications within applications.

Another major problem with MOM is that there is little in the way of standardization. In 1993, a group of suppliers formed the MOM Association (MOMA) to promote common interests. Key members include IBM, Digital, Novell, Peer Logic and Software AG. MOMA is not a standards-making body, which means MOM products are essentially proprietary in nature. MOMA does lobby standards bodies with an interest in middleware. It has ties to the Open Software Foundation (OSF) and the Object Management Group (OMG) in its work on object-oriented computing. MOM suppliers argue with some justification that the simplicity of MOM calls means that rigid standards are unnecessary. There are some individual initiatives aimed at promoting interworking both between different MOM products and with non-MOM middleware such as OSF's DCE remote procedure call (RPC) technology, which was discussed earlier in the chapter. Many third-party products also provide links to IBM's CICS to ease the migration path from legacy systems to client/server.

As MOM expands to resolve these problems, it will inevitably become more complex and start to resemble other approaches to middleware, such as transaction processing and RPC. Finally, like many other solutions to the middleware problem, tools that help create application systems around MOM and subsequently manage them are needed. Momentum Software offers one of the most promising solutions with its modeling and simulation software that sits on top of Message Express.

Available MOM Products

The leading MOM products inevitably come from the established systems suppliers, with IBM and Digital having the highest profile. IBM's MQSeries, originally developed for IBM's main platforms (Mainframe MVS, OS/400 and AIX, and IBM's UNIX), now supports a wide range of non-IBM hardware platforms such as Sun Solaris, Tandem, and AT&T GIS. MQSeries is a group of products that uses IBM's message Queue Interface (MQI) to provide communications between mixed computer platforms. IBM has begun to spread MQSeries to a wide range of platforms and environments, giving it the most comprehensive coverage for any MOM product. In addition to supporting all of IBM's key platforms, MQSeries accommodates all of the major computer languages (COBOL, C, Visual Basic) and network protocols (SNA, TCP/IP, Decnet, and IPX). Front-end client support covers Microsoft Windows, MS-DOS, and OS/2. MQSeries goes much further than many MOM products in providing support for transactional messaging and all of its associated benefits. This support includes features such as two-phase commit, security, and restart and recovery, which would normally be found in transaction management software.

Digital's DECmessageQ also supports a wide range of other vendors' operating systems. In addition to the proprietary DEC VAX VMS and Alpha platforms, DECmessageQ covers the leading UNIX implementations (IBM, SUN, HP, SCO) and Microsoft's Windows environments. Languages supported include COBOL, C, FORTRAN and ADA, Visual Basic, and C. Digital includes a wide range of queue processing features designed to help systems management. In the future, DECmessageQ will support multiple APIs and standards for formal message queuing as they emerge from standards bodies.

Among the third-party suppliers, Peer Logic's Pipes is one of the leading contenders. It supports the main platforms of DEC, IBM, and Hewlett Packard. Again, most of the major languages and network protocols are supported. Peer Logic's position as an independent has let it build relationships with other major vendors, particularly IBM. The two companies are working to integrate the Pipes software into IBM's Distributed System Object Model (DSOM) and to provide bridges between Pipes and MQSeries. Momentum Software's Message Express and X-IPC products are also widely used.

Transaction Processing Monitors

Before client/server had developed as a concept, the concept of middleware was very much in place within transaction processing systems. Transaction Processing (TP) monitors were first built to cope with batched transactions. Transactions were accumulated during the day and then passed against the company's data files overnight. Originally, TP monitor meant teleprocessing monitor—a program that multiplexed many terminals to a single central computer. Over time, TP monitors took on more than just multiplexing and routing functions, and TP came to mean transaction processing.

By the 1970s, TP monitors were handling online transactions, which gave rise to the term Online Transaction Processing that then became a part of the majority of legacy business systems in place today. Transaction Processing systems pass messages between programs. They operate, store, and forward queues, and they send acknowledgments. They have advanced error trapping procedures and restart and recovery features in the event of a breakdown that have evolved over the past 30 years from the requirements of mainframe integrity. IBM has defined a *transaction* as an atomic unit of work that possesses four properties. These properties are atomicity, consistency, isolation, and durability. These properties are often referred to as ACID properties.

Atomicity effectively provides the transaction recovery needs. A transaction must be completed as a whole, or the transaction is not completed at all. Therefore, the system must have full restart and recovery capabilities such that any transaction that goes bad can be automatically reversed. Consistency means that the results of a particular transaction must be reproducible and predictable. The transaction obviously must always produce the same results under the same conditions. Isolation means that no transaction must interfere with any concurrently operating transaction. Finally, durability means that the results of the transaction must be permanent.

As you can see from these definitions, the software required to achieve these properties is essential for robust client/server systems, yet also it is inevitably complex. The robustness of TP systems, as discussed earlier, has evolved over many years as companies have demanded strong, secure mainframe systems. Client/server still has a long way to go to match this robustness.

IBM has been in the forefront of moving TP from its mainframe roots to client/server. IBM's CICS is perhaps one of the best examples of a Transaction Processing system. CICS began in the late 1960s as the Customer Information Control System (not Covered In Chocolate Sauce as was initially rumored!), a robust and reliable piece of software with a great range of OLTP functionality. It has traditionally been used on mainframes, yet recently it has also been ported to OS/2 as CICS OS/2 and the RS/6000 UNIX machines as CICS/6000.

The CICS OS/2 product brings the traditional terminal emulation product and a new External Call Interface (ECI) together at the client for processing across a network to a TP server. IBM uses a technique called function shipping that enables TP tasks to be moved around a network. The ECI technology is the crux of the system because it provides a high level of communication between the client and server components of the TP application that is required to support function shipping. Function shipping works in a similar fashion to RPC as outlined in the DCE section. The benefit for CICS users is that the CICS API is the same across all the platforms, so, in theory, a mainframe CICS application could run on either CICS OS/2 or CICS RS/6000.

IBM and other TP suppliers have recognized that their products have an enormous role to play in the new era of client/server computing. Their experience in the TP world, coupled with the maturity of the product, can teach the client/server world significant lessons as development goes forward. As a result, TP products such as CICS from IBM, Tuxedo from Novell, and Top End from NCR are beginning to meet the demands of client/server developers who need the robust, secure, and controllable features available in these products. Without a doubt, the biggest reason for not moving to client/server is that developers fear that the systems (sometimes rightly) do not have the integrity of the 30-year old legacy systems. In comparison to these legacy systems, client/server is a newborn babe. Yet now more than ever, client/server systems based on workgroups and LANs are considerably more viable than the traditional centralized mainframe processor operating dumb terminals.

The main drawbacks of a TP system for client/server are that it is still considerably more expensive than other forms of middleware and that TP suffers from a lack of standards, similar to MOM. As companies diversify their client/server systems and move from their legacy systems to client/server, they will benefit from using TP.

Queued, Conversational, and Workflow Models

Most TP monitors have migrated from a client/server basis to a three-system model in which the client performs data capture and local data processing and then sends a request to a middleman called a request router. The router brokers the client request to one or more server processes. Each server in turn executes the request and responds. This design has evolved in three major directions: queued requests, conversational transactions, and workflow.

Queued TP is convenient for applications in which some clients produce data and others process or consume it. E-mail, job dispatching, EDI (Electronic Data Interchange), print spooling, and batch report generation are typical examples of queued TP. TP monitors include a subsystem that manages transactional queues. The router inserts a client's request into a queue for later processing by other applications. The TP monitor may manage a pool of applications servers to process the queue. Conversely, the TP monitor may attach a queue to each client and inform the client when messages appear in its queue. Messaging applications are examples of queued transactions.

Simple transactions are one-message-in, one-message-out client/server interactions, much like a simple RPC. Conversational transactions require the client and server to exchange several messages as a single ACID unit. These relationships are sometimes not a simple request and response, but rather small requests answered by a sequence of responses (for example, a large database selection) or a large request (such as sending a file to a server). The router acts as an intermediary between the client and server for conversational transactions. Conversational transactions often invoke multiple servers and maintain client context between interactions. Menu and forms-processing systems are so common that TP systems have scripting tools to quickly define menus and forms and the flows among them. The current menu state is part of the client context. Application designers can attach server invocations and procedural logic to each menu or form. In these cases, the TP monitor (router) manages the client context and controls the conversation with a workflow language.

Workflow is the natural combination of conversational and queued transactions. In its simplest form, a workflow is a sequence of ACID transactions following a workflow script. For example, the script for a person-to-person e-mail message is compose-deliver-receive. Typical business scripts are quite complex. Workflow systems capture and manage individual flows. A client may advance a particular workflow by performing a next step in the script. A developer defines workflow scripts as part of the application design. Administrative tools report and administer the current work-in-process.

Advanced TP

Modern database systems can maintain multiple replicas of a database. When one replica is updated, the updates are cross-posted to the other replicas. TP monitors can complement database replication in two ways. First, they can submit transactions to multiple sites so that update transactions are applied to each replica, thus avoiding the need to cross-post database updates.

Second, TP systems use database replicas in a fallback scheme—leaving the data replication to the underlying database system. If a primary database site fails, the router sends the transactions to the fallback replica of the database. Server failures are thus hidden from clients, who are given the illusion of an instant switch over. Because the router uses ACID transactions to cover both messages and database updates, each transaction will be processed once. The main TP monitors available today are CICS, IMS, ACMS, Pathway, Tuxedo, Encina, and Top End.

ODBC

Open database connectivity (ODBC) is Microsoft's strategic interface for accessing data in a distributed environment made up of relational and nonrelational DBMSs. Based on the Call

Level Interface specification of the SQL Access Group, ODBC provides an open, supposedly vendor-neutral way of accessing data stored in a variety of proprietary personal computer, minicomputer, and mainframe databases. ODBC alleviates the need for independent software vendors and corporate developers to learn multiple application programming interfaces. ODBC now provides a universal data access interface. With ODBC, application developers can allow an application to concurrently access, view, and modify data from multiple, diverse databases. ODBC is a core component of Microsoft Windows Open Services Architecture (WOSA). ODBC has emerged as the industry standard for data access for both Windows-based and Macintosh-based applications.

The key salient points with respect to ODBC in the client/server development environment are as follows:

- ODBC is vendor-neutral, allowing access to DBMSs from multiple vendors.

- ODBC is open. Working with ANSI standards, the SQL Access Group (SAG), X/Open, and numerous independent software vendors, Microsoft has gained a very broad consensus on ODBC's implementation, and it is now the dominant standard.

- ODBC is powerful; it offers capabilities critical to client/server online transaction processing (OLTP) and decision support systems (DSS) applications, including system table transparency, full transaction support, scrollable cursors, asynchronous calling, array fetch and update, a flexible connection model, and stored procedures for static SQL performance.

The key benefits of ODBC are the following:

- It allows users to access data in more than one data storage location (for example, more than one server) from within a single application.

- It allows users to access data in more than one type of DBMS (such as DB2, Oracle, Microsoft SQL Server, DEC Rdb, and Progress) from within a single application.

- It simplifies application development. It is now easier for developers to provide access to data in multiple, concurrent DBMSs.

- It is a portable application programming interface (API), enabling the same interface and access technology to be a cross-platform tool.

- It insulates applications from changes to underlying network and DBMS versions. Modifications to networking transports, servers, and DBMSs will not affect current ODBC applications.

- It promotes the use of SQL, the standard language for DBMSs, as defined in the ANSI 1989 standard. It is an open, vendor-neutral specification based on the SAG Call Level Interface (CLI).

- It allows corporations to protect their investments in existing DBMSs and protect developers' acquired DBMS skills. ODBC allows corporations to continue to use existing diverse DBMSs while moving to client/server-based systems.

The ODBC Solution

ODBC addresses the database connectivity problem by using the common interface approach outlined previously. Application developers can use one API to access all data sources. ODBC is based on a CLI specification, which was developed by a consortium of over 40 companies (members of the SQL Access Group and others) and has broad support from application and database suppliers. The result is a single API that provides all the functionality that application developers need and an architecture that database developers require to ensure interoperability. As a result, a very large selection of applications use ODBC.

How ODBC Works

ODBC defines an API. Each application uses the same code, as defined by the API specification, to talk to many types of data sources through DBMS-specific drivers. A driver manager sits between the applications and the drivers. In Windows, the Driver Manager and the drivers are implemented as dynamic-link libraries (DLLs). Figure 11.5 shows how the ODBC driver for Windows 3.1 and Windows for Workgroups works. Windows 95 and Windows NT work in a similar fashion, but as they are both 32-bit operating systems, they can use a 32-bit version of ODBC.

FIGURE 11.5.

The ODBC architecture.

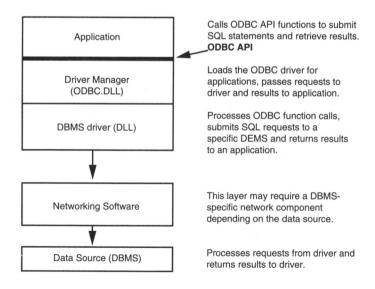

ODBC Architecture

Application — Calls ODBC API functions to submit SQL statements and retrieve results.
ODBC API

Driver Manager (ODBC.DLL) — Loads the ODBC driver for applications, passes requests to driver and results to application.

DBMS driver (DLL) — Processes ODBC function calls, submits SQL requests to a specific DEMS and returns results to an application.

Networking Software — This layer may require a DBMS-specific network component depending on the data source.

Data Source (DBMS) — Processes requests from driver and returns results to driver.

The application calls ODBC functions to connect to a data source either locally or remotely, send and receive data, and disconnect. The Driver Manager provides information to an application such as a list of available data sources, loads drivers dynamically as they are needed, and provides argument and state transition checking. The driver, developed separately from the application, sits between the application and the network. The driver processes ODBC function calls, manages all exchanges between an application and a specific DBMS, and may translate the standard SQL syntax into the native SQL of the target data source. All SQL translations are the responsibility of the driver developer.

Applications are not limited to communicating through one driver. A single application can make multiple connections, each through a different driver, or multiple connections to similar sources through a single driver. To access a new DBMS, a user or an administrator installs a driver for the DBMS. The user does not need a different version of the application to access the new DBMS. This is a tremendous benefit for end users and provides significant savings for IS organizations in support and development costs.

How ODBC Benefits the End User

End users do not work directly with the ODBC API; its configuration and setup is handled during installation. Users benefit in several ways when they use applications written with ODBC:

- Users can select a data source from a list of data source names or supply the name of a data source in a consistent way across applications.

- Users can submit data access requests in industry-standard SQL grammar regardless of the target DBMS. This capability makes ODBC ideal for what-if analysis.

- Users can access different DBMSs by using familiar desktop applications. When users need to access data on a new platform, they will have a common level of functional capabilities while accessing the new data with familiar tools. Similarly, if data moves to a different platform, only the ODBC definition needs to change; the application can stay the same.

Figure 11.6 shows that a user may be running two applications accessing three different data sources through ODBC. The three sources may be on three completely different systems elsewhere on the network, yet they are seamlessly linked into the applications on the desktop of the client.

What ODBC Means to Application Developers

ODBC was designed to allow application developers to decide between using the least common denominator of functionality across DBMSs or exploiting the individual capabilities of specific DBMSs. ODBC defines a standard SQL grammar and set of function calls that are called the *core grammar* and *core functions*, respectively. If an application developer chooses only to use the core functions, he doesn't need to write any additional code to check for specific capabilities of a driver.

FIGURE 11.6.
A possible ODBC setup.

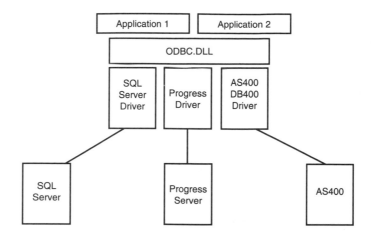

A Possible ODBC Setup
Client

Using the core functions, an application can do the following:

- Establish a connection with a data source, execute SQL statements, and retrieve results
- Receive standard error messages
- Provide a standard logon interface to the end user for access to the data source
- Use a standard set of data types defined by ODBC
- Use a standard SQL grammar defined by ODBC

ODBC also defines an extended SQL grammar and set of extended functions to provide application developers with a standard way to exploit advanced capabilities of a DBMS. In addition to the preceding features, ODBC has extensions that provide enhanced performance and increased power through the following:

- Data types such as date, time, timestamp, and binary
- Scrollable cursors
- A standard SQL grammar for scalar functions, outer joins, and procedures
- Asynchronous execution
- A standard way for application developers to find out what capabilities a driver and data source provide

Finally, ODBC supports the use of DBMS-specific SQL grammar, allowing applications to exploit the capabilities of a particular DBMS. ODBC has a vast number of supported databases available including IBM DB2/6000, IBM DB2/400, SQL Server, dBASE, Interbase, DEC Rdb, Microsoft Access, IBM DB2, and Progress.

ODBC is a powerful tool for providing end-user access to data stored in a wide variety of databases without requiring SQL or custom programming. It provides an excellent interface for creating client/server applications that are portable across multiple databases and even across multiple client platforms. The widespread industry (practically every database vendor has an ODBC driver for their product) acceptance of ODBC has resulted in many drivers, programs, and tools offering an outstanding array of features and capabilities.

Summary

Providing seamless access from your client machines to your distributed servers is a very complex process that is prone to difficulty. Each of the middleware types discussed in this chapter has taken a major share of the market. As time goes on, other products and techniques will emerge. Because the requirements for client/server vary considerably from company to company, it is not easy to choose one overall best technique or type. The main considerations when choosing your middleware types have to be ease of integration, ease of use, integrity to your needs, and the ease of development use. It is, after all, of no value to choose a product that you cannot develop your business applications on top of!

If, however, you think (wish may be more accurate) that a perfect middleware solution will become available, I am afraid that you are in for a long wait. It is perhaps best to take advantage of the existing products outlined in this chapter, develop your initial systems, build your experience, and then revisit your middleware requirements, changing products if you need to.

Communications

12

by Vinay Nadig

IN THIS CHAPTER

Communications services provide the "glue" in client/server architectures. Just as networking provides device-to-device connections, think of the communications component as providing software connections. Client applications talk to server data or applications using one of the various means of communications. In Chapter 9, "Networking," I discussed a wide variety of protocols briefly. I will revisit them in this chapter whenever appropriate.

The Basics

Basically, you can study the communication aspects of client/server architecture in two segments: within a local network and outside a local network (telecommunications). Inside or within a local (area) network, client applications communicate to servers using the protocol suites of the LAN. Cross-platform connectivity is established by APIs (Application Programming Interface), database access specifications (ODBC, WOSA, and so on), and interprotocol connection software services (for example, gateways).

When data is communicated over huge distances and spanning many local networks, telecommunications plays an important role. From the POTS (Plain Old Telephone System) analog services for serial modems to emerging methods like SONET and ATM, the telecommunications networks provide a variety of ways for your applications to communicate. Communications also plays an important role in remote access to local area networks. The distance may not be great, but telecommunications still plays a role.

Communicating in a Local Area Network

In client/server architecture, you can essentially boil down communications to a client communicating with the server; viewed from another angle, the client application communicates with the server data/application. Of course, there will be many clients and many servers with different applications talking to different databases. Figure 12.1 shows a simplified model of client/server communications.

FIGURE 12.1.

Client/server communications model.

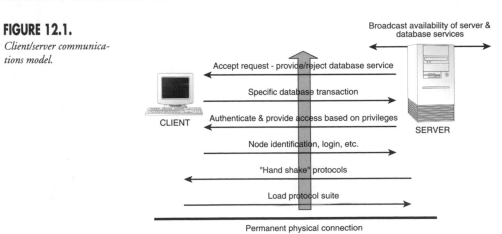

Broadcast availability of server & database services

Accept request - provide/reject database service

Specific database transaction

Authenticate & provide access based on privileges

CLIENT

Node identification, login, etc.

SERVER

"Hand shake" protocols

Load protocol suite

Permanent physical connection

In this model, the client and the server are connected over a physical wire (this wire may contain cables, gateways, switches bridges, and so on). When the server goes live on this network, it begins to broadcast its services and any database services that are available. (All network operating systems may not handle this process exactly the same, but for this example, assume that this is true.) A client goes live when it is switched on and the network start procedures are initiated; for example, loading VLMs in NetWare 4.1, loading NETx in NetWare 3.xx, loading TCP/IP in UNIX, and so on. When a client goes live, protocols are verified and the client establishes software contact with the server. Think of this contact as the telephone ringing on the other end when you call someone. At this time, you know that your connection is good, although you still don't know what services are available to you.

In the next step, the user logs into the client sending usernames and passwords to the server. The server authenticates them and provides the services according to that particular user's privileges (which are previously determined). Then the user boots up a specific application (for example, an order-entry application tied to a sales database on the server). At this time, client application-to-server database connection is established through one of various means (ODBC, native database API, gateway, and so on). This connection is more or less transparent to the user (however, if the connection is not established, the user will get an error message indicating that the connection to the database failed). From this point on, the user can send specific database transactions (such as additions, deletions, SQL queries), and they will be processed by the server and returned to the client.

Understanding Telecommunications

From 9.6 Kbps dial-up lines to 2.5 Gbps SONET fiber, telecommunications plays an integral role in establishing communications between your applications and data. As businesses become global and workers more mobile, your client/server applications must communicate over even larger geographical areas. You need to understand a number of basic telecommunications topics before you begin to design your client/server communications.

Analog Communications and Modems

Most people are familiar with the *modem* (*MOdulator/DEModulator*). It is a device that connects serially to a computing device and is able to send and receive data over a POTS connection. Speeds ranging from 2400 bps to 115.2 Kbps are possible with emerging standards of data compression. Modems still use analog transmission. What does this mean? Well, computers, when taken to the lowest level of data communications (bits and bytes), talk in 0s and 1s. Essentially, this communication is digital in nature, but phone lines typically were built to carry analog signals (due to a number of electrical characteristics of copper, and so on). Therefore, to transmit data over phone lines, modems have to convert the digital signal from computers to analog. The data then is transmitted as analog signals over the phone line to the receiving end, where another modem converts it back to a digital signal before feeding it to the receiving computer or network.

With *asynchronous transmission modems*, data is usually broken into bit-packets, with a start and a stop bit. In asynchronous communications like this, one bit is usually used as a control point: the *parity* bit. The sending modem breaks each byte of data into start bits, actual message portions, stop bits, and parity bits. The receiving modem receives data in a continuous stream of bit-packets, which it then puts back together with the information from the parity bits. Although this process builds overhead as far as speed is concerned, error checking is built in.

Synchronous transmission modems synchronize time stamps each time they are in Send or Receive mode. So in any transmission, you may have a number of times when the modems stop to synchronize and begin transmission again. These types of modems never really caught on, although the differences between synchronous and asynchronous modems are almost insignificant now.

As far as standards are concerned in asynchronous modems, you should be aware of the V.32bis and the V.33 standards that apply to the 14.4 Kbps modems. The new V.34 and V.FAST standards apply to 28.8 Kbps modems. With data compression and high-quality phone lines, 28.8 Kbps modems (if they are on both ends) can achieve theoretical speeds of up to 115.2 Kbps. Realistically, you can probably count on maximum speeds ranging between 38.4 Kbps and 57 Kbps.

When Dial-Up Is Not Enough

Dial-up connections and asynchronous modems may suffice for simple file transfer and electronic mail functions. What happens when you want to build robust, fault tolerant communications for your applications? If your application is going to span a number of databases in many sites, with user access from many geographical points both for data entry and as decision support, dial-up communications over modems will not fit the bill. That's when the Wide Area Network (WAN) comes into play. Although telephone lines were leased and WANs were in place in the mainframe-centric environments, most of them were for facilitating data entry and, in some cases, file transfer. However, today's WAN requirements are far more complex. Data replication, synchronization, remote access, video, and so on require more bandwidth, speed, availability, and reliability. What choices do you have, and what do you have to understand to make informed decisions?

The first and earliest way of guaranteed increased bandwidth was *leased lines*. Here you leased a telephone line of a certain bandwidth, and the telephone company granted you that "circuit" between two points for your exclusive use. You pay a set amount per month regardless of usage.

In *circuit switching*, a temporary pathway or *circuit* is established between two points for the duration of the transmission. This channel is exclusive to the two points for the duration of the transmission. You pay for the connection time.

In *packet switching*, data gets broken into packets of specified size (bits), with header, source, and destination information. Depending upon the protocol (Frame Relay/ATM), these packets are called *frames* or *cells*. Then these segments of data travel over circuits along with data segments from other transmissions and arrive at their destinations, where they are reassembled. Special hardware devices are required both at the telecommunications company's network and the end user's premises. Though data travels over shared circuits, it appears like a dedicated circuit to the end user. This seemingly dedicated circuit is called a *virtual circuit.*

How Fast Can You Go?

With all the different choices available, how fast can your data fly through these networks? Again, you have different levels according to the type of technology (leased line, ISDN, ATM) you choose.

On the leased-line front, a common and popular standard is called *T-1*. It is readily available from all telecommunications carriers and is rated at 1.544 Mbps. T-1 is divided into 24 channels of 64 Kbps each. To facilitate higher bandwidth needs in leased lines, the telecommunications companies came up with *T-2* and *T-3*. Rated at 6.3 Mbps, T-2 is equal to four T-1s. T-3, an emerging technology, is equivalent to 28 T-1s, so the theoretical maximum bandwidth is close to 45 Mbps. To achieve speeds like that, data has to be transmitted over fiber or microwave signals.

In the circuit-switched arena, *Switched 56* provides 24 simultaneous channels of 64 Kbps through regular dial-up. Connections are established over standard telephone lines, but you use special modems and CSU/DSU hardware. You can achieve a maximum throughput of 1.5 Mbps by multiplexing all the channels.

ISDN (Integrated Services Digital Network) in one of its flavors is a circuit-switched technology that can use existing telephone lines but provide greater bandwidth to you. It is catching on quickly as the phone companies begin to deploy ISDN hardware more comprehensively. Basically, a *Basic Rate Interface (BRI)* ISDN connection gives you two 64 Kbps connections (2B) and one 16 Kbps connection (1D), so BRI is rated as 2B+D. The D channel is used for call setup information and is not available for your use. You can multiplex voice and data over the two B channels, so the BRI connection gives you a throughput of 128 Kbps. But another significant difference is that data transmission is digital, not analog. Data signals are not converted into analog signals when they originate from your computer network. Rather, they are slightly modified to suit the ISDN hardware and are then transmitted. At the higher end, ISDN comes in a *PRI (Primary Rate Interface)* connection that gives you 23B+D channels. This gives you close to 1.5 Mbps. But the real advantages of ISDN lie not in bandwidth alone but the quality of data transmission, ease of setup, and reliability of the circuits.

The frame and cell (packet) switching technologies are pushing the envelope of data transmission as bandwidth needs continue to increase. As discussed earlier in this chapter, data is broken up into packets of specified bit-lengths and streamed over a virtual circuit to the destination. Each of these packets is equipped with control information that determines where it is going.

The oldest packet switching technology available today is *X.25*. Usually, you install an X.25 "pad" at each site on the WAN, which then connects to the telecommunications provider's network cloud, as shown in Figure 12.2. X.25 is not a WAN protocol but sits between the LAN and the WAN. Maximum throughput is 64 Kbps. With the newer packet switching technologies becoming widely accepted, X.25 is rare for new installations.

FIGURE 12.2.

X.25 packet switching.

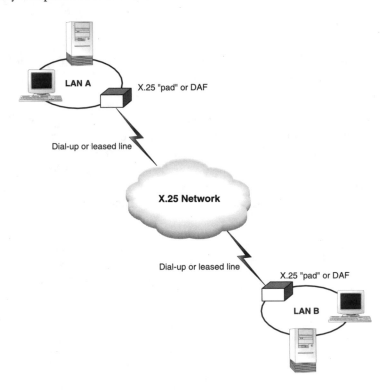

Frame Relay is a reliable and popular protocol for interconnecting LANs. In fact, it was designed with LAN-to-LAN connectivity in mind. Frame Relay is not the actual WAN protocol. When data leaves the LAN, it is transmitted to the WAN media in *frames*. These frames (similar to cells or packets) can then travel through the WAN cloud in any of the cell-based technologies: ATM, SONET, Broadband ISDN, and so on. The hardware device at the recipient LAN takes care of the protocol conversion. Frame Relay excludes much of the error protection present in X.25, thereby providing a faster means of transmission. Because Frame Relay and the newer methods rely more on digital rather than on analog technology, error correction built into the protocol is superfluous.

Switched Multimegabit Data Service (SMDS) provides a dedicated hardware link at your site. SMDS is the phone companies' answer to your needs for a secure, private network. Because dedicated links are used, your network is secure and data transmission speeds of T-1 (1.544 Mbps) to T-3 (44.7 Mbps) can be achieved.

Asynchronous Transfer Mode (ATM), though enjoying a lot of attention at the LAN level, is fast becoming a viable option for connecting LANs. ATM is a cell-based transmission technology, where data is streamed in cells over the physical wire. When a data stream is transmitted from one point to another, ATM establishes a "virtual connection." To you, it seems like a dedicated leased line. ATM can multiplex several virtual connections over a single physical wire. Error correction overhead is greatly reduced providing for faster transmission. ATM also allows the switching of voice, video, and data over the same switching infrastructure. Another advantage ATM provides is a "virtual path" where a group of virtual connections in the same direction are multiplexed over the same path. This allows for simplified network architecture and simulated private networks for end users like you.

Synchronous Optical Network (SONET) is the high-bandwidth, fast-throughput wave of the future in telecommunications. SONET, based on digital fiber technology, offers potential bandwidths ranging from 55 Mbps to 2.5 Gbps. SONET is also an accepted international standard. You will see the telecommunications providers building SONET infrastructure and providing transmission services over it for your existing protocols (ATM, FDDI, and so on). To build private SONET networks will be prohibitively expensive for some time to come.

Design Considerations

From a communications perspective, client/server architects and designers must consider three main factors: LAN protocols and communications issues, WAN protocols and communications issues, and application design issues (see Figure 12.3). With an understanding of the various protocols and telecommunications methods, it is now important to apply that knowledge to design your applications.

Localized (within a LAN) Considerations

Primary issues to consider in this area are the LAN protocols you use to communicate. Novell's NetWare has a large share of the LAN file-serving market. But UNIX has traditionally led the database server market. Microsoft's Windows NT Server 3.51 is fast becoming a viable alternative for database and application serving. Even within these various network operating systems, you can use the same protocol (TCP/IP) or different ones. With the explosion of the Internet and the integration of databases over the World Wide Web (WWW), TCP/IP is a strong contender for your enterprise-wide networks. The Internet was built on TCP/IP and still runs on TCP/IP. So, if your applications need integration with the 'Net, TCP/IP may become very important in your design considerations.

FIGURE 12.3.

Design considerations.

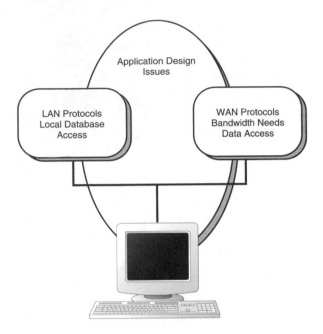

To implement databases in a NetWare environment, you will have to run the database as an *NLM (NetWare Loadable Module)* on the file server. You can have a dedicated "database server," but you still implement the database as an NLM. What this means is that communication between the database server and the network is established by Novell's *SAP (Service Advertising Protocol)*, which constantly broadcasts the presence of the database. The actual transactions between the client and the server will ride on the IPX/SPX protocol.

Is this the best method for database communications in a client/server architecture? Unfortunately, the answer is not straightforward. Technically, IPX and NetWare are probably suited for file sharing. Running database services as NLMs has certain disadvantages, although Novell has striven to minimize those in NetWare 4.1. Look at your existing network infrastructure. Are you heavily invested in NetWare networks? Can you get away with running your mission-critical databases as NLMs? What kind of fault tolerance do you need as far as uptime is concerned? Many packaged third-party solutions offer NLM versions of their back-end databases. For example, almost all the leading financial software packages offer NLM versions of their databases. If integrating your mission-critical client/server applications smoothly with your productivity applications is a significant goal, seriously consider NetWare, IPX/SPX, SAP, and the NLM platform for client/server communications.

UNIX has traditionally been vendors' and consultants' favorite platform to establish client/server communications between database server and client application. All the leading database vendors offer robust, reliable, and tested UNIX versions of their products. This is partly due to the networking features built into UNIX from the ground up and the robustness of

TCP/IP as a protocol. *TCP/IP* or *Transaction Control Protocol/Internet Protocol* breaks data into packets with a header and a footer denoting destination and source. When a TCP/IP client makes a request to a TCP/IP host or server, a *socket* or pathway is opened between the two, and communication is established. TCP/IP is the de facto standard on the Internet. TCP/IP is the protocol you should choose if you have heterogeneous platforms, including mainframes, UNIX-based minicomputers, PC-based LAN servers, and different databases (relational, hierarchical, and so on). It is definitely the protocol of choice for cross-platform integration. Even in NetWare and NT networks, it is relatively easy to grant access to UNIX-based servers from PC clients. From a Windows-based PC or application, you would implement Microsoft's WinSock architecture to talk TCP/IP and establish communications. When building a Wide Area Network (WAN), it is more realistic to assume that you would talk TCP/IP over the wire rather than IPX/SPX. So where does that leave you in your design?

Again, the salient point to ponder here is the architecture of your existing network. Are you heavily dependent on UNIX? Do you have a number of platforms that are not going away any time soon? And do the Internet and WANs play heavily into your client/server architecture? If so, TCP/IP is definitely a strong contender in your network. However, note that as vendors strive to include native TCP/IP support in their network operating systems you may not necessarily be tied to UNIX.

For example, Microsoft's systems strategy for you is to run your applications (databases) on Windows NT Servers. Your client applications are probably running on Windows PCs anyway.

To facilitate cross-platform integration, the native protocol of this NT-based network could either be IPX or even TCP/IP instead of Microsoft's NetBEUI (a modification of NetBIOS). So, from Microsoft's point of view, you cannot lose! As usual, though, the answer is a little more involved than that. Windows NT Server 3.5 is beginning to establish a strong presence. But there are no long-term operational performance results as a UNIX-based, mission-critical implementation can provide. So, although "Windows everywhere" can sound really attractive, your business requirements should drive your client/server communications strategy. Will your database be many gigabytes in size? What kind of response will your users need to run the business? Again, what kind of data sources and destinations will you use? TCP/IP is not a chatty protocol like IPX/SPX is. Therefore, there are definite speed benefits in using TCP/IP for dial-up connections. Also, most database development is done first on UNIX. Then when it is completed or almost completed, it is ported over to Novell. So if staying on the leading edge is important, keep in mind that UNIX products usually come out first.

Wide Area Considerations

When your client/server architecture needs to scale the enterprise, issues like the number of sites, mobility of your users, method of telecommunications, and network service provider selection crop up. Figure 12.4 illustrates how your client/server communications framework could evolve.

FIGURE 12.4.

Client/server communications evolution framework.

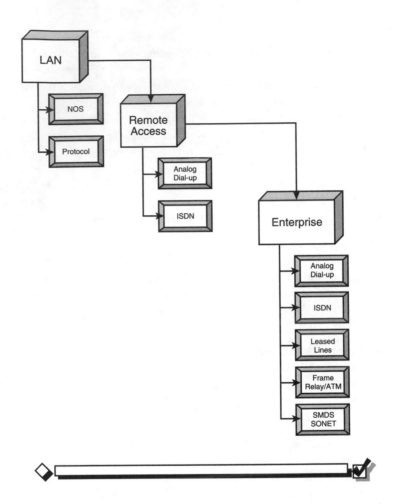

It is useful to view the framework in three steps or phases: the *LAN phase*, which has already been discussed; the *remote access phase*; and the *enterprise phase*. Depending upon the nature and scope of your application, you may have to consider all three phases simultaneously.

Remote Access

The first logical step to extending your application beyond its LAN is to grant remote access. For my purposes here, I define *remote access* as accessing application/data residing on a LAN by mobile users. It is characterized by users who are probably part of the LAN some of the time, and roving in the field the rest of the time. A two- to three-user branch office may also make use of remote access. Remote access is usually facilitated by *remote control* or *remote node*. In remote control, your remote user will dial in and take control of a physical PC connected to the LAN. From that point on, only the screen refreshes and keystrokes are transmitted over the phone line. In *remote node*, your remote user will load the LAN protocol on his or her PC and send it over the phone line to a remote access server (a dedicated hardware component or the server itself) and become a node just as if on the LAN, only over a phone line. There are advantages and disadvantages to both, and your application will determine this choice in most cases. My objective here is not to compare the two, but to discuss the communications components required to facilitate remote access.

The simplest form of communications is, of course, to use an analog modem to dial up the LAN. With 28.8 Kbps modems (which can go up to 57 Kbps with data compression), this method does provide an efficient way of communicating. However, your application requirements will determine whether you choose this route. For simple file transfers, data entry, and electronic mail, analog dial-up solutions may suffice. But if you are allowing your remote users to access databases and perform ad hoc queries, you may find yourself looking for the next step up very quickly.

Analog modem technology has reached its technical limits. You will not see a widespread vendor release of a 56 Kbps modem, for example. Speeds such as 56 Kbps and 115 Kbps are touted by vendors with data compression using only 28.8 Kbps modems. But the telephone companies are banding together to market their answer to this: ISDN. Capable of running over existing phone wires, ISDN provides two channels of 64 Kbps and one channel of 16 Kbps in a Basic Rate Interface service. Telecommunications providers still have to install switching equipment in their networks, but full deployment is slated by 1996-97. With data compression, it is possible to achieve speeds of up to .5 Mbps with ISDN. Due to its digital technology, the quality of the line is much superior to analog phone lines. ISDN requires special terminal equipment at your site as well as your remote users' sites. But the prices for this equipment as well as for ISDN services are falling rapidly. If your applications demand higher bandwidth, more reliability in communications, and constant access for remote users, seriously consider ISDN.

Enterprise

If you are truly considering client/server architectures for the enterprise, you are really looking at making your applications communicate to a number of sites in addition to remote users. Your enterprise needs will probably involve site-to-site communications, database-to-database communications, real-time transaction processing, and batch-mode file transfers. This is where you must decide whether your WAN can survive on dial-up analog lines and modems, leased line X.25 networks, or cell-based (ATM, Frame Relay, and so on) private or public networks.

For all but the simplest of applications, dial-up WANs probably will not suffice, mainly due to bandwidth and reliability needs. So as you scale your application across the enterprise, you are looking at WAN protocols and methods that must give you sufficient bandwidth, be reliable, and ideally be built on more modern cell-based technologies.

You may choose to segregate segments of your network with heavy usage and use the more modern technologies like ATM or Frame Relay, while still using dial-up capabilities at the lesser-used segments. ISDN may prove to be a good evolution from dial-up analog lines for you. Depending upon the bandwidth needs of your application, you may decide to step up to T-1 or ATM networks. You must understand the performance characteristics of your application under varying access loads. If some of your sites rely on your application only to enter order-processing data, you may decide on dial-up lines. But note that if your application is accepting real-time updates, you cannot permit your users to drop, and thereby stop, business. This may prompt you to consider leased lines of 56 Kbps or even T-1 capacities. If your users generate a large number of SQL queries, you should definitely start from either a 56 Kbps leased line or a switched 56 Kbps line, preferably using Frame Relay. Building private T-1 and T-3 networks can become expensive very quickly, so vendors offer the use of their networks to you. CompuServe, AT&T, and Sprint are among a few that will contract out their networks and services to you. You can remove yourself from the hassle of managing the network because the vendors will do that for you. As public networks begin to deploy SMDS and SONET, multi-gigabyte transfer speeds will become efficient, and transparent database access could be a reality.

Application Considerations

Your application's architecture affects the communications framework in client/server architectures. How your applications access databases, how your databases replicate and synchronize, whether you will allow users online access, whether you are going to use a two-phase commit process, and how you are going to use messaging will all affect the communications decisions you make.

A Primer on Distributed Computing

Distributed computing typically involves multiple servers, networks, and databases functioning to solve a set of business needs. In doing so, databases may be split across geographically dispersed servers. Sharing of resources is done over a network, introducing significant communications challenges. Some standards/specifications you must become familiar with are the OSF's DCE (Distributed Computing Environment), Microsoft's Distributed OLE (Object Linking and Embedding), IBM's SOM (System Object Model), and the multivendor CORBA (Common Object Request Broker Architecture).

DCE provides integration and interpretability across multiple-platform LANs and WANs by making use of a "global namespace" or directory tree. This namespace, hierarchical in nature, is accessible by a directory services API. Using this API, your application can use any resource (data, services, and so on) found on the global namespace.

CORBA is a distributed architecture for building three-tier client/server applications, where application (user interface), business rules, and data are partitioned into three segments. CORBA provides the "object brokers" that allow your application to manipulate the data according to the business rules. *SOM* is IBM's variation of CORBA.

Distributed OLE is proprietary to Microsoft and is an extension of the OLE 2.0 specifications. Just as OLE 2.0 turns discrete sets of documents (containing applications, data, and business rules) into objects that can be accessed by OLE-compliant applications on a local PC, distributed OLE is slated to provide the same services over a network.

A Primer on Data Access

Data or database access is usually provided in one of two ways: by using a native database API or by using a data access specification like ODBC or ODAPI. Some other issues you need to understand are database replication and online access.

In a native database API scenario, you would use the database vendor-provided API to let your application access that database. For example, if your application ran on the Sybase database platform and you wanted to go the native API route, you would use the Sybase API from your application to make calls to the database. This API manifests itself as an extra set of drivers (DLLs in Windows, sometimes DOS-based requesters) loaded on the client PC. Figure 12.5 shows an illustration of this concept.

FIGURE 12.5.

Data access using native database API.

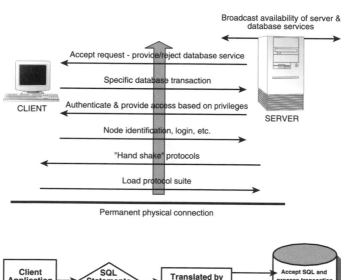

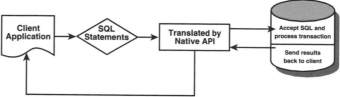

Native database APIs are primed for their databases and can provide extremely fast and reliable communication. Consequently, network stress will be less. But as you move into multiple databases (from different vendors), you will find that your client application and PC need to work that much harder, with a number of APIs.

If you use a common data access specification like ODBC (Open Database Connectivity), you would load a set of ODBC drivers for the databases you are going to access. For example, if your application is going to access a Sybase and an Oracle database, you would load those ODBC drivers. See Figure 12.6 for an illustration.

FIGURE 12.6.

Data access using ODBC.

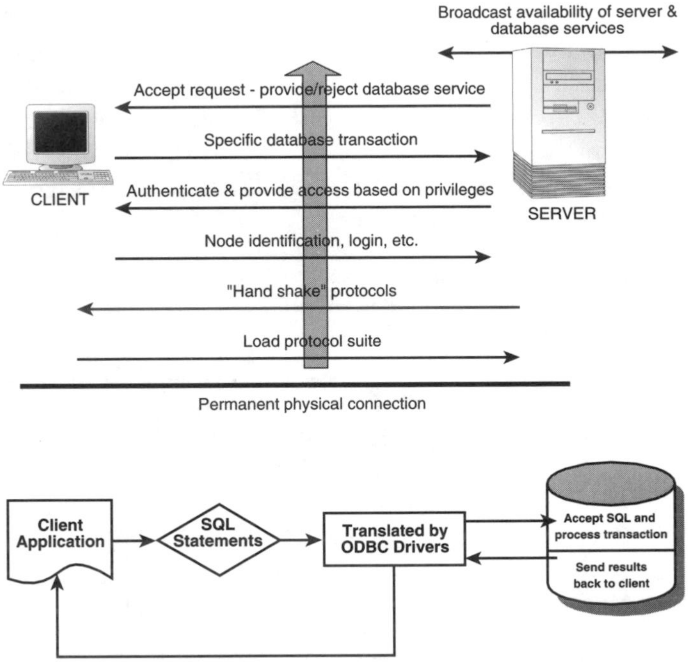

Microsoft provides these drivers; third-party vendors like Q+E make robust ODBC drivers also. The advantage of using ODBC is that you get instant multidatabase access without your client application knowing a whole lot about each database's idiosyncrasies. The downside is that if ODBC is not implemented properly, it can drastically affect performance. Some vendors implement ODBC in its higher levels (0 and 1), which tends to introduce a lot of hand shaking and emulation leading to decreased performance. Level 2 is the most robust and clean for ODBC data access. When vendors tout ODBC compliance, make sure that you understand at which level ODBC will function.

Another important feature of your application that will affect your communications framework is whether your users will be online over wide areas all the time hitting centralized databases, or whether you will distribute databases and have users access them only through their LANs. Essentially, the online model is from the mainframe era, where all the processing took place in a centralized location. Some data may have been downloaded into LANs, but it was not "live" data for transaction processing. But the whole concept of client/server pushes to a more distributed model, where processing needs to be decentralized. So what happens to databases? How do you make sure that your users at well spread-out regional and branch offices are looking at real-time or real-enough time data on their LANs? Do you build a communications framework wherein all your users (from hundreds to thousands) are live and "online" all the time? The impact that such a framework would have on your WAN bandwidths is almost unthinkable. You are essentially going against the basic tenet of client/server computing, where you distribute processing!

Enter database replication. Essentially, database vendors provide replication capabilities that allow you to replicate changes from "parent" databases to "child" databases. Note that replication is usually associated with server-to-server database distribution. (Although Lotus Notes uses replication for server to remote client also.) The replication can take place based on the time frequency you determine. It may be overnight or twice a day, if your business can allow that. And it can be replicated with a few seconds lag, called *real-enough time* replication, if your business demands that. See Figure 12.7 for an illustration.

FIGURE 12.7.

Database replication.

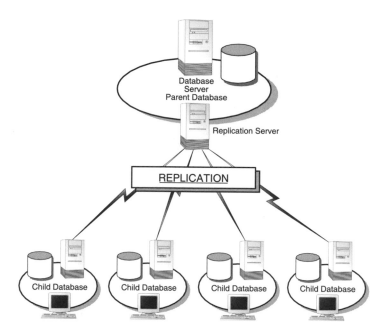

There are still issues like synchronization, roll backs, two-phase commit implementations, and so on that are not completely trouble free, but replication is here to stay. Products like Sybase System 10 and 11 and Lotus Notes provide sophisticated and robust replication features. If replication is in the scope of your application architecture, make sure you understand how it affects the communications framework, both in terms of protocols and in terms of bandwidth needs.

Summary

Understanding the communications components in your client/server architecture is key to the success of your application development efforts. Your applications will tend to evolve on the communications framework from the LAN to the enterprise. Therefore, you must design your communications infrastructure so that it can scale well. Issues that you must consider are the type of protocol you will use within a LAN, the telecommunications framework you will use to connect sites, and the methods you will use for data access and database distribution. A comprehensive background in these areas should be represented in your client/server development teams.

Essential Techniques

13

by Ellen Gottesdiener

This chapter examines the techniques to use when building, migrating, or enhancing client/server applications. These techniques facilitate achieving the desired outcome for every client/server application: speedy deployment of a quality application that meets business needs.

The Need for Techniques

Today, companies are pushed to get products and services to market quickly. Simultaneously, client/server technology promotes rapid delivery of the information systems that support these products and services. Vendors of client/server tools and related technologies promote the perception that client/server applications can be created and deployed quickly. But the "just do it" approach yields client/server applications that have a very short life of usage and that ultimately do not scale up for additional users, functionality, and/or data requirements. Moreover, the applications tend not to address the real business opportunities and problems.

The following frameworks and processes are needed to ensure long-term usability of both tactical and strategic client/server applications.

Client/server applications, because of the added difficulties of integrating multiple components, the complexities of the technical infrastructure, and design challenges like application partitioning, are *more* difficult to develop than traditional applications. Today's client/server applications become legacy applications that need to be maintained and enhanced. If properly addressed, the methods and the processes that they use, which are discussed within, are essential to ensure success with your client/server application efforts.

Methodologies

Methodologies are collections of techniques and guidelines for managing the complex, interrelated steps involved in building a software product. The complexity, high cost, and immaturity of client/server technology require a disciplined, proven, repeatable set of processes to assist in reducing the risk of embarking on a client/server project. Methodologies serve this role. They are guidelines for the process of developing a system and are an important tool in risk reduction. The guidelines contained in a methodology vary in the level of detail, but most define steps, tasks, subtasks, roles, objectives, deliverables, and estimators for each phase of the system development life cycle.

Methodologies can be purchased from a vendor or built within the organization. Companies that develop and market methodologies use the actual project experiences of their clients and consulting staff to establish workable, proven guidelines. Some IT (Information Technology) organizations choose to "roll their own" methods, based on their in-house experience and culture. However, many IT organizations today have abandoned or never used a methodology because it is perceived as being too cumbersome and difficult to use.

There is an increasing respect for these methodologies as evidenced by recent trends in the IT industry. The methodologies now provide features that make them easier to use. For example, many methodologies come with multiple paths or routes so a project team can pick a framework that more closely matches the scope and complexity of the application they are deploying. Many methods are now packaged as a hypertext tool installed on a workstation or a network rather than being stored in multiple volumes of manuals. And finally, some methods have the capability to assist in project management tasks such as planning and estimating.

Waterfall Methodology

Most traditional methodologies are rooted in structured or information engineering approaches. These *top-down* or *waterfall* methods are largely based on the premise that the results of one phase directly feed the next. The goal during each phase is to do such a good job at any given phase that the team does not need to go back "up" to revisit a completed phase. At the end of the whole set of phases, the software product is completed (see Figure 13.1).

FIGURE 13.1.

The waterfall methodology. (Source: EBG Consulting, Inc.)

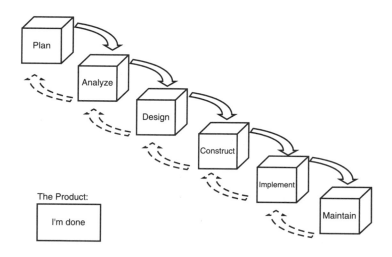

Waterfall methods are criticized as being too slow, inflexible, and costly. In addition, they presume that design activities, such as selecting a technical platform or creating a prototype, will occur later in the project life cycle. This traditional waterfall method is indeed not appropriate for client/server applications. It does not lend itself to exploiting the technology through prototyping and evolving application models. Nor does it emphasize the critical role of the application user and sponsor. Because the waterfall method assumes that requirements can be known in the early phases of a life cycle, it does not need to have risk-assessment built into the process. This method also assumes that the technical infrastructure is in place and operational, and it has no provisions for the logical design challenge of partitioning functions and data between client and server.

Client/Server Methodologies

Client/server methodologies are just emerging. They all make use of the idea of *iterative prototyping* (or *concurrent engineering*) techniques such as Joint Application Design (JAD), shorter releases and/or versions of applications, and early definition of the technical architecture. Iterative prototyping is a process in which the development team switches between prototyping the application with a development tool, creating application models (data/process/object), and reviewing the prototype with customers. Some client/server methodologies are adapted from structured, information engineering, rule-based, or object-oriented approaches. Others are "home grown" methods. All use some form of data or object modeling and process modeling.

All client/server methods make use of a technique known as *iteration*. Iteration is the process of repeating something multiple times, with each repetition being closer to the desired goal. For example, the user interface will be designed in an iterative fashion with end users reviewing versions of the interface for a fixed period of time or for a fixed number of versions. The application models (data, process, event, object) will be developed in a similar iterative fashion.

The idea of *concurrent engineering* is also employed in most client/server methodologies. This is the same concept as that used in manufacturing whereby a concept team creates the models for the product *at the same time* as the design team, thereby producing a manufactureable, usable product. Applied to client/server methods, the application models will be built concurrently with the user interface prototypes. In this way, each component (model and interface) will validate the other. This method of development relies highly on IT standards that should be already in place. These standards help stabilize both models and code, reducing the variations that might otherwise occur in both human understanding and software execution.

There are essentially three *process models* for software methodologies. A process model is an approach or style within the methodology for people to work on the end product. These models are incremental, evolutionary, or waterfall. Because the waterfall process model is most often not appropriate for client/server, the focus of this chapter will be on the incremental and evolutionary styles. In addition, *rapid application development*, or *RAD*, which combines these two approaches and adds some variations, will be covered.

Incremental Process Model

An *incremental process model* is one in which the client/server application is delivered in a series of releases whereby each release, or version, builds upon prior releases while increasing the functionality. An *increment* is a subset of usable functionality that is delivered to the customer in pieces. Other terms used in the software industry for increment include: *release, version, feature set, cycle, fragment, phase, segment, build, cluster, use case,* and *chunk*. Each increment is deployed in a short period of time—for example 4, 6, or 12 months—and is fully functional. The first increments are targeted to provide the customer with the most important business functionality, thereby giving the customers some relief quickly. Thus, the whole software product is not delivered at once, as in the waterfall process model, but is delivered in pieces by order of business importance.

This approach is rooted in Barry Boehm's *spiral* method of software development, which recommends the use of concurrent activities and successive releases of the software product. A "divide and conquer" approach is followed whereby multiple development cycles are performed, each using this spiral approach. Each cycle broadens the scope of the spiral thereby adding more functionality (see Figure 13.2).

FIGURE 13.2.

The incremental process model. (Source: EBG Consulting, Inc.)

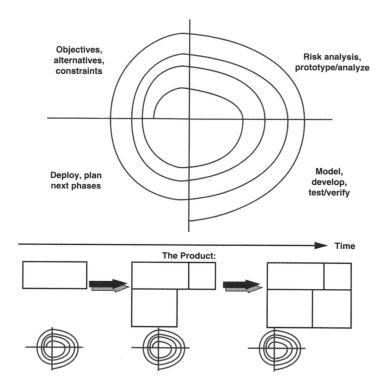

Another key concept in the spiral process is to reduce project risk. Risk analysis forces the team (including the customer as part of the team) to consciously make choices between time and risk. Risks may include such issues as complexity of processing, newness of the technology, commitment by end users, number of dependencies between processes, interfaces to existing applications, and pressures for very quick delivery time. When objectively evaluated, the project team can determine which processes will deliver the highest business value while simultaneously understanding the risks associated with satisfying that business need. This risk analysis is conducted most frequently in the early phases of the spiral, where the biggest payback can be gained.

The incremental model thus makes use of an iterative process by which the team melds prototyping with more formal modeling techniques. This combination, in conjunction with an orientation to early delivery of some core functionality with the first increments of the software product, is essential to ensuring both quality and speed of delivery.

Evolutionary Process Model

In an *evolutionary process*, the product changes over time as it is exposed to the environment. Applied to software development, the evolutionary process model makes use of successive releases of the application with the intent of refining the system with greater functionality, performance, and structure. Learning and adapting to the environment is the key to evolution. By exposing the software product to the environment quickly, customers critique, review, and provide feedback on a prototype. Then the application team can make changes to the software to allow for better adaptation to the future production environment. The evolutionary process model is similar to the incremental process model. The product releases, however, are intended to fundamentally change rather than build upon a prior increment.

Such an approach requires an application architecture, tools, and technology that is highly adaptable. The best technology to use for an evolutionary process model is object-oriented technology in which object classes can be fundamentally redesigned and extended in subsequent product deliveries by a well-trained team of designers and developers (see Figure 13.3).

FIGURE 13.3.

The evolutionary process model. (Source: EBG Consulting, Inc., adapted from OMG, 1992.)

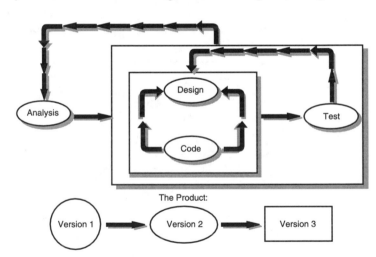

RAD (Rapid Application Development)

Rapid Application Development is a variation of the incremental and the evolutionary process models that facilitate deploying a customer's software needs within a short period of time. This predefined time frame is called a *timebox*. Like the incremental process model, the software product is not delivered at once but is delivered in pieces by business priority at predetermined points in time. Each timeboxed increment typically takes three to six months. Like the spiral model, each cycle within the timebox is completed multiple times to evolve the application closer to completion based on continual customer feedback.

RAD makes heavy use of prototyping techniques to test, confirm, and critique the application under development. The RAD process thus requires a small team of highly skilled individuals (including customers) to work together using tools that accelerate the testing, prototyping, and construction artifacts of the software product. Successful delivery of a product is based on the skills and ability of the team to learn about customer requirements as the software product is being built.

The RAD process defies a linear series of steps carried out in a sequence. RAD begins by defining the desired product in an initial planning phase. During planning, a definition of the project scope is performed along with some preliminary data/process analysis, architectural definition, risk assessment, and estimating. After a timebox is chosen, a spiral process occurs involving prototyping, modeling, architectural design, construction, and testing (see Figure 13.4). After each timeboxed delivery, a planning session is conducted to determine the next timebox. These timeboxes can be arranged in sequence, in parallel, or staggered to create the whole application, as shown in Figure 13.5.

FIGURE 13.4.

The RAD process model. (Source: EBG Consulting, Inc.)

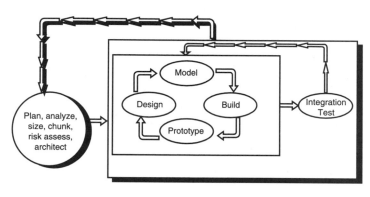

FIGURE 13.5.

Timeboxes can be arranged in sequence, in parallel, or staggered. (Source: EBG Consulting, Inc.)

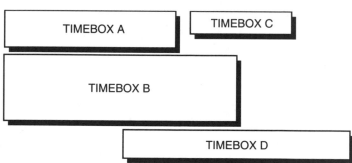

RAD emerged in the mid-1980s, not out of the PC or client/server world, but from the midrange DEC/VAX environment and MVS environments in which code generator tools were used to virtually eliminate the manual steps involved in the construction phase of software development. RAD's inventor, Scott Shultz (then at DuPont), devised the technique as a unique combination of tools, methods, and people to deliver systems quickly to customers. His approach was later popularized by James Martin's 1991 book, *Rapid Application Development.* Other RAD practitioners began by using tools in a mainframe environment while also changing the development methodology.

Tools are indeed a critical part of the RAD process. Beyond the typical tools associated with RAD—those that build the GUI interface, for example—are tools that capture the application models, document the development process, create test scripts enabling the whole testing process, generate and build code, and assist in software configuration management. In addition, the quality of the application is dependent upon maintaining a stable "memory" of the product structure. This is accomplished through the use of models underlying the interface design. Although the tools are very critical to the RAD approach, the tools alone will not create a stable, scalable software product.

RAD requires a very different approach to project management. Project development in our industry has been notoriously late, over budget, and particularly susceptible to creeping requirements. The timebox is a mechanism to control resources and delivery scope and provides a dramatically different way to manage a project. It forces the team to anticipate reducing the scale of product delivery, requires focus on customer priorities, assumes continual change will occur, and imparts to the team a sense of urgency. In a RAD process, the scope of the functionality will be pared down to meet the time frame. In a more traditional project management approach, the end date would be extended.

Elements for successful use of RAD are:

- Strong management support
- Use of tools to make the process quicker, traceable, and verifiable
- A small team of knowledgeable business and IT people
- A well-understood methodology for accomplishing results

RAD projects typically last three weeks to six months and are therefore very time-driven. The team is given the authority to decide what will be accomplished in the predetermined time frame. They may follow up that RAD project with another and successively add functionality to the original core system. In the end, the team must have the power to balance the use of iterative prototyping tools with modeling and continual feedback and determine what will be achieved for each timebox.

Defining the Technical Infrastructure

Prior to client/server computing, IT projects could make certain assumptions about which technology would be used for a system being developed, enhanced, or bought. If there were choices to be made, there were only a few. Now, things aren't so simple. Hundreds of options exist when combining such technical components as operating systems, hardware, and software. These are layered on both client and server components. Each of these choices needs to be determined for all the physical locations where users and/or hardware exist (see Figure 13.6). For each client/server application, as part of the planning process, the technical infrastructure must be outlined. Ideally, it will incorporate aspects of an existing enterprise architecture.

FIGURE 13.6.

Client/server technical infrastructure components. (Source: EBG Consulting, Inc.)

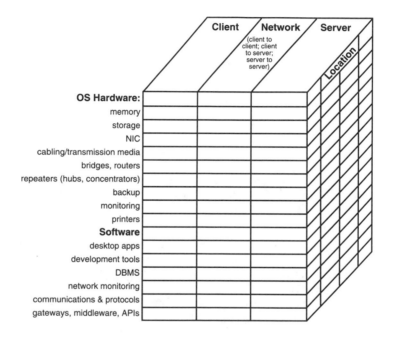

This architecture should include the components needed not only to develop the client/server application, but also the execution environment. To accomplish this, IT may need to inventory the current technologies available, factoring in capacity, cost, usage, and network forecasts. Additionally, the team needs to realize that certain aspects of the architecture may need to be adjusted as the project progresses. Early definition of a working technical architecture is a critical component for successful client/server projects. Most client/server methodologies recognize this fact and have early technical architecture definition as a main activity.

JAD (Joint Application Design)

An essential technique to use in client/server efforts is *facilitated group sessions*. Most IT professionals refer to this technique as *JAD (Joint Application Design* or *Joint Application Development)*, a term coined by IBM Canada in the late 1970s. JAD requires getting the right people together at the right time with a skilled, unbiased facilitator to accomplish specific objectives. IT and business clients gather together in facilitated meetings for half a day to as many as five days, with a specific, planned agenda. Facilitated sessions are most often needed during the definition and design stages, permitting IT and business partners together to accomplish the following: conduct risk analysis, determine project scope, create requirements (events, models, and scenarios), and generate "low-tech" interface prototypes.

Removing errors originating in the requirements and design constitute up to 60 percent of the cost of any application. Errors originating from the requirements stage, such as not understanding them, account for 45 percent to 65 percent of the errors in delivered systems. As a means to reduce risk, enhance quality, and increase productivity, JAD has proven to be extremely useful. Due to the critical nature of continuous end-user involvement in the client/server development process, JAD is an essential technique to gather information in an effective and efficient way.

JAD has the effect of decreasing the lapse time for gathering and validating application requirements. Team and management commitment to the process along with skilled facilitation are key ingredients for JAD success. The technique should not be used if the team is not cohesive, if there is poor management support, if authority will not be delegated to the team, and/or if there are no facilities made available for the JAD process. In an appropriate situation, JAD is a technique that naturally pushes customer requirements to center stage, as does client/server computing. Perhaps most importantly, JAD promotes teamwork and mutual accountability, crucial factors when people are under pressure to quickly learn, adapt, and act.

Recent research by metrics guru Capers Jones demonstrates that JAD, along with prototyping, significantly decreases the risk of creeping scope, reduces application defects, and increases productivity. Jones focuses on metrics for IT, which are measures and quantification of all aspects of software development. His research also shows that projects using JAD are unusually resistant to the creeping scope problem, reducing the frequency from 80 percent to 10 percent.

An experienced, knowledgeable facilitator is key to successful JAD, where planning, conflict management, and client/server technology requires sophisticated facilitation and modeling skills. To maintain energy, creativity, and motivation, the facilitator must orchestrate the use of interactive as well as parallel group activities. These activities should promote mastery of the sometimes difficult details of the session goals. The facilitator should work with the project sponsor to ensure the following JAD critical success factors are met:

- **Right people.** Cross-functional, knowledgeable, skilled, motivated, and empowered people with decision-making authority for the JAD goals by their management and the project sponsor.

- **Distinct project/JAD sponsor.** A person who is the key stakeholder, who has final decision-making power if any conflicts cannot be resolved by the JAD team.

- **Skilled facilitator.** A neutral individual with no stake in a single point of view, experienced in group facilitation, knowledgeable about the JAD methodology, group dynamics, and the products being developed in the JAD; the facilitator manages the JAD session so that it starts and ends on time, enhances teamwork and cooperation, enforces ground rules, and promotes creativity.

- **Planned agenda.** The agenda is communicated in advance, is realistic for the time allotted to the JAD, uses no business or technology acronyms, and uses effective individual and group techniques to accomplish the session objectives.

- **Dedicated scribe.** Not a participant, but a person whose role is to capture and later synthesize the products for later feedback and validation of the JAD session.

- **Relaxed setting.** Usually an off-site location with no distractions, interruptions, or cancellations permitted; the JAD is the single priority of the participants while it is conducted.

- **All prior work is proposed.** Any documents, communications, presentations, or assumptions are not cast in stone and are only "working" definitions; this frees participants to "think out of the box" if necessary.

- **Uses visual and text tools.** Tools used during the JAD are "hands-on" and interactive; they can be "low-tech" tools like flipcharts, markers, whiteboard, and overheads, or "high-tech" like group meeting software or prototyping tools.

- **Follow up.** A complete record of the session is sent to all participants soon after each JAD session is completed to correct, enhance, and validate all JAD products.

JAD is a tremendously flexible tool that can be successfully applied to all phases of the system development life cycle. It is portable to any system development methodology (structured, information engineering, client/server, object-oriented) and scalable to any size effort (see Figure 13.7). It assists in obtaining commitment, consensus, trust, partnership, and motivation to the risky business of client/server software development.

Prototyping

Although *prototyping* is associated with software tools, it is really a technique, not just a tool. *Mock-ups*, or *prototypes*, provide a concrete example of some system artifact, usually an interface screen, and allow the end users and IT to test the viability of that artifact and then continually refine it. Prototyping permits showing a requirement, rather than just saying or writing it. This mimics how people think—going from concrete to abstract understanding.

FIGURE 13.7.

JAD usage in the client/ server development life cycle. (Source: EBG Consulting, Inc.)

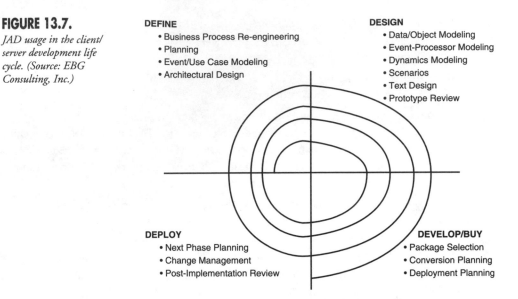

DEFINE
- Business Process Re-engineering
- Planning
- Event/Use Case Modeling
- Architectural Design

DESIGN
- Data/Object Modeling
- Event-Processor Modeling
- Dynamics Modeling
- Scenarios
- Text Design
- Prototype Review

DEPLOY
- Next Phase Planning
- Change Management
- Post-Implementation Review

DEVELOP/BUY
- Package Selection
- Conversion Planning
- Deployment Planning

When you use prototypes, systems are easier to use and learn. End-user satisfaction is greater, and requirements are better communicated. Systems using prototypes also require less code, and projects have less deadline pressure. Productivity is increased and defects are decreased when projects combine JAD and prototyping.

Prototypes can be classified into different types, each appropriate in different circumstances, as shown in Table 13.1.

Table 13.1. Types of prototypes and their usage.

Type	Appropriate Usage
Performance	Test high-volume data
	Test high-frequency function
	Test critical-response time
Usability	New technology
	Wide base of users
Feasibility	New technology
	New software
Requirements	Conflicting requirements
	New requirements

Most client/server projects use prototyping for usability testing and requirements definition. This starts with the GUI prototypes. Early GUI prototypes can be built on flipcharts, whiteboards, or pads of paper. These early paper-based prototypes test the overall metaphor of the GUI. A metaphor mimics a real-world object or task, forming the mental model of the process. This mental model is conveyed by the application's icons and window navigation. After the metaphor and early prototype is satisfactory, the prototypes should be designed and reviewed to test the details of the interface.

The scope of a prototype can be wide (horizontal) or narrow (vertical). A *horizontal prototype* tests the overall facade, showing the broad window and menu structure without taking the end user through a specific event process. A *vertical prototype* is deep, yet narrow in character, testing a specific portion of the interface such as a specific event process like "customer places an order," "employee changes department," or "supplier unloads shipment."

Prototypes can be designed to be *throwaway*, which will never be implemented, or *evolutionary*, which will grow and change into the actual production product. Throwaway prototypes are quick and dirty, have little rigor, are geared toward optimizing time, and tend to be utilized for only the tough parts of the system. Evolutionary prototypes have more rigor, are constructed for the well-understood or frequently used parts of the system, start and build on a solid foundation for the system, and are optimized for usability and performance. Client/server tools facilitate evolutionary prototyping. Most client/server prototypes are evolutionary to better exploit time and customer commitment to the prototyping process.

The team responsible for arranging the prototypes must ensure that the following prototyping critical success factors are met:

- **Right people.** The actual end users of the application participate in prototyping session definition and review.

- **Skilled designers.** The IT team members responsible for the prototyping are trained not only in the prototyping tools but also in the art and science of effective GUI design.

- **Cooperation and understanding.** The end users understand the purpose of prototyping, are willing and able to provide useful feedback on the prototypes, and understand that the product they are reviewing is under development; developers also must apply discipline in creating a prototype that is not a "play" thing but one that will evolve into a working portion of the client/server application.

- **Appropriate planning and scheduling.** The prototype review sessions are planned and integrated into the development life cycle; enough time is provided for developers to design and test the prototype prior to customer (end user) review sessions.

- **The process is controlled.** Techniques are used to prevent the prototyping session from lapsing into a "prototype forever" syndrome, for example, time period, number of iterations (timebox the prototype), or time between iterations.

- **Usability testing is performed.** The prototype seeks and records end-user reactions to specific features of the design, for example, ease of menu and window navigation, mirroring of actual workflow, understandability of the icons, ease of use and learning, support of accelerated users (speed bars, hot keys), consistent error messages and feedback messages, effective use of color and empty space.

- **A method is used to record usability features.** Usability tests should employ one or more techniques to capture the results; some of the methods include videotaping users, using test scripts, using a form, automated recording of keystrokes, and observation.

Certain techniques can be used to conduct the process of prototyping: *dueling prototype* or *iterative prototype*. Dueling prototypes involve multiple clients moving between multiple developers to test a horizontal or vertical navigation path. Developers adjust and create alternative screens based on feedback from the users. Iterative prototypes are useful for verifying and refining requirements. They often start with a whiteboard, then add interface screens, then small amounts of data, then minimal edits, and finally server access. The goal with prototyping is to get bad news early, or "act early, act small."

Process Improvement

Process management has its roots in the teachings of W. E. Deming, a statistician considered by many to be the father of *total quality management (TQM)*. TQM is an Americanized name for the techniques he taught and that were adapted by post-World War II Japan. Deming believed that products will be less expensive, easier to create and fix, and have better quality if the *process* of production is analyzed, quantified, and continually improved. By tracking and analyzing data from the product development process, a business can continually improve the methods and procedures of developing that product. Deming thus taught business to focus on the process of developing products and using feedback from metrics for continually improving on those processes.

Unlike project management, which is an event with a beginning and an end, process management is cyclical and ongoing. In the IT world, the recognition of the key role of process in product delivery is leading more and more IT organizations to have a *process orientation*. This orientation includes such things as establishing and using a methodology, baselining and tracking metrics, establishing customer contracts, inventorying software assets, installing configuration management activities and tools, and training staff on effective project management and modeling techniques.

Process Management Tools

Process management software tools extend development methodologies by addressing the planning, development, deployment, and maintenance of an application. These tools facilitate application development by providing a repository of not only the method but also project tasks, activities to manage the workflow, standards, roles, and responsibilities, estimation assistance, metrics, and even project tracking. These tools are in a hypertext format and provide a path through the methodology's templates, or frameworks. Some process management tools launch a CASE (computer-aided software engineering) tool and/or a project management tool. Examples of some process management tools are LBMS' Process Engineer, Coopers & Lybrand's Summit Process, Advanced Development Methods' SCRUM, Ernst & Young LLP's Navigator, and Knowledge Structure's RADical Software Development Framework.

Software Maturity

The *Software Engineering Institute (SEI)* was created by the Department of Defense to help advance the state of the art of software development and reduce variability and unpredictability in the software design process. The Capability Maturity Model, shown in Figure 13.8, was first published in 1987. It describes how organizations mature as they improve their software processes. The study, done by the SEI at Carnegie-Mellon University, showed that most of the IT organizations function at the Initial (ad hoc) level. The five levels of process maturity are characterized as follows:

- **Initial (also know as "chaotic").** Software process is ad hoc or semi-chaotic; project success depends on individual effort (estimated to be 75 percent of all IT organizations).

- **Repeatable.** Basic management control is performed on projects that are familiar to the organization through planning, tracking and reporting of costs, schedules, and requirements; some software configuration management and QA (quality assurance) exists.

- **Defined.** All projects make use of an organized, documented, and standardized set of activities that are institutionalized throughout the organization; they include such activities as peer reviews, product engineering, use of CASE tools, and use of testing standards and configuration management throughout the life cycle.

- **Managed.** Detailed metrics are collected for both process and quality and used to quantitatively manage software processes; the organization is focused on quality and has a metrics database, tools, and training to support the quality focus.

- **Optimized.** Continuous process improvement is achieved through metrics feedback; sophisticated methods of defect prevention such as inspection and walkthroughs are utilized; an automated metrics collection process is in place; new ideas and technology are continually tested.

FIGURE 13.8.
The capability maturity model. (Source: Software Engineering Institute.)

Level of
Process
Maturity

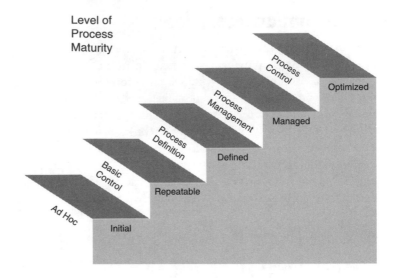

Many IT organizations are interested in this model. They are addressing some of the activities that comprise the "next level" up for them in an attempt to improve their own processes. Studies indicate a 5:1 to 8:1 return on investment for moving from one SEI level to the next.

Testing

Client/server applications involve a wide variety of hardware, software, and connectivity components to be combined in new ways. This combination tends to yield unexpected results. Many client/server projects see these results during integration testing, when performance and interconnectivity is first experienced. Client/server technologies require a much higher attention to testing than do traditional applications. There are many levels of testing needed: requirements, user interface, unit, integration, regression, client acceptance, integration, and performance. The scope and nature of the application will dictate the depth and degree of testing, but one key to successful and timely implementation is to plan for testing at the beginning of the client/server application development effort.

Scenarios are a powerful technique to use and are applicable to many types of client/server testing. Scenarios describe how end users (or groups of users) interact with the system to perform tasks and what the expected outcome is. At a more granular level, scenarios form multiple test cases, which in turn, form multiple test scripts. Scripts are the detailed actions and steps undertaken during execution of the scenarios.

Scenarios can be used as the basis for testing the user interfaces, functionality, interfaces with other applications, and/or performance modeling. For example, scenarios applied to performance modeling would yield details such as transaction rates, server throughput, utilization, and average response time needed for each scenario.

Testing of client/server applications should be a life cycle process, not an afterthought during integration testing. Tools should be used to assist in testing the GUI interface, such as tools that create test scripts and can be replayed and compared against expected results.

Testing thus provides quality-related metrics both during development and after deployment. Tracking things such as defects by delivery cycle, priority of defect correction, assigned developer, and defect status provides useful project control information. It measures application quality by identifying, categorizing, and planning how to fix defects.

Configuration Management

Configuration management is the identification and control of all the components of the software development and maintenance process. The goal of configuration management is to assess the business priority and technical viability of changes to an application, minimize the risk of introducing change to the software environment, ensure implementation of the correct component(s) during deployment, and track and control all versions of an application both during development and after initial installation. Configuration management is done for both new and existing applications.

Configuration management is especially critical for client/server applications because of both the volume of components and number of components that must be managed. Some of the components include the following: project requests, change requests, priority of the request, programs, DML (data manipulation language), tables, indexes, stored procedures, APIs (application programming interfaces), DDL (data definition languages), GUI objects, GUI scripts, dialogs, protocols, RPCs, directory files, operating system files, and macros.

Configuration management is more than just software, as evidenced by the list in the preceding section. It also emphasizes planning changes to the software environment, and managing these changes through various processes such as logging, authorizing, prioritizing, staging, and installation. Configuration management steps are:

- Configuration identification (know the source, file, test files, database, and so on, and where they are located)
- Configuration control (authorize and prioritize any modifications to the components)
- Status accounting (who, what, when, where for any component change)
- Auditing/reporting (for production assurance)

The framework of configuration management, with its emphasis on version releases of the application, is a highly effective method for controlling diverse changes that can have compound, unpredictable results in production. Some software configuration tools include Optima Software's ChangeMAN, Legent's Endevor, and Intersolv's PVCS.

Quality Assurance (QA)

Quality assurance is the process of evaluating, conducting risk assessment, testing, and authorizing changes to the software environment to prevent errors and defects. It occurs *before* the changes are made; quality control (QC) occurs *after* the changes are made. QA is harder to establish, but it has bigger payback than QC. The overall goal of QA is to control and minimize risk. For this reason, many successful client/server projects have an established role for a QA analyst. This person's attempt to "break" the software prevents defective application software from being deployed.

Quality Function Deployment (QFD)

QFD is a series of product improvement techniques that are customer-oriented. QFD is an extension of TQM and is borrowed from the Japanese business methodology that helps teams make decisions based on customer needs. It involves a series of phases called design, details, process, and production during which the team focuses on the "whats" (what the customer requirements are) and the "hows" (means of achieving them).

The QFD method is based on the philosophy that products and services should be designed according to customer requirements, and therefore the customer should be part of the process. Detailed analysis is done on different types of customers, what the requirements are, how important and risky building the requirement will be, and how to objectively measure whether a requirement is met. QFD uses evaluation and analysis techniques that can be used during JAD sessions with customers. An example of a QFD ranking form in shown in Figure 13.9 in which the "whats" for the requirement (on the horizontal axis) are assessed against the "hows" (on the vertical axis) to evaluate how important the process is to the overall customer requirement.

Because client/server technology is so often used to meet a critical business need, these techniques can be very useful for prioritizing functionality, application versions, and keeping the team on focused.

Metrics

"That which cannot be measured cannot be improved," said W. E. Deming, father of Total Quality Management (TQM). *Metrics* are objective criteria for measuring the results of the application process (*results metrics*) or criterion used to predict the time and effort to create the application (*predictor metrics*). Results metrics are gathered after a project is completed. Predictor metrics are based on the premise that application artifacts, noted early, have a strong correlation to later results.

Metrics can be any of the following: lines of code, software science (Halstead metrics based on language operand volume), cyclomatic complexity (McCabe metrics based on the flow of control in a program), CoCoMo (Boehm's constructive cost model based on lines of code), function points (discussed later), number of defects found during testing, number of defects delivered, degree of complexity, and time to complete.

There is no industry standard with which to measure software, although function points seem to be a de facto standard or foundation for capturing productivity and defects in software. *Function points* is an objective software metric originated by A. J. Albrecht of IBM in 1979; it is derived by synthesizing five characteristics of software applications: inputs, outputs, inquiries, logical files, and interfaces. Function points is a technique that is supported by an active user group (IFPUG: International Function Point Users Group).

Metrics programs are highly controversial. In one study of metrics programs by metrics guru Howard Rubin, only 16 percent of the 500 IT organizations attempting to put measurement in place were successful. Only IT organizations that establish a baseline of metrics and use them to improve the software process will mature, however, as indicated by the capability maturity model. In cases of more sophisticated IT organizations, metrics like function points will be used to estimate and control change requests. It may also be useful to consider such issues as skill level and experience when using metrics as a predictor for client/server projects.

People Management Maturity

In early 1995, the Software Engineering Institute (SEI) drafted a people maturity capability model outlining how an IT organization can mature in managing their greatest asset: people. This model represents an important evolution in our industry's traditional lack of interest and attention to the "peopleware" issues that accompany software development. Because of the complexity and scope of skills needed to make client/server technology work, and the fact that the client/server skills gap is in many cases the greatest obstacle to achieving client/server success, this new people management model provides a framework for IT organizations to strive toward. The five-stage model, similar to the capability maturity model, includes the following stages:

- **Initial (also know as "chaotic").** Human resources management is inconsistent and unpredictable; people are considered "overhead."
- **Repeatable.** Policies, practices, procedures, and plans are established and used for managing people.
- **Defined.** Human resource management is customized and aligned to business plans (both tactical and strategic).
- **Managed.** Measurable objectives are established for tracking and growing human talent; a database is used.
- **Optimized.** The organization focuses on continuous improvement of people management processes and is able to experiment with new and innovative practices.

Client/Server Critical Success Factors (CSFs)

In the early 1990s, most Information System organizations were piloting client/server; by 1994, most were actively implementing client/server applications. Although initial applications have been decision-support and data-access applications, transaction-oriented applications are now being built. How do you know if your organization is "ready" to move to client/server? One model produced by one client/server consulting company incorporates these elements:

- Capability to handle technical complexity
- Company readiness
- End user willingness to accept change and risk
- Relationship between the business and Information Systems
- Experience

Additional research into companies using client/server technology to run mission-critical client/server applications showed the top issues to be the following: system and network management, systems security, and multivendor complexities. Some of these issues will dissipate as the technology evolves. The key elements continue to be skilled people and committed end users. A summary list of the critical success factors for client/server success is:

- Project objectives that are strongly linked to critical business needs
- Early definition of the technical (infrastructure) architecture
- A well-defined methodology that uses an approach that balances model-driven requirements with iterative prototyping
- Use of accelerated group techniques like JAD
- Use of project control facilities like configuration management, standards (naming, GUI, use of features like stored procedures), metrics, timeboxing, and attention to process improvement
- Early testing and performance modeling
- Defining a shorter development life cycle
- Committed end users who are involved throughout the entire client/server project
- Well-trained and motivated IT staff

The techniques listed here are essential for making client/server work. The human factor is the most critical, however. Due to the complexity of client/server technology, the knowledge, skills, and motivation of all the people involved in the effort is the single most important determinant for success.

FIGURE 13.9.

QFD ranking form.

CUSTOMER-PROCESS IMPORTANCE RANKING

OBJECTIVE: What are the important customer response features for the _____ function?	Relative Importance Rating (1-5)	Process (how):	Process (how):	Process (how):	Process (how):	Process (how):
		Rank: Overall Rank:	Rank: Overall Rank:	Rank: Overall Rank:	Rank: Overall Rank:	Rank: Overall Rank:
Composite Score (total for all rows):						
Relative Importance Ranking:						

Note: Rank for each process (1-5) for the degree to which the process contributes to the objective. Then obtain an overall ranking by multiplying the process ranking by the objective's relative importance ranking.

Summary

Being successful with client/server technology requires more than technical skills and knowledge. It requires changing the behavior of all the players—developers, IT and business management, and end users. Iterative prototyping, timeboxing, JAD, RAD, configuration management, and GUI testing are examples of essential new behaviors and techniques that enable success with client/server.

Using CASE

14

by Charles Wood

CASE stands for computer-aided software engineering. In the broad sense of the word, CASE is any tool that helps you develop a computer application. In fact, the definition of CASE is constantly changing, but currently I would view a CASE tool as a tool that helps with at least data modeling and at most helps you generate the source code needed for your application.

Many CASE tools are available to help client/server data modeling. This chapter uses S-Designor for CASE design as shown in Figure 14.1, with a little ERwin thrown in for comparison and contrast. Although I like S-Designor, my use of it as an example in this chapter is not intended to be an endorsement, but rather an illustration of how a CASE product might work and the capabilities of CASE.

FIGURE 14.1.

Today's CASE tools concentrate on data modeling, as shown by this very simple data model.

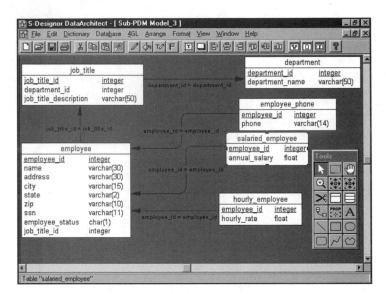

Although this chapter is not designed to be a tutorial for any CASE product, this chapter is designed to give you an overview of what CASE tools can do for you as a client/server developer. In this chapter, you will read how CASE came about as well as how to use CASE for data modeling, process modeling, and application generation.

NOTE

Before beginning this chapter, you may want to read Chapter 16, "Database Design," and Chapter 17, "Object-Oriented Development with Client/Server." An overview of design topics may help your understanding of CASE.

The Evolving Role of CASE Tools and System Developers

CASE means many things to many people. Earlier versions of CASE were geared toward functional development, whereas later CASE products focused on data modeling. Now, many CASE tools are taking an object-oriented approach by stressing data modeling and incorporating functions needed to work on the data model.

Early design methodologies stressed functionality over data. Methods like structured programming and structure charts, top-down design, data flow diagrams, flow charts, and functional decompositions were used to document what a system was supposed to do. Often, data was considered a byproduct of functional design; where the data flowed in and out of a system was the developers' only concern. The database used to be considered by many developers as a side-effect of functional design. The database was merely a container for inputs and outputs of functions inside a system.

CASE tools from this era (such as Knowledgeware) concentrated on functionality and code generation. Systems developed using these early CASE tools were hard to use, expensive, and consisted of what many developers considered bad code. Although companies saved on development time after extensive training, often companies that thought CASE was a magic wand to develop systems became disillusioned and dropped out of CASE almost immediately after starting to use CASE tools.

Now, the prevailing (and correct) wisdom is that the data is the most important part of the system. Data describes all possible states and attributes of an entity. Functions, on the other hand, are what is needed to process data from one form to another or from one entity to another. Newer CASE tools (such as S-Designor, ERwin, and EasyCase) did an about-face and evolved to become data-centric. They started concentrating on data modeling rather than functionality. Many developers found CASE to be of great value in this task and started to use CASE to model databases. CASE found its home in the client/server data model.

Today, many CASE tools are starting to add code generation to their suite of tools to allow you to develop windows in client/server database tools like PowerBuilder, C++, Visual Basic, and other languages based on your client/server data model. Still, whereas older CASE tools tended to concentrate on delivering programs, newer tools center their product around a data model. Only now is functionality creeping back into newer CASE tools.

Using a CASE Tool

CASE tools can generate data models, as mentioned previously. They are also great for creating database documentation and data dictionaries, "reverse engineering" an existing database into a data model, migrating from one database to another, and generating SQL from a data model.

Generating a Data Model

Today's CASE tools make data modeling a lot easier. This section will discuss how CASE tools can be used to enhance data modeling, including adding tables, adding columns to those tables, and defining indexes, keys, and relationships.

Tables

As you can see by Figure 14.2, most CASE tools have a method for adding tables to your database design. S-Designor has a toolbar where you pick a table icon and then click in your environment. Using this method, you can generate the tables needed for your data model.

FIGURE 14.2.

To define tables in a CASE tool, click a table icon and then click somewhere on the data model.

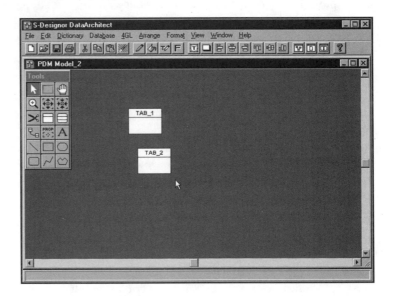

Usually by double-clicking, right-clicking, or selecting an item from a menu, you can open a dialog box of properties of a table to customize its name and to define its other attributes. In Figure 14.3, the name of the table is switched from *Tab_1* to *employee*.

CASE tools allow you to add comments to your tables as well. In Figure 14.4, a notes area in the property sheet of my employee table allows me to enter freeform documentation about the table. Comments are important. They will appear on certain CASE reports and can aid you greatly in system documentation as well as training new developers.

FIGURE 14.3.

Changing the default name to a more appropriate name.

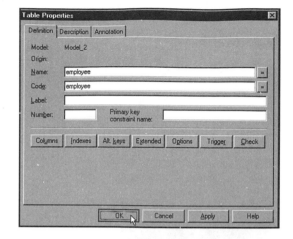

FIGURE 14.4.

CASE tools allow you to add comments to each table. These comments let other developers know the table's purpose.

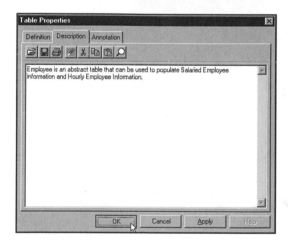

Columns, Data Types, and Primary Keys

Columns, also called attributes or data elements, are the data that makes up a database table. Columns that uniquely identify a row in a table are called *primary keys*. You can add columns to tables using your CASE tool. This section shows how two different CASE tools, ERwin and S-Designor, handle column definition.

Defining Columns with ERwin

Using ERwin, you enter columns when you double-click on a table. In ERwin, columns are separated into key and non-key attributes, as shown in Figure 14.5.

FIGURE 14.5.

ERwin from LogicWorks lets you enter each attribute in either a Primary Key or Non-Key list.

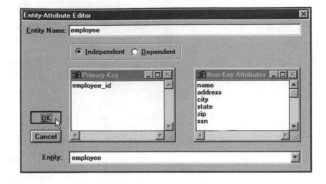

You then can view the table with a column list inside, as shown in Figure 14.6. By right-clicking the table, you can cause a pop-up menu to appear. If you choose the Database Schema option, you can display the Column Property Editor, as shown in Figure 14.7. In this editor, you can choose data types for your table columns. You can also set other column properties such as defaults, validation rules (also called rules or checks), and whether the column is allowed to contain a NULL value.

FIGURE 14.6.

Entity models in ERwin can show a list of attributes.

As you can see in Figure 14.8, ERwin can also display data types in the entity diagrams if you click Display, Physical Schema Level on the menu bar.

FIGURE 14.7.

The Column Property Editor in ERwin allows you to choose data types for your columns.

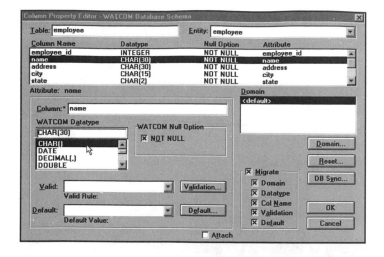

FIGURE 14.8.

Data types can also be displayed in the entity relation diagram with ERwin.

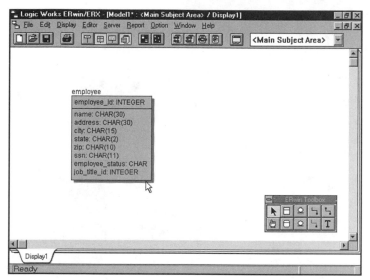

Most CASE tools allow you to enter comments for each column and table. To enter comments about an attribute in ERwin, right-click the entity in the data model (as shown in Figure 14.6) and choose Attribute Definition to open the ERwin Attribute Definition Editor. You can then define the attribute definition (another name for column comments) in ERwin, as shown in Figure 14.9.

FIGURE 14.9.

*You can enter ERwin
attribute definitions
(column comments) in the
ERwin Attribute
Definition Editor.*

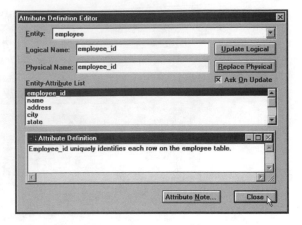

Defining Columns with S-Designor

With S-Designor, you double-click a table to display the table property sheet, as shown in Figure 14.3. From there, you can click the Columns button to open the Columns of Table dialog box, as shown in Figure 14.10.

FIGURE 14.10.

*S-Designor lets you assign
primary keys and attributes
from the same lists.
Primary keys require that
you click the P check box.*

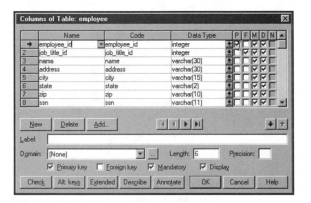

S-Designor lets you enter all your attributes on a single list. In Figure 14.10, notice the list of check boxes to the right of the column name. These check boxes allow you to describe the attribute. Check boxes allow you to chose primary keys, foreign keys (discussed later), whether the column is mandatory, whether the column can be displayed, and whether it can be NULL. As you can see, S-Designor did a great job of allowing you to enter all your information in one place.

To enter comments about an attribute, select that attribute and click the Describe button to open the Description of the Column dialog box shown in Figure 14.11.

FIGURE 14.11.

The Description of the Column dialog box allows you to enter comments about each column in your database.

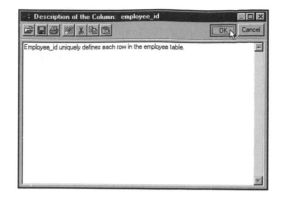

By clicking the Check button in the Columns of Table dialog box (refer to Figure 14.10), you open the Check Parameters dialog box shown in Figure 14.12. The Check Parameters dialog box enables you to enter rules about each of the table columns.

FIGURE 14.12.

The Check Parameters dialog box allows you to enter rules about each column in your database table.

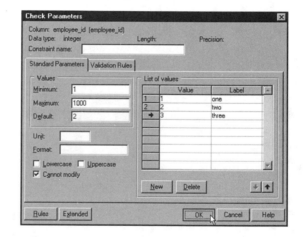

As you can see in Figure 14.12, you can use the Check Parameters dialog box to declare minimums, maximums, defaults, or a list of values. S-Designor even allows you to specify the format and modifiability of a table column.

Indexes

Indexes are a special type of key. Although they aren't used to uniquely define a row on a database, they are defined to speed up database searches. Every data-modeling CASE tool provides some way to create an index for a database. To define an index in S-Designor, you right-click a table and choose Indexes from the pop-up menu that appears, as shown in Figure 14.13.

FIGURE 14.13.

Right-clicking a table opens a pop-up menu. From here, you can choose Indexes to define indexes for a table.

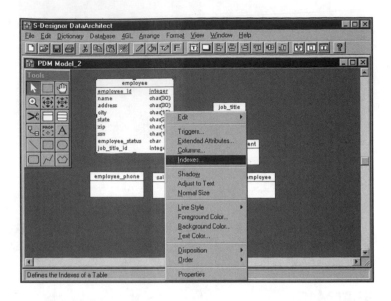

Choosing the Indexes command opens the Indexes of the Table dialog box. From this point, you name the index, and then you click the Add button to add columns to form your index, as shown in Figure 14.14. (Your CASE tool may look different, but it's probably similar in implementation.)

FIGURE 14.14.

The Indexes of Table dialog box enables you to create or modify indexes in your data model.

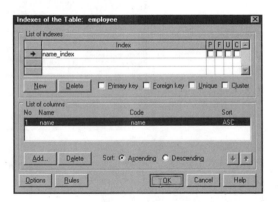

> **NOTE**
>
> Although indexes speed up SELECT statements considerably, they tend to slow down UPDATE, INSERT, and DELETE statements. If you have a highly volatile table, you may want to carefully consider the consequences and perhaps benchmark performance before gratuitously adding indexes to a table.

Relationships

Relationships refer to how two tables (also known as *entities*) are related to each other. These relationships are expressed using foreign keys. If Table 1 has a foreign key to Table 2, you could say that Table 1 is *dependent* on Table 2.

Every data modeling tool has the ability to express foreign keys using some type of methodology. In S-Designor, you define a foreign key by clicking the Reference icon, and then clicking the dependent table and dragging the mouse (with the left button down) to the table that is referenced. The end result should be an arrow from the dependent table to the referenced table, as shown in Figure 14.15.

FIGURE 14.15.

Dependent tables have some type of connection drawn between them in a CASE tool.

Reference icon

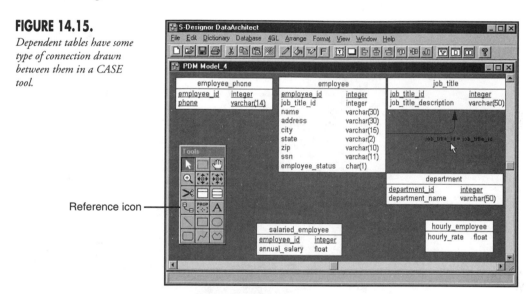

Different CASE tools use different methodologies. ERwin uses the IDEF1X methodology, which consists of a line connecting two related tables with a black circle attached to the dependent table, as illustrated in Figure 14.16.

Many CASE tools support a CHEN or CHEN-based design (often called crow's feet design), as shown in the S-Designor conceptual data model in Figure 14.17.

Although there are many different ways to draw an entity relation diagram, few true differences exist between the different methodologies. All will develop a cohesive design. However, methodologies should be considered when implementing a CASE tool for the first time. A CASE tool that matches your existing methodology will be easier to learn and implement than a CASE tool that uses a foreign methodology.

FIGURE 14.16.

ERwin uses an IDEF1X design methodology to show relationships between entities.

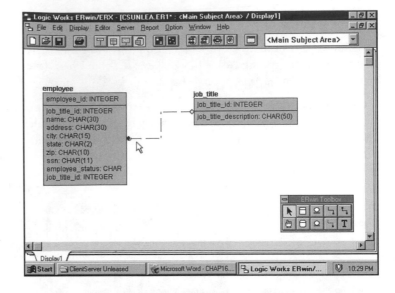

FIGURE 14.17.

The CHEN, or crow's feet, methodology is popular in many IS shops.

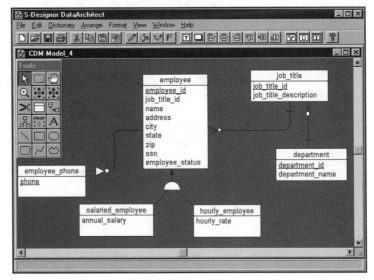

Reverse Engineering the Database

Newer databases have the capability to generate a data model from an existing database. This capability is called *reverse engineering*. Reverse engineering is an important step when it comes to documenting an existing database with a CASE tool. Reverse engineering enables you to start using a CASE tool even after a system has been implemented and to keep the data model and the entity relation diagram in sync.

To reverse engineer a database into a data or entity model, you must first connect to your database. CASE tools aid that connection by letting you use ODBC definitions to link to your database, thereby allowing a drop-down list for database connection, as shown in Figure 14.18.

FIGURE 14.18.

You must connect to a database before reverse engineering it into a data model. Here, I connect to the Client Server Unleashed database.

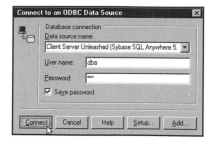

Some sort of database table listing will then appear, as shown in Figure 14.19. From this listing, you can choose tables that you want to reverse engineer as well as options on what database constructs (like views, procedures, and triggers) that you want to reverse engineer.

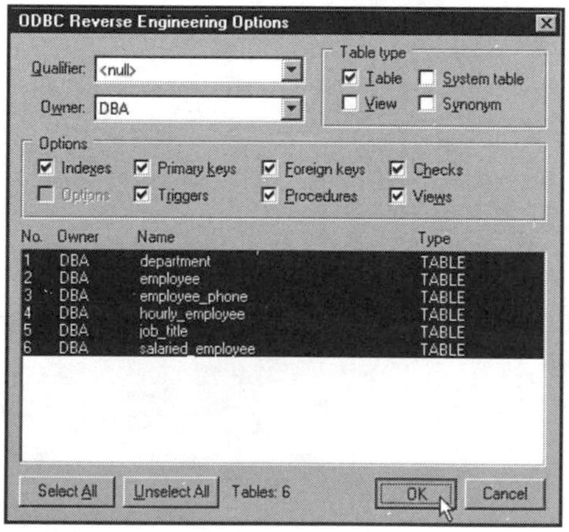

FIGURE 14.19.

Choose the tables and items you want to reverse engineer from your database to your CASE data model.

When finished, you can see the final data model, which will look something like Figure 14.20. All tables and all relationships between tables are defined. Even views are listed as data model constructs.

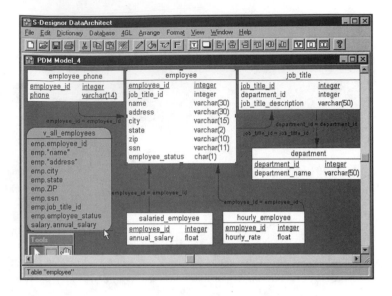

Generating a Database or SQL from a Data Model

One of the beautiful things about most CASE tools is their capability to migrate from one database to another. After you develop your physical data model, you can choose or change your target database and generate your database. As shown in Figure 14.21, CASE tools let you choose which database options to create, and some even let you generate SQL rather than implement a database. This feature is a also a great way to migrate between databases using CASE tools.

FIGURE 14.21.

CASE tools allow you to generate an entirely new database or SQL to create a database from a data model.

As mentioned previously, you can migrate data models in CASE from one database to another. You can also take an existing model and change databases anywhere throughout the development cycle. CASE is database-independent. No matter which database you're using now or in the future, you can (hopefully) count on your CASE tool to aid in your database administration.

The Benefits of CASE tools

Using CASE tools has many benefits. These benefits include cohesive design, time savings, and database independence. Furthermore, with functionality not found in most databases, CASE caters to database developers and database administrators.

Cohesive Design

Several CASE tools can catch you if you try to make a database mistake. In Figure 14.22, I tried to make `job_title` dependent to `employee` after making `employee` dependent on `job_title`. ERwin correctly generated an error message informing me that I was attempting an operation on the data model, which was not the correct way of doing things.

FIGURE 14.22.

ERwin stopped me from joining a dependent table. Such an error would cause an illegal cycle, which is the relational database equivalent of an infinite loop.

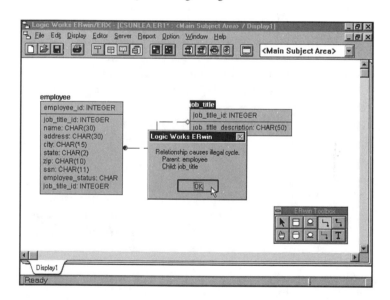

Data Model Report Generation

Reporting and documentation have become standard features in CASE tools. Many CASE tools, like S-Designor, let you customize your report with an extensive set of predefined modules, as shown in Figure 14.23.

FIGURE 14.23.

S-Designor lets you pick the objects you want your report to contain.

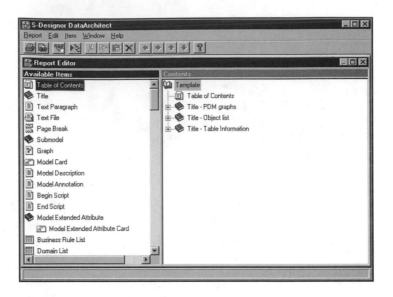

With customizable reporting tools, CASE products let you easily create and use any number of reports, from data dictionaries to a list of business rules.

The Changing Role of the Database Developer

Database developers used to manipulate their databases using SQL and a text editor. Database administration was difficult, and it was hard to get a good picture of the entire database without laborious hand drawings. Now, because of the many advantages to using a CASE tool, many database developers and client/server shops don't allow any alteration of the database without the use of a CASE tool. CASE tools can make database development and administration a lot easier.

With the development of ODBC, database-independent development tools (like Delphi and PowerBuilder), data warehousing and replication, departmental databases, and CASE, often the database developer is now not only asked to develop and/or administrate multiple databases, but also to make data flow across databases in a seamless manner. As shown in Figure 14.24, CASE products can support a multitude of databases.

Database developers and administrators are starting to leave the low-level database alone and concentrate on high-level tools that are database-independent. These high-level tools make the job a little easier and let developers use tools to contend with multiple databases rather than having to administrate several databases separately.

FIGURE 14.24.
Most CASE products work with most popular databases.

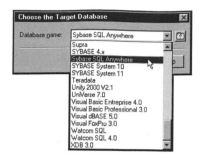

Time Savings

With features like reverse engineering, documentation support, immediate error checking, and other important features, CASE products can save the developer a lot of time. Whereas older design methodologies required that you use a separate product from your modeling tool (often a word processor or text editor) to generate a data dictionary, or that your business rules be kept separate in a 3-ring binder, or that your process design and your database design be kept separate, newer CASE tools can be a huge savings in both development and administration because they handle all these items in one place.

Other Functions of CASE Tools

CASE is growing into a complete development environment. CASE products can aid you in conceptual (business) modeling, process analysis, and even application development in popular tools like Visual Basic and PowerBuilder.

Conceptual Modeling

Data models are derived from conceptual models. A data model shows how the data will reside on a database. By this point, issues like business rules, entity categories, attribute arrays, and the like have all been resolved using normalization. (See Chapter 16 for a detailed look at database normalization.) Figure 14.25 shows a conceptual model.

Attribute Arrays

Conceptual models allow arrays of elements. For instance, phone would be an array of employee in the example shown in Figure 14.25. Many CASE tools, like S-Designor, do not yet support arrays of elements in their conceptual models. These tools still force you to do a little normalization of your own to separate arrays into their own related tables, as shown by the phone entity in Figure 14.25.

FIGURE 14.25.

Data models are often derived from conceptual models.

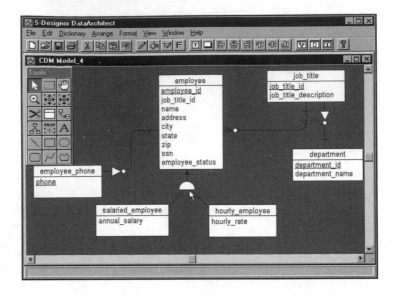

Arrays cannot exist as columns in a database and must be normalized at some point. However, the data model won't tell you how many entries are allowed (through screen design or business rules) in a dependent category. Data models assume that the number of entries in a dependent table is infinite. The conceptual model can tell you how many elements are allowed in a table.

Categories (Inheritance)

Object-oriented inheritance is the expression of categories. (See Chapter 17 for more details.) In Figure 14.25, `salaried_employee` and `hourly_employee` are inherited from `employee`. That is to say that `salaried_employee` contains everything that's in `employee` plus specific salaried information.

Inheritance is a powerful way of expressing a situation and is one of the major components in object-oriented development. However, data models can't handle inheritance because they have no way of distinguishing inherited entities from dependent entities. However, in a conceptual model, you can tell that `employee` has two categories: salaried and hourly. A conceptual model allows you to specify inheritance, and the inheritance is converted with your CASE tool to either separate tables or one parent table with dependent child tables.

Business Rules

Business rules are system requirements that affect the way you model data and the way you develop a system. CASE tools allow you to define and store business rules, and then to apply them to the appropriate entity. For instance, in Figure 14.26, a business rule is declared. Extensive notes can then be made about the business rule, as seen in Figure 14.27.

FIGURE 14.26.

CASE allows you to define business rules.

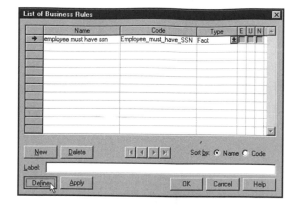

FIGURE 14.27.

CASE tools let you enter freeform text about a business rule once the business rule is declared.

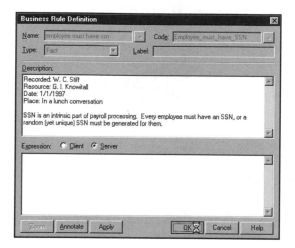

After you have defined the business rule, you can assign this business rule to the appropriate entity or entities in your conceptual model, as shown in Figure 14.28. That way, models are documented with the appropriate business rules.

Process Analysis

Process analysis is used to define processes within a design. You can use CASE tools to develop a process analysis document using the entities defined in the data model and conceptual model. Data flow diagrams, flow charts, functional decomposition, and structure charts are often used when analyzing processes, but data flow diagrams seem to be the most common.

FIGURE 14.28.

Business can be assigned to a specific table.

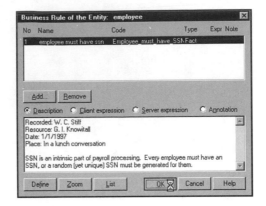

Defining Data Flow Diagrams

Figure 14.29 shows a data flow diagram.

FIGURE 14.29.

Data flow diagrams track how data flows through a system.

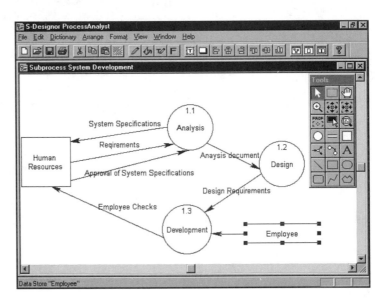

A data flow diagram consists of four objects:

■ *Processes* describe the functionality of a system. Processes are usually illustrated as a circle or a rounded rectangle.

■ *Data stores* are the equivalent of tables. Data stores are where the data is kept for use by the processes. Data stores are usually illustrated as an open-ended rectangle on one or both sides.

- *External entities* are people or objects (like departments or other systems) that exist outside the system. The input into the system and the output from the system always go to the external entities. External entities are often shown as boxes.

- *Data flows* occur any time data is moved to or from a process, entity, or data store. Data flows always flow into or out of a process. Data flows are shown as arrows from a process, entity, or data store to another process, entity, or data store.

CASE tools can help you generate a data flow diagram by using your conceptual model or data model as data stores. CASE tools can even make sure that all the data elements on your entity are captured and used in your processes. Data flow diagrams are great way to make sure you have processes available for every data element in your system.

Defining Stored Procedures and Triggers

A *stored procedure* is a set of SQL with some additional commands (like IF and CHOOSE CASE) that can be called from a program (or another stored procedure) to do a set of required SQL. *Triggers* are stored procedures that are automatically executed when an event occurs and are not explicitly called. For example, often you'll want the database to perform some automatic check or function based on an UPDATE, INSERT, or DELETE command that is issued against the database.

One of the hardest tasks of a DBA in a shop that uses a lot of stored procedures is tracking, documenting, testing, and administering these stored procedures. A good CASE tool can make stored procedure development a little easier. Good CASE tools allow you to create stored procedures in a database. These stored procedures would be automatically generated when you create a database. In Figure 14.30, I generated a stored procedure to select all employee information.

FIGURE 14.30.

Using a CASE tool helps you with stored procedure development and administration.

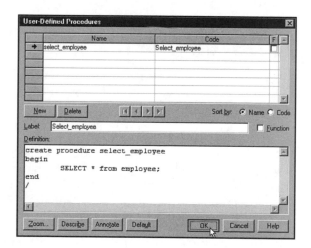

Application Generation

Application development from a data model is the next step in CASE design. Already, several CASE products offer C++ code generation. Others have gone on to PowerBuilder, Visual Basic, and other popular development environments. Figure 14.31 shows the many options you can use when developing a PowerBuilder application in S-Designor's AppModeler module.

FIGURE 14.31.

You can define a lot of your application in your CASE tool.

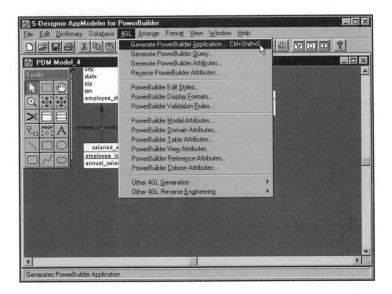

If CASE products do a good job with development, CASE may very well become the centerpiece for all client/server development. Individual tools will be by preference only and will even be changeable when a better tool comes along.

Future Developments with CASE

In the future, CASE will become even more prevalent in development. CASE vendors are trying to enhance their products right now to develop for other popular languages like Java and Delphi. Already, MIS shops are starting to make standards for CASE development, and some shops even require that all database work be done through a CASE tool.

Many CASE products right now are walking a fine line between being a tool to aid development languages and being a full-fledged development environment in their own right. Some CASE vendors may jump the fence and start billing their easy-to-use products as an alternative to traditional programming.

Conversely, many development tools are starting to become more CASE-like. Delphi and PowerBuilder generate code in other languages. There are rumors that Borland is trying to put a Delphi front end on other language development environments, making multilanguage support a part of Delphi. PowerBuilder and Delphi both work with several databases using techniques that are often easier to use than the environment that comes with the database. What this means for us, the developers, is that client/server development is going to improve even more to make analysis, design, and programming for client/server environments easier.

Summary

This chapter shows what can be accomplished with a CASE tool. However, no CASE tool is a replacement for design knowledge. Without design knowledge, your CASE tool may seem difficult or impossible to work with. Check out Chapters 16 and 17 for information on database design and object-oriented design methodologies. Chapter 18, "Applications Development," is also a must-read for those of you who are using CASE to develop applications.

Workflow

by Neil Jenkins

Client/server systems aim to improve the business areas that use them. In doing so, these systems must be effective and efficient in providing ease of use, quick response, and accurate data. The systems should mirror the way that the business area should work to provide its function to the overall organization. The development of good client/server systems must take into account improvements in the business areas' workflow.

Workflow can be defined as the activity or group of activities that need to take place for a business transaction to be completed. You can break down almost everything in daily life into workflow patterns. Consider making a pot of coffee. The overall transaction would consist of a full pot of hot coffee, yet the following activities are required to achieve that result:

1. Empty out old coffee.
2. Replace filter.
3. Add coffee to filter.
4. Add water to coffee.
5. Allow coffee to percolate.
6. Completion.

Anyone can achieve the completion of a full pot of hot coffee by following the simple steps. Workflow systems can be broken down in this fashion to achieve a set of activities that can be used to develop client/server systems. In this chapter, you will see how to analyze workflow and apply that knowledge to improve your completed systems.

The Workflow Principle

In all computer system development, a well-designed, user-friendly system will have a far superior impact on a business area than a badly crafted one. The benefits can include reduced training time, more productive users, lower overheads, fewer automated and manual errors, and better staff motivation. When was the last time that you delivered a system that delighted your user community as well as delivered those essential business benefits? The major difference in client/server between a good system and a bad one can be as simple as the way it looks, the way it operates, or the way it interacts with the user to get the transactions completed.

Automation of a current business transaction should take into account how the business should work rather than how it works today. For example, if a customer would like to purchase a holiday from a travel company through the telephone, the business area will work more effectively if the travel company can service all the customer requirements in one telephone call to one staff member. Customer satisfaction can quickly disappear if the customer is transferred from a sales department to another sales department to purchase each piece of his/her vacation. In this example, a client/server system has to be able to satisfy 95 percent of the customer requests if it is to be successful.

A customer telephone call can be enormously complex because people do not think in a logical, step-by-step way. Consider the last telephone call that you had. It is unlikely (though not impossible) that it was structured in a logical fashion. You probably found yourself asking questions, requesting more information, probing for details, and asking for confirmation in order to figure out what the customer wanted. In the travel example, a customer might call with one or more of the following questions:

- "Hello, can you provide a safari?"
- "Can I get a cruise added to the end of my Bahamas trip?"
- "What is the weather like in the Bahamas at that time of year?"
- "What is the likelihood of a hurricane?"
- "Is the price fully inclusive?"

Human nature is to be inquisitive and ask many varied questions. Client/server systems need to be flexible in meeting end-user information demands so that the user in turn can complete the business transaction. In this example, the transaction may culminate in the purchasing of a vacation from the travel company. The information needs of both the end user and the customer have been satisfied and the transaction achieved. In today's proactive, demanding business arena, business flow cannot normally be identified as a simple step-by-step process. In the travel example, the user has to jump around many areas of information in order to get the sale. Most of us would find it unacceptable to be told, "I'll answer that question after I've completed the booking," if our decision to book is based on the answer. However, most legacy systems are developed in a step-by-step way. Figure 15.1 shows an example of a step-by-step system.

FIGURE 15.1.

A step-by-step process.

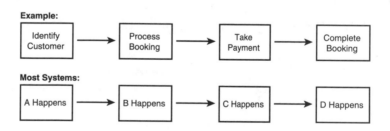

Clearly, systems that are expected to deliver flexibility and enhance business flow can no longer continue to be built this way unless there are definite business rules that dictate their structure. In a customer service environment, such rules rarely exist because good customer service is a result of meeting the customers' needs quickly and with quality.

As a result of changing business focus to more business process-driven organizations and to the flexibility of client/server systems, companies are developing applications that model their business flows. Such applications present a considerable challenge to the systems division in so far as new techniques and tools are required to produce workflow systems. Systems staff must learn and apply new techniques to model the workflow so that prototype systems demonstrating workflow can be created. In time, these prototype systems may evolve into production client/server systems.

There are tools that can be used to create, test, and modify workflow prototypes to gain understanding and knowledge about how a completed system might operate. A prototype does not involve months of development time. Creating a first-cut prototype should take no more than a man-week. After this step, the prototype must be enhanced as the user community experiments with different variables of a workflow system. Indeed, the beauty and value of rapid prototyping of workflow is that it allows the users to get a feel of how a completed system can appear much earlier in the development cycle. It also allows the users to feel part of that cycle. This feeling is beneficial in that it develops "ownership" of the application in the business area.

Because of the short time frames that should be insisted upon when prototyping workflow, complex client/server development systems such as Microsoft Visual C++, Omnis, and Progress should not be used at this stage. Your teams can be far more efficient using smaller departmental development tools, such as Visual Basic from Microsoft or Delphi from Borland. Prototypes can be created in these tools without having to prebuild database structures or create application logic to any great degree. Sure, it could be argued that these things are beneficial to the developers building the application, yet the user does not need to know or understand these areas. In essence, you should concentrate on the flow of the work through the application and provide ease of access to other applications (to enable the user to jump about) and to the look and feel of the system.

Techniques for Building Workflow Systems

Two fundamental techniques are needed to develop workflow systems that will delight your user base. These techniques are called *goal modeling* and *event response modeling*. At a high level, goal modeling can be defined as creating a logical view of what activities need to be handled to successfully complete the business process you are modeling. To start goal modeling, you first need to ask what activities must be handled, regardless of sequence. Then break down these high-level activities into more detailed activities; repeat this procedure until you have a realistic model of the process you are trying to perform successfully.

Event response modeling is a logical view of what occurs when an activity takes place, what work gets done, and what the response is. If you make the decision to develop using event response modeling, you can begin by building an event response environment into your applications and client/server systems. The event response model is what helps the user jump into other areas of information. Popular GUI operating systems, such as the Windows family (3.x, NT, and 95), OS/2, Apple System 7.x, and X Window, operate along the principle of event response, so building systems on these platforms is easier in the development stage than using single-tasking systems like Microsoft DOS.

If you apply these modeling techniques to the travel example, a better picture begins to emerge. When a customer calls, the user can identify the customer and begin the booking activities. If the customer requests different information during the booking activities, the user may trigger an event (such as pressing a Get More Information button), which generates work to be done in the computer and results in the display of information (the response to the event) without leaving the booking activity. Figure 15.2 shows this process.

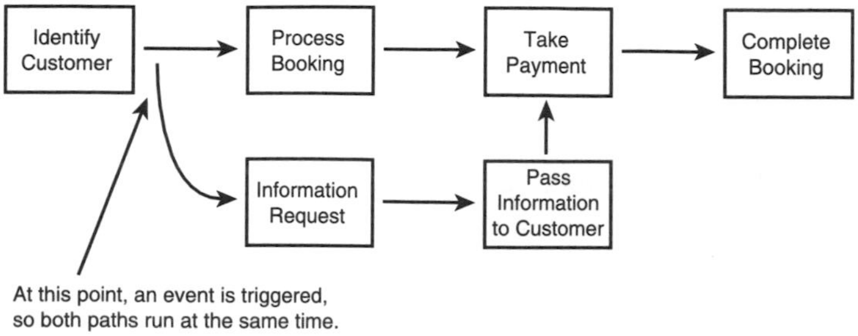

FIGURE 15.2.

An example of an event-based workflow.

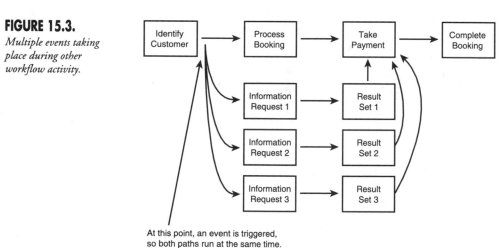

Extrapolating this idea can lead to tremendous benefit. If the customer required a best price quote, for example, the system might connect seamlessly to other systems and retrieve all the pricing information while the user is working and adding the customer information to the booking area. Figure 15.3 shows a system in which multiple events are running at the same time.

FIGURE 15.3.

Multiple events taking place during other workflow activity.

Each event might generate multiple pieces of work that can be run as separate applications or threads that eventually return to the main application. This setup is considerably shorter than doing each activity in succession. If you're making a cup of tea, for example, getting the cup, milk, and sugar while the kettle is boiling makes better use of the available time than waiting until the water has boiled to get the cup, then get the milk, and then get the sugar.

Goal Modeling

Goal modeling requires the client/server developer to think somewhat differently than he/she has been used to. I once heard the phrase "thinking out-of-the-box," which I think sums up the concept quite well. You need to think at a high level about the business function and what is required to meet this function. The goal model of a business function must represent the activities that need to be completed to achieve a successful result. I use the word *successful* because it implies a higher level of achievement than any current system and because I believe you should strive for continuous successful improvement in the client/server systems that you develop. These are, after all, the main reasons for developing systems using the client/server models.

Goal modeling involves four basic steps:

1. Define the overall business process in one statement. This statement is the goal.
2. Break down this statement into the three or four constituent parts that make up the overall process. These parts are the subgoals.
3. Divide the subgoals into the three or four procedures required to complete them. These procedures are the workflow tasks.
4. Detail the various activities in the current system and those that will exist in the new system that enable a user to completely finish each of the workflow tasks. These activities are known as the detailed activities.

Occasionally when you are developing a large client/server system, you may find it impossible to identify the workflow tasks because there really are too many subgoals. In this case, add an intermediary step to break down the subgoals into a much more manageable set of tasks. Call these tasks the high-level workflow tasks, and then move onto Step 3.

Defining the Goal

The first step is to identify the one-line statement that meets the success criteria for the business area at a high level. This statement provides the focus for the client/server system you are going to develop and implement (successfully!). The following are examples of good first-cut goal models for different business areas:

- Achieve customer satisfaction
- Sell more of our products
- Increase response to marketing campaigns

The first goal can often be answered by asking the business area the question, "At a high level, deliberately avoiding detail, what are you trying to do that will seriously improve the business of this area, the areas that you interact with, and the company as a whole?" The initial answers should be discussed, debated, and refined until everyone involved feels comfortable with the encompassing statement. This process will take time because everyone involved must review the statement to ensure that it is valid.

> **NOTE**
>
> Note that goal modeling is not a perfect science because you are trying to determine the key business objectives from users who have not experienced anything like what you are asking them to do. Also expect yourself to have to go through this process several times before you become experienced enough to feel comfortable.

Establishing the Subgoals

The second step of goal modeling is to break down the goal into its three or four component parts. Ask your business users the question, "To meet this goal, what are the three or four activities or parts, in order, that need to be done?" Remind users to focus their efforts at the high level and avoid detail.

Again, you are looking to find the activities needed to achieve the function, but, in reality, you are adding more detail to the first high-level statement and getting an understanding of what makes it up. You are doing this step so that the business areas and users involved are forced to think about the long-term goal they are trying to achieve and its cycle, which you will turn into a workflow-based client/server system. All too often the user community finds itself concentrating on today's details rather than tomorrow's business. It can be hard for a client/server developer to rein in the users to concentrate on the longer term business. Goal modeling helps this effort by avoiding the detail until the very final stages.

Consider the first sample statement, "Achieve customer satisfaction." This example is the goal for a customer service area. Suppose this area, which is responsible for handling the customer correspondence for a major store chain, is preparing to develop a new client/server business system based on new improved workflow for the current users. Figure 15.4 shows a valid set of subgoals for this business area.

FIGURE 15.4.

Sample subgoals for customer service area.

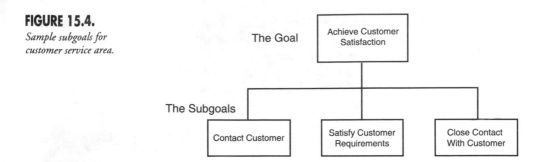

Setting Up the Workflow Tasks

The third step is to break down the subgoals into their main component parts. Don't concentrate on just three or four parts, but concentrate on the number that you feel most comfortable with. This number may be one or two or perhaps four or five. If, however, you feel that you need more than five in every task, you probably need to have high-level workflow tasks, and you should add an extra step to your goal modeling process. You need to ask your users, "How would you like to get things done? What are the main areas of each task going to be?" In the example in Figure 15.5, the Contact Customer subgoal becomes the Identify Customer and Correspond with Customer workflow tasks. The other subgoals are also broken down into their workflow tasks. The systems you design will be much larger than this example and contain many more steps, of course.

FIGURE 15.5.

Sample workflow tasks for the customer service area.

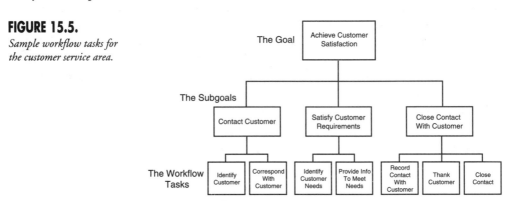

Listing the Detailed Activities

Finally, the fourth step is to list each of the different ways that the workflow tasks can be done. These ways are straightforward descriptions of the items that need to be entered in the system to complete the transaction. These items tend to be the specific types of business that the function does. In the customer service example, the Provide Information To Meet Needs workflow task may become the list of products the company supplies. If you added this further level of information to the example, the finished goal model would look like Figure 15.6.

FIGURE 15.6.

Completed goal model for the customer service area.

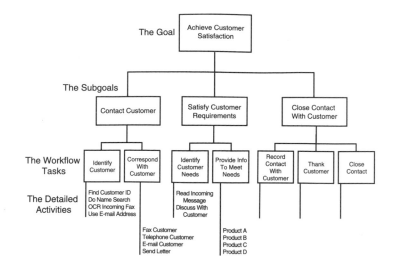

Event Response Modeling

Event response modeling works on the principle of how different pieces of information flow through the goal and how the information changes as it flows through the process. You need to check the event response model against the goal model to ensure both are accurate and do not miss any part of the business process. The best way to approach event response modeling is to take the first workflow task of the goal model and identify the information pieces of that task. Then discuss how that information flows into the business area and out again, be it through e-mail, phone, letter, or fax. Chart how that piece of information flows through the company and how it is modified. Make specific note of any changes to the information, any delays in the information, and any areas that the information is stored in. Figure 15.7 shows how a complaint letter arrives in a customer service department.

FIGURE 15.7.

Partial sample event response model for a letter arriving.

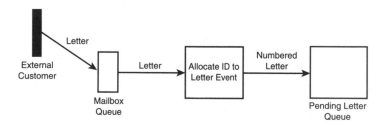

The letter may first go into a physical mailbox, and then be allocated a correspondence number. The allocated letter (note the information has now changed) may go into a pending letter queue being handled by a customer services representative. The letter may be held for a period of time before it is accessed. Figure 15.8 shows the next steps in the process.

FIGURE 15.8.

Partial sample event response model for a letter arriving.

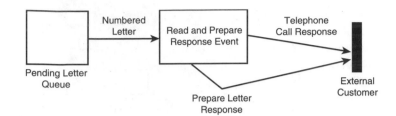

Note that the Read and Prepare Response event may become one of two branches based on the decision of the representative. The interaction with the external customer may then take place. For the purposes of this example, you can see how the information flowed through the business process, where it was changed along the way, and the various places it may have been held along the way.

By repeating this exercise for each type of information feed, such as fax and e-mail, you can build a complete picture of the information flow. Figure 15.9 shows the completed event response model for a letter arriving into a customer service department.

FIGURE 15.9.

An sample event response model for a letter arriving.

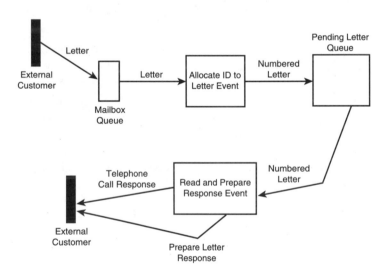

In a workflow environment, you should develop your client/server system so that each information feed is automated; documents and letters can be scanned in, incoming faxes can be automated with optical character recognition software, and e-mail can be fed directly into your system. Each queue should become a physical database or modified data within a physical database, and each event should become a piece of application logic that is either automatic (such as the allocation of a correspondence number when the letter is scanned) or is controlled by the user (such as a click on a More Information button).

The Benefits of Event Response Modeling

The benefits of event response modeling are numerous. It provides a detailed picture of how information flows through the business area. It gives a graphic view of what is going on (which is often easier to understand than lengthy text-based reports), and it can be used to test the viability of adding functions to the system. Above all, it provides a means to create improved information flow. For example, you might review your event response model to determine how queues of data might be reduced, decreasing the time it takes to get a response back to the customer. Once you create a detailed diagram of the event response model for the client/server system, you can use it with the goal model to create a workflow prototype.

How to Build a Workflow Prototype

Good prototypes need to be modeled on the workflow tasks of the goal model. The workflow tasks should be readily available to the user of the system. By placing the workflow tasks on a menu bar within a system, the user can quickly navigate through the system using this bar, as per the design principles in Chapter 19, "Developing Mission-Critical Applications." A customer service system might have a menu bar environment like that shown in Figure 15.10.

FIGURE 15.10.

A sample workflow-based menu bar.

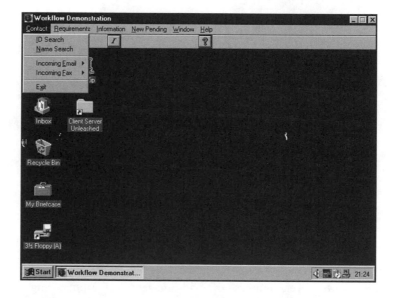

The workflow tasks are the individual menus under which the detailed activities reside. The Contact menu may have ID Search, Name Search, Incoming Fax, and Incoming E-mail options. Each option would cause an event to occur to get the information record from the queue holding that particular piece of information. In the case of the two searches, a form might appear asking the user to enter the appropriate information before the system searches the database. Each event accessed then generates the next step in the application, and the subsequent information follows along the lines of the event response model, causing the workflow tasks of the goal model to be completed until the overall business transaction is completed.

Develop your prototype so that it handles each event at some point and covers each of the workflow tasks. Sometimes you may find that the workflow tasks are at too high a level. If this situation occurs, revise your goal model. This is, after all, an iterative process of development.

When the prototype is complete, run through a number of scenarios with your users, making sure that the workflow steps are correct. If they are not, revisit the models and the prototypes as necessary. If the models highlight an area of immediate improvement that the users would like, then put it in also. The next stage is to try the prototype with a number of novice users. This stage demonstrates flaws in the workflow. You are looking to develop the easiest system that achieves the business function. With feedback from these users, refine both the models and the prototype. Occasionally, the users will overrule you on a workflow issue; do not feel bad about this situation as it normally means that they had not created the models correctly initially. After the models have been revisited and the prototype created, you can begin to build the production system.

Advantages and Disadvantages of Workflow

Workflow has a number of advantages for client/server systems:

- Provides an easy-to-use environment
- Mirrors how the business area works
- Can automate complex manual tasks
- Can reduce overheads and manual mistakes
- Can streamline how the business area works

There are, however, a number of disadvantages to developing using workflow techniques. Perhaps the biggest disadvantage is that workflow techniques as outlined in the last few sections cannot be used to correct a business process that is fundamentally flawed. If the business process does not work correctly, is costly to run, or requires a lot of manpower to complete, automating the existing process will bring little or no benefit. You should spend time working with the business area users developing a new system that overcomes these problems, which means that the business area has to change its way of working.

The second disadvantage is people's natural reluctance to change. People find change very difficult, and providing an improved workflow system to users can cause this difficulty to surface. It may be in the form of reluctance to take on the new system, questioning why the change to the new environment is necessary, or outright hostility. The only way of bypassing this problem is to ensure that the users are involved every step of the way in the development of the models and the prototype.

When developing these systems, you should ask the users the following questions to determine what changes you can make to the prototype that may improve workflow:

- Does the system look right?
- Can you access all the detailed activities to achieve the business transaction?
- Is there enough online help?
- Does the system flow? Are you spending too much time trying to find options?
- Do the color and sound designs make the application appealing?

If you find it difficult to develop the workflow systems, you can always use external specialists who use these design principles to develop client/server systems. Hiring external help for the first few projects until you get used to the techniques is often a good way to establish the skill levels of your own systems department.

Summary

The most effective client/server systems built today are based on workflow. By using workflow as the foundation of an automated system, the organization can develop a competitive advantage over systems that are not workflow-based. Workflow systems benefit businesses in several key areas. The primary business benefits are gained from ease of use, quicker training paths, reduced errors, improved functionality, and better morale of the users.

The main focus when developing a workflow-based system should be on the new improved business process, concentrating on how the business should run rather than how it operates today. Trying to automate what is already there will only cause further difficulties.

The tools for successful workflow creation are goal modeling, event response modeling, and prototyping. You must use these tools in conjunction with each other. The prototyping process should be iterative.

Developing workflow-based systems takes time and effort; you may not get it exactly right the first time. You will always do it better the next time around! If you need help, you can always get external help from specialists who understand the key concepts outlined in this chapter. These specialists will help you increase your skills by training and assisting you in your development. At the end of the day, a client/server system is often successful based on the quality of its implementation of workflow within a business area. Spending time and effort on this workflow will seriously improve the systems you develop.

Database Design

by Paul Hipsley

16

IN THIS CHAPTER

After analysis of the users' functional, data, and systems requirements, the logical data model is defined to support these requirements. Whether you use a CASE tool or not, the logical data modeling process is important for a good database design and a successful project.

The first part of this chapter will review topics associated with logical data modeling, including:

- Normalization
- Integrity
- Naming conventions
- Entities
- Domains
- Attributes
- Unique identifiers
- Relations
- Entity/relationship diagrams
- Reviewing the logical data model

Physical database design will be reviewed in the last part of this chapter. The physical design process takes the information gathered in logical data modeling and maps the objects in the data model to objects in the physical model, including the following mapping processes:

- Entities to tables
- Attributes to columns
- Relations to foreign-key columns
- Primary keys to primary key constraints
- UIDs to unique constraints
- Values required to not-null constraints
- Restricted values to check constraints
- Relations to reference constraints

As this chapter progresses through physical database design, it will establish the conventions that will be used for naming the physical objects. Then it will discuss views, indexes, and tablespaces. This chapter concludes by doing the module-to-table and module-to-column mapping.

Logical Data Modeling

The logical data model is abstract. This means that the model is independent of the database, operating system, or hardware. It also means that the data model can include components that have been designed and implemented, as well as components that have not. In addition, this abstraction enables us to work on a data model that has been implemented without any immediate impact on the current implementation.

The creation of the database using the database definition language (DDL) is concrete. This means that the DDL is dependent on the vendor's implementation of the SQL language on the database. Even with the standardization of the SQL language, most database companies still use different syntax in their DDL. You will find much similarity, and the proprietary differences are eroding. But as in any computer language, there is a big difference to the compiler between *similar* and *identical*.

Normalization

During the logical data modeling process, it will be important to understand a certain amount of relational theory and the practical application of that theory. The subjects of normalization and integrity are among the more significant components of relational theory for most database practitioners. In addition, it is necessary to understand the definition of entities, domains, attributes, unique identifiers, and relations.

This section reviews the three forms of normalization that are most commonly known and practiced. I will include a single statement of the form and a description of what it means.

1NF (first normal form): All entities have a primary key and no repeating groups.

All entities must be able to be uniquely identified by one or more attributes that will never be null. When more than one unique identifier exists, one of them must be nominated as the primary key. In addition, the same attribute cannot exist within the same entity more than once. If an attribute is repeated, it must be removed and associated with another entity.

2NF (second normal form): Complies with 1NF, and all attributes depend on the key.

All of the attributes associated with the entity must have a direct dependency on the primary key in order for their value to have meaning. If an attribute has meaning independent of the primary key, it must be removed and associated with another entity.

3NF (third normal form): Complies with 2NF, and no attributes are dependent on other attributes.

None of the attributes associated with the entity can have a dependency on another attribute. If an attribute has a dependency on another attribute, both attributes must be removed and associated with another entity.

Third normal form is generally the expected and accepted degree of normalization that is needed and useful to create a database without redundancy—that is, one that has integrity. You may hear the expression "the key, the whole key, and nothing but the key" used to describe third normal form.

Denormalization is the process of undoing some amount of the normalization process, and it is sometimes suggested for performance or ease of use.

A data model that is not normalized or is unnormalized is different than one that is denormalized. A data model that is not normalized may not have been normalized to begin with, while a data model that is denormalized was originally normalized.

CAUTION

Resist the temptation to denormalize. Do not compromise the integrity of the data model. If you do denormalize, be sure to document the impact on integrity and provide management for the restoration of the integrity in the physical design and implementation. For example, if you have redundant data, you could create a database trigger to update one of the columns from the other.

NOTE

For more information on normalization, refer to one of the many books available on relational databases.

Integrity

Integrity in a relational system means that the data will be consistent and reliable. There are four basic types of integrity found in a relational system:

- Entity
- Referential
- Column
- Business rules

A system has entity integrity when no entities can contain nulls in their primary key. Referential integrity exists when each foreign key references a primary key. Column integrity means that the values in the columns conform to the data type and format defined. Business-rule integrity means that anything and everything that the user defines as rules are enforced by the system.

The Oracle database provides declarative support for entity, referential, and column integrity, as well as support for business rules through the use of check constraints, database triggers, database functions, database procedures, and database packages. There is a variety of methods used during physical design and implementation to provide integrity. Other DBMSs have similar features.

This discussion was included in this chapter because the process of providing integrity begins in the logical data model.

Naming Conventions

The purpose of establishing naming conventions is to create a consistent point of reference for the user community and the project staff. The names of all types of objects should be simple and meaningful. Avoid the use of jargon and acronyms unless they are very familiar and intuitive to everyone.

Using standard class words in attribute names is invaluable in creating a consistent convention. The following list is a good example of useful class words:

> Amount
> Code
> Date
> Description
> Indicator
> Id
> Name
> Number

Attributes may contain class words, but they may need additional words for further clarification.

Create and maintain a list of all class words and standardized abbreviations to be used by the entire project. Make the list accessible to everyone, but appoint a custodian to manage the list. If you are not using a CASE tool, create a table list for recording the words and abbreviations. For example, you can create a table like the one shown in Table 16.1.

Table 16.1. Abbreviations.

Word	Abbreviation
Commission	Comm
Customer	Cust
Department	Dept
Department Name	DName
Employee	Emp
Identifier	Id
Location	Loc
Manager	Mgr

continues

Table 16.1. continued

Word	*Abbreviation*
Number	No
Order	Ord
Percentage	Pct
Received	Recd
Report	Rpt
Sales Representative	Rep
Salary	Sal

Abbreviations of entities should be used for short names, and abbreviations of attributes should be used for creating column names during physical design.

Entities

An entity is an object or thing of significance, and it is usually a noun. Entities should be given names that are singular, brief, and meaningful. One of the first steps in modeling the logical database is to identify the entities that are needed to support the data requirements of the application system. You may have an existing system that is being extended to include additional functionality.

Entities may be supersets or subsets of other entities. A *supertype* is an entity that contains other entities called *subtypes*. And likewise, subtypes are contained within a supertype. Supertypes contain attributes that are common, and subtypes contain attributes that are specific. For example, you could define the customer entity as a supertype with some basic attributes. Then, within the customer entity, you could define the government customer and commercial customer entities. Each of the subtypes would contain attributes that support and/or describe their respective entities.

> **NOTE**
>
> Supertypes and subtypes can be implemented using one of three different methods:
> - One table
> - Separate subtype tables
> - A supertype table and separate subtype tables
>
> In the first method, a single table is defined for the supertype, and any specific attributes belonging to the subtypes must be added as columns to the supertype. Then an additional column is added to indicate the subtype.

In the second method, a table is created for each subtype, and the attributes belonging to the supertype are added as columns to each of the subtype tables.

In the third method, tables are created for the supertype and subtypes, and an additional column is added to the supertype to indicate the subtype. Then a single foreign-key column is added to the supertype.

While identifying entities, it can be useful to associate a short name with each entity. Also, list any other names that the entities may have in a list of synonyms. For example, a customer is sometimes called a client, as shown in Table 16.2.

If you are not using a CASE tool, create a standard template for recording the entity names, short names, and synonyms. For example, you can create a simple table with the appropriate column headings, as shown in Table 16.2.

Table 16.2. Entities.

Entity	Short Name	Synonyms
Contact		
Customer	Cust	Client
Department	Dept	
Employee	Emp	
Employee Audit	Emp Audit	
Report Audit	Rpt Audit	
State		

NOTE

To provide management for time, which may be historical data or auditing information, you will need to add additional entities and attributes to the data model.

Domains

When several attributes share a common data type, length, and format, a single definition is created, called a domain. The domain is then associated with each attribute that it supports. Domains may also contain a range, or list of valid values. This use of domains will result in a more consistent definition of the data items in the system, and in some instances it will provide standard validation.

If you are not using a CASE tool, create a standard template for recording each domain. For example, you can create a simple table with column headings for the domain name, data type, length, format, and values, as shown in Table 16.3.

Table 16.3. Domains.

Domain	Data Type	Length	Format	Values
Amount	Number	7,2	$999,990.00	
Code	Character	2		
Date	Date	9	DD-MON-YY	
Id	Number	4		
Blob	Long Raw			
Name	Character	30		
Percent	Number	3	990	
UserId	Character	30		

Notice in Table 16.3 that at this time none of the domains are restricted to a given range or list of values.

> **TIP**
>
> Consider the data types and format masks supported by the system when defining your domains.

Notice the Employee Audit entity in Table 16.4 uses domains for every attribute.

Unique Identifiers

Every entity must be uniquely identified by one or more of its attributes. When no natural unique identifier exists, or the nominated UID could change value, create a sequence number for the primary key. Indicate which attributes comprise the unique identifier(s), as well as the primary key as shown in Table 16.4. Use a number to indicate the UID and a Y for the primary key. The number is used for the UID so that multiple UIDs in the same entity may be supported.

Attributes

An attribute describes the entity or provides information about the entity. After each of the entities has been defined, identify all of the attributes for each entity. Identify the data type, the maximum length, and whether or not a value is required for each entity.

Again, if you are not using a CASE tool, create a table or spreadsheet to record all of the attributes associated with each entity. For example, Table 16.4 contains the entity, relation, attribute name, data type or domain, maximum length, value required, unique identifier, and primary key.

Table 16.4. Entities and attributes.

Entity Contact	Relation	Attribute Name	Data Type or Domain	Max Len	Value Req'd	UID	PK
	Employee				Yes	1	Y
	Customer				Yes	1	Y
		Contact Date	Date		Yes	1	Y
		Type	Character	5	Yes		
		Subject	Character	20			
		Action	Character	20			
		Location	Character	20			
		Phone	Character	20			
		Received By	Userid				
		Message	Blob				
		Success	Character	1			
		Direction	Character	1			
		Priority	Character	1			

Entity Customer	Relation	Attribute Name	Data Type or Domain	Max Len	Value Req'd	UID	PK
		Id	Id		Yes	1	Y
		Name	Name				
		Address	Character	40			
		City	Character	30			
	State						
		Zip	Character	9			
		Area	Number	3			
		Phone	Character	9			

continues

Table 16.4. Continued

Entity Customer	Relation	Attribute Name	Data Type or Domain	Max Len	Value Req'd	UID	PK
	Employee				Yes		
		Credit Limit	Number	9,2			
		Comments	Long				

Entity Department	Relation	Attribute Name	Data Type or Domain	Max Len	Value Req'd	UID	PK
		Number	Id		Yes	1	Y
		Name	Name				
		Location	Character	13			
		Increase	Percent				

Entity Employee	Relation	Attribute Name	Data Type or Domain	Max Len	Value Req'd	UID	PK
		Number	Id		Yes	1	Y
		Name	Name				
		Job	Character	9			
		Hire Date	Date				
		Salary	Amount				
		Commission	Amount				
		Increase	Percent				

Entity Employee Audit	Relation	Attribute Name	Data Type or Domain	Max Len	Value Req'd	UID	PK
	Employee				Yes	1	Y
		Change Date	Date		Yes	1	Y
		Old Salary	Amount				
		New Salary	Amount				
		Updated By	Userid				

Entity Report Audit	Relation	Attribute Name	Data Type or Domain	Max Len	Value Req'd	UID	PK
		Report	Character	8	Yes	1	Y
		Run By	Userid		Yes	1	Y
		Run	Date		Yes	1	Y

Entity State	Relation	Attribute Name	Data Type or Domain	Max Len	Value Req'd	UID	PK
		Code	Code		Yes	1	Y
		Name	Name		Yes		

NOTE

Notice in the contact, customer, and employee audit entities that the relations appear in the list. This method facilitates a better overall understanding of the entities and attributes without compromising the data model.

CAUTION

Foreign key columns are not attributes, just as calculations and derived data are not attributes. In fact, no columns are attributes. Columns only exist in the physical design and implementation of the database. Foreign key columns are represented in the logical data model as relations.

Relations

Relations describe how one entity is associated with another entity, and they should contain verbs. A relationship is the combination of two entities and two relations. There are five basic types of relationships:

- One-to-many
- Many-to-many
- One-to-one

- Mutually exclusive
- Recursive

The one-to-many relationship is the most common and represents the concept of the repeating group. The many-to-many relationship is common in the basic logical model, but it must be resolved to include an intersection entity for the detailed data model. The one-to-one relationship is very rare and usually not appropriate in a correct data model. The occurrences of the entities in a relationship is sometimes called cardinality. A mutually exclusive relationship exists when an entity has a relation to one entity or the other, but never to both entities. A recursive relationship exists when an entity has a relation to itself.

After defining the entities in the application system, define the relationships between them. There are several methods of defining relationships. Entity/relationship diagrams are very common, but they require the symbolic structure to be translated before the meaning of the diagram can be understood. One alternative method is to use a sentence structure, as appears in Table 16.5. A sentence structure is usually an effective way to communicate to management and end users, as well as members of the design team and development staff.

Table 16.5. E/R sentences.

Each	Entity	May or must	Relation	One or many	Entity
Each	Contact	must	involve	one	Customer
Each	Contact	must	involve	one	Employee
Each	Contact	must	be received by	one	Employee
Each	Customer	may	be involved in	many	Contacts
Each	Customer	must	reside in	one	State
Each	Employee	may	be involved in	many	Contacts
Each	Employee	may	receive	many	Contacts
Each	Employee	may	be the subject of	many	Employee Audits
Each	Employee Audit	must	be auditing	one	Employee
Each	State	may	have	many	Customers

Entity/Relationship Diagrams

Entity/relationship diagrams appear to the untrained eye as a bunch of boxes with names, lines with symbols, and verbs in between. The key then for making effective use of E/R diagrams is training the people using them to understand the symbolic representation.

There are two common types of E/R diagrams: the basic E/R diagram and the detailed E/R diagram. The basic E/R diagram supports a high-level view of the data model and includes the major entities and their relations. It may contain many-to-many relationships and does not necessarily even have to show cardinality or optionality.

The detailed E/R diagram is the type of diagram you usually see that has been created using a CASE tool. It defines a much lower level of detail in the data model. Detailed E/R diagrams contain all entities and their relations. They have their many-to-many relationships resolved into intersection entities, and they must show cardinality and optionality. Some detailed E/R diagrams will even include the attribute(s) that have been nominated for the primary keys of the entities. You may even see the attribute list for each entity in a detailed E/R diagram.

NOTE

Not every entity has to be placed on a single detailed E/R diagram. In fact, it is quite common for larger systems to have many separate but related detailed E/R diagrams.

A mutually exclusive relationship is usually displayed in a detailed E/R diagram as an arc that crosses the lines of the two relations. A recursive relationship is generally displayed in a detailed E/R diagram as a looping line that returns to the entity where it originated.

CAUTION

Entity/relationship diagrams may use different syntax, depending on the method or system being used. Also, E/R diagrams may be difficult for end users to understand because of their schematic nature, so be careful not to make them any more difficult to read than they already are.

TIP

Align the entities vertically and horizontally to create sight lines, use straight lines for the relationships, and use white space to avoid clutter. Be brief but meaningful when naming entities and relations. And include a legend in the data model documentation folder.

Review of the Logical Data Model

The user representatives should be reviewing the logical data model during the definition and at the conclusion of the process. The review should include all of the component parts of the model that were just reviewed in this chapter.

In addition, during initial review of the data model, the entities should be mapped to the functions they support. Then, as the data model is completed, the entities and attributes should be mapped to the functions they support.

Function to Entity Mapping

Sample functions are listed here (Tables 16.6 through 16.8) along with the supporting entities. The functions are grouped by function type.

Table 16.6. Maintenance functions to entities.

Maintenance Function	Entity
Contact Management	Contact
	Customer
	Employee
Maintain Customers	Customer
	State
Maintain Salary Increases by Department and Employee	Department
	Employee
Maintain States	State

Table 16.7. Report functions to entities.

Report Function	Entity
List Customers	Customer
	State
List Contact Messages	Contact
	Customer
	Employee
List Contact Priorities	Contact
	Employee
List Contact Totals	Contact
	Employee
List Contact by Employee	Employee
	Contact
	Customer

Report Function	Entity
List Employees by Department	Department
	Employee
Sales Employee	Department
Salaries and Commissions	Employee

Table 16.8. Program functions to entities.

Program Function	Entity
Audit Salary Increases	Employee
	Employee Audit
Audit Reports	Report Audit
Annual Salary Increases	Department
	Employee

Function-to-Attribute Mapping

Sample functions are listed in Tables 16.9 through 16.11 along with the supporting entities and attributes. The functions are grouped by function type.

Table 16.9. Maintenance functions to attributes.

Maintenance Function	Entity	Attributes
Contact Management	Contact	Contact Date
		Type
		Subject
		Action
		Location
Phone		
		Received By
		Message
		Success
		Direction

continues

Table 16.9. continued

Maintenance Function	Entity	Attributes
		Priority
	Customer	Name
	Employee	Name
Maintain Customers	Customer	Id
		Name
		Address
		City
		Zip
		Area
		Phone
		Comments
	State	Name
Maintain Salary Increases	Department	Number
by Department and Employee		Name
		Location
		Increase
	Employee	Number
		Name
		Job
		Increase
Maintain States	State	Code
		Name

Some of the attributes in the report functions are calculations. When the calculations involve attributes, the attributes are referenced.

Table 16.10. Report functions to attributes.

Report Function	Entity	Attributes
List Customers	Customer	City
		Name

Report Function	Entity	Attributes
		Phone
	State	Name
List Contact Messages	Contact	Message
		Contact Date
	Customer	
	Name	
	Employee	Name
List Contact Priorities	Contact	Priority
	Employee	Name
List Contact Totals	Contact	(count)
	Employee	Name
List Contact by Employee	Employee	Name
	Contact	Contact Date
	Customer	Name
List Employees by Department	Department	Name
		Location
	Employee	Name
		Salary
		Commission
Sales Employee	Department	Name
Salaries and Commissions	Employee	Name
		Salary
		Commission
		(Salary+Commission)

Table 16.11. Program functions to attributes.

Program Function	Entity	Attributes
Audit Salary Increases	Employee	Salary
	Employee Audit	Change Date
		Old Salary
		New Salary
		Updated By
Audit Reports	Report Audit	Report
		Run By
		Run Date
Annual Salary Increases	Department	Increase
	Employee	Increase
		Salary

Physical Database Design

After the logical data model is complete, physical database design can begin. The physical database design is the transition from the abstract logical model to the concrete physical implementation.

Tables

Tables are defined by mapping the entities identified in the logical data model. Document the definition of the existing tables, as well as each of the new tables. To identify all of the tables and synonyms for the database, begin with the list of entities from the data model. Use the plural form of the entity name or the plural form of the short name as the table name. Replace the spaces with underscores. Base your decision about whether to use the short name on the general principle of keeping the table names brief and meaningful.

If the table already exists in the current system, keep the table name as it is, unless you are doing a complete make-over of the database. Be consistent in naming your tables. If the existing table names have not been pluralized, as in the example, then keep the new table names singular as well. At least this way the naming convention is consistent for the entire system.

Entity	Table	Synonym
Contact	Contact	Cont
Customer	Customer	Cust
		Client
Department	Dept	
Employee	Emp	
Employee Audit	Emp_Audit	EmpA
Report Audit	Rpt_Audit	RptA
State	State	St

If the short name is too brief, use the short name as a synonym. Make the Entity to Table and Synonym list accessible to everyone on the project, but appoint a custodian to manage the list.

Supertype/Subtype Options

If the data model contains supertyped and subtyped entities, you must choose which method will be used to implement them. There are three options:

- One table
- Separate subtype tables
- A supertype table and separate subtype tables

In the first method, a single table is defined for the supertype, and any specific attributes belonging to the subtypes must be added as columns to the supertype. Then a column is added to indicate the subtype.

In the second method, a table is created for each subtype, and the attributes belonging to the supertype are added as columns to each of the subtype tables.

In the third method, tables are created for the supertype and subtypes, and a column is added to the supertype to indicate the subtype. Then a single foreign-key column is added to the supertype.

> **CAUTION**
>
> Using the second and third methods means that a union must be used to access the complete set of data for the supertype. Also, you will not be able to directly insert, update, or delete data.

Mutually Exclusive Relationship Options

If the data model contains mutually exclusive relationships, you must choose which method will be used to implement them. There are two options:

- The generic
- The explicit

In the first method, the relation is added as a single foreign-key column, and an additional column is added to identify which relation the foreign key is associated with. In addition, each of the primary-key columns that map to the foreign-key column must have the same data type. In the second method, each primary key is added as a foreign-key column.

> **NOTE**
>
> The generic implementation method for exclusive relationships is also the third implementation method for subtypes.

Data Types

Before defining the columns for our tables, we need to consider the data types that are supported by the database. Then we will map each of the domains and logical data types to their corresponding physical data types.

In addition, we will add to the list of domains from the logical data model to include existing physical implementations that are different and still need to be adhered to. For example, CreditLimit was in the Amount domain in the logical data model, but the existing physical implementation has a different precision. The same is true for CustId and DeptNo; that is, they were both in the Id domain, but their physical implementation is different.

Domain	Logical Data Type	Physical Data Type
Amount	Number	Number(7,2)
Blob	Long Raw	Long Raw
Code	Character	VarChar2(2)
CreditLimit	Number	Number(9,2)
CustId	Number	Number(6)
Date	Date	Date
DeptNo	Number	Number(2)
Id	Number	Number(4)
Name	Character	VarChar2(30)
Percent	Number	Number(3)
UserId	Character	VarChar2(30)

Another example of variation in the logical and physical data types exists when the version of the database is considered. For example, Oracle6 uses the CHAR data type to support character data, and its maximum length is 255, whereas Oracle7 uses the VARCHAR2 data type, which has a maximum length of 2000. A simple list of the mapping between the logical data type and the physical data type clarifies this issue.

Logical Data Type	Physical Data Type
Character	VarChar2
Long	Long
Number	Number

Columns

From the Entities and Attributes list created in logical data modeling and the relationships that we documented in the E/R Sentence table, we define the columns for our tables.

The process of naming columns is fairly straightforward. Use the attribute name for the column name, unless it is not brief enough, in which case you should use the list of abbreviations to create the appropriate name. Replace the spaces with underscores. For columns that will be created from relations, use the primary key column from the table being referenced, such as DeptNo in the Emp table. If this method does not create a brief and meaningful column name, then consider the following guidelines:

- Use the table name for codes, such as State in the Customer table
- Use the relation for recursive foreign-key columns, such as Mgr in the Emp table

The following is a list of each of the tables with the columns mapped from the attributes and relations:

Table Name	Column Name	Data Type	Not Null
Customer	CustId	Number(6)	Yes
	Name	VarChar2(45)	
	Address	VarChar2(40)	
	City	VarChar2(30)	
	State	VarChar2(2)	
	Zip	VarChar2(9)	
	Area	Number(3)	
	Phone	VarChar2(9)	
	RepId	Number(4)	Yes
	CreditLimit	Number(9,2)	
	Comments	Long	

Table Name	Column Name	Data Type	Not Null
Dept	DeptNo	Number(2)	Yes
	DName	VarChar2(14)	
	Loc	VarChar2(13)	
	Increase_Pct	Number(3)	

Table Name	Column Name	Data Type	Not Null
Emp	EmpNo	Number(4)	Yes
	EName	VarChar2(10)	
	Job	VarChar2(9)	
	Mgr	Number(4)	
	HireDate	Date	
	Sal	Number(7,2)	
	Comm	Number(7,2)	
	DeptNo	Number(2)	Yes
	Increase_Pct	Number(3)	

NOTE

Notice that the Increase_Pct columns have been added to the existing Dept and Emp tables.

Table Name	Column Name	Data Type	Not Null
Contact	EmpNo	Number(4)	Yes
	CustId	Number(6)	Yes
	Contact_Date	Date	Yes
	Type	VarChar2(5)	Yes
	Subject	VarChar2(20)	
	Action	VarChar2(20)	
	Location	VarChar2(20)	
	Phone	VarChar2(20)	
	Recd_By	VarChar2(30)	
	Message	Long Raw	
	Success	VarChar2(1)	
	Direction	VarChar2(1)	
	Priority	VarChar2(1)	

Table Name	Column Name	Data Type	Not Null
Emp_Audit	EmpNo	Number(4)	Yes
	Change_Date	Date	Yes
	Old_Sal	Number(7,2)	

| | New_Sal | Number(7,2) | |
| | Updated_By | VarChar2(30) | |

Table Name	Column Name	Data Type	Not Null
Rpt_Audit	EmpNo	VarChar2(8)	Yes
	Run_By	VarChar2(30)	Yes
	Date_Run	Datc	Yes

Table Name	Column Name	Data Type	Not Null
State	Code	VarChar2(2)	Yes
	Name	VarChar2(30)	Yes

Naming Constraints

One of the most powerful features of a database is its capability to support declarative constraints. The proper identification, definition, and maintenance of declarative constraints is essential to the success of the project. Defining standard naming conventions for the constraints is therefore extremely important.

The following are the guidelines that are used for naming constraints in this chapter:

- The constraint name begins with the table name.
- If an abbreviation is needed for the table name, use the short synonym.
- The table name is followed by the two-character constraint type. Primary key is PK, unique key is UK, foreign key is FK, not-null is NN, check range is CR, and check condition is CC.

> **NOTE**
>
> The system table contains constraint types for primary key (P), unique key (U), reference (R), and check (C). The two-character constraint types we are using add further clarification that is not possible with just the single character.

- When the constraint type is PK, UK, NN, CR, or CC, it is followed by the column(s) defined in the constraint.
- When the constraint type is FK, it is followed by the referenced table name and column(s) defined in the constraint.
- If an abbreviation is needed following the constraint type, use the synonym for the table name or the abbreviation from the Abbreviation table for column names.
- If the abbreviation is not available from the Abbreviation table, create one and add it to the table.

■ If an abbreviation is required in any constraint name for a given table, the same abbreviation must be used for the second and subsequent references to the name that was abbreviated in the current constraint, as well as any other constraints for that table.

Primary Key and Unique

The conventions for naming primary-key and unique constraints are identical, with the exception of constraint type. Consider the following primary-key constraint:

Type	Table Name	Constraint Name
P	Contact	Cont_PK_EmpNo_CustId_Cont_Date

The constraint type is P, for primary key. The constraint name is restricted to 30 characters. Therefore, we must abbreviate the table name using the synonym we defined earlier. The synonym is followed by the two-character constraint type. The primary-key constraint for this table is a multicolumn key, consisting of EmpNo, CustId, and Contact_Date. The columns that define the primary key follow the two-character constraint type. Again, an abbreviation was used for space consideration and consistency.

Check

The conventions for naming not-null, check-range, and check-condition constraints are identical, with the exception of constraint type. Consider the following not-null constraint:

Type	Table Name	Constraint Name
C	Contact	Cont_NN_EmpNo

The constraint type is C, for check. A previous abbreviation was used. Therefore, the abbreviation is used again for the table name. The synonym is followed by the two-character constraint type. The column that is defined in the not-null constraint follows the two-character constraint type.

Reference

Consider the following reference constraint:

Type	Table Name	Constraint Name
R	Contact	Cont_FK_Emp_EmpNo

The constraint type is R, for reference. A previous abbreviation was used. Therefore, the abbreviation is used again for the table name. The synonym is followed by the two-character constraint type. The table and column that are defined in the reference constraint follow the two-character constraint type.

> **TIP**
>
> Start with the longest constraint name first. The primary-key constraint name for a multicolumn key is usually the longest. This way, if an abbreviation is needed, you can apply it to the subsequent constraint names as well.

The aim is to create meaningful names that will be unique. By using the method described here, you will achieve both of these goals.

Identifying Constraints

Now that we have a convention for naming constraints, we can define each of the constraints needed to support our data model.

Keep in mind that:

- UIDs that are also PKs become Primary Key Constraints
- UIDs that are not also PKs become Unique Constraints
- Values Required become Not-Null Constraints
- Restricted Values become Check Constraints
- Relations become Reference Constraints

Start by using the list of Entities and Attributes from our logical data model, and group the constraints by constraint type.

> **TIP**
>
> Using the list of Entities and Attributes will simplify the process of identifying constraints—especially since that list includes, PKs, UIDs, Required Values, Domains, and Relations.

The existing constraints will be left unchanged for now. Once we can categorically verify that no reference exists anywhere in the system to any of the existing constraint names, we can change them to conform to our naming convention. Alternatively, once all the references have been discovered, a separate project could be initiated to change them (a project which is outside the scope of this book). This is what the tables' constraint names will look like:

Type	Table Name	Constraint Name
C	Contact	Cont_NN_EmpNo
C	Contact	Cont_NN_CustId
C	Contact	Cont_NN_Contact_Date
C	Contact	Cont_NN_Type
P	Contact	Cont_PK_EmpNo_CustId_Cont_Date
R	Contact	Cont_FK_Emp
R	Contact	Cont_FK_Customer
C	Customer	Customer_NN_CustId
C	Customer	Customer_CK_CustId
P	Customer	Customer_PK_CustId
R	Customer	Customer_FK_State_Code
C	Dept	Dept_NN_DeptNo
P	Dept	Dept_PK_DeptNo
C	Emp	Emp_NN_EmpNo
P	Emp	Emp_PK_EmpNo
R	Emp	Emp_FK_Emp_EmpNo
R	Emp	Emp_FK_Dept_DeptNo
C	Emp_Audit	Emp_Audit_NN_EmpNo
C	Emp_Audit	Emp_Audit_NN_Change_Date
P	Emp_Audit	Emp_Audit_PK_EmpNo_Change_Date
C	Rpt_Audit	Rpta_NN_Report
C	Rpt_Audit	Rpta_NN_Run_By
C	Rpt_Audit	Rpta_NN_Date_Run
P	Rpt_Audit	Rpta_PK_Report_Run_By_Date_Run
C	State	State_NN_Code
C	State	State_NN_Name
P	State	State_PK_Code

Having seen where we are going may help put things in perspective, but we will still go through the process of identifying each constraint type for each table. We will review and document the constraint names for the existing tables, as well as the new ones.

Primary Key

Attributes that were unique identifiers and were nominated as primary keys will be assigned primary-key constraints. The tables with primary keys are as follows:

Table Name	Column Name	Constraint Name
Contact	EmpNo CustId Contact_Date	Cont_PK_EmpNo_CustId_Cont_Date
Customer	CustId	Customer_PK_CustId
Dept	DeptNo	Dept_PK_DeptNo
Emp	EmpNo	Emp_PK_EmpNo
Emp_Audit	EmpNo Change_Date	Emp_Audit_PK_EmpNo_Change_Date
Rpt_Audit	Report Run_By Date_Run	RptA_PK_Report_Run_By_Date_Run
State	Code	State_PK_Code

Unique

Attributes that were unique identifiers and were not nominated as primary keys will be assigned unique constraints. The table with a unique constraint is:

Table Name	Column Name	Constraint Name
State	Name	State_UK_Name

Not Null

Attributes that had values required will be assigned not-null column constraints. The tables with not-null constraints are as follows:

Table Name	Column Name	Constraint Name
Contact	EmpNo CustId Contact_Date Type	Cont_NN_EmpNo Cont_NN_CustId Cont_NN_Cont_Date Cont_NN_Type

continues

Table Name	Column Name	Constraint Name
Customer	CustId	Customer_NN_CustId
	RepId	Customer_NN_RepId
Dept	DeptNo	Dept_NN_DeptNo
Emp	EmpNo	Emp_NN_EmpNo
	DeptNo	Emp_NN_DeptNo
Emp_Audit	EmpNo	Emp_Audit_NN_EmpNo
	Change_Date	Emp_Audit_NN_Change_Date
Rpt_Audit	Report	RptA_NN_Report
	Run_By	RptA_NN_Run_By
	Date_Run	RptA_NN_Date_Run
State	Code	State_NN_Code
	Name	State_NN_Name

Check Range

Attributes that have restricted values may be assigned check-range or check-condition column constraints. The table with a check-range constraint is as follows:

Table Name	Column Name	Constraint Name
Customer	RepId	Customer_CR_RepId

Check Condition

Again, attributes that have restricted values may be assigned check-range or check-condition column constraints. The table with a check-condition constraint is as follows:

Table Name	Column Name	Constraint Name
Contact	Priority	Cont_CC_Priority

Reference

Relations become reference constraints. Reference constraints are often called foreign-key constraints and serve to enforce referential integrity. The tables with reference constraints are as follows:

Table Name	Column Name	Constraint Name
Emp	EmpNo	Emp_FK_Emp_Mgr
	DeptNo	Emp_FK_Dept_DeptNo
Contact	EmpNo	Cont_FK_Emp_EmpNo
	CustId	Cont_FK_Customer_CustId
Customer	State	Customer_FK_State_Code

For each reference constraint, you must choose a mode of cascade processing. Keep in mind that the first two options are declarative, and the first one is the default, while the last three will require the use of database triggers to implement. The five choices are as follows:

- Cascade Restrict
- Cascade Delete
- Cascade Null
- Cascade Default
- Cascade Update

Cascade Restrict means that no delete of the parent will be permitted while dependent children exist.

Cascade Delete means that all rows that are dependent on the reference will be deleted when the parent is deleted.

Cascade Null means that the value in the foreign-key column will be set to null when the parent is deleted.

Cascade Default means that the value in the foreign-key column will be set to a predetermined default value when the parent is deleted.

Cascade Update means that when the value in the parent is changed, the corresponding children will automatically be updated.

The first two can be defined decoratively, whereas the third, fourth, and fifth require additional procedures and database triggers to implement.

Views

During the physical design process, you can define views. A view may be useful if, in reviewing the table and column requirements for the reports and displays, you discover a frequently used join condition. Views are sometimes thought of as stored queries. Views are documented as a special PL/SQL module type and mapped to the tables and columns that are used to create them.

Some developers might suggest that views are bad and create performance problems in the system. It is true that views are vulnerable to performance issues, but views are not inherently bad. For example, a view designed and built to support queries and/or reports may be very useful. They can standardize and simplify the use of several tables that are commonly used together.

When views are involved in performance problems, it is usually because an execution plan chosen by the optimizer is not optimal. This can happen when you are using a where clause against a view. This results in additions to the where clause of the total query. But, if the views are well-designed and implemented, and these issues are understood and taken into consideration, views will not adversely affect performance.

Indexes

Indexes will automatically be created to support the unique and primary-key constraints. But additional indexes may be needed to increase performance associated with querying on columns that are not already indexed. The appropriate use of additional indexes depends directly on the specific details of the system (and is therefore outside of the scope of this book).

Tablespaces

During the physical design process you can begin to define the space requirements for the database. Depending on the size of the database and the physical characteristics of the database server, different approaches may be taken.

For smaller projects, the User Data tablespace can be used for tables and indexes. But for larger projects, the DBA is likely to create new tablespaces for the project tables, indexes, rollback segments, and redo logs. As with indexes, the appropriate use of tablespace depends directly on the specific details of the system and is therefore outside of the scope of this book.

Review of the Physical Database Design

The user representatives and project team should periodically review the physical database design, and the review should include all of the component parts reviewed in this chapter.

In addition, during the initial review of the physical database design, the tables should be mapped to the modules they support. Then, as the physical database design is completed, the tables and columns should be mapped to the modules they support.

Module-to-Table Mapping

The modules that will support the functions described earlier are listed here along with the supporting tables. The modules are grouped by module type.

Forms Description	Module Name	Table(s)
Contact Management	contact	Contact Customer Emp
Maintain Customers	customer	Customer State
Maintain Salary Increases by Department and Employee	dept_emp	Dept Emp
Maintain States	state	State

Reports Description	Module Name	Table(s)
List Customers	customer	Customer State
List Contact Messages	cont_msg	Contact Customer Emp
List Contact Priorities	priority	Contact Emp
List Contact Totals	con_tot	Contact Emp
List Contacts by Employee	econtot	Emp Contact Customer
List Employees by Department	dept_emp	Dept Emp
Sales Employee Salaries and Commissions	sal_comm	Dept Emp

Database Triggers Description	Module Name	Table(s)
Audit Salary Increases	Emp_Audit	Emp Emp_Audit

Database Procedures Description	Module Name	Table(s)
Annual Salary Increases	annual_sal_update	Dept Emp

SQL Scripts Description	Module Name	Table(s)
Audit Reports	rptaudit	Report Audit

Views Description	Module Name	Table(s)
Contact List	contlist	Contact Customer Emp

Module-to-Column Mapping

The modules that will support the functions described earlier are again listed here along with the supporting tables and columns. The modules are grouped by module type.

Forms Description	Module Name	Table(s)	Column(s)
Contact Management	contact	Contact	Contact_Date Type Subject Action Location Phone Received_By Message Success Direction Priority
		Customer	Name
		Emp	EName

Maintain Customers	customer	Customer	CustId
			Name
			Address
			City
			Zip
			Area
			Phone
			Comments
		State	Code
			Name
Maintain Salary Increases by Department and Employee	dept_emp	Dept	DeptNo
			DName
			Loc
			Increase_Pct
		Emp	EmpNo
			EName
			Job
			Increase_Pct
Maintain States	state	State	Code
			Name

Some of the columns in the reports are calculations. When the calculations involve columns, the columns are referenced.

Reports Description	Module Name	Table(s)	Column(s)
List Customers	customer	Customer	City
			Name
			Phone
		State	Name
List Contact Messages	cont_msg	Contact	Message
			Contact_Date
		Customer	Name
		Emp	EName
List Contact Priorities	priority	Contact	Priority
		Emp	EName

continues

Reports Description	Module Name	Table(s)	Column(s)
List Contact Totals	con_tot	Contact Emp	(count) EName
List Contacts by Employee	econtots	Contact Customer Emp	Contact_Date Name EName
List Employees by Department	deptemp	Dept Emp	DName Loc EName Sal Comm
Sales Employee Salaries and Commissions	sal_comm	Dept Emp	DName EName Sal Comm (Sal+Comm)

Database Triggers Description	Module Name	Table(s)	Column(s)
Audit Salary Increases	Emp_Audit	Emp Emp_Audit	Sal EmpNo Change_Date Old_Sal New_Sal Updated_By

Database Procedures Description	Module Name	Table(s)	Column(s)
Annual Salary Increases	annual_sal_update	Dept Emp	Increase_Pct Increase_Pct Sal

SQL Scripts Description	Module Name	Table(s)	Column(s)
Audit Reports	rptaudit	Rpt_Audit	Report Run_By Run_Date

Views Description	Module Name	Table(s)	Column(s)
Contact List	contlist	Contact	Contact_Date
		Customer	Name
		Emp	EName

Summary

This chapter reviewed the principles of logical data modeling, including:

- Normalization
- Integrity
- Naming conventions
- Entities
- Domains
- Attributes
- Unique identifiers
- Relations
- Entity/relationship diagrams
- Reviewing the logical data model

In addition to mapping the objects in the data model to objects in the physical model, the following mapping processes were reviewed in this chapter:

- Entities to tables
- Attributes to columns
- Relations to foreign-key columns
- Primary keys to primary-key constraints
- UIDs to unique constraints
- Values required to not-null constraints
- Restricted values to check constraints
- Relations to reference constraints

We established naming conventions for the physical objects. We discussed views, indexes, and tablespaces. And we concluded by doing the module-to-table and module-to-column mapping.

Object-Oriented Development with Client/Server

17

by Charles Wood

Object-oriented development and client/server development are two relatively new technologies. The challenge of many client/server developers is understanding how to integrate client/server technology with object-oriented design.

Many languages, like C++, Object Pascal, and even GUI development tools like PowerBuilder and Delphi, support object-oriented techniques. Some languages, like Java and SmallTalk, even demand that all code be encapsulated inside an object class.

> **NOTE**
>
> You can implement object-oriented design when not using an object-oriented language. It's just a little bit harder to do because that language won't support some neat features like inheritance. Still, you can mimic all the object-oriented features in any computer language.

Object-oriented development consists of object-oriented analysis to determine the objects and what they contain in your system and object-oriented design to implement your analysis into a database. This chapter first discusses object-oriented analysis, and then it discusses how object-oriented design and programming can be implemented inside a database. Finally, this chapter talks about the future of object-oriented development.

Defining Object-Oriented Development

The term *object-oriented* has been one of the more overused and misused technical computer terms. OOD is so ambiguous that many environments, languages, and programs claim to be object-oriented but have little if any of the criteria for being object-oriented.

> **NOTE**
>
> Some development packages are referred to as "object-based" rather than object-oriented. This term means that these packages incorporate some, but not all, of the features found in true object-oriented development tools.
>
> Often object-based tools evolve into fully object-oriented programming tools. For instance, PowerBuilder in version 2.0 was object-based because it didn't have a means to encapsulate code well and only supported limited inheritance. Now in version 5.0, it supports all of the object-oriented features found in other object-oriented development tools.

Object-oriented development is the practice of developing and coding modules in a system that behave independently of other modules. This practice involves tying data more closely to the functionality of the system programs. To understand OOD, you need to understand the definition of an object, how OOD grew into a viable technology, and what you gain when you use OOD as opposed to traditional, non-OOD methods to develop a program.

What Is an Object?

One of the hardest questions to answer when using object-oriented analysis is exactly what an object is. When discussing object-oriented development, an *object* is a collection of data that is grouped together with the functionality needed to view, create, delete, and manipulate that data.

Simply put, an object is variables and functions tied together. These objects often mimic real-world roles where people's jobs include processing data from one point to another. This point will be made clearer in the "Object-Oriented Analysis" section later in this chapter.

The Growth of Object-Oriented Development

Through the early '90s, MIS areas used tools that stressed functionality above data. Concentration on functionality rather than data led to the following programming techniques:

- Top-down design
- Structured programming
- Control break programming

This concentration on programming techniques took away from the real importance of a system: namely, the data that the system contains and conveys. Data was *passive,* meaning that the data stayed in data stores waiting for functions to query or update it.

As stated earlier, an object is simply a class or group of attributes that also contains functions needed to manipulate that data. You *could* view all programs as object-oriented because they all contain functions to work on data, yet most traditional, non–object-oriented languages tend to separate the data from the program code. Object-oriented development allows the data to be *active* by tying functionality to the data.

For example, an employee system could tie employee row retrieval functions to the actual employee data. If you were to write such a retrieval function using C (a non–object-oriented language), you would place all data either in some type of local or global variable or an argument. Any data stores are placed inside `structs`:

```
EXEC SQL INCLUDE SQLCA;
struct {
    int employee_id;
    char name[31];
    char address[31];
```

```
        char city[16];
        char state[3];
        char ZIP[11];
        char ssn[12];
        int department_id;
        float annual_salary;
} employee;
```

Then, using ANSI standard SQL, you would add functions to manipulate those structures:

```
void select_employee( int emp_id) {
    EXEC SQL BEGIN DECLARE SECTION;
        short int employee_id;
        char name[31];
        char address[31];
        char city[16];
        char state[3];
        char ZIP[11];
        char ssn[12];
        short int department_id;
        float annual_salary;
    EXEC SQL END DECLARE SECTION;
    employee_id = emp_id;
    EXEC SQL    SELECT name, address, city, state, ZIP, ssn, department_id,
annual_salary
                INTO :name, :address, :city, :state, :ZIP, :ssn, :department_id,
:annual_salary
                FROM mytable
            WHERE employee_id = :employee_id;

    employee.employee_id = employee_id;
    strcpy(employee.name, name);
    strcpy(employee.address, address);
    strcpy(employee.city, city);
    strcpy(employee.state, state);
    strcpy(employee.ZIP, ZIP);
    strcpy(employee.ssn, ssn);
    employee.department_id = department_id;
    employee.annual_salary = annual_salary;
}
```

It seems pretty complicated just to access a client/server SQL database to fill in some employee information. This complexity is due to the fact that SQL DECLARE SECTION statements in most databases don't allow structures to be used as host variables and most don't allow a period operator (.) to be present in a host variable. To load a structure, you have to perform the following steps:

1. Define a struct with the proper variables.

2. Define local SQL variables in your function with a DECLARE SECTION statement.

3. Use the SQL SELECT statement to move your variables into the local SQL variables.

4. Copy the values of the SQL variables into the struct.

Contrast the `struct` construct in C with the object-oriented `class` construct found in C++:

```
EXEC SQL INCLUDE SQLCA;
class employee {
    EXEC SQL BEGIN DECLARE SECTION;
        short int employee_id;
        char name[31];
        char address[31];
        char city[16];
        char state[3];
        char ZIP[11];
        char ssn[12];
        short int department_id;
        float annual_salary;
    EXEC SQL END DECLARE SECTION;
    void select_employee( int emp_id){
        employee_id = emp_id;
        EXEC SQL    SELECT name, address, city, state, ZIP, ssn, department_id,
annual_salary
                    INTO :name, :address, :city, :state, :ZIP, :ssn,
:department_id, :annual_salary
                    FROM mytable
                WHERE employee_id = :employee_id;
    };
};
```

Because I can use `class` variables with C++, the SQL functions I'm using to act on the class don't need to use the period operator or to refer to a different `struct`. When you use `class` objects in C++, you have to perform these steps:

1. Define a class with the proper variables, functions, and a DECLARE SECTION statement for SQL variables.

2. Use the SQL SELECT statement to move your variables into the local SQL variables.

I don't think anyone could argue that this C++ code is easier to understand, develop, and modify and is less prone to errors than the C code. However, for now you can forget about which one is easier and instead consider the basic differences between the code.

When you coupled C code with SQL, each group of functions needed its own variables to work with. If you wanted to store the variables inside a `struct` construct, you then had to move them there. In contrast, using `class` objects in C++ allowed the data and functionality of the C++ code and the SQL to be combined. Because functionality is centered around data, it's easier to manipulate data into a logical, easy-to-use program.

The Benefits of Object-Oriented Development

Both OOD and non-OOD methods can deliver systems that are required by the end user. However, OOD has some benefits that other development methods can't effectively deliver:

- OOD eventually leads to a repository of objects. These objects, if coded correctly, can be used in other programs. Instead of recoding thousands of lines of code for each new system, OOD allows you to code few lines of code that are used to implement existing modules. If a new module needs to be written, that module becomes part of the existing repository and is available for reuse in other programs.

- Maintenance of existing code is often more efficient. Because modules are independent, they tend to be encapsulated from each other, making it easy and inexpensive to track down bugs and/or add enhancements. What occurs in one module will probably not affect other modules so maintenance on existing programs is faster to develop, easier to test, and more bug free.

- Iterative development is easier to accomplish. Any new modules can be inherited from other similar modules to make the addition of needed modules easier.

Object-Oriented Analysis

Object-oriented analysis allows you to define real-world objects for your system. These objects will contain both attributes (data) and functions. Any analysis should be independent of the actual tool used to develop your system, so this part of the chapter doesn't involve code.

Object-oriented analysis consists of entity relation analysis, identification of entity attributes, and identification of entity functions. After you complete the object-oriented analysis, you can then move on to actually design your database and define the tools you'll be using for development.

Throughout the rest of the chapter, an *extremely* simplified payroll system is developed. This system is developed using object-oriented techniques, and then is placed on a relational database during the design stage.

Searching for Entities

Like in normal database analysis, the first step in object-oriented analysis is to find and define all possible entities in a system. (Soon, as you will see, object-oriented analysis will diverge from normal database analysis and design.) Entity definition consists of finding the real-world entities that a system is to facilitate or replace. In the case of a payroll system, assume you only defined the employee entity. Of course, a real payroll system would have several entities.

Identifying Entity Attributes: Object Normalization

As you would expect with database design, you must now define all attributes (variables) of all your entities. Figure 17.1 illustrates this step.

FIGURE 17.1.
As with database design, object-oriented design begins with declaring all entities and defining all the attributes in an entity.

Employee	
string	name
string	address
string	city
string	state
string	zip
string	phone(2)
string	SSN
float	pay_rate
string	department
string	job_title

Typical normalization uses normal forms to make sure data is properly placed on the database, as explained in Chapter 16, "Database Design." However, object-oriented analysis is different than database design, so I coined the term *object normalization* and use normalization steps rather than normal forms to give you a step-by-step view of object-oriented analysis.

CAUTION

Don't think that you no longer need to do database design when you do object-oriented design. Database design is *always* necessary when placing data on a relational database. When employing object-oriented development, do the object-oriented analysis, then the database design, then the object-oriented design, and finally the object-oriented development.

Object Normalization Step 1: Making Objects Unique

In database design, first normal form deals with eliminating all duplicate rows. However, in object design, this is not necessarily something you want to do. In fact, many times objects can be exact duplicates of each other. However, in an employee's case, common sense dictates that you can't have two identical employees, so an `employee_id` item is added to ensure uniqueness, as shown in Figure 17.2.

Therefore, Object Normalization Step 1 is to make sure that each object is unique *if applicable*. This step is a little less binding than first normal form in database design, which doesn't allow any duplicate rows.

Employee	
int	**employee_id**
string	name
string	address
string	city
string	state
string	zip
string	SSN
string	phone(2)
float	pay_rate
string	department
string	job_title

Object Normalization Step 2: Placing Subobjects into Contained Objects

When viewing the Employee object in Figure 17.2, notice that both `department` and `job_title` are listed as strings and are probably used to enter this employee's department and title within that department. However, there is an indication of a problem with this design. There is no guarantee that the department entered for an employee exists. Also, there is no guarantee that the title listed for an employee exists in the department where the employee is employed.

Figure 17.3 shows the object diagram with two more objects added to the model: `Department` and `Job_Title`. A good test for each attribute in the `Employee` object is to consider whether the attribute would exist if the employee did not. The employee name, employee address (address, city, state, and zip), the employee SSN, and the employee pay rate would not exist if the employee did not. However, the department would still exist if the employee were never hired, and the job title would still exist, but would have other employees fill it.

Object Normalization Step 2 is to remove all attributes that are not dependent on their containing object into their own objects.

> **NOTE**
>
> When one object (entity) is listed in another object as an attribute, you say that one object is contained in another object.

FIGURE 17.3.

Object Normalization Step 2 requires placing subobjects into their own objects.

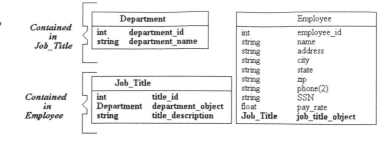

> **NOTE**
>
> Notice that Department and Job_Title are unique identifiers. You need to renormalize when using objects with each step to keep a cohesive object model.

Object Normalization Step 3: Inheriting Subcategories

Now look at the model in Figure 17.3. The pay_rate attribute in Employee is ambiguous. This attribute could be a salaried amount, in which case it needs to be paid regardless of attendance or hours spent on the job. It also could be an hourly amount in which the amount paid is directly dependent on the amount of time spent on the job. The type of pay rate depends on the type of employee: salaried or hourly.

Categories of entities should be split apart during the third step of object orientation into their own objects, with a link to the object they came from, as shown in Figure 17.4. This link is called *inheritance*. Salaried_Employee and Hourly_Employee are inherited from Employee, which means that Salaried_Employee and Hourly_Employee contain not only their own attributes, but all the attributes in Employee as well.

> **NOTE**
>
> With the addition of two employee categories, you now can say that the Employee object is *abstract*. This means that it doesn't make sense to talk about an Employee object by itself and that Employee will *never* be contained within another object or declared in a program. Rather, either a Salaried_Employee will be contained or Hourly_Employee will be contained in other objects or declared in programs. Abstract objects are for building other objects only.

Object Normalization Step 3 is to put all object categories into their own inherited objects.

FIGURE 17.4.

Entities that are categories of other objects need to be inherited from those objects.

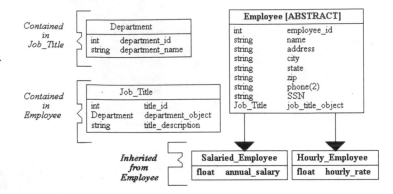

Adding Entity Functions

The next step in object-oriented analysis is to identify the functions of each of the objects you've described so far, as shown in Figure 17.5. Adding functions to your data-centric objects ties functionality to the data. This is the final step in building an object model during object-oriented analysis.

FIGURE 17.5.

Defining functions in your object model finishes object-oriented analysis.

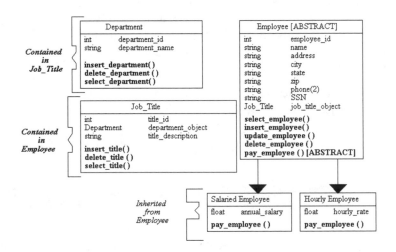

Understanding Situations to Avoid During OOA

There are other rules that you may need to or want to follow during object-oriented analysis. First, don't let two objects contain each other. This is an object-oriented version of an infinite loop (or perhaps an object-oriented paradox). When two objects contain each other, neither object can be declared until the other object is declared.

You *can* have one object inherited from more than one object. This situation is called multiple inheritance. Figure 17.6 shows the C++ file structure in which an input file and an output file are both inherited from a file object, and the IO file is then inherited from both the input file and the output file, making multiple inheritance intrinsic to the C++ language. However, although a few languages (like C++) support this feature, others (like Java and PowerBuilder) don't. Usually multiple inheritance leads to problems during development, and you should avoid it when possible.

FIGURE 17.6.

C++'s file structure implements a form of multiple inheritance, although most developers believe that you should try to avoid multiple inheritance.

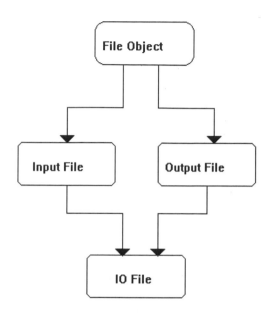

The New Role of Data in an Object-Oriented Program

Now that object-oriented analysis is finished, consider the difference between OOA and traditional structured system analysis. In traditional analysis, you would do the following:

1. Determine the entities in a system.
2. Determine the attributes (or data) of each entity.
3. Determine the functions those entities perform. (This step is often called a process model.)
4. Balance the process model with the data model to ensure every function has the data it needs to process.

With this process, you'll end up with a function-driven design. Contrast this process with the steps involved in OOA:

1. Determine the entities in a system.
2. Determine what attributes (or data) make up those entities.
3. Determine the functions needed to process these attributes.

With OOA, you end up with a data-centric model, as opposed to a function-centric model. Often, OOA can clarify *why* certain functions are needed in a system. Because the functions and the data are so closely tied together, you'll often end up with a system model that is closer to what the end user has requested.

The Three Components of Object-Oriented Development

The three components of object-oriented development are as follows:

- Encapsulation
- Inheritance
- Polymorphism

These components affect the entire object-oriented development process and are described in the following sections.

Encapsulation

Entities in OOA are encapsulated. That is, the object functions affect the data only within their own object. Furthermore, no other object should directly access or change the attributes of another object, but rather you should call that object's functions (also known as *methods*) to change the attributes of an object.

If you properly encapsulate your objects, you gain several benefits:

- Development becomes clearer. You know that when you develop an object, all you need to write are functions that handle the object's attributes. If your object contains another object, you'll need to make calls to the contained object's functions to change the attributes of the contained object.

- Maintenance becomes much easier. When you make a change to an object, you only need to worry about that object during testing. Other objects should function the same as before the change and should only need minimal testing.

- Debugging becomes much easier. When an error occurs in an object, at best you know exactly where the offending function is. At worst, you need to set a breakpoint in your object to determine why you have a bug. Contrast this process with searching through thousands of lines of code to find a bug, and then searching through another thousand lines of code after fixing the error to make sure other objects aren't affected.

An OOA diagram only has lines between child objects and their parent objects. Data modeling requires that you establish relationships between entities. Object modeling, on the other hand, requires that each object is independent from other objects whenever possible. Each object should be encapsulated from other objects. Because of encapsulation, OOA makes data flow diagrams somewhat obsolete. Instead of functions passing data around, as is done in a data flow diagram, objects invoke a data set's functions.

Inheritance

Inheritance is a great way to categorize an entity. When you invoke inheritance, the child objects contain all the functionality of the parent objects, plus any additions required to distinguish them from other categories. Inheritance is an extremely powerful tool in analysis as well as development. Inheritance is revisited later in this chapter.

Polymorphism

Polymorphism is when a "child object" changes the functionality of a "parent" object. For instance, in the example, the `pay_employee()` function is callable from `Employee` (the parent object), but the code that actually gets executed is either the `Salaried_Employee pay_employee()` function or the `Hourly_Employee pay_employee()` function. In this case, the child objects changed the way that an employee was paid, depending on the circumstances of the individual child object.

Understanding Object-Oriented Design

Object-oriented design takes object-oriented analysis and implements a database design as well as programming specifications needed to program a system. Implementing an OOA into a relational database design can be tricky. An alternative might be to use an object-oriented database (OODB), but using an OODB has some serious pitfalls that may make using a relational database preferable.

Using an Object-Oriented Database

Object-oriented databases (OODBs) support inheritance, arrays with tables, and container data types and are typically better suited to object-oriented development. However, there are some problems with these databases.

Because OODBs are relatively new, OODBs don't support some neat features found in established databases, a fact which will probably make them unpalatable to most client/server systems:

- Performance is usually a lot worse with OODBs when storing and retrieving character- and numeric-based data, sometimes by a factor of several hundred times slower than a comparably priced relational database.
- Features such as referential integrity and BLOBs (binary large objects, often used for storing pictures) are often lacking in OODBs.
- Database administration is difficult, and security is often nonexistent in OODBs.

- Most OODBs require you to access their data through an object-oriented language like C++. Most relational databases, on the other hand, give you utilities to access data from within most major languages, as well as independently with a database browser written expressly for the relational database.

- Finally, some relational databases are adding features that make their databases more object-oriented. Stored procedures, triggers, and rules bring functionality closer to the data and allow for a more OOD approach to development no matter which language is used for the end-user front end.

Because of OODBs' limited success so far, as well as their lack of features, OODBs right now are only usable in a stand-alone environment. For client/server development, relational databases are currently the only option. However, animals like stored procedures, triggers, and checks bring some of the object-oriented world into relational databases.

Using OOD with a Relational Database

You may be tempted to simply make all your objects developed in OOA into individual tables when trying to design your database. However, you'll soon find out that translation from an object-oriented model to a relational database model can be somewhat complicated. This is because constructs found in objects do not translate well into a relational design.

Handling Nonunique Instances of Objects

As mentioned previously in this chapter, instances of objects are not necessarily unique, although every object in the sample payroll system is. Take, for instance, a `Sale` object at a cash-and-carry card shop. A simplified object model of a sale may look like Figure 17.7.

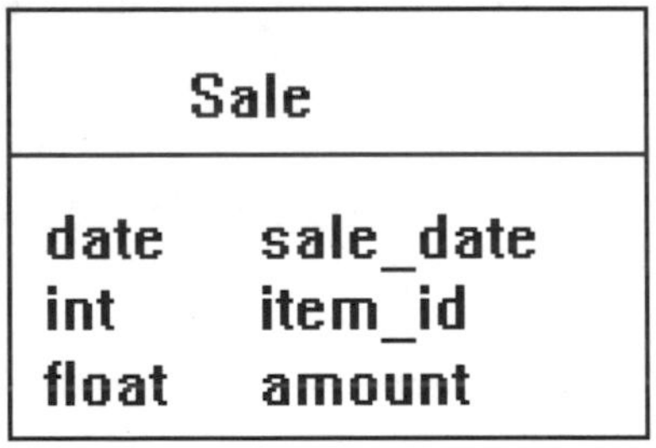

FIGURE 17.7.

Duplicate instances of objects are OK.

Sale	
date	sale_date
int	item_id
float	amount

Notice that if you sold the same item for the same amount on the same day to two different people, you would have a duplicate instance of a Sale object. This is not necessarily a bad thing! Many developers would argue that you have to be able to tell one sale from another, but if there's no business rule requiring uniqueness, don't force uniqueness into an object-oriented design.

Although having duplicate instances of an object is OK, duplicate rows in a relational database are not OK. (Duplicate rows violate first normal form, as discussed in Chapter 16.) To resolve this conflict, you need to add a sequence number or date/time stamp on the corresponding database table to force uniqueness, as shown in Figure 17.8.

FIGURE 17.8.

Date/time stamps are often a good way to resolve duplicate entries in a table.

```
┌─────────────────────────────────┐
│          sale table             │
├─────────────────────────────────┤
│  datetime    sale_date (PK)     │
│  int         item_id            │
│  float       amount             │
└─────────────────────────────────┘
```

Handling Iteration within an Object

An object can contain an array of attributes. The `phone` attribute in the `Employee` object shown in Figure 17.9 allows two phone numbers. Although multiple items for an object attribute are acceptable in object-oriented programming, iterative components violate the second normal form of database design and are hard to work with when using a relational database.

FIGURE 17.9.

Array attributes inside objects must be converted if used in a relational database.

```
┌─────────────────────────────────────┐
│       Employee [ABSTRACT]           │
├─────────────────────────────────────┤
│  int          employee_id           │
│  string       name                  │
│  string       address               │
│  string       city                  │
│  string       state                 │
│  string       zip                   │
│  string       phone(2)              │
│  string       SSN                   │
│  Job_Title    job_title_object      │
├─────────────────────────────────────┤
│  select_employee( )                 │
│  insert_employee( )                 │
│  update_employee ( )                │
│  delete_employee ( )                │
│  pay_employee ( ) [ABSTRACT]        │
└─────────────────────────────────────┘
```

You can handle this situation one of two ways. The first way is to individually list each attribute in the data model. For example, phone1 and phone2 are shown in Figure 17.10. Although this technique violates second normal form, it often is acceptable when dealing with small, fixed-length arrays.

FIGURE 17.10.

Although it may be a minor violation of second normal form, array elements can be listed individually inside a database table.

employee table	
int	employee_id (PK)
string	name
string	address
string	city
string	state
string	zip
string	**phone1**
string	**phone2**
string	SSN
Job_Title	*job_title_object*

NOTE

Violating a normal form should always set off warning flags when doing a design. However, in the case of separating phone(2) into phone1 and phone2, the efficiency and performance gains may outweigh the normalization rules. You would no longer have the overhead of two tables, and you would automatically enforce that the end user is only allowed two phone numbers per employee.

You can also separate array elements into their own table. Figure 17.11 shows a phone table that relates to the employee table. This is a good way to convert arrays, and it does not violate second normal form like listing them separately would. However, the overhead of using two joined tables may make the solution in Figure 17.11 inefficient.

FIGURE 17.11.

Using two related tables is often a good way to resolve arrays inside objects. Arrays form dependent tables.

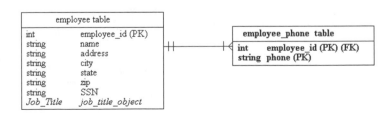

Handling Contained Objects and a Relational Database

Notice in Figures 17.10 and 17.11 that `job_title_object` is still present in the data model. However, `Job_Title` is not a valid data type and needs to be resolved. As you might have guessed, contained objects are resolved by making foreign key relationships with all joined tables. For instance, there is no longer a `Job_Title` table as well as a `Department` table. Figure 17.12 shows the new data model.

FIGURE 17.12.

Contained objects can be made into separate tables. Objects that contain other objects are made into dependent tables.

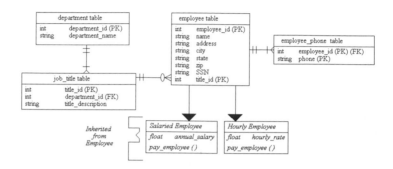

Each contained object becomes a table, and all object data types are then resolved before data modeling can continue.

Handling Inheritance and a Relational Database

Figure 17.12 shows inherited objects (`Salaried_Employee` and `Hourly_Employee`) that need to be resolved. There are two ways to handle inheritance in a relational data model. First, a method called *rolling down* makes separate tables out of each inherited object. Each table contains all the attributes of the parent table as well as the child table, as shown in Figure 17.13. As you can see by the model in Figure 17.13, all dependent tables (the `Phone` table, for example) need to be duplicated for each table.

FIGURE 17.13.

Separating inherited objects into their own tables is a viable option for relational databases, but often will be too cumbersome.

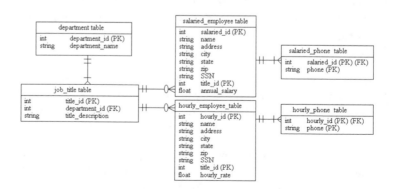

You could also make a table out of the parent object and make dependent tables out of each inherited object. This method, as shown in Figure 17.14, is called *rolling up* and is preferable to *rolling down*.

FIGURE 17.14.

Making inherited objects dependent tables of a parent object's table is often used to model inheritance.

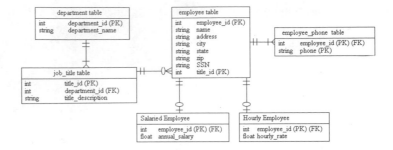

Both methods have their place. Rolling down so that inherited objects are separate, nondependent tables typically results in a more cohesive data model. However, certain functionality (such as getting lists of all employees and searching through the employee tables) is more difficult. Also, it's cumbersome to duplicate any dependent tables.

Conversely, rolling up seems more intuitive, as well as easier to manipulate, in this case, all employees at once. However, certain rules (like every employee must be either a salaried employee or an hourly employee) must be enforced outside the data model. Still, rolling up is usually the preferred method because it seems more intuitive and doesn't multiply the dependent tables like rolling down tends to do.

Object-Oriented Features of Relational Databases

It can take a lot of work to bring an object-oriented design into a relational database. However, relational databases are adding many features, like stored procedures, triggers, and checks (rules) to try to make themselves more object-oriented. No longer are client/server databases to be treated as data repositories only. Now, some functionality can also be encapsulated on the database, making many relational databases somewhat object-oriented.

Checks

Checks allow only certain values in a database. For instance, if you had added the Employee_Status column to the Employee table with valid values of A (Active), S (Sabbatical), Q (Quit), or F (Fired), you would have to make sure every developer added only valid fields to your database.

Checks (also called rules) allow you to specify valid values in a database for a given variable. For instance, using an SQL Sybase Anywhere database, you could add the following ALTER TABLE statement for your new Employee_Status column:

```
ALTER TABLE employee
MODIFY employee_status
CHECK (employee_status IN ('A', 'S', 'Q', 'F'));
```

Now, no developer or end user can put a value in `Employee_Status` that is not one of the four accepted values.

Stored Procedures

A *stored procedure* is a set of SQL with some additional commands (like `IF` and `CHOOSE CASE`) that can be called from a program (or another stored procedure) to do a set of required SQL. For instance, you can create the stored procedure call to `SELECT` all employee information with Sybase SQL or Microsoft SQL Server and this code:

```
CREATE PROCEDURE select_employee AS
SELECT name, address, city, state, ZIP
    FROM mytable
 WHERE employee_id = :employee_id;
```

You can then use the host language to execute prewritten SQL, as shown by this C++ piece of code:

```
EXEC SQL DECLARE my_cursor CURSOR FOR CALL select_employee;
...
EXEC SQL OPEN my_cursor
EXEC SQL FETCH my_cursor INTO :name, :address, :city, :state, :ZIP;
WHILE (SQLCA.SQLDBCode == 0) {
    //Code processing here
    ...
    EXEC SQL FETCH my_cursor INTO :name, :address, :city, :state, :ZIP;
}
...
EXEC SQL CLOSE my_cursor;
```

> **NOTE**
>
> You may wonder why you would use a procedure instead of an embedded SQL `SELECT` statement here. Often, stored procedures are more efficient than embedded SQL because stored procedures are precompiled before they are placed in the database. Therefore, the database needs to do less work when processing a stored procedure than it would when processing SQL. In other words, most databases actually *encourage* you to encapsulate your SQL with your database, or you'll pay the price in performance.

Stored procedures are an example of true functionality being tied to the database. Rather than just using a database to store data, now you can use a database to store data as well as procedures that act on that data. Coupling data with functionality is the entire basis for object-oriented development.

Triggers

Triggers are stored procedures that are often used when rules cannot be used. Often, business rules are stored as triggers to prevent developers from violating business rules. For instance, say the Human Resources department (the end user for your Employee system) insists that you cannot delete an active or sabbatical employee. If an employee is to be deleted, the employee must either quit or be fired.

Using the `Employee_Status` column defined earlier (again with the Sybase SQL Anywhere database), you could define the following trigger:

```
CREATE TRIGGER check_employee_status
        BEFORE DELETE ON employee
        WHEN (employee_status IN ('A', 'S'))
     FOR EACH ROW
   BEGIN
        DECLARE delete_not_allowed EXCEPTION FOR SQLSTATE '53W06';
        MESSAGE 'You cannot delete an employee who is Active or on Sabbatical';
        SIGNAL delete_not_allowed;
END
```

Now, an error will be signaled whenever anyone tries to delete an active or sabbatical employee. Triggers are very handy because they ensure data integrity no matter what the developer tries to do.

Developing with Object-Oriented Programming

Now that you have your design, you are ready to start programming. I've separated programming out into two categories, graphical and nongraphical, because many graphical languages, like Delphi, Visual Basic, and PowerBuilder, often have somewhat object-oriented constructs that tie a database with general functionality (create, insert, update, and retrieve). These constructs not only should change the way you code using a graphical language, but they also make your life a little bit easier when developing a system.

Using the Database During Development

You can often use a database to make your life a little easier before or during the development process. Before beginning development, I created a view using the following SQL:

```
CREATE VIEW v_all_employees (    employee_id,
                 name,
                 address,
                 city,
                 state,
                 ZIP,
                 ssn,
                 job_title_id,
```

```
                      employee_status,
                      pay_rate
)
   AS
   SELECT      emp.employee_id,
        emp.name,
        emp.address,
        emp.city,
        emp.state,
        emp.ZIP,
        emp.ssn,
        emp.job_title_id,
        emp.employee_status,
        salary.annual_salary
     FROM      employee emp,
        salaried_employee salary
    WHERE      salary.employee_id = emp.employee_id
   UNION
   SELECT      emp.employee_id,
        emp.name,
        emp.address,
        emp.city,
        emp.state,
        emp.ZIP,
        emp.ssn,
        emp.job_title_id,
        emp.employee_status,
        hourly.hourly_rate
     FROM      employee emp,
        hourly_employee hourly
    WHERE      hourly.employee_id = emp.employee_id;
```

You can now use this view to display information on all employees, whether they are salaried or not.

OOP with Nongraphical Languages (C++)

The first thing you should notice when developing with an object-oriented language and a relational database is that your data model doesn't match your object model. To get around this problem, you'll need to create *another* object that can take your class data and convert it for use in your database.

First, you'll need a set of objects to talk to your database. Here is a small sample of the C++ code you'll need in your new object:

```
EXEC SQL INCLUDE SQLCA;
class employee_database {
    EXEC SQL BEGIN DECLARE SECTION;
        short int employee_id;
        char name[31];
        char address[31];
        char city[16];
        char state[3];
        char ZIP[11];
        char ssn[12];
```

```
        char employee_status;
        char phone1[15];
        char phone2[15];
        short int department_id;
        char department_name[51];
        short int title_id;
        char title_description[51];
        float pay_rate;
    EXEC SQL END DECLARE SECTION;

    void get_info_from_database( int emp_id){
        employee_id = emp_id;
        select_employee( );
        select_phones ( );
        select_title( );
        select_department( );
    };
    void select_employee( ) {
        EXEC SQL SELECT     name,
                address,
                city,
                state,
                ZIP,
                ssn,
                title_id,
                pay_rate
            INTO     :name,
                :address,
                :city,
                :state,
                :ZIP,
                :ssn,
                :title_id,
                :employee_status,
                :pay_rate
            FROM     all_employees
            WHERE     employee_id = emp.employee_id;
        check_for_SQL_error();
    };
    void select_phones( ){
        EXEC SQL SELECT MIN(phone)
            INTO :phone1
        WHERE employee_id = :employee_id;
        check_for_SQL_error();
        EXEC SQL SELECT MIN(phone)
            INTO :phone2
        WHERE employee_id = :employee_id
            and phone <> :phone1;
        check_for_SQL_error();
    };
    void select_title( ){
        EXEC SQL SELECT     department_id,
            title_discription
            FROM    job_title
        WHERE     title_id = :title_id;
        check_for_SQL_error();
    };
    void select_department( ) {
```

```
        EXEC SQL SELECT     department_name,
            FROM    department
        WHERE     department_id = :department_id;
        check_for_SQL_error();
    };
    void check_for_SQL_error() {
        if (SQLCA.SQLDBCode != 0) {
            issue_sql_error(SQLCA.SQLErrText);     //Function for SQL errors
        }
    };
};
```

The preceding code only handles selected information from the database. (Adding UPDATE, INSERT, and DELETE functions would have taken several more pages.) The retrieval from the object then has to be written to assign the variables from this class to the variables in the Employee abstract class. As you can see, using object-oriented methods with relational databases incurs some overhead.

OOP with Graphical Languages (PowerBuilder)

Graphical development environments have taken some of the tedium away from writing thousands of lines of code. PowerBuilder contains a DataWindow that already encapsulates an interface to a database with functionality needed to add, change, delete, and retrieve information. After building my database, I went into PowerBuilder to develop my DataWindow. After a couple of mouse clicks, PowerBuilder asks you which tables you want to use, as shown in Figure 17.15.

FIGURE 17.15.

PowerBuilder lists the available tables in your database for you and lets you choose which tables you want to use.

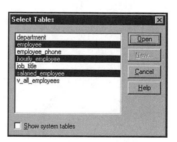

Because I wanted to SELECT, UPDATE, INSERT, and DELETE from the Employee, Salaried_Employee, and Hourly_Employee tables, I selected those as my data source. Then PowerBuilder lets me select which columns I want to select. It even lets me specify the WHERE criteria or SQL computed columns, all the while displaying the SQL being built, as shown in Figure 17.16.

After I click an icon, PowerBuilder builds my DataWindow, as shown in Figure 17.17. This process is a whole lot faster than building windows from text-based function calls. PowerBuilder also lets you select which tables and columns to UPDATE when an update function is invoked, as shown in Figure 17.18.

FIGURE 17.16.

Now you can graphically build the SQL needed to select rows from your database.

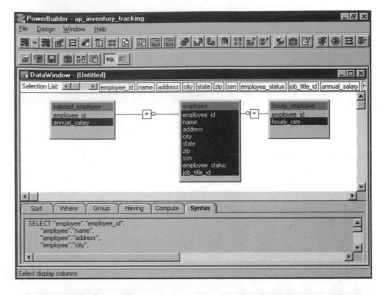

FIGURE 17.17.

PowerBuilder can quickly build DataWindows that you can use as reports or data-entry windows.

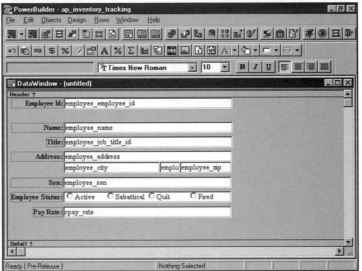

Finally, PowerBuilder is object-oriented itself. You could not only implement your OOA design, but also implement class libraries or prototypes that allow you to control standards and make programming easier. For instance, by inheriting your DataWindow, you only need to code error handling routines once. The rest is inherited into descendent DataWindows.

FIGURE 17.18.

*PowerBuilder gives you fine
control over what gets
updated in a
DataWindow.*

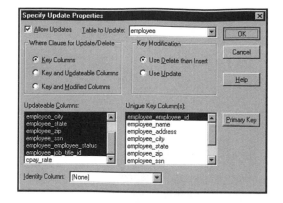

The Future of Object-Oriented Development

Object-oriented programming is not just a way of grouping your functions. Object-oriented development not only makes development easier to create and maintain, but it also makes any new development less prone to bugs. Two trends in the current development market will make OOD much more common:

■ Databases are getting more object-oriented. Right now, most relational databases support triggers, checks, and stored procedures. In the future, perhaps inheritance will also be supported.

■ Development environments are quickly becoming object-oriented. PowerBuilder has surpassed Visual Basic in new development at the corporate level. Delphi is making huge inroads in the personal development market. There are plans (or possibly rumors) to make object versions of BASIC and even COBOL. Operating systems soon will be optimized for object-oriented development.

Current developers will have to rethink the way they program. New developers won't know any other way. Systems will not only be easier to develop and maintain, but programming languages will become easier to learn. (Of course, this may spell disaster for client/server salaries in the future, but time will tell.)

Summary

Object-oriented development and client/server development can work quite well together if you understand the theories underneath each technology. New tools that integrate data with functionality are becoming common. Relatively new languages, like Delphi, PowerBuilder, C++, and Java are all object-oriented and have gained immediate, wide acceptance by developers everywhere.

This chapter covered how to integrate object-oriented languages into a cohesive relational data model. Be sure to check out Chapter 16, "Database Design." Remember that object-oriented design supplements rather than replaces database design and normalization.

Application Development

18

*by Ellen
Gottesdiener*

Portions of this chapter are derived from the course "Client/Server Analysis & Design," ©
EBG Consulting, Inc., 1996.

This chapter examines client/server application development. Business events are the driving force for defining and detailing client/server applications. By using multiple application models, iterative prototyping, application usage information, and knowledge of the technical infrastructure, an effective and efficient application can be designed and developed.

Client/server application development should combine the best attributes of the client with the best attributes of the server. The client-based interface should be easy to use, increase end-user productivity, and facilitate efficient end-user workflow. The server should enforce data integrity and security, promote business rule reuse, and exploit the technical infrastructure. Access to the server from the client should be transparent to the end user. Underlying all of these is the fact that analysis and design activities are needed more than ever, encompassing a clean data design but using a new model—one that is iterative, event-driven, and job-/role-oriented. The result should be an application architecture that conforms to project and technical constraints while achieving business goals.

Framework for Application Development

One of the benefits of client/server systems is their capability to mirror how the business responds to real-world events; therefore, business events are used to define and detail the client/server application. These events, along with the definition of the context in which the application will reside, are the basis for the application models. Business events trigger a series of processes that affect data collected about the business and change the states of that data. These ingredients—process, data, and states—are tightly interwoven within the application and thus make up the key components of an effective application model.

For thousands of years, humans have used models to represent concepts. In the world of information systems, models are best expressed by using both visual representations and text. Visual models convey concepts quickly, while text models convey the same concepts with accuracy. Modeling permits both information systems and end-users the opportunity to define requirements. The process, data, and state models serve as a focal point for iteratively discovering details about the application and transforming those details into application software.

Each singular model, or view, is designed to validate the other possible views, thereby populating the details of the application. Details from each model are added to an event table. The event table is a model that contains information on what events are within the scope of the application (domain) and how the application should handle those events. It is built concurrently with the application models and prototypes. The event table is thus a repository for details about the application's behavior, data, and usage.

Interface prototypes, application code, and data structures are built from the models. Usage characteristics for each model are needed to design an appropriate application and technical architecture. Module, integration, and performance tests can be used to prove the viability of the application (see Figure 18.1).

FIGURE 18.1.

Framework for client/server application development. (Source: EBG Consulting, Inc.)

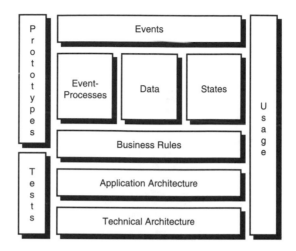

Events

The guiding principles for a client/server application are the real-world events to which the end user must respond. The term "event-driven" is greatly overused and misunderstood. Events have two different contexts. The first context is a *business event*, such as a customer calling to check the status of an order. The second context is a *GUI (graphical user interface) event*, that is, an action that "drives" the application like a mouse click or a menu selection. Application development starts with determining the business events within the application domain. Through the iterative process of modeling and prototyping, GUI events emerge naturally. Business events are therefore transformed into GUI events when they are brought to their most granular form.

The process of modeling events involves creating a list of events and an accompanying context diagram, which show the events to which the system must respond. The other application models (process, data, and state) are built based on satisfying *responses* to the events. In this way, events are used to control project scope. The events that must be defined are *business events* and *temporal events*. Both business and temporal events cause processes to be triggered within the application (see Figure 18.2).

FIGURE 18.2.

Events trigger activities within the application.

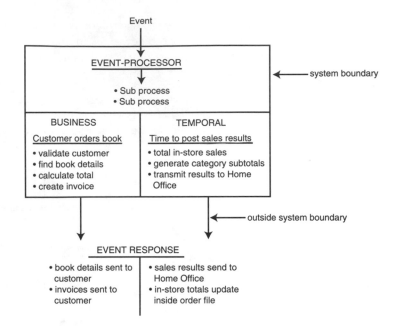

Business Events

Business events are things of importance to the business that happen *outside* of the context of the system and require a response by the system. These business events are also called *external* events. They serve as triggers, or messages, which cross the application boundary and provide the stimulus for generating actions inside the application (refer to Figure 18.2). The system must create one or more planned responses each event. Business events happen continually, and the timing and frequency of them is unknown. What is known is that the application must respond to them in a predictable manner.

The format for describing events is Subject + Verb + Object. For example:

- Customer requests price
- Patient wants to schedule appointment
- Supplier transmits invoice
- Claimant submits claim
- Engineer inspects pipeline
- Marketing department establishes sales targets
- IRS changes deduction amounts

There are other events that happen in the real word that *indirectly* affect the system. *Indirect events* trigger Subjects (as in the preceding format) to take action. They do not interface with the applications themselves. Because they do not directly cross the application boundary, these types of events are called *out-of-scope*. For example:

- Earthquake damages building
- Accident damages car
- Patient has a toothache

There are many things that happen *inside* the application. *Internal activities* are not events per se: they are not used to define the *application domain*. (The application domain is the environment in which the application lives.) Rather, internal activities are the processes that occur inside the system in response to a business or temporal event, such as validate customer order, update customer address, or generate invoice. These activities will be modeled by using event-processors (event-partitioned *DFDs, data flow diagrams*).

Temporal Events

Temporal events are initiated by the passage of time and are therefore predictable. These time-based events often generate reference documents for objects in the event list. They are best described in the following format: "Time to...." For example:

- Time to send 1099 (to IRS)
- Time to send out course catalogue (to students and to vendors)
- Time to post sales results (to management)

Temporal events do *not* trace back to business events but meet a business need that is time-sensitive. They do not have to result in responses to the outside environment; a temporal event like "Time to purge retired employees" will result only in data being changed within the application itself.

Application Domain

Application development is risky. It is particularly vulnerable to creeping, or gradually expanding, user requirements. Client/server adds to that risk because of the following:

- The added complexities of the technology
- The unpredictability of integrating different software and hardware elements
- The traditional aversion that IT (Information Technology) holds toward working with end users
- The general lack of skills required to work with the technology

In addition to using essential client/server techniques (which are covered in Chapter 13, "Essential Techniques"), a well-defined application scope is needed.

Event List

Application domain, or scope, is defined by using a list of business and temporal events. These events drive all requirements' definitions and design activities. Events from the *event list* are used to create the *event table*, discussed later. The event table is supplemented with a visual model called the context diagram. Together they define the application domain. The domain, or subject matter of interest, shows the scope of the business problem and/or opportunity to be addressed by the client/server application.

Context Diagram

The *context diagram* is an environmental model that depicts the scope of the system by showing the interfaces between the system and the outside world (see Figure 18.3). The single bubble on the context diagram is like a "black box." The details of what happens inside the black box are not important to this model because the process, data, and state models will represent those details.

FIGURE 18.3.

Context diagram for a bookstore special-ordering client/server application. (Source: EBG Consulting, Inc.)

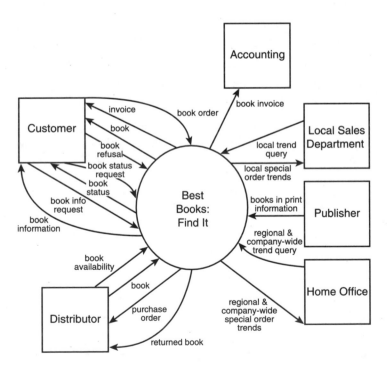

All input to and output from the application is shown. Senders and receivers of that information and/or real-world things (the boxes on the diagram) are known as *terminators*, *agents*, or *external entities*. Terminators are the people, places, other systems, or any other object in the world that communicates with the system in some way.

Information flows or products moving *to* the system indicate a business event. Those moving *away* from the system signify a response to a business event *or* a response to a temporal event. The context diagram does not depict *how* the interfaces occur, just *which* interfaces exist.

The process of discovering events and creating the context diagram should be very dynamic. Events and the context diagram can be created separately or concurrently, but they must be balanced with each other. A balanced set of models will show all business events as information flows going into the system on the context diagram. Their predictable responses are shown as information flows or real-world things (for example: forms, files, reports, letters) going out of the system. Temporal events that generate external responses will have information flows going *out of* the system on the context diagram.

Event Table

The *event table* shows all external and temporal events within the scope of the project in an easy-to-read format of columns and rows (see Table 18.1). The event table is an analysis and design tool and acts as a central location for showing all event responses within the application domain. Additional details about how each event is handled in the application are added iteratively as the team is prototyping and modeling the application (see Table 18.2). The event table provides a text-based account of how the application handles events: who, what, when, where, how quickly, and how importantly.

Table 18.1. Event Table (partial): Best Books—book store special-ordering client/server application.

Event	Event Category	System Response
Customer requests book information	External business	Book information given to customer
Customer orders book	External business	Purchase order sent to distributor Customer receives invoice Book invoice sent to accounting

continues

Table 18.1. continued

Event	Event Category	System Response
Customer asks for book status	External business	Customer receives status information
Customer refuses book	External business	Book returned to distributor
Sales manager queries local (special-order) buying trends	External business	Manager receives trend information
Home office queries (special-order) buying trends (regional and company-wide)	External business	Home Office manager receives trend information
Time to update books in print	Temporal	N/A
Time to update distributor availability	Temporal	N/A

Table 18.2. Columns used in the event table.

Column	Discovery Phase
Event name	Scope/project domain definition
Event category	Scope/project domain definition
System response	Scope/project domain definition
Event-processor	Process modeling
Roles/Users	Process modeling
Location of Roles/Users	Process modeling
Frequency baseline	Process modeling
Frequency of usage	Process modeling
Event-processor dependencies	Process modeling
Response time requirements	Process modeling
Business priority	Process modeling
Data entities and CRUD*	Data modeling
Data entity freshness	Data modeling

*CRUD is an acronym for Create, Read, Update, and Delete, the essential actions performed on data.

NOTE

Details such as data entity start-up volume and growth are stored with the data model.

Document of Definition

Application scope is one essential part of a mutual agreement between IT and the business. Changes to scope are inevitable, so each project needs to have a predefined mechanism for handling such occurrences. Additionally, a clear definition of goals and roles must be understood by all team members. This information is best captured in the *Document of Definition* (also called Project Initiation or Project Charter). It acts as a contractual agreement between all project players. It should comprehensively address application development infrastructure needs and project goals. It is a powerful tool to manage the project. Table 18.3 is a list of potential elements to include in a Document of Definition.

Table 18.3. Application Document of Definition contents.

Project Definition Element	*Purpose*
Business Purpose	Description of the business reason for the project; reference should be made to the current situation, desired situation, obstacles in achieving the desired situation, and the changes desired.
Business Objectives	Discrete, measurable goals that will result in reducing operating costs, increased profits, better customer service, more competitive positioning, and/or satisfying regulatory requirements.
System Objectives	Discrete, measurable goals that IT must achieve in order to facilitate satisfying the business objectives; these are SMART: Specific, Measurable, Attainable, Realistic, and Time-based.
Critical Success Factors	Elements in the business and project environment that must be in place for the project to succeed.
Project Constraints	Order of priority for time, cost, and scope. The order of these competing priorities will determine the most appropriate methodology to use and how the project should be managed.

continues

Table 18.3. continued

Project Definition Element	Purpose
Locations	Physical place where an activity or activities of interest to the business scope is performed and/or where hardware for the application will be located; includes locations of end users who access the application.
Data Entities in Scope	Major subject areas of interest to the project scope, roughly equivalent to Subject and Object components from the Event List.
Event List/Event Table	Complete list of all the business and temporal events within the application domain.
Context Diagram	Environmental model showing the interfaces and information/products the application gets and gives.
Business Rules	English-like description of business rules within scope (to be maintained by the system); details of these rules should be defined during prototyping and modeling data, states, and processes.
Preliminary Technical Architecture	Details of the operating system, hardware, and software elements to be used on the client, server, and network components of the application; defined for all locations where the application will be deployed.
Project Infrastructure	Activities that support the project and promote effective utilization of resources: people, software, and hardware (see Table 18.4).

Table 18.4. Client/server project infrastructure.

Infrastructure Activity	Definition
Security	Defines allowable access to interfaces, data files, and execution of procedures; for example, which end users are granted authorization to read, update, add, and/or delete certain tables; defines who must approve security access and who implements it.

Infrastructure Activity	*Definition*
Programming Standards	Module, data name, variable, table, object, window naming standards.
Reuse Standards	Defines which application components are the focal point for reuse (for example, high-level and common windows such as printer selection, pick-lists, and output viewing windows); if stored procedures and/or triggers are to be used, which functions will be done using this DBMS feature; outlines methods for promoting and rewarding reuse.
Repository Standards	Where and how products created in analysis, design, and iterative prototyping are kept up to date, shared, and protected; (the repository is often a combination of a CASE or drawing tool along with word processing, presentation, and spreadsheet files); describes how (if) the repository will be kept updated after deployment; addresses how repository contents will be useful to the rest of the enterprise.
GUI Standards	Defines a corporate-wide and consistent "look and feel" for the graphical user interface; defines GUI guidelines.
Network Tuning	Defines how network performance will be tested, monitored, and tuned; outlines network support resources needed.
Training	Defines what education and skills end users, applications developers, designers, IT management, and business management need.
Conversion/Migration Plan	Defines what interfaces to existing applications exist, how those interfaces will be managed, and how any data conversion will be performed.

continues

Table 18.4. continued

Infrastructure Activity	Definition
Testing	Defines how and when the application will be tested; provides a plan for defining test scenarios, scripts, and criterion; details goals for user-interface testing and addresses integration, regression, performance, and acceptance testing; defines the platforms and files needed, who will conduct the tests, criterion for accepting test results, test tracking procedures, and end-user roles in testing.
Change Control/Configuration Management	Defines how changes will be handled; (for example, change to any application artifact such as requirements models, software modules, data tables, and nodes); details the migration strategy for moving software components to different levels (for example, test to acceptance to production); defines the software and hardware platforms needed for configuration management; defines change control and monitoring mechanisms (such as a change control board).
Database Administration and Tuning	Who, when, and how of physical database design, installation, and tuning.
Help Desk/Support	Defines what problem and technical support will be provided to both application developers and end users; determines source and resources for that support, such as availability, constraints for usage, costs, access, and location of the support.

Multiple Application Models

A synthesis of three application models is appropriate to manage the complexity of client/server applications. These models, or views, are *orthogonal* (at right angles) to each other and are built in an iterative fashion. They are the event-processor, data, and state models.

As orthogonal views of the application, each provides an independent axis of understanding (see Table 18.5). Yet, when combined together, they provide a complete picture of the application. Each view responds to a well-defined set of events and is constrained by *rules*, guidelines or protocols that govern the process, data, or state (see Figure 18.4).

Table 18.5. Orthogonal views of the client/server application.

Axis of Emphasis	Visual Model
Process/Function/Action	Event-Processors or Data Flow Diagram (DFD)
Data/Information	Entity Relationship Diagram (ERD)
Dynamics/Behavior/Time-Sensitive	State Transition Diagram (STD)

FIGURE 18.4.

Multiple application views handle events and are governed by rules. (Source: EBG Consulting, Inc.)

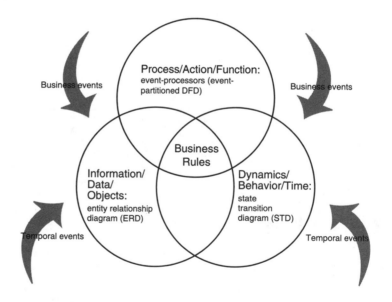

The *data-oriented view* defines what data will be stored in the database and the constraints that apply to the data. The *process-oriented view* defines the actions performed by the system (human and automated) in transforming the data to accomplish the action. The *dynamic-oriented view* shows how the system undergoes change over time by describing the states that data experiences and the conditions that give rise to the transition from one state to the next. Each view is needed for a comprehensive understanding of the application.

Because all models are defined by the same business events, their order of creation is not important. In fact, they can be developed concurrently. By doing so, the models can be used to validate each other (see Figure 18.5), giving the project team the flexibility of not having to determine all the in-scope events at the very start of the development effort. Although an initial list of business events, along with the context diagram, is generated early in the project, new events are likely to be discovered. The team will then add these events to the event list and context diagram. The data, process, and behavior needed to support those events are also modeled.

FIGURE 18.5.

Application models validate each other. (Source: EBG Consulting, Inc.)

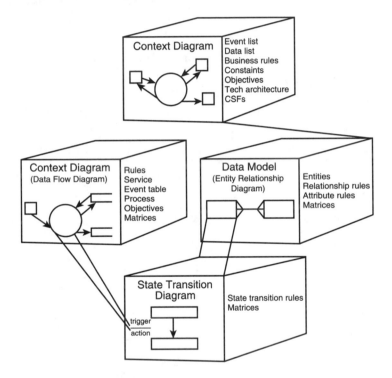

Business Rules

Business rules are constraints, tests, or conditions that describe business policy. They can be expressed in nontechnical natural language (such as English), which means that nontechnical business subject matter experts can specify them. As statements of business policy, they are universally enforced by the business regardless of the technology applied to them.

Rules can be found by examining how the business experts discuss the business, within written policy and procedure documentation, and in other forms of business such as graphs, charts, and tables. Because rules are so fundamental, they span the three dimensions of analysis: information, process, and dynamics (see Figure 18.4). The following are some examples:

- An order cannot be placed unless credit has been approved.
- Every customer must have approved credit.
- Orders must have an order-taken date.
- Orders for less than $100 cannot be changed.
- Books on reserve cannot be renewed.
- Salespeople under age 21 cannot cash out alcoholic beverages.
- Each video returned after the due date is charged 99 cents a day.
- People cannot be added as new customers unless they have a current state license.
- Bills unpaid for 32 days will be marked past-due.
- Customers with past-due bills will receive a past-due notification.
- Hardcover books on the *New York Times* best-seller list have a net price of regular retail cost less a 20 percent discount.

Each application model may represent multiple business rules. The event-processor model will have processing rules such as formulas for derived information and validation logic. The data model will have rules that include entity definition, relationship and attribute derivation, existence, and dependencies. The state model will have rules about the triggers for new states and allowable state transitions.

One rule may apply to multiple models. For example, the rule "products must be ordered from approved suppliers" implies the following:

- A data relationship rule (products are related to suppliers)
- A data type rule (suppliers can be approved)
- A processing rule (certain actions are performed to approve a supplier)

Eventually, rules will become application code. Those rules that enforce referential integrity (maintaining relationships between entities) may take the form of code (such as database triggers) or may be handled by the DBMS (for example, declarative referential integrity). In any case, all rules should be captured and documented along with the model to which they apply.

Event-Processor Model

An *event-processor* is a subset of activity that happens in response to a real-world event. It is depicted by using the symbols and notation rules of the DFD, or data flow diagram. Each event-processor depicts what happens inside the application in response to an external or a temporal event (for example, "customer places order" or "time to restock inventory"). Looking "inside" the context diagram, there are sets of event-processors responding to all the business and temporal events in the scope of the system. The context diagram is in this sense the highest level of processing abstraction (see Figure 18.6).

FIGURE 18.6.

Looking "inside" the context diagram at event-processors. (Source: EBG Consulting, Inc.)

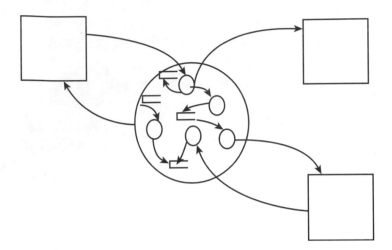

Event-processors show the flow of data throughout the system and how it is transformed en route. Every business and temporal event defines one event-processor. In this way, event-processors are naturally partitioned by event. Each event-processor should be complete in and of itself, containing all the transformations needed to respond to that event. It may also contain one or more "bubbles" to handle a single business or temporal event (see Figure 18.7).

The visual DFD model is supplemented by a text-based description of the process rules. Both visual and text models should be stored in the project repository. (The repository is like an encyclopedia for all project information: visual and text models, plans, and all documents of definition.) Process rules explicitly define how the event-processor should be carried out. These rules include constraints ("only an approved policy has policy pages issued") and computation rules ("net price is equal to regular retail price less standard hardcover discount"). These specifications will be physically implemented as code and data access routines.

Event-Processor Dependencies

Event-processors depend upon each other for data. Dependencies between event-processors should be modeled. Chaining event-processors into sets provides the logical sequencing for the physical design, construction, and testing of the application. These sets can be used to generate lists of possible scenarios for testing the application. (*Scenarios* are descriptions of possible ways to interact with the system based on business events.) For example:

- Customer asks to add the special order cost to books she is buying now
- Customer adds another copy of the book to special order
- Customer wants a copy of the invoice before the book is received

Chaining event-processors also helps determine what post-deployment backup and recovery procedures should be created.

FIGURE 18.7.

One event-processor for each business and temporal event. (Source: EBG Consulting, Inc.)

Business Event: Student requests course prerequisite info

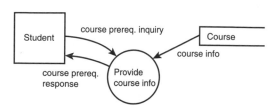

Temporal Event: Time to produce overdue notices

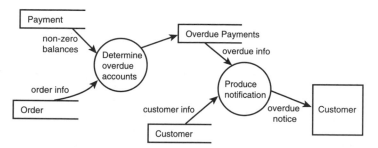

Validating Event-Processors

Event-processor models should be validated for completeness. Validation contributes to better quality: the processes do what is required by the business, use correct business rules, and all the data needed for input and output data is defined. Because there is a direct link between events (in the event table) and event-processors, these models can cross-check, or validate, each other.

Completeness checking should be done by using *matrices*. A *matrix* is an intersection diagram used to cross-check models and/or components of models. A check mark, x, or some form of documentation inside a cell of the matrix indicates that an interrelationship exists between the x and y axis. Validating event-processor models involves creating matrices of event-processors against events from the event list, roles, and locations (see Table 18.6).

Table 18.6. Sample matrices for validating event-processors.

Event-Processor : Role (partial)

Research Book Details

Event-Processor / Role	Order Book	Find Buying Trend	Handle Status Query	Update Books in Print	Update Distributor Availability
Help Desk Technician	X		X		
Special Order Technician	X		X	X	
Sales Clerk	X		X		
Sales Manager	X	X	X	X	X
Home Office Buyer		X			X

Event-Processor : Business Event (partial)

Research Book Details

Event-Processor / Role	Order Book	Find Buying Trend	Handle Status Query	Update Books in Print	Update Distributor Availability
Customer requests book information					
Customer orders book	X				
Customer asks for book status			X		
Customer refuses book					
Manager queries buying trends		X			
Time to update books in print				X	
Time to update distributor availability					X

Data Model

A *data entity*, or *object*, is a person, place, or thing about which the system must store information. The system uses this to adequately respond to business and temporal events. A data entity can be *uniquely identified* and described with one or more *facts*, or *attributes*.

Data entities within the application domain are modeled by using an *Entity-Relationship Diagram (ERD)*, which shows the entities and their business relationships with one another (see Figure 18.8). Details such as attributes and attribute rules must be defined and stored in the project repository. The data model also should be *normalized*, a data model refinement process that optimizes the data structures by removing redundancies and inconsistencies. During application implementation, some data structures may need to be *denormalized* because normalized data structures can affect response time, particularly if the application has many complex queries.

FIGURE 18.8.
Data Model (ERD - Entity Relationship Diagram). (Source: EBG Consulting, Inc.)

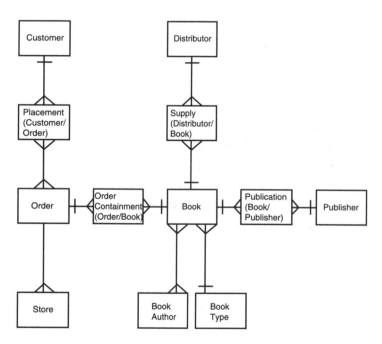

Data analysis, using the ERD as a discovery tool, provides the team with a global view of the system memory, or persistent data, used by the event-processors. The ERD depicts the *logical*, or *conceptual*, structure of the data rather than the physical structures. The entities of the ERD are converted into physical schema in order to implement data files for the application's DBMS of choice.

With client/server applications, prototyping should be used to populate and validate the data model. Many details about data will be discovered as end users see the proposed interface screens. Data modeling itself is an iterative process, where candidate attributes may be added while entities are defined. Relationship existence criteria (for example, an Order entity must have one and only one Customer) may be determined along with relationships and cardinality (number of expected records occurring for each entity in a relationship). The ERD can be defined concurrent with the event-processor model.

Data rules should be added to the repository. These rules include a business definition for each entity. Rules defining relationships between entities are also specified and will translate in *referential integrity* constraints, insuring that valid linkages are maintained in the database. (This is accomplished by guaranteeing that when a business rule relating two entities is present, there will be a data attribute, called a *foreign key*, which is a unique data attribute, called a *primary key*, in the related entity.) Attribute rules are also used to determine the following:

- Whether the attribute is required
- If the entity depends on the attribute to exist
- Any domain values for the attribute
- Derivation rules, like calculations
- Any dependencies that exist between attributes

Validating the Data Model

As with event-processors, the data model is synchronized with the other application models. Business and temporal events require both event-processors and data. Event-processors require data, and vice versa. That is, each should use one or more data entities in some way. Data instances (rows or records) are

- **C**reated (born, or inserted, same as SQL INSERT command)
- **R**ead (accessed, same as SQL SELECT command)
- **U**pdated (attribute values are changed, same as SQL UPDATE command)
- **D**eleted (die, or are removed from the file, same as SQL DELETE command)

These actions result in the acronym CRUD. CRUD matrices are used to validate data entities (see Table 18.7). These matrices include: Data Entity: Business Event; Data Entity: Event-Processor; and Data Attribute: Event-Processor.

Table 18.7. Sample data model validation matrices.

Data Entity: Business Event Matrix (partial)

Event \ Data Entity	Customer	Store	Order	Book	Publisher	Distributor
Customer requests book information				X	X	X
Customer orders book	X	X	X	X	X	
Customer asks for book status			X			X
Customer refuses book	X		X	X		
Store Manager queries buying trend		X	X	X	X	X
Time to update books in print				X	X	X

Data Entity : Event-Processor CRUD Matrix (partial)

Event \ Data Entity	Customer	Store	Order	Book	Publisher	Distributor
Research book				R	R	R
Order book	C,R,U	R,U	C,R,U	R	R	R
Find buying trend		R	R	R	R	R
Handle status query	R	R	R	R	R	
Return refused book	R,U	R,U	R,U,D			
Update books in print				C,R,U,D	C,R,U	C,R,U
Time to update distributor availability			R	R	R	C,R,U

State Model

Over time, data entities change. These changes are observed as orderly patterns of behavior, which together describe the life cycle of an entity. Each stage of the life cycle puts the entity in a *state,* a period of time during which an entity exhibits some observable behavior or characteristics. For example, states for a Book Order entity might be

- Open
- Filled
- Received
- Paid
- Archived
- Returned

The *state transition diagram,* abbreviated STD (or eSTD, for entity STD) is a model of the time-dependent behavior of entities. Each basic entity (one that existed before, as well as after, data normalization) will have an STD created. The STD depicts the finite number of states in the application scope for that entity and the sequence of the allowable state changes. The STD also defines the conditions, or triggers, that cause state changes (see Figure 18.9), that may be abrupt.

FIGURE 18.9.

State transition diagram. (Source: EBG Consulting, Inc.)

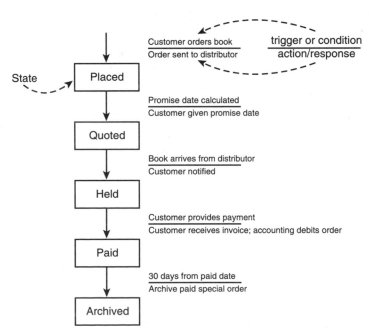

Triggers are business events, temporal events, or the completion of an event-processor within the application itself. One or more responses to a trigger correspond to the individual bubbles (elementary processes) making up an event-processor. For example, when a customer requests a book (trigger), the application must execute the event-processors "add new order," "check stock," and "obtain billing information."

Capturing the time-oriented changes of the client/server application is an excellent way to assure that all the attributes have been defined (such as those needed to define each state) and to validate that all the necessary event-processors will be developed.

Rules about states must also be defined. These rules include a definition of each entity state (what attributes values and relationships are present indicating a particular state), what the trigger is that stimulates a state change, state transition sequences that are allowed, and what the response (processing) to the detection of a trigger will be. The repository should contain the values, or domain rules, for any attributes associated with an entity state. For example, an attribute such as *status* may define the allowable domain values for an Order entity (for example, open, filled, received, paid, canceled, and archived).

State Model Validation

Matrices are used to validate the state model. An Entity State: Event-Processor matrix validates that all of the states have event-processors (or elementary processes within an event-processor) to support the transition to that state. It also validates that each event-processor is used in at least one state of at least one entity in the system's scope. An Entity Attribute: Event-Processor validates that each attribute is used in at least one entity state.

Application Usage Information

Specific characteristics of how the application will be used must be known in order for the project team to determine which architecture, or combination of architectures, is the most efficient. These characteristics include: number of end users, locations of end users, event locations, business priority of the event-processors, frequency of each event, response time required for the process, data required to process each event, data currency (how up-to-date the data must be), volume of transactions and/or queries, amount of concurrent access to the same data, and type of data access required by location.

This usage information is gathered as the application models are built and is also added as columns to the event table (see Table 18.8). This is necessary to analyze design scenarios for the application.

Table 18.8. Usage information.

Usage Information	Application Development Discovery Activity
Locations	Project Domain Definition (Scope) Document
Roles	Project Domain Definition (Scope) Document
Event Location (physical or geographic location that triggers an event)	Event-Processor Model
Business Priority	Event-Processor Model
Response Time (how soon after execution must the output be received)	Event-Processor Model
Volatility (frequency of change)	Event-Processor Model, Data Model
Volume and Growth (initial number of instances and physical sizing information derived from the creation/insertion and deletion/removal of entity instances; defined for all locations)	Data Model
Data Sharing (locations requiring the same data entities—rows and columns—and type of access required: C, R, U, and/or D)	Data Model
Retention	Data Model
Currency (how fresh the data must be and still satisfy the business need—lag time tolerance between propagating updates)	Data Model

Usage information is needed to bridge from the logical to the physical design of the application. Technical choices are made based on the physical requirements of the application. For example, if there is a tolerance for older data (and response time delays), data distribution options like replication and fragmentation are possible. Non-instantaneous response time permits using less network bandwidth and more flexible data synchronization schemes. On the other hand, if many high priority event-processors are required at all locations, or if the processing is highly volatile, technical options like stored procedures or *TP* (*transaction processing*) monitors should be considered. The distribution of data is an important consideration, as well. For example, data used only by a given location should be partitioned only to that location. Highly volatile data might be centralized, as opposed to distributed. This usage information, in conjunction with the models to which it applies, is needed to determine the best application design.

Application Design Challenges

In the end, client/server application development involves the careful management of trade-offs. These trade-offs deal with balancing the application's performance requirements with the end users' need for security, integrity, and maintainability (see Figure 18.10). It is necessary to understand the capabilities of the technologies that are planned or in place. For example, if the application requires high levels of data currency at all sites, response time may suffer. When transaction processing speed is critical, allowing data to be a little old (for example, hours, ½ day, day) may be needed. Application design requires balancing the needs of the end user, the project and technical architectural constraints, and the characteristics of the problem at hand. These are complex issues leading to challenging "techno-business" decisions that should be made together by IT and business.

FIGURE 18.10.

Design challenges. (Source: EBG Consulting, Inc.)

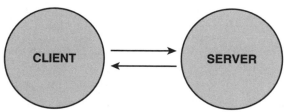

- minimize network traffic
- maintain data integrity
- enforce security
- exploit existing hardware
- push location-specific logic to that user and location
- promote reuse
- provide maintainable design architecture
- provide usable interface design
- stay within limits of technical constraints

Data Distribution

In distributing data in a client/server application, it is desirable to do the following:

- Place the data closest to the end user
- Make data available in multiple locations

■ Eliminate a single point of failure
■ Permit efficient data access
■ Balance network traffic
■ Meet data currency needs

There are several ways to distribute, or partition, data across clients and servers (or even servers and servers). Data can be distributed by using a variety of techniques: manual extract, snapshot, summarization, replication (or mirroring), fragmentation, or two-phase commit (see Table 18.9). In addition, nonrelational legacy data can be accessed from remote locations using a database gateway. The database gateway translates SQL generated at the client workstation into the access method of the legacy files, such as VSAM and QSAM. If actual data distribution is used, knowledge about how the application is to be used (refer to Table 18.8) and of the technical architecture is needed to determine which data distribution technique is optimal.

Table 18.9. Data distribution techniques.

Data Distribution Technique	Description
Manual Extract	Data is logically centralized and copied from a central location to multiple locations via an extract process; the central site may initiate the extract, which loads the remote tables, or the sites may issue the extract request.
Snapshot	The distributed database management system is capable of issuing extracts of predefined data (tables and the necessary columns) at a predefined time or frequency.
Summarization	Different levels of summarized data are stored at different locations; "rollups" or consolidations of the data will vary according to site needs.
Replication/Mirroring	Multiple sites have copies of the same data tables and are periodically updated by a central site coordinator. Data is kept consistent via a synchronous process (all sites have the same data at all times) or an asynchronous process (data is not exactly the same for a period of time, such as minutes, hours, or days).
Fragmentation	Portions of nonoverlapping data are stored at different locations and periodically refreshed via snapshots; data can be fragmented vertically (rows) or horizontally (columns).

Data Distribution Technique	Description
Two-Phase Commit	A highly synchronous protocol which assures that data is consistent at all locations at all times; a database change is committed or aborted at all sites; the process uses a commit coordinator site to 1) check all locations for availability to accept the transaction (prepare) and 2) issue the COMMIT command, which will be ROLLBACKed if any site did not respond affirmatively (commit).

Client/Server Architecture

An *architecture* is a set of definitions and protocols for building a product. A *computer architecture*, like that of a building, is a broad plan for the overall shape of the system. A *client/server architecture* encompasses both the technical and the application architecture, defined next.

Technical Architecture

The *technical architecture* is the infrastructure upon which the application is built. It is a detailed inventory of all the hardware, software, and network elements that reside on the client and server components for all locations in the application (see Chapter 13, Figure 13.6). This inventory includes such elements as

- Operating systems
- DBMSs
- Memory
- Network schemas
- Database schema (physical layout of the databases including Data Definition Languages)
- Space allocations
- Index definitions
- Security and locking
- Program packaging
- Network protocols

- Physical hardware devices (workstations, servers, wiring, bridges, routers)
- Network operating systems
- Network monitoring and tuning software
- Gateways and connectivity software (APIs, ODBC, messaging, ORBs, RPCs, and so on)
- Application development tools
- TP monitors
- Security software
- Configuration management software

Because of the unpredictability associated with mixing a variety of application components together, the technical infrastructure can make or break a project. "Test early and often" should be the motto of all client/server project team members.

Application Architecture

Client/server technology affords the designer and end user great flexibility in how to allocate functions and data between client and server. The scope and complexity of the application architecture is determined by the number of locations, size of the databases, volume of data, and amount of concurrent data access (see Figure 18.11).

FIGURE 18.11.

Elements in application scope and complexity. (Source: EBG Consulting, Inc.)

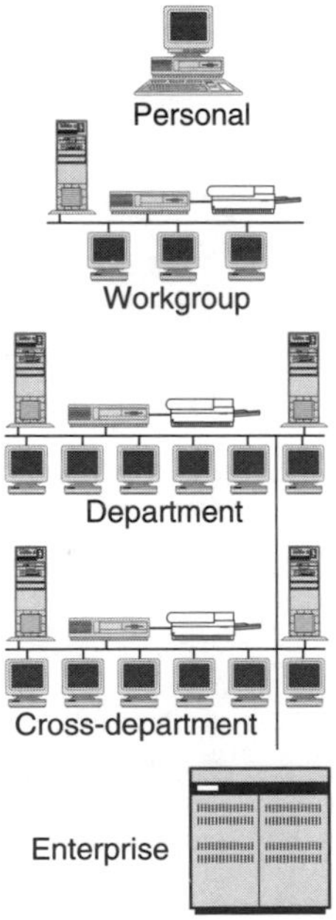

	Concurrency	Volume	Database Size	Location
Personal	none	low	low	single
Workgroup	few	low	small to medium	same building
Department	business unit	medium large	medium to large	same building
Cross-department	multiple departments	medium to large	medium to large	multiple departments, maybe multiple cities
Enterprise	high	high	large	multiple buildings, cities, continents

An application architecture specifies how application components are distributed between clients and servers. These components represent conceptual layers that are allocated (partitioned) to different physical or hardware components. Essentially, three layers need to be distributed: *presentation, business rules/logic,* and *data management* (see Figure 18.12).

FIGURE 18.12.

Application layers to be partitioned. (Source: EBG Consulting, Inc.)

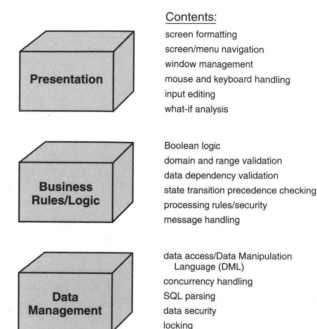

Contents:

screen formatting
screen/menu navigation
window management
mouse and keyboard handling
input editing
what-if analysis

Boolean logic
domain and range validation
data dependency validation
state transition precedence checking
processing rules/security
message handling

data access/Data Manipulation
  Language (DML)
concurrency handling
SQL parsing
data security
locking

The *presentation* layer furnishes the user interface for the overall system. It permits end users to enter and manipulate data, analyze information, and navigate throughout the system. It may also interact with existing applications on the desktop. This layer should mask the complexity of the overall system and provide an easy-to-use interface. Validation and verification logic is often needed in this layer to edit input values and selections.

The *business rules/logic* layer processes the policies and constraints that the application is responsible for enforcing. This includes: decisions ("Can we schedule this course for next Tuesday?"; "Can this account be approved?"), policy enforcement ("Credit approval is required for orders exceeding $10,000"), and resource management decisions ("The limit of class size for workshop courses is 20 students"). These are collections of business rules ascribed to the data, state, and event-processor models.

The *data management* layer maintains consistent and secure data through the enforcement of referential integrity and data security. Transactions and queries against the database are managed in this layer and include the following:

- Accessing
- Matching
- Updating
- Inserting
- Locking
- Retrieving
- Security
- Logging
- Backup
- Recovery

Some of these tasks are performed by the DBMS.

Client/server allows you to implement these layers in a modular fashion for the appropriate physical location. This permits the flexibility to change locations if business needs or performance problems so require. The presentation, business rules, and data management layers of the applications can be partitioned in a variety of ways. Some possible application architectures have been suggested by the Gartner Group (see Figure 18.13). The Gartner model views an application in three layers: presentation, business rules and logic, and data management. Each layer, or combinations of layers, resides at client and server components. In some cases, portions of a single layer, such as business rules, may be split between multiple physical layers. For example, both the workstation and the application server machine may contain business rules.

FIGURE 18.13.

Client/server design architectures. (Based on work by the Gartner Group.)

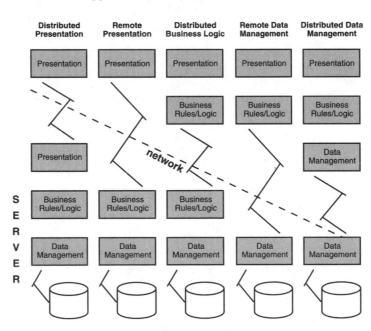

Tiers

Tiers are the physical platforms on which client and server application layers reside. A first generation of client/server applications utilizes two collaborating computing platforms. The front-end application, residing on an end user's workstation, provides the application interface and most of the business processing. The back-end application component, residing on one or more hardware processors, provides the database services including data access, management, and integrity services, and some business rule processing in the form of stored procedures and triggers. *Stored procedures* are a relational DBMS feature that provides processing capability on the server. They have the advantage of centralizing business rules, enforcing security, and reducing network traffic by allowing access only to the procedure code, as opposed to the data itself. *Triggers* are stored procedures that can be used to maintain referential integrity and are executed when the database is updated by an INSERT, UPDATE, or DELETE command.

In *two-tiered applications*, application clients invoke the database server by using an interface like ODBC or by invoking dynamic SQL. Clients are built by using application development tools like Microsoft Visual Basic, Powersoft's PowerBuilder, or Centura's SQLWindows applications (up to 20 or perhaps 50, depending on the hardware infrastructure). Because business rules may be executing on the client as application logic, they are known as *fat clients* or *client-centric*. For many applications, this is a cost-effective and relatively simple architecture.

A more scalable but complex physical architecture uses three or more tiers. Rather than employing server-based application logic that is part of database services, business logic is insulated from the database services by placing them on their own tier (see Figure 18.14). In this way, the raw data is separated from the business logic layer. The business logic will operate on its own platform. It will run under the control of its own operating system, TP monitor, or some form of middleware.

Today, object-oriented tools such as Dynasty's Dynasty and Forté's Forté provide drag-and-drop, multi-tier partitioning. Newer versions of tools like PowerBuilder and Visual Basic are evolving to enable three (or *n*) tier partitioning using OLE (object linking and embedding) in conjunction with RPCs (remote procedure calls) technology.

In *three-tiered architectures*, an *application server* is the new third tier and is used to access multiple heterogeneous databases. It generally executes quicker than stored procedures and removes the need to use a proprietary language (like stored procedure SQL). It facilitates reuse of application logic and allows application code to reside on a variety of platforms. Maintaining business rules is easier; instead of redeploying application logic to multiple end-user workstations where application logic resides in a two-tiered architecture, the logic is updated only on the server(s) in which it resides.

The three-or-more-tiered application architecture is a more complex environment involving additional hardware, software, and vendors. However, the usage needs for the application may require this second-generation client/server architecture.

FIGURE 18.14.
Three-tiered client/server design architecture. (Source: EBG Consulting, Inc.)

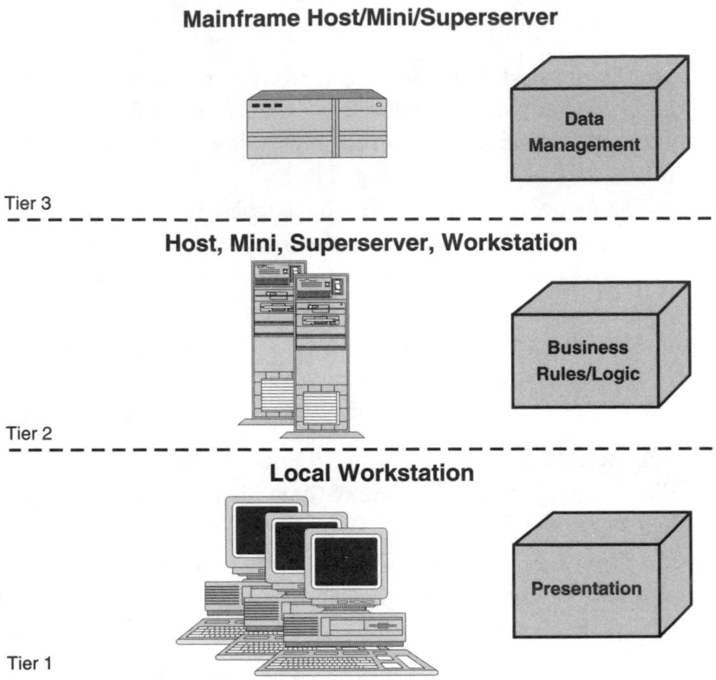

Mainframe Host/Mini/Superserver

Data Management

Tier 3

Host, Mini, Superserver, Workstation

Business Rules/Logic

Tier 2

Local Workstation

Presentation

Tier 1

OLTP and Three (n)-Tiered Client/Server

Online Transaction Processing (OLTP) is a processing environment appropriate for high-volume concurrent updating. The TP monitor, as it is abbreviated, is highly sophisticated software that manages a processing environment with large volumes on concurrent transactions. It balances the workload, locates and synchronizes data, and provides fast response time. In the mainframe world, IBM's CICS (Customer Information Control System) is the most commonly used transaction processing (TP) monitor. OLTP for client/server requires software that handles a number of concurrent tasks:

- Balancing the workload
- Locating and synchronizing the data
- Giving very fast response time
- Providing for reliable transaction completion
- Offering administrative support (installation, configuration, monitoring)

For these transactions to succeed in the distributed environment, they must pass the pass the ACID test:

A:	Atomicity	(The entire transaction, as a unit, is completed or aborted)
C:	Consistency	(The database is kept up-to-date completely, leaving it in a consistent state)
I:	Isolation	(The transaction's effect is not known to other users until it is complete)
D:	Durability	(Failures can be recovered through features like logging and application restarts)

In a three-tiered design, using a TP monitor may be necessary for an application that involves high-volume transaction processing and a large number of users. The client application invokes the TP monitor, the middle tier, which in turn acts as a client to the back-end database engine. The TP monitor is dedicated to scheduling and balancing the workload of multiple servers, managing distributed transactions or distributed requests, and providing an environment for the execution of the application logic. Unlike stored procedures and triggers, which perform similar functions, TP monitors are database-independent. TP monitors, which have been used in the mainframe world for many years, are known as *TP-heavy*. Stored procedures and triggers are known as *TP-lite*. TP monitors excel at managing additional clients while not having to simultaneously increase the power of the database server. Software from vendors like BEA System's Tuxedo, NCR/AT&T's Top End, Transarc/IBM's Encina, Tandem's Pathway, UniKix Technologies' UniKix, Digital's ACMS, and IBM's CICS all offer these features.

Usage Analysis

In many client/server applications, partitioning is accomplished through guesswork—a slow, expensive, and frustrating process. The best architecture is based on the expected behavior of the user roles and business events to which those user roles must respond. It anticipates the execution environment and expected application workload. It requires detailed examination of information about the locations and characteristics of application processing and data, for example, usage information (refer to Table 18.8).

Usage analysis is the process of scrutinizing these details with a series of matrices and visual techniques (see Table 18.10) and is a complex, iterative process. Data distribution guidelines are also used when analyzing data usage information (see Table 18.11 in following section). Distributed data placement should be based on the following:

- What needs to be done
- With what data

- Where it needs to happen
- How often it will occur
- How accurate the data used in the process must be

Table 18.10. Usage analysis techniques.

Technique	Purpose
Event: Event Coupling Matrix	Analyze the percentage of time that events occur together
Event-Processor: Role Frequency Matrix	Understand which business roles (who) perform which activities (what) and how often (when)
Data Access: Location Partition	Determine which locations need which partition of data entities
Data Placement: Location	Analyze and summarize read and update access needs for each location and each data entity
Data Distribution Network Traffic Scenario Comparison	Analyze network traffic for various data-entity placement scenarios based on access required
Data Distribution Guidelines (Table 18.11)	Provide guidelines for data distribution based on volatility and concurrent usage of data
Visual Partitioning Scenarios	Analyze trial partitioning strategies using the event-processor models

Performing usage analysis allows the application designer to formulate a best-case architecture. The proposed architecture should be tested within the technical environment intended for the application.

Data Distribution Guidelines

High-level recommendations for how data is distributed are based on data currency, volatility, and the source of updates to the data. Other issues such as volume, response time, and retention must be factored into the data distribution strategy (see Table 18.11).

Table 18.11. Data distribution guidelines.

Volatility \ Currency Level	High Currency (Synchronization Required, (for example, up to the second)	Low to Medium Currency (for example, hours old)
Infrequent updates from one source	Data distributed to database servers with distributed updates (such as two-phase commit or synchronous data replication)	Extracts, snapshots, or asynchronous data replication
Infrequent updates from geographically dispersed sources	Centralized database or distributed with updates distributed (such as extracts or snapshots from central source, two-phase commit, or synchronous replication)	Extracts, snapshots, or asynchronous replication
Frequent updates from one source	Same as above	Data centralization or distributed with batch updates or asynchronous replication
Frequent updates from multiple geographically dispersed sources	Centralized database or transaction server (such as CICS, Tuxedo, Top End, Transarc or synchronous replication)	Same as above

GUI Development

The GUI is the presentation layer of the client/server application. An effective and usable GUI interface is a substantial improvement from hierarchical, character-based menus. It also allows end users to interact in new ways with their applications, ultimately allowing them to better serve business customers.

GUI development should be focused on creating usable interfaces based on the behavior of the end user, not the system. The interface should be built based on the behavior of the user in response to the real world. This premise is directly supported by event-driven modeling and development.

GUI Definition

GUIs use bit-mapped displays and contain elements such as the following:

Windows	Rectangular areas in which actions occur; windows can be nested
Menus	List of items for users to select
List boxes	Mini windows in which items are listed for selection
Icons	Pictures representing actions (cut, paste) or application objects (Word-Processor, E-Mail, Repair, Billing, Calendar, and so on)
Toolbars	Horizontal or vertical areas with icons for initiating actions like cut, paste, draw, undo, print, and so on
Push buttons	Selection icon for common actions like OK, Cancel, and Exit
Check boxes	For multiple selections
Radio buttons	For single selections
Data fields	For input and display of data

GUI interfaces are comprised of WIMP (Windows, Icons, Menus, Pointers) and NERD (Navigation, Evaluation, Refinement, and Demonstration) components. Well-designed GUIs confirm the assertion that a picture is worth a thousand words.

Object-Action Interface

An important distinction between CUI (Character User Interface) and GUI is how the user interacts with the screen. In a CUI interface, the user determines the *action* needed and then selects the *object*. The interface typically takes the user through the actions, or procedures, step by step. In a GUI interface, the user first identifies the *object* needed, such as policy, order, account, customer, VCR, or part, and then performs *actions* upon that object. For example, the user has to respond to some real-world event, such as a customer wanting to cancel a book order. The Book object is selected, followed by Cancel. Thus, the GUI interface is *object-action* oriented (see Figure 18.15).

FIGURE 18.15.
CUI versus GUI interaction. (Source: EBG Consulting, Inc.)

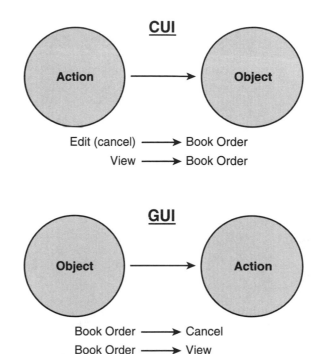

GUI Events

Within the GUI world, there are one or more windows. Within a window, actions are performed on objects. The window actions are also called *events*. Like business events, GUI events happen in the real world but occur within the context of the GUI window. They are business events at their most granular level. They include the following:

- Mouse events (clicks, points, drags)
- Keyboard events (typing, key combinations)
- Menu events (selection)
- Window events (resize, minimize, maximize, update)
- Activate/Deactivate events (icon open, close; window activate, deactivate)
- Initialize/Terminate events (application open, close)

GUI events are managed by some combination of interface software, programmer logic, and predefined routines known as *application programming interfaces (API)*.

Human-Computer Interface Design

The *human-computer interface*, also called *human-computer interaction* (or *HCI*) is the study of what happens when a human user and computer system get together to perform tasks. Traditional interface design uses screens, menus, and dialog boxes based on what the system needs to accomplish. The system acts procedurally, according to predefined processing needed by the application. The design is effectively accomplished from the inside-out.

The HCI perspective is user-centric, building the interface from the outside-in. It is concerned with the modeling, building, and testing of interfaces to directly match the tasks performed by the user. The design must be usable. *Usability* implies that an interface

- Is easy to learn
- Facilitates quick task completion
- Minimizes errors during usage
- Reinforces the user's ability to retain interface knowledge
- Satisfies the user (positive subjective evaluation)

GUI design is both art and science. It requires that you understand and appreciate *human learning factors* such as predictability, metaphors, visual and auditory clues, and feedback. It must exploit traditional features in the development process, such as using standards and basing the design on sound models of behavior. It requires the GUI designer to consider the users' level of expertise (new, novice, casual, knowledgeable worker) and the workflow of tasks to be performed.

Locate Application Interfaces

The *location of interfaces* in the client/server application should be determined by the event-processors. GUI interfaces are needed when an event-processor shows a terminator sending or receiving information (see Figure 18.16). The application developer must know if that event-processor (or single bubble within an event-processor) will be *automated* or *manual*. If it is automated, the information on the data flow needs to be used in the interface windows and validated during interface prototyping.

The GUI designer should gain a good understanding of the actions, objects, and flow of processing which will be contained in the GUI interface. Using these techniques (see Table 18.12), a look and feel can be designed. Details should be filled in by the prototyping process itself.

FIGURE 18.16.
Locating GUI interfaces using event-processors. (Source: EBG Consulting, Inc.)

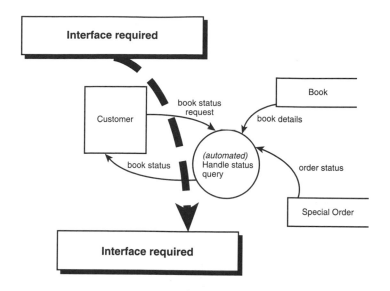

Table 18.12. Techniques for modeling user interface.

User Interface Modeling Technique	Purpose
Window Navigation Flow	Visual model (similar to DFD) showing how an end user can navigate through the window structure
Task Analysis	Table listing GUI objects, interface action, and next action performed
GUI event-processor: GUI Object Matrix	Matrix showing what event-processors are invoked when a GUI object is selected
Event Coupling Matrix (see Table 18.13)	Matrix showing the percentage of times processes occur together for a particular end-user role
User Profile (see Table 18.14)	Profile of types of users accessing the interface
User Interface Notation	Text specifications of specific user actions and interface feedback provided for each action

Table 18.13. Example event-processor coupling matrix.

User Role: Help Desk Technician

Event-Processor ⟍ Event-Processor	Research Book	Order Book	Handle Status Query	Return Refused Book
Research book	100	65	45	40
Order book		100	55	20
Handle status query			100	10
Return Refused Book				100

Table 18.14. User profiles.

ROLE	Sales Manager	Help Desk Technician	Special Order Technician	Sales Clerk	Home Office Buyer
TYPE OF USER	Access User	Access User	Access User	Speed User	Access User

Object-Oriented Modeling

An alternative way to model, architect, design, build, and implement a client/server application is to use object-oriented techniques and technologies. Object-oriented technology evolved apart from client/server, yet many client/server tools make use of object-based concepts such as classes, messaging, and encapsulation. Object concepts promote reuse and extensibility. (*Extensibility* is the ability to add and modify an object design or implementation.) They may be a more natural way for end users to think about requirements. Rather than examine application views—data, process, and states—as orthogonal, an object-oriented approach is concerned with abstracting and implementing "objects." Objects have data, state, and behavior components. They are categorized into classes and communicate using messages.

There is much debate about which modeling technique is "better." Object-oriented techniques make use of diagramming and requirements gathering techniques similar to those forwarded in this chapter (for example, class inheritance models, object messaging diagrams, class relationship models, and object state models). They are *extensions* of these models. Object-oriented technologies and techniques are relatively new. There are no standard notations for expressing object-oriented analysis and design artifacts. The technology is complex and requires developers to use new patterns of thinking.

There is a growing body of analysis and design techniques from object-oriented leaders (such as Booch, Coad/Yourdon, Jacobson, Rumbaugh *et al*, Shlaer/Mellor, Wirfs-Brock *et al*). Yet most client/server application development efforts do not use object-oriented methods unless "true" object-oriented technologies are being used throughout the application life cycle. This means object-oriented languages, tools, and/or DBMS are being used for implementation of the client/server application. For a more in-depth look at object-oriented programming, refer to Chapter 17, "Object-Oriented Development with Client/Server."

Successful Client/Server Development

Client/server development requires IT to marry the best of the PC and mainframe worlds. A balance must be achieved between the benefits of prototyping and the advantages of careful exploration of requirements. The end user must be at center stage during client/server application development, continually involved in defining and validating models and prototypes, and testing the developed system. An event-driven development approach provides a solid foundation for an effective business system and an efficient iterative development methodology. Architectural and design choices must be made using the application models and usage information associated with those models. Techniques must be practiced that promote teamwork, quality, speed, and application integrity and longevity (see Chapter 13).

REFERENCES AND RECOMMENDED READING

Barker, Richard, *Case*Method: Entity Relationship Modeling*, Addison-Wesley, England, 1989.

Barker, Richard and Longman, Cliff, *Case*Method: Function and Process Modelling*, Addison-Wesley, England, 1992.

Berson, Alex, *Client/Server Architecture*, McGraw Hill, 1992.

Davis, Alan, *Software Requirements: Objects, Functions, and States*, PTR Prentice Hall, 2nd ed., 1993.

Dewire, Dawna Travis, *Client/Server Computing*, McGraw Hill, 1993.

Fleming, Candice and Von Halle, Barbara, *Handbook of Relational Database Design*, Addison Wesley, 1989.

Hackathorn, Richard, *Enterprise Database Connectivity*, John Wiley & Sons, Inc., 1993.

Hay, David C., *Data Model Patterns: Conventions of Thought*, Dorset House Publishing, 1996.

Hix, Deborah and Hartson, H. Rex, *Developing User Interfaces: Ensuring Usability Through Product & Process*, John Wiley, 1993.

McMenamin, Stephen M. And Palmer, John F., *Essential Systems Analysis*, Yourdon, Inc., 1984.

Orfali, Robert, Harkey, Dan, and Edwards, Jeri, *Essential Client/Server Survival Guide*, Van Nostrand Reinhold, 1994.

Redmond-Pyle, David and Moore, Alan, *Graphical User Interface Design and Evaluation*, Prentice Hall, 1995.

Robertson, James and Suzanne, *Complete Systems Analysis*, Dorset House Publishing, 1994.

Shlaer, Sally, and Mellor, Stephen J., *Object Lifecycles: Modeling the World in States*, PTR Prentice Hall, 1992.

Simsion, Graeme C., *Data Modeling Essentials: Analysis, Design, and Innovation*, Van Nostrand Reinhold, 1994.

Smith, Patrick N. with Guengerich, Steven L, *Client/Server Computing*, 2nd ed., Sams Publishing, 1994.

Sully, Phil, *Modeling the World with Objects*, Prentice Hall, 1993.

Vaskevitch, David, *Client/Server Strategies: A Survival Guide for Corporate Reengineers*, IDG Books, 1993.

Wilkie, George, *Object-Oriented Software Engineering: The Professional Developer's Guide*, Addison-Wesley, 1993.

Yourdon, Edward, *Modern Structured Analysis*, Yourdon Press, 1989.

Yourdon, Inc., *Yourdon™ Systems Methods: Model Driven System Development*, Yourdon Press Computing Series, 1993.

Summary

Developing a client/server application that meets business needs requires a solid understanding of the application's requirements and a complete knowledge of the performance expectations for the application. Business events provide a powerful and easy-to-understand framework for modeling the scope, data, process, and interface design of the application. Business rules must be captured along with these application models. Details about data, locations, and processing—along with an appreciation of data and processing distribution schemes—need to be captured in order to design an effective client/server architecture.

Developing Mission-Critical Applications

19

by Neil Jenkins

Although client/server has been readily accepted as the main systems development environment for low-risk situations such as data warehousing and online reporting, only a small percentage of companies have shifted a mission-critical application (like inventory management, purchasing, or tele-sales) off the main centralized system and deployed it enterprise-wide into a new client/server environment. Why hasn't the shift to client/server computing happened more rapidly? The reasons are numerous. They include the following:

- Security
- Adaptability
- Lack of skills
- Complexity of client/server
- Lack of understanding about the business benefits of client/server
- Reluctance to change
- Lack of maturity in the toolsets

The primary issue behind all these reasons is risk. It is a risk at present to bet your core business environment on a distributed technology that is relatively new compared to the tried and tested LAN-based or centralized systems in place in the market today.

This chapter explains how building mission-critical applications differs from building other types of applications. These applications form the cornerstone of businesses and are the main revenue and profit earners. Because they are so important to the business, they need to be treated differently than smaller, lesser risk applications. In this chapter, I cover the risks associated with building applications of this type, the different ways in which an existing mission-critical application can be moved to client/server, and the painful additional issues that so often arrive as a result of the complexity of this type of project and people.

Risk

Placing application logic is fairly straightforward when you are using a mainframe and dumb terminals. The application and everything that goes around it runs on the central processor and nowhere else. The mainframe environment has been around for over 20 years; its weaknesses and, more importantly, strengths are well-known, well-understood, and well-documented. To take away those known strengths by building or porting a core business system to client/server is to move into an uncertain environment.

The peripheral applications within a company, those that are important yet not direct revenue earners, such as payroll, online reporting, and EIS, are much more likely to be readily transferred to the client/server environment. Using these low-risk (relatively) applications to develop your experience in client/server development and implementation is a good approach. However, the real benefit to the organization will be to take advantage of client/server systems in the core business areas. Improved workflow, removal of redundant and inefficient processes, greater usability and flexibility, and improved functionality, which are all results of a successful client/server system, can lead to serious productivity improvements that in turn lead to more money on the bottom line either by reducing overheads or by increasing revenue.

Before jumping blindly into client/server, a company should consider the successes and failures within the client/server arena. The unprepared company typically only has a 50-50 chance of a successful client/server implementation when inadequate time is invested into the planning and analysis of the project. This figure gets worse when the company also has little or no experience in the development of client/server systems. Tackling your main business area as the first client/server project is not wise!

If you pick up any computer magazine, the news section is likely to tell the woes of at least one company who has given up on client/server. Many client/server systems are considered failures because the cost of development and implementation went over budget. When developing a core business application, you must keep track of costs. Be aware that in most cases the education costs surrounding a client/server application are twice that of the programming it takes to create your software. Research on the Internet has shown that most client/server applications are delivered over budget.

Most companies who have implemented client/server have not tracked costs because their accounting practices are inadequate and their focus has been on speed of delivery. This focus has caused them to miss the fact that staff costs dominate most client/server projects. Because of these cost issues, make sure that any critical development is clearly and correctly budgeted and that any issues with justifying the project (such as estimating the business value it is intended to return) are completely agreed upon before project commencement. This rule reflects a somewhat perfect development world, but remember that many projects have failed due to not returning business value or return on investment (see Chapter 5, "Considerations for Migrating to Client/Server").

The best way to manage the risk involved in implementing client/server is to understand the potential business benefits and advantages that a client/server system can bring to the company. Developing a mission-critical application requires a high level of understanding of the business drivers. In many industries, for example, market share is not determined as much by the availability of different features as by the speed or quality with which some activity can be performed. Examples might include customer service, where the nature of service may be almost indistinguishable between different vendors, so the speed and way in which the service is delivered becomes crucial. Failing to understand or even identify these key business drivers makes client/server development very difficult. Without the understanding of business drivers, the main thrust of development work becomes the minor changes and incremental updates rather than the real leaps that would improve the business benefit. Users may say, "We need to improve by 5 percent," when they really want to know how the company can improve by 500 percent.

The level of risk involved requires you to have your development personnel work with a group of main corporate users who believe in the move to client/server. Having a development team focused on moving the core business onto client/server will get the system built, but having a user base that is keen to move the business forward is what will make the system work.

Client/server computing also can provide an evolutionary approach to integrating your older legacy systems with your new client/server systems. New applications can be written to access the old data sources in more productive and responsive ways. As time and budget allow, the data can be moved to more cost-effective platforms, and applications can continue to function entirely (or at worst, largely) unchanged.

As discussed in Chapter 3, "Business Process Re-engineering," the key to long-term competitiveness is the ability to rapidly and effectively respond to change—change in the legal environment, change in business practices, change in the competitive environment, and change in the structure of the organization. These changes force frequent re-engineering of business processes, which requires a continual re-engineering of the underlying information systems. Information systems must support changes in business or risk becoming an obstacle to company growth. The flexibility of client/server allows a company to make changes relatively quickly. In comparison, the rate of change on a mainframe system is much slower.

Mission-Critical Move to Client/Server

When a company understands what business drivers support the move to client/server, and when the company has reached the consensus that a move to client/server would deliver benefits to the business, the company can make the move to client/server in five ways:

- Renovate
- Relocate
- Rewrite
- Replace
- Re-engineer

The following sections describe each of these ways.

Renovate: Make It Look Nice

Renovating an application typically means updating the user interface to a GUI environment such as Windows or OS/2. This technique involves providing terminal emulation of some kind at the desktop and using a development tool to sit on top of the application and present a new face to the user. In addition, this technique allows the application to be easily integrated with other applications on the desktop. The downside to this approach is that the application and its functionality remains largely unchanged, and a strong link still exists between the application and its environment. The inherent problems of the application, such as being unfriendly, hard-to-use, and inflexible, remain.

Renovation is usually seen as a short-term tactical move that is designed to relieve the pressure on the IS department as much as anything else. The main thrust of this development would be to begin to migrate the mission-critical application. This step represents no more than the first crawl on the way to true business benefit. The return on investment with this method (assuming major process changes are not put in place) is likely to be very small indeed.

This step can provide good business benefit if the mission-critical application is integrated with new applications to create an almost superset system. However, the business benefit rarely comes from the renovation; the benefit is much more likely to be a result of the accompanying integration and process changes.

Relocate: Put the Beast in a Smaller Cage

Downsizing has caused many companies to investigate and possibly move applications from mainframe environments to supposedly lower cost open systems platforms. The application is taken almost as is, and ported to the smaller platforms. Structure, functionality, and processes are rarely altered (often due to time constraints), and the benefits are rarely realized quickly. The realities of downsizing usually mean that the cost of migration tends to destroy any other cost savings. As there has been no functionality or process improvements, the new system usually does not deliver any benefit to the end users either.

This technique is often best avoided unless you improve functionality and processes at the same time. Regretfully, these improvements also increase the complexity and the risk (who said it was easy?).

Rewrite: Build It How We Really Want It

Rewriting an application can involve relocating, renovating, and enhancing functionality. Combine this rewrite with improvements to the business processes, and you will see significant business benefits. Rewriting an application also provides an opportunity to implement client/server architectures and specifically to make the application environment-independent. Using software tools that support GUIs, a sophisticated repository, environment independence, and an object-oriented approach is essential. Rewriting a mission-critical application from scratch is best attempted after you have cut your teeth on less risky projects.

Replace: Buy It Off the Shelf

Replacing a mission-critical application with a new package is an increasingly popular alternative. Applications that use client/server techniques and technologies in a multitude of industry areas are now being sold. The advantage of such a package is that it can be up and running in a much shorter period than any rewrite. In addition, such a package is likely to be well-supported and well-developed, reducing the need for your staff to fully understand the complexities of client/server. However, most of the packaged applications in the marketplace are tied to specific resources such as a database program, user interface, and operating system. True openness is hard to find.

Most applications have a supported range of platforms, but normally Jenz's Law of Systems Integration says that yours isn't one of them! Finding an application, however, that meets 100 percent of your business requirements for your core business area is going to be nearly impossible. You are lucky if the application meets 80 percent of your requirements. Invariably, you will need to consider paying for modifications (and normally the resultant testing of these modifications) to gain the functionality that you need. Often this approach is preferable to the complexity of a rewrite, but both approaches should be discussed and reviewed side by side. Another approach is to purchase pieces of the application. For example, you could purchase the inventory control module and adapt or fit it into your complete system. This method adds the functionality you require but may also introduce additional difficulties in costs, integration, and implementation.

A note of caution is that although the primary driver in package evaluation and implementation is the business need, client/server principles must be adhered to as well. This adherence is particularly important as it applies to the support of your environment. Consider a company that might try to get its five main business systems migrated to package solutions, each of which had a particular nuance concerning infrastructure. The resulting underlying infrastructure would consist of many components and would thus be very complex and unstable. The effect of this unstable infrastructure would be difficulties in support and troubleshooting, ultimately leading to user problems. A happy medium has to be maintained between business functionality and infrastructure; sacrificing either one can create difficulty.

Re-engineer: Create the Ideal

Creating client/server applications as part of a business re-engineering exercise clearly provides the greatest opportunity for business advantage, and it also presents the greatest risk. The graphical interfaces and network topologies that client/server supports provide valuable business opportunities. The re-engineering process should focus on how the current business strategy could be modified by supporting client/server technologies.

Client/server is the only effective way of implementing the rapidly changing business process models, particularly if the business models can be independent of the application environment and the application environment can be independent of the technical infrastructure. Developers must respond quickly to rapidly changing business needs without disrupting day-to-day business processes. Gone are the days when entire applications would be replaced after a multiyear development effort. Remember the chaos and loss of user productivity while the new system settled into place? Today's new applications must fit in with the existing environment, support the re-engineered processes, and provide a competitive advantage.

Re-engineering a mission-critical application involves ripping apart the very essence of the company. It is not to be entered into lightly. Those companies that have re-engineered themselves successfully have enjoyed enormous returns. Development using this technique results in new processes, new information, new information flows, new look and feel, new infrastructure (if required), and new training.

Building Your Business

The very heart of a good client/server system is the understanding of the business at an organizational level rather than just the narrow view of any one particular area. Integration of systems is born from the integration of business areas and/or business processes. The functional view of an organization can no longer be used when building mission-critical client/server systems. You have to look at the business system in its entirety, regardless of the organizational structure of the company. Building a client/server system that only meets the need of one business function will not deliver the required return on the investment and will not encourage acceptance of the techniques and technology. Building mission-critical applications requires a lateral thought process across the organization rather than the vertical functional thought process that was required to build all the old legacy systems. This method is sometimes called *circular thinking*.

To successfully develop a mission-critical application, use the techniques and processes outlined in Chapter 6, "Steps for Migrating to Client/Server" with the additional requirements born from the added complexity, importance, and risk of the mission-critical environment. The following sections describe these requirements.

Build a Good Team

The successful development or delivery (regardless of type) of a mission-critical application is dependent upon the use of a focused and enthusiastic team. This team forces the change to the new environment, is supported and encouraged by the business, and never gives up. Choose a small team of enthusiastic and capable people who are open-minded enough to understand the promise of the new technology, skillful enough to use it creatively, and strong enough to champion it throughout the organization.

When building mission-critical applications, the team should be made up of staff from within the company. You may, where applicable, add new blood into the team, perhaps by hiring new recruits to fulfill a particular need or taking from your existing staff. Using existing staff gets the best results because existing staff members have a very valuable asset that cannot be found outside your company—knowledge of the business. Beware of the steady string of consultants promising to deliver just what your business needs after they have spent six months understanding what it is you do. Most new recruits also take at least three to six months to get a grasp on the environment. A mission-critical application project needs a team of people who can be productive on day one.

The team should include natural leaders who are well-respected within the company. Respected does not mean feared. The transition of a business from legacy system to new client/server requires continual selling. The people doing the selling have to have credibility and responsibility. Leaders who lack these assets will not get recognition and neither will the project; the result will be an uphill struggle all the way. This team manages the development of the client/server application with the goal of exemplifying the new way of doing business. You will know that your team is a success when people comment on the pleasure of working with it!

Train Existing Staff

You will push staff members into new areas. You will ask them to tackle projects of large risk to the company. You have to give them the toolset to do the job. Team members usually must learn new skills to adapt effectively to the change from mainframe to client/server computing. Typical training involves the mastery of programming languages, such as Progress; new operating systems, such as UNIX; and database management languages and systems, such as SQL and RDBMS. Team members also need to master networking and tuning and become familiar with windowing technologies and new application development tools. Education is crucial to the success of a project.

Perhaps the biggest lack of knowledge will be in the areas so important to the transition to client/server. How do you move core components of the mainframe to client/server? How do you integrate the new system with the older legacy systems? This type of information and training is usually left to the consultants groups. Have your staff trained before the development begins, in the planning stages, so they are ready to go straight into analysis.

Integrate Users into the Team

The team must include end users who can ensure that the system fulfills the business requirements and can aid in promoting the product within the organization. Experience shows that mission-critical application development projects are best served by having full-time user involvement.

Piloting and prototyping help users to easily understand a design and participate in application development. End users can now contribute to the development cycle in ways that were not possible before. Your end users normally have better and more detailed information about their area of work than anyone else does, and in a perfect world, they would be the application designers. Consider giving them design tools backed by an intelligent automatic application developer. In this way, end users and application developers can talk in terms of working prototypes because it is no longer necessary to discuss the application in the abstract while developers code reams of code. Active involvement from key users plays an important role in obtaining the support from other areas of the business.

Retrain End Users

If the new client/server systems are to succeed, they will inevitably change the way your business works. This change should ideally be in the form of improved workflow and process-oriented work. Systems can only be successful if the end users accept them, so considering users' interests is vital.

End users will be viewing very different screens from those to which they are accustomed as your new systems improve the users' workflow. They must have training in the new systems and the new front-end software. If end users are moving from terminals to PCs or workstations, particularly if they are moving from "Green Screen" to GUI, they will need training in this technology as well. Many of them will fear the move, as it can be very unsettling if they have been using the same system for years. As with the programming team, the best way of achieving success is to find early advocates of the new technology who can both train and create enthusiasm among end users. Although the newer processes and user interfaces are superior to the old, overcoming initial resistance may be necessary. Untrained users can't exploit the new features of the client/server system. Half-hearted acceptance of the new system means slow death for the system and possibly a serious delay in the general acceptance of client/server computing within the corporation. End users who are highly trained and use the system to capacity are an invaluable source of suggestions for enhancements and requirements for future systems.

Use Consultants Wisely

One of the most difficult questions is how to use consultants to support your development. In the early days of analysis, training and knowledge transfer consultants have a major role to play if required. Of course, this benefit does not come without cost, and control of external consultants imposes an additional management burden.

The use of consultants can range from management and design assistance to almost complete replacement of internal staff. If a company wishes to retain some client/server expertise, then technology transfer from the consultants is critical. In this role, consultants working alongside in-house staff can provide a level of education impossible to achieve in any other way. As with all uses of external consultants, look for a group that already has the skills you need. Don't pay to train the consultants so that they can train your staff! When the consultant is only two pages further ahead of you with this book, you know you've got problems. At the end of the day, the consultant walks away. Make the consultants earn their money. Be aware, however, that you must focus the consultants; it is not in your interests to keep changing your requirements of them (particularly when they are on-site and charging you).

Mad COWs: Manageable Chunks of Work

A specific challenge is migrating a mainframe mission-critical application to client/server. To minimize the risk of failure of the mission-critical application, it is best to migrate from the older mainframe technology gradually. Replacing large systems overnight is now practically impossible, not to mention undesirable. Instead, concentrate on partitioning the application on the mainframe into manageable chunks of work that can be approached somewhat separately.

By approaching the task in this way, you can begin to develop mission-critical applications that provide new functions or processes without disturbing the other older legacy systems. The partitioning enables the teams to focus on their particular pieces, and this approach is much more acceptable to upper management. The remaining systems can be altered and moved to client/server as time and budget allows. You could take the brutal approach and ban all old system development and concentrate on providing all new systems through client/server, in time switching off the mainframe functions. This approach has been successful in organizations, but it requires real support and commitment across the company, something only you can determine.

Give Yourself Enough Time

The premise of client/server is flexibility, rapid enhancement, and change. With experienced team members and good company support, you can expect short time frames and high user satisfaction. However, in the early days, the picture is somewhat different when applied to the development activities surrounding the transition of a mission-critical application. Most organizations find that the time frame is longer than they had anticipated due to the reasons and issues identified at the start of this chapter. Don't fool yourself into thinking that a mission-critical application can be converted to client/server computing quickly (in other words, in approximately 10 months). Many companies on the Internet have related that it takes about a year to thoroughly absorb the technology while building a number of no-risk pilot applications and prototypes. This year is also taken up building technical infrastructures and data models. When the level of experience begins to rise, the time frames begin to come down.

When you develop an application in which the processes cut across several departments, an increased level of interaction is required to achieve completion. There will be differing sets of views as to the real focus of the application. Take, for example, an operational call center. The accounts department will be keen to focus on actual sales and moneys generated. The operational team, however, may be focused on the customer service aspect in order to ensure repeat business and long-term customer relationships. Neither view is wrong, yet together they will demand more of your time than if you tackled them individually. As the number of departments involved increases, so does the amount of time you will have to put in with each department. This area is where the main amount of internal politics begins to surface, and your real role of business integrator begins to emerge.

Mission-Critical Issues

Mission-critical applications by their very nature generate issues. Some of the main issues that you will face are outlined in the following sections.

Skepticism: "It'll Never Work; Don't Even Try"

Regardless of how well you explain the benefits of client/server computing, you will encounter skeptics, some in senior positions, some from your own IS department, who must be convinced. The reality is that the only effective convincing is by doing. Often the mainframe skeptics voice the opinion, "You can't take core business and put it on a distributed server. We do 28 million I/O transactions a day!" They often fail to realize that these transactions may only relate to 10,000 real business transactions! After you build and develop a successful mission-critical application, your skeptics should go away; if they don't, then perhaps they're the wrong people for the way the company is heading.

Readiness: You Are, the Company Is Not

Ask yourself the question, "Is this company ready for the impact of client/server?" You may be developing a new mission-critical application that will fail because the company is just not ready to receive it. The first pilots and prototype applications will be closely watched, and if they demonstrate problems or fail to deliver a working system on time, they may be scrapped completely. For this reason, you must set expectations correctly and avoid any temptation to oversell. A working prototype is only that—it is not a fully working, industrial-strength system. Don't let your users think it is.

Rewrite, Rewrite, Rewrite

Your mission-critical application will need to be rewritten every couple of years. Through each iteration, you will be able to effectively enhance and improve the business system to correspond with how the business changes. Believe it or not, this rewriting is often seen as an issue because previous development mentalities said a system should last a good 20 years. Continual competitiveness in business comes from the continual evolution of your core business applications. The rewrite will also demonstrate the much lower maintenance costs of the system compared with the maintenance costs of older legacy applications.

Unexpected Dependencies

Over the years most mainframe systems have been enhanced to such an extent that it is very difficult to distinguish the main component parts of each business function. You will probably unravel a whole host of interdependencies with the piece that you are assigned to develop. Worse still, you will find that these dependencies are not documented or sometimes even known about! When planning your project, allocate some time for discovering and solving interdependencies.

Cutting Time and Quality

When you embark on your mission-critical development project, time will run short, and quality can often be the first casualty of tight deadlines. If this does occur, work on justifying the extra time. No senior manager (who is any good) will want an application that is of dubious quality. As project manager, your responsibility is to change time frames as you see fit to ensure a successful project. Do not under any circumstances sacrifice training or quality. With such a key application, the results of such sacrifices could be disastrous.

The Pain of Politics

As already discussed, the major challenge of client/server is to create effective systems in response to the rapidly changing business world. Client/server computing provides an IS infrastructure that is scalable and can be reconfigured easily. One of the main difficulties that will surface as you begin to develop a mission-critical application is that the IS structure itself needs to be more flexible. The IS group itself must first make the change to the client/server model. This change is complex and subject to political attack, so it requires careful management. The rigidity of the IS structure does not show when dealing with the first few small client/server projects, probably because the systems are small enough to be considered almost inconsequential in the greater scheme of things. Yet when an IS department begins the move to transition the company to client/server, its own structure begins to crack!

Commonly, and most unfortunately, most political problems involve the mainframe division or department. This department has spent years running a high-performance, centralized system whose role has never really been questioned. Risk aversion is common in this environment. Midrange IS organizations tend to be more risk aware and flexible. The other end of the spectrum tends to be the client developers, who often are gung-ho in approach and a little too risk-oriented!

The role of centralized IS has to shift drastically to support the new business climate, and this shift is troubling to those who may feel anxious about their futures because their roles are inexorably linked to the mainframe environment. Do not make the statement that the mainframe is going to disappear overnight. Usually it will have a continuing role, at least in the medium term. Over time, its role will change as will that of most staff within the department. Focusing on the better aspects of change and change management will help. The company must recognize the need to retrain mainframe developers who want to move to the client/server environment. Experienced mainframe developers are very knowledgeable about the business and its systems, so an investment in their education can offer an excellent return. You will lose staff that are unwilling to change, but this is not a bad thing because they are no longer going the same route as the company. (You might consider assisting them with obtaining positions in companies that have not or are not moving to client/server.) IS staff members now need to focus on helping you to develop core business systems as robust and resilient as the centralized systems while maintaining the integrity of the core mainframe systems as you migrate. This task adds a level of complexity far more challenging than their current roles require.

The complex task of integrating a mainframe application and its data may require the agreement of many people across the organization. One of the basic questions is whether to give the client/server system access to the mainframe applications or to the data itself. In many older applications, semantic information about the data is held only in the applications, so it is difficult to integrate the raw data. In such cases, a good connectivity architecture should make it possible to execute a mainframe program in exactly the same way as a stored procedure on another relational database. Because few mainframe data management packages support integrity constraints within the database, mainframe database administrators are reluctant for remote clients to have more than read access. If clients can access and update data only through preprogrammed mainframe applications, however, remote clients can also have write access to the data. This is the only way to fully integrate most legacy applications.

The role of IS becomes a business integrator. Because of the process and workflow values that are brought with client/server, IS departments find themselves working to assist the users in understanding the impact and value of moving to a business based on processes that span organizations rather than ones that are self-contained within a department. As a result, IS staff members play a major role as the catalysts of change within the company. In this way, IS retains its professional role as expert in major portions of systems methodology while recognizing that much of the expertise in the new technologies will be in the development teams.

In a perfect company, everyone would stand behind the move to client/server. More frequently though, many employees are confused and possibly anxious about the change to client/server computing, and skeptics may hold a more conservative technological view. As with any other important internal change, you must pay attention to selling the new ideas throughout the organization. Selling the new technology to end users, senior management, and the central IS department is essential.

For end users, the immediate effect is likely to be a dramatic improvement in application presentation. End users will appreciate the new functionality of the planned applications, which will make them more productive while providing them with a more pleasant screen environment. Many new applications built for client/server systems let end users easily perform tasks that used to be difficult, perhaps making better use of inventory, perhaps satisfying customer calls faster and more accurately, or integrating information that was previously difficult to compare.

Senior management is interested primarily in two things: increasing competitiveness and reducing overheads. Savings are difficult to predict, especially early in the project, though expenditures and savings should be carefully tracked to create a knowledge base to support future estimates. Improved ability to perform business tasks is easier to define and quantify, so this data is often more acceptable to management. Another concern to senior management is risk management. A shift to client/server (particularly from a centralized base) by an IS department is a high-profile event. The inclusion in the task force of outside consultants with experience in such transitions can significantly reduce the risk of making poor decisions through ignorance of the power and limitations of the new technology.

As with any technology change, it is vital to obtain acceptance from all the interested parties: business management, end users, IS staff, and system administrators. Some will be reluctant converts who will need to see a successful implementation before being convinced. For the mission-critical application, it is essential that all who help determine its success have signed up for the program. Too many great projects that are complex enough in their own right get sabotaged through foot dragging, political maneuvering, or other wasteful behavior.

Tools and Standards

The mission-critical application requires toolsets and standards that are robust and industrial-strength just like the tools and standards that make up your core systems today. The following sections detail the considerations required when developing mission-critical applications with regards to tools and standards.

Standards

As discussed throughout this book, standards play an important role in client/server development. Aim to set your standards quickly and efficiently in the early stages of the project. Many companies and sources of information can help you with this task. Keep in mind that standards take time to become standards within the industry and continually evolve. Try to establish those standards that are right for your business, adhere to them, and move on rather than spending months deciding which standard to adopt before doing. The normal IS practice of standardizing names and data formats for key corporate data elements should continue.

Visual Standards

As companies adopt new GUI application environments, they need to set up GUI interface and design standards. Determine a style that you like from the preferred products available on the market and discuss with your users all the areas associated with good visual design. Microsoft publishes a *Visual Design Guide*, as do other tool vendors. Remember that design is one area where the user is normally right. You, after all, do not have to sit and operate the application all day. Look and feel must remain consistent in the use of icons, buttons, and any other visual on-screen control. With reduced training and users moving between different applications, consistency is key. The strength of many of the integrated office suites, such as Microsoft

Office and Lotus SmartSuite, is that the icons within each application mean the same thing. Figure 19.1 shows how an integrated suite has very similar look and feel. You should aim to achieve the same kind of consistency.

FIGURE 19.1.

Microsoft Office's consistent look and feel.

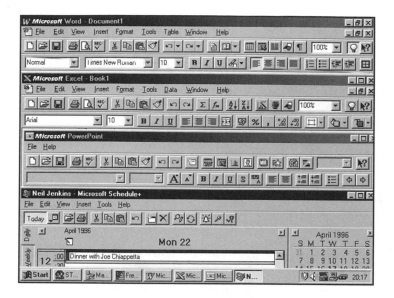

Location Standards

Most mission-critical applications require the developers to decide where to put the business rule and relationship integrity mechanisms. In most circumstances, these mechanisms should be on the main data server alongside the data. Putting this information with the data encapsulates the data to some extent. It frees application developers from concern with basic integrity issues and gives system managers confidence that no application can wreak havoc on the data at this basic level.

Tools for Mission-Critical Applications

Client/server application development environments are evolving very rapidly. Newer CASE tools integrate with the database, automatically generating much of the data definition and basic integrity code. Highly productive fourth-generation languages aid programmers in producing complex workflow and event-response applications.

Object-oriented application development technology is also coming of age, as discussed in Chapter 17, "Object-Oriented Development with Client/Server," delivering remarkable increases in productivity and quality. By the late 90s, technology will enable application developers to work at the design level, leaving application development tools to generate most of the procedural code. The best programmers become fantastically productive in such environments.

For the first time, a population of power users of client/server applications will exist. The power users' application development paradigm will be browsing, prototyping, and redesigning! This new technology will have to be harnessed and controlled, yet the ability to integrate new functionality and business processes will be unsurpassed.

In my opinion, the main toolsets that focus on these levels of development and technique are the following:

- Dynasty 2 from Dynasty Technologies
- Forté 2 from Forté Software
- Progress 8 from Progress Software
- Uniface from Compuware
- Unify Vision 2 from Unify

The Mission-Critical Client/Server Database

Mission-critical applications introduce a new set of considerations for application developers related to databases. Developers need to understand that all applications, even those on PCs, become multiuser applications because they are sharing access to database servers. The databases that support the mission-critical application must have the integrity, robustness, and security of databases on mainframe and midrange systems. Client/server databases must also have the following attributes:

- **Interoperablity**. They must work with any combination of networks and client systems that you use.
- **Scalablity.** They must cater to the small regional office of five users and operate at the headquarters that copes with hundreds of online users.
- **Affordablity.** They must be cost-effective at either end of the scale.
- **Data Integrity.** Entity, domain, and referential integrity are maintained on the database server at all levels.
- **Accessibility.** Data can be accessed from WANs, LANs, and multiple client applications simultaneously.
- **Performance.** Performance may be optimized by both hardware and the database itself.

Because of these issues, the most critical technical decision in building mission-critical applications is the choice of database. Provided the RDBMS maintains open interfaces, it should not preclude tools or application choice. If you make a large investment in different but similar tools and database products that don't work together and cannot be used interchangeably, the money will have been wasted. Tools that work well with one database may not be able to be used with another. Hardware that economically runs the systems you choose will enhance the migration. Hardware price/performance ratios move constantly, so no absolutely correct long-term hardware solution exists.

Although many tools and databases have some of these requirements, you should investigate and ensure that the products you purchase and use fit the long term strategy of your organization. A new system, no matter how state-of-art, will become tomorrow's legacy system. You have to ensure that you can maintain and change it. Otherwise, your client/server world will become just as restricted as your centralized one, yet with additional complexity! Regardless of your selection criteria, you want full access to the features and functionality provided by the database from the development tools that you use. Tools that claim to support database-independent development but do so at the expense of giving up the features and functions of the database are no use at all in the mission-critical environment. Sure, they are of value in the smaller, less risky development scenarios but in the key development areas of the business, they are best avoided.

Summary

For organizations, the move to client/server computing has become the greatest mission of IS professionals. Companies are absolutely committed to this new model of computing, working feverishly to get to client/server. But at the same time they are asking, "What are the barriers?," "Where do we gain and lose?," "Can we afford to fail?," "Do we have to add or modify pieces to make them viable?," and "How easy is this versus rewriting to a new standard using our existing equipment?" At the same time, the business is demanding rapidly changing, customer- and client-focused applications that can be delivered in less and less time.

The dilemma is that to get these applications you need to use client/server. Yet client/server only comes from the investment and support from the business users. These same users are also adverse to the risks of changing the core business applications. The only way to achieve the transition to client/server and to use the environment as a means to build mission-critical applications is to embrace today's increasingly tough business environment, to become more competitive, and to reduce IS costs at the same time. The reason that client/ server has become the dominant computing model of the late 90s is that it provides an architectural solution to this dilemma. The benefits of client/server computing are persuasive: significant cost savings, much greater architectural flexibility, better integration across distributed enterprises, and access to more productive development environments. Without these qualities, the business-critical applications will remain unchanged, unmanageable, and constraining.

PART

The Big Move

Upgrading to Client/Server

by Neil Jenkins

IN THIS CHAPTER

A company moving from an existing centralized system to a new client/server environment has to go through a number of changes. Previous chapters covered aspects of this transition, such as the reasons for moving to client/server, the steps and considerations involved to do it successfully, and the way in which technologies and techniques can help you move to client/server. This chapter covers more fundamental aspects of the delivery of client/server by looking at the upgrade issues and changes that may be required in moving from an older legacy system to a new client/server system.

After you have identified what your business objectives are in developing a new system, this chapter helps you examine the available hardware, software, and networks that a client/server will need and identify some key areas that will help you upgrade smoothly.

What Do You Have?

Take a look at the current systems that you have in place. Do you run a centralized mainframe environment? Do you have attached local area networks? Is there stand-alone equipment in your organization that provides a business function? Is there any communication or interconnectivity between any of these systems?

What is the level of integration within your organization at this point? Without a doubt, moving your organization to client/server will force areas to be more tightly integrated.

How upgradable are the hardware and software that currently run your business? Can the machines be upgraded to meet the extra disk and processor requirements that you are to place on them? Are your PCs capable of running the latest operating systems, such as UNIX, Windows 95, or OS/2, or do the PCs need to be upgraded?

What about your software levels? Are your operating system versions stable and up-to-date? What changes will need to be made? Will you have to obtain SQL for your AS/400? Will you have to get the latest version of Oracle? What protocol will be used (for example, TCP/IP)? By finding out the answers to these questions, you should begin to see how big of a task the move to client/server is.

What business applications can you reuse within a new business system created using client/server techniques? Can you "screen scrape"? Can you integrate these legacy applications alongside the new business applications?

With each of these questions, you're trying to find out what effect client/server will have on the current environment. You must understand the answers because they indicate which areas are most in need of change, what areas can stay pretty much the way they are, what areas will need to be changed before you start the move to client/server (such as hardware upgrades), and what areas just won't work!

What Can You Do with the Legacy Application?

Each legacy application is different; however, for the purposes of this book, I have outlined some general recommendations from experience that should be considered against your particular projects.

Integrate It

If the legacy application is centralized and based on nonrelational database structures, try to integrate these legacy applications into your new systems using screen scraping and presentation techniques (see Chapter 1, "Information: The Driving Force"). Begin to analyze and plan for the eventual replacement of the legacy system with new client/server systems based on relational data structures.

The new client/server application could contain both the old legacy application and the new client/server systems. Figure 20.1 shows how a new client/server system might sit alongside an older legacy system.

FIGURE 20.1.

Integrating those applications that cannot be changed.

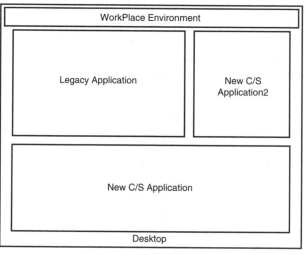

In this way, you can build added functionality around existing systems to deliver business benefit without changing the application. This technique is particularly useful if the application cannot be modified for any reason. Reasons why you wouldn't modify an application include the following:

- The application is not based on relational databases.
- The application is not a long-term requirement.
- The application is to be superseded soon.
- The application is considered to be too risky to change.
- Internal political reasons prevent a change or don't permit a high investment.

Integrating the new system with the current system eases your initial migration to client/server and is a good first step to developing the experience required to develop larger, more complex systems.

Reuse It

Ask yourself if there are complete systems or pieces of systems that you can reuse in the new system? Is there data that you can reuse in the new system (both current and historical)?

If the application is centralized and based on relational database structures (that are well-known and documented), plan to develop client/server systems around these structures. Identify the best places (as per the five client/server models) to store the application logic, and also identify where additional data structures may be needed.

Applications that already exist may be built around data structures that are still valid in a client/server environment. For example, if an application resides on an IBM mainframe in DB2 databases in a well-defined, relational structure, it may be beneficial to leave these databases as they are and move the application logic to PCs linked to these databases. Figure 20.2 shows how this transition might occur. In the first setup, the application is completely housed on the mainframe. As long as the databases on the mainframe are relational, tools can be used to migrate the application off of the mainframe and onto intelligent workstations.

This migration is first achieved by implementing workstations connected to the mainframe. The next stage is to implement an interface to the mainframe on each workstation. This interface is normally in the form of middleware. After an active communication environment is established from the workstation to the mainframe, you can establish direct data access from a workstation through the middleware and into the relevant databases on the mainframe. The final step is to develop your business application around this middleware, thus operating the application at the workstation while retaining the data on the mainframe.

You can save time and effort if you can reuse portions of your existing applications. Take this fact into consideration as you plan your move to client server. Because you still use existing systems effectively, you can do the work in phases instead of implementing the new system all at once.

FIGURE 20.2.
Reusing systems already in place.

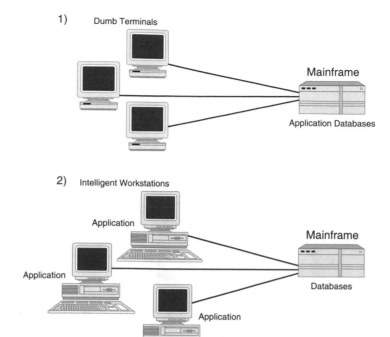

1) Dumb Terminals

Mainframe

Application Databases

2) Intelligent Workstations

Application

Application

Application

Mainframe

Databases

Renew It

The majority of systems in place began with the centralized approach of the 1960s and 70s, and then shifted to minicomputers in the 1970s and 80s. These systems do not fit the decentralized, workgroup computing environments at the desktop. The primary goal of client/server computing is to provide timely and easy access to information so users can quickly respond to change. The ideal client/server solution allows easy access to every potential information source by any authorized user. The older systems were built around users doing functions within their specified roles; users tended to have information availability dictated to them and could not move around within their applications. Providing the flexibility in the new systems allows companies to reap the benefits of client/server computing.

Detailed analysis of your current systems may show you that the applications themselves (rather than the databases) can be renewed and used within one of the client/server models discussed in Chapter 1, "Information: The Driving Force." The likelihood, however, is that these applications would probably take as long to rewrite as it would to develop a new application utilizing all the new client/server techniques. If using the current application is the preferred option, then you are best off using the technologies and toolsets you already have and standard development techniques rather than trying to move the application to a client/server model.

Add to It

If the application is already a GUI application using relational database techniques distributed in a workgroup environment, take a vacation! Seriously, examine and plan how the workflow and business processes can be improved through this application. Add new data structures and business functionality where applicable to support this goal.

Throw It Out and Start Over

Inevitably, most applications that are centralized cannot be re-engineered to support client/server. Those that have tried to do so have faced lengthy time frames or have had projects that have failed dismally. When dealing with such applications, the only choice is to start again and build a new system. Having to start from scratch is usually not a result of mismanagement of the project but rather a reflection of a business's change in focus or direction. This change coupled with old technology being used (particularly data structures) leads to a major re-engineering effort that interferes with the rapid change of client/server that is outlined in Chapter 3, "Business Process Re-engineering."

There is normally tremendous resistance to this kind of major re-engineering effort because you are, in effect, developing new core business systems when the current systems may do the job well. However, if the company is to evolve, improve, and develop, the IS applications must do the same. Progress cannot be made by continuing to rely on systems that are years out of date.

Upgrading Hardware to Client/Server

Client/server systems by their nature are distributed workgroup systems that use the latest equipment at the desktop and the most robust, resilient servers at the back end. The software on these systems is relatively new, complex, highly configurable, and capable of providing very diverse applications across many application types. Client/server systems are found in all areas of business, including medicine, manufacturing, retail, customer service, science, leisure, and, if you consider iD Software's latest program QUAKE, in the Games industry. Because these systems are so advanced, there is an inevitable impact on both the hardware and software within your organization as you move to client/server.

Upgrading Client Machines

Client machines requiring upgrades will need to be upgraded dependent on the client/server application. An application that requires fast mathematical computation may need a fast processor or a fast math coprocessor. An application that needs to handle large volumes of graphic data may require a faster graphics adapter and a large monitor.

Upgrading the Hardware

You should purchase computers that have an upgrade path. The upgrade path should include the ability to add hard disk storage inside the PC, easily add faster processors (through Zero Insertion Force (ZIF) sockets), and add additional RAM. Likewise, it is good policy to ensure that the various adapters needed for the machine can also be upgraded. This upgrading may involve adding a 100 MB Ethernet LAN adapter to replace the existing 10 MB card, or adding a new PCI graphics adapter and removing the existing ISA one.

Eventually you will reach a point where the PCs within your organization can no longer be upgraded, or the cost of replacement may become the same or less than the upgrade. When this occurs, try to use the older machines elsewhere in the company to prolong their lives and value to the organization. Typically, you can use older 386-based PCs for the lesser roles, such as print servers, fax servers, and mail gateways.

For your client/server systems, try to get the fastest computers you can realistically afford. When you upgrade these computers, make sure you are getting the best possible performance from the components. Realistically, the minimum specification you should be looking at is a Pentium-based PC with a PCI motherboard, 8 MB RAM, a fast hard disk over 800 MB capacity, and a 32-bit or 64-bit graphics adapter with on-board graphics acceleration. You shouldn't attempt client/server on any machine less powerful than an Intel 486 DX/2 66Mhz because the performance will be too slow for all but the smallest applications.

Upgrading File Servers

The file server is normally a local area network-based PC or UNIX server running a number of applications and controlling the printing, file sharing, and security of the local area network. A file server contains software that forms a shell around the client machine's normal disk operating system. This shell software filters out commands to the file server before the operating system can receive them.

The file server also maintains its own file system. When a workstation demands a specific file, the file server already knows where the file is because of its own internal, high-performance file system. It sends the file directly to the client. The client maintains a connection table of logically designated mapped drives or resources that point to file system directories or available resources in the file server. The user makes a request, and the file server responds with the file or resource.

Your file servers may need to have additional memory placed in them to support the requirements of your client/server system. For PC-based file servers in a client/server environment, consider the following upgrades:

- Additional RAM and processor cache
- Pentium or Pentium Pro processors

- Symmetric multiprocessors (if the network operating system takes advantage of them)
- Improved bus capabilities of PCI
- High-performance disk drives, such as SCSI
- Disaster upgrades such as RAID, mirroring, and UPS
- High-performance network interface cards (NICs)

For your minicomputer-based file servers, consider the following upgrades:

- Additional RAM
- Disaster upgrades, such as RAID, mirroring and UPS
- High-performance network interface cards (NICs)
- Multiple network interface cards to balance load

Centralized and Distributed File Servers

For most small-office networks, a single file server, known as a *centralized server*, is more than adequate. It functions like a minicomputer; one unit handles all the file serving, and each workstation waits its turn.

If the LAN is designed to handle several different departments or a larger network, adding more file servers to the network is usually more efficient than using a centralized server. These additional units are known as *distributed file servers* because they divide (or distribute) the file serving duties for the entire network. For example, all accounting department workstations use the same accounting programs and access the same data. Sending this information several hundred feet away to a file server is inefficient. A distributed file server located in the accounting department can speed access time and reduce the load on the rest of the network. This approach maintains optimum speed for other network users as well. Accounting personnel no longer need to request files from a central file server that also services other users' requests. Because the accounting department's distributed file server is only concerned with accounting files, it has fewer files to search. It can find and deliver requested information much more quickly. The workload is more evenly distributed across the servers.

Distributed file servers have one other important advantage. If one file server becomes inoperative, the LAN is not necessarily shut down. Another distributed file server (provided it has sufficient disk space) can service the entire LAN temporarily.

Although distributed file servers can provide a number of advantages, they can make security more difficult. The network administrator must now ensure that all file servers' hard disk drives are protected from unauthorized entry.

Dedicated and Nondedicated File Servers

A *dedicated file server* is a microcomputer or minicomputer used exclusively as a file server. By dedicating all its memory and processing resources to file serving, the particular computer usually provides increased network speed and efficiency. In the business world, dedication was not always prized; it was very expensive. However, with the price of minicomputers and microcomputers continually falling, companies are using dedicated file servers.

When a file server is *nondedicated*, it is used as a workstation along with its file-serving functions. The RAM in a nondedicated file server must be partitioned so that some of it is available for running programs. A network workstation might also have to wait for a file to be sent while the file server user loads a program from memory using the machine's microprocessor. The faster the microprocessor, the faster the server can perform its tasks. Because file servers generally are the fastest and most expensive computers in the network, deciding whether to dedicate the unit is difficult. Money that might be saved by making the machine nondedicated is lost many times over by the degradation of the entire LAN. The time lost by users of the other workstations in the network soon shows the folly of trying to economize on this very critical network element. Generally, a centralized file server for more than three or four workstations should be dedicated. It is not wise to use a nondedicated file server in a client/server environment because you need the best performance and reliability you can get from the various servers on the network. Using a nondedicated server will create no end of problems for you. For example, a user may be operating an application on the same machine that is responsible for serving a production database to 25 other users; what happens if the user hits the on/off button by mistake?

Database Servers

The function of the database server is different than the function of the file server. In fact, the database server may not be housed on the file server and may even be on a completely different system, such as an IBM AS/400. The database server's function is to provide the database engine to the client machines requesting work to be done. When upgrading the database server, consider those aspects that improve the performance of a database engine. The database server is your most valuable asset within your corporate network because it controls your organization's data; you should therefore use the best disk facilities that you can on this machine.

The upgrades listed in the section on file servers are still valid, but take special note of the hard disks in the machine. Because the database is continually accessed, the drives are running most of the time. You should therefore consider protecting drive systems by using techniques such as mirroring, duplexing, and RAID.

Mirroring means supporting two duplicate hard disk drives with a single hard disk controller. Every time the database server performs a disk write function, it mirrors this image on its duplicate hard disk. It also verifies both hard disk drives to ensure complete accuracy. If a hard disk fails, the system switches to the mirrored drive and continues operations with no inconvenience to users.

In *duplexed* systems, virtually all the hardware is duplicated, including the disk controller and interface. If a disk controller or disk drive fails, the system switches automatically to the duplexed alternative and records this switch in a log. The performance of a duplexed system is far superior to that of a single system because of *split seeks*. If a certain file is requested, the system checks to see which disk system can respond more quickly. If two requests occur simultaneously, each drive handles one of the disk reads. In effect, this hard disk protection technique greatly enhances the database server's performance.

Novell's NetWare has a feature known as the *transaction tracking system (TTS)*, which is designed to ensure the data integrity of multiuser databases. The system views each change in a database as a transaction that is either complete or incomplete. If a user is in the middle of a database transaction when the system fails, the TTS rolls the database back to the point just before the transaction began. This action is known as *automatic rollback*. A second procedure performed by the TTS is roll-forward recovery. The system keeps a complete log of all transactions to ensure that everything can be recovered in the event of a complete system failure.

Systems managers are very concerned about their systems' fault tolerance. If a database server disk drive fails, they want to know that data will not be lost. A solution today that is growing in popularity is known as *redundant arrays of inexpensive disks (RAID)*. RAID can be implemented at either the hardware level or software level. Hardware RAID is most efficient. A RAID system consists of multiple disk drives used in parallel. This arrangement provides the network with redundancy because parity bits spread across the entire range of disks make it possible to reconstruct the data found on a specific disk should it be damaged. Although not all levels of RAID provide complete redundancy of data, they do provide enhanced I/O performance over a single, very large file or database server. Six different levels of RAID are available.

RAID 0

Data is striped (spread) across several disks to improve I/O performance. Unfortunately, this level of RAID does not provide any data redundancy. The failure of a single disk will result in lost data.

RAID 1

RAID 1 consists of disk mirroring. Data is written simultaneously to a pair of drives. If one drive fails, the data can be retrieved from the mirrored drive. The disadvantage of RAID 1 is that a network with an expensive, very large file server would require an expensive second drive with the same capacity to act as the mirrored drive.

RAID 2

In RAID 2, error correction is implemented to provide fault tolerance. A failed disk can be rebuilt from the error correction data spread across several disks.

RAID 3

With RAID 3, error correction is included in drive-controller hardware as well as with a parity drive. Data is transferred to the array disk drives one byte at a time; parity is calculated and stored on the dedicated parity drive. A single drive controller is used for reads and writes so that only one write to an array drive takes place at a time. RAID 3 is best suited for handling very large blocks of data.

RAID 4

RAID 4 is similar to RAID 3 except that it offers better performance with less fault tolerance. Reads and writes can take place independently on any of the array drives. One disadvantage of RAID 4 is that parity information must be updated for every write to every drive.

RAID 5

RAID 5 spreads data and parity information across all the drives in an array. No single dedicated parity disk performs error checking. Performance is boosted because it is possible to have simultaneous reads and writes of data. RAID 5 is better suited for handling smaller files.

Print Servers

Just as a network file server permits the logical sharing of network resources, a network print server can enable dozens of workstations to share various types of printers. A manager might use a laser printer for his daily correspondence, but once a month he might need a wide-carriage dot-matrix printer to print a critical spreadsheet. An accountant on the same network might use a wide-carriage dot-matrix printer daily to produce balance sheets, financial reports, and charts. Once or twice a month, he might need to write a business letter using a laser printer. With a LAN and its print server software, both the manager and the accountant may choose any printer on the network.

A network print server may be a dedicated microcomputer running print server software only, or it may be a piece of software running on the network file server. To speed up the network printing process, many network managers often install printers with their own NIC. Such printers can receive data from the network at the rate of several million bits per second. They are particularly useful for printing large graphics files containing so much data that they can congest other network traffic while printing. Because these printers are connected directly to the network rather than to a computer, they can usually be positioned anywhere within an office.

Not every model of printer can support a network card. External print servers are available that have parallel ports connected off them to make any printer a network printer.

Using print server software doesn't mean that a workstation can't have its own dedicated printer. Suppose that a marketing analyst uses a thermal color printer almost exclusively to print transparencies of charts for presentations. This printer, connected by a parallel interface and cable to the analyst's workstation, can remain a dedicated local printer and not a network printer so it is always available to the specific user. If the analyst needs to produce a letter-quality report, he can send his word processing file through the network to a laser printer.

Another major reason for dedicating a printer to a particular workstation and not including it as part of the network is that a user may need to print special preprinted continuous-feed forms. A purchasing agent, for example, might need to print dozens of purchase order forms, or an accounts payable clerk might need to print continuous-feed company checks. It would be a lot of trouble for these individuals to have to remove the continuous-feed forms in order to print an occasional letter. Security and confidential company documents are usually the most common reasons for stand-alone printers.

The network administrator ensures that when a program is installed on the network, it is installed with a default printer driver. This default means that usually the program's files are printed on a particular printer. Word processing programs, for example, might routinely send files to the office letter-quality printer or a laser printer. Spreadsheet programs might send files to a wide-carriage dot-matrix printer.

Printer-sharing software should contain a *print spooler*, which is software that creates a buffer for storing print jobs that are waiting to be printed. Think of this buffer as a list of print jobs. As each file is printed, the next file in line takes its place. Sophisticated print spoolers have additional capabilities, including moving a job to the front of the line if it requires immediate printing. On a large office network, time-consuming printing jobs such as daily reports often are placed in the print spooler to be printed in the evening so they don't tie up a printer during peak hours.

Increasing the reporting and viewing capabilities of the user environment can lead to the generation of numerous extra reports. You should strive to make sure that the printing requirements are valid. After all, if the aim of the client/server system is to make information readily available online, you don't want reams of additional printing to be produced. You may need to localize more of your printing capabilities in the user areas by using dedicated workgroup printers. To do this, use the aforementioned printer network interface cards, such as the Hewlett Packard JetDirect for the HP LaserJet series.

Communications Servers

LANs are being used more and more to connect microcomputers to the larger minicomputers and mainframes within a company. Because these larger computers do not run the same operating systems as microcomputers, some translation has to be done between the microcomputer and the mini/mainframe. This translation enables the microcomputer to talk to the larger computers.

This translation can be handled by each microcomputer or it can be handled by a *network communications server*, also called a *gateway*. A network communications server can allow many microcomputers to communicate with a single mini/mainframe computer. Gateway servers allow easy access to mainframe data and simply require a file server computer running specialized software. An example of this software is Novell's NetWare for SAA.

If your client/server system needs to use a communications server, you should have this server operate as a dedicated machine. This way, you are partitioning the servers available on your network and having dedicated servers provide specific functionality to the client/server system. This arrangement can be more costly from an implementation viewpoint, but it also can make the client/server network more resilient because there is no single point of failure for the entire system. If you intend to increase the load on your communications servers with your client/server system, identify the main areas of the server that need to be upgraded. Invariably on a PC communications server, the amount of RAM needs to be increased, as does the available throughput on the network interface cards to both the LAN and the computer that the communications server is talking to.

Other Servers

New types of servers are beginning to appear. In nearly all cases, these servers are specifically configured to manage a particular function. For example, a fax server is essentially a fax machine running on a microcomputer. This server's function is to send and receive faxes. When this server is implemented in a client/server system, users could be able to fax documentation directly to their customers and clients. Incoming faxes could be automatically scanned by the fax server and integrated into a work queue being operated by a business unit. Other notable examples of servers include mail servers, which act as mailboxes on the network, graphics servers, which handle and transport high-quality images around the network, and Internet Web servers, which provide access to and from the Internet.

Most high-performance modern file servers can adequately handle all the server functions outlined previously. From a management and ease-of-use viewpoint on larger networks (typically over 100 users), it is practical to split these functions onto distributed servers.

Upgrading Software to Client/Server

When you move to client/server, you may find that the operating systems and network operating systems in use within your organization need upgrading. The operating systems on both the client machines and the server machines form the heart of your client/server system. Like your own heart, they have to be looked after. They need regular checks as the load placed on them gets heavier. The software on any good client/server system will need upgrading also. As new patches and versions of software packages and operating systems are released, assess in a controlled fashion the impact of such upgrades on your system. If the impact is positive, plan and implement the upgrade.

Upgrading Operating Systems

When looking at upgrading operating systems, say Windows 3.1 to Windows 95, consider the cost of the upgrade versus the business benefits that should be realized. In a perfect world, companies would upgrade operating systems only when there was great benefit to doing so. However, in the current climate, support from vendors for older versions of operating systems rapidly disappears, as does the continued development of packaged applications, as everyone begins developing for the latest version of the operating system. For the client/server world, this trend is something of a double-edged sword. The benefit is that you get better and better operating systems, such as Windows 95 and OS/2, to develop on. The problem is that you risk finding bugs and "undocumented features" of the operating systems in their early stages. You need the new features such as multithreading, 32-bit device access, and more robustness, but you face the dreaded .0 release, incompatibility problems, a rush of quick upgrades to application packages, and general uncertainty about the reliability of the products.

The best way to approach this dilemma depends on your situation. If you are prepared to add the research of new products, such as the operating system, into your client/server project or as a project in parallel, you can uncover the answers to some of the uncertainties. If your client/server system depends on some of the functionality of the new operating systems, then obviously you have little choice other than to make sure your testing and development is particularly thorough.

If you can avoid upgrading, you may take the view that there is less risk by staying with what you know and operate today. This approach is entirely valid and eases complications that may arise within the project plan. However, if there is a competitive advantage to be gained by being at the new level, you will miss out this time around. You may realize that the operating system you are on today has its faults also.

This decision is a difficult one for any company. You have to ask yourselves the questions, "Can we stay or must we move on? If we move on, what are the risks and how do we plan and contain them?"

Upgrading Database Software

When moving from a centralized system to a client/server system, the biggest decisions to be made are those concerning the database server and database engine. Production-capable client/server database engines must be able to provide a similar operational environment to that found in the database engines available on the minicomputers and mainframes of today's centralized environments. Capabilities to be compared include performance, auditing, and recovery systems.

The following features are almost essential in any system:

- Performance tools
- Optimization tools
- Transaction backout and recovery
- Commitment control
- Audit file recovery
- File repair tools
- Mirroring capability
- Remote distributed database management features
- Proper locking mechanisms
- Deadlock detection and prevention
- Multithreaded application processing

Database systems for client/server include the DB2 family from IBM, CA-Ingres from Computer Associates International Inc., Microsoft SQL Server from Microsoft Corporation, Oracle from Oracle Corp., Progress RDBMS from Progress Software Corp., and Sybase SQL Server from Sybase Inc.

Upgrading Networks to Client/Server

The problem with networks is that they never go away once you implement them! Regardless of what you initially spend on a network, you will spend considerably more than that amount to maintain it. Networks grow; they do not shrink, and they have this uncanny ability to link to other networks! This growth causes problems as you upgrade. As your network grows, consider the components of the network and how these may need to change.

Upgrading Cabling

You will need to upgrade and modify existing cabling to allow faster traffic such as 100 MB Ethernet, ATM, and fiber speeds of over 600 Mbps. Cabling will have to be put in place if the system is completely new and no cabling is currently available.

There are no particularly good ways to upgrade cabling if your existing cabling is old and will not support newer, faster network topologies. If the cabling systems cannot operate at higher speeds of 100 Mbps using cabling such as Category 5, you are best off replacing the cabling structures with new cabling. If your cabling is reasonably modern, look into segmenting the networks in order to partition off those areas of cabling that require upgrading. This is considerably easier than replacing the whole lot!

Upgrading Bandwidth

The bandwidth capability of your networks will definitely need to increase (as certain as death and taxes). The 10 MB Ethernet shared between 50 users will no longer be enough. Upgrades to the bandwidth result in high-speed links to the desktop, such as fast Ethernet switching of 100 MB and ATM. The requirement for faster and faster access to the Internet will also increase the demand for more bandwidth. Dedicated bandwidth specifically for communication between server should also be a consideration as your systems are distributed across the world.

The WAN bandwidth will also need to be examined, and it's likely that this bandwidth will need to increase over time. With the advent of managed network services such as Frame Relay and ATM, faster WAN environments are getting easier to implement, manage, and control.

Upgrading Network Operating Systems

Your network operating systems will evolve over time, and like the client and server operating systems, there is no easy way to determine whether to upgrade this technology. The best approach to take is to upgrade only when there is a driving business need to do so. For example, if there is no reason for your organization to move from Novell NetWare 3.12 to 4.1, don't do it until there is a sound return on investment. Moving from one operating system to another is a major project in itself and is not to be taken lightly. Ensuring that you have a sound business need and justification for the upgrade is the only realistic way of moving forward.

The Upgrade Checklist

The list in Table 20.1 will give you a good start as to how your new client/server system will affect your technical environment. When used as a checklist, this list can help to identify the changes that need to be planned. Your client/server system will affect each of these technical areas and may also need to be modified because of them. This list is by no means complete and is intended as a beginning guide only.

Table 20.1. An upgrade checklist.

   I. Hardware

  A. Client Computers

      1. What is currently on hand (brand, configuration)? _____

      2. Number of additional workstations required: _____

         a. IBM compatibility? _____

         b. RAM requirements: _____

         c. Number of disk drives required: _____

            i. For security reasons, do you prefer no disk drives and a remote boot PROM chip? _____

    ii. If disk drives are required, what size and capacity (720KB, 1.2MB, 1.44MB, 2.88MB)? _____

  d. Is a hard disk required? _____

    i. Size (megabytes): _____

    ii. Mounted in what kind of microcomputer? _____

    iii. Formatted with which operating system and version? _____

    iv. What bus type (SCSI, IDE, EIDE)? _____

  e. Number of monitors and monitor adapter cards: _____

    i. Color or monochrome? _____

    ii. Resolution capability? _____

    iii. Size? _____

    iv. Dual mode? _____

    v. Graphics capabilities? _____

    vi. Other features required (Video Acceleration): _____

  f. Other required I/O cards

    i. Parallel or serial cards and cables? _____

    ii. Multifunction cards? _____

    iii. Accelerator cards? _____

    iv. Sound cards? _____

    v. CD-ROM drives? _____

    vi. Others: _____

B. File Servers

  1. Amount of RAM required: _____

  2. Hard disk and cache sizes required: _____

  3. Processing speed: _____

  4. Additional specialized system fault tolerance? If so, what kind? _____

  5. Number of tape backup units: _____

  6. NOS required: _____

  7. Number of concurrent connections required: _____

  8. Other features required: _____

C. Connections to Other Networks

  1. Other networks to be connected: _____

  2. Adapter cards and cabling required: _____

  3. Software required: _____

continues

Table 20.1. continued

    4. Communications servers required: _____

    5. Bridges and routers required: _____

  D. Backbone Networks Required to Connect Networks

    1. Description of networks to be connected: _____

    2. Processing speed required: _____

    3. Protocols to be supported: _____

  E. Gateways to Mini/Mainframe Environments

    1. Local or remote connections? _____

    2. Protocols required: _____

    3. Number of concurrent sessions required (licensed connections): _____

    4. Terminal emulation hardware or software required: _____

    5. Local printer emulation required: _____

    6. Amount of activity to be handled: _____

  F. Minicomputers

    1. What's currently on hand (brand, configuration)? _____

    2. Does information need to be integrated with LAN? _____

    3. Network adapters required: _____

    4. Protocols and network links to be established: _____

  G. Mainframe Computer

    1. What's currently installed (brand, configuration)? _____

    2. Does information need to be integrated with LAN? _____

    3. Network adapters required: _____

    4. Protocols and network links to be established: _____

  H. Printers

    1. What's currently on hand (brands, buffers, accessories)? _____

    2. Number of additional printers needed: _____

      a. Speed required: _____

      b. Type (laser, dot-matrix, and so on): _____

      c. Are printer drivers available? _____

      d. Connection type(parallel, serial): _____

      e. Distance from workstations: _____

    f. Other special features

        i. Special language or downloadable fonts: _____

        ii. Letter-quality and fast dot-matrix modes: _____

        iii. Which workstations/areas will need to access which printers? _____

        iv. Any unusual printing requirements (color, multiple copy, specific accounting forms, and so on): _____

        v. Do any software packages require a specific printer? _____

I. Modems

    1. What's currently on hand (brand, speed, special features, and so on): _____

    2. Number of additional units needed: _____

        a. Transmission mode required (simplex, half duplex, full duplex): _____

        b. Interconnections required (point-to-point, multiple drops): _____

        c. Special features needed

            i. Auto-dial? _____

            ii. Auto-logon? _____

            iii Auto-dial-back-on-answer? _____

            iv. Rackmounted? _____

            v. Other: _____

J. Plotters

    1. What's presently on hand (brands, configuration)? _____

    2. Number of additional units required: _____

        a. Speed: _____

        b. Number of colors: _____

        c. Programs to drive plotters? _____

K. Optical scanners

    1. What's currently on hand? _____

    2. Number of additional units required: _____

        a. Speed: _____

        b. Types of documents to be scanned: _____

        c. Which programs will need access to this data?

        d. Full page and/or color? _____

continues

Table 20.1. continued

L. Other Required Hardware

    1. Number of cash registers required (for retail environment): _____

        a. Connection type (serial, parallel): _____

        b. Compatibility with which point-of-sale accounting program? _____

    2. Number of badge readers required (for manufacturing environment): _____

        a. Will employees clock in and out of several jobs in the same day? _____

        b. Must this information be interfaced with an accounting program's payroll module? _____

    3. Number of multiplexers required: _____

        a. Devices to be attached: _____

        b. Device location: _____

        c. Type of transmission required: _____

        d. Speed required: _____

    4. Number of protocol converters required: _____

        a. Devices to be attached: _____

        b. Protocols involved (SNA, IPX, BSC, ASCII, and so on): _____

    5. Power protection required (UPS): _____

        a. Voltage regulation? _____

        b. Limits sags, surges? _____

        c. Prevents common-mode noise? _____

        d. Provides battery backup? _____

II. Software

A. Operating System and Utility Programs

    1. Operating system

        a. Which system and version? _____

        b. Multiple versions on the network? _____

    2. Electronic mail program

        a. Menu-driven? _____

        b. Help screens available? _____

        c. Displays messages? _____

        d. Distribution lists? _____

        e. Message receipt notification? _____

      f. Message forwarding? _____

      g. Ability to define multiple user groups? _____

      h. Ability to print and file messages? _____

      i. Ability to attach files including graphics, sound, and video? _____

      j. Other features desirable: _____

  3. Network calendar

      a. Can all workstations access calendar features? _____

      b. Ability to schedule rooms and hardware resources? _____

B. Network Management

  1. Ability to perform diagnostics? _____

  2. Ability to add and delete user groups? _____

  3. Password protection? _____

  4. Ability to maintain user statistics? _____

  5. Ability to handle remote dial-in users? _____

  6. Ability to handle multiple operating systems? _____

  7. Ability to handle bridges to other networks? _____

  8. Ability to add and delete printers? _____

  9. Security provided

      a. Log-in level (time, station, account restrictions)? _____

      b. File system (directories and files; attributes)? _____

      c. Printing system? _____

  10. Menu-driven, but sophisticated users may bypass the menu and use commands? _____

  11. Log-in scripts or other facilities (such as batch files) permitted to make it easier for novice users to log in? _____

  12. Printer server software: _____

      a. Number of printers supported by print server: _____

      b. Print queues? _____

          i. Storage location on the server: _____

          ii. Multiuser/operator capable? _____

          iii. Can users control own print jobs? _____

      c. Printer redirection commands available to network users? _____

          i. Are there commands for setting parameters of specific print jobs? _____

continues

Table 20.1. continued

        ii. Are there commands for disabling network sharing of printers temporarily? _____

    d. Printer types supported

        i. Parallel? _____

        ii. Serial? _____

        iii. Laser? _____

        iv. Line printers? _____

        v. Direct network attach? _____

13. File server software: _____

    a. Size and number of volumes supported: _____

    b. Network drives permitted (mapped drives)? _____

    c. Virtual drives (transparent to users)? _____

    d. Restore tape to disk capability? _____

    e. Directory and file allocation tables duplicated for fault tolerance? _____

    f. Directory and file allocation table caching for performance? _____

14. Network communications server software: _____

    a. Protocols supported

        i. IPX? _____

        ii. TCP/IP? _____

        iii. SNA? _____

        iv. AppleTalk? _____

    b. Ability to handle call-back modems? _____

    c. Automatic dial-out? _____

    d. User statistics provided? _____

C. Current Software Standards

    1. Word processing: _____

    2. Spreadsheets: _____

    3. Graphics: _____

    4. Accounting: _____

    5. Other application software: _____

Summary

Upgrading your existing systems to client/server should be part of the client/server project itself. The magnitude of the work to be done in upgrading is very much dependent on the state of the systems you already have. Failure to adequately upgrade your computer systems may cause your client/server project to fail due to poor response times, sluggish components, and user despair! Your client/server systems are only as strong as their weakest link; if that link is the technical infrastructure of any of the three main components, you will have problems. As outlined in Chapter 6, "Steps for Migrating to Client/Server," plan the upgrading of the infrastructure as part of the project. Upgrading is just as important as any coding or testing, and should be treated as such. Through proper upgrading, you can turn a good system into a great one.

Supporting Client/Server

21

by Neil Jenkins

IN THIS CHAPTER

Users of large mainframe systems rarely experience downtime of a critical nature in their well-built systems. They also do not expect data loss on a mainframe system; when a transaction completes, the data is reliably stored away. PC users, however, have had different experiences. When a system hangs, a virus activates, or the power fails, users are not normally surprised that they have lost their data.

Companies that move towards client/server require mainframe-like support and robustness. There are, therefore, significant challenges in supporting the client/server environment. This chapter covers the main areas to consider when setting up a support system. After a client/server system is implemented, there are steps you can take to ensure that it is always operating effectively and downtime is kept to a minimum. In this chapter, you learn about establishing a support routine that keeps your client/server system in a healthy state. When trouble does strike, this chapter provides tips and describes tools that will make you a true troubleshooter.

Availability

Your system uptime is its *availability*. Availability is the capability of the system to be available for processing information and doing its expected work. In the midrange or mainframe environment, availability is typically above 95 percent. In order to get to these levels, a combination of good technology and procedural steps is required. Procedural steps are required because most failures today are caused by human error. To minimize human error, IS departments implement rigid change management procedures for all areas of the main computing systems.

Client/server systems must be able to provide the appropriate levels of availability required by the business need. Providing the same technology features or procedural steps is not as easy as it is in the mainframe world because the client/server environment consists of many diverse machines located geographically rather than one large machine located centrally. If your system is in a major city with fast repair service, you can get by with fitting client/server systems with technology such as redundant power supplies and battery backup to protect data in case of a sudden shutdown. However, in smaller sites, perhaps in remote locations around the world, you may need to purchase duplicate equipment for swap out because it might be impossible to get (or guarantee) quick response times from a service contract supplier. You also probably won't be able to justify the cost of supplying technical resources at all locations of a client/server system, so remote management becomes another necessity.

The Initial Build

Client/server systems should be built by trained staff and trained installers. Most configuration problems that arise could have been avoided by getting the installation right the first time. It is therefore important to ensure that the client/server hardware is specified and tested prior to implementation. The hardware should be configured to the organization's specification. Software should be loaded by trained staff and tested to ensure that it works as expected. If you buy PCs that come with pre-bundled software that won't be used in the system, remove the software so that it doesn't cause confusion.

The Help Desk

Providing support to the user community on client/server systems is best done through a help desk. A help desk is a set of systems and procedural steps used by technical and applications staff to provide support to end users in areas ranging from basic how-to and problem determination to advanced troubleshooting and diagnosis. This support is normally provided by telephone, but it may also be provided by on-site visits or remote PCs. A professional help desk can seriously improve the credibility of installed client/server systems. Effective implementation of a client/server system depends on the availability of immediate support when problems occur.

The majority of problems, typically 75-80 percent, should be solved within the initial contact period with the user. Of the remaining problems, 15 percent should be dealt with and resolved within the hour. The remainder should be solved or a workaround found within 24 hours. PC software users expect ease of use, intuitive navigation, and recovery within their software. If a client/server system does not have these characteristics internally, the help desk must be available at the first sign of trouble. And users want more than just a voice mail number to call!

Help desk personnel must be able to sympathize with the frustrated user. They must also be clear and concise when solving the problems. Most users want to know why their systems went wrong and discussing this subject can improve the relationships between IS and the users. End users are usually very upset when the crash or problem results in loss of data and their valuable time. The help desk personnel should be able to defuse these situations and not lose the confidence of the end user in the client/server application.

Help desk problems must be tracked. Many help desk tracking packages are available on the market today, so it is probably not worth your while to build your own because most of these products meet the needs of most organizations. Tracking problems enables you to identify common problems and find a resolution so that the problems do not occur again. These problems might be because of a bug, faulty configuration, or lack of user training. Tracking gives help desk staff the tools to cure the problem rather than just fix the symptom.

Remote Management

Support for geographically dispersed systems can be greatly improved through the use of remote systems management tools. Such tools effectively allow support staff to connect by LAN, WAN, or modem to users at other sites to diagnose problems. The support staff takes over the remote client machine and can reconfigure, reinstall, or modify it. These tools are particularly important when a remote site does not have staff employed to support the technical environment. The tools are also helpful when the remote staff members are in another country where they do not speak your native tongue.

Preventative Maintenance

A client/server system needs regular care to make sure that it operates smoothly and efficiently. Preventative maintenance is a group of activities done over a period of time that ensure that your client/server system gives you, the Systems Manager, a minimum amount of problems. These activities are best arranged on a weekly, monthly, quarterly, and yearly basis. Feel free to modify the timeliness of these activities to your own, or the company's, needs, adding or modifying the list as you deem appropriate. The support team within your IS organization normally handles these activities. In a new IS organization, as discussed in Chapter 10, "System and Network Management," this team would be the Service Delivery team.

Weekly Maintenance

The weekly maintenance activities include daily and weekly backup, as well as housekeeping. Daily backup is a daily activity normally done overnight. Weekly backup and housekeeping are weekly support activities normally done at the end of the week.

Daily and Weekly Backup

Each day you should back up the system using the media you have. The backup does not need to be a full backup, but it should at least be an incremental backup of files that have changed since the previous day. Nearly all backup systems allow you to make an incremental backup. Avoid those systems that don't.

At least once during the week, make a full system backup, including the network operating system and its file areas. Always make sure that you use high-quality tape or disk media; using cheap tape or disk may result in an inability to restore at a later date.

It is good practice to cycle tapes or disks over at least a three-week duration. This technique is normally called *Grandfather-Father-Son* data storage and enables you to have several complete backup sets in case any one should fail. Also, if possible, try to store at least one set of backups off-site. If a small fire or other problem occurs, you can recover the majority of your data from the off-site backup. Data security companies offer this type of storage as a service. Using a data security company keeps staff from having the responsibility of taking data home, which is not ideal.

Always test the backup you have made by using your backup software's compare feature. Testing ensures that you can restore from the backup at a later date. Too many restore procedures fail because the backup was not tested. This task is often overlooked; companies assume that the backup has been successful only to realize at a later crucial time that the backup has errors.

> **NOTE**
>
> A network requires an effective server backup system to ensure that valuable files are never destroyed.

Several companies, including Palindrome, Cheyenne Systems, and Emerald Systems offer backup software. Palindrome Corporation's The Network Archivist (TNA) is an example of specialized software that helps a network manager manage and control network backups. TNA enables a network manager to establish a backup schedule, indicate when tapes should be rotated, and schedule an unattended backup. The program maintains a backup history for each file so that the network manager can restore a specific version of a file. This feature is useful when a user needs an earlier version of a file that has been overwritten. The network manager can restore an individual file, a directory, or the entire server.

Housekeeping

Housekeeping entails spending time on the clients, servers, and network making sure that standards are adhered to and files available for use are being regularly accessed. A file server can quickly become a dumping ground for users' temporary data. If such an area is required, make one available, but let all the users know that the files in the area will be deleted at the end of each week. It is not good practice to have huge data areas filled with files that people can't identify.

Keep a consistent naming standard for user names, network addresses, and configuration files. This standard will help you save time when problems occur. System management is considerably easier when you have a good knowledge of the standards in place. These standards should be documented and widely available to the support staff.

To improve housekeeping, try to restrict users' access to only the areas that they need. This restriction keeps the files that they use in the correct locations. Audit files so that when data areas get large you can see which files belong to whom and therefore have a contact name to see whether the files are still required. Finally, make it policy to back up and archive file server data files (not application files) that are older than two years and have not been accessed within that time.

Within the client machine, you should restrict access to the parts of the operating system that the users do not need access to. For example, you can use Windows 95's policy and system registry editor to restrict the applications and settings a user can access. If you remove access to the Control Panel, users will be unable to change their network addresses. Sometimes it can also be beneficial to restrict the "user fun" sections such as the ability to change colors, backdrops, and wallpaper and play supplied games.

Also, ensure that the client machines only have the hardware they need. This advice may sound strange, but in these days of PCs being supplied with CD-ROM drives, sound cards, and various other peripherals as standard, your support environment workload can increase dramatically. Do you want to spend your time making sure a user in the accounts department can listen to his music CDs at the right volume? You must at some point ask what the business benefit is.

Monthly Maintenance

The following sections cover the tasks you should do monthly.

Virus Scanning

In a perfect world, there would absolutely zero risk of viruses infecting your network systems and potentially damaging your data. Regretfully, users may deliberately, or more often, inadvertently bring a virus in to the company. Some simple steps can significantly reduce the chances of this happening.

Aim to have all floppy disks scanned before they are used in the company. Invest in a virus scanning tool, such as McAfee's Scan Virus, Norton Anti-Virus Toolkit, or Dr. Solomon's Anti-Virus Toolkit. All these products are regularly updated and can deal with most types of virus. The file server should be scanned at least monthly. In most cases, weekly scans are recommended. Be careful, however, because some virus scanning software can slow network performance if run all the time on a file server. Check with the appropriate vendor prior to purchase to see whether this is the case with its product.

Purging the Server's Hotfix Area

On a monthly basis, you should run the purge utility on your server. This tool removes salvageable files from the deleted file listings. In a Novell environment, this utility is the Purge tool. On an AS/400, this utility is the Reclaim Storage command. Other platforms have other names for this utility.

Peer-to-Peer Hard Disks

Main machines that are shared in a client/server peer-to-peer network should have the hard disks checked monthly. This check involves running the Scandisk and Defrag utilities under MS-DOS or Windows 95, for example. Running these utilities will rebuild and correct any errors in the file allocation tables of these machines and also write the data files sequentially. These actions keep the disk organization correct and reduce disk I/O on these machines. By using the Windows 95 policy tools, you can have these utilities run automatically at the time you set.

Quarterly Maintenance

The following sections describe the maintenance activities you should do each quarter.

Cabling

Cabling has an uncanny ability to come free of its connector or socket, and it's probably fair to say that the majority of networking problems are attributable to cabling. Each quarter, examine your cabling connectors and cabling for loose connections and wear and tear. Replace worn or damaged cabling. Where possible, make sure that cabling is firmly screwed into position, but not so tightly that you need Arnold Schwarzenegger's arms to remove it again!

Powering Hardware

Most modern server equipment is designed to run and operate 24 hours a day. It rarely gets switched off. It is a good policy to power off server systems in a controlled manner once a quarter. Turning off the power allows the diagnostic routines in the machine to run when the power is switched back on. These routines can often identify problem areas in a machine before that area fails (often during a very critical time in the working month). If you use this method, any problem can usually be fixed in a controlled manner rather than the panic state that often comes about when a LAN crashes. Taking down the system in a controlled manner involves notifying all users that the system will be shut down in *x* amount of time and asking them to log off or disconnect. Ensure that all users are off of the system just prior to shutdown. Shut down the particular server components in the order recommended by the hardware vendor, and then power off the system.

Fixes and Patches

Once a quarter, discuss with your product vendor what patches and fixes have been brought out for the particular operating systems that you are running. These may be patches and fixes for the client, server, or network operating system. Obtain a copy of these patches and see whether they improve or correct any difficulties that you may be experiencing. Test patches on a test machine before updating large numbers of users, and then apply any patches in a controlled manner.

Obtaining updated patches and fixes to operating systems can be valuable, particularly when the system is connecting to a midrange or mainframe computer through emulation and middleware. CompuServe and the Internet are valuable information networks for this type of information and are also very useful as support tools.

Yearly Maintenance

The following sections describe yearly maintenance tasks.

Hardware Maintenance

Physical hardware maintenance contracts are usually reviewed annually. These contracts are for you to have a backup plan if the PCs and servers in your company fail. Usually, you pay a fixed price contract for the year to a third-party maintenance company who guarantees repair or replacement of a particular machine within a contracted period. The period of time can vary significantly dependent on the following things:

- The equipment to be repaired
- The physical location of the equipment
- The contract

Most companies settle for a next-day fix on LAN workstations and a four-hour fix on LAN servers. This kind of agreement means that the maintenance company will arrive and fix the server within four hours. It is very important in any contract situation that you make sure that the maintenance company has the correct parts for your server in the event of failure. You have a real problem if your 4GB NT server is under a maintenance contract with a maintenance company that can only fix 1GB hard drives. Verify that any third-party support staff is authorized by the server vendor to repair the failed hardware. This authorization gives you some degree of comfort that the support engineers know what they are doing to the machine holding all your corporate data (which you backed up…didn't you?).

Network Operating System Support Contract

In addition to a hardware maintenance contract, you may want to take out a Network Operating System Support contract. This contract is usually placed with the vendor of the NOS or a recognized support vendor. Typically, this is an annual contract providing you with regular monthly updates, patches, fixes, press releases, unlimited telephone support for a few designated individuals, and sometimes a number of visits from the support vendor to check your LAN environment. This type of contract can usually be extended to provide support coverage and additional resources from the support vendor if needed.

Server Hardware

At least once a year have the server hardware checked by removing memory and adapter cards, removing dust inside the machine, and reseating all adapters and memory. Do not attempt to do this check if you are not authorized to repair the machine. Your hardware maintenance company will usually do it for a nominal fee.

Troubleshooting Network Problems

Many network managers spend a disproportionate amount of their time troubleshooting network problems. A user calls to report that she is unable to print, and a second user calls to complain that he is unable to access a particular database. A third user might call to complain that he is unable to log into the network. The network manager diagnoses the user's problem by asking a series of questions—just as a doctor asks several questions to diagnose a patient's illness.

First, the network manager must determine whether the problem is hardware- or software-related. Is the problem limited to a single user's workstation, or is it a problem with the client/server program itself? Is the user's local network interface card defective, or is the network connector linking the workstation to the network loose?

Some network managers utilize a program such as Closeup, which enables them to take over a local workstation and view that workstation's screen from their own monitor. The network manager might take over the workstation of the user who complained about not being able to print to see whether the correct printer has been selected. The network manager might take over the workstation of the user unable to access the database to ensure that the appropriate middleware is installed.

Maintaining Network Hardware and Software Documentation

Network documentation is a very important part of a network manager's daily responsibility. When a new release of a network application appears, the network manager must install this software promptly so that the software vendor can provide accurate technical support should it be needed.

Another major maintenance chore for the network manager is to create and maintain network documentation. If a user's network interface card becomes defective, the network manager must have documentation available that shows when the card was installed, the card's serial number, and the warranty expiration date. If a server goes down, the network manager must know whether it is covered by a 24-hour service contract or an 8-5 contract. Similarly, the network manager must keep accurate documentation on other network equipment (such as printers, bridges, routers, gateways, and tape backup units).

The network manager should be able to access this information rapidly so that the equipment's manufacturer or vendor can be called quickly. Technical support departments usually require the equipment's serial number, warranty expiration date, and detailed information about the

LAN's topology, including the version number of the network operating system. This type of critical information often should be placed in a network log book to provide clear audit trails of all network changes. Password changes, alterations in user access, software updates that have been installed, and program additions or deletions can be noted and dated. Without such an administrative tool, the network represents a disaster waiting to happen. This log book should be locked up when not being used.

To reduce the number of calls from frustrated users, the network manager must provide users with accurate and easy-to-read network documentation. How can users direct a document to a specific printer? How can a user copy several network files from one directory to another directory? How can a user customize his operating system if allowed? These are the types of questions that must be answered in network documentation.

Periodically, a network manager must walk the network to check the LAN's cabling, as discussed in the section on preventative maintenance. Checking the cabling can determine if connectors are coming loose, cabling is cracking or is pinched, or hubs are operating properly. Some network managers report they have to reset network devices such as hubs at least a couple of times a week to keep them operating efficiently.

Because so many network devices now have diagnostic lights to indicate how they are performing, a network manager can quickly determine whether traffic is flowing smoothly or whether access collisions are taking place or a channel is not operating properly. Many modern file servers are running 24 hours a day, seven days a week. To make the server go through its diagnostic routines and self test, a network manager will normally shut down the file server and then power it up again. The messages generated by the diagnostic routines and self-test are very useful in determining whether components are failing on the server.

The Network Supervisor's Tools

A network supervisor should have a number of tools and materials on hand, including both standard and Phillips screwdrivers, as well as needlenose and diagonal-cutters pliers. A volt-ohm meter or digital voltmeter is useful for cable testing.

When workstations suffer hardware failure, often it is because of a bad interface board, a defective floppy disk drive, or some bad memory chips. Although companies probably have in-house technicians to handle these problems, a network supervisor might find it expedient to keep some replacement parts on hand. The supervisor should also keep an ample supply of printer ribbons, printer paper, extra formatted tapes for file server backups, toner cartridges for the network laser printer, and certainly a box (at least) of formatted floppy disks.

A Protocol Analyzer

A *protocol analyzer* provides information to help you understand why a network is not running at top efficiency. Protocol analyzers analyze the packets of information flowing across a network and provide very valuable statistics. Although several major protocol analyzers are on the market, I will focus on one of the major contenders, Network General Corporation's *The Sniffer*.

The Sniffer is attached to a network as if it were a workstation and listens to every transmission that goes by. The Sniffer is a self-contained computer with its own network adapter card, hard disk, operating system, and software. If you exit from the Sniffer program, the machine becomes a standard DOS-based Compaq microcomputer or Toshiba portable. While running the Sniffer, however, the machine has two major functions: to capture frames and to display information.

The large amount of information passing through a protocol analyzer is usually filtered by establishing parameters. The user may want to select information by station address, protocol, or particular frame pattern.

The Sniffer uses a bar graphic to display traffic density as kilobytes per second, as frames per second, or as a percentage of the network's available bandwidth. You can display in linear form or logarithmic scale. The Sniffer also displays traffic statistics by using counters that reveal the number of frames seen, the number of frames accepted, and the percentage of the capture buffer (the area in the Sniffer's memory that holds captured packets) in use.

For each station that is contributing to network traffic, the Sniffer is able to display (in real time) a count of frames per second or kilobytes per second. The machine also displays pair counts for each pair of workstations communicating information. Figure 21.1 illustrates both a summary and a detailed display of an exchange between two stations. Notice that the Sniffer identifies the two stations communicating from its own name table; apparently user Dan is communicating with the NetWare SERVER. The conversation you are eavesdropping on consists of a response from the NetWare file server regarding its LOGIN file.

Notice also that this protocol analyzer provides some detailed file directory information about the file being accessed. You are able to observe the file's length, its creation date, the last access date, and the last update date/time.

As this brief discussion of the Sniffer illustrates, protocol analyzers have proven to be invaluable tools for network managers. With some practice, a network manager can read and analyze his reports with relative ease and uncover a good deal of information regarding the network's general health. Other protocol analyzers include Watchdog and Lananalyzer for Windows.

FIGURE 21.1.

A report from The Sniffer (reprinted with the permission of Network General Corporation).

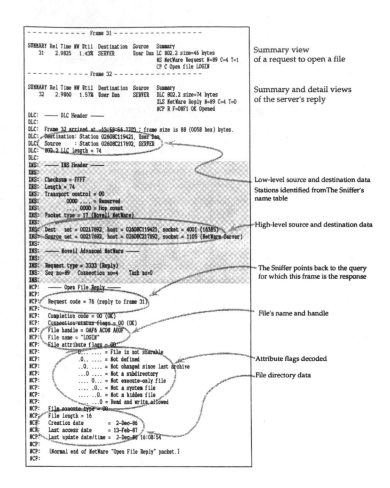

Summary

Supporting a client/server system requires considerably more thought than supporting a centralized system. Proper planning of the network and systems management activities will improve the support and levels of response that you can give to your user base. Following a schedule of preventative maintenance chores may seem tedious, but such chores can prevent serious problems.

Performance Tuning and Optimization

22

by Neil Jenkins

Good performance from a client/server system comes from a number of things, but it is mostly the result of a combination of good design, excellent development and testing, and a continual emphasis on optimization. Applications developed for client/server may achieve substantially greater performance when compared with traditional workstations or host-only applications.

One reason for this difference is the difference in complexity between client/server and other types of systems. As shown in Figure 22.1, a typical centralized system may have several applications and databases, but it has only one operating system, one communications protocol (SNA for example), and one main computer.

FIGURE 22.1.

The complexity of a centralized system.

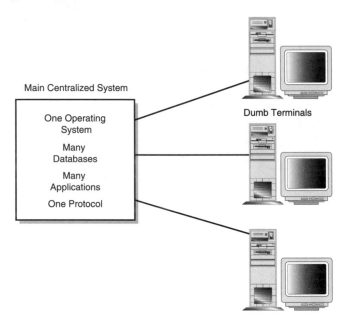

By comparison, Figure 22.2 shows a picture of the complexity of a client/server system. Because the number of distinct components has significantly increased, the level of complexity has also significantly increased. Because you are using intelligence at the client level, you have to cater to an operating system and applications at this level. You may also have to deal with many protocols at the network interface and local databases residing on the client. Figure 22.3 shows how this complexity is further increased by running client/server across a WAN.

Figure 22.4 shows how the complexity of a system can sharply increase when the number of components in a system reaches a certain amount. As complexity increases, so do potential performance problems or bottlenecks. By concentrating on these bottlenecks, you may be able to come up with some ways to optimize the system's performance.

In general, a client/server system will always fall foul to its weakest component. As your experience grows, you will begin to be able to spot and remedy these weak areas. The constituent parts of a client/server system can be identified individually as the clients, the servers, the databases, and the networks. This chapter looks at each of these parts.

#### Chapter 22

FIGURE 22.2.

The complexity of a client/ server system.

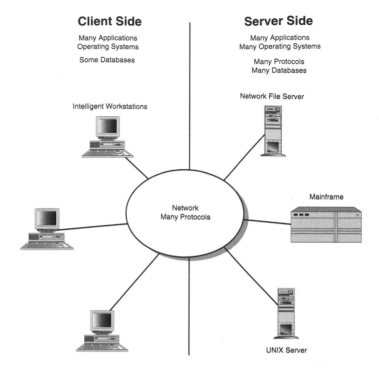

Client Side

Many Applications
Operating Systems

Some Databases

Server Side

Many Applications
Many Operating Systems

Many Protocols
Many Databases

Intelligent Workstations

Network File Server

Network
Many Protocols

Mainframe

UNIX Server

FIGURE 22.3.

The complexity of client/ server across a WAN.

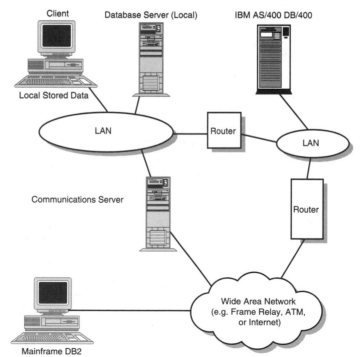

Client

Database Server (Local)

IBM AS/400 DB/400

Local Stored Data

LAN

Router

LAN

Communications Server

Router

Mainframe DB2

Wide Area Network
(e.g. Frame Relay, ATM,
or Internet)

FIGURE 22.4.
Complexity in relation to the number of components.

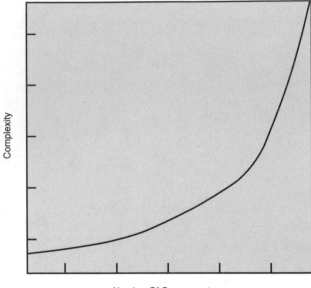

The Client Performance

Performance in client/server systems can be improved in many ways. In theory, you could spend forever and a day improving the performance of each component, be it client, server, or network. This section focuses on the attributes you can examine in order to improve the performance of a client machine.

Hardware

The performance of the client workstation is to a certain extent dictated by the physical hardware within the client. The client machine's performance will be improved by improving any of its major subsystems. In a PC, these subsystems would be the amount of available RAM, the processor speed, the video graphics speed, the disk I/O speeds, and the speed of the network interface card.

NOTE

When purchasing client machines, the best strategy is to buy the fastest, most reliable machines available. In today's market, the price of machine components is dropping so quickly that unfortunately the month after you make a purchase, something better will have come along.

It is rare to see a client/server system's performance significantly boosted by major changes at the client workstation level unless drastic changes are made. The majority of improvements come by altering the client such that it runs the application and the underlying operating systems better. A hardware upgrade can sometimes have this effect. For example, increasing the amount of client RAM from 8 MB to 16 MB will have a significant performance improvement on applications created for Windows 95 and OS/2.

Regular maintenance of the machines also keeps performance at a high level. These tasks include deleting redundant temporary files and defragmenting the hard disks and are covered in more detail in Chapter 21, "Supporting Client/Server."

Software

The software on the client workstation is broken down into two areas for performance reasons. The first is the operating system that runs on the client. This software may be products such as Windows 3.11, Windows 95, Windows NT, OS/2, Linux, or X Window. The second area is the client application or applications themselves. The following sections discuss these areas in more detail.

Operating System

Because workstation users have become more sophisticated, the capability to be simultaneously involved in multiple processes is an essential requirement for client/server systems. Independent tasks can be activated to manage communications processes, such as electronic mail, electronic feeds from news media and the stock exchange, and remote data collection (downloading from remote servers both internally and externally). Multiple personal productivity applications, such as word processors, spreadsheets, and presentation graphics, can be active. Several of these applications can be dynamically linked together to provide the desktop information processing environment. Functions such as DDE and OLE permit including spreadsheets dynamically into word processor documents. These links can be hot so that changes in the spreadsheet cause the document in the word processor to be updated. The business applications operate seamlessly with these purchased off-the-shelf products to deliver integrated business systems.

Doing all these activities in parallel requires a real multitasking operating system such as OS/2, Windows 95, or Windows NT. These operating systems require better hardware than their predecessors. Workstation performance can be improved by adding additional levels of RAM to the workstation. In addition, any improvements you make at the hardware level, as outlined earlier, will improve performance.

Most multitasking operating systems today are 32-bit. Therefore, you should, whenever possible, use tools, purchased applications, and products that are also 32-bit. Using only 32-bit applications ensures that the machine does not have to worry about running 16-bit code, which will operate slower than the same product running as a 32-bit application. Keeping your development work at a level that is the best for your client workstation will keep performance at a high level.

New releases and service packs that become available for operating systems should be treated with caution as they are something of a double-edged sword in that they can improve or slow down performance depending on the application. The worst case scenario is that they cause incompatibility problems and stop applications from working at all. Make sure that you test all new software before implementing it on the system.

Search out configuration and optimization tips and techniques on your particular operating systems from information sources such as CompuServe, AOL, and the Internet.

Applications

The client application is normally where the largest improvements can be made. The development team created the client application to deliver a business system and in so doing realized (but obviously did not implement due to time constraints) new techniques and ways of improving the systems. By making changes in the way the application processes information after the system is implemented, you can greatly improve performance.

In general, GUI-based applications that are developed for the client can be improved in a number of ways. The best way of determining problem areas is to ask users what areas of the application they consider slow. The first answer will likely be all of it! Subsequent answers will help you zero in on the main areas of concern and the real areas of need.

Performance at the client level is very difficult to judge because each user's perception of response is different. Users who were used to the subsecond response of their previous mainframe screen complain that all screens are slow; the fact that you spent months streamlining the process so that the overall process takes two screens rather than 20 won't enter into the conversation. On the other hand, some users will be delighted with the system and won't highlight shortfalls that require attention. Whatever responses you decide to use, prioritize them based on value to the business and make the further enhancements in a version x.1 release. The areas outlined later on database access are equally relevant to the client if local data is housed on the client.

You also can make a few adjustments that improve the user's perception of the application's performance. For example, in a GUI environment, application screens should appear on the client before they are populated with data. This technique makes the screen appear faster, and the user perception is that the application is operating faster. Likewise, when a business process requires several seconds to complete, indicate this fact to the user in the form of a bar graph that fills up as process goes through its cycle. This graph shows the user that something is happening and gives an idea of how long the user has to wait. This method always makes a transaction appear to finish faster because the brain is concentrating on how much has been done and how much is left.

Search out optimization tips and techniques on your particular development language from information sources such as the original vendor, CompuServe, AOL, and the Internet. Alternatively, you could employ a consultant who is well-versed in your particular language to have a look at your source code and recommend improvements or ask others who have done the same thing for advice. The Internet opens all sort of opportunities for finding out whether someone has solved your problem already. Just as a note, if you take help from people off the Internet, try giving some of your knowledge back in return.

The Server Performance

Just as it is important to fine-tune client machines, tuning the server machines can lead to large performance gains. This section concentrates on performance gains and improvements you can make at the server.

Hardware

Upgrading server hardware, just like upgrading client hardware, can improve the performance of the client/server systems you operate. The points highlighted in the client section are equally applicable here. Using multiple network interface cards within a server can also improve performance by moving the network load from one overburdened card to two or more balanced cards.

Within file servers and PC-based database servers, high-performance file systems using technologies such as SCSI-2 and RAID offer dramatic performance improvements over older ISA and EISA drive technologies. Use these technologies to ensure data integrity and speed on your PC-based systems.

Software

Database and communications processing should be offloaded to a server processor. Some applications also may be offloaded, particularly for a complex process that is required by many users. The advantage of offloading is realized when the processing power of the server is significantly greater than that of the client workstation. Shared or enterprise-level databases or specialized communications interfaces are best supported by separate processors so the client workstation is available to handle other client tasks. Database searches, extensive calculations and queries, and stored procedure execution can be performed in parallel by the server while the client workstations deal directly with the current user needs. These benefits are obviously best realized when the client workstation supports multitasking.

Several servers can be used together, each performing a specific function. In this way, performance of the individual components can be improved. For example, a system may be broken down into a file server, a communications server, and a database server rather than having one completely overburdened single server trying to do all three tasks. By splitting the tasks (particularly the database function from the file serving function), you can gain performance benefits because the optimization of each task is somewhat different.

Choosing servers that support symmetric multiprocessors gives performance gains over single processor models. Operating systems such as Windows NT support multiprocessors, and server performance can be improved by using such technology.

The Database Performance

A book of this type cannot possibly cover all the issues related to database performance. Instead, this section covers the major areas of optimization that can be used across most departmental and enterprise-level database systems. To make client/server database applications perform well, you have to follow two simple rules:

- Minimize network traffic
- Process data on the fastest, most appropriate box

Implementations that store large databases on network servers but use logic that's only embedded in the PC client to perform analysis violate both of these rules and rarely perform well. These rules are the reason why most things written about using tools with ODBC data sources go to great lengths to explain what portions of a query are and aren't evaluated on the server. These rules are also the reason why three- or two-tier implementations with the data and logic encapsulated together generally outperform two-tier implementations with the user interface and logic encapsulated together.

In any real-world client/server implementation, some data will be stored locally on the client for performance reasons. This data is often static tables such as those used in list boxes for selecting options, but the application may require that data be stored temporarily on the client PC. For example, in some decision support applications, users might specify a first cut at the data they are interested in. The application retrieves that data from the server and places it in local tables. Subsequent analysis is performed on the local data, minimizing network traffic and the load on the server while providing the user with faster response to subsequent queries.

Most well-known commercial database programs are capable of very high performance on large databases. To fulfill this performance potential, you must use efficient database design, indexes, and queries. These areas are the best candidates for obtaining significant performance improvement. Experimentation with indexes is especially suggested. A methodical approach in analyzing performance problems will often yield very significant improvement for relatively little time investment.

Efficient Database Design

Normalization of the logical database design yields the best performance improvement of anything you can do to your database. A greater number of narrower tables is characteristic of a normalized database, and a lesser number of wider tables is characteristic of a non-normalized database. Some of the benefits of normalization include faster sorting and index creation, narrower and more compact indexes, and fewer indexes per table (which helps the performance of the updating process).

In an ideal world, the database would be completely normalized. However, a highly normalized database is usually associated with complex relational joins, which can hurt performance. For products such as SQL Server, normalization will often help performance rather than hurt it. Normalization increases the number and complexity of joins required to retrieve data. Microsoft suggests carrying on the normalization process unless it causes many queries to have over four-way joins. You will need to use your database staff's experience to determine the extent to which you normalize the database.

If the logical database design is already fixed and total redesign is not feasible, you may be able to selectively normalize a large table if study shows that a bottleneck exists on this table. If access to the database is conducted through stored procedures, this schema change could in theory take place without affecting applications. If not, you may be able to hide the change by creating a view that presents the illusion of a single table.

Efficient Index Design

Unlike many nonrelational systems, relational indexes are not considered part of the logical database design. Indexes can be dropped, added, and changed without affecting the database schema or application design in any way other than performance. Efficient index design is foremost in achieving good database performance. Experiment with different forms of indexes in order to find the optimum use.

SQL Server's Optimizer reliably chooses the most effective index in most cases. With this particular product, the strategy should be to provide a good selection of indexes to the optimizer and trust it to make the right decision. This strategy reduces analysis time and gives good performance over a wide variety of situations.

You shouldn't have more indexes than are absolutely necessary to achieve adequate read performance because of the overhead involved in updating those indexes. However, even most update-oriented operations require far more reading than writing. Therefore, don't hesitate to try a new index if you think it will help. You can always drop it later.

Efficient Query Design

Some types of queries are inherently resource-intensive. This fact is related to fundamental database and index issues common to most RDBMSs. These queries are not inefficient, just resource-intensive, but the set-oriented nature of SQL may make them appear inefficient. They are intrinsically costly when compared to a simpler query.

Most people are aware that normalizing data into the two-dimensional tables that constitute the heart of the relational model results in more entities. Suppose you were working with a contacts database. In a nonrelational environment, repeating groups of data would be used to hold multiple contact names and phone numbers within an organization. However, in the relational environment, you would create three tables (or files) that contain company, contact name, and contact phone information. This increase in entities affects performance quite severely. More files have to be opened, more disk I/O is carried out to store and retrieve data, and programming becomes more difficult.

This simple example does not demonstrate the magnitude of the problem as it exists in reality. Where 50 or so entities in a nonrelational environment might be adequate, you might typically find 300 are required in a relational system that represents an enterprise-level client/server system. As the system increases in size, so the number of entities increases. This increase is what causes database systems to fail if they were designed from a departmental view and are scaled up to try to fit the enterprise view. Far from enhancing productivity, this situation causes a drop in productivity because of the number of files that have to be manipulated at the same time. Fine-tuning such large systems also becomes increasingly difficult; using proprietary database optimizers can be helpful in such situations.

As a direct consequence of the increasing number of entities that are implemented in the relational environment, you create more relationships using foreign keys. For example, the company code in the contact table would be a means of associating contacts with companies. In systems where hundreds of entities are involved, you may end up implementing thousands of foreign keys. These keys are almost always indexed, which means you might end up creating thousands of indexes.

Unfortunately, most RDBMS have no way of directly representing a relationship hierarchy other than the use of foreign keys. As a result, these keys can get quite lengthy, being composed of multiple fields. For example, the telephone number record in the contacts example requires a company code and contact code to identify it. This proliferation of foreign keys is probably the most significant problem associated with RDBMS. From a mathematical point of view, if n entities exist, there are $n(n-1)/2$ possible relationships between them. Thankfully, not every entity is related to every other entity, but there is a tendency for the number of relationships to grow geometrically.

From the large number of foreign keys that have to be implemented within a RDBMS, another problem occurs, which is an associated increase in data volumes. This problem is particularly serious where a deep natural hierarchy exists. Many of the foreign keys may have several fields to specify them, and you can quickly reach the situation in a database where the greatest part of the data volumes is associated with foreign keys. The actual data held in rows is one problem, but don't forget that there is a data volume overhead associated with the indexes related to such data also.

The only really effective way around these problems is to use effective design techniques as outlined in previous sections. One thing to keep in mind when designing queries is that large result sets are costly on most RDBMSs. Try not to return a large result set to the client for final data selection through browsing. It is much more efficient to restrict the size of the result set and allow the database back end to perform the function for which it was intended. In addition, the creation of calculation tables can sometimes decrease the query loads on a server.

The Network Performance

When you are analyzing the performance of a client/server system, consider the following items with regards to the network:

- The application development should include development, performance testing, and system testing across the network.

- The network design should be completed and documented as part of the development process.

- Look at the current utilization of the networks and see whether this utilization is causing bandwidth and/or response time problems.

- Reduce the number of users per LAN or increase the bandwidth available to each client if bandwidth or response time problems exist. If you make these changes, ensure that you have adequate lead time to implement them before the client/server system goes live. This lead time reduces complications that may be network-based when you are troubleshooting problems with the application.

Excessive network traffic is one of the most common causes of poor client/server system performance. Designers must take special care to prevent this problem by minimizing network requests and easing the strain on network resources.

Minimize Network Requests

In the centralized host environment, network traffic is reduced to the input and output of presentation screens. In the client/server models, significantly more network traffic may be introduced to the system if detailed consideration is not given to the requester-server interface.

In the file server model, which is implemented by many database products such as dBase IV, Foxpro, Access, and Paradox, a search is processed at the client workstation. Record-level requests are transmitted to the server, and all filtering is performed on the workstation. As a result, rows that cannot be explicitly filtered by primary key selection are sent to the client workstation for rejection. (Now where is the sense in that? Hey, let's transport what we don't want down to the client and have it rejected!) In a large shared database, this action can be devastating. Records that are owned by a client cannot be updated by another client without integrity conflicts. An in-flight transaction might lock records for hours if the client user leaves the workstation without completing the transaction. For this reason, the file server model breaks down when there are many users or when the database is large and multikey access is required.

However, with the introduction of specific database server products in the client/server implementations, the search request is packaged and sent to the database server for execution. The SQL syntax is very powerful, and when it is combined with server trigger logic, it enables all selection and rejection logic to execute on the server. This approach ensures that the answer set returns only the selected rows and reduces the amount of traffic between the server and client on the LAN. (To support the client/server world, small database languages such as dBase and Foxpro have been retrofitted to be SQL development tools for database servers.)

Online transaction processing (OLTP) in the client/server models requires products that use views, triggers, and stored procedures. Products such as Sybase, Ellipse, and Ingres use these facilities at the host server top join, to apply edit logic prior to updates, calculate virtual columns, or perform complex calculations. Wise use of OLTP can significantly reduce the traffic between client and server and use the powerful CPU capabilities of the server. Multiprocessor servers with shared memory are available from vendors such as Compaq, Hewlett Packard, and Sun. These servers enable execution to be divided between processors. CPU-intensive tasks, such as query optimization and stored procedures, can be separated from the database management processes.

Ease Strain on Network Resources

Using application and database servers to produce the answer set required for client manipulation will dramatically reduce network traffic. There is no value in moving data to the client when it will be rejected there. The maximum reduction in network overhead is achieved when the only data returned to the client is that necessary to populate the presentation screen. Centralized operation, as implemented in minicomputers and mainframe environments, requires every computer interaction with a user to transfer screen images between host and the workstation. When the minicomputer or mainframe is located geographically distant from the client workstation, WAN services are invoked to move the screen image. Client/server applications can reduce expensive WAN overhead by using the LAN to provide local communications services between the client workstation and the server. Many client/server applications use mixed LAN and WAN services. Application design must evaluate the requirements of each application to determine the most effective (not necessarily cost effective!) location for application and database servers.

Summary

Performance and optimization in client/server systems involve all the components of the overall system. The very nature of the integration of client/server systems causes potential bottlenecks to appear in any component. By having a structured approach to tuning each of the individual components, you can make performance improvements. Experience on individual systems plays a part in being able to make improvements, yet it is also important to take every opportunity to reflect, redesign, and fine-tune the system. Helping staff to understand the other areas of the client/server system that differ from their skill sets will help them to improve their components for the good of the whole system.

Securing a Client/Server System

23

by Neil Jenkins

Imagine spending months building your organization's new core client/server system. It is implemented to great success, providing your company with significant competitive advantage. The money starts rolling in, and your promotion looks guaranteed because of a job well done. Then one quiet summer's night a computer virus begins its damaging work, eating its way through the main databases. The unknown (and uninvited) program takes control of your system, and within a matter of minutes, the virus has spread to every single computer on your network, across buildings, network links, and geographic regions. You reach for your keyboard to stop the onslaught, but you are locked out of your own workstation. You sit there helpless as the system is slowly, painstakingly, and methodically deleted.

Or imagine your company is responsible for arranging the vacations of your four million members, yet the responses to your telemarketing campaign begin to go down because your prices are considered too expensive. Some analysis of your membership base reveals that all four million members have received an offer from a rival company on the same vacation at 20 percent cheaper than your own prices. You wonder how this could happen; you took all the right precautions. Your systems are secure. How could anybody gain access to your information systems?

Regretfully, the client/server systems that you develop are more susceptible to damage from computer viruses, fraud, physical damage, and misuse than any centralized computer system. The reason for this susceptibility is because a client/server system is distributed. As a result, equipment is also distributed. Hackers can deliberately misuse this equipment to gain company information if the system security is inadequate.

Security is a concern from both a technical and management viewpoint. It is therefore critical to examine your business needs and develop a security policy that addresses both of these issues. Without an effective security policy and a strategy to implement that policy, you may be assuming more risk than you realize. Effective computer security comes through an understanding of what can happen and what has happened on your systems. Without this knowledge, it is only a matter of time before you experience a serious breach of security.

Information is major business asset, and the protection given to this information should reflect its value to the company. Computers and advanced network technology allow your business to develop, process, and transfer information around the world. From concept to production, your business is online. Your networks link you to valuable information from stock market reports to customer credit histories. With a comprehensive security policy, architecture, and implementation, your business benefits from appropriate access while locking out intruders.

The Changing Information Technology Environment

New technologies, such as satellite and mobile communication, portable laptop computers, image processing, multimedia, and object-oriented solutions are evident in all industries: banks with shared, automated teller machine networks; manufacturing firms with electronic data interchange arrangements with suppliers and customers; doctors and health care services with electronic connections to laboratories and diagnostic specialists; companies marketing products on the Internet; and corporate executives traveling with laptop PCs, to name a few. Unfortunately, unauthorized access to computing systems is a bigger threat than ever before, and it is on the increase all the time.

Today's open distributed information technology environment presents many challenges for effective security management. Securing the centralized system of the '70s and '80s was difficult enough, but now system managers are faced with multivendor systems and, ultimately, multiple security issues. In the distributed era of the late '90s, security must encompass host systems, PCs, LANs, workstations, and global WANs. These new configurations are creating an environment of increased security concerns and add complexity to the development of a company-wide comprehensive security solution. The following sections discuss some of the issues influencing this new environment and their effect on security.

More Sophisticated Users

Today's users are more sophisticated than users of the past. They have powerful desktop workstations with access to private and public networks. They have a host of end-user publications and easy-to-use software at their fingertips. Their sophistication advances with technology, resulting in increased productivity and value to the business. Although sophisticated users can be helpful for your business, you need to be sure a security system is in place to prevent the possibility of any unauthorized access to resources.

The Open Environment

Whether you planned for it or not, your organization is most likely comprised of multivendor information processing resources. Shared applications as well as advancements in networking technology have made interoperability a necessity in even the smallest companies. Security must now reach beyond the closed system and offer high-quality protection in the open, interconnected world of systems. This kind of security is particularly relevant if your business wishes to conduct business with users of the Internet.

Today's Security Threats

Threats in an open distributed environment reach far beyond those encountered in the centralized system. Because each individual piece of the network and system can be linked to many other networks and systems, a single unauthorized event could have far-reaching impact. Some possible threats in a distributed environment include the following:

Viruses infect unsuspecting programs and often cause damage. Their most dangerous attribute is their ability to self-propagate. They can be passed from user to user through diskettes or can infect hard disks and network file servers. Viruses can be found on most of the major operating systems, particularly DOS-based systems.

Worms are programs that replicate themselves to destroy data or usurp system resources.

User fakes are common in an environment where trust is based on identification rather than authentication. The intruder takes control of a workstation by faking the identification of a trusted user. The resultant damage is tracked back to the unfortunate user rather than the intruder.

A **Trojan horse** is a piece of damaging code slipped inside a useful program by an unauthorized user. When the program is executed, the unwanted Trojan horse is executed also. Trojan Horse programs can range in what they actually do. Common ones wipe out data; more complex ones can save company data to other locations for later collection.

The **back door** often refers to a specific hidden word that a programmer may use to directly access the programs, bypassing the security systems. Hackers search endlessly for such a lapse in your security system. If a hacker finds a back door, he may alter some security program to enable unauthorized users to bypass access controls established on your system. This term was made even more popular by the film *Wargames*.

Evaluating Your Information Assets

Not all information assets are equally valuable or equally exposed. Therefore, you need to manage your information assets like any other aspect of your business. Each asset or class of assets needs to be identified and assessed in terms of value and risk.

Your business will typically have some data that requires more protection than other data. Information related to payroll, personnel, customers, research and development, strategies, and roll out schedules are considered valuable assets. Although information about company policy, stock prices, and health care plans is important, it presents less risk to your business if it reaches the public domain. The information assets you identify must be assessed in terms of their value to your business and the impact or damage they would have if their security were compromised. Similarly, these same assets require further analysis to determine their level of security.

Although all employees need to have access to information, and some employees need to have access to sensitive information, rarely does any employee need access to all information. Information has degrees of sensitivity that can be measured by the effect the loss, exposure, or modification of the information would have on your business. It may be more advantageous to audit access to some information instead of strictly limiting access. In general, types of data requiring additional security are those that could do one or more of the following:

- Have an immediate negative effect on your business if viewed or changed by any unauthorized means

- Cause legal problems for your company if viewed or changed by any unauthorized means
- Require their origin or authenticity verified
- Contain confidential employee information

The Challenge of Client/Server Security

Security capabilities exist to varying degrees on many of today's stand-alone platforms. The IBM AS/400 operating system, for example, has robust user-level and database-level security, but its ability to monitor the activity on the attached Novell LAN is somewhat limited. The Novell LAN is unable to provide security to the AS400. The client/server environment introduces a totally new dimension of considerations as systems from different vendors using different formats and protocols must now interoperate with each other seamlessly. Keeping these systems secure poses new challenges beyond the security capabilities of any one of the individual platforms. Synchronizing clocks and time stamps and integrating resource directories of the different systems are just a couple of the problems that need be addressed. As your IS structure migrates to this type of environment, you must understand and address the distributed security requirements that arise.

The Main Areas for Security

A typical client/server system requires security across its different sets of resources. Figure 23.1 shows these levels of security and some of the harmful activities associated with each level.

FIGURE 23.1.

Computer security on a client/server system.

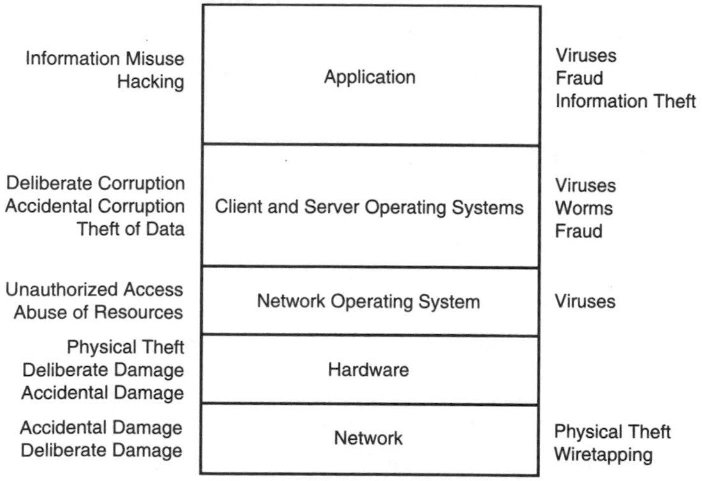

Harmful activities (left)	Resource level	Harmful activities (right)
Information Misuse / Hacking	Application	Viruses / Fraud / Information Theft
Deliberate Corruption / Accidental Corruption / Theft of Data	Client and Server Operating Systems	Viruses / Worms / Fraud
Unauthorized Access / Abuse of Resources	Network Operating System	Viruses
Physical Theft / Deliberate Damage / Accidental Damage	Hardware	
Accidental Damage / Deliberate Damage	Network	Physical Theft / Wiretapping

Hardware security requires you to protect the physical components of the system. For example, you may prevent unauthorized users from starting the PCs on a LAN by requiring entry of a power-on password. Most systems have mechanisms to prevent users from opening the case of the system, and others protect the system against addition of unauthorized components or cables. You can house the physical machines in lockable cabinets with only the monitors and keyboards accessible. As the theft of computer memory and computer chips continues to grow, this option becomes more and more attractive. Larger servers and minicomputers are increasingly being housed in centralized computer rooms that protect the systems from physical harm.

You can use the operating system to protect resources in a single stand-alone system. For example, the operating system protects files on local disks from unauthorized access through the file system interface. Operating systems such as OS/2, with its restricted Workplace Shell, and Windows 95, with its System Policy Editor, can further restrict access to the client machine. Both operating systems provide the toolkit for the systems administrator to provide end users with only the access required to do their job.

The network has to have protection against unauthorized use. Network security mechanisms include link encryption and gateway authentication. Link encryption can protect the network cabling against passive wiretapping, and gateway authentication protects the network against the introduction of packets by unauthorized users.

The network operating system protects distributed resources. Because files in a distributed file system frequently reside in caches on various machines, you need to protect the caches as well as the server disks, even if the caches are transparent to users. The network operating system also provides validation of all users logging onto the LAN.

At the application level, you need to protect against misuse of information by providing the users with only the systems required to do their jobs, where possible. You can restrict productivity tools in various ways to avoid misuse, and electronic mail systems can provide encryption that protects messages against disclosure to anyone except the intended recipient.

Integrating Platforms

Because few distributed systems are alike across all platforms, the security systems of each platform are likely to have been designed independently. To produce manageable, secure systems, you must understand the security mechanisms of all the platforms to be integrated. These mechanisms include the different server operating systems, the client operating systems, the network operating system, the application security, and the physical hardware security.

This variety of security mechanisms creates an increased opportunity for security breaches, be they deliberate or accidental. Configurations where the security mechanisms of the different platforms are not designed together often have the security concerns discussed in the following sections.

Compromised System Integrity

Because the security mechanisms of the different platforms were not designed to work together, they do not protect each other. This lack of protection could result in attacks at the seams between the different security platforms.

Multiple Logons

Each platform usually has its own user database and its own logon procedure. These databases and procedures may create a very complex environment for the user who has many different identities and many different passwords. The typical LAN user using a normal system invariably only connects to one file server. However, in a client/server system, the user may need to connect to many different servers on a frequent and infrequent basis. Figure 23.2 shows how client/server users may need to log onto four computer systems to get access to their complete system.

FIGURE 23.2.

Logging on to a client/server system.

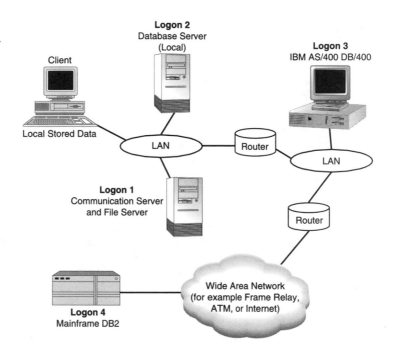

In such a system, the user is often presented with a bewildering array of logons, passwords, and user IDs to all the different systems. If users are required to access an AS400, Novell LAN, mainframe, and a UNIX server, they may have four logons that are all different. There are two schools of thought on how client/server access should be handled.

The first states an idealistic view that one logon and password should seamlessly connect users to all the systems that they require. Each of the major network operating systems is trying to move towards this approach, including NetWare 4.1 with its NetWare Directory Services. This approach does have its problems. The main one is that it involves a major security risk. Once a hacker or rogue user knows another user's password and user ID, she can access all the associated computer systems. In this environment, if I knew your single password and user ID, I would be immediately logged onto the AS400, Novell LAN, mainframe, and UNIX server with your clearance. The access could not be tracked back to me. Any misuse would be considered to be done by you! If there were different passwords or IDs for each system, I would only have access to one system.

The second method is to force users to have distinctly different passwords for each system. This method gives the best security, but it does increase the amount of times a user has to log on to the different systems. If I knew your Novell LAN password and user ID, I could access the LAN, but I wouldn't be able to access the other systems. This method is therefore less risky. In both cases, periodic password changes should be implemented to provide even better security.

Dissimilar Audit Logs

Each platform uses its own audit log, audit event formats, and auditing interface. Each audit log knows only its version of a user's identity, making correlation of events in different platform logs difficult. Different platforms may not have consistent ideas of system time, further complicating the correlation task and making the sequence of events difficult or impossible to reconstruct. If a security problem arose that crashed both your production AS/400 and your attached Novell LANs, you would need to access both the systems log of the AS/400 and the server log of the Novell file servers. Neither log, however, would contain information on the other. The net result being that you would have to go through a painstaking, manual comparison to try to identify the source of the problem.

Building Your Security Requirements

A client/server environment brings with it new security requirements beyond those found in a stand-alone system. In a minicomputer or mainframe system, the operating system can be trusted to protect resources from unauthorized access. This is not the case in open distributed systems. Communications take place over an accessible network where messages between machines can be observed or forged. A new security system is required in order to control access to resources in a distributed environment.

Your organization will have its own specific set of security requirements. The following is a list of common security requirements for client/server systems. This list is by no means exhaustive:

Secure sign-on—When users connect themselves to the network and client/server system, passwords should not flow in clear text. Encrypted passwords are required to reduce the security risks in this area.

Client security—Security on the client has requirements beyond those typically needed on a mainframe. Mainframes are typically in a secure location, are too large to carry away, and have tightly controlled access to their operating systems and applications. Client workstations are often in accessible locations, with portable data and applications, and are small enough to carry away. At incredible risk are the laptops that are left lying around on desks. Pay particular attention to the security needs for these machines because they are very easy to steal.

Security management—Security management is the administration, control, and audit of your organization's security policy. Security management goes beyond password and access control administration. An important requirement centers around the registration and enrollment of system users and the management of programs, data, and security information.

Secure electronic commerce—With the advent of public networks like the Internet, secure electronic commerce has become a major security requirement. Firewall protection can aid in securing your network gateways while your business takes advantage of electronic commerce. You should use a secure firewall gateway between your organization and the Internet.

System integrity—System integrity is the ability of your operating system to prevent the circumvention of its security, auditing, or accounting controls. IBM was the first and main software vendor to commit to this objective.

Antivirus protection—Protecting your assets from infectious viruses, worms, and other damaging programs is now an essential requirement. Exposure sources are public networks such as the Internet, diskettes and other outside media, and, regretfully, unscrupulous employees.

Accountability—You should be able to monitor specific security events using a single audit function. This audit function should allow you to monitor the system and generate reports, and it should help you assess the adequacy of established controls in accordance with your organization's stated policies.

End-to-end security—It is not enough to secure the ends or gateways of your network; you need to be sure all points in between are secured as information flows from point of origin to point of destination.

Building a Security Solution

Your security solution will be born from the platforms that you use in your client/server systems. Define your requirements based on the availability of tools and techniques for these platforms, taking into consideration the requirements that are outlined in the previous section and those that are additional or different for your organization. By identifying your requirements, you can begin to build your security solutions.

In the initial stages of client/server development within your organization, you may decide to use those systems that are already in place across the different platforms that you use. This decision is quite common as companies begin to move to client/server. As you become more experienced in client/server development, however, you will realize that by using existing systems you waste time trying to keep the various diverse systems integrated manually.

After you define your requirements, you can develop a security policy and implement a security solution. IBM's proven security methodology, for example, consists of the following tasks:

- Assessing and managing risks as your business and the environment change
- Defining your security needs and policies
- Implementing the products and services that align your security and business objectives
- Administering the security policies and practices for your organization
- Auditing your security controls
- Repeating the life cycle processes to maintain the vitality of your security solution

Information Security Issues

To take full advantage of networking opportunities, you need to be able to verify the authenticity of all users, both internal and external, to your system. Customers accessing the system need to be sure that the servers are real and not impostors and that the data and programs are reliable and not modified by an unauthorized party. The competitive advantage in the late 1990s will go to the companies that can deliver the most cost-effective services while ensuring secure transactions and access to confidential information.

When implementing an information security system, you need to take three main information security issues into consideration:

- Confidentiality is the most obvious benefit of information security. Maintaining confidentiality involves ensuring that staff members have access only to the data that they are allowed to see and modify. When deciding the level of confidentiality required for a system, consider the cost of compromise of data to the company. The cost to a company could be loss of market share for the disclosure of trade secrets or a lawsuit for failing to protect personal data.
- Integrity means that data should remain in its originally intended format and should not be vulnerable to inadvertent or malicious changes. Integrity is not the same as accuracy. Accuracy, as discussed in Chapter 8, "Data Warehousing," cannot be guaranteed. You can have integrity without accuracy, but you cannot ensure accuracy without integrity.
- Availability is ensuring that systems and data are available to those who need them. For example, an airline booking system needs greater availability than an office mail system because the airline loses sales when a booking system is unavailable.

User Awareness

A crucial area of information security that is frequently overlooked is user awareness. Staff do not genuinely understand the cost of damage to computer systems as a result of misuse. For example, the casual play of the latest game infected with a virus could wreak havoc on the network, causing hours of work to be lost. You should begin developing good security practices by educating the user base as to the policies that are in place within the organization. The education should stress the importance of information to the business. Individuals may not be aware of the value of trade secrets, which, if revealed to competition, could jeopardize the business. Likewise, the corruption of a database could bring down a production line.

The following are a few guidelines you might want to include in your policy:

- No games
- No photographic images other than those supplied with applications
- Regular cycling of passwords
- No software other than those programs specified as a company standard
- No use of software from magazines or brought in by individuals
- All diskettes must be regularly scanned for viruses

The key to the most secure systems is the password, so time spent educating users about nontrivial passwords is well spent. Some simple rules apply to passwords:

- Never pass them on or write them down (how many times have you seen passwords taped to monitors?)
- Choose nondictionary words
- Change passwords regularly (you may want to force this in the operating systems)
- Do not use personal information (for example, names, car type, or favorite film)
- Mix letters and numbers or use at least one nonalphabetic character (for example, $CWAR*ENEG@ER). If you have a NOS, such as UNIX, that allows mixed-case passwords, use both uppercase and lowercase.

All security issues should be included in an awareness program so that the message is delivered across the company. The program should not take long and should also be placed within a company's staff handbook. Ideally, try to make a security awareness program part of any new employee induction process also. The program should contain information on responsibilities, threats, controls, and solutions, including disciplinary procedures, which should be explained to all employees during recruitment. Staff should be made aware of the dangers of viruses and encouraged to scan all incoming and outgoing data to prevent proliferation. Passing on a virus to another company could be a major blow to your corporate image, especially if you are a software house.

Security for the Clients and Servers

Companies have heavily invested in information systems and the people managing this technology. No company can afford to ignore these investments and start from scratch. Client/server security implementations must include current applications and operating environments. Investments in popular heterogeneous environments need to be protected as you ensure the security of your distributed system. The following sections explain the areas you need to focus on when protecting your clients and servers.

The Client

The client machines pose the greatest threat to security because they connect to the servers that are elsewhere in the organization. The client machines also are easily accessible and easy to use.

In order to provide good security at the client level, you need to consider the role of the client machine. The client machine provides access to all the servers that the user needs to do her or his job. As such, client machines are normally located within easy access for the users who use them day to day. These locations are typically offices that are designed to be open and friendly for staff and visitors. Regretfully, these offices can provide the same cozy atmosphere for thieves and hackers. It is not possible to lock away your client workstations in tight, secure rooms like you can your servers, so it is wise to consider the location of these client machines in your security plans.

Physical Security

There are number of measures you can take to protect the client machine physically:

- Use diskless workstations to protect against software piracy and viruses

> **NOTE**
>
> Diskless workstations have often been criticized as not being flexible enough. If you agree with this view, consider buying one of the various types of diskette locks on the market that give as much protection as the diskless workstation.

- Lock the PC cases of the client machines
- Set alarms to go off if the client is moved
- Set smoke alarms inside the PC cases to go off if the case is opened by unauthorized staff
- Lock the client machine into a small case attached to the user desk that only allows access to the keyboard and monitor and effectively houses the PC case
- Use power-on passwords

As the number of computer thefts per year shows no sign of declining, protecting your computer investments in these ways can save you time, money, and stress!

Network Security

Once turned on, the client machine will connect to some form of network. At this point, you can implement a number of security measures. First, the network server must receive a valid user ID and password from the client machine and authenticate the user against the valid user list held on the server machine. You can tighten this security by only allowing users to log on to specific client workstations. You handle this by building a user workstation list on the authenticating server. When a user logs onto the network, his user ID and password are recognized by the server; but the network address for the client machine is also checked. If the user ID and network address are a valid combination, access is granted. If not, access is revoked.

Windows 95 has security features that enable you to lock out the local hard drive of the client workstation if the network authentication fails. This feature is particularly useful if you have built a client/server system that houses some production data on the client workstation. When a user signs onto a Windows 95 system attached to NetWare, the system can be set up so that authentication is immediately done at the server. If authentication fails, then access to the operating system on the client is revoked. As systems improve, more systems will provide access security in this way.

If you are running a system that requires the user to log on to each of the individual servers that create your client/server system, you will need valid user IDs, passwords, and possibly network addresses for all these servers.

Application Security

Once the user has access to the main client/server application, you can add levels of security to the application. For example, you might tie the network user ID to a security access table within the application. If Tony signs onto the customer application, he is only allowed to view customer details, whereas Kevin can update the customer details. These access rights are taken from the network user ID and are then used within the application. When setting up this type of security, keep in mind the information in Chapter 15, "Workflow," which discusses the business processes surrounding this application. It may be wise to allow users to update all data that they can view to improve the business process.

The application can have varied levels of security based around the user using the system. A call center environment, for example, might have something called supervisor clearance to handle those calls from customers that are special in some way. If the supervisor is the only one that can use this clearance, customers may be kept waiting while staff members try to track down the supervisor for help. Instead, you may want to let the normal staff use this special clearance.

You then can monitor the usage of this clearance and record each event. If you build supervisor access type functionality into an application, everyone signs on with the supervisor's password before long anyway.

The Servers

Server security is different from client security. Whereas the emphasis for client security is biased towards physical security, the bias for server security is software, data, and network security. These issues are covered in the following sections.

Physical Security

Most organizations handle the physical security of the servers well. They recognize the value of the servers and house them either in custom-built computer rooms or in lockable rooms near the client machines. In addition to this separate room, server machines can have the same security attributes as the client, with the exception of the diskless workstation! You should use a lockable diskette drive to the server.

The servers should be operated on by authorized personnel only and should be attached to an Uninterruptable Power Supply (UPS). A UPS protects the machine by filtering the power supply to the server. It prevents power spikes and power drops from reaching the server. If the power does fail, the server detects the UPS has kicked on, and the UPS notifies the server. The server then shuts itself down in a controlled manner to protect data.

Software Security

All servers should be protected with the right levels of password security applicable to your business. The passwords to gain access to the servers should be cycled regularly, and if there are complications with any IS employees leaving the company, the passwords to the servers should be immediately changed. Upgrades to the software should be planned, monitored, and controlled. Virus protection should also be active on all your PC-based servers.

Most servers have auditing capabilities to show when and how events occurred. Take advantage of these audit trails; they will help you to track security problems when they arise.

The Network

Network security is often overlooked. The main area for network security is physical aspects. Where possible, all network cabling should be in ceiling compartments, cable-managed desks, and under false floors. Concealing the cabling in this manner makes it more difficult to be wiretapped and also significantly reduces the number of network failures due to damaged cabling or cabling that has been kicked out of its sockets.

By using intelligent hub technology from companies such as Cabletron and Bay Networks, you can also restrict access to the network for workstations connecting to the hub. For example, you may not want a particular group of client machines attaching to the network between 9 PM and 7 AM. By using the management features of the intelligent hubs, you can restrict access in this way. See Chapter 21, "Supporting Client/Server," for additional notes on network cabling.

Security and the Internet

In the last 10 years, the Internet has grown from 50 to well over 10,000 networks. In 1988, the National Science Foundation estimated that there were over half a million users; today that organization estimates that more than 20 million people around the world use the Internet, and the number is growing daily and rapidly.

One of the Internet's key strengths, and one of its key weaknesses, is that no one agency or organization is responsible for its overall management. Thus, it has been free of any official control and regulation. Management is decentralized and informal, residing primarily at the host site and the individual network levels. Early in the Internet's development, responsibility for managing and securing host computers was given to the organizations, such as college campuses and federal agencies, that owned and operated them. It was believed that the host sites were in the best position to manage and determine a level of security appropriate for their systems. Each of the Internet's thousands of networks maintains operational control over its own network, whether it is a backbone network, regional network, or local area network.

This presents a number of security risks. An organization's Internet access can be compromised if the passwords become known. The reliance on the use of passwords is the biggest challenge. Intruders can capture information on user IDs and passwords for subsequent access to company hosts and accounts. This is possible because the password is used over and over and the password passes across the network in clear text.

Secure Business on the Internet

The Internet, and other such public networks, offer businesses and their customers links to valuable information and to each other. These networks will be by far the most popular way for business to be done throughout the late 1990s. People ask for business e-mail addresses and home page locations nearly everyday. It is now almost considered essential that a company has a presence on the Internet. If you deny access to the Internet, you are limiting your ability to reach customers and access valuable tools like Telnet, FTP, Gopher, and the various Web browsers such as Internet Explorer, Mosaic, and Netscape. Therefore, you need a way to provide your employees and customers access to the Internet (and each other) without compromising system security. You need ways of restricting the incoming flows of Internet mail to protect against viruses, and you need to be able to stop users from using the Internet for their own purposes on company time. Firewalls are normally used to provide this security.

Firewall Options

Some commercial organizations who are conducting business on the Internet have turned to electronic firewalls to insulate the organizations' vital information systems from outsiders yet permit the organizations to securely transfer and receive information through the Internet. These firewalls offer varying degrees of security, however. Figure 23.3 shows how these various firewalls work and differ.

FIGURE 23.3.

The different types of Internet firewalls.

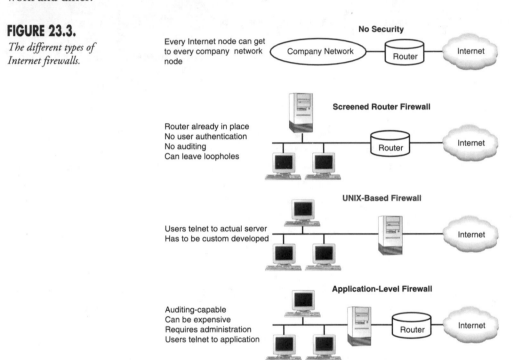

You can configure a screening router firewall, for example, with a set of access rules to filter out many would-be intruders. Using a router as a screening firewall is convenient because it is usually already in place, but this method of controlling access cannot be customized to specific network environments, does not authenticate users, and has no audit capability. If not properly set up, this type of firewall may have loopholes through which intruders can enter.

A UNIX-based firewall, a server with UNIX-programmed filtering, security, and auditing, is effective in allowing users to telnet directly to an application server. However, the network administrator must create and maintain the security architecture and program it for every possible exposure.

Application-level firewalls, offered by vendors such as ANS, Raptor, Trusted Information Systems, Digital, BNTI, Checkpoint, SOS, and Technologic, allow users to telnet to an application-level prompt and include a high level of preprogrammed, customizable network and security functionality. Application-level firewalls can be configured to be virtually impenetrable, but they can be expensive and difficult to administer. Most firewalls still rely upon static passwords as a means of authenticating a user's identity. An unauthorized user may gain access to a system using a dummy password and then create a back door for future access, thus reducing firewall security levels.

Industry Standards and System Security

Adherence to standards is important because it provides the framework to migrate client/server applications into future environments with minimal cost and impact. Many organizations have created standards to address the complexity of securing a client/server environment. You can use these standards as a means to evaluate and compare security products and to foster interoperability. The following organizations create such standards:

- International Standards Organization (ISO)
- Object Management Group (OMG)
- American National Standards Institute (ANSI)
- Institute of Electrical and Electronics Engineers (IEEE)
- National Institute of Standards and Technology (NIST)
- European Computer Manufacturers Association (ECMA)
- Open Software Foundation (OSF)
- X/Open

Information on these organizations is widely available on the Internet.

Summary

Securing a client/server system is a complex challenge due to the diversity of the various systems that form it. By reducing the number of different servers, you may ease your security burden, but you may also complicate the business process. The levels of security you place within your networks, servers, clients, and applications should be beneficial to your organization and easy for the user base to use. Bear in mind also that as you increase the complexity of the security systems you put in place, you also increase the complexity of the ongoing support, management, and modification of those security systems. Only you and your organization can set the appropriate level of security for your system.

Attacks on networks, whether LANs, WANs, or the Internet, have one thing in common. The intruders are able to penetrate those networks by exploiting passwords. You must educate your user base on the value of frequently changing their passwords; do not give in to those users who complain that they have to change it every 30 days.

Social Considerations and Problems

24

by Vinay Nadig

Is changing the computing platform enough? Are you assured of a return on investment, just because you implement client/server technology? Client/server computing demands a different way of doing things, both for the MIS organization and the end-user organization. Consider the facts: End users are presented with a radical new interface (the *graphical user interface* or *GUI*); MIS managers are told to forgo lengthy design and development phases to develop mission-critical systems in six months; application developers struggle to come to terms with a completely new paradigm of systems development; executive management wants to know why MIS cannot show tangible returns on investment; add to these facts the ever-changing business landscape and the evolving information technology industry, and you get a chaotic mix. Although client/server computing does significantly affect end-user organizations (especially if preceded by business process re-engineering), this discussion will attempt to analyze how the MIS organization can cope with the challenges of client/server computing.

End users are empowered with data and information access; your mission-critical databases are distributed; your business rules are isolated; and your MIS staffers will have to be more like systems integrators than old-time coders. Can all this be done with your existing MIS organizational structure? Typical MIS departments are usually centralized and functionalized according to various disciplines. Application developers and systems folks rarely talk to each other, and until recently, end users were an afterthought. With the new paradigms, end users assume paramount importance not only from a requirements definition standpoint but also from an application development standpoint. The "ivory tower" or the "glass house" mentality so pervasive during the birth and growth of MIS organizations can no longer work in today's fast-paced environment.

But what about the people? What about their skills, insecurities, and fears? That's where this issue is multifaceted. Not only do you have to structure your organization to follow your strategies, but you also have to "retool" or "reskill" people to fit the new strategies and structure. In this chapter, I discuss existing MIS organizations and the fears associated with moving to client/server. I then propose a framework for the "new" IS/IT organization, a dynamic and distributed structure that can stand the stress of today's challenges. Hopefully, you will get a starting point for the rebuilding that is inevitable. With client/server applications, old-world programmers will need to become programmer/analysts. All applications used to run on the same servers. Now part of the application design is to determine which server best fits the project. These new tasks will require a more versatile employee.

Structural and Organizational Aspects of Existing MIS Departments

Most MIS departments are based on the mainframe era of computing. Progressive companies have also tried to evolve the structure to include end-user computing, PCs, and LANs. There is a lot of press right now about the move to "recentralize" IS. Essentially, these reports say that client/server computing is so complex that the need for centralized IS is more important than maintaining a decentralized, "departmental" type of IS organization. Amazingly, the same mistakes seem to be repeated: focusing more on the technology and its maintainance, rather than focusing on the business value of technology and how to implement solutions and applications of technology. Progressive companies avoid this mistake. This group of companies is tearing down all vestiges of traditional IS structure and building a flexible organization, where core IT staff and distributed IT staff with end users form the IS department. Again, the idea presented in this chapter is that the move to "consolidate" or "recentralize" IS is wrong, and developing a dynamic, if somewhat chaotic, distributed IS organization is a better way. To fully understand the issues in this chapter, you must understand existing structures and their evolution.

Existing MIS Structures

In the past, most companies did a pretty good job of structuring their MIS organizations based on their computing strategies. Mainframe computing demanded centralized maintenance of data, applications, hardware (for the most part), and systems software. So, all the expertise required was also centralized in central MIS organizations. These have come to be called "glass houses" and "ivory towers." Trying to optimize the maintenance and operational efficiencies of these huge mainframe investments, MIS easily forgot about the end user. Take a look at two models of existing structures: one the Gartner Group calls the "IS Organization of the Past" (this discussion calls it the *centralized IS organization*) and the other, more recent *decentralized IS organization*. Chronologically, you can also view this as an evolution.

Centralized IS Organization

Centralized IS organizations are just that—centralized; therein lies the crux of the problem! Figure 24.1 illustrates a centralized IS organization.

FIGURE 24.1.

A centralized IS organization.

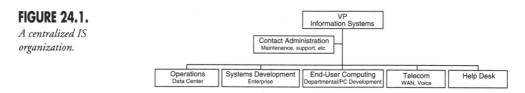

Typically, you have a VP or CIO heading up the department with discrete functional groups for operations, systems (application) development, end-user computing, telecom, and support (help desk). Briefly, the operations department manages the mainframe, minicomputer, and even LANs; backs up data; installs and updates software; runs reports; and generally tries to keep users under control. Systems development folks immerse themselves in developing many hundreds of lines of code. These lines run your organization! From mission-critical order-entry systems to utility batch routines, these people do it all. But they probably don't communicate to the data center at all. They communicate with the user community, but it is too few times with a lot of time in between. End-user computing or information centers were an outgrowth of the spurt in LANs in the mid '80s. Some organizations experimented with information centers in the early '80s. Basically, end-user computing is central IS's benign acceptance of end-user importance. But information centers were built to fail because they are staffed with people who know a lot about technology but are not equipped to properly manage it.

Central IS pushed end-user computing groups to the departments, hoping to quiet users down with cosmetic updates and macro-driven applications. But the crucial feedback loop between end-user computing and central IS never happened. End-user computing became (and is) islands of automation. The ubiquitous help desk is probably the only well-structured unit of central IS. Typically, centralized help desks have been more accessible to users, and IS has kept costs down and productivity up. The telecom group has traditionally managed voice applications in companies. Until recently, telecom staff thought of themselves as the "phone" or "voice" people. Neither central IS nor these professionals saw any need for integration. However, in these days of computer telephony and voice/data/video/fax integration, integration between the software groups and the telecom groups assumes significant importance. There's probably an administration group handling the myriad details of mainframe and minicomputer hardware and software maintenance, contract details, purchasing, and so on.

Decentralized IS Organization

With the explosion of LANs and end-user computing, centralized IS organizations were faced with some perplexing problems. Business end users were buying hardware and software without IS's consent or approval. Nonstandard hardware cropped up everywhere. Users brought in productivity tools on their own and introduced a host of file compatibility and data access issues. Users also wanted to know why the order-entry system (on the mainframe/mini) could not show a graph of orders for their best customers, but their spreadsheet on the PC could do it in two mouse clicks! IS thought that pushing a unit of their own staff into the user departments would solve most of these problems. Figure 24.2 shows a conceptual view of a decentralized IS organization.

FIGURE 24.2.

Decentralized IS organization.

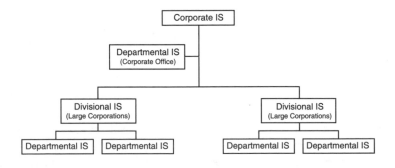

Now users could interact with their own "mini MIS" departments for immediate resolution. IS still maintained control, especially on the mission-critical applications and data running in the glass house. The so-called "islands of automation" structure continued to flourish because there was still no integration—no enterprise plan, as it were. So LANs grew, hybrid databases abounded, and IS was forced to integrate platforms. This forced integration started the move to recentralize or consolidate IS again. But there is enough evidence to prove that recentralizing IS is not the answer—distributing it is. More about that later.

As you try to understand existing MIS organizations, you must also understand the skill sets of existing staff. What kind of skills do people in these different groups possess? As the new organization is discussed, the focus will be on how these skill sets fit and how they compare to the skill sets that are currently required.

Existing Roles and Skills

Although the roles and skills of existing staff may not fit into the new organization, they are inherent to the structure. So logic suggests that when you change the structure, you will also be able to train and adapt your existing staff. This is true for all those who wish to make the transition. But you must understand the existing roles and skills to facilitate effective transition. This section will take an objective look at existing staff skills. A succeeding section will address required new skills.

In most IS organizations, the two most important functions have been systems development and operations. This chapter explores these two groups. Figure 24.3 illustrates staff skills in a typical development (applications development) group.

FIGURE 24.3.

Existing development staff roles and skills.

Project Managers/Group Leaders	DBA	COBOL Programmer	Programmer Analyst	Systems Analyst
❖ Staff supervision ❖ Budget control ❖ Resource scheduling	❖ Hierarchical database design ❖ Relational database design	❖ Comprehensive procedural programming skills ❖ Advanced COBOL skills	❖ Structured programming techniques ❖ 4GL skills ❖ CASE skills ❖ Beginning to advanced PC database (xBASE) skills	❖ Structured systems analysis (design) skills ❖ Systems development life cycle skills ❖ CASE skills ❖ Training skills

Figure 24.4 illustrates staff skills in a typical operations group.

FIGURE 24.4.

Existing operations staff roles and skills.

Data Center Manager	Computer Services	Systems Programmer	LAN/Mini Support
❖ Staff supervision ❖ Limited capacity planning ❖ Cost allocation	❖ Tape mounting ❖ Job scheduling ❖ Report production & distribution ❖ Back up ❖ Change management	❖ Batch/JCL programming skills ❖ OS configuration skills ❖ Database dump/rollback/recover skills	❖ NOS skills ❖ Backup/restore skills ❖ Basic RDBMS maintenance skills ❖ LAN troubleshooting ❖ Local bridges/routers maintenance skills

Some other skills that a typical IS organization would possess are the phone system skills of telecom staff and limited business analysis skills of end-user computing staff. Before launching into a discussion of a proposed IS organizational framework, the following section takes a look at the real and perceived productivity barriers (or fears) of IS managers, IS staff, and the end-user community in the face of client/server computing. Armed with an understanding of existing skills and barriers associated with the move to client/server computing, you will be ready to design and implement the new IS organization.

The Human Impact

Your most significant challenge in client/server computing will not be integrating diverse computer systems, but managing client/server's human impact. Client/server computing threatens the order of the day at each step. For the end-user community, it means tremendous insight into corporate data and hence the corporation itself; such insight results in empowerment and increased responsibilities. For IS, it means new tools, new skills, new ways of developing and deploying systems, and a shift from mainframe-/server-/data-centric computing to user-centric computing. Will everyone welcome these changes? Does IS have a readily available pool of skilled resources to handle these challenges? Probably not.

Barriers Facing IS Managers

For people conditioned to think about maintaining smooth data center operations, developing large systems with discrete phases, supervising staff versus coaching them, and generally viewing end users as an unpalatable but necessary entity, client/server computing poses enormous challenges. IS managers' lack of PC/LAN/WAN/RDBMS and GUI tool technology knowledge places them at a distinct disadvantage. Their staff and outside contractors/vendors either mistrust their capabilities or spend inordinate amounts of time educating (misleading?) them. Due to this lack of knowledge, insecurities creep into these managers' mindsets. This leads to a lack of trust between them and their staff. This mistrust is usually embodied as "analysis by paralysis"—continually researching and evaluating options without making decisions. Managers constantly question everything their staff does, without letting them have enough freedom.

Another aspect that IS managers have mastered in the mainframe world is the art of scheduling resources and supervising employees. They usually viewed their staff as bodies capable of x number of work hours in a year. Then they broke up a project into discrete parts and assigned their people without much regard to skills, qualifications, and so on. The only factor that would be considered was the time each staff member was allotted for the project. In client/server computing, empowerment of IS staff is key, and teams usually are the norm. This kind of environment necessarily means that the IS manager has to let go and coach, cajole, and guide his or her team, which is a far cry from withholding the big-picture information and trying to drive a group of people solely by deadlines. This "letting go" creates a lot of anxiety in the IS manager. As he or she gives up the position of the information filter between top management, the business users, and IS staff, the IS manager experiences a feeling of diminished power. Naturally, all these factors make IS managers resist the move to client/server computing. Although IS managers may not be able to overtly voice their opposition against client/server computing itself, they may try to use old methods of management to implement it, which will have disastrous results. In summary, technological obsolescence, insecurities about abilities, and lack of trust are the main barriers to IS managers contributing in your organization's client/server efforts.

Barriers Facing IS Staff

Not all IS staff welcome the new technologies either. Due to the lack of skills required (4GL/ GUI programming, NOS skills, RDBMS skills, LAN-WAN integration, business knowledge, and so on), certain staff resist the move, citing different reasons. Some may state that the "PC guys" don't know anything about procedures, security, reliability, and so on. They may also resent the fact that they would be giving up the power of controlling the information from end users. End users can now create reports by relatively simple actions in less than an hour. These reports may have taken weeks and required heavy IS involvement before. IS staffers definitely feel a loss of power when the task of creating reports goes away. Some may also feel threatened about their jobs.

As companies shift from developing in-house systems to customizing third-party software packages, there is a fear of layoffs. This leads to a drop in productivity and a paralysis of learning. Another unpalatable fact that you must consider is that there simply may be a limited supply of qualified people in the whole industry. As you try to force-fit your staff into learning about and implementing new technology, they may find that they cannot go to anybody in-house for expert advice. This creates a burden that many may not want to bear. Some staffers fear empowerment and increased responsibilities. Being told that they are now accountable as a team for achieving results without managers to blame is daunting for a lot of staff. Griping about their managers' inefficiencies was one thing; doing something to solve the problems is quite another. Lack of appropriate skills, resistance to change, and apprehension about increased responsibilities and accountability are the significant barriers to productivity.

Barriers Facing the End-User Community

Resistance to change, new ways of doing business, and lack of training act as barriers to the end-user community. End users (the business) are now considered to be central to the IS organization's objectives. Users are taking a more active role in all phases of new systems' implementation. This new role means that they participate in IS decision-making and have to take some responsibility for the decisions made. Some users balk at this responsibility, preferring to hold IS solely responsible for all mishaps (if any). Client/server computing pushes change in workflow, business processes, and daily operations. Some users not wanting to change how they have always done things will resist new systems. These employees are afraid that their hard-earned skills (of old systems, old workflow, and so on) can no longer be used and that they will lose their power and influence as a result. A significant segment of end users will resist new systems and new ways simply because they don't know how to use them. This segment can be easily turned around by focused training.

The New IS Organization

If neither centralized nor decentralized organizations work, what do you do? Client/server computing calls for a flexible and dynamic approach. I believe this can be achieved by a distributed IS organization. Structuring the IS organization and retooling the people who fill the slots in this structure are the two keys to the new IS organization.

A Distributed IS Structure

The sample IS organization in this chapter is neither desktop-centric nor data/server-centric: it is user-centric. The central values around which the new IS organization revolves are business users' needs and requirements, as shown in Figure 24.5.

FIGURE 24.5.

Distributed IS structure.

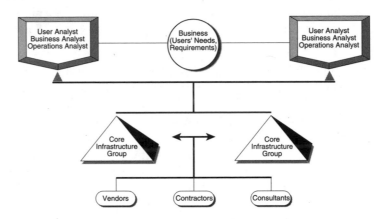

The new organization will be built from the center outward, instead of from the top down or from the bottom up. In each business unit, you will establish the distributed component of IS, the *Business/IS Arm*, which is a formal group made up of the following:

- **A User Analyst.** An analyst drawn from the user community of that workgroup/ business unit.

- **A Business Analyst.** A hybrid IS/Business unit type who is hired and managed by the business unit manager. IS can help the business unit define job requirements and recruit the business analyst, but he or she will be an employee of the business unit.

- **An Operations Analyst.** An IS employee permanently positioned in the business unit.

All three positions report to the business unit manager. The User Analyst will be the catalyst of business/IT based solutions. This position—a position where different staff can rotate in and out—will generate new systems needs and help communicate business requirements. These duties will be a formal part of this person's job. The Business Analyst will help translate the business needs into IT specifications. He or she will help the business unit understand the technology, spot opportunities for technology integration, and help optimize end-user productivity. The Operations Analyst will optimize business unit LANs, systems, WAN connections, databases, and so on. The Operations Analyst will spot unique systems integration opportunities. This group is in constant communication with the central part of IS, or the "core" part. This core is divided into the *Core Architecture Group* and the *Core Infrastructure Group*.

The Core Architecture Group is made up of DBAs, systems architects, senior internal consultants, and senior systems development gurus. This group sets the IT strategies for the company, based solely on business goals and objectives derived from feedback from the distributed business/IS arms. This group sets standards, weighs outsourcing options, evaluates new technologies, and provides personnel and project management expertise.

The Core Infrastructure Group is made up of senior network integration specialists, LAN/WAN specialists, capacity planning experts, and the centralized help desk. Though the business/IS arms provide local support, the existence of the centralized help desk provides for another level of help-call escalation, for purely technical issues. This group also has major input in determining the company's client/server platforms. Supporting these two core groups are vendors, contractors, and consultants. No longer can these entities be viewed as "external"; they have to be integral to your IS organization. At any given time, it is not uncommon to have a vendor/contractor/consultant on-site with a physical office at your site(s). As you move to deploying third-party software packages and integrating separate systems, you have to leverage outside expertise as if it were your own.

How Does the New IS Organization Function?

Figure 24.6 illustrates the life cycle of a project in the new IS organization.

FIGURE 24.6.

Distributed IS organization in action.

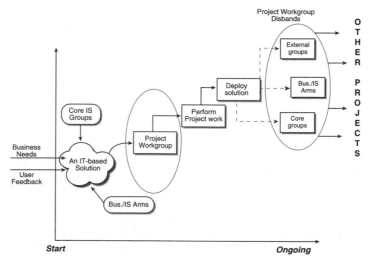

All work has to become discrete projects. You and your staff have to become primed to do project work and achieve your goals and objectives. The only way you can conduct this type of work is by frequent, quick forming and disbanding of teams or project workgroups. This gives you the advantage of a variety of skills and expertise that you can use to complete projects. As business needs are solidified into a request for an IT-based solution, a project workgroup composed of the right components quickly forms. This workgroup may include members from the core groups, the business/IS arms, and external entities, depending upon the scope and complexity of the project. This newly formed project workgroup is completely responsible for project completion, and they are empowered to make all the relevant decisions. IS and business senior management will have already set budgeting and architectural guidelines. If they are communicated properly, and your staff is trained effectively, the project workgroup will need no "supervisors." The project workgroup proceeds to perform all requisite work, deploys the solution, and quickly disbands, ready for the next project. At the right points in the project, Core Infrastructure Group members and the Operations Analysts begin the process of infrastructure maintenance, and the Business Analysts begin the process of enhancements and feedback to the core IS groups.

Roles and Skills in the New IS Organization

It's time to look at the roles and skills of IS professionals in the new IS organization. The new structure can function only with the right people. You must understand the roles and skills necessary for successful deployment of the new IS organization, as shown in Figure 24.7.

FIGURE 24.7.

Roles and skills in the new IS organization.

Business Analyst	Operations Analyst	Core Architecture Group Member	Core Infrastructure Group Member
❖ Business Process Reengineering skills ❖ Business Process Analysis skills ❖ User interaction skills ❖ CASE tool skills ❖ Macro language application development ❖ LAN-based RDBMS design and development skills ❖ Marketing skills ❖ Consultative skills ❖ Business knowledge ❖ Training	❖ LAN/WAN skills ❖ LAN-based RDBMS configuration skills ❖ Internet skills ❖ Telecommunications set up and maintenance ❖ Business knowledge ❖ Training	❖ RDBMS skills ❖ Object-oriented DBMS skills ❖ GUI programming ❖ 4GL skills ❖ CASE tool skills ❖ Coaching skills ❖ Technology vision ❖ IS strategy ❖ Knowledge of industry trends ❖ Multivendor coordination skills ❖ Marketing skills ❖ Consultative skills ❖ Business knowledge ❖ Object-oriented analysis skills	❖ NOS setup, configuration, and architecture skills ❖ RDBMS skills ❖ Telecommunications knowledge and skills ❖ Internet skills ❖ WAN analysis and setup skills ❖ Desktop and client OS skills ❖ Consultative skills ❖ Business knowledge

Organizational Migration—Is It Possible?

Even if you are convinced that the new IS organization will work, can your organization make the transition? Can you and your staff evolve into the new roles and acquire the skills required? Do you have to completely revamp your staff and hire new people? The answer lies between the extremes. Some of your staff will be able and willing to make the transition. They will accept more responsibilities, acquire new skills, and generally prove themselves invaluable in your client/server efforts. Some staff will resist change and will become obstacles for progress. You will have to accept this fact and find a mutually beneficial way out; usually this is to counsel and help resistant employees find suitable employment elsewhere. For the employees who are willing and for the new hires, you will need a migration plan. Willingness does not translate into ability. So you must chart out a plan wherein your IT strategy drives your IS structure, which in turn is populated by employees with the appropriate skills.

A Migration Plan

The migration plan detailed in this section will help you effectively implement the new and improved IS organization:

1. Define the new skills required for each position in your new IS organization.

2. Evaluate existing skill sets of employees. Do you have all the skill sets required? If not, do you have a partial set? When you are finished with this step, you will be able to get a very accurate picture of existing skill sets.

3. After your skill evaluation, compare them against the skills you defined in Step 1. The difference in skills gives you the gap. You have to fill this gap if you want the right mix of employee skills.

4. Develop strategies to fill or reduce this gap. These may include focused technology training, team training, coaching, and project management skills. After training, re-evaluate your employee base again and decide opportunities for layoffs and/or new hires.

All these steps constitute a generic migration plan. Your migration plan will have to be customized according to your company's corporate culture, budgetary constraints, and the type of employee resources you have. But this generic plan should give you a place to start. Figure 24.8 illustrates the migration plan and its different steps.

FIGURE 24.8.

Migration plan for IS staff transition.

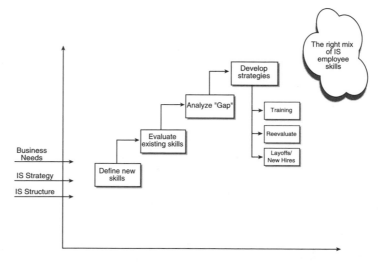

Summary

Client/server computing poses more than technical challenges. It affects your organizational fabric by causing you to question old ways of doing things. Critical to the success of your client/server efforts is the structure of your IS organization and the skills and knowledge of your IS staff. Existing IS structures do not provide the flexibility and the quickness required for client/server computing. A distributed IS organization provides the right structure for meeting and triumphing over today's computing challenges. IS staff retooling is an integral part of repositioning the IS structure. IS staff members have to be reskilled in new technology and management methods. Charting out a migration plan for this transition helps you migrate your staff smoothly.

The Great Skills Gap

by Ellen Gottesdiener

IN THIS CHAPTER

Client/server technology requires people to master new tools, operating systems, languages, connectivity products, and DBMSs (database management systems). In addition, new concepts, techniques, and methods of working are essential. Competent staff is needed to leverage these technologies. One of the greatest problems in implementing client/server technology is the gap that exists between the skills needed to design, migrate, develop, and maintain client/server technology and the skills that exist in IT (Information Technology) organizations today.

This chapter examines the sources of this skills gap, how roles have changed as a result of client/server computing, and presents effective ways to approach the retooling of IT and end user staff.

Continuous Learning

Client/server technology, with its multiple components and heterogeneous platforms, requires knowledge and skill in a wide variety of topics. Not only are the combinations of products and technologies complex, but they are also undergoing continual change. New methods of working are also needed, such as iterative prototyping, working in facilitated group sessions, negotiation and consensus building, event-driven analysis and design, architectural planning and design, application partitioning, and human/computer interface design. These are major transitions for most IT organizations (see Figure 25.1).

FIGURE 25.1.

The client/server skills transition. (Source: EBG Consulting, Inc.)

Traditional	Transitioned
Procedural	event-driven
character interface (CUI)	graphical interface (GUI)
file/program	data/object model
COBOL, C, ALC, PL/1	SQL, GUI 4GL, mm C++/Smalltalk
unit/mod testing	prototyping
waterfall method	spiral/iterative method
single environment	network design/tuning
single protocol	multiple/layered protocol
silo application focus	cross-functional/business process reengineering

Industry analysts describe the idea of "reskilling" and "retooling" as a monumental effort. Bridging the skills gap is possibly the single biggest obstacle to transition to client/server. Like the work effort itself, migrating to client/server will take years in many organizations. Reskilling IT and end user staff will occur concurrently with that migration. Training thus plays an important role in facilitating to client/server.

Training for client/server is an ongoing and iterative process, much like effective client/server application development methods. More training, rather than less, is needed to position staff for continual learning. Learning should not be perceived as one-time event. It is an ongoing, continuous process facilitated by effective curriculum and learning methods (see Figure 25.2).

FIGURE 25.2.
Continuous learning.
(Source: EBG Consulting, Inc.)

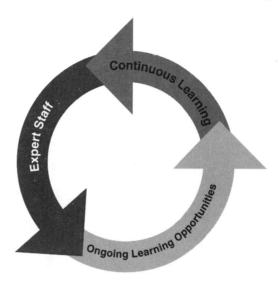

In traditional system development efforts, analyst/programmers were trained in a set of fairly static skills that were useful for five or more years. Project plans addressed the training of end users, which was timed at the end of project and geared toward training them to use the new application once it was deployed.

Training can no longer be an afterthought with client/server computing. End users are intimately involved in the design of the application by participating in planning and prototyping the application. Moreover, IT staff is likely to have major skills deficiencies in using the technology. Often, re-education is also needed to boost business knowledge and interpersonal skills.

New Roles for Client/Server

Traditional roles, or job activities and responsibilities, are gradually being replaced with a more complex and interdependent set of skills. IT professionals need to be generalists in many skill and knowledge areas, and specialists in a subset of client/server products and processes. One individual may play multiple roles, depending on the size of the organization and the scope of the technologies. Some of the roles for participants in client/server are

- GUI designer
- Business analyst

- Application architect
- Client/server tester
- Quality assurance analyst
- Application developer
- Application modeler
- JAD facilitator
- Project manager
- Business sponsor
- Customer advocate
- Network administrator
- Network architect
- Data administrator
- Database administrator
- Help Desk analyst
- Client/server trainer

Management's Role

To accelerate the skills migration process, IT organizations are tempted to hire people already possessing the needed skills. A similar option is to use system integrators, outside sources ("outsourcers"), and/or consultants. By itself, this is not a good solution. It is expensive, but more importantly, the skills needed for client/server technology are hard to find. A significant negative factor in this approach is that external hires or consultants lack the knowledge and experience of the business and company culture. Because the organization has invested much by infusing its own employees with these competencies, staff retraining fosters a mutual sense of goodwill and investment in the future. Skills along with motivation make for a productive workforce (see Figure 25.3).

FIGURE 25.3.
Formula for success.
(Source: EBG Consulting, Inc.)

Skills = knowledge + experience

Productivity = skills * motivation

Business and IT management must communicate that retraining and retooling is necessary for corporate and individual survival. Humans find change difficult. Some staff will not desire or be able to make the transition to the new work processes and technical skills required by client/server computing. Predictions for the number of casualties of the transition process range from 5 to 30 percent of existing staff (including managers). The good news is that mainframe and traditional skills are still needed. The legacy applications now running on the mainframe will not disappear but will cohabitate with client/server technology (and in many cases, be one component of the technical infrastructure). Therefore, the organization still needs to maintain some mainframe skills.

Skills assessments, peer and management performance review, customer ratings, and results from training or college courses will help to determine which staff will be more successful with the transition. A balance is needed between the new skills and enthusiasm that new hires might bring and the business savvy and organizational knowledge that the professionals already on staff have.

Transition to client/server requires a major commitment by management in providing the money and time to reskill staff. It requires innovative thinking on the part of training and development staff on how to effectively facilitate the process. In addition, it requires a learning attitude on the part of IT professionals who need to understand a wider breath of topics and skills to be effective application developers and designers.

Organizing to Exploit Specialty Skills

Due to the need for many specialized skills, application areas cannot expect individual developers to be adept at all skills. One solution is to have specialists as resources to projects on an as-needed basis. Together, these specialists form a core of infrastructure support to the project and act as adjunct team members. Their role is to provide expertise, mentoring, and project assistance.

These specialty units, or centers of competency, have in-depth expertise in such skills as database administration and tuning, data/object/process modeling, JAD facilitation, software engineering practices (testing, configuration management, quality assurance, project management), network design and management, middleware, architectural design, user interface standards and guidelines, workgroup computing, and systems redevelopment.

Individuals with these specialized skills serve not only as internal consultants and contributors to projects, but also as mentors to application areas. Part of their role is to promote knowledge transfer. These specialists are masters in their skill areas. Application developers do not need to be masters in these areas, but they need to have an awareness or working knowledge of the skills. The specialty units should be responsible for promoting knowledge transfer through their tour of duty on application projects throughout the organization.

The Client/Server Learning Cycle

A comprehensive curriculum for client/server addresses the concepts, techniques, and products of the technology. *Concepts training* provides learners with an overall understanding of what the technology entails and the benefits and difficulties in using it. IT professionals need to understand what is truly different in client/server and perhaps object-oriented environments, and why it is different. This understanding provides a foundation for subsequent training. *Technique training* involves learning what processes are used to build and migrate applications to a client/server or object-oriented system. This includes such processes as RAD (Rapid Application Development), JAD (Joint Application Design), analysis and design techniques, requirements validation, application partitioning, GUI design, and modeling data, state, process, event, and/or objects. *Product training* covers the vendor-specific tools that make up the client/server and object-oriented architecture. This training includes application development tools and languages, DBMSs, network systems, communications protocols, middleware, operating systems, and the tools used for testing and debugging, configuration management, and network management.

Although concepts training should have to occur only once for each trainee, learning client/server and the object-oriented techniques that often accompany client/server computing may require multiple training events. Product training may need to be "chunked" into beginning and advanced topics and retaken as product upgrades are installed in the organization.

Varying Skill Levels

Different roles will require a variety of skills, which in turn may require different degrees of competency, such as mastery, working knowledge, and familiarity. For an example, one role, a GUI designer, needs a variety of skills with different competency levels (see Table 25.1).

Table 25.1. Sample skills/skill competency levels for the role of GUI designer.

Skill Needed	Degree of Competency Required
GUI design	Mastery
GUI tool (PowerBuilder, SQLWindows, Forté, Visual Basic)	Mastery
SQL	Working Knowledge
Object-oriented concepts (polymorphism, inheritance, encapsulation)	Working Knowledge
Operating System (Windows, NT, OS/2, UNIX)	Working Knowledge
Messaging, OLE, APIs, CORBA	Working Knowledge
Data, Process Modeling	Familiarity
DBMS (Sybase, SQL Server, Oracle)	Familiarity
Object-oriented language (Smalltalk, Visual C++, C++)	Working Knowledge (if needed at all)
Event/user task modeling	Mastery

GUI design skills are essential for the GUI designer. Creating user-centered interfaces requires skills such as understanding when to use which WIMP components (windows, icons, mouse, pull-down menus) and how to decide what GUI framework is appropriate for the specific user task that needs to be performed. GUI design requires developers to be parsimonious in the myriad of interface choices that exist and to provide a natural workflow for the user. These design skills do not come naturally or by virtue of being trained in the GUI development tool alone.

Categories of Learning

Today's serious developers need to learn possibly dozens of interrelated disciplines. A combination of personal/transferable, business, and technical skills and knowledge are needed. These disciplines, in turn, need to follow the learning cycle of concepts, techniques, and product-specific learning (see Figure 25.4).

FIGURE 25.4.

Interlocking skill needs along a learning continuum. (Source: EBG Consulting, Inc.)

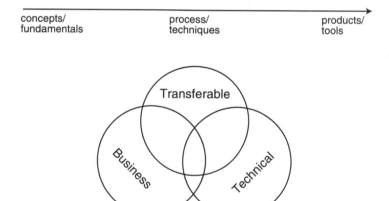

concepts/ fundamentals   process/ techniques   products/ tools

Transferable

Business

Technical

Transferable Skills

Effective use of client/server and object-oriented technologies requires IT professionals to behave in new ways. They must work with end users consistently, be able to negotiate, build a consensus, and have a customer and product orientation toward IT services. To make client/server technology work, a relationship of trust between IT and business people is necessary. IT professionals must be able to understand the competitive pressures facing their internal customers and take a more customer service approach to satisfying business needs. This means being able to listen and communicate with business partners without being distracted by jargon or being biased toward technology versus business solutions. Good communication skills are essential. These skills are known as *transferable skills*.

Transferable skills, also called "soft" or interpersonal skills, include: oral communication, written communication, conceptual thinking, giving presentations, running meetings, project management, negotiation, feedback, ability to work in a team, and delegating. Unlike technical client/server skills which are often tactical in nature, transferable skills (and business skills, addressed next) are strategic. They are necessary regardless of specific job responsibilities.

Today's teams and organizations are flatter and less hierarchical. This structure means that managers must learn to relinquish tight control of individuals and people must work more collaboratively. Teamwork, recognition of individual differences, conflict resolution, peer review, and provision of feedback to others are skills that are also critical in this setting. Project management skills for the client/server environment are also required for individuals playing a management role.

Business Skills

IT professionals must have a better understanding of the business problems and opportunities that exist. Without an understanding of the competitive, tactical, and strategic issues facing the business, IT cannot facilitate the best technical solution. A solid appreciation for the details of business life cycles such as research and development, sales and marketing, manufacturing, distribution, financial, administration, and human resources is important.

Technology is being used to facilitate achieving breakthroughs in business. Business process re-engineering (BPR) is based on the premise that dramatic improvements in how processes occur is only possible by using technology in newer and smarter ways. BPR, which should precede client/server application development efforts, must also be understood by IT professionals.

Technical Skills

Technical skills span the operating system, hardware, and software elements that make up the client, server, and network portions of client/server computing. Among the greatest challenges for implementing client/server technology is the establishment and maintenance of a solid infrastructure for client/server. Infrastructure issues are like the foundation and floorboard of a house: without solid ones, the whole building can collapse. In addition to the tools and techniques of application development, technical infrastructure training includes the following:

- System and network management
- Systems security and auditing
- Network configuration and installation
- Software configuration management
- Change management
- Disaster recovery
- Backup and recovery
- Methodology

- Data architecture
- Capacity management
- Database administration and tuning

A comprehensive training curriculum should address the specific skills and knowledge needed by each client/server role to develop a working competency. In addition, it will have the depth needed in skills required by an individual in a specific role (see Figure 25.5).

FIGURE 25.5.

Sample technical training for the role of application developer. (Source: EBG Consulting, Inc.)

concepts/ fundamentals	process/ techniques	products/ tools
client/server fundamentals interface design network concepts reengineering fundamentals object-oriented thinking overview	data modeling, event modeling, object modeling client/server methodology e.g. incremental, evolutionary, RAD JAD, facilitated techniques client/server analysis & design object-oriented analysis & design	database: e.g. Sybase, Oracle, SQL Server operating systems: NT, OS/2, Nextstep development environment & tools: e.g. Windows, OS/2, PowerBuilder, Oracle 2000 languages: e.g. C++, SQL Smalltalk, Delphi data access/access tools: e.g. ODBC, SQL*Net, EDA/SQL

End-User Training Explosion

In addition to the obvious need to train IT staff in client/server technology, there is the explosion of knowledge, both technical and strategic, needed by the end-user community. This includes using the GUI interface environment, desktop suites (word processing, spreadsheet, graphics), groupware, personal information managers, and e-mail systems in addition to new client/server applications. The industry research firm Gartner Group reported in 1994 that many organizations do not provide enough user education.

Formalizing peer support for end users is a necessary element of client/server technology. One study found that for every full-time staff person, there are up to three end users providing support. End users spend countless hours "futzing" with the technology, seeking answers for specific tasks being performed in an application. Studies support the notion that even if end-user support structures, such as Help Desks, are in place, they are not meeting the growing demand. Often computer-savvy end users fill in the gap. However usefully this solution appears to meet short-term needs, it is actually more time-consuming, costly, and counter-productive in the long term.

Informal peer support does not help formal support functions to effectively conduct problem management. The support unit must know what the questions and skill gaps are in order to address the need. In addition, the people providing informal help tend to be less efficient and effective than individuals who are formally trained and knowledgeable in the art of computer support.

Consequently, IT must survey the end-user community to discover the degree and depth of informal peer support that exists and begin to address the lack of support by formalizing support resources and providing timely training along with tips and techniques education.

Business management needs to understand the capabilities and limitations of client/server technology. They need to know why and how active business support is required for client/server application development. This requires a solid understanding of client/server concepts by business management, which commissions the projects. Business analysts need both client/server concepts and techniques training in order to actively participate in client/server projects. The training and support infrastructure needed by the end-user community is serious business.

Skill Gap Analysis

A planned approach to migrating IT and end-user skills is needed. Some IT organizations are approaching the transition by performing detailed skill needs analysis of current staff. By knowing what the client/server environment will be, skill needs can be predicted. A survey can be designed to assess individuals' familiarity and experience with a variety of skills, including those needed by the organization. Conducting a detailed assessment of existing skills will outline what the skill gaps are and help to define what the curriculum must contain to bridge those gaps. The organization also learns about current skills that it may not know exist (see Figure 25.6).

FIGURE 25.6.

Skills gap analysis. (Source: EBG Consulting, Inc.)

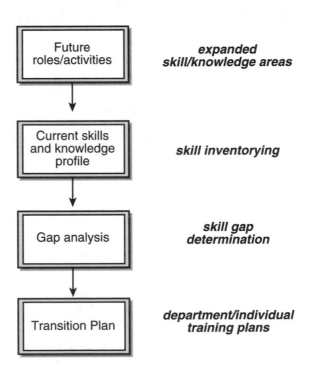

Transition Planning

Some companies are bridging the skills gap on a project-by-project basis, addressing training needs as they arise. Others are managing the migration to client/server by creating a strategy for reskilling IT staff that combines a variety of training methods, beginning with client/server concepts and methods. In either case, a proactive, comprehensive, and timely training program is essential for making a productive transition to new skill sets.

Costs of Reskilling

Training costs are the greatest single expenditure in the move to client/server. The Gartner Group estimates that two-thirds of the expenses of client/server computing are related to labor-related activities. Therefore, any investment in training to create more skill competency will pay off. According to Dataquest, U.S. companies spent $3 billion in 1994 alone on training executives, IT staff, and end users. This figure will grow to $5 billion by 1998, making education and training expenditures 4.8 percent of all IT services. Forrester Research, Inc., reports that training costs for the Fortune 1000 have increased by 50 percent since 1995 and will continue to increase by that amount for the next several years. This increase is due to insufficient client/server skills, particularly among veteran application developers.

The costs are significant. Forrester estimates that a company might spend as much as $600 million over two years to retrain 200 developers. In general, expectations of costs should range from 10 to 20 percent of salary per developer. For example, the cost of training a software engineer can be as much as $10,000 to $15,000 per year. A 1995 study by Olsten reported that training for client/server amounted to 22 percent of the overall IT budget, whereas mainframe computing training amounted to 11 percent of the overall budget. Many system integrators, who specialize in migrating applications to client/server computing, recommend that training dollars should make up 25 percent of the overall cost of system integration.

Training costs can be measured in a variety of ways: number of days of training, cost per student day, costs for Help Desk support, cost for peer support of the "futz" and "fiddle" factor. Another way to view costs is to assess the price of *not* providing effective training. Traditionally, education and training have been viewed as overhead or perks. This view is no longer valid.

Time for training must be built into project plans, individual performance objectives, and reskilling plans. IT staff who need very specialized skills, such as networking, database administration, connectivity tools, and so on, may need to have five to eight weeks of time dedicated to learning. Developers who need to learn tool sets and have a working knowledge of new languages and DBMSs may need up to five weeks allotted for learning. One IT organization (Motorola in Bangalore, India) that was rated as Level 5 in the Software Engineering Institute's Capability Maturity Model (see Chapter 13, "Essential Techniques") provides its IT staff with 42 days of initial training and as many as 80 to 100 days of ongoing training per year.

Training Methods

A variety of mechanisms to deliver training exist. Organizations are coupling instructor-led training with media such as CBT, video, and self-study material. A learning or resource center can be made available to obtain training materials, self-study workbooks, and work-in-study rooms. Learning can also be accomplished by assigning people the task of creating an original article or paper on a technology or product that needs to be researched by the organization. This assignment serves the dual purpose of creating a positive learning experience while also providing the company with the information it needs on the product or service.

The need for feedback, quick answers, advice, and coaching, while applying new skills in a real project, has led some organizations to establish formal mentoring programs. This kind of program is most effective when both the mentor and the "apprentice" have a formal agreement about their roles, mutual expectations, and time commitment. A variation of mentoring is "tag team" training whereby one or more staff members becomes the lead/expert in a particular tool, DBMS, or methodology. This person is then responsible for cross-training the other staff in that area.

Another type of tailored training is to conduct learning labs in which an expert facilitates solving specific work problems by using the techniques and/or tools that trainees have recently learned about. This reinforces the learning, permits trainees to see how to apply the technique or tool to real-world problems, and establishes a mentor relationship between experts and new learners.

Object-oriented training programs require special attention because of the dramatic shift in thinking that objects require. Working with objects truly represents a major paradigm shift for most developers. Object-oriented training must include not just the principles, but the language and tools of choice, object class libraries, frameworks, interoperability mechanisms (such as object request brokers), and object-oriented analysis and design.

Learning Styles

Effective training, whether instructor-led or technology-delivered, activates all the human senses and exploits human learning preferences. There are three principle modes of taking in information, as shown in Table 25.2.

Table 25.2. Learning styles.

Learning Style	Percent of Population Preference	Characterized by
Visual	60 to 72 percent	Prefers seeing; pictures and images help with concepts and information; tends to create mental pictures; typified by the statement, "I see your point"

Learning Style	Percent of Population Preference	Characterized By:
Kinesthetic	18 to 30 percent	Prefers to touch, feel, and do; feel actions by using the body; typified by the statement, "I feel we are moving in the right direction"
Auditory	12 to 18 percent	Processes what is said or needs to hear him/herself; explanations, sounds, listening are important; typified by the statement, "I hear what you are saying"

Training Delivery Options

A summary of some available methods for training is shown in Table 25.3.

Table 25.3. Training methods.

Method	Cost	Pluses	Minuses	Interesting Points
Instructor-led/ workshop	Moderate to expensive (per student costs are much lower for in-company training than public courses)	Human interaction with both a knowledgeable and skilled instructor and other learners can be beneficial; usually accompanied by good quality assurance and control	The instructor is most critical, along with course materials	Best if just-in-time; in-class questions and workshops can accelerate learning
Computer-based	Inexpensive to moderate (depending on the site license and maintenance contract)	Just-in-time; if in-house CBT exists, examples and workshops can be from the workplace; learner gets involved by controlling the pace and answering questions	No person to facilitate the process and answer questions	Can deploy enterprise-wide education via a network-based CBT program

continues

Table 25.3. continued

Method	Cost	Pluses	Minuses	Interesting Points
Video-based	Moderate to expensive	Just-in-time; exploits all senses but kinesthetic	Must repurchase new material if the content changes frequently; no learner interaction involved	May be valuable for some concepts education
CD-ROM	Moderate to expensive	Sensory rich (text, graphics, audio, video); learner gets involved	Must have appropriate hardware; new so few products available	Extends CBT with more presentation options (video, audio)
Mentoring	Inexpensive	Uses available expertise; provides new development experience for the mentor; provides continuum to the learning process	Takes time away from the mentor to do actual development work; mentor/ apprentice relationship is key (personalities must match)	Commitment by mentor and learner is critical; the relationship should be formalized
Immersion projects	Moderate (increases project time/costs due to adding learning curve time to the project)	Trial-by-fire can be exciting and motivating to some individuals	Can risk project quality or timeliness; without formal training or mentoring, can be frustrating	Tests the capabilities of the learners to learn and apply new skills quickly and under pressure
Original article or paper	Inexpensive	Allows learner to research topic they may be interested in; provides the organization with details it needs	Without guidance for the research process, can be frustrating and time-consuming	Provides opportunity for recognition; provides a written communication development experience
Facilitated learning labs	Inexpensive	Just-in-time; problems are tailored to the student	Must have experts made available and trained in facilitation and training skills	Opportunity to "test" the skills

Method	Cost	Pluses	Minuses	Interesting Points
Tips/techniques "theaters," new product overview presentations, training newsletters	Inexpensive	Goes a long way in promoting learning and sharing of learning as a valued activity; provides means of giving individuals recognition and development opportunities (by writing and presenting to peers)	Needs to be managed and professionally delivered	May provide an informal means of training needs analysis
None	Expensive	No monetary outlay; no time needed to plan and manage in the process	Doesn't leverage existing human assets	Client/server migration may not have started the organization, or there is no business support for it; promotes view that reskilling is not important

The best approach is to use a variety of methods. The existing infrastructure to support the various media must be in place. Individualized training plans should be developed and managed to ensure proper sequencing and reinforcement of the learned skills and knowledge. Techniques and product training should be conducted "just-in-time." Just-in-time training provides the learner with the knowledge and skills needed to perform tasks for a project just prior to the project commencing. In this way, learning is better retained. All training, regardless of media, should be preceded by pretraining preparation: notification to the student of the contents and prerequisites, expected time to complete, and notification to the manager about the training. Post-training evaluations should include not just "smile sheets" (forms evaluating the course), but also a follow-up within a month to determine the usefulness of the training in reducing the learning curve for skills utilization.

Future Trends in Computer Training

The landscape of computing training is changing. Some trends to anticipate include the following:

- Increase in options and sources for technology-delivered learning (for example, CD-ROM, networks, multimedia technology, the Internet)
- Shorter, "bit-size" modules
- Distance learning (satellite, educational TV, Internet)
- Use of electronic performance support (EPS)—training integrated in the actual application

Skills Assessment and Tracking

The greatest asset a company possesses is the people who work there. Just like the need to track all the physical assets owned by a company (buildings, equipment, computer hardware, software, desks, chairs, and so on), organizations need to track and manage their skills assets. The most sophisticated companies not only track employee skills but their skill levels, career paths, salaries, and promotions, and are able to automatically generate suggested training curriculum and learning paths.

Tracking skills against job responsibility is one way to ensure that the appropriate skills are being acquired and that training money is spent on the right skills. It permits just-in-time placing of the right people with the right skills on new projects, cutting down the time needed to get the people in place for new projects and thus reducing start-up costs. It helps to first identify which skills gaps exist. Managers whose span of control in today's flatter organizations have widened, or who are responsible for staff in diverse locations, can more readily track and control personnel movement and training.

Skills inventorying not only helps redeploy people appropriately, but can also provide a mechanism for manager/employee skills feedback, skills competency recommendations, job posting, and even online registration.

Tracking and Planning Tools

Products that manage skill assessment, curriculum planning, and test skills are offered in both stand-alone PC and client/server form. Examples are Bensu, Inc.'s Skills Management System; SkillView Technologies, Inc.'s SkillView; People Sciences' Skill Quest; Computer Training & Support's Skills Assessment Tests; Individual Software, Inc.'s Skill Assessment Software; KnowItAll's ProveIt! Testing Software; Park City Group's ActionForce; SHL Kee Systems, Inc.'s Aequitas, and BSG Consulting's BSG Smarts:Skills. Because of the need for strong problem-solving and communication skills, some organizations are also utilizing psychological testing, such as Cambridge Assessment Centre's Cambridge Assessment Method, which tests for traits such as problem-solving, creativity, and coping with change.

Certification

Skill certification is promoted by training and tool vendors as a means of endorsing the learning achievements of an IT professional and/or technology trainer. Certification may involve attending and satisfactorily completing one or more client/server training courses and, in some cases, passing a series of multiple-choice examinations. Vendors such as Powersoft, Microsoft, and Novell have exams that must be taken (for a fee) and passed in order to receive the certification in their product (for example, PowerBuilder, NT/AS, or NetWare). In those cases, certification can be time-consuming (up to a year or more) and costly (up to $3000 to attend courses and take the tests).

The trend toward becoming certified in a product or product-set will continue to grow. In addition, there will be an increasing trend to award certifications for multivendor skills. Being certified for most IT organizations is indeed desirable, but it is not a substitute for real-world experience or transferable skills like interpersonal skills and verbal communications. Little qualitative evidence exists that shows that certification correlates with on-the-job-performance competency. Few organizations measure the benefits of having a certified professional on staff but perceive that they get more value from these individuals.

Competency Testing

Very few products on the market test technical skill competency. Less than 10 percent of surveyed management conduct competency testing. Rather, they rely on interviewing and references. Although these tests can weed out individuals who do not accurately portray their experience, technical competency testing, like certifications, does not test for the nontransferable and business skills that are also critical to today's client/server roles.

The Learning Organization

An organization that will excel in using client/server technology is proactive in addressing retraining and displays the following characteristics:

- The training department's mission is linked to organization-wide, computer-related skills and learning.
- It has the ability to track all training costs: formal, informal, help desk, on-the-job, and peer support.
- Training dollars are not managed like overhead, but as capital investments.
- The training budget has increased from the prior year.

■ Training occurs in a "just-in-time" manner.

■ Centralized procurement of training purchases is performed.

■ Skills inventorying and tracking are performed regularly.

■ The organization conducts skills gaps analysis and planning.

■ Individualized training plans are created and tracked.

■ The company attracts technically competent developers.

■ Training schedules are linked to project plans.

■ Training specialists are involved during new project planning.

■ Job promotions are linked to retraining.

■ A variety of skills training methods in use: instructor-led, VBT, CBT, CD-ROM, formal mentoring, learning labs.

■ Pretraining information is sent to trainee and manager.

■ Post-training evaluation and testing of skills is performed.

■ Formal training needs analysis is conducted to evaluate the training needs of both IT and the end-user departments.

■ Regular peer-support, technical sharing presentations, overviews, and tips/techniques sessions are provided.

■ Individuals with the right skills are readily rotated to projects that need those specific skills.

■ End-user training is provided that addresses concepts and techniques in addition to tools.

■ Support structures are in place for both IT and end-user technical assistance; skills needs are identified by these units, and the needs are integrated into the learning programs managed by the training department.

The technologies associated with client/server require a complex and interrelated set of skills and knowledge by both IT and end users. They require using new techniques and behaviors. Training for technical skills must occur just-in-time. The business and soft skills training needs must also be addressed. Traditional learning methods should be combined with newer training delivery modes.

The most successful business organizations are those that take a proactive approach to retooling their human resources—both IT and business—and that systematically define and bridge the skills gaps that exist in their organizations. Planning the retraining of staff must be carried out as seriously as any enterprise strategy. It must be managed as closely as any other corporate asset. The whole organization is responsible for establishing and maintaining a positive learning environment.

Summary

In many ways, client/server is more about psychology than technology. The psychology of grasping new concepts, tools, and ways of thinking and interacting has a huge impact on people and the whole organization. Training is essential in bridging the gap between the old ways and the new ways. Training can be accomplished in a wide variety of formats. Cost-effective training must be planned and managed like any other corporate resource.

The Future of Client/Server

26

by Neil Jenkins

IN THIS CHAPTER

After reading the preceding chapters, you probably have realized that client/server computing is very much becoming the norm for most commercial organizations. It brings value and business benefit to those that use it. Yet inevitably it will become the norm for the computing industry also, and the vendors and resellers will move on to more advanced systems and techniques that will ultimately replace even the newer client/server systems that you use today.

This chapter discusses the major areas that will ultimately bring about improvements to the client/server environment and systems that you build. The essence of this chapter is that client/server will get bigger, better, and faster!

Improvements at the Client

Perhaps the most unknown area to you, the systems manager, is the robustness of the client. The client is, after all, the area in which you are expecting to place the business systems, yet you require it to operate at the level of your centralized midrange or mainframe computer. The client workstation will continue to improve in its capability as a strong, reliable business computer. This improvement will require changes in the components of the hardware itself, the operating systems, and the applications.

The Hardware

Client hardware continues to change at a rapid pace; performance escalates while prices plummet. A Pentium 75Mhz was once the norm; now the 120Mhz level is best for your normal machines. Everything about PC hardware is getting bigger and faster. The architecture is also becoming more user-friendly, with the advent of technologies such as Plug-and-Play, and more integrated, with the advent of integrated cards containing audio, fax, modem, and voice mail capabilities on a single card. Network interface cards are becoming smarter; they now can power on the machine, if required, so that updates can be made without user intervention. This capability will increase as the integration of networking software and client machines improves, making for a more tightly knit systems environment.

In time, the role of the traditional personal computer may become only that of a very intelligent graphical workstation attached to a very large, powerful client/server system. Then the client/server environment will have turned full circle and returned to a somewhat centralized architecture. The machine at the desktop will be a powerful network computer with its own processor, GUI, and memory capacity, yet the applications and data will all be stored on a central server. Although this scenario may occur, I cannot help thinking that the loss of that personal aspect may be too much for most companies to utilize this approach.

The Operating Systems

With the likes of Windows 95, Windows NT V4.0, and OS/2 Warp, desktop operating systems have become more and more reliable. They have also taken onboard more and more of the advanced technologies, such as multithreading, multitasking, security, and communications, normally found in larger systems. As time goes on and these operating systems evolve further, you will continue to see improvements that will benefit the client/server environments that you build. These products will continue to have built into them the features normally found within large-scale operating systems.

Also, you will begin to see a complete integration of Internet and Intranet support within the operating systems. Navigating and browsing the Internet will become as easy as moving between folders on a hard disk. Further out, improvements in voice recognition and voice activation will allow the human voice to control the operation of the computer rather than the more traditional keyboard and mouse.

Just as object orientation has proliferated through the application development tools, it also will move into the operating systems. Object orientation in an operating system is not a necessity, but as advancements are made in operating system functionality, you will see this functionality delivered as objects.

Companies demand compatibility with their existing installed environments. The challenge for the operating systems vendors is to build in state-of-the-art advancements yet still maintain the compatibility. They must provide an ever-increasing number of new features and support for advanced 32-bit applications, but they must also tailor the systems to certain usage requirements. The operating systems also have to offer maximum compatibility with older drivers, older applications, and older equipment.

The Application Development Environment and Programming

The future of the development tools for C/S is somewhat uncertain. One thing, however, is certain; programming will never be the same as it has been over the past decade. The meteoric rise in tools capable of providing C/S developments has to come to an end. A significant number of tools have developed into robust, reliable toolkits that can build your client/server systems. These products include Visual Basic 4, Delphi 2, Magic, Progress, Obsydian, and PowerBuilder. Over time, the toolsets will be split into those recognized as providing adequate capabilities for department-level systems and those capable of providing large, scalable, enterprise systems.

All the tools available will move to true object orientation. The use of objects within the development tools will allow developers to make the switch to true object-based systems. The strengths of the development tools will become their capability to deliver business systems built from pre-built objects joined together by business analysts and business users. The development toolsets will allow access to significant numbers of both relational and object-based databases. This kind of access will become essential as more and more companies move to information bases built on objects that include textual, numeric, graphical, and sound data. Tools, such as Progress, that allow independence from databases will increase in both market share and capability to the point that companies can truly mix and match requirements without losing the necessary processing requirements of housing application logic and data at the server. Currently, most toolsets provide database independence by splitting the presentation and application at the client and the databases on the servers.

The move to object orientation and then further to object fabrication, in which an object may be built from many different low-level toolsets such as C++ and Assembler, brings up an interesting issue concerning the role of the traditional programmer. The trend is now beginning to appear that more and more companies are recognizing that the days of employing large numbers of language programmers in the likes of COBOL, RPG, and C are beginning to disappear. Because it is now more effective to outsource application development or use lower numbers of skilled internal staff with object-based tools or CASE systems, companies no longer require the numbers of detailed programmers that they once had. As the tools themselves become more object-oriented, systems may begin to be built from off-the-shelf objects pieced together by key users.

Information systems staff will become systems integrators. More and more of the developers' time will be spent leading or joining in RAD (Rapid Application Development) projects, quickly assembling objects and interacting with users. These developers will form the nucleus of the IS department. They will be multiskilled—knowledgeable in the business and skilled at programming using a wide range of techniques, and they will probably use some form of 4GL or 5GL. The problem for staff currently in this area is their ability to absorb knowledge of the business, particularly if they have been back-room developers protected from the whims of users by the ranks of business analysts.

So where will all the traditional programmers go? As the demand for business objects increases, software houses will need more programmers capable of building packaged business objects. Most detailed programmers will find themselves working for companies that provide systems rather than building the systems themselves.

There will also continue to be significant growth in technical coding. *Technical coding* is the low-level programming of components, such as device drivers and ROM chips, that make up the software piece of most commercial hardware. Also, as society's thirst for better and better technology expands to household items such as video recorders, televisions, and dishwashers, there will be an increasing need for development staff in these areas. Ultimately, the television as we know it today will be replaced with a very high-resolution monitor, Dolby or THX sound capabilities, an integrated telephone, fax, Internet repository, and a rewritable CD-ROM capable of storing cinema-quality video and sound, effectively turning into a high-capacity personal computer. Someone will have to program the components, won't they? Although most programmers with technical coding skills will likely move to product-based companies, other kinds of companies will probably still need programmers of this type for quite some time because the development industry probably will not move fast enough for these companies to do without them.

Departmental tools also will become more object-oriented and more user-friendly to the point where the departmental systems will be built by the users in the departments using object-based development toolsets as part of the product ranges that they use. This already happens to a certain extent when departments use Microsoft's Visual Basic for Applications to provide integrated office automation systems using Access, Excel, and Word. Staff who are not necessarily employed to program will be expected to solve their business problems by being occasional programmers and using the tools available to them.

Improvements at the Server

Like programming languages and systems development, the commercial database also will move to an object base. The future business systems running on distributed systems will be based on object-oriented database management systems (ODBMSs). The continual demands for different information types has slowly been strangling the existing relational database market. The organizations requiring different types of data, fast performance, and integration of these data types and wanting to standardize on an object-oriented programming tool are looking to ODBMSs to fulfill their needs. The object-based systems that are beginning to appear are better suited to handling complex data types and transactions, particularly across different platforms and environments. The benefit of the object within the object database as opposed to the record within a relational database is that the object is made up of both data and methods, or behavior, for that object. An object's data can be graphics, video, or even code, as well as a number of other complex data types. Relational databases of today exist as tables of rows and columns, normally of fixed length, and the data is typically text or numeric fields. Some databases provide support for large binary objects, but they are not effective in handling the likes of video clips, application programs, or CAD diagrams.

Improvements on the Network

How will networking change during the next few years? The need for more bandwidth is leading the industry toward much greater transmission technologies such as fast Ethernet as a standard for LANs and asynchronous transfer mode (ATM) as a standard for WANs. Applications such as multimedia will require extensive bandwidth. In addition, companies will begin to create networks that can provide them with bandwidth on demand. This capability allows a company to pay for a guaranteed bandwidth capacity but, at peak times, burst into a higher bandwidth amount with no cost implications. For example, a company based in California may purchase a 1 Mbps WAN link to their offices in Stony Stratford, England. This link may have a 2 Mbps bandwidth-on-demand capability. During normal daily activity, the line is used to its 1 Mbps capacity, yet at the end of the day when there is a high transfer rate due to object database updates or video transfer, the line bursts into the 2 Mbps capacity. Because this is sporadic in most cases, the company can negotiate a lower cost of supply for the link from their WAN vendor.

As networks become larger, more users will be dialing in from remote locations. Furthermore, an increasing number of users will have mobile computers and will use wireless network links. As companies link LANs throughout the country and world to form wide area networks, integrated services digital network (ISDN) will finally find a receptive audience. These systems are costly to install for the average network, yet as prices continue to come down and new technology improves, these systems will become the normal working infrastructure.

The Movement Toward Higher Bandwidth

Network applications continue to become more complex and include more use of video and picture images. Furthermore, as companies migrate mainframe applications down to the network level, network applications tend to be much larger than in the past. The result of these trends is a growing customer demand for greater network bandwidth with which to carry data associated with these applications.

When Ethernet was designed, its 10 Mbps bandwidth and contention media access approach seemed more than adequate. Unfortunately, the *bursty traffic* (short bursts of information exchange such as an inquiry and brief response) that Ethernet has been designed to handle has been replaced by traffic that often is uniformly heavy on large LANs. Although Token Ring topology was created as a noncontention network approach to handle heavy traffic, its maximum of 16 Mbps bandwidth is already proving inadequate for some companies with larger, heavily used LANs.

Fiber Distributed Data Interface (FDDI)

Some companies have opted to prepare for the future by installing LANs with *fiber distributed data interfaces* (FDDI), which are able to provide 100 Mbps bandwidth. FDDI has been accepted as a standard since 1990, yet its high cost has meant that companies have not implemented it widely, preferring to use it only on their LAN backbones. A broad range of FDDI products is currently available from a variety of vendors including Cisco, 3Com, Hewlett-Packard (HP), and DEC.

Copper Distributed Data Interface (CDDI)

The high cost of FDDI adapters has caused many companies to look at a twisted-pair wire alternative to FDDI, copper distributed data interface (CDDI). *Copper distributed data interface (CDDI)* is a network topology that is based on the FDDI standard and enables FDDI packets to be transmitted over twisted-pair wire. With a price per port under $995 and 100 Mbps bandwidth, CDDI has attracted some interest. Unfortunately, though, many large companies have chosen to wait for a high bandwidth topology offering an even better price/performance ratio: fast Ethernet.

Fast Ethernet or 100 Base T

What makes fast Ethernet so appealing to many large companies is that users retain existing Ethernet software compatibility and, in many cases, are able to keep existing cabling. Only the network adapter cards and hubs must be modified. The idea of being able to increase network bandwidth from 10 Mbps to 100 Mbps with network adapter cards that are likely to be priced under $400 is intriguing to network managers faced with increasing network traffic congestion generated by client/server systems. Fast Ethernet cards are now readily available, and this technology can be implemented. Because of the ease of transition from existing Ethernet to fast Ethernet, a lot of companies will take this approach.

100VG-AnyLAN

The 100VG-AnyLan networking technology is supported by AT&T, IBM, and HP. 100VG-AnyLan is a logical system upgrade to both Ethernet and Token Ring. It is based on a star topology at both the physical and logical levels. It places intelligence in the central hub to provide network management. 100VG-AnyLAN products are available from Hewlett-Packard.

Asynchronous Transfer Mode (ATM)

Asynchronous transfer mode (ATM) is already having an impact on local area networks. This cell-based transmission technology will have an even greater impact on both LANs and WANs in the near future. ATM, with its specifications developed by both the CCITT and by an ANSI committee, uses a cell-switching technology to achieve transmission speeds from 1.544 Mbps to 1.2 Gbps. A virtual circuit is established between network users, which is very much like the approach used by a telephone system. As much bandwidth as is necessary can be allocated for these circuits through which ATM's cells are transmitted. Cells consist of 48 bytes of user information and a 5-byte header.

A major advantage of ATM is that because all cells are the same 53-byte size, network delays can be predicted so that this type of transmission can be used to carry real-time information such as voice and video. Because ATM is a switch-based technology, it is scalable. Greater traffic can be handled by adding additional switches.

Another major advantage of ATM is that it is independent of upper-layer network protocols. A variety of protocols, including FDDI, can be used at the physical layer. What really appeals to many network managers, though, is the prospect of using ATM with a minimum transmission speed of 155 Mbps as a common ground for a single, global infrastructure, as well as a high-speed backbone for enterprise networks. The advantage of using ATM on a LAN as well as on a WAN is that the interface between the two is seamless. A group of vendors known as the ATM Forum is working on a complete set of ATM specifications that will cover all key elements, including the LAN/WAN interface.

Multimedia and the Future LAN

True multimedia on LANs is still in its infancy, but already industry experts are predicting that it will become a significant network application by the end of 1997. The hardware required for this technology is almost in place. Intel's higher level Pentium chips and some of the new RISC chips offer the processing power to create and transmit video images over a LAN. Until there is widespread acceptance of bandwidth over 100 Mbps, the use of multimedia in everyday applications will not be a reality for most companies, however.

Multimedia on a LAN will probably use special multimedia servers. These servers will have the most powerful processing chips available, fast-access, high-capacity storage devices including CD-ROMs and optical jukeboxes, and video compression chips. It is likely that fast Ethernet and ATM switches will be used to ensure that video information is transmitted rapidly enough so that users can view it in real time.

One way to glimpse what multimedia will look like on future LANs is to examine the LAN industry leader's vision of how this application will function under NetWare. Among the major uses of multimedia on the LAN envisioned by Novell are education, corporate training, kiosks with which to view information, video messaging, video conferencing, and even cable TV-based information services. To optimize transmission of multimedia information over a NetWare 4.1 LAN, Novell has announced enhancements to its network operating system including 64 KB block sizes, burst mode, and special NetWare multimedia directory services. Burst mode refers to Novell's method of sending several packets followed by an acknowledgment rather than requiring an acknowledgment every time a NetWare packet is transmitted over a network. Novell has developed network loadable modules (NLMs) called NetWare Video that run on the server and optimize the disk and network I/O subsystems for use as a video server.

An interesting question to ask is "When desktop video conferencing becomes widespread reality, what will happen to the telephone?" As soon as it is possible to call your family or friends through your home PC and see and discuss and interact with them no matter where they are, it would seem reasonable to suggest that the telephone will begin to seriously change functions. Similarly, when a PC can present video at the same audio and picture quality as the best laserdisc players, video recorders, and movie theaters, what happens to the television? It will probably become a PC monitor with a built-in, dedicated PC for video. Downloading the latest blockbuster from the video store rather than going out in the rain will become a reality, and the store won't run out of copies!

The Growth of Remote Networks

A significant number of corporations have installed large local area networks at their headquarters. Gradually, more and more branch offices are being equipped with smaller LANs. One of the major trends in networking is the growth of remote LANs. In order for a remote LAN to communicate efficiently with a LAN installed at the corporate headquarters, it needs a remote bridge or router and some kind of dial-up modem line or leased line, depending on the amount of traffic on the network. The corporate LAN must be equipped with the appropriate dial-in communications software and the remote LAN must also run communications software for users on the remote LAN to be able to have all the network benefits of local users on the corporate LAN.

The two most common network protocols currently found on networks are NetWare's IPX and TCP/IP. Several network operating systems, including IBM's LAN Server and Microsoft's LAN Manager, utilize the NetBEUI transport protocol. Unlike IPX and TCP/IP, however, NetBEUI cannot be routed over interconnected LANs and WANs. A PC user communicating with a remote LAN using the NetBEUI protocol must operate via a direct link that, in effect, is a bridged extension of the LAN. What this means is that a remote user with NetBEUI protocol cannot dial into a local LAN node and then be routed to a remote destination LAN through the network.

Wireless LANs and Mobile Computers

Today, wireless LAN technology is at a serious competitive disadvantage when competing against conventional LAN cable technology. The low price of cabled LANs, particularly Ethernet, has restricted wireless LANs to specific market niches. Companies with isolated reception or warehouse buildings, for example, install wireless LANs in these areas and then bridge them to existing cabled LANs. Other current users of wireless technology include field auditors who move from location to location and salespeople who need to become local users of their corporation's LAN whenever they visit headquarters.

As the visual displays of mobile computers continue to improve and battery life increases, the convenience of these machines will encourage users to request them for their desktop computing. A standard interface for these computers, the PCMCIA (Personal Computer Memory Card International Association) specifications, has made it possible for vendors to introduce network interface cards using the PCMCIA credit card footprint.

Network operating system vendors, including Novell and Microsoft, currently are working on extensions to their directory services to make it easier for a mobile computer to become a network node through a wireless LAN connection. For example, drivers have been developed that enable two notebook computers with PCMCIA cards and Windows 95 installed to communicate through wireless connections.

One possible result of the explosive growth of mobile computers is that these units eventually will probably include wireless LAN connectivity built-in as well as having peer-to-peer LAN software installed in their firmware. This means that when these machines are turned on, they will immediately be ready to link to any other computers in the area that are similarly equipped. Artisoft, as an example, already has designed Ethernet chips that include the LANtastic network operating system.

ISDN and the Future Office

Study Group XVII of the CCITT worked four years (1980-1984) to develop a set of standards for future voice and data integration. Taking a broad view of future global telecommunications, the committee planned an architecture that would provide integrated access to circuit-switched and packet-switched networks, as well as end-to-end digital transport of data. The resulting model—the Integrated Services Digital Network (ISDN)—represents a network of the future. It includes truly integrated voice, data, and even video traveling smoothly (over the same pathways) from one type of network to another.

The ISDN concept of a universal interface means that each terminal will understand every other terminal. It will be possible to send information such as interactive videotext and facsimiles at the relatively high speed of 64 Kbps. ISDN standards define a digital interface divided into two types of channels: B channels for customer information (voice, data, and video) and D channels for sending signals and control information. These D channels utilize a packet-mode layered protocol based on the CCITT's X.25 standard.

The CCITT committee defined two major interfaces that use these B and D channels. The Basic Rate Interface (BRI) is used to serve devices with relatively small capacity, such as terminals. A second interface, Primary Rate Interface (PRI), is used for large-capacity devices, such as PBXs. Both interfaces utilize one D channel and several B channels, transmitting at 64 Kbps.

Because ISDN can be used for a variety of data types, voice, video data and so on, it can be applied to a variety of applications. As Figures 26.1 through 26.6 show, ISDN can be applied to many different computer applications scenarios.

FIGURE 26.1.

Leased-line backup server-to-server.

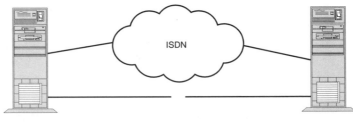

FIGURE 26.2.

Leased-line backup via routers server-to-server.

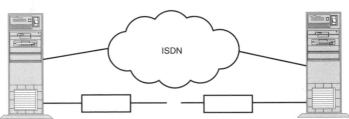

FIGURE 26.3.
Database access.

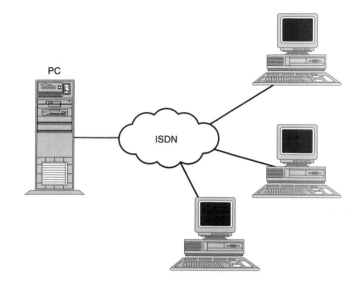

FIGURE 26.4.
Internet connectivity.

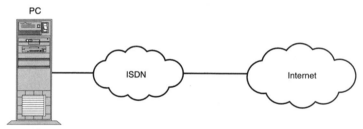

FIGURE 26.5.
Desktop videoconferencing.

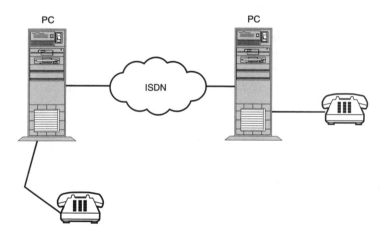

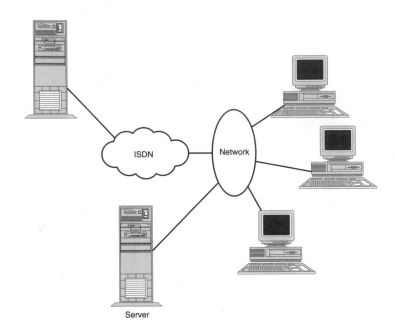

FIGURE 26.6.

Remote LAN access.

The Growth of Enterprise Networks

A trend that will continue for the next few years is the linking of one company's several different networks to form enterprise-wide networks. Many companies have realized that their computing environments consisted of several different isolated network islands. A mainframe might use PROFS for its electronic mail while handling the company's manufacturing computing. A Digital Equipment Corporation VAX minicomputer might be part of a DECnet network that handles the same company's accounting activities as well as its research and development computing tasks. Finally, the newest addition, a local area network, might link together that company's PCs and Macintosh computers to share productivity software such as word processing, spreadsheet, and database programs and also share expensive laser printers. Finally, the engineering department might have several Sun workstations linked through Ethernet to share computer-aided engineering (CAE) and computer-aided design (CAD) files.

The network manager in the late 1990s has been charged with creating a single enterprise-wide network of all these diverse computing elements. Every employee under such a network would have access to the resources available on any one of these previously isolated computing networks, assuming that this individual has the appropriate security clearance. The access must be seamless, timely, and reliable.

As part of this enterprise-wide network, users can expect to see a more uniform graphical user interface regardless of hardware platform. Furthermore, the end user will eventually not need to even know what computing platform contains specific software. By clicking an icon representing a specific business task, the user will be able to call up an application regardless of where it is physically located. Similarly, many large databases will be dispersed on different servers that could be located in different cities. Once again, all the complex computing required to make these functions work will be invisible to end users. Mainframe programs will appear on a user's PC screen looking identical to PC-based programs. No longer do network users need to be forced to learn how to use a keyboard that is functioning under mainframe or minicomputer terminal emulation mode.

Network Management Software

> **NOTE**
>
> Enterprise network management across multiple locations and multiple platforms is still in its infancy, yet it will develop quickly as companies require structured management of their systems. This is the currently the largest problem faced by companies moving to client/server. It is therefore also one of the main areas being developed.

Today, several software programs are available to manage networks, but several problems remain. On enterprise networks, it is likely that a mainframe might be managed by a comprehensive network management program such as NetView. Hewlett-Packard minicomputers are likely to be managed by the company's OpenView program. In addition, dozens of programs are currently available that utilize the Simple Network Management Protocol (SNMP) to receive information from network devices and report on their status.

Although SNMP-based network management programs are very common in networks where UNIX is used, many managers have hesitated using this protocol to manage their PC LANs because it would add additional overhead to run a second protocol (TCP/IP) over a LAN that more than likely is already running NetWare's IPX protocol or LAN Manager's NetBEUI protocol.

Many current LAN management programs manage only a small portion of a network. Some programs manage PCs attached to a hub, for example, and other programs might only manage file server activity. It is sometimes necessary for network managers to run several different LAN management programs to provide comprehensive coverage. On an enterprise network, information from the LAN devices must still be integrated with information regarding the status of devices on minicomputers and mainframes.

Today, companies typically use a variety of products to manage their enterprise network. Yet increasingly there are a number of comprehensive network management programs that can track all types of LAN devices, as well as integrate information from mainframe and minicomputers. Because networks are becoming increasingly more complex and larger, network management software continues to grow in popularity. As the network management software of the future becomes more and more powerful and robust, companies will feel much more comfortable moving to client/server.

Here Comes UNIX!

UNIX is gaining popularity on PC-based LANs. UNIX does offer several advantages over current network operating systems. It offers symmetrical multiprocessing, meaning that several processors can divide up the processing load of a server. Microsoft's Windows NT offers this feature as does VINES, but NetWare still does not provide this feature. UNIX also offers built-in communications, a powerful script language, and program portability from one UNIX hardware platform to a second hardware platform. Perhaps equally important, UNIX was designed specifically for large networks and for providing security on such networks.

Historically, UNIX has failed to dominate the LAN NOS market because it required very fast processors and extensive memory resources, both of which were very expensive until recently. Also, UNIX is complex enough to require a very well-trained support person as well as users who have been trained it its basic commands. UNIX will grow in popularity on PC-based LANs because it now can overcome its heretofore most serious limitation, its reputation for being a very user-unfriendly environment. The use of X Window and Motif has allowed users to move from the more familiar Microsoft Windows environments to those of UNIX. More and more throughout the late 90s, LANs will also include UNIX servers as part of their structure, providing server resources to a variety of client workstations. In the initial stages, this inclusion will be in the form of database servers, such as Informix, but as traditionally PC-based companies become more familiar with the UNIX systems, the roles will increase to business systems such as graphical repositories, transaction processors, systems management consoles, and data warehouse/statistical analysis systems.

Summary

As is the case with most information systems areas, the future of client/server looks both exciting and challenging. Whereas in years past computing environments have gone through major changes with the passing of every 10 years, client/server and distributed computing presents the formidable task of changing every two years! This constant change is an advantage in that the technology will not stagnate or stop being developed, yet it also presents big headaches for you, the systems professional.

At the end of the day, the future of your client/server systems is based on the future of your business. The client/server models can help your business get to where it wants to go. As your business evolves and improves, you can use the more advanced technology highlighted in this chapter to enable the business to achieve its goals.

Intranets

IV

PART

Designing an Intranet

27

by Tim Evans

This chapter is about the process you will use to design your Intranet. Although you will no doubt find that your design will change as you implement your Web, and the people who use it will want further changes, you should nevertheless go through this process before you begin the nuts-and-bolts work of putting it together. Planning your Intranet now will result in building it more effectively and in less overall time.

This chapter assumes only that you have used a World Wide Web browser (like Mosaic or Netscape) and that you therefore have a general familiarity with the Web as a whole. You'll learn about the tools you can use to implement your server. You'll also do the following:

- Learn what an Intranet is and how it is different from what you've seen on the World Wide Web
- Identify the customers in your company for whom your Intranet is designed
- Determine the kind of information you will make available on your Intranet
- Decide who in your company or organization (or what organizational component) is best as the keeper of your Intranet
- Consider high-level issues about the design and organization of your Intranet server(s)
- Identify and target your Intranet's customers and sell them on the idea of an Intranet

You'll find that these subjects are closely interrelated and that your decisions in one of these areas inevitably affect the others. As a result, the process of designing an Intranet won't turn out to be the linear process these bulleted items seem to suggest.

The What and Why of an Intranet

This book uses the term *Intranet* to refer to organizations' use of World Wide Web and related Internet technology to do their essential work, that of helping to produce the goods or services the organizations exist to produce.

In the rush to get on the Web, most organizations think in terms of making information available to people outside the organization. Many companies have installed Web servers and made them accessible on the Internet with the idea of making corporate information available to others or of selling things on the Web. Interestingly, though, the initial objective of the Web pioneers at the European Particle Physics Lab (CERN) in Geneva, was to create a means by which CERN scientists could more easily share information. Thus, the first Web was an Intranet designed to distribute information *within* an organization to the organization's own people. Without detracting from the proven business value of World Wide Web services in making information available to those outside organizations and companies, this book focuses on how Web and related technology may be used purely within an organization to further the purpose for which the organization exists.

Your Customers

Given this premise, the definition of those who will use your Intranet is sharply different than that of those who use a company's public Web. Traditionally, when a company sets up a Web server, the intended audience is one or more of the following: the general public, current and future customers, stockholders, and even competitors. What all these people have in common, of course, is that all of them are *outside* the business. Figure 27.1 shows a typical business home page offering public information, news releases, and the like about a major international company.

FIGURE 27.1.

The Conoco home page.

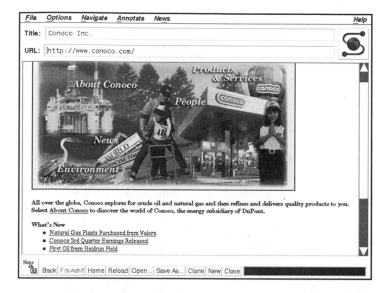

Although many of Conoco's employees may have an interest in this Web site, you can see that its primary focus is on presenting information to outsiders. General information about the company is available, as are public news releases about company earnings and activities. There's even a page about the company's people and its community service activities and another about company environmental activities. Both contain valuable public relations information. Clearly, the potential audience of this Web site is external to that company.

By contrast, Figure 27.2 shows the home page for the University of Kansas campus-wide information center. Here the focus is on those people inside or closely associated with the organization: students, faculty, and administrators of the university. You see information about the university's campuses, calendars of events, course listings and schedules, departmental and campus organization information, and information such as the campus phone book.

FIGURE 27.2.

KUFacts, the University of Kansas Online Information System.

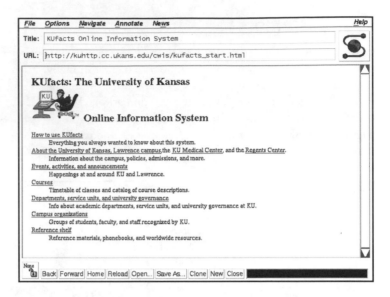

Although some of the information available on this Web server would be useful to people outside the university, its primary audience is clearly campus insiders. The campus phone book or the football schedule may be of wider interest. On the other hand, the History department's fall schedule of classes (see Figure 27.3) showing that History 565, Imperial Russia and the Soviet Union, taught by Professor Alexander (a course the author took with the same professor in 1969!), meets on Mondays, Wednesdays, and Fridays at 11:30 in Room 4002, is probably of interest only to a few history students at the university who are trying to fulfill graduation requirements and/or fit a course into their schedule.

FIGURE 27.3.

KU History department schedule of classes.

NOTE

Note the decidedly nongraphical approach taken by the university's Web site. KU is the home of lynx, a text-only Web browser that is freely available and widely used. Nongraphical browsers are important in situations in which users have dumb terminals or other nongraphical devices that cannot display the images and other graphical features of the Web. Intentionally unable to support graphics, lynx and other plain-text browsers provide the ability for users to follow hyperlinks, download files, send e-mail, read and post Usenet news articles, and access other Internet services, pretty much just as the more fortunate of us who have access to Netscape or Mosaic. Figure 27.4 shows the same KU History department class schedule as Figure 27.3, this time viewed in lynx. More information about lynx is available at the following URL:

`http://www.ukans.edu/about_lynx/about_lynx.html`

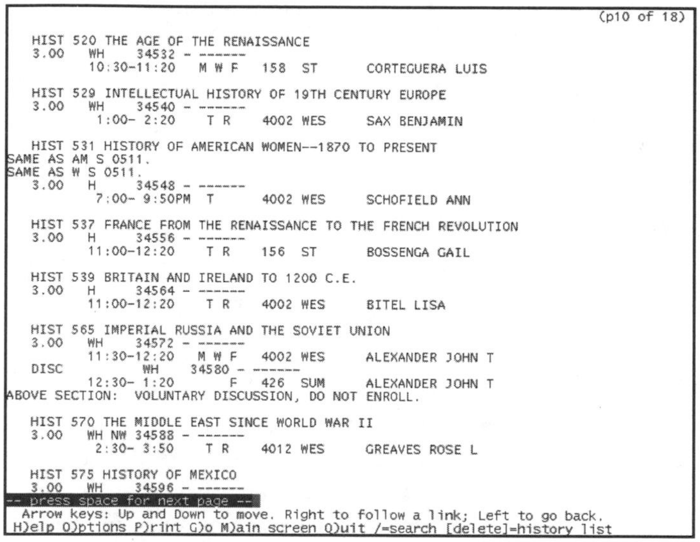

```
                                                              (p10 of 18)
   HIST 520 THE AGE OF THE RENAISSANCE
   3.00    WH     34532 - ------
           10:30-11:20    M W F   158  ST       CORTEGUERA LUIS

   HIST 529 INTELLECTUAL HISTORY OF 19TH CENTURY EUROPE
   3.00    WH     34540 - ------
            1:00- 2:20     T R    4002 WES      SAX BENJAMIN

   HIST 531 HISTORY OF AMERICAN WOMEN--1870 TO PRESENT
SAME AS AM S 0511.
SAME AS W S 0511.
   3.00    H      34548 - ------
            7:00- 9:50PM  T       4002 WES      SCHOFIELD ANN

   HIST 537 FRANCE FROM THE RENAISSANCE TO THE FRENCH REVOLUTION
   3.00    H      34556 - ------
           11:00-12:20     T R    156  ST       BOSSENGA GAIL

   HIST 539 BRITAIN AND IRELAND TO 1200 C.E.
   3.00    H      34564 - ------
           11:00-12:20     T R    4002 WES      BITEL LISA

   HIST 565 IMPERIAL RUSSIA AND THE SOVIET UNION
   3.00    WH     34572 - ------
           11:30-12:20    M W F   4002 WES      ALEXANDER JOHN T
   DISC           WH     34580 - ------
           12:30- 1:20        F   426  SUM      ALEXANDER JOHN T
ABOVE SECTION:  VOLUNTARY DISCUSSION, DO NOT ENROLL.

   HIST 570 THE MIDDLE EAST SINCE WORLD WAR II
   3.00    WH NW 34588 - ------
            2:30- 3:50     T R    4012 WES      GREAVES ROSE L

   HIST 575 HISTORY OF MEXICO
   3.00    WH     34596 - ------
-- press space for next page --
  Arrow keys: Up and Down to move. Right to follow a link; Left to go back.
 H)elp O)ptions P)rint G)o M)ain screen Q)uit /=search [delete]=history list
```

FIGURE 27.4.
KU History department schedule of classes viewed in lynx.

Insiders Are Your Customers

The distinction between the intended audience of the two Web servers you've examined should now be clear. When you begin to consider the design of your Intranet, your first consideration must be a clear definition of your intended audience, your customers, if you will. As you've seen, KUFacts' customers are clearly different from Conoco's. The university's primary business is education and research, with its primary customers being students, educators, and researchers, all of whom are members of the organization. KUFacts supports those business objectives by providing information services primarily to those customers. Conoco's primary business is exploration for and production of energy products (oil, natural gas, and the like); its Web site customers are primarily the very same people who consume the company's products, the vast majority of whom are outside the organization.

Although your company may already have a World Wide Web server with a constituency like Conoco's, your Intranet will take on the primary characteristics and orientation of KUFacts. Your organization's primary business might be the manufacture of ball bearings, the provision of health insurance services, or the payment of government benefits, but your Intranet's customers are not the same as the customers who buy or receive those products and services. Rather, in this case, your customers are the people inside your organization. Further, your customers are the people who make those products or provide those services.

These critical distinctions must be kept in view when conceiving and designing your Intranet. How you design your Intranet and what information it contains must be based on your target audience: your customers on the inside. Later in this chapter, you'll consider further focusing the definition of this audience. Accordingly, this book uses the term *customer* from here on to refer to people inside your organization, company, or agency.

Your Business Is Providing Services to Your Customers

Your company provides services of one or more kinds for its employees (customers). These services may cover a wide range:

- Human resources (personnel) services
- Materiel and logistical services such as office space, equipment (desks, telephones, computers, machinery, and so on), supplies, and all the physical services involved in operating an organization
- Information systems services

Most businesses have a formal or informal organization that reflects these services, with Materiel and Logistical, Human Resources, Information Systems, and other similar departments providing services to insiders. Whether your organization is a small shop, multinational corporation, government agency, or other institution, one of its business activities is the provision of these kinds of services. Looking at them is the first major step toward defining the content and layout of your Intranet.

This book takes a frank, strong customer-is-always-right point of view. Just as your business is all about selling goods or services to your outside customers, your Intranet is all about doing the same with your inside customers.

Information and Services Your Customers Need

The people in an organization can be seen as customers of some of the organization's goods and services. The provision of those goods and services also can be seen as a business activity. To bring those two ideas together, think about the sorts of things that might go into an Intranet by using the major breakdown of business activities listed previously. Just what specific things among those goods and services might fit on an Intranet?

Human Resources Services

Whether or not your company has a formal personnel department, a great deal of paperwork is involved in activities relating to employees. Much of that paperwork is information your customers need. Some examples of this paperwork are the following:

- Employee manuals, codes of conduct, information about health insurance plans, pay and vacation information, and procedures for buying things or getting reimbursed for expenses
- Company bulletin boards papered with government notices about minimum wages and nondiscrimination policies, job announcements, work schedules, training courses, cafeteria menus, softball schedules, and for-sale notices
- Employee records of time, attendance, vital information (marital status, home address, and so on), and performance reviews
- Employee newsletters with company announcements and other communications
- All the varied substantive and procedural documents a Human Resources department might use to hire, fire, promote, transfer, train, keep records on, and otherwise manage the employment and benefits of employees

Here is a veritable treasure trove of information for an Intranet! Imagine how your Human Resources department might provide these kinds of information in a more up-to-date and more easily accessible way with a World Wide Web server. You may even already have some of this information in some kind of electronic form. Employees then can use their Web browser to retrieve for themselves current copies of the documents you've previously stored in file cabinets, saving both the employee's and your own time and money.

Suppose an employee wants to know whether the company health insurance plan covers a particular surgical procedure. If the health plan brochure is available on your Web server, the employee can look it up herself at her own convenience and in a confidential, private way. Again, the employee nearing retirement age may want information about the pension plan, possibly even a benefit computation. Why not make it possible for him to get this information himself? Similarly, how about giving your people the opportunity to file trip reports, including requests for reimbursement of travel expenses, or apply for a job vacancy? How about providing the company phone book or the old-fashioned suggestion box online? Your Personnel department is a rich source of information for your Intranet.

Materiel and Logistics Services

Every organization, large or small, provides to its customers desks, telephones, computers, office supplies, trash removal, cleaning services, and a whole host of other related services. Fire extinguishers are serviced, parking lots and sidewalks are maintained and cleared of snow, mail is picked up and delivered, equipment and furniture is moved and repaired, and goods and services are purchased. Records are kept of all these things, some of which (Occupational Safety and Health Administration records, for example) are required by government agencies.

These items are another source of information and services your Intranet can provide, as described in the following examples:

- A Web-searchable listing of excess office furniture, machinery, or computer equipment can save money in a large company by matching people and excess equipment.

- A nested, clickable image of building blueprints available to building services staff can display increasingly detailed architectural/structural drawings of buildings and their rooms. Ditto for engineering drawings of industrial equipment and all of the underground facilities (water, heat, electricity, network connections) at a large campus.

- Similar, but less detailed, image maps can provide a graphical front end to the company telephone book allowing employees to locate each other easily. Clicking a building on a campus map can bring up the building's phone book; clicking a room in a building can bring up the names of its occupants.

- A wide range of fill-in forms for searching and updating inventories, filling orders, locating and ordering supplies, maintaining required records, and a hundred other tasks, can be provided on your Intranet.

As you can see, these Intranet uses can range from administrative trivia (locating a used file cabinet) to essential company services. The last idea listed is especially intriguing. You've seen fill-in forms on the Web that allow you to sign electronic guest books and do searches on the Web using Web search services such as Yahoo (`http://www.yahoo.com/`) or Lycos (`http://www.lycos.com/`). Because a fill-in form is merely a means of collecting information and passing it off to a computer program for processing using the Common Gateway Interface (CGI), you can now provide a Web interface to a plethora of services that must be requested. Bureaucracies already have hundreds of forms employees must fill out to get things or to get things done. Figure 27.5 shows a simple Web fill-in form that could be a replacement for the paper purchase order or requisition form.

Generated in a few minutes with just over 40 lines of very simple HTML markup, this form, when backed up with an equally simple CGI script, can take the information the user enters and e-mail it to data entry personnel in the Purchasing department. With a more elaborate back-end CGI script, the very same simple form could be used to enter the order directly into an electronic ordering system, debit the orderer's charge code, update company inventory if the order is for capital equipment, and fire off a return e-mail message acknowledging the order. In fact, leaving questions of authorization aside, the information in the fill-in form could just as easily be sent through Internet e-mail or fax directly to the supplier, bypassing company purchasing altogether (though you'd probably want the program at least to leave a copy for them).

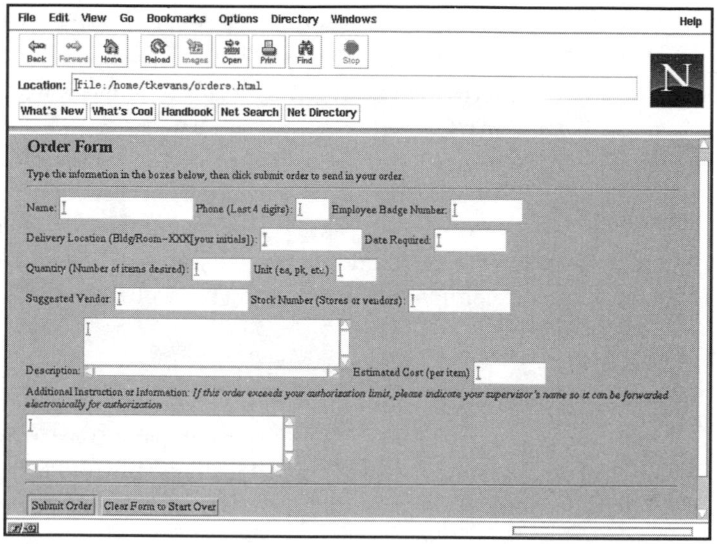

FIGURE 27.5.

A simple order form.

Information Systems Services

Your organization's Information Systems department, if you have one, is already in the business, at least in part, of providing data processing services to customers inside the company. (The term Information Systems Services is used here to mean any information your organization has stored on computers, all the way from the MIS mainframes to your desktop PCs, and any services these computer systems provide.) As a result, you'll find crossover between Information Systems Services and the two other broad categories already mentioned in this chapter. Your Personnel department, for instance, surely uses some data processing services in doing its work whether those services are on the company mainframe or on desktop PCs. All the potential customers of your Intranet, because they must have computers to access it, are already users of some of these services.

Accordingly, this area is perhaps your most fertile source of resources for your Intranet. These services will then form most of the meat of your Intranet. The following are some ideas:

■ If computer use is widespread in your company, you may have a help desk staff that answers phone calls from users about hardware, software, and other related matters. People operating help desks know there are questions that come up over and over which, not surprisingly, have the same answers. How do I set up my modem so I can dial into the office from my home PC? How do I change my password? How do I print mailing labels with my word processor? Canned answers to common questions can form the heart of an Intranet Help Desk. Using Netscape or Mosaic, your Help Desk staff can use fill-in forms like the ones on Yahoo or Lycos to search for answers (and create new ones). Taken a step further, there's no reason you can't make the Intranet Help Desk available directly to users, allowing them to search for the information they need at their own convenience.

■ Web-based interfaces to both commercial and homegrown database applications are available. No matter what you may use a database for, it has two major functions: entering or updating information and retrieving information. While your database application may have special screens for users to perform these functions, both of these functions can just as easily be done with Web fill-in forms and back-end CGI scripts that access the database. The advantage? Users see an interface they recognize and with which they're comfortable, because you've implemented it for many purposes in your Intranet.

■ Existing word processing documents, spreadsheets, and other application data files can be shared using Web technology. Proper set up of your Web server and your users' Web browsers can, for example, allow a company executive to click on a hyperlink and open current sales or operational data directly into his spreadsheet program for what-if analysis, then graph the results for inclusion into presentations or word processing documents.

■ Scientists, engineers, and technicians can share data files from their computer applications on your Intranet. Chemists can fire up molecular modeling programs just by clicking on a hyperlink pointing to a data file and engineers can bring up CAD drawings in the same way.

■ You can wrap an entire custom computer application program your company uses inside a Web interface with Netscape as its interface and with built-in help for its users.

As you've read this section, you've no doubt thought about existing Information Systems resources in your company that might be made accessible on your Intranet. Just this brief listing of possibilities can lead you to think about legacy information (that is, existing documents and other data) that will be an immediate source of data you can tap to get your Intranet up and running quickly.

Who Will Do This?

In earlier years, when MIS departments had a monopoly on data and data processing, assigning responsibility for Intranet setup and design would have been easy: the MIS department would do it, of course. Today, though, the Web is based on distributed computing, and MIS can't control everyone's desktop PC or workstation. This situation presents a terrific opportunity for the consumers of Information Systems Resources, who presumably know the most about what they need to take an active role in the design and construction of your Intranet. Web server setup and HTML are not rocket science. With freely available Web server and supporting software, it's easy for almost anyone with a PC or workstation to create a Web home page and make it available.

Central Control or No Control?

This ease of setup can be both a blessing and, the MIS folks will be quick to remind you, a curse. If anyone can set up a Web server and/or a home page, who will control your Intranet? This question is valid not only from an authoritarian point of view (after all, people are supposed to use their computers to do their jobs) but also from other points of view as well. Here are some issues you may have to deal with:

- Will you want your Intranet to have a common organization and look or is substance all you care about?

- Will someone approve each and every piece of information before it goes on your Intranet, or can anyone put up anything they like?

- If people are free to put up anything they like, will you be concerned about inappropriate material and/or inappropriate use of your organization's information systems and personnel resources?

- Will you accept and welcome the inevitable evolution of your Intranet as you and its users figure out new things it might do?

If you've used the World Wide Web to any extent, you've recognized it as the world's largest vanity press; people can, and do, put anything they want on it. You can find truly amazing (in all senses of the word) things on the Web, many of which may be offensive (again, in all senses of the word). How you feel about this sort of anarchy will inevitably color how you approach assigning responsibility and setting standards for your Intranet. At the same time, the fundamental nature of the Web as a distributed service provides unparalleled opportunities for individual and organizational development, and imposing a rigid, authoritarian structure on your Web might well inhibit the sort of creativity that can bring about breakthroughs in your company's work.

Organizational Models

Based on the philosophical approach you decide to take in assigning responsibility for your Intranet, there are several models you can follow. This section focuses on the following three:

- The *centralized model* has a single Web server administered by a specific organization in your company; it also has a formal process for developing and installing new services.

- In the *decentralized model*, everyone is free to set up a Web server and place resources of their choice on it.
- The *mixed model* has elements of both the centralized and decentralized models.

Centralized Model

In this top-down model, all Web services are centralized. Just one computer system in your company runs a Web server. You have a specific individual or group responsible for the setup, design, and administration of the server. All Web pages (documents, forms, and so on) are designed centrally at the request of customers. Thus, if the Personnel department wanted to put employee benefit information on the Web, a formal request would be required, including content and design requests. The Web staff would, in consultation with Personnel, design and refine the employee benefits page and, when the process was complete, make the page available on the Web server. Figure 27.6 shows the centralized model of Web administration with all Web-related development funneled through an approval process before any information is placed on the central Web server.

FIGURE 27.6.

Centralized model of Web administration.

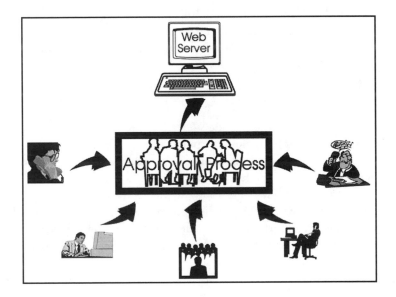

This approach is sound for a number of good reasons. First and foremost, by focusing Web server administration, page design, and production in a single person or group, you can develop a consistently designed Intranet. You can develop and use common Web page templates to ensure layout consistency as well as use a standard set of substantive and navigational images. Users will see a coherent, well-thought-out Web server with each part consistent with your overall design, layout, and content standards.

Another strong argument in favor of the centralized model is that it simplifies the setup and administration of your Intranet. Only one computer system runs the server. All updates, both Web pages and server software, need only be applied once. Security (see Chapter 29, "Intranet Security") can be focused on the single machine, which can also be physically secured. Backups are easy to do because everything that needs backing up is on the one system.

Unfortunately, there are equally strong reasons this approach is the wrong one to take. From a philosophical point of view, it runs counter to pretty much everything that's happened in data processing over the past two decades. With the rise of the personal computer and workstation, data processing has moved out of the glass-walled MIS data center and onto people's desks. Taking the centralized approach to your Intranet may satisfy the MIS diehards, but it also contradicts everything the Web stands for.

More practically speaking, bureaucratized administration of your Intranet's development can choke it to death before it ever gets off the ground as endless memoranda about standards circulate before any real development takes place. Your primary objective in setting up an Intranet is to get information to your customers. Centralized administration can easily get bogged down in organizational and turf matters, cutting off the potential of rapid response to your customers.

> **TIP**
>
> Because your target audience is inside your company, not outside, the standards you'd apply to the former will probably be very different from those for the latter. The employee looking for help in setting up his PC probably doesn't care whether the help document he finds on your Intranet has the correctly proportioned corporate logo on it. Rather, he's interested in the substance of the document. Your company's outside Web server, aimed at a completely different audience, can—and probably will—be subject to a more rigorous set of standards.

Finally, the centralized model places all your Web eggs in a single basket. If the computer system running your Intranet server goes down, everyone is cut off. This policy requires a decision between potentially expensive downtime and expensive duplicative hardware—another hot, spare computer ready to run in the event the main system goes down. This adds not only the extra cost of the hardware and software for the system but introduces a new aspect of the administration of the system, that of making sure all changes to the primary system get mirrored to the backup.

Decentralized Model

At the other end of the spectrum lies the decentralized model. In this model, Web server software, which is widely available both commercially and as freeware or shareware, runs on desktop

PCs (including both Windows PCs and Macs) and on UNIX systems. This software is relatively easy to set up and run. The HTML language, the markup language used to create Web pages with all their nice formatting and image and hyperlink capabilities, can be learned by just about anyone in a couple of hours. Using free software or shareware, even a moderately experienced PC user can have a Web server up and running with some HTML documents in an afternoon. Figure 27.7 shows the decentralized model of Web administration with users free to develop their own Web documents and even set up individual Web servers.

FIGURE 27.7.

Decentralized model of Web administration.

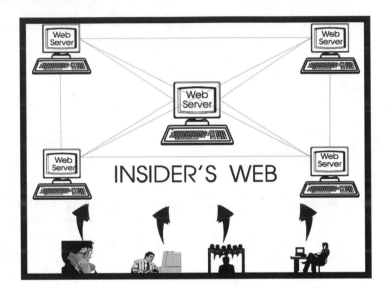

As with the centralized model, the decentralized model has both strong and weak points. The most compelling argument for this model is that the user who sets up her own Web server (and who is also one of your Intranet's customers) may be the single best person to do so because she knows precisely the service she wants to provide. That is, if an engineer wants to share engineering drawings and technical reports with her colleagues, she and her colleagues are in the best position to decide what is to be shared and how it is best presented. In the centralized model, this customer with information to share has to negotiate the standards process before being able to get the information to her colleagues. Similarly, the personnel specialist who has new pension information to make available or the office manager who wants to announce the staff holiday party is more concerned about getting the information posted than whether it's properly formatted according to some standard or whether the proper colors are used in the corporate logo.

In other words, the main advantage of the decentralized model is that it allows those who have information to share to share it quickly and with a minimum of fuss. If you're running a Web server on your PC, for instance, you can put up a new Web page on some subject in your area of expertise in just a few minutes. This advantage can also be seen as a disadvantage. The fact that it is so easy to set up Web pages lends itself to what may best be termed anarchy, with uscrs putting up related or unrelated (who decides which is which?) Web pages all over the company. A casual walk around the World Wide Web shows how this anarchy can and does lead from the sublime to the absurd to the downright obscene.

> **TIP**
>
> The overall tone of a Web server can lead to increased or decreased support from both its customers and its sponsors. Too much anarchy often turns off users, and they just stop using the service. And, of course, few things could be worse for the overall health of your Intranet than to have the president of the company stumbling across a particularly inappropriate or offensive link on some junior researcher's home page.

The nature of your organization will help you evaluate this model. Academic and research institutions may find the intellectual freedom of their researchers outweighs the high noise level of the Web created under this model. Businesses may want a tighter focus on the work at hand, finding this sort of anarchy has too much potential for abuse and/or misdirected time and effort. I have seen numerous examples of otherwise useful, well-focused Web pages with just one clinker of a hyperlink pointing off to some other Web page that's egregiously unrelated to the rest of the page, and inappropriate to any conceivable purpose of the page.

Mixed Model

Somewhere between these two extremes is probably where most organizations will land when setting up Intranets. For example, you may want to establish a broad policy that your Web's primary purpose is to support a specific group of your customers and that anything consistent with that purpose is permitted. In this case, you'd rely on that part of the centralized model that dictates the overall direction and purpose of your Web but use those aspects of the decentralized model that leave most details to your customers. There will inevitably be gray areas or even outright violations of the overall policies, but you can deal with them on a case-by-case basis as management issues, just as you do with, say, misuse of company telephones or time and leave abuse.

Please don't make firm decisions on a model for administering your Intranet quite yet. You still need to focus on its primary objectives, and doing so will help you focus your decision-making on these administrative issues. In the following sections, you'll look at these questions as well as lay out some of the technical possibilities for implementing the mixed model.

Design and Layout of Your Intranet

Having considered the foregoing administrative matters, it's now time to turn to more interesting things: the substantive design and content of your Intranet.

What Is the Purpose of Your Intranet?

So far in this chapter, you've established a framework that should help you bring your ideas about an Intranet into clearer definition. This chapter has so far covered the concept of thinking of the potential users of your Intranet as customers and provided some possibilities based on this concept. Next, this chapter discussed some of the high-level administrative aspects of setting up and running an Intranet. By now, you perhaps have a clearer focus on who your potential customers are and some definite ideas on the sorts of information you want to make available.

Statement of Purpose

Putting your ideas together into an Intranet statement of purpose is your first concrete step toward realizing your ideas. The following sample statements of purpose are based on the possibilities listed under the previous heading "Information and Services Your Customers Need."

- ■ Provide customers with information about their employee benefits.
- ■ Give customers access to a searchable database of PC hardware and software technical support information.
- ■ Provide customers with a Web browser interface to the corporate inventory and ordering database.
- ■ Use Web technology to enable customers to share data files from common applications.

As you can see, each of these statements is both specific and limited. Developing your statement of purpose allows you to define the task ahead of you in terms both you and your potential customers can easily grasp. There is, of course, no reason you can't write a larger statement of purpose that incorporates several of these (or other) purposes, such as "Provide customers with Human Resources, materiels and logistics, and information system services using World Wide Web technology." Such a far-reaching statement of purpose is certainly acceptable, provided that you're able to clearly define the objectives that fall under it, possibly using lower-level statements of purpose for each of the major subdivisions, Human Resources, Materiel and Logistics, and Information Systems. Some people may want to start out with more limited statements of purpose like those listed, and then expand on them later. The method you choose depends on your own ideas as to what you want your Intranet to accomplish.

Besides giving you a pole star toward which to steer in developing your Intranet, your statement of purpose also implies some substantive choices about the work you're cutting out for yourself. For example, it's one thing to take a batch of Microsoft Word documents and put them up on a Web server as a boilerplate library for customers to browse and grab. Most computer-literate people can put such a library together and generate the HTML code to index it. It's quite another thing, though, to develop the CGI scripts to back up forms-based data entry and retrieval (see Chapter 30, "Web Access to Commercial Database Applications"). The order form example earlier in this chapter is quite simple, but the program that it executes will not be. You'll need competent programmers to write the scripts in whatever programming language you choose on your system.

Implementation Goals

Once you have a statement of purpose, particularly if yours is a broad one, you'll need to develop more concrete *implementation goals*, or specific objectives for the information and services your Intranet will provide to your customers. If you were using the employee benefits statement of purpose, you might define the following series of goals:

- Provide online health benefits information
- Provide online job vacancy announcements and give customers the capability to read both summary and detailed information
- Allow customers to enter change-of-address and/or family status information using fill-in forms
- Allow customers to calculate an estimated pension benefit based on their years of service and projected earnings between now and retirement age using a fill-in form

In order to implement and manage your implementation goals, translate them into clusters of specific tasks to be performed. For example, if your job vacancy announcements are created using your word processor, they can be quickly saved in plain text form (or converted to HTML by a conversion package), and then placed on your Web server. As they expire, old announcements can be removed and replaced by new ones. You'll need to designate someone to be responsible for managing the job announcements and, if necessary, train that person to use HTML. Depending on the administrative model you've chosen for managing your Intranet, you may also need to train the individual in the process of placing the job announcements on the Web server so they become available.

Purposes and Goals Evolve

As you develop your overall purpose statement and implementation goals, bear in mind that once a Web server starts getting hits (that is, customers start using it), you and they will start thinking of new ideas you could implement using Web technology. Accordingly, you shouldn't cast your plans in stone. Rather, you'll want to leave room for evolution. Good ideas often beget other good ideas, so don't lock yourself out with a purpose statement that's too restrictive to allow new goals.

The job vacancy announcement goal example used above is a good illustration of how such a seemingly specific goal might evolve over time. You might start out with simple one-line announcements and find customers wanting more information about the positions. Adding more details to the announcements helps, but sometimes people want to be able to communicate with a real person to ask questions not covered in the announcements, so you add contact information to the announcements. Later, someone asks about using the *mailto* Uniform Resource Locator, and you realize you can add hyperlinks to the job announcements that allow your customers to send e-mail to the contact person just by clicking on a hyperlink. Still later, customers ask why they can't just go ahead and apply for the job directly using a Web fill-in form.

Web Design and Layout

With your statement of purpose and implementation goals ready, you can turn to the design and layout of your Intranet. It's useful to break this process down into two related pieces: logical and physical.

Logical Design of an Intranet

The logical design and layout is the process of arranging the information on your Intranet according to some overall plan. (Later you'll see how you can reflect your logical design in your physical design.) Much like you begin the process of writing a book by organizing your material with an outline that places major subjects placed into some sort of logical arrangement, your Intranet design should begin with some organizational layout. The information you're planning on placing on your Intranet often naturally breaks down into logical chunks, so you can reflect these natural divisions in its logical design. You might do well to start out with a traditional outline of the material. Use the statement of purpose to generate a brief outline, as in the following example:

> Statement of purpose: Provide customers with Human Resources, Materiel and Logistics, and Information System Services information using World Wide Web technology.
>
> I. Human Resources Information
>   A. Employee benefits information
>   B. Job announcements
>   C. Other HR information
> II. Materiel and Logistics Information
>   A. Inventory database
>   B. Purchase orders
>   C. Building and grounds plans
>   D. Other M&L information
> III. Information Systems Services Information
>   A. Computer hardware and software help desk
>   B. Boilerplate libraries
>   C. Spreadsheet data libraries
>   D. Other IS information

IV. Other Departments
    A. Engineering
    B. Research
    C. Manufacturing

Looking at this short summary outline (most of the details have been left out for space reasons of course), it's easy to see how you can organize the overall logical structure of your Intranet. The following collapsed outline makes this clear:

ABC Company Home Page

Statement of purpose: Provide customers with Human Resources, Materiel and Logistics, and Information System Services information using World Wide Web technology.

Major subdivisions of this Web:

Human Resources information
Materiel and Logistics information
Information systems services
Other departments

You've laid out not only the overall design of a Web, but also all but written its home page, which is shown in Figure 27.8.

FIGURE 27.8.

Simple home page.

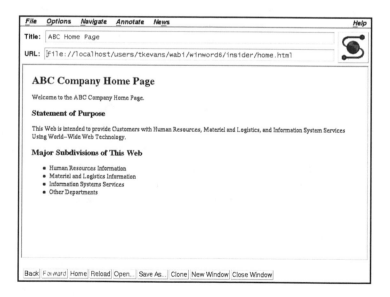

> **TIP**
>
> Your network capabilities and your customers' hardware capabilities can provide important cues to help you in your Web's logical design. For example, if all your customers have high-speed network connections and graphical Web browsers such as Mosaic or Netscape, you can plan on using graphics heavily in your Intranet. If some of your customers work with dumb terminals and/or some have only modem dial-up connections to your network, you'll want to downplay graphics and make sure your Web pages are accessible to the graphics-impaired.

Hierarchies and Hypertext

Within this design, as you no doubt have guessed, each of the ABC Company's major subdivisions also has a home page with the information and services to be offered. For the sort of high-level layout you're considering here, this simple hierarchical structure is a good way of beginning your own Intranet design. Within your Intranet, though, you'll want to take advantage of the ability to create hyperlinks to other pages so your customers can get around easily and intuitively. Rigid adherence to some purely hierarchical design can limit you in Intranet design.

Books are usually designed to be read sequentially, page by page, from front to back, and hierarchical design is apparent in such an arrangement. People who pick up a book expect this arrangement. On the other hand, the World Wide Web has introduced the concept of hypertext, a most assuredly nonhierarchical element. Through the use of hyperlinks, users can jump from place to place on the Web with little attention to page hierarchies or other structure. As a result, Web pages (and Web servers themselves) lend themselves to more human design. Users follow hyperlinks based on their own interests, predilections, and the needs of a given moment.

As you design your Intranet, the nice, neat hierarchical design you might lay out at the top level can handcuff you when you get down into the meat of your Web. You'll want to therefore be receptive to using nonlinear design as your Intranet develops. For example, you should include hyperlinks on pretty much every page (or every major page, at least) that allow the customer to jump back to the top-level page from anywhere without having to backtrack. Cross-references among documents are also great things to use as hyperlinks. If a document mentions another document, the user may want to see the referred-to document, and a hyperlinked cross-reference allows this.

At the same time, your overall design decisions can set limits on where hyperlinks might take your customers. Many people like hypertext because it seems somehow more like how they think, but others are more literal in their thinking and prefer a well-organized, hierarchical structure to things. In either case, total reliance on hypertext features without any overall organization can lead to confusion and frustration and to the loss of your Intranet's customers.

Personal differences concerning hypertext is one reason why it's critical for you to involve your customers early in the process of designing your Intranet, as well as keeping them involved by getting their feedback throughout the process. It's difficult, if not impossible, for you to anticipate what your customers will and will not like about their Intranet, so it's critical for you get them involved in issues like design and layout.

Physical Design of a Web

There are a number of ways to lay out the physical aspects of your Intranet. Your decisions on the administrative and logical aspects discussed in this chapter can give you important clues here as well. As suggested earlier, a single computer running Web server software lends itself well to the centralized administrative model. If you're using this model, you need not be concerned about the physical layout of a Web in which multiple servers in multiple locations operate; your server is inside a secure room, accessible only by its administrators. All the administration and configuration of your server and your Web pages takes place in one location. This kind of organization vastly simplifies server administration, maintenance, system backups, and, of course, server security.

Paradoxically, the decentralized model of Web administration, where anyone is free to set up and maintain their own Web server as part of an Intranet, is also simpler for you to administer because you don't have to do anything. Just by making the administrative decision that any user can set up a Web server and place anything on it, you've washed your hands of all the issues of physical layout, design, and server administration. Users are free to set up servers, placing documents on them according to whatever logical design they find applicable, and are responsible for doing so, as well as for maintaining their servers and documents. Any central administration can be limited to maintaining an overall home page for your Intranet with hyperlinks pointing to all the other servers. This administrative (and physical) layout can further suggest hardware and software requirements; if all your central Web server does is serve a home page with links to other servers, you don't need a powerful computer to run it.

As you can probably surmise, the mixed administrative model provides the most flexibility in both the logical and physical layout of your Intranet while retaining your ability to manage its structure. For example, you might design an Intranet with a main server and several departmental servers. The sample Intranet used in this chapter lends itself to this setup. Each of the major subdivisions of your Intranet, corresponding to the major administrative departments of the ABC Company, can be hosted on a separate computer system running Web server software. Thus, the Personnel department would run and manage a Web server devoted to human resources information, and the Materiel and Logistics department would run another server. Having delegated the administration of those logical pieces of your Web to the departments, you can also, if you choose, delegate the physical ones. As with the decentralized model, this choice can affect your needs for hardware.

Personnel may not want the responsibility of physically maintaining a computer system, however. The decentralized model can still allow the logical layout of your Web to allow Personnel to maintain its own substantive Intranet content. The HTML language is not difficult to learn, and ABC's departments could share a single computer system running a Web server physically maintained by a dedicated individual or staff but still maintain their own documents on that server. Departments can create and/or edit HTML documents using almost any editing tool on desktop PCs, and then upload them to your main Web server. You can even use file-sharing mechanisms to make Web server administration completely transparent. Through appropriately secured use of Appleshare, Novell NetWare, or UNIX-based Network File Systems (NFS), your Web server's filesystems can be shared so users see them as local volumes or filesystems with HTML documents directly accessible for editing. As far as the user is concerned, he's just creating or editing documents on his own PC, yet the documents are available to everyone else on your Intranet.

As with most three-choice models, your actual implementation of an Intranet is unlikely to be as clear-cut as described here. The mixed model described in this section is recommended, but there is virtually an infinite number of variations possible. The neat logical and/or physical division of ABC's departments probably won't fit your needs. It's more likely that Personnel will need one sort of setup, and Engineering might need a completely different one because the two groups have different skill sets and interests. You may find that one department wants their piece of your Intranet rigidly administered with all sorts of preset standards and procedures, and another department wants a completely decentralized model. Fortunately, you can accommodate both. Intranet server design and setup are known for their flexibility, and what you start out with may well change as you gain experience.

Selling Your Intranet

This final section explains how you can get your customers to buy into your Intranet. Web technology, or, more properly, the things Web technology makes possible, is very seductive. The ongoing explosion of the Internet has been driven in very large part by the Web. People really like using Mosaic or Netscape to find interesting things on the Web. As many managers are recognizing, there's a seductive, recreational aspect to the World Wide Web, as the widely used terms *playing Web* and *surfing the Web* indicate. The Web, in large respect, sells itself. This section is about using this seductive technology on an everyday basis in your company's work.

Defining Your Audience

Defining your audience might seem like a no-brainer. After all, your Intranet is for people within your company. Although this is generally true, a closer look reveals the fact that you need to fine-tune your definition. First, unless everyone in your company has a computer (or access to one), your audience is immediately defined as the group of users who will have some sort of access to your Intranet. Even this, however, isn't a true audience definition; it's a definition of your potential audience. You still need to break this audience down based on common characteristics. The kind of work a group of individuals do can help you define their needs as customers of your Intranet. Members of a clerical pool, for example, constitute an audience for a sort of boilerplate library of documents. Your scientists and engineers comprise a completely different group who'll have more interest in using your Web in their own scientific and technical applications. Both these groups, however, fall into the larger audience of company employees with an interest in the sorts of human resources and/or materiel and logistics information and services described in this chapter.

Hardware Considerations

Your larger potential audience also breaks down in another way based on the capabilities of the computer hardware they'll use to access your Web. Do they all have graphical Web browser capabilities and high-speed network connections? This question raises further questions that go to both the substantive content of your Intranet and to its physical and logical nature (that is, hardware capabilities and the concomitant limits they may place on the logical design of it).

Computer use is widespread, but not nearly universal, in organizations. Millions of people have computers on their desks at work or at home, but millions more don't. This obvious fact acts to define your Intranet's audience. Further, though, even among the group of people who do have computer access, there can be a wide variation in both access and hardware capabilities. Some users have PCs or UNIX workstations with full graphical capabilities, but others may be using dumb terminals with little or no graphics. In either case, a number of users may be sharing these machines.

These important audience characteristics speak not only to the relative ease by which your customers can access your Intranet but also to what they can see when they do access it. The user with a dumb terminal can't see graphics and can't use clickable image maps, so your Web design decisions must take this limitation into account. Do you do so by not using graphics at all, dragging that part of your audience with graphical Web capabilities down to the lowest common denominator, or do you attempt to design a Web that everyone can use even with their hardware limits? Similarly, if large numbers of your customers share PCs or terminals, on a factory floor, for example, the timeliness and immediacy of your Intranet's information is affected because not everyone will have easy, immediate access.

As with each of the other major subjects covered in this chapter, the characteristics of your intended audience can provide valuable help in the overall development of your Intranet.

Web Users, Web Mockups, and Focus Groups

You can help focus your audience definition as well as generate valuable information that can contribute to the design and content of your Intranet by involving potential customers in its development process using *focus groups*. Getting your customers involved early—and keeping them involved—generates an investment on their part in your Intranet. This investment will pay dividends by helping you create the right Intranet, the one your customers want.

Mockups and Demos

Before you get your focus group(s) together, be sure you have something to show them. Getting a group of people together to shoot the bull about getting an Intranet going without your first having prepared some sort of presentation is a poor way of starting out. You may have a few people who have Web experience, and some of them may already have ideas you can use, but as much as two-thirds of your focus group may never have seen the World Wide Web. If you don't have something to show them, they'll have a great deal of trouble understanding what it is you want from them. To a person with no experience of the Web, even the crude home page shown in Figure 27.8 is a dramatic demonstration, particularly if there are hyperlinks to similar home pages for the major divisions shown on the page and an actual document or two linked into them. Even a simple demonstration can let you use that Web seductiveness to spark interest in your Intranet and get your customers to invest in it early.

Encourage your demonstration participants to discuss possibilities based on what you've shown them. Even Web novices know the information they want from their organization. Showing them real information as well as the potential capabilities of an Intranet will surely stimulate ideas on their part. Your focus group(s), also including your organization's information providers, should provide a lively and useful means by which you'll further define your audience and its interests. This definition, in turn, will help you pin down the kinds of information your customers will want, thereby generating audience investment and support in your Intranet.

Users and Focus Groups

You probably already have a good deal of experience with the World Wide Web and have based your own ideas about your Web on things you've seen. If you have good ideas from your own Web experiences, it's a good bet that others in your company have ideas too, or would have if you asked them to think about it. Experienced Web users who are also your potential customers are in the unique position of both knowing a lot about the capabilities and possibilities of Web technology and of knowing what they, as potential customers of your Web, want to see. Get these customers together, informally or in formal focus groups, to talk about your ideas and theirs.

Don't limit your focus groups to those with Web experience, though. The employees of a company or the members of an organization have definite ideas about the information they want. Even if they've never seen a Web browser, they can give you information that's important to your Intranet design. Similarly, don't forget to include people you might call Intranet information *resellers*. This chapter has used the example of employee benefits and other personnel-related information in this chapter as potential Intranet content. The people in your Human Resources department who provide this information now, and who will be providing it on your Intranet, should also be part of your focus groups. They know the information they provide and probably have a good idea of how often their customers ask for it.

Summary

This chapter, part hardware, part philosophy, dealt with the overall process of designing an Intranet. It covered a number of major, interrelated, topics, including the following:

- What an Intranet is, and how it is different from what you've seen on the World Wide Web
- Identification of the customers in your company for whom your Intranet is to be designed
- Determination of the kind of information you will make available on your Intranet
- Decisions on who in your company or organization (or what organizational component) is best as the keeper of your Intranet
- Consideration of high-level issues about the design and organization of your Intranet
- Targeting your Intranet's customers and selling them on the idea of an Intranet

For more detailed information on these topics, you may want to check out *The World Wide Web Unleashed,* by John December and Neil Randall, published by Sams.net (ISBN 0-672-30737-5). For information on this and other Sams books, see the World Wide Web URL http://www.mcp.com, or check your bookstore.

The next chapter discusses Intranet infrastructure, the hardware and software tools you'll need to get started building your Intranet.

Tools for Implementing an Intranet Infrastructure

28

by Tim Evans

IN THIS CHAPTER

The last chapter was devoted to high-level issues involving the overall design and objectives of your Intranet. In this chapter, you'll turn from abstract consideration of purpose statements and audience definition to some hardware and software specifics. Here you'll survey the software and hardware tools you need to get set up. Mentions of specific commercial software packages are examples only and don't imply any endorsement of them by the author or by Sams.

The following list of chapter objectives will help you get oriented to the material to be presented; you may want to refer back to this list as you work your way through the chapter. This chapter covers the following topics:

- TCP/IP (Transmission Control Protocol/Internet Protocol) networking and its essential role in any Web

- Computer hardware suitable for running a Web server, ranging from desktop PCs to UNIX systems

- World Wide Web server software for a variety of computer systems ranging from desktop PCs to UNIX systems

- Software tools for creating documents in the Hypertext Markup Language, the language of the Web

- World Wide Web browser software for a variety of computer systems ranging from desktop PCs to UNIX systems

- Common software packages, called helper applications, that work in conjunction with Web browser software

- How to integrate other office and/or technical applications you may use with your Intranet

- Other network services accessible using Web technology and how they might fit into your Intranet

This chapter is an overview. Although it highlights the set up of World Wide Web server software, many of the technical details of Web server software are beyond its scope. Similarly, it refers to other Internet standard software you can integrate into your Web, but leaves details to other references. Although this chapter provides a good deal of specific setup information about several Web browser software packages, this book is not a complete reference on those packages. You'll find a variety of book-length treatments of these subjects in your favorite bookstore. For information about other Sams or Sams.net books relating to the World Wide Web and the Internet, access the Macmillan Computer Publishing's Information SuperLibrary at World Wide Web URL `http://www.mcp.com/`.

TCP/IP Networking Required

If you're already using the World Wide Web, you're already using TCP/IP, the fundamental Internet networking protocols. Only the TCP/IP networking protocols, the foundation of the worldwide Internet, support the Web over local area and wide area networks, including both the Internet and your LAN. In order for you to set up an Intranet, you must be running TCP/IP networking on your network. Without TCP/IP, there would be no Internet and no World Wide Web; without it on your LAN, you'll have no Intranet. Designed from the very beginning to operate over different communication media, TCP/IP works on Ethernet and token ring LANs; it even operates over ordinary telephone lines using modems, as you may know if you have a home Internet access package, such as CompuServe's *Internet in a Box* or Apple's *Internet Connection Kit.*

A Brief History of TCP/IP and the Internet

In the 1970s, the United States Department of Defense (DoD) contracted with researchers at the University of California at Berkeley and a company named BBN to develop networking for DoD computers worldwide. The primary objectives of the research project were to develop computer networking that

- Worked on a variety of computer hardware
- Operated over different communications media to link both individual computers and computer networks
- Was robust enough to automatically reconfigure itself in the event of network failures

More than after-the-fact Cold War speculation, the last of the points relates to the then-real possibility of large parts of the DoD network disappearing in a nuclear war and the need for the network to withstand it. Today's Internet meets this objective; if a large portion of the network were to disappear because of some massive hardware failure, the rest of the network would find a way around the service interruption and keep on working.

Even though the DoD funded most of the development of what came to be known as TCP/IP networking, the free thinkers at Berkeley managed to get permission to redistribute the network software they developed and the specifics of its protocols written into the contract with DoD. At about the same time, Berkeley was developing its own revised version of the UNIX operating system software, which it had licensed from AT&T (where UNIX was invented) as a research project. In short, TCP/IP networking was dropped right into BSD (Berkeley Software Distribution) UNIX, which was then made available to other academic institutions, also for research purposes, for the mere cost of a computer tape.

The wide distribution of these BSD tapes to other colleges, universities, and research institutions was the beginning of the Internet. TCP/IP networking not only allows individual computers to be linked into a network, but it also allows networks of computers to be linked to other networks with the illusion that all the computers on all the linked networks are on the very same Internet. Universities began building local networks, linking them together, and then they moved toward connecting their local networks with remote networks at other locations or other institutions, laying the foundation for today's Internet explosion. The DoD built its own private Internet, called MILNET, using TCP/IP, and many other U.S. Government agencies set up networks as well, some of which eventually became part of the Internet.

TCP/IP Implementations

Because the implementation nuts and bolts of TCP/IP networking (that is, the detailed descriptions of the network protocols themselves) were publicly defined in documents known as Internet *Requests for Comments*, software companies and individuals were free to develop and sell or give away their own TCP/IP software. For example, the first implementation of TCP/IP for the IBM PC was a university Master's thesis project and the resulting software was given away; the authors went on to found ftp Software, Inc., makers of one of today's leading TCP/IP software packages, *OnNet* (formerly called PC/TCP), for IBM PCs and compatibles. Dozens of other vendors sell TCP/IP software for PCs, and Microsoft's Windows 95 has it as a standard feature. Most modern UNIX systems have TCP/IP networking built in as a standard feature. Apple and other vendors sell TCP/IP networking software for the Macintosh PC. Even mainframe computers like IBM and DEC machines can and do run TCP/IP software in addition to, or in lieu of, the vendors' proprietary networking products like DECNet or SNA.

Several vendors, including IBM, have announced plans to develop inexpensive computing devices that will have TCP/IP networking built in. Not full-blown PCs, but also not dumb terminals, these *Internet appliances* would include not only TCP/IP, but also graphical capabilities and World Wide Web browser software. These appliances could prove to be a valuable part of your Intranet because they'd give users access to any Web services you might make available and at substantially lower cost than full-capability PCs or workstations.

Hardware for Your Web Server

You're just about unlimited in selecting a kind of computer system hardware on which to run a Web server. Almost any modern computer system equipped for networking, including TCP/IP network software, can host a Web server. The most widely used systems for Web servers are UNIX machines, such as Sun, IBM, Digital, and Hewlett-Packard workstations or servers. According to a University of Arizona survey (see Figure 28.1, or for details, see the survey's Web page at http://www.mirai.com/survey/), more than half of all Web servers are UNIX systems, with the largest share being Sun Microsystems machines. This is no surprise because multitasking UNIX systems with mature TCP/IP software built in are particularly well-suited to being Web servers. Surprisingly, perhaps, the second leading platform for Web servers in this survey, with a share of about 17 percent of the market, is the Macintosh. IBM compatibles came in third in this survey with 15 percent.

The hardware you select for your Intranet server(s) is dependent on a number of factors, including your anticipated traffic levels, ease of setup, your in-house technical expertise, and other requirements. Macintosh and Windows server software is quick and easy to set up with a good deal of point-and-click configuration. You can have a Web server running on a Mac or PC in just a few minutes, just as you can with many other PC and Mac software packages. This ease of use can be a strong attraction to organizations with lower levels of technical experience or who simply want to stay with PC platforms. Also, if you choose to use the decentralized or mixed models of Web administration described in Chapter 27, "Designing an Intranet," individual users can easily take advantage of this software on their own desktop PCs.

FIGURE 28.1.

World Wide Web servers by operating system.

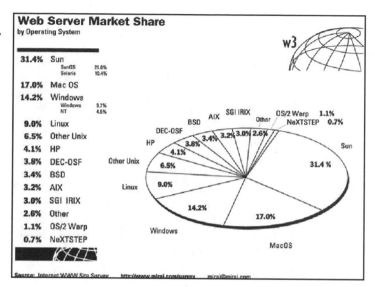

If you don't expect your Web server to have high traffic, you may find that dedicating a Mac or Windows PC to it will meet your needs. Except for personal Web servers, you should not, however, plan on running a Web server on a PC that is also somebody's everyday desktop machine. If you expect a high level of traffic, or plan to use common gateway interface scripts heavily, you'll do better to set up camp on a UNIX system.

> **TIP**
>
> As you consider Web server hardware platforms, don't neglect PC-based UNIX systems such as Sun's Solaris for x86, SCO UNIX, Novell's UnixWare, or even Linux, the freeware UNIX clone for Intel-based PCs. UNIX is natively multitasking and, having built-in TCP/IP networking and running a PC UNIX without all the overhead of a graphical user interface (for example, Microsoft Windows), you can put a relatively underpowered 386 PC to work as a useful Web server, although you'll want a system with at least 8 MB of RAM.

Software for Your Web Server

Two Web server software packages dominate the UNIX share of the market: the Apache and the NCSA httpd (hypertext transfer protocol daemon) servers. The former, based on the latter, has, in fact, the largest share of any Web server, with about 31 percent of the market. Both of these packages are freely available at no cost. The leading commercial Web server for UNIX systems is *Netsite* from Netscape Communications, maker of the Netscape Navigator Web browser. (You should expect these figures to change, especially as Netscape is aggressively marketing its several server packages available for both UNIX and Windows NT/Windows 95 with no-cost, 60-day test drive promotions, available at `http://www.netscape.com/comprod/ server_central/test_drive.html`.)

If you are concerned about security in your Web server (see Chapter 29, "Intranet Security"), you will probably want to consider the Netscape Commerce Server, which supports secure, encrypted communications. MacHTTP, formerly a shareware package but now commercially marketed by StarNine Technologies under the name WebStar, is the leading server package for the Macintosh. MacHTTP/WebStar is available for 30-day demos at URL `http:// www.starnine.com/machhttp/machhttpsoft.html`.

Windows httpd is licensed free of charge for personal and noncommercial use and may be used on a trial basis for 30 days in a business or commercial application. For more information about Windows httpd, see the URL `http://www.city.net/win-httpd/`. Bob Denny has upgraded his Windows httpd package into an on-the-move commercial package for Windows NT and Windows 95 under the name Website. Evaluation copies of Website are available from O'Reilly & Associates (`http://website.ora.com/`), and the complete program is widely available, sometimes at discounted pricing, in major bookstores.

According to `http://www.netcraft.co.uk/survey`, the leading Web server software packages, with relative market share are:

1. Apache (UNIX)	31.4 percent		4. CERN (UNIX)	7.8 percent	
2. NCSA (UNIX)	25 percent		5. WebSite (WinNT)	4.5 percent	
3. Netscape (all)	16 percent		6. Microsoft IIS (NT)	2.6 percent	

HTML Editors and Tools

You can create Web pages with the HTML using any text editor you want, including generic UNIX vi or emacs, an X Window graphical editor such as Sun's textedit, Microsoft Windows' NotePad, MS-DOS edit, Macintosh TeachText, or your favorite word processor in plain text mode. Although HTML documents are plain ASCII text with simple markup codes, you may want to use a specialized HTML editor or conversion tool. These tools cover a wide range of these tools, and they can be broken down into several categories:

- Wordprocessor add-ons (style sheets, templates, and macros) that allow you to use your own word processor to more easily create documents with HTML markup

- Stand-alone HTML editors, some of which provide WYSIWYG (What You See is What You Get) capabilities, that create your HTML markup as you go

- Tools to convert one sort of legacy document or another into HTML

You'll find a long listing of all sorts of HTML-related tools at the URL `http://www.w3.org/WWW/Tools`. Figures 28.2 and 28.3 show a couple of examples: the HoTMetalPro editor from SoftQuad and Microsoft's Internet Assistant for Word, respectively.

FIGURE 28.2.

SoftQuad HoTMeTaLPro WYSIWYG editor.

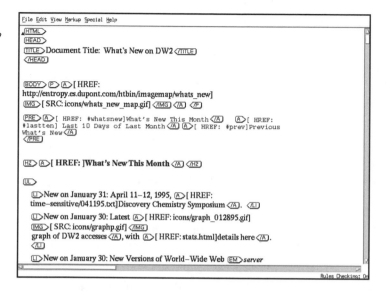

FIGURE 28.3.

Microsoft Internet Assistant for Word.

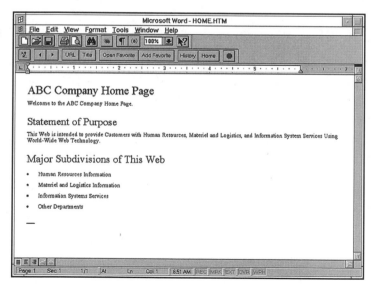

World Wide Web Browsers

NCSA Mosaic and Netscape Navigator are the two most widely used Web browser packages. Both are available for PCs running Microsoft Windows, Macintoshes, and for a wide variety of UNIX systems. Figures 28.4 and 28.5 show Netscape and Mosaic, respectively. NCSA Mosaic is free software. You can get a copy, if available, over the Internet at URL `ftp://ftp.ncsa.uiuc.edu/Mosaic/` or through anonymous FTP at `ftp.ncsa.uiuc.edu` in the `/Mosaic` directory. Netscape is a commercial package, but you can download a copy from the Netscape home page, `http://home.netscape.com/`, or via anonymous FTP at `ftp.netscape.com`. Netscape is free for people in educational and nonprofit institutions and for personal use. Commercial users must pay for the package if they use it beyond an evaluation period. For details, see the licensing information that comes with the Netscape software.

Both Netscape and NCSA Mosaic are highly capable Web browsers, and many users hold near-religious views on which is best. Netscape tends to be flashier, and its Release 2 version has a number of unique features, including support for the emerging Java technology. Netscape also implements a number of proprietary *extensions* to the HTML language that improve document formatting, but these extensions aren't compatible with other Web browsers. (If you use these extensions in creating Web pages for your Intranet, be sure to view the pages with other browsers to ensure they're readable unless your organization standardizes on Netscape for all users.)

Mosaic has been licensed for commercial resale by Spyglass, Inc. This company sells the rights to its enhanced Mosaic (now called Spyglass Mosaic, but previously marketed as Enhanced Mosaic) to other companies for resale or corporate use. Although you cannot buy individual copies of Spyglass Mosaic, several commercial Web browsers are in fact rebranded versions. In addition, a number of large corporations and other organizations have contracted with Spyglass for mass redistribution of Spyglass Mosaic within their company. As a result, if you're interested in standardizing on a commercial-quality Web browser, this is an alternative to Netscape.

You can get more information about the Spyglass Mosaic and download an evaluation copy at URL `http://www.spyglass.com/` (a good example of a poorly laid out Web server, incidentally, as you'll see when you connect). Spyglass' contractual arrangements with NCSA are unique in that, although Spyglass is a commercial company with a commercial product, enhancements to Mosaic are to be made available back to NCSA for incorporation in the no-cost version of Mosaic.

FIGURE 28.4.

Netscape version 2.

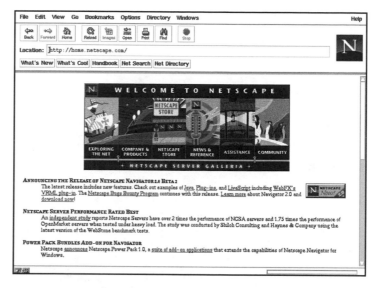

FIGURE 28.5.

NCSA Mosaic version 2.7 beta.

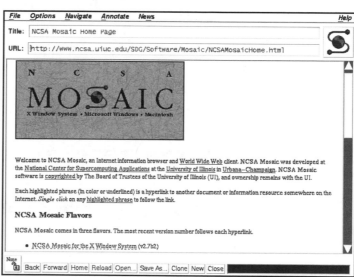

A number of lesser-known Web browsers are also available. For example, lynx (Figure 28.6) is the nongraphical browser from the University of Kansas. This package is freely available and runs on UNIX systems. A special version of lynx, called doslynx, is available for IBM PC compatibles; it runs under MS-DOS, not Microsoft Windows, and includes TCP/IP networking built in. This version can be an important addition to your Intranet because it can give users with very old PCs the ability to access it. For more information on lynx, see the URL `http://www.ukans.edu`. The Arena graphical Web browser (Figure 28.7) is being developed by the W[3] Consortium as a reference platform for the still-developing HTML version 3 standards. Still in prerelease, Arena runs on UNIX systems and is also freely available. For more information or a copy of the software, see the URL `http://www.w3.org/`.

FIGURE 28.6.

The lynx nongraphical browser supports the graphics impaired.

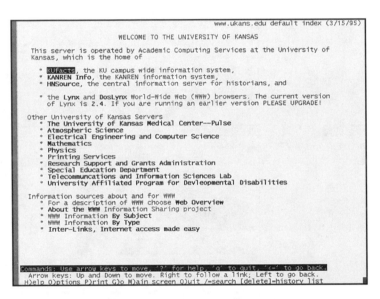

> TIP
>
> The W[3] Consortium is an industry cooperative that exists to develop common standards for the evolution of the World Wide Web. Operated jointly by the Massachusetts Institute of Technology's Laboratory for Computer Science and the French National Institute for Research in Computer Science and Control (INRIA), the Consortium is funded by its members, which include a large number of high-tech companies. The Consortium has taken over the work formerly done at CERN, the European Particle Physics Lab, which includes, among other things, the CERN httpd World Wide Web server, the CERN line-mode browser, a nongraphical Web browser similar to lynx, and the Arena graphical browser.

FIGURE 28.7.

The Arena browser functions as W[3] testbed.

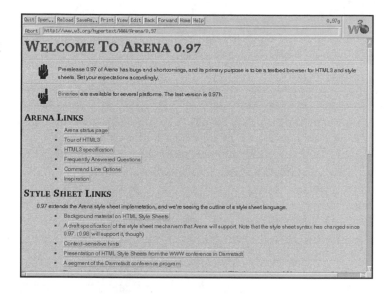

Selection of a Web Browser

Some of the decisions you make with respect to the design of your Intranet may have implications in Web browser selection and vice versa. Netscape, for example, supports a significant set of semiproprietary extensions to HTML standards, including special capabilities for image placement and font selection, along with version 2's Java and frames support. These extensions may not be supported in other browsers, so you'll need to consider whether to use them in your Web server's HTML documents. This, in turn, affects your choice of a browser. Specifically, if you want to take advantage of Netscape's HTML extensions on your Web, you'll probably want to standardize on Netscape as a browser. To turn this statement on its head, if you like Netscape and decide to standardize on it, this gives you additional capabilities you can implement on your Web. If, at the other extreme, your Web will have large numbers of customers who don't have graphical capabilities, you may want to standardize on the *lynx* browser. This, choice, too, has implications for your Web design because you must deal with the inability of many users to view images while still providing more than plain text services to those who do have graphical browsers. The emerging Internet appliances with built-in Web browser software can also be of relevance here.

Whether you choose to standardize on a particular browser also is a function of how you choose to administer and lay out your Intranet. The decentralized and mixed models described in the last chapter inevitably result in a wide range of Web services, some of which may use Netscape HTML extensions, for instance, while others use no special features at all. As a result, you may want to leave the choice of a Web browser to individuals.

Web Browser Helper Applications

Web browser software usually can display graphical images found on the World Wide Web, as previous figures show. Other kinds of data, however, require the use of helper applications, also known as *external viewers*. Web technology—that is, both Web servers and browsers—uses a common mechanism called MIME (Multi-Part Internet Mail Extensions) to match up types of data with helper applications. As a result, for example, although your Web browser may not itself be able to play an audio file you find on the Web, it can pass off that audio file to a sound-playing application on your computer when you click the file's hyperlink in your Web browser. Figure 28.8 shows a video helper application (xanim) being used with Netscape on a UNIX system. As you can see from the screenshot, Netscape is still running in the background as xanim is called up. The video data came from clicking a hyperlink on the weather page shown while in Netscape; the incoming data stream, recognized as video data, was passed off to xanim for display. Once the user is finished viewing the video (with xanim, there are VCR-like controls to play, rewind, fast-forward, and so on), control passes back to Netscape.

FIGURE 28.8.

The xanim video helper application.

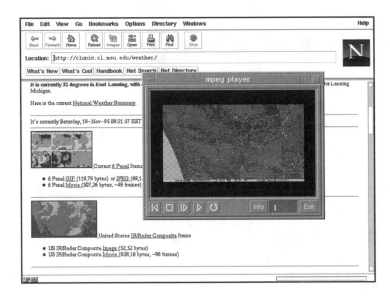

Based on MIME, the helper application mechanism using MIME is almost infinitely flexible. You'll find extensive lists of common Web helper applications downloadable with your Web browser at these URLs:

- ■ `http://www.ncsa.uiuc.edu/SDG/Software/XMosaic/faq-software.html` (for UNIX systems)

- ■ `http://www.ncsa.uiuc.edu/SDG/Software/WinMosaic/viewers.htm` (for PCs running Microsoft Windows)

■ `http://www.ncsa.uiuc.edu/SDG/Software/MacMosaic/helpers.html` (for the Macintosh)

Other Office Applications

Integration of everyday office applications into your Intranet is easy to do and allows your customers to point and click using their Web browser to access live corporate information for use in their daily work. Moreover, they'll be able to do much more with that information than just look at it. Statistical data can be provided in the format your company's favorite spreadsheet package uses, for example. Managers can use their Web browsers to access this data and bring it directly into their local spreadsheet application for what-if analysis, graphing, or other manipulation of the data. Figure 28.9 shows Microsoft Excel used as a Web helper application in NCSA Mosaic on a PC running Windows.

FIGURE 28.9.

Microsoft Excel as a helper application.

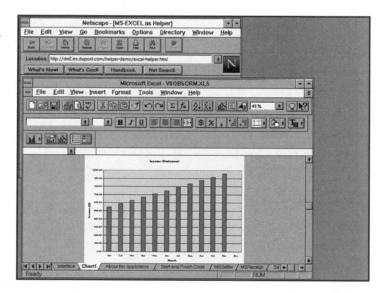

All the user had to do to bring up the data in her local copy of Excel was to click on a Web page hyperlink. Mosaic received the data, identified it as Excel spreadsheet data, and handed it off to Excel for display. It's important to note a couple of things about this.

■ The user is not just passively looking at this data. All the features of the spreadsheet package are available to use on the data; it can be manipulated, changed, recalculated, saved, printed, graphed, whatever.

■ The data on the Web server, which the user downloaded into Excel, is not changed. The user's copy is a temporary one.

Other Services Accessible via Web Technology

Besides the rich set of possibilities for your Intranet using helper applications, there's a wide variety of TCP/IP-based network services you can integrate into your Intranet. Although these services are commonly seen as over-the-Internet services, there's no reason you can't implement and use them locally as part of your Intranet even if your organization is not connected to the Internet. The ability to use these services is a major dividend of your investment in the TCP/IP networking that underlies your Intranet. Without TCP/IP networking capabilities, you wouldn't be able to use World Wide Web services, but having installed it, you now also have access to a much wider range of services that will extend and enrich your Intranet.

Web browsers know about many Internet services, including, but not limited to

- The file-transfer protocol (FTP) service used for transferring files between computers
- The Gopher service, which is a search-and-retrieval service based on hierarchical menus
- Usenet news, which is the mother of all bulletin board systems
- Several data indexing facilities, including WAIS (Wide Area Information Servers)
- Access to electronic mail (e-mail) using a Web browser
- Remote login and terminal emulation services to enable users to access other computer systems and use them from their own desk

Summary

This chapter has been a survey of the basic hardware and software infrastructure you'll need to implement an Intranet in your organization. You've learned about

- TCP/IP networking and its essential role in any Web
- Computer hardware suitable for running a Web server
- World Wide Web server software for a variety of computer systems
- Software tools for creating documents using the HyperText Markup Language
- World Wide Web browser software for a variety of computer systems
- Common software packages, called helper applications
- How other applications you use can be integrated as helper applications
- How other network services that are accessible using Web technology might fit into your Web

Intranet Security

by Tim Evans

29

You might think that there is little reason to be concerned about security in an Intranet. After all, by definition an Intranet is *internal* to your organization; outsiders can't access it. Also, since one of your objectives in setting up your Intranet is to provide your customers with access to a wide variety of public documents, there might seem little need to secure access to them. These are strong arguments for the position that an Intranet should be completely open to its customers, with little or no security. You may not have considered your Intranet in any other light.

On the other hand, implementing some simple, built-in security measures in your Intranet can allow you to provide resources you may not have considered possible in such a context. For example, you can give access to some Web pages to some people without making them available to your entire customer base with several kinds of authentication. In this chapter, you'll learn how simple security measures can be used to widen the scope of your Intranet.

The following list of chapter objectives will help you get oriented to the material to be presented; you may want to refer back to this list as you work your way through the chapter. In this chapter, you'll do the following:

- Consider the overall security aspects of your Intranet
- Learn how implementing security on your Intranet can broaden the ways in which the Intranet can be useful in your organization
- Learn how to set up username/password authentication to limit access to resources on your Intranet
- Learn how to provide secure access to Intranet resources to groups of customers
- Learn how to restrict access to sensitive resources based on customers' computer hostnames or network addresses
- Learn about the security aspects of CGI-bin scripting
- Learn about using encrypted data transmission on your Intranet to protect critical information
- Learn important information about securing access to your Intranet when your corporate network is attached to the Internet
- Learn how to provide—and limit—secure access to your Intranet from outside your immediate local network

Intranet security is a multifaceted issue with both opportunities and dangers, especially if your network is part of the Internet. This chapter walks through the major ones, with detailed information on using built-in Intranet security features.

> **WARNING**
>
> Except in the sections of this chapter that are specifically devoted to Internet security issues, it's assumed your Intranet is not accessible from outside your organization. If

you are on the Internet, the Intranet security measures discussed in this chapter may not be sufficient to secure your system. If you want to make the services and resources of your Intranet accessible from the outside, you'll need to take significant additional steps to prevent abuse and/or unauthorized access. Some of these steps are described at the end of this chapter in the section "Your Intranet and the Internet."

Why Security?

Many people view computer and network security in a negative light, thinking of it only in terms of restricting access to services. One major view of network security is "that which is not expressly permitted is denied." Although this view is a good way of thinking about how to connect your organization to the Internet, you can, and possibly should, view Intranet security from a more positive angle. Properly set up, Intranet security can be an *enabler*, enriching your Intranet with services and resources you would not be able to otherwise provide. Such an overall security policy might be described as "that which is not expressly denied is permitted."

This chapter takes the latter approach, presenting Intranet security in terms of its opportunities for adding value to your Intranet. For example, some of your customers may have information they'd like to make available, provided access to it can be limited to a specified group—for example, confidential management or financial information. Without the ability to ensure that only those who have the right to see such information will have access, the custodians of such data will not be willing to put it on your Intranet. Providing security increases your organization's ability to use the important collaborative aspects of an Intranet.

The more defensive approach, preventing abuse of your Intranet, is also given play, however. Organizations' needs for security in an Intranet can vary widely. Businesses in which confidentiality and discretion is the norm in handling proprietary information and corporate intellectual property have different needs than a college or university, for example. Academic institutions generally tilt toward making the free exchange of ideas a primary interest. At the same time, though, the curiosity (to use a polite word) of undergraduates imposes strong needs for security. Keeping prying sophomores out of university administration computing resources is a high priority, for example; students have been known to try to access grade records (their own or those of others) for various reasons. Even simple adolescent pranks take on new dimensions on a computer network.

What Are the Security Features of an Intranet?

Before this chapter goes into a great deal of detail about how you can use security to enhance your Intranet, the following sections take a high-level look at what security features are available to you. These features break down into three main categories. First, you can take steps on your Web server to set up security. Second, you can take steps with the other TCP/IP network services you've set up on your Intranet to enhance their security. Third, you can secure customers' Web browsers themselves to limit what they can do with them.

Web Server Security

There is a wide range of very flexible security features you can implement on your Web server(s):

- Access to Web servers, individual Web pages, and entire directories containing Web pages can be set to require a username and password.

- Access to Web servers, individual Web pages, and entire directories containing Web pages can be limited to customers on specific computer systems. (In other words, access will be denied unless the user is at his or her usual computer or workstation.)

- You can organize individuals into groups and grant access to individual Web servers, Web pages, and entire directories containing Web pages based on group membership.

- You can organize computers into groups, and grant access to individual Web servers, Web pages, and entire directories containing Web pages based on group membership.

- CGI-bin scripts on your Web server(s) can use any of the preceding access restrictions, though you must take care in writing them to ensure you don't make security-related mistakes.

- Some httpd server software is capable of communicating with compatible Web browsers in a verifiably secure, encrypted fashion, defeating even network-level sniffers and ensuring confidential data transmission across your Intranet.

You can combine these features in a number of ways, such as requiring a password and limiting access to a group of users who must access your Web server from a specific group of computer systems. You'll see a good deal of detail about Web server security setup in this chapter.

Security in Your Other Intranet Applications

In addition to the access controls you can set up on your Web servers, you can implement security in some of the other network servers. Here are some of the steps you can take:

- Access to your anonymous FTP server can be limited in several important ways, much like with your httpd server, while still enabling authorized customers to upload files to it.

- Access to your Usenet news server can be limited in much the same way.

- Access to searchable Intranet indexes and databases (see Chapter 30, "Web Access to Commercial Database Applications") can be controlled through password-protected Web interfaces.

■ Access to Gopher services can be controlled based on TCP/IP network addresses, and separate browse, read, and search permissions can be set on a per-directory basis.

Refer to the documentation for these network packages to learn about how to handle access control and other security features in them.

Securing Customers' Web Browsers

Some Web browsers can be set up in kiosk mode, which limits the features of the package that users can access. Available primarily in NCSA Windows Mosaic and Mosaic-based browsers, kiosk mode runs the browser with a limited set of features. Users cannot save, print, or view the HTML source of Web pages, and hotlist/bookmark editing is not allowed. The user cannot even exit from the browser and restart it in normal mode without exiting from Windows altogether. Even the overall Mosaic window cannot be minimized or maximized, and the normal pull-down control-menu box for Windows is missing.

Figure 29.1 shows NCSA Mosaic for Windows in kiosk mode, and Figure 29.2 shows the same page in standard Mosaic for your comparison. As you can see, many of the normal toolbar buttons are missing, as is the Options menu. The remaining pull-down menus are also limited in the available features. Kiosk mode is primarily for use in library or trade-show environments, where users need to be limited in what they can do, but you may find a use for it in your Intranet if you need to limit what some customers can do with the package. The Netscape Navigator browser does not have a kiosk mode.

FIGURE 29.1.

NCSA Mosaic for Windows in kiosk mode.

FIGURE 29.2.

*NCSA Mosaic for
Windows in normal mode.*

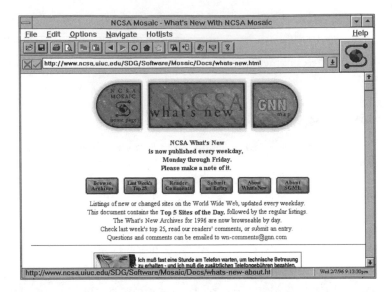

Resourceful users will quickly figure out they can manually edit their PC's `autoexec.bat` file or Web browser `.ini` file to override kiosk mode, undoing the limitations you've placed on them. If you're concerned about such things, you'll need to place user startup and Windows and browser setup files on a file server to which users have read permission only. You'll also need to limit access to the Mosaic startup command itself, or else users would simply use the Windows Program Manager's Run command to start another Mosaic session. As a result, kiosk mode may not be worth your trouble except in limited situations, such as at a trade show.

It's Your Call

It's your responsibility to determine the level of security you need on your Intranet, and, of course, to implement it. Putting most of the security measures mentioned into place, as you'll learn in the following sections, is not difficult. Your primary concern will be explaining to customers how Intranet security works, not so much as a limiting factor but as an opportunity for increased use and collaboration using your Intranet. Assuring decision-makers that they can make information available on your Intranet in a secure fashion can go a long way toward making your Intranet a success. At the same time, it's important to make sure both information providers and their customers understand a number of critical aspects of Intranet security, so they don't inadvertently defeat the purpose of it.

There are network security commonplaces, unrelated to Intranet security specifically, that need your attention. All the security precautions in the world can't protect your Intranet from overall poor security practices. Poor user choices on passwords always lead the list of computer and network security risks. If Bob uses his own name as his password or his significant other's or pet's name, password-guessing is simple for anyone who knows him. Some people write their passwords down and tape them to their keyboards or monitors—so much for the security of those passwords. You can limit access to a sensitive Web resource based on the TCP/IP network address of the boss's PC, but if the boss walks away and leaves his PC unattended without an active screenlock, anyone who walks into the empty office can access the protected resources.

In other words, the same good security practices that should be followed in any networked computing environment should also be made to apply in your Intranet. Not doing so negates all the possible security steps you can take and reduces the value of your Intranet. Even in the absence of malice, the failure to maintain any security on your Intranet will inevitably result in an Intranet with little real utility and value to its customers.

Security on Your Web Server(s)

It's useful to break the overall subject of World Wide Web server security down into three pieces and discuss them separately, This section does this by covering user/password authentication, network address access limitations, and transaction encryption. Bear in mind throughout the discussion of these separate pieces that you can combine them in various ways to create flexible and fine-grained access control. In fact, combining two, or even all three, of these methods provides the best overall security.

Controlling Access Globally and Locally

Whichever individual security mechanism(s) you implement on your Web server(s), the first thing you need to know is that you can implement them at either or both of two levels. First, you can specify high-level access control in a Global Access Configuration File (GACF), specifying overall access rules for your server. In the NCSA httpd server, and those which are derived from it, such as the Windows httpd and Apache servers, the GACF is called `access.conf`. The CERN/W[3] server doesn't have a separate GACF; rather, all access control information is in the main server configuration file, `httpd.conf`. The Netscape servers have a graphical interface (actually, Netscape Navigator itself) for overall server administration, including setting up access control. If you feel more comfortable editing configuration files, the Netscape server does allow them, calling them Dynamic Configuration Files. Although you can do both global and local configuration using the graphical tool, a top-level Netscape Dynamic Configuration File can be created and hand-edited to function as a GACF.

Second, you can set up per-directory access control using local ACFs (LACFs) for each directory or subdirectory tree. Usually named `.htaccess` or `.www_acl` (note the leading periods in the filenames), LACFs lay out access control for an individual directory and its subdirectories, although subdirectories can also have their own LACFs. The CERN/W[3] server can even extend protection to the individual file level using LACFs. In the Netscape server, lower-level Dynamic Configuration Files serve as LACFs. You can change the names of LACFs in both the NCSA and Netscape servers, but you're stuck with `.www_acl` in CERN/W[3].

With a few important exceptions, you can do everything with an LACF you can do with a GACF. Although you can control access to every directory in your Web server document tree from the GACF, you'll probably not want to do so, especially if your needs for access control are complex. It's easy to make mistakes in a lengthy configuration file like the GACF, and you'll get unexpected, unintended results when you do. These mistakes may be hard to track down and may not even show up without extensive testing. Overall, it's better to use your GACF to establish high-level security policy, and then set up lower-level, simpler controls using LACFs.

> **NOTE**
>
> The CERN/W[3] server's LACF files have a completely different format than its GACF. Most of the examples in this chapter apply only to the format of the GACF.

What's the GACF for, then? Most Webmasters use the GACF to establish a general access policy for their Web servers. For example, if your Web server is accessible to the Internet at large and you're not using a firewall system (see later sections) to limit access to your network from the outside, you may want to establish a policy in your GACF that only computers with TCP/IP network addresses that are inside your network can access your Web server's document tree. Similarly, you can use the GACF to segregate public and private areas on your Web server according to some criteria and require usernames and passwords for access to the private area(s).

After you've established your overall policies, you can implement LACFs to fine-tune your setup. In doing so, you can selectively apply different access controls to the directory or directories controlled by the LACF. Earlier, exceptions to the statement that you can do everything with an LACF you can do with a GACF were mentioned. The following is a quick, incomplete list of these exceptions; you'll want to consult detailed server documentation for comprehensive explanations of these exceptions and others. The first one applies to all httpd servers, but the last three refer only to UNIX servers:

- If you want to control all access on your Web server with your GACF, you can use it to prohibit the use of LACFs altogether.
- You can deny use of a potentially dangerous and CPU-hogging feature called server-side includes, which cause the server to execute outside commands each time a page containing them is accessed, in user Web pages.

■ You can limit access to CGI-bin scripts in the server's main CGI-bin directory, preventing users from creating potentially dangerous ones in their own Web directories.

■ You can prevent potential security problems that can come from following UNIX symbolic links.

With respect to symbolic links, confidential files on the system that are completely outside of your Web server tree could be compromised by a naive or malicious user. For example, if a user created a symbolic link in her home directory pointing to the UNIX /etc/passwd file, which contains usernames and encrypted passwords, outside users could obtain a copy of that file using their Web browser, and then run a password-cracker on it offline. Of course, a malicious user can grab /etc/passwd himself and run the cracker directly or e-mail the file to someone else for the same reason, but that's no reason to make it easy to do so via your Intranet. (The UNIX System V /etc/shadow file is not readable by non-root users, nor is the IBM AIX /etc/security/passwd file.) See "The Common Gateway Interface (CGI) and Intranet Security" later in this chapter for discussion of CGI-bin and server-side includes security issues.

Username/Password Authentication

The first major element of Web server security is username/password authentication. To kick off this discussion, look at what the Web browser user sees when he encounters a Web page that requires username/password authentication for access. Figure 29.3 (part of NCSA's excellent access control tutorial at http://hoohoo.ncsa.uiuc.edu/docs/tutorials/) shows a Prompt dialog box asking for a username. After the username is entered, a new dialog box asks for a password, as shown in Figure 29.4.

FIGURE 29.3.

The user is prompted to enter a username on a protected Web page.

FIGURE 29.4.

The user is also prompted for a password on a protected Web page.

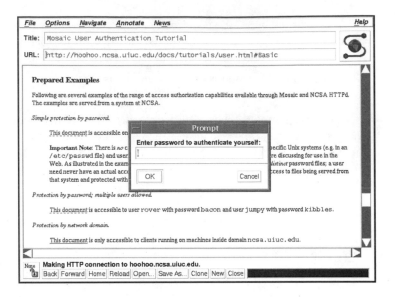

As you can infer from Figures 29.3 and 29.4, there are three aspects of username/password authentication: the username, the password that applies to that username, and what is permitted to that user when a correct username and password are supplied. Usernames and passwords are meaningless unless you specify a directory, directory tree, or filename to which your username/password access restrictions apply.

Suppose your httpd server's DocumentRoot directory contains three main subdirectories, named public, management, and personnel. Using your GACF, you can specify that access to the management and personnel subdirectory trees requires username/password authentication, and public is left wide open for anyone to access without being prompted for username and password. You can also set up LACFs within the protected subdirectories to further limit access to particularly sensitive documents by using usernames and passwords.

Setting Up Username/Password Authentication in a Netscape Server

Setting up username/password authentication is easy in a Netscape server. The Netscape servers use the Netscape browser itself as a graphical interface for administering the server, providing a set of private Web pages and configuration scripts to do so. Using the Server Manager page, you can easily enter new users and their passwords into what Netscape calls the user database. (You must first create an empty user database before you can add any users and passwords to it.) Figure 28.5 shows the User Database Management screen. Notice that you must give an administrative password as well as a username and password for the user being added to the database. After you've entered this information, click the Make These Changes button.

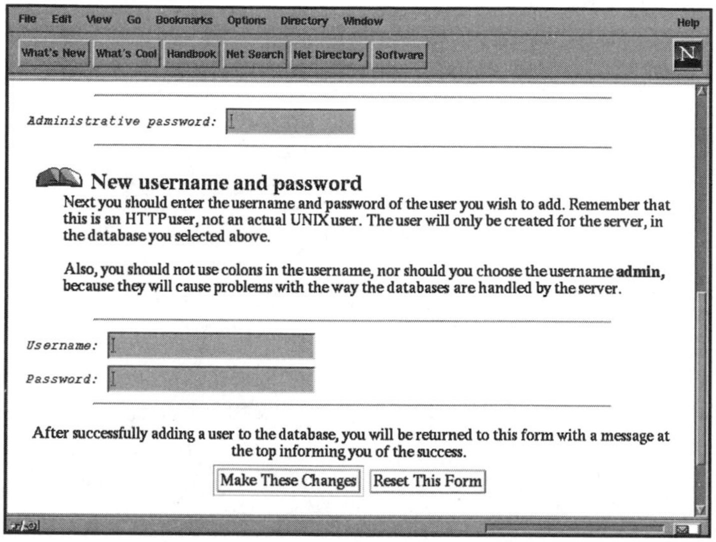

FIGURE 29.5.

The Netscape Communications Server Add User form.

Once you've set up one or more users, you can continue to use the Server Manager to apply access control rules to users. You can associate groups of users together for purposes of authentication and define access control rules that apply to groups as well as to individuals. With group access controls, users must still provide their own usernames and passwords, but access to a specified area of the server filetree (Netscape calls this a *realm*) can be controlled by requiring that a user be a member of a group for access. Even if a user provides the correct username and password, he may be denied access based on group access control rules if he is not a member of that realm's group.

Setting Up Username/Password Authentication in the CERN/W[3] httpd Server

The CERN/W[3] httpd server uses a UNIX-like password file (but with only three colon-separated fields) containing usernames, encrypted passwords, and users' real names. The password file is controlled using the htadm program that comes with the httpd server software. This program enables you to create and delete user accounts, as well as change and verify existing passwords. Although you can provide all the information htadm needs on the command line, it's easier to let the program prompt you for it. For example, to add a new username and password, use this line:

```
# path/to/htadm /path/to/passwordfile
```

You must specify the name of the password file on the command line, but htadm will prompt you for the function you want to perform and the actual username, password, and user's real name, as appropriate. (You can use multiple words in the realname field to include a full name and/or other information.) If you're in a hurry, or have a long list of users to add or delete, you can take advantage of specifying all the `htadm` command-line arguments at once, like one of these examples:

```
# htadm -adduser passwordfile joeuser joespassword Joe User
# htadm -deluser passwordfile baduser
```

The first example creates the user `joeuser` with the password `joespassword`, and the second example deletes the user `baduser`. This feature enables you to do mass account deletion using shell looping and/or to take username, password, and realname input from a file. You'll need something like the `expect` package (described in Chapter 30, "Web Access to Commercial Database Applications") to do automated, mass account creation. The `-passwd` and `-check` command-line arguments for `htadm` enable you to change and verify passwords, respectively.

As with the Netscape server, the CERN/W[3] httpd server also enables you to associate individual users with groups. You can set up group authentication rules in LACFs that control access to portions of your Web server document tree. CERN/W[3] uses a group file, the format of which is based on the standard UNIX `/etc/group` format, but it has an added feature for defining access control rules and for recursive inclusion of groups into metagroups. A simple group file, which is used for examples in this chapter, might be something like this:

```
management: tom, mary, joan
personnel: anne, joe, jerry
staff: management, personnel
public: All, Anybody
```

In this example, four groups are defined. The first two each contain a list of several individual usernames, but the last two are groups of groups. (Two special groups, All, meaning all authenticated users, and Anybody, meaning anyone, authenticated or not, are predefined by the CERN/W[3] httpd server software and refer to anyone who might access the server; see the server documentation for details on the distinction between All and Anybody.)

After setting up your password and group files, you can add access control protection to your server. As previously noted, high-level rules go in `httpd.conf`, the GACF. Access control rules in `httpd.conf` use the Protect directive and associated protection rulesets. Here's a simple Protect directive, based on the group file shown previously. It implements the sample division of your Web server's document tree into public, management, and personnel subtrees:

```
Protect /personnel/* Personnel
```

This example indicates that all subdirectories and files in the `personnel` subtree of your Web server `DocumentRoot` are subject to the rules in the protection ruleset named `Personnel`. (You can name protection rulesets with any name you want, but it makes sense to use meaningful names.) According to this Protect directive, the ruleset itself also appears in the GACF under the label `Personnel`, and might look like the following:

```
Protection Personnel {
    AuthType    Basic
    Passwordfile /usr/local/etc/httpd/passwd
```

```
    GroupFile     /usr/local/etc/httpd/group
    GetMask       personnel
}
```

> **NOTE**
>
> Your Protect directive can specify the protection ruleset be read from a file rather than from another part of the GACF. In this case, the directive would look like the following:
>
> ```
> Protect /personnel/* /usr/local/etc/httpd/acls/Personnel
> ```
>
> Here, the absolute pathname to the file named `Personnel` (not relative to the server `DocumentRoot`) is specified. This example assumes you've created a special subdirectory (`/usr/local/etc/httpd/acls`) in which to store all your access control information. If you use individual files like this to define your protection rulesets, you need not enter the curly braces that are required in the GACF.

This simple example applies username/password authentication access control to all files and subdirectories in the `personnel` directory, using the following criteria, all of which must be met before access is granted:

- Users must enter a username and password.
- Usernames and passwords are validated against the file `/usr/local/etc/httpd/passwd`.
- Authenticated usernames are checked for membership in the group named `personnel` in the groups file `/usr/local/etc/httpd/group`.

Going back to the previous sample group file, you can see only users Anne, Joe, and Jerry will be granted access to files in this directory tree. Even if Tom provides his correct password, he will not be given access.

This has been a very cursory look at user authentication in the CERN/W[3] httpd server. Your Protect directives and protection rulesets can be quite detailed, including other features not described here. In addition, you can set up both a default protection ruleset and progressively more limited protection rulesets according to your own criteria, adding access control all the way down to the individual file level. For details, check out the World Wide Web Consortium's online CERN/W[3] httpd documentation at `http://www.w3.org/pub/WWW/Daemon/User/Admin.html`.

Setting Up Username/Password Authentication in the NCSA httpd Server

The NCSA httpd server, along with those derived from it (WinHttpd for Windows and the Apache package for UNIX systems), provide similar username/password authentication mechanisms. Except where differences exist among these packages, this section discusses them as a group.

These packages use authentication methods that are similar to the methods used in the CERN/ W[3] httpd package. Most importantly, the NCSA packages support both GACFs and LACFs, enabling you to set high-level policy at the server level and then fine-tune it at the directory and subdirectory levels. In addition, both individual user and group authentication are provided for. Finally, some configuration commands affecting critical items listed earlier, such as `AllowOverride`, may only appear in a GACF. You can also preclude the server-side includes use and symbolic link following, for example, as described earlier.

The GACF in the NCSA packages is the file named `access.conf` (`access.cnf` in WinHttpd) and is located in the `conf` subdirectory of your Web server's file tree. On UNIX systems, the server is usually installed in `/usr/local/etc/httpd`; on Windows systems, the server is in `c:\httpd`. In both cases, there exists a `conf` subdirectory in the top-level httpd directory. The layout and syntax of the `access.conf` file is significantly different from the GACF in the CERN/W[3] httpd server, however.

The NCSA file is divided into sections, one for each directory to be controlled. Each directory section in `access.conf` looks something like this:

```
<Directory /absolute/directory/path>
[ Various configuration commands ]
</Directory>
```

Like HTML markup, each `Directory` (the literal word `Directory` must appear) section is marked off by the `access.conf` tags `<Directory>` and `</Directory>`, surrounded as shown with angle brackets. Case is not significant in the word `Directory`, though it may be significant in the actual directory name.

It's important to note the directory path here is an absolute pathname and is not relative to either the Web server's `ServerRoot` or `DocumentRoot` directories. If you mean `/usr/local/etc/htdocs/`, for example, you must specify it in full and not just use `/htdocs`. Within each `Directory` section of the file, you specify one or more options, or configuration commands, which the server will apply to the specified directory. There are a number of different options, but you're concerned here with username/password authentication.

Of course, before you can apply an username/password access control, you need to have established users and passwords on your server. Usernames and (encrypted) passwords are stored in a special httpd password file. NCSA provides a utility program, `htpasswd`, for creating this file; you'll find it in the `support` subdirectory of your NCSA httpd server file tree, and you may need to compile it. The syntax of the `htpasswd` command is substantially simpler than that of the CERN/W[3] `htadm` command, as are its capabilities. To add a user to your password file, or change his password, use this syntax:

```
# htpasswd /path/to/passwordfile username
```

If you don't already have a password file, you need to modify this command a bit:

```
# htpasswd -c /path/to/passwordfile username
```

The -c argument creates a new password file, so you use it only once. If you use it again, you'll erase your current password file. You can name your password file anything you like. You can't remove a user from your password file with the htpasswd command. Instead, you'll have to hand edit the password file with a text editor and delete the user's entry. The format of the file is quite simple, with just two fields in each record separated by a colon:

```
tkevans:TyWhfX9/zYd7Y
```

Obviously, the first field is the username. The second field is the encrypted password. Permissions on the password file must be set so as to be readable by the system user under whose user ID the httpd server runs (usually, the no-privileges user nobody), so passwords are not stored in clear text.

Besides the httpd password file, the NCSA servers also respect a group file, in which you can define groups of users. Groups can be treated like individual users with respect to access control, so the group file can both add capabilities and save data-entry time. For the most part, syntax of the NCSA httpd group file is exactly the same as that shown earlier in this chapter for the CERN/W[3] group file. There is one significant difference in what the two group files may contain, however. As noted previously, the CERN/W[3] group file can include group entries that consist of other groups. The NCSA group file can include only individual users as members of groups. Thus, the recursive staff group consisting of all the members of the personnel and management groups is not possible in NCSA. To create such a group, you'd need to re-enter each user's name in the group entry for staff.

Now that you've set up your password and group files, you're ready to add username/password authentication in your GACF or LACFs. Take a look at this example:

```
# Anybody in the personnel group can get to the top level
# of the personnel filetree
<Directory /usr/local/web-docs/personnel>
AuthType Basic
AuthName Personnel Only
AuthUserFile /usr/local/etc/httpd/userpw
AuthGroupFile /usr/local/etc/httpd/ourgroup
<Limit GET>
Require group personnel
</Limit>
</Directory>
```

This GACF file limits access to the top level of the personnel tree of the Web server. Only members of the predefined group personnel (defined in the ourgroup file) are allowed to GET (access) files in the directory tree, and they must provide a valid username and password, verifiable against the encrypted password in the userpw file.

Most of the lines in the example are clear, but a couple need a little more explanation. `AuthName` is just an arbitrary label for your rule; you should put something there that'll make sense when you read the rule a year from now, and you can use a phrase here. The `<Limit GET>` subsection of the file is, of course, the critical section, in which you specify who has access. Note that you can also include comments in the file, as indicated by the first two line where the # symbol is used.

As previously noted, you can use LACFs to refine the access rules in your GACF. The following is an example of an NCSA httpd LACF: a file named `.htacces` in the `personnel/executive` subdirectory. See if you can translate its meaning:

```
AuthType Basic
AuthName Anne Only
AuthUserFile /usr/local/etc/httpd/userpw
AuthGroupFile /usr/local/etc/httpd/ourgroup
<Limit GET>
Require user anne
</Limit>
```

You're right—this rule limits access to the `executive` subdirectory to a single user: `anne`. The heart of this rule is, of course, the matter between the `<Limit>` and `</Limit>` tags near the end of the file. Other users, including the other members of the `personnel` group, are denied access, even if they give a correct password for themselves. A dialog box will demand Anne's username and password. Notice that this LACF file, which controls access to a single directory (`personnel/executive`), does not require the opening and closing `<Directory>` and `</Directory>` tags required in the server's GACF because there are no subdirectories in this directory.

Important Warnings About Username/Password Authentication

Unless the access rules change (that is, new LACFs are encountered) as a user moves around on your Intranet Web pages (as with the `personnel/executive` subdirectory in the example above), he will be prompted only once in his browser session for a username and password. As long as he continues his browser session, he can access all of the files and directories available to him under the most recent access rule, without being prompted again for his password. This is for convenience's sake; customers shouldn't have to repeatedly provide their usernames and passwords at each step of the way when the access rule hasn't changed.

However, this situation has important ramifications if you follow it out logically. Suppose Anne, having authenticated herself to access the `executive` subdirectory, leaves her Netscape or Mosaic session running, as most of us do. Her privileged access remains open to all the files protected by that one-time, possibly days-old, authentication. If she leaves her workstation, PC, or terminal unattended when she goes to lunch or goes home for the day without any sort of active screen or office door lock, anyone can sit down and browse the files and directories that are supposed to be limited to Anne's eyes only. This potential security breach is one that you as Webmaster can do little about. This is really no different from a user who leaves his workstation unattended without logging off. Although you can try to educate your customers about such everyday security matters, even though they have very little to do with your Intranet, you'll agree a security breach like this can be potentially harmful to all your work.

As a further technical note, user passwords are transmitted over your network by most Web browsers in a relatively insecure fashion. It is not terribly difficult for a user with a network snooper running to pick out the httpd network packets containing user passwords. Although the passwords are not transmitted in clear text, the encoding/encryption method is a very old and widely used one. Every UNIX system, for example, has a program (uudecode) that can decode the encrypted password in a captured httpd packet. If you believe this may be a problem on your Intranet, you'll want to consider the secure Web servers and browsers that encrypt user-transmitted data, as discussed in the section, "Secure/Encrypted Transactions," later in this chapter.

Authentication Based on Network Hostname or Address

All the Web servers discussed in this chapter provide an additional authentication method that uses the TCP/IP hostname or numerical network address of customer workstations or PCs as access criteria. In the context of CGI-bin programming, every Web browser request for a document or other Intranet resource contains the numerical IP address of the requesting computer. Servers look up hostnames using these addresses and the Domain Name Service. You can set up rules in your GACFs and LACFs based on either of these, making a considerable amount of fine-tuning possible.

Hostname/Address Authentication in the NCSA Servers

Because the format of the NCSA access.conf file is still fresh in your mind from the last section, this section looks at this one first in the context of hostname/network address authentication. As you'll accurately presume, you'll place your rules for this sort of authentication within the <Limit> and </Limit> tags of the server's GACFs or LACFs <Directory> sections. Do this with several new access control directives, including:

- Order, which specifies the order in which the other directives in the file are to be evaluated
- Allow, which permits access based on a hostname or IP address
- Deny, which denies access based on a hostname or IP address

Here's a simple example limiting access to the personnel subtree of your Web server. (The opening and closing <Directory> tags have been left off so as to cut right to the chase). For purposes of this example, say your company's TCP/IP network domain is subdivided along operational lines and that there is a personnel subdomain in which all of the computers have IP addresses beginning with 123.45.67.

```
<Limit GET>
order deny,allow
```

```
deny from all
allow from personnel.mycompany.com
allow from 123.45.67
</Limit>
```

In plain English, this example rule says "access is denied to all hostnames and IP addresses *except* those in the subdomain `personnel.mycompany.com` and those in the numerical IP address family `123.45.67`. Notice that both the subdomain name and IP address family are wildcards that may match many computers; you can also use individual hostnames or addresses for even finer control.

You might wonder why both `allow` and `deny` statements are used in the example. The World Wide Web was built with openness in mind, not security. The server therefore assumes, without instructions to the contrary, all directories are accessible to all hostnames/addresses. (This is the same as the username/password authentication. In the absence of a username/password requirement, all directories and files are accessible to all users.) Without a `deny` directive, the rule might just as well not exist. The server assumes, in the absence of a `deny` directive, that all hostnames/addresses are allowed access. Why have any rule at all, then, since all are allowed access? In other words, it makes no sense to have rules with `allow` directives without `deny` directives.

Because you must have both `deny` and `allow` directives in order to have meaningful access rules, the order in which the rules are evaluated is important. One way to do this is to follow the order in which the directives appear in the file, but it's easy to make mistakes with this approach. Instead, NCSA httpd uses the `order` directive so you can explicitly instruct that your directives be processed in the order you want. The example uses `order deny,access`, indicating all incoming requests are to be tested against the `deny` directive(s) first, and then tested against the `allow` directives. In the example, you set up a general `deny` rule, and then make exceptions to it. The `order` directive can also be turned around, with `allow` rules processed first. Using this sequence, you can make your server generally available, and then add selective denials, as in the following example:

```
<Limit GET>
order allow,deny
allow from all
deny from .mycompetitor.com
</Limit>
```

Here, you're granting access to your server to everyone *except* your competitor. For more information about hostname/IP address authentication, see the authentication tutorial at NCSA's Web site, `http://hoohoo.ncsa.uiuc.edu/docs/tutorials/`.

Hostname/Address Authentication in the CERN/W[3] Server

You can also impose hostname/IP address access control with the CERN/W[3] httpd server. Although you can accomplish the same ends as with the NCSA server, the method of doing so is different, and the access control file formats are different. As you'll recall from the earlier username/password authentication, the CERN/W[3] httpd server uses protection rulesets in the GACF or LACF. A modification of the earlier example, in which you limited access to the `personnel` portion of your Web server by groupname, can illustrate hostname/IP address authentication. For purposes of this example, assume your company's TCP/IP network domain is subdivided along operational lines, and that there is a `personnel` subdomain in which all of the computers have IP addresses beginning with `123.45.67`.

```
Protection Personnel {
    AuthType      Basic
    Passwordfile  /usr/local/etc/httpd/passwd
    GroupFile     /usr/local/etc/httpd/group
    GetMask       @*.personnel.mycompany.com,@123.45.67.*
}
```

As you can see, the only thing changed about this ruleset is the `GetMask` line. In the earlier example, you used `GetMask` to limit access based on membership in a defined group of usernames, `personnel`. This example shows two methods of access control limitation. First, an Internet Domain Name Server (DNS) subdomain name (`personnel.mycompany.com`) is specified. Second, the rule contains a numerical IP address family. In both cases, a special wildcard syntax is used; note the use of both the @ symbol and the asterisk (*). You can think of the string `@*.personnel.mycompany.com` as meaning any computer in the personnel subdomain. Similarly, `@123.45.67.*` refers to any computer with an IP address beginning with `123.45.67`.

As all computers in the personnel subdomain have IP addresses in the `123.45.67` family, you may be wondering why both rules are included. This is done for a couple of reasons. The first reason, obviously, is to show that you can use either symbolic host/domain/subdomain names or numerical IP addresses.

The second reason is a more technical one. In some cases, your httpd server won't be able to resolve the hostname of a computer making a request for a document from the numerical IP address it receives in the browser request. The reasons for this inability vary, but they usually involve out-of-date or inaccurate DNS information. In growing networks, newly networked computers may not get added to the database promptly. Errors in DNS configuration, such as misspelled hostnames, can also result in unresolvable hostnames. To be safe, placing both symbolic host/domain name and numerical IP address information in your `GetMask` is a good idea; there's nothing like having the boss's brand-new PowerMac being denied access to your Intranet's Web server on his very first try because its DNS entry hasn't been made by the network operations staff yet.

Hostname/Address Authentication in the Netscape Server

As with most aspects of Netscape Communications server administration, you can set up hostname/IP address access control using a graphical interface. Start up the Administration Manager, and select Restrict Access From Certain Addresses. This command opens a document with extensive instructions for setting up access restrictions. You'll find fill-in boxes in this document for hostname/IP address restrictions. Figures 29.6, 29.7, and 29.8 show the essential parts of this form. You have all the same choices here for restricting access that you saw in the NCSA and CERN/W[3] httpd servers.

FIGURE 29.6.

The Netscape Communications Server Host Restriction (Part 1).

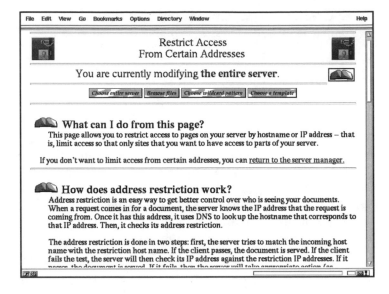

Your first step is to select what Netscape calls a *resource* to which you'll apply hostname/IP address restriction. For this purpose, a resource can be the entire Web server tree, a particular part of it, or one or more individual files. Clickable buttons (as shown at the top of Figure 29.6) enable you to select the resource you want. In the example, your resource would be the `/usr/local/web-docs/personnel` subdirectory of your httpd server tree. After you've selected your resource, scroll down the form to the headline `What To Protect` (see Figure 29.7). Here, you'll make two important choices.

If you like, you can accept the default of protecting everything in the selected resource. Or, if you prefer, you can specify a wildcard filename pattern to match the files you want to protect. Notice the hyperlink labeled `wildcard pattern`, which takes you to a detailed document describing how wildcard pattern-matching works in the Netscape servers. (Essentially, it's standard UNIX shell filename expansion, but it has some additional features.)

For the purposes of the example, you need not enter anything because you're going to accept the default restriction to all files and directories in the `personnel` resource. However, you could have entered the wildcard pattern for the files to which you wanted to apply your hostname/IP address restrictions in the boxed labeled Pattern of files to protect. The Addresses to allow section, which starts in Figure 29.7 and ends in Figure 29.8, tells you how to enter hostnames and IP addresses.

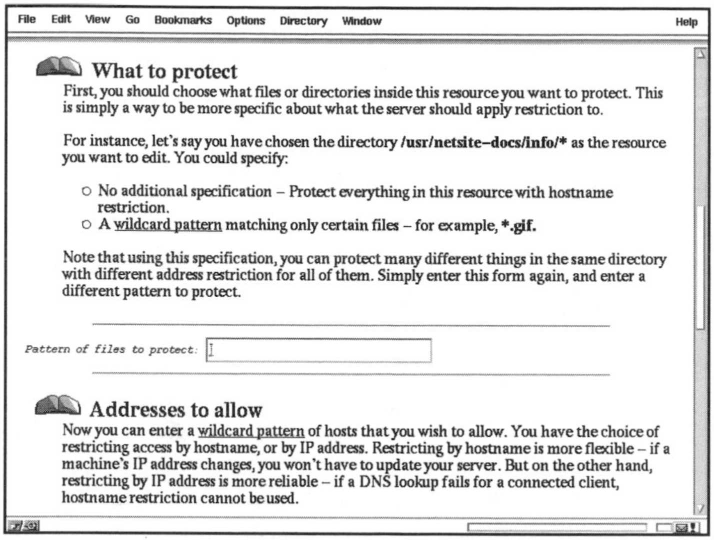

FIGURE 29.7.

*Netscape Communications
Server Host Restriction
(Part 2).*

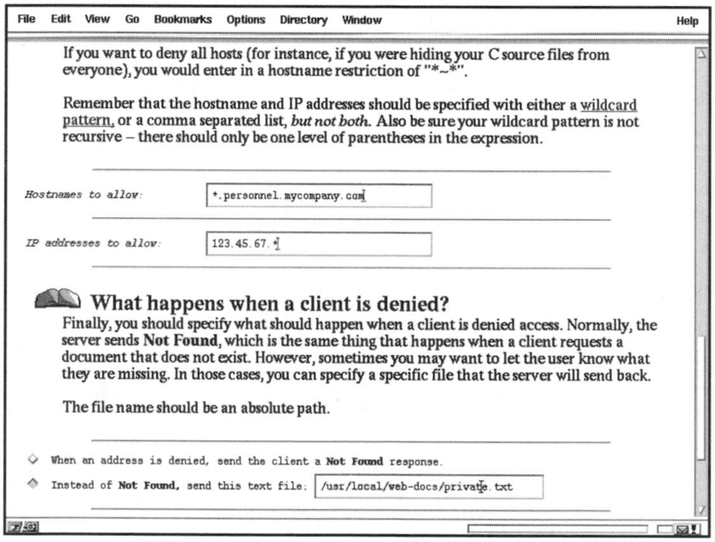

FIGURE 29.8.

*Netscape Communications
Server Host Restriction
(Part 3).*

As with filenames, you can enter either specific individual hostnames or IP addresses or wildcard patterns that match multiple hosts. The Hostnames to allow and IP addresses to allow boxes are shown in Figure 29.8 with the personnel example filled in.

The bottom of Figure 29.8 shows how you can set up a custom message to users who try to access restricted resources, giving them a reason for the denial of their request. You need not use this feature, but it can be friendlier than the generic Not Found message most httpd servers return. The example has things set up so the contents of the file /usr/local/web-docs/ private.txt will be returned. This file could explain politely, for example, that access to per- sonnel resources on the Web server is limited to the Personnel Department. When you're fin- ished with the form, scroll all the way to the bottom (not shown in Figure 29.8) and click Make These Changes to apply your restrictions.

An Important Warning About Hostname/IP Address Authentication

All of the Web server software described in this chapter trustingly accepts the word of a re- questing computer when it sends its IP address. There is no possible verification of this infor- mation. It's relatively easy for a user to change the hostname/IP address of a UNIX system and laughably easy to change that of a PC or Mac. A curious, mischievous, and/or malicious per- son can reconfigure his computer to impersonate someone else's by changing the IP address of his own. Although this is an overall network security issue, not specifically one for your Intranet, it's important you know about it because it can affect the security of your access-controlled documents. Security-minded network administrators can use special hardware and software to prevent this sort of IP spoofing, but for your Intranet's purposes, you'll probably want to com- bine hostname/IP address authentication with username/password authentication, as outlined in the following section.

Combined Authentication

Now that you understand how username/password and hostname/IP address authentication work separately, this section gets you thinking about how you can combine the two to beef up your access control.

Combined Authentication in the Netscape Server

Netscape's scanty $40 documentation for the Communications server doesn't address the sub- ject of combined authentication directly, but you can infer from it how to implement com- bined username/password and hostname/IP address authentication. As you learned earlier, the Netscape server uses one or more user databases to store usernames and passwords, and you can apply access control limits based on both individual usernames and on group membership. Also, the Netscape server can restrict access by hostname/IP address, as described in the previous section. Although the Netscape Communications server manual, and its essentially identical online help, describe these two methods as an either-or choice, it would appear that applying both kinds of access control to a single resource would result in both methods being applied. In other words, you can do the following:

- Define a set of users, such as the sample `personnel` group, in the Netscape user database

- Apply username/password authentication, such as to the `personnel` resource, limiting access to the members of the `personnel` group in the user database

- Apply hostname/IP address restrictions, such as to the same `personnel` resource, limiting access to those computers in the `personnel` subdomain (or even to the individual computers of the members of the `personnel` group)

Because the documentation doesn't say what happens in such a situation, including whether there is an order of precedence in the testing of the access control rules, check very carefully how things work when you set up intersecting access control rules of this sort. For example, it isn't clear if the username/password authentication rule would be applied first, prompting the customer for a username and password, only to have the hostname/IP address rule kick in to deny access even to an authenticated user, or whether the latter rule would be applied first, which should be the case.

Fortunately for those who want to have their access control rules perform exactly as they want them to, Netscape provides another means of access control by using Dynamic Configuration Files (DCFs). You can think of Netscape's DCFs as what this chapter has called LACFs— access control files that apply to a single directory or subdirectory on your Web server. Normally named `.nsconfig` (note the leading period in the filename), DCFs are organized into discrete sections with HTML-like markup. Each section is marked off by the tags `<Files>` and `</Files>`, in between which are access control and other rules that apply to the files specified. You can do many things with Netscape DCFs. The following example replicates the combined username/password and hostname/IP address access control to the personnel section of the sample Web server:

```
<Files *>
RequireAuth dbm=webusers userpat="anne¦joe¦jerry" userlist="anne,joe,jerry"
RestrictAccess method=HTTP method-type=allow ip=123.45.67.*
dns=*.personnel.mycompany.com
</Files>
```

This DCF, which goes in the top level of the `/usr/local/web-docs/personnel` directory, applies to all files and subdirectories in that directory tree. It requires username/password authentication, limiting access to users `anne`, `joe`, and `jerry` listed in the Netscape user database named `webusers`. It further limits access by both numerical IP address and symbolic hostname, both using wildcards. Notice that it's not necessary to specify both `allow` and `deny` rules; Netscape's server takes a more conservative approach to access restrictions than do NCSA and CERN/W[3].

TIP

Netscape DCFs in lower-level directories take precedence over the rules in a DCF in a higher-level directory. Thus, by creating a `.nsconfig` file in the `personnel/executive` subdirectory, you can limit access to files in that directory to the user anne, as you did earlier in this chapter. Such a DCF might look like this:

```
<Files *>
RequireAuth dbm=webusers userpat=anne userlist=anne
RestrictAccess method=HTTP method-type=allow ip=123.45.67.89
dns=annspc.personnel.mycompany.com
</Files>
```

You can enable Netscape DCFs using fill-in forms similar to those shown earlier for setting up hostname/IP address access control. For example, you can enable a DCF for a given server resource, and the graphical interface will create a skeleton `.nsconfig` file. However, you'll need to use a text editor to add your own detailed access control and other directives.

Combined Authentication in the NCSA Servers

Combining username/password and hostname/IP address authentication in the NCSA httpd servers is fairly simple. You'll extend the rules in the `<Limit>` section(s) of either the GACF or LACF. The following is the now-familiar personnel example modified to combine the two access control methods:

```
AuthType Basic
AuthName Personnel Only
AuthUserFile /usr/local/etc/httpd/userpw
AuthGroupFile /usr/local/etc/httpd/ourgroup
<Limit GET>
order deny,allow
deny from all
allow from personnel.mycompany.com
allow from 123.45.67
Require group personnel
</Limit>
```

As you can see, all that was needed was to pull in both of the two sample methods shown in the earlier NCSA examples. Notice that order counts in the `<Limit>` section. In this example, the hostname/IP address access control rules are applied first (using the deny and then allow sequence). Once those rules are satisfied, the user is prompted for a password as the username/password authentication is applied. Based on this example, it's easy to modify this rule for a LACF in the `personnel/executive` subdirectory simply by replacing `Require group personnel` with `Require user anne`.

Combined Authentication in the CERN/W[3] Server

The CERN/W[3] Server is similarly capable of combining username/password and hostname/ IP address authentication. Here, you'll modify the GetMask directive in your GACF. Again, the following is the modified personnel example, this time limiting access using both methods.

```
Protection Personnel {
    AuthType     Basic
    Passwordfile /usr/local/etc/httpd/passwd
    GroupFile    /usr/local/etc/httpd/group
    GetMask      @*.personnel.mycompany.com, @123.45.67.*,
                 personnel
}
```

As with the NCSA example, this one applies hostname/IP address access control first (because it appears on the GetMask line first), and then username/password authentication. Both rules must be satisfied before access is permitted. To further restrict access, you'll need to develop LACFs for individual directories and subdirectories. As noted earlier, the CERN/W[3] LACF file's format is completely different from that of the server's GACF. Here's one (note the file must be named .www_acl) that can be placed in the personnel/executive directory to limit access to the subdirectory to user anne, and only from a specific hostname/IP address:

```
*  :  GET  : anne@annspc.personell.mycompany.com,
ann@123.45.67.89
```

This simple file has just one rule. (The rule is usually a single line, with colon-separated records, but it can be wrapped, as shown above, after a comma.) No one other than the user anne (who must give a password under the rule in the previous example) can access any files in the personnel/executive directory. Moreover, anne must be accessing the files from her normal PC to be granted access, even if she gives the correct password. For more information on CERN/ W[3] LACFs, check out the online documentation at http://www.w3.org/pub/WWW/Daemon/User/ Admin.html.

Secure/Encrypted Transactions

You can further enhance security on your Intranet by encrypting Web transactions. When you use an encryption facility, information submitted by customers using Web fill-in forms—including usernames, passwords, and other confidential information—can be transmitted securely to and from the Web server.

There are a wide range of proposed and/or partially implemented encryption solutions for the Web, but most are not ready for prime time. Of the several proposed methods, only two have emerged in anything like full-blown form. This chapter looks at the Secure HTTP (S-HTTP) and Secure Socket Layer (SSL) protocols. Unfortunately, the two are not compatible with each other, though compatibility is possible. Worse, Web browsers and servers that support one method don't support the other, so you can reliably use one or the other only if you carefully match your Web server and customers' browsers.

S-HTTP

Secure HTTP was developed by Enterprise Integration Technologies and RSA Data Security, and the public S-HTTP standards are now managed by CommerceNet, a not-for-profit consortium that is conducting the first large-scale market trial of technologies and business processes to support electronic commerce over the Internet. (For general information on CommerceNet, see `http://www.commerce.net/`.) S-HTTP is a modified version of the current httpd protocol. It supports the following:

- User and Web server authentication using digital signatures, and signature keys using both the RSA and MD5 algorithms
- Privacy of transactions, using several different key-based encryption methods
- Generation of key certificates for server authentication

EIT has developed modified versions of the NCSA httpd server and NCSA Mosaic (for both UNIX systems and Microsoft Windows) that support S-HTTP transactions. Although the licensing terms allow for NCSA to fold EIT's work into its free httpd server and Mosaic browsers, there's been no public indication of NCSA's plans to do so. Meanwhile, the CommerceNet secure NCSA httpd server and Mosaic browser are available only to members of CommerceNet. You'll find information about both packages, including full-text user manuals, at the CommerceNet home page `http://www.commerce.net/`.

SSL

S-HTTP seems to have been engulfed in the 1995 Netscape tidal wave. Unwilling to wait for widely-accepted httpd security standards to evolve (as it was with HTML as well), Netscape Communications Corporation developed its own Secure Sockets Layer encryption mechanism. SSL occupies a spot on the ISO seven-layer network reference below that of the httpd protocol, which operates at the application layer. Rather than developing a completely new protocol to replace httpd, SSL sits between httpd and the underlying TCP/IP network protocols and can intervene to create secure transactions. Netscape makes the technical details of SSL publicly available. In addition, C-language source code for a reference implementation of SSL is freely available for noncommercial use.

The Netscape Navigator Web browser has built-in SSL support, as does the Netscape Commerce server; the Netscape Communications server does not support SSL. Given Netscape's share of the Web browser market, it's hard to see how S-HTTP has much of a chance at becoming widely available. With the exception of NCSA Mosaic, most other Web browsers have—or have promised—SSL support. Some of them are Spry's Internet in a Box, that company's newer product, Mosaic in a Box for Windows 95, and Release 2 of Microsoft's Internet Explorer for Windows 95 and the Macintosh. By the time you read this, all these packages may have completed their SSL implementations.

> **NOTE**
>
> Even though a browser may support secure transactions using SSL or S-HTTP, no transactions are secure except those between the browser and a compatible Web server. Thus, using Netscape, for example, won't provide any security unless you're also using the Netscape Commerce server. It's also important to note that most mechanisms for passing Web services through network firewalls (proxying, for example) don't support secure transactions unless both the proxy server and the destination server do.

As noted in the preceding section, the Netscape Commerce server supports the company's SSL security mechanism. Other packages that support SSL include the Secure WebServer package from Open Market, Inc. (http://www.openmarket.com/), which also supports S-HTTP, and IBM's Internet Connection Secure Server, which runs under IBM's UNIX, AIX Version 4, and OS/2 Warp. (Evaluation copies of Secure WebServer for several UNIX systems are available at the Open Market Web site.)

Both Secure WebServer and Internet Connection Secure Server are based on Terisa Systems, Inc.'s SecureWeb Client and Server Toolkit. This package provides source code for developers building secure Web servers and browsers. The Terisa Toolkit supports both SSL and S-HTTP. For more information about the package, visit Terisa's Web site at http://www.terisa.com/. Open Market's promotional announcements about Secure WebServer state that the package supports secure transactions through Internet firewalls, but no details on just how this works are provided.

The Common Gateway Interface (CGI) and Intranet Security

CGI is the mechanism that stands behind all the wonderful, interactive fill-in forms you'll want to put on your Intranet. You need to be aware, though, CGI-bin scripting is susceptible to security problems. You must take a good deal of care to do your scripting to avoid them.

You can minimize much of your risk for security breaches in CGI-bin scripting by focusing in one particular area: include in your scripts explicit code for dealing with unexpected user input. The reason for this is simple: you should never trust any information a user enters in a fill-in form. Just because, for instance, a fill-in form asks for a user's name or e-mail address, there is no guarantee that the user filling in the form won't put in incorrect information. Customers make typographical errors, but probing crackers, even those inside your organization, may intentionally enter unexpected data in an attempt to break the script. Such efforts can include UNIX shell metacharacters and other shell constructs (such as the asterisk, the pipe, the back tick, the dollar sign, the semicolon, and others) in an effort to get the script to somehow give the user shell access. Others intentionally try to overflow fixed program text buffers to see if the program can coaxed into overwriting the program's stack. To be secure, your CGI-bin scripts have to anticipate and deal safely with unexpected input.

Other problems inherent with CGI-bin scripts include

- Calling outside programs, opening up potential security holes in the external program. The UNIX sendmail program is a favorite cracker target.

- Using server-side includes in scripts that dynamically generate HTML code. Make sure user input doesn't include literal HTML markup that could call a server-side include when your script runs.

- Using SUID scripts, which are almost always dangerous, whether in a CGI-bin context or not.

Paul Phillips maintains a short but powerful list of CGI-bin security resources on the Web. Check out `http://www.cerf.net/~paulp/cgi-security`, where you'll find a number of documents spelling out these and other risks of CGI-bin scripting. For an extensive list of general CGI-related resources, go to Yahoo's CGI page, at `http://www.yahoo.com/Computers_and_Internet/Internet/World_Wide_Web/CGI___Common_Gateway_Interface/index.html`.

Your Intranet and the Internet

Is your Intranet accessible from the Internet? If so, all of the security problems of the Internet are now your Intranet's problems too. You can, however, connect safely to the Internet and still protect your Intranet. You can even use the Internet as a means of letting remote sites in your company access your Intranet.

Firewalls

It's a fact of Internet life that there are people out there who want to break into other people's networks via the Internet. Reasons vary from innocent curiosity to malicious cracking to business and international espionage. At the same time, the value of the Internet to organizations and businesses is so great that vendors are rushing to fill the need for Internet security with Internet firewalls. An Internet *firewall* is a device that sits between your internal network and the outside Internet. Its purpose is to limit access into and out of your network based on your organization's access policy.

A firewall can be anything from a set of filtering rules set up on the router between you and the Internet to an elaborate application gateway consisting of one or more specially-configured computers that control access. Firewalls permit desired services coming from the outside, such as Internet e-mail, to pass. In addition, most firewalls now allow access to the World Wide

Web from inside the protected networks. The idea is to allow some services to pass but to deny others. For example, you may be able to use the Telnet utility to log into systems out on the Internet, but users on remote systems cannot use it to log into your local system because of the firewall.

Here are a couple of good general Web resources about Internet firewalls:

- Marcus Ranum's Internet Firewalls Frequently Asked Questions document at `http://www.greatcircle.com/firewalls/info/FAQ.html`

- Kathy Fulmer's annotated list of commercial and freeware firewall packages (with many hyperlinks to firewall vendor Web pages) at `http://www.greatcircle.com/firewalls/vendors.html`

If your company is also connected to the Internet, you'll want to know how to make sure your Intranet isn't generally accessible to the outside world. Although you learned earlier in this chapter about denying access to your Web server using hostname and IP address authentication, the fact that IP addresses can be easily spoofed makes it essential that you not rely on this mechanism as your only protection. You'll still want to rely on an Internet firewall to protect your Intranet, as well as all your other network assets. Moreover, in all likelihood, unless your corporate network is not connected to the outside world at all, you'll want to ensure the security of your other Intranet services, including not only your Web servers, but also your FTP, Gopher, Usenet news, WAIS, and other TCP/IP network services.

Virtual Intranet

More and more companies with widely distributed offices, manufacturing sites, and other facilities are turning to use of the Internet to replace private corporate networks connecting the sites. Such a situation involves multiple connections to the Internet by the company and using the Internet as the backbone network for the company. Although such an approach is fraught with security risks, many organizations are using it for nonsensitive information exchange within the company. Using a properly set up firewall, companies can provide access to services inside one site's network to users at another site. Still, however, the data that flows across the Internet backbones between the corporate sites is mostly unencrypted, plain text data that Internet snoopers can easily read. Standard firewalls don't help with this situation.

A number of firewall companies have recently developed Virtual Private Network (VPN) capabilities. Essentially, VPN is an extension of standard firewall capabilities to permit authenticated, encrypted communications between sites over the Internet. That is, using a VPN, users at a remote site can access sensitive data at another site in a secure fashion over the Internet. All the data that flows on the public Internet backbones is encrypted before it leaves the local network, and then decrypted when it arrives at the other end of the connection.

The most mature VPN product comes from Raptor Systems (`http://www.raptor.com/`), part of the company's Eagle family of products; others are available from Checkpoint (`http://`

www.checkpoint.com/) and Telecommerce (http://www.telecommerce.com/).

Figure 28.9 shows a schematic drawing of a VPN reprinted with the permission of Raptor Systems, Inc. The cloud represents the Internet, and the firewall system, local network, and remote site are shown as workstations. The broad line connecting the workstation at the remote site to the local workstation illustrates the VPN. Such products make it possible for you to extend the availability of your Intranet to remote company sites without having to set up a private network.

FIGURE 28.9.

A virtual private network.

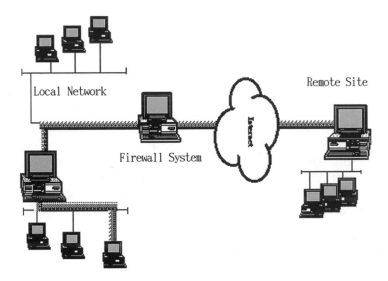

Summary

This chapter has dealt with implementing security on your Intranet. Although an Intranet is, by definition, internal to an organization, security is important not so much because it prevents things, but because it enables them. Judicious use of built-in security features of Web servers and other Intranet resources can add value to your Intranet by making new things possible. In this chapter, you have done the following things:

- Considered the overall security aspects of your Intranet
- Learned how implementing security can broaden the ways in which your Intranet can be useful in your organization
- Learned how to use username/password authentication to limit access to resources on your Intranet
- Learned how to provide secure access to Intranet resources to groups of customers

- Learned how to restrict access to sensitive resources based on customers' computer hostnames or network addresses
- Learned about the security aspects of CGI-bin scripting
- Learned about encrypted data transmission on your Intranet to protect critical information
- Learned important information about securing access to your Intranet in the case where your corporate network is attached to the Internet
- Learned how to provide—and limit—secure access to your Intranet from outside your immediate local network

Web Access to Commercial Database Applications

30

by Tim Evans

As with so many other computer applications' vendors, commercial database vendors are racing to provide Web-accessible front ends to their packages. If you've struggled to build useful, user-friendly database applications using the tools your database vendor has provided, or using custom programming, you'll no doubt welcome the idea of using a Web browser and fill-in forms as an alternative to building user interfaces from scratch or with vendors' application-building tools.

In this chapter, you'll learn about a number of commercial database vendors' Web front ends, third-party database interfaces that are Web-enabled, and several no-cost Web/database interfaces. You'll also learn about creating custom CGI-bin scripts for accessing your database applications.

In this chapter, you'll do the following:

- Review important information about the Web's Common Gateway Interface (CGI) to get a bird's eye view of how Web access to UNIX databases works
- Learn about no-cost and commercial gateways to UNIX database packages from Oracle, Informix/Illustra, and Sybase, as well as those from third-party vendors
- Learn about developing your own Web front ends to these and other UNIX database packages
- Learn about accessing PC database applications using a Web browser front end

This chapter does not touch on designing and developing the database applications themselves. Consult your database package's documentation for that information. In this chapter, it's assumed you're already running some database package and that you have an application you'd like to access using your Web browsers. Of course, once you start accessing your database with your Web browsers, you may want to change the database's design. This is no different from the traditional database application development process, in which you use the application for a while to see how you want to change it.

Accessing Large Commercial Database Packages—The Big Picture

Whatever UNIX database package you use on your Intranet—and whatever bells and whistles it provides for developing database applications, entering queries, and generating reports—database access boils down to two broad processes:

- Formulating and submitting structured query language (SQL) queries or data-entry statements to the database engine
- Receiving and processing the results of the query

These two processes are, of course, traditional database processes: query and report and data entry. Whether the user hand-edits SQL queries or fills in an on-screen query or data-entry form, the objective is the same: to pass the query or new data to the database back end. Similarly, when the database spits out the results of a query or data entry, an application has to receive it and generate human-readable output (on screen or on paper) or machine-readable output in some specific format.

Web access to these databases involves exactly the same two processes, with important differences:

- Your customers perform queries and data entry using fill-in Web forms (created with HTML), in which they enter query keywords or other search criteria through menu selections, click buttons, free-form text blocks, or fill-in-the-blanks.

- CGI-bin scripts take the information entered in the form and bundle it up into valid SQL queries or data-entry updates. They then pass it off to the database back end.

- The same CGI-bin scripts receive the results back from the database engine after processing. They format the report in HTML and pass it back to the customer's Web browser for display.

To Thine Ownself Be True—An Example

HTML fill-in forms take the place of the database vendor's graphical interface, your laboriously painted custom graphical interface, or your text-based input forms. Similarly, CGI-bin scripts take the place of the custom programming you've done using the database vendor's development tools, a stand-alone programming language such as C, or other custom tools.

Focusing on a near-hypothetical SQL query can help you get oriented. Figure 30.1 shows what might be a Web-based interface to a database application. Although this form is actually a front end to the Glimpse search engine, assume for the sake of this example that it's an interface to an Oracle, Informix, or other commercial database application.

> **NOTE**
>
> Because this HTML form is so terrific, you may want to look at the source for it with your Web browser (at `http://the-tech.mit.edu/Shakespeare/search.html`). In Netscape, open the View menu and select Document Source; in Mosaic, open File menu and select View Source. Or save and print the source for reference if you'd like.

First, notice how the page's author has used several features of standard HTML forms markup to create this striking and quite complex form. At the same time, the form is easy to grasp at a glance. You see small and large fill-in boxes, radio buttons, and form housekeeping buttons (such as Begin Search and Reset Form).

More importantly, occupying most of the center of the form are four independent menu selectors, three of which have scroll bars for viewing choices. You can select any or all of them to create an almost infinite number of quite complex queries. Take a look at Figure 30.2, where a famous line (*To thine ownself be true*) has been entered in the keywords box. Also, several possible works are selected. Among the possible sources selected for the line are two of the tragedies, one history, and all the sonnets. This quotation, which is one of Shakespeare's most famous lines, is not (the widespread 1970's Me-First belief to the contrary) one of the Ten Commandments, nor is it from anywhere else in the Bible.

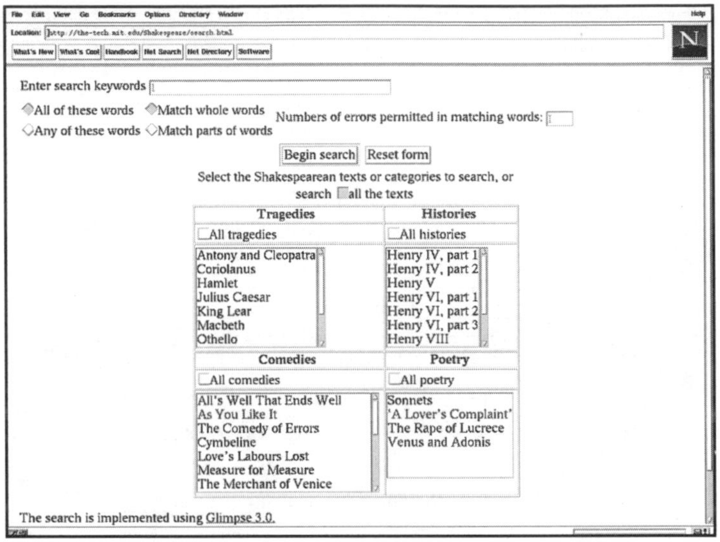

FIGURE 30.1.

A Shakespeare Web search form.

FIGURE 30.2.

A complex search on a Shakespeare Web form.

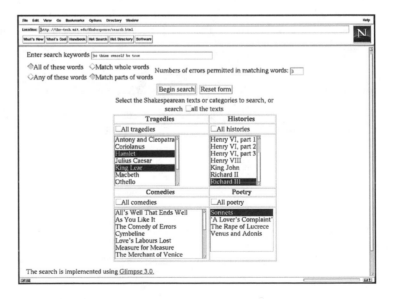

Of course, you could have just taken the defaults and had the search hit all the works, but stick with the program for just a little longer. Look at the form, and then consider the SQL statement that you would need to produce the same query in a traditional relational database application. Something along the lines of the following might do it:

```
select speaker, title, act, scene from (( tragedies where (title = "King Lear" or
title = "Hamlet"))
or ( histories where title = "Richard III" ) or verse from (poetry where title =
"sonnets"))
and line = "to thine ownself be true"
```

Now, the above may be illegal, even doggerel SQL that would be rejected by any self-respecting database application's query parser, even if it does have the right number of opening and closing parentheses. Nevertheless, you get the idea. For even the most computer-macho of your customers, the simple, intuitive fill-in form shown in Figure 30.2 beats handcrafting such an SQL query every time. Your first job as a Web CGI-bin scripter is to build scripts that will take the user input from these fill-in forms, convert them into truly legal SQL syntax, and then pass them off to the database engine.

But wait, you've only done half your job. What do you do with the results that come back from the query? The not-too-terribly-complex Shakespearean sample query has a simple, four-word answer. Your customer's Web browser, however, is powerless to read it unless your script both passes it back to the browser and does so in a format the browser can recognize.

Just as you have had to negotiate your database's report writer to format the output of queries into something meaningful and attractive, you'll need to do the same with the data your CGI-bin scripts pulls from the database. The happy news is that you get to use HTML in formatting this output, something you've already learned in building your Intranet. As a result, you're all set to use something like the following perl code in your CGI-bin script to return the answer to your customer in HTML. (The matter to the right of the # signs is commentary.)

```
print "Content-type text/html\n\n"; # send a MIME data type/sub-type header and a
blank line
print "<HTML><HEAD><TITLE>Query Response</TITLE></HEAD>";
# send necessary beginning HTML markup and a document title
print "<BODY><H1>Results of Your Query</H1>"; # more HTML markup; print a Level-1
HTML headline
print "In Shakespeare's <EM>$play</EM>, Act $act, Scene $scene, Speaker $speaker
said \"$line\"\n";
# send back the data, with variable substitution
print "</BODY></HTML> # close up the HTML document with concluding markup
```

This fragment is pretty self-explanatory, but it's your second major key to providing your Intranet's customers access to your database application through their Web browsers. In this example, you're dynamically creating a complete HTML document line by line, using perl's print command. (HTML markup appears in uppercase.) The script uses variables that it assigned earlier when it received the data your customer entered into the fill-in form. The data, in the form of variables, was passed off to the database engine. Data coming back is assigned to your variables, and then hot-plugged into the HTML output for viewing in your customer's Web browser. Figure 30.3 shows what such an output would look like.

FIGURE 30.3.

The HTML results of the Shakespeare query.

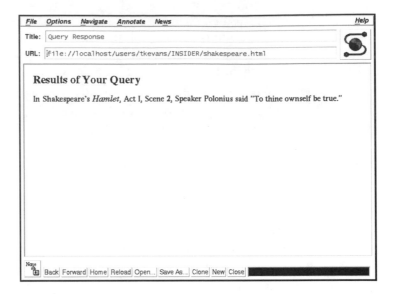

Polonius' Point

It doesn't matter that the Shakespeare database you searched in this example is a Glimpse index, not an Oracle database. What *does* matter is that you're taking and processing user input using a standard, ready-to-use, interchangeable set of tools, almost custom made for your Intranet:

- The Form subset of the HyperText Markup Language
- The Web's Common Gateway Interface, with its standard methods of receiving data from a form, passing it off to an external program, and getting the results back, using environment variables
- The use of HTML to dynamically format and return the results of the customer's query to his Web browser for viewing

You could take the Shakespeare search form and its underlying CGI-bin perl script and have the hardest half of the work of interfacing your database with your Intranet already done. (As with other things you find on the Web, be sure you don't violate copyrights when you steal them.) Nearly every freeware and commercial database gateway package uses the same basic CGI-bin approach; scripts may or may not be in perl (although most are), but the basic ideas behind them are just what you've been learning.

Important CGI Basics

It's time to leave Hamlet behind and take a quick look at some CGI basics. All are relevant to Web database application interfaces, and you'll want to bear them in mind as you work your way through the rest of this chapter.

■ Each piece of data your customer enters into an HTML fill-in form (query keywords or new data entry) is available to be passed, as UNIX standard input, directly to your database engine by your CGI-bin script.

■ You can include additional data in form output using the INPUT TYPE=hidden HTML markup. You can hard-code this information into your forms or you can dynamically set it based on user behavior or other factors that the customer doesn't see but that your CGI-bin script might need for processing.

■ CGI-bin scripts carry with them a good deal of standard information in the form of environment variables. The variables include not only the customer's Web browser type, but also the TCP/IP address and hostname of the user's computer, his user ID and access authentication (if the server is configured to provide it), and the MIME data type/subtypes supported by the browser.

If you're using the NCSA httpd server, you'll find a useful CGI-bin test script comes with the software, which you can run with your browser to get a feel for this script. The script should be in the `cgi-bin` subdirectory of your Web server software tree under the name `test-cgi`. You may also find `test-cgi.tcl`, an alternative version. Figure 30.4 shows part of the output of the latter, run from the NCSA Mosaic X Windows (UNIX) browser.

FIGURE 30.4.

The output of the NCSA test-cgi.tcl script.

TCL/TK

The `test-cgi.tcl` script is not written in perl, but rather in John Ousterhout's *Tool command language* (Tcl). Tcl is an embeddable scripting language, and it comes with a companion graphical user interface builder toolkit called Tk. Tcl/Tk is not as widely used for CGI-bin scripting as perl, but it has a growing and fanatical user base, and it's being used for both CGI-bin scripting and general use.

Development of Tcl/Tk continues at Sun Microsystems Labs, with frequent updates, so check the Tcl/Tk home page at `http://www.sunlabs.com/research/tcl`. Ousterhout has also written a book about the package, *Tcl and the Tk Toolkit*. Its home page is at `http://www.aw.com/cp/Oust.html`. If you're interested in pursuing Tcl/Tk for your CGI-bin scripts, you'll want a copy, as well as a copy of the NCSA library of Tcl/Tk routines from `ftp://ftp.ncsa.uiuc.edu/Web/httpd/Unix/ncsa-httpd/cgi/tcl-proc-args.tar.Z`. You can find further Web-related Tcl/Tk resources at `http://www.sco.com/Technology/tcl/Tcl.html#Tcl-NetandWeb`.

To continue this digression just a bit further, Don Libes' package *expect* is an important Tcl/Tk application for automating ordinarily interactive procedures. Although you probably won't use it for CGI-bin scripting, you may find it an otherwise useful tool in maintaining your Intranet. Libes' book *Exploring Expect*, which has a compact introduction to Tcl/Tk, is on the Web at `http://www.ora.com/gnn/ora/item/expect.html`.

CGI-bin Environment Variables

To get back to Figure 30.4, although you can't read the fine print, you can see a partial listing of the standard set of CGI-bin environment variables. This is CGI-bin solid gold. You're free to use and manipulate all this ready-rolled information with your scripts to supplement the customer's query or data-entry data, which the script also, naturally, passes.

CGI-bin scripts often generate fill-in forms on the fly, based on such things as the initiating user's Web browser type (Netscape, Mosaic, or lynx, for example). You can tailor your input screens based on the customer's browser type. For example, you might use Netscape's proprietary HTML extensions where appropriate, but not for browsers that don't handle them correctly. (Tables and font changes are two important examples.) You can set and use hidden variables in these scripts for many reasons, not the least important of which is to track the customer's complete session with the database package. (This maintenance-of-state is how the ubiquitous shopping cart CGI-bin scripts you may have used for shopping on the Web work, incidentally.) With perl (and with Tcl/Tk), these environment variables can be read into programming arrays for fast and efficient handling.

CGI-Bin Interaction with Your Database Engine

All this information—both the customer-entered data or query information and the CGI-bin standard environment variables—can be processed as needed, and then handed off to your database engine. Data coming back from the engine is also subject to the same sort of manipulation by your scripts. In this context, it's critical that you have an intimate understanding of your database package's operation, as well as the table and record-and-field structure of your databases. Most importantly, you must know precisely how your database engine accepts and processes UNIX standard input. You need to know how queries have to be formatted, what to do with long lines, whether there are confirmation dialog boxes that have to be negotiated, and the like.

This knowledge can help you craft your CGI-bin scripts so they output SQL queries or data-entry commands that are compatible with both your database package and the database itself. Just as important, you must have a complete understanding of the raw data your database may spit out in response to queries or data entry passed by standard input. CGI-bin scripts must be able to properly parse your database package's output. Thus, if your database returns, say, a stream of line-oriented records, with colons separating the fields of each record, your CGI-bin script will need to separate the records and fields, associate them with the input variables initially generated based on the customer's Web form input, and then reformat and return everything to the customer's Web browser in HTML. Keep all this in mind as you read about the capabilities of the software packages described later in this chapter.

If you're an experienced DBA (database administrator), all this information sounds quite familiar to you. Your CGI-bin scripts replace the standard vendor interfaces to database applications. Instead of separate data-entry, query, and reporting mechanisms, you use the HTML fill-in forms and the CGI mechanism to send and receive data to the database application and process its output for the customer. Keep this in mind as you read the following sections that describe some actual Web-based interfaces to commercial database applications.

Gateways to Oracle Database Applications

The Oracle Corporation has aggressively embraced Web technology with a complete suite of Web/Oracle products. Oracle has WebSystem, a comprehensive package that includes the Oracle7 database server, an enhanced httpd server, a Web browser, a custom development package called WebAgent, and a connectivity (middleware) package called the Web Listener. You can also add Web services to an existing Oracle7 database server using Oracle's add-on product Web Server Option.

> **TIP**
>
> The httpd server and Web browser that Oracle provides appear to be enhanced versions of the NCSA server and browser packages from Spyglass, Inc. Free, fully functional copies of the Spyglass Server for several UNIX systems are available at `http://www.spyglass.com/`.

In addition, via Oracle's Web Listener package, you can integrate existing httpd servers with your Oracle7 database server. Integrated with this suite are tools for creating and editing HTML documents and creating clickable image maps. The Oracle WebSystem package has enhanced security and file handling, including the ability to cache frequently accessed documents for faster response to customer queries. Also, the server has read-ahead caching, in which the server tries to make intelligent guesses at documents about to be retrieved based on those already retrieved and/or in the cache. Finally, Oracle's WebSystem supports automatic national language and httpd file type negotiations. For example, if your Web browser isn't capable of displaying a particular kind of image, WebServer will detect this and send you an image you can display.

Oracle's products are, the company says, completely compatible with CGI-bin standards, and the WebAgent package enables you to use your existing stored Oracle PL/SQL procedures. Although WebAgent is implemented using CGI, you don't have to directly create CGI-bin scripts. Instead, you can develop applications using PL/SQL (with which you may already be familiar), and WebAgent will take care of making them work via CGI. As a result, the company indicates, your development work can access not only the Oracle WebServer, but any CGI-compliant Web server. Your WebAgent-developed applications become standard Oracle7 database objects, with portability across your Intranet. The user simply clicks hyperlinks using her Web browser, and your Oracle procedures run.

WebAgent supports extensible HTML encapsulation procedures that run on your Oracle7 server, which can dynamically create HTML documents in response to Web browser requests. Such procedures can even output different HTML formatting in response to the capabilities of the Web browser making the incoming request.

There's an online demonstration of WebSystem that you can access at `http://support.us.oracle.com:8000/tr/owa/tr.splash`. This page is a travel game in which you're given a set amount of play money and try to get the most miles out of it by traveling among a list of available destinations. Figure 30.5 shows its startup page. Although this demonstration is not particularly instructive, note the login and password boxes on the fill-in form, indicating that database security is a major feature.

> **NOTE**
>
> In early 1995, Oracle made a free Web Interface Kit available on their Web site. This package is apparently no longer available, with WebServer and related products now for sale. You can, however, order a CD-ROM containing WebServer for a 90-day evaluation. See `http://www.oracle.com/products/websystem/html/webSystemOverview.html` for specifics. This page also has links to a good deal of detailed documentation on the Oracle packages.

FIGURE 30.5.

The Oracle WebSystem Demo startup screen.

> **NOTE**
>
> At the time of this writing, Oracle had just announced its Universal Server, calling it "the world's first all-purpose server." Universal Server features an underlying Oracle database engine, Web server, text management, messaging, and multimedia support. Details can be found at http://www.oracle.com/products/oracle7/ Oracle_Universal_Server.

Oracle's PowerBrowser for PCs

Before leaving Oracle's products, this section takes a look at what the company calls its "PowerBrowser browser and application development environment for personal computers." PowerBrowser is a suite of integrated packages, including a Web browser that's programmable (using old-fashioned BASIC, not Visual Basic), an HTML editor with drag-and-drop features, a personal PC httpd server, and a personal database manager called Blaze. Users can build small Web applications with these packages and share them over the network with others, as well as being able to access standard Oracle databases and WebServer. To read more about the PowerBrowser product, see http://www.oracle.com/products/websystem/powerbrowser/html/ index.html.

GSQL, a Free Gateway to Oracle Databases

As you no doubt realize from a close reading of the preceding discussion of Oracle's Web-related products, particularly the emphasis on CGI standards, you can build your own CGI-bin interfaces to Oracle databases. Moreover, you can do so without having to buy any new products. Your own grounding in CGI-bin scripting, using perl, Tcl/Tk, or other languages, will enable you to access your databases directly. In fact, one of the very first CGI-bin gateways to relational databases can be used with Oracle databases. Early in the period of CGI development at NCSA, NCSA programmer Jason Ng developed the NCSA GSQL Toolkit, generic C language tools for database access. GSQL works by reading special configuration files you create called proc files. Proc files contain the following:

- References to the structure (tables and fields) of your database application
- HTML setup information for specifying how forms and retrieved data are to be formatted
- User authentication information

The GSQL program first creates an on-the-fly Web fill-in form based on the proc file's HTML setup information. A sample GSQL-generated form appears in Figure 30.6, which shows a trouble ticket database system. Users accessing the database application fill in the form with database query keywords. GSQL then takes the user-entered data and the proc file's information about the database application's structure and creates a formal SQL query. The reformulated query is shipped off to another of the package's programs, sqlmain, for the actual query submission to the database engine. Returned data from the database engine once again passes through GSQL, which uses the proc file for HTML formatting information, and then returns to the user's Web browser in HTML for viewing.

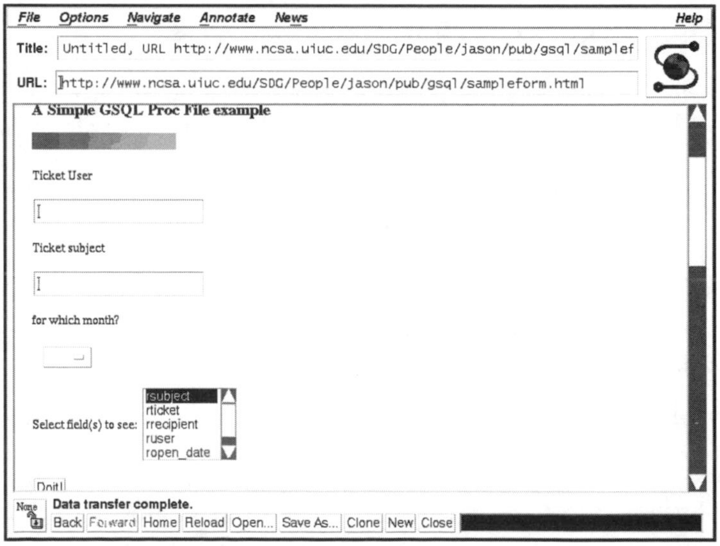

FIGURE 30.6.

A GSQL-generated database search form.

You'll find basic information about GSQL, along with links to several demonstration databases that use it, at `http://www.ncsa.uiuc.edu/SDG/People/jason/pub/gsql/starthere.html`. These demonstrations include Sybase, Interbase, Illustra/Informix, and Windows NT MS-SQL databases, but they don't include an Oracle demonstration. The GSQL source code, however, includes Oracle-specific code and examples, as well as pointers to Oracle-related GSQL work done at Georgia Tech University in the United States (`ftp://cc.gatech.edu/pub/gvu/www/pitkow/gsql-oracle`) and at IGD Darmstadt in Germany (`ftp://ftp.igd.fhg.de/pub/packages/oracle`).

Gateways to Sybase Database Applications

At the time of this writing, Sybase did not have formal Web-related products, although it was beta-testing a package called web.sql. You can download the beta at `http://www.sybase.com/`. Sybase has taken a different approach than Oracle to enabling Web access to its databases through proprietary extensions to HTML. With web.sql, Web pages can include hyperlinks to special Sybase HyperText Sybase (HTS) format files, stored directly in Sybase databases.

HTS documents can contain standard HTML markup and are rendered by Web browsers normally. The format, however, allows Sybase-specific markup. HTS documents can contain literal Sybase Transact-SQL statements or perl code. These blocks of code are executed when the user's Web browser loads the document by passing it through the web.sql middleware package. If your Web server is a standard httpd server (such as the NCSA or CERN servers), the perl code is executed using web.sql CGI-bin scripts. If you're running the Netscape Communications or Commerce servers, however, the Transact-SQL code gets passed directly to the web.sql executable using the Netscape Application Programming Interface (NSAPI), rather than using CGI-bin scripts. In either case, the results of the included code runs are sent back to the user's Web browser (in HTML, of course).

> **NOTE**
>
> Sybase claims dramatically better performance with web.sql and the Netscape servers through use of the NSAPI. HTS queries go directly to the Netscape server, which has direct access to web.sql, rather than being passed through perl scripts first.

What's Special About web.sql?

The web.sql package is not being marketed as an overall set of Web tools for Sybase databases, but rather as a means of customizing and dynamically updating the customer interface to databases. Accordingly, you can build customer profiles that create individualized views into the database application. In addition, you can track customer activity and update the custom profiles dynamically based on the activity. Sybase's web.sql home page (`http://www.newmedia.sybase.com/interact/web_spec.html`) uses one of the company's customers to illustrate these features. Virtual Vineyards (Los Altos, CA) is an Internet wine shop, specializing in small vintner's wines. You can order wines using your Web browser. (The Virtual Vineyards home page is at `http://www.virtualvin.com/`.)

Figure 30.7 shows part of Virtual Vineyards' Personal Account creation form. The form goes on for several screens and is not particularly remarkable as far as forms go. What's unique about setting up personal accounts at the Virtual Vineyards Web site is the use of Sybase's web.sql to maintain information about your account. Each time you order wine, your customer profile is updated, including the history of your purchases. In addition, you can annotate your account with your own wine taste preferences, using an online Virtual Vineyards Tasting Chart. Later, when you access the Web page again, you'll see startup pages and special offers based on your purchase history and your expressed wine tastes and preferences.

It's the use of these customization techniques that can be of value to your Intranet, not the potential ability to order wine, of course. As customers interact with your databases via CGI-bin scripts, you'll be able to provide custom views of the database based on their habits, which Web browser they're using, and other identifiable data your scripts can pull out of the transactions. As a result, every customer, or group of customers, will have a different view of your database application that is customized to their every use of the application, their Web browser, and their work habits.

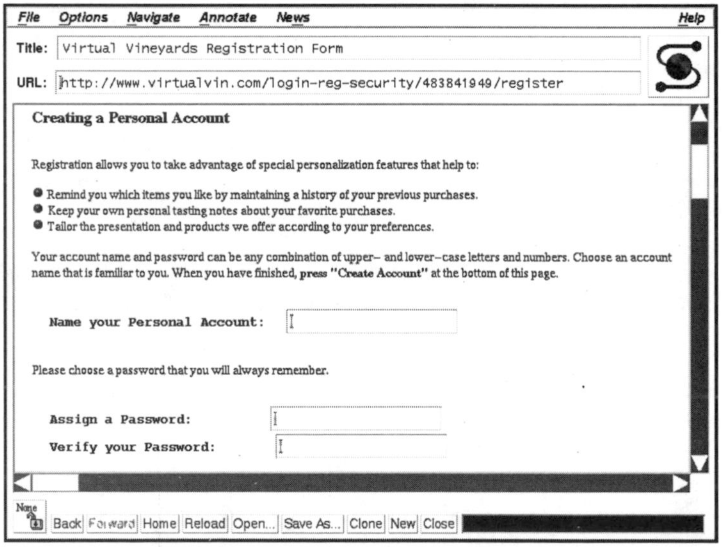

FIGURE 30.7.

Virtual Vineyards Personal Account Creation form.

Other Sybase Database Web Interfaces

Besides its own work with web.sql, Sybase tracks the activity of others in building Sybase Web gateways. You'll find a list of them at `http://www.sybase.com/WWW/`. You've already read about the NCSA GSQL Toolkit, which supports several database packages including Sybase. The following sections take a look at a couple of the others.

Sybperl

Michael Peppler of the Swiss firm ITF Management SA has developed Sybase-specific extensions to perl called sybperl. Sybperl adds Sybase's db_library API calls to the perl language. Peppler indicates that the combination of perl with the Sybase API creates an "extremely powerful scripting tool for Sybase DBAs and programmers." As with perl itself, sybperl is useful for those situations when interacting with Sybase's isql in the UNIX shell is too limited, but when you are writing C programs, sybperl is the proverbial sledgehammer in search of a fly.

WDB

WDB, a Web-to-database interface, is based on sybperl. The sybperl package, then, can be used as a tool in the construction of higher level Sybase databases. WDB was developed by programmers at the European Southern Observatory (ESO), an astronomical consortium that operates observatories in South America.

As a perl CGI-bin script, WDB enables dynamic creation of HTML fill-in forms for database access. Perhaps more importantly, WDB enables the data retrieved from Sybase databases to be converted to clickable Web hyperlinks, allowing data to be retrieved by customers' Web browsers using the point-and-click technique. To turn this statement on its head, the WDB FAQ states, "The entire database system can be turned into a huge hypertext system." Sybase databases also can include hyperlinks to outside World Wide Web resources and/or to resources in other databases. Figure 30.8 shows a WDB fill-in form for an ESO telescope schedule database.

Like GSQL (described previously), WDB uses a high-level form definition file to create views into a database. With the package comes a utility for querying a database application for its table structure and using the results to build template form definition files.

NOTE

Besides Sybase databases, WDB also supports Microsoft mSQL and Informix databases.

FIGURE 30.8.
WDB query form.

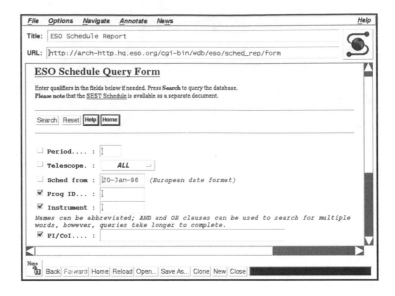

Web/Genera

Stan Letovsky's Web/Genera is a set of tools for integrating Sybase databases with the World Wide Web. The package is based on a high-level schema file you'll write that describes both the Sybase database application table-and-field structure and the HTML format to be created when queries are run. Web/Genera was created for scientific purposes in the U.S. Government-financed Human Genome Database (GDB) project. GDB, centered at the Johns Hopkins University in Baltimore, supports biomedical research, clinical practice, and scientific education by providing human gene-mapping information. Web/Genera databases can be queried directly using Web URLs; the extracted data is formatted into HTML on the fly for display in your Web browser. You can do queries not involving SQL through fill-in forms. Figure 30.9 shows part of a quite lengthy Web/Genera query form that accesses an agricultural science database at the University of Missouri.

Finally, you can use Web/Genera to dump the contents of Sybase databases to flat-text files, based on the same schema files used for the Web gateway interface. These text files can, in turn, be indexed using indexing utilities like WAIS and Glimpse to provide additional means of Web-based search-and-retrieval.

FIGURE 30.9.

A Web/Genera query form (partial).

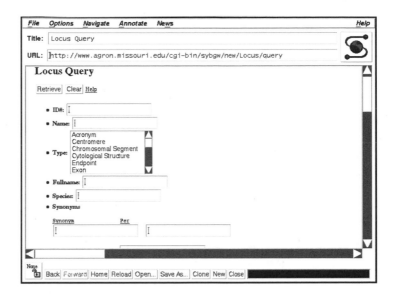

Informix and Illustra

Long-time UNIX relational database leader Informix acquired Illustra Information Technologies, Inc. in late 1995. Both companies previously produced Web-based interfaces to their database applications, so you'll see the two companies' products separately in this section. By the time you read this, though, the products may have merged in some way. It's not clear if the Illustra product will disappear into Informix, or if it will have a continued separate life, but you can expect at least some of its features to turn up in Informix sooner or later.

Informix

Informix has two free Web interface kits available for its Informix-ESQL/C and Informix-4GL products. Of course, you must already own the underlying Informix database application. Both kits are squarely based on the CGI standard.

The Informix-ESQL/C CGI Interface Kit is a ready-to-compile library for simple Web access from applications developed in ESQL/C. It reads and decodes HTML forms and displays both text and Informix BLOBs (binary large objects) to Web browsers. The Informix-4L CGI

Interface Kit performs the same functions for Informix-4GL database applications. The Informix kits have been certified on Sun, SGI, HP, and IBM UNIX systems, and the company is confident that the packages will build on most other modern UNIX systems. You can download both kits at `http://www.informix.com/informix/dbweb/grail/freeware.htm`. The distributions include sample source code for database access. Documentation, however, is quite sparse.

> **NOTE**
>
> In February 1996, Informix announced its own Universal Server package, also calling it the first such package. Based on the combined resources of Informix and its recently acquired Illustra package (see the next section), the product is called a "fully extensible relational database management system" that supports numbers, images, maps, sound, video, Web pages, and user-defined rich data types. The package, or parts of it, may be available by the time you read this.

If you have Informix database applications in place, but would prefer to use other means of Web interface, Informix tracks several freeware gateway packages, providing links to them at the URL listed above (though with a lot of negative commentary). First, as noted previously, the WDB package supports Informix databases.

Informix-Online database users may be interested in the isqlperl subroutine library written by Bill Hails. A set of reusable Version-4.036 perl subroutines, isqlperl is due to be folded into a successor package, DBperl, which is currently under development and which will support several vendors' database packages, including Informix. (Information on both isqlperl and DBperl is at `ftp://ftp.demon.co.uk/oub/perl/db/`.) Informix-CISAM users may want to check out CISAMperl, available at `http://www.singnet.com.sg/~mathias/software/`. This package implements an interface to the Informix C-ISAM library for indexed sequential access methods search. Also based on perl 4.036, this package, like isqlperl, is quite old and may no longer be maintained.

Another commercial interface to Informix databases comes from SQLweb Technologies, Inc. The company's product, SQLweb, provides "an intelligent, adaptive, and dynamic connection" between Web servers and Informix (and several other) relational database products. It supports all database functions (queries, data entry, and canned procedures). Like the Sybase product, SQLweb features customized user interfaces that can be based on users' past activity in the application.

SQLweb is based on standard CGI principles, but the company claims no perl or other scripting is required. Rather, the product adds proprietary extensions to the HTML markup language. Special database entities called SQLweb pages support HTML and the company's CURSOR, IF, and INCLUDE extended markup tags to accommodate its features. SQLweb pages, when accessed with a Web browser, trigger database queries, updates, and the like. Figure 30.10 shows a schematic diagram of how SQLweb works.

FIGURE 30.10.

SQLWeb interfaces with Informix databases.

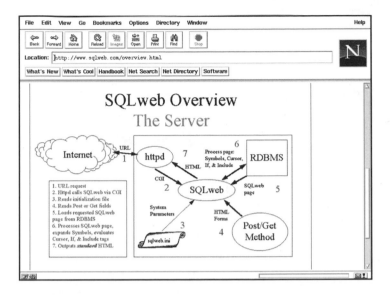

SQLweb has one additional feature that sounds interesting, although current company literature does a poor job of explaining it. The SQLweb Toolkit enables reverse engineering of existing HTML documents, presumably enabling conversion of standard HTML to SQLweb pages with extended markup. You'll find more information about SQLweb at `http://www.sqlweb.com/`.

> **NOTE**
>
> Besides supporting Informix databases, SQLweb also supports Oracle, Sybase, and Microsoft OBDC database products. In addition, the company indicates that the product will support any relational database package that has what the company calls an "adequate" C language API.

Illustra

The Illustra database server, which the Illustra company calls "the database for cyberspace," is an object relational database management system. It handles alphanumeric, character, text, video, image, and document data types in a single database repository.

The company describes the package as the first relational database with object-oriented extensions. In any event, the quoted slogan suggests strongly that Illustra databases are meant to be Web-accessible. Illustra's home page (`http://www.illustra.com/`) contains a link to a page of Illustra demonstration applications. Figure 30.11 shows one of these demonstations: an imaginary, searchable catalog of Sun-logo, noncomputer products (mugs, T-shirts, and the like). In

Figure 30.11, a search on the keywords *purple* and *sun* has been done using a fill-in form. As you can see, the search comes back with several clickable buttons. Clicking one would bring up details about the selected product.

FIGURE 30.11.

The Illustra demonstration database search results.

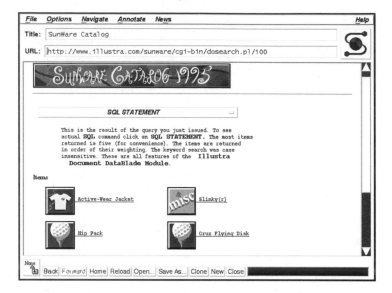

A particularly interesting thing about this demonstration is that you can ask to see the SQL statement that your query used. Notice the SQL STATEMENT button near the top of the screen. Clicking it generates Figure 30.12.

FIGURE 30.12.

The Illustra SQL statement the query in Figure 30.11 used.

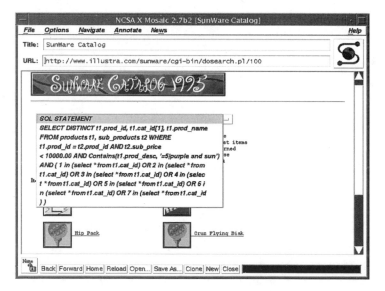

Illustra does not support standard CGI-bin scripting, sniffing at it as something somehow old-fashioned. Instead, it implements its Web interface using an add-in module (called a DataBlade) to the main database server.

The module works something like that described previously with respect to the Sybase HTS product. You can embed literal SQL code in special HTML documents stored directly in the database. These pages, called Application Pages, directly execute queries, data entry, or stored procedures when loaded with a Web browser. (If you run the search shown in Figure 30.10 and 30.11 yourself, and then use your Web browser's View Source capability, you'll see the SQL code in the source document.) Illustra has provided for yet more proprietary extensions to HTML markup. The extensions go further, adding conditional capabilities that enable you dynamically turn on and off support for different browser capabilities, such as HTML Version 3 tables and other browser-specific features, such as Netscape Frames and image support.

Other Commercial Products

New products for accessing corporate databases using Web technologies are rolling out of third-party software shops all over the Internet. This section can't possibly survey them all, but here are brief descriptions of a few of them.

Spider

Supporting Oracle, Informix, and Sybase database products, the Spider Technologies product is a two-part package. First, a visually oriented development tool enables you to build HTML forms to interface with a database application using point-and-click. The interface enables you to view your database structures, selecting tables and relationships, and then build HTML forms and underlying SQL queries dynamically.

Spider 1.5's graphical form-building tool is shown in Figure 30.13. Note the access both to HTML markup tags and to the underlying database application's structure through click buttons, pull-down menus, and the like. You would think this form could be more Web-like in its appearence and operation.

The second part of the package is a middleware program that interacts with the database application to run queries, enter data, and so on. As middleware, Spider's back end does the following:

1. Receives queries from both CGI-bin scripts and from Web browsers through the httpd server
2. Reads special database application files
3. Queries the underlying database
4. Relays the results back to the user's Web browser, in HTML, for viewing

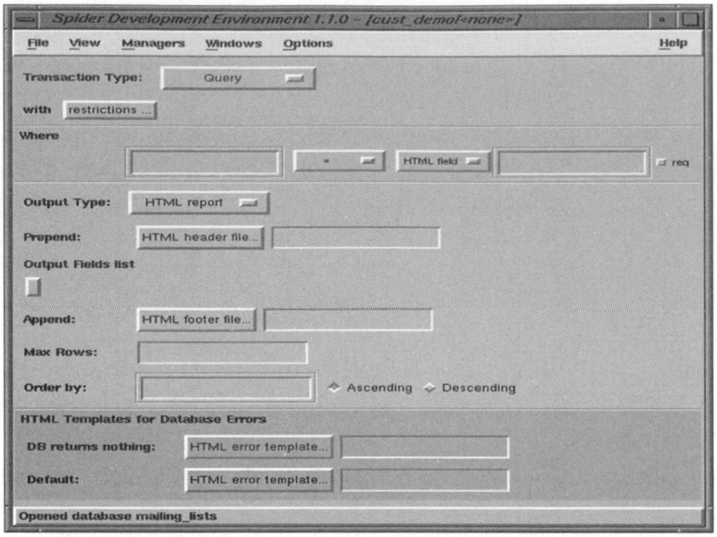

FIGURE 30.13.

The Spider 1.5 graphical form-building tool.

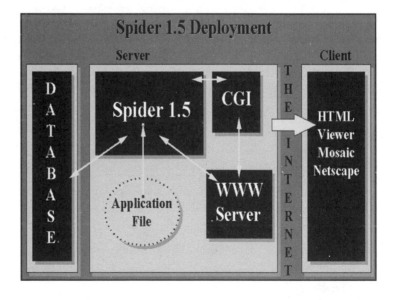

Figure 30.14 shows this process displayed graphically. You can get more information about Spider at `http://www.w3spider.com/`. While you're there, you can pick up a 30-day evaluation copy of the package at no charge.

FIGURE 30.14.

A diagram of Spider 1.5 deployment.

Sapphire/Web

Informix, Oracle, and Sybase users may also want to check out Bluestone's Sapphire/Web database interface. Sapphire/Web's claim to uniqueness is its capability to automatically produce CGI-bin scripts based on a combination of existing HTML documents and fill-in form templates. Like several of the other packages reviewed in this chapter, this one has a graphical front end (shown in Figure 30.15), which is also decidedly un-Weblike. Called the Bind Editor, this tool enables you to drag-and-drop objects from the underlying database and the HTML documents/templates to create CGI-bin code (in C or C++) that can access database contents, including stored procedures. Press reports quote Bluestone as hoping Sapphire/Web will become the "PowerBuilder for the Web," referring to the successful Windows product from Powersoft.

FIGURE 30.15.

The Sapphire/Web graphical Bind Editor.

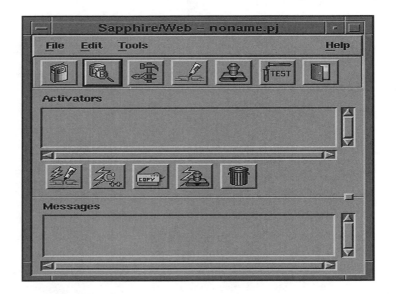

Sapphire/Web is based on Bluestone's existing graphical database interface builder, db-UIM/X. As a result, code built with the former works directly with your database applications, rather than through any sort of middleware. If you're already using db-UIM/X, you can use your legacy code with Sapphire/Web. No-cost evaluation copies of Sapphire/Web are available at `http://www.bluestone.com/products/sapphire`.

VisualWave

Described by Parcplace-Digitalk as the "first object-oriented application development environment (ADE) for building live applications," VisualWave supports Sybase, Oracle, and DB2, as well as object-oriented databases, with add-on products. The package's Web Delivery System promises to automate coding of interactive, adaptive Web applications with graphical drag-and-drop tools.

VisualWave's GUI interface, shown in Figure 30.16, produces both HTML documents and CGI-bin scripts. The package is written in the SmallTalk programming language. Interactive Web Applications built with the package retain state between transactions (HTTP is a stateless protocol, with each transaction completely separate from every other one), unlike many standard CGI-bin scripts. Intelligent program flow is thereby possible based on user input, Web browser capabilities, and the like. (In this connection, VisualWave features an image-conversion feature that creates GIF files, supported in all graphical Web browsers.)

Developers will like the package's features for testing and debugging Web applications, as well as its reusable application framework and built-in personal Web server for quick and easy application testing. Parcplace-Digitalk promises Java support and OLE support in later versions. For more information about VisualWave, see `http://www.parcplace.com/`. At the time of this writing, evaluation copies of VisualWave were not available on the company's Web site, and the site's promised on-line demonstrations were not yet active.

FIGURE 30.16.

VisualWave Interface Painter.

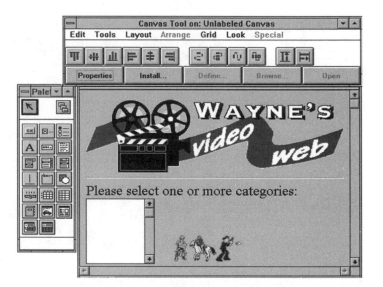

Generic UNIX Database Gateways

Besides the several more-or-less generic database gateway packages noted in the preceding sections, (GSQL, WDB, and isqlperl), you may want to look at a number of additional packages. All of them are based on CGI standards, and all are either perl scripts or perl extensions.

oraperl and oraywww

Arthur Yasinski, formerly of the Canada Department of Natural Resources' Forest Service, has developed two perl interfaces to Oracle databases, oraperl and oraywww. The former is much like other perl scripts you've seen in this chapter, building a fill-in form dynamically and then taking user input and passing it off to the Oracle back end. With oraywww, nonprogrammers can access Oracle databases and interactively build query and data-entry forms, as well as access prebuilt forms. Since the release of oraywww, Yasinski has taken a position with Oracle; presumably his work is reflected in the Oracle Web products described earlier, and his oraperl and oraywww packages are no longer being developed or maintained. You can read about oraperl and oraywww at `http://www.nofc.forestry.ca/features/features.html`.

Other perl Scripts/Extensions

You'll find a collection of perl scripts/extensions at `http://sunsite.doc.ic.ac.uk/packages/dbperl/perl4`. Among the database packages for which you'll find scripts (of varying degrees of currency and utility) are Ingres, Interbase, Postgres, and Unify. You'll find some of these to be quite old, pre-dating the Web. As a result, they are more suitable for stand-alone operation than as CGI-bin scripts and would need substantial overhaul to turn them into CGI-bin scripts. You may be able to modify them or use chunks of them on your Intranet, but they're more likely to be useful as building blocks than as ready-made scripts.

Tim Bunce is working on a standard perl DBI (database interface) and has plans to include support for Oracle, Ingres, mSQL, Informix, Interbase, and DB2. You'll find more information about the ongoing DBI project at `http://sunsite.doc.ic.ac.uk/packages/dbperl/`. You may also want to check out the University of Florida's perl archive at `http://www.cis.ufl.edu`, where you'll find a wide variety of perl-related resources. You can also check out the Comprehensive Perl Archive Network (CPAN), a very busy FTP archive of perl resources at `ftp://ftp.cis.ufl.edu/pub/perl/`.

WebLib

Tobin Anthony (of NASA) and Erik Dorfman, Jim Gass, and Pradip Sitaram (all of Hughes STX Corporation) are developing WebLib, a package that, if brought to fruition, will provide access to distributed relational database systems in a network. The package can also access WAIS and other document-based indexes. Simple configuration files define the structure of databases that WebLib can access, including the creation and passing of SQL queries to database back ends and the HTML formatting and return of results to Web browsers. Figure 30.17 shows the results of a query on a demonstration WebLib database. Check for later releases, as well as updated documentation, on the WebLib home page at `http://selsvr.stx.com/~weblib/`.

FIGURE 30.17.

WebLib online demonstration search.

Access to PC Databases

You can configure your Web server to serve complete Access databases, just as it serves any other file on the server. Your customers' Web browsers can then use their own copies of Access as a Web browser helper application to load them for data search and retrieval and/or export to other Microsoft applications. Figure 30.18 shows an Access database loaded using this approach.

FIGURE 30.18.

Microsoft Access as a helper application.

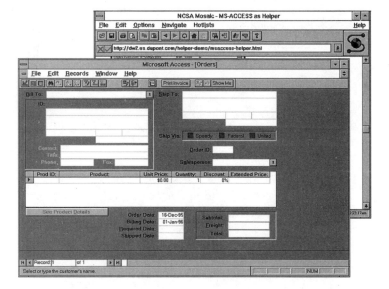

It's important to note that such helper application access to a database application should be considered read-only because the Web browser downloads a temporary copy of the database to the local system. All queries made by your customer are based on the temporary copy, and any changes that he might attempt to make will not be reflected in the master copy on your Web server. Similarly, updates made to the master server won't get propagated to any client unless the client reloads the database from the Web server. Thus, you'll want to limit the capabilities of such an arrangement to running queries, generating reports, and exporting data from the application.

This limitation is more than offset by other capabilities, however. For example, if your company uses other Microsoft products, such as Microsoft Office or its individual components, you'll be able to use their capabilities to move data from one application to another. You can import information in Access databases, for example, into Word or Excel (and vice versa).

Windows CGI Scripting

You'll also want to develop your own CGI-bin scripts for Windows access to databases. Although you can use PC versions of perl, or custom programming in C or C++, you'll probably want to do your scripting in Visual Basic (VB). The Professional Edition of Visual Basic has built-in hooks for native access to database applications in Access, dBASE, Paradox, FoxPro, and Btrieve. Beside this direct access, VB supports the ODBC (Open Database Connectivity) and SQL standards. Databases that are accessible via ODBC and/or SQL include several of the preceding, plus Lotus Approach. Finally, VB's crossover access via Microsoft's DDE and OLE enables access to those databases that support these standards, as well as to other applications that do so.

CGI-bin scripting in Windows (and in DOS) is problematic, though. This is mainly because there's no easy way to throw all the environment variables CGI scripts use and need around as easily as you can on UNIX systems. Most Windows CGI-bin approaches, such as the examples provided with the Whttpd Web server, write environment information out to temporary files, and then read them back when the information is needed for formatting output and such. This system is clearly inefficient and tends to support the argument for the retention of major CGI-bin functions on true multitasking systems, such as UNIX or NT systems.

FoxWeb for FoxBase Access

FoxPro users will want to look at a new product from the Aegis Group called FoxWeb. This software tool interfaces Windows Web servers with FoxPro data and programs. FoxWeb overcomes the limitations of other Windows CGI-bin approaches, which read and write temporary files to pass environment variables between processes. It works by running multiple, backgrounded Visual FoxPro instances simultaneously, each one of which can handle CGI interactions. CGI environment variables are placed into FoxPro arrays and objects for manipulation. All programming is done in FoxPro rather than in an external scripting language like perl, so your investment in FoxPro programming can be both preserved and leveraged. You can even store reusable HTML code directly in FoxPro databases for easy retrieval with intelligent branching capabilities.

Aegis claims substantially faster database access compared to ODBC database transactions, although ODBC database applications can access FoxPro databases, as noted earlier. FoxWeb requires Visual FoxPro, Version 3.0. FoxWeb includes login/password security features. Figure 30.19 shows a FoxWeb fill-in form, with access to a job-search FoxPro database at the University of California. For more information about FoxWeb, including a no-cost, 30-day evaluation copy of the package, see `http://www.intermedia.net/aegis/`.

FIGURE 30.19.

An example FoxWeb application.

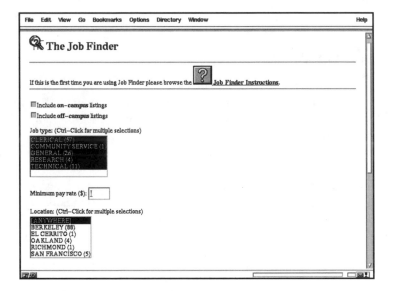

WebBase

ExperTelligence, Inc. offers WebBase for all Microsoft Windows platforms. This package is a 32-bit httpd server with built-in hooks for accessing databases without the use of CGI scripting. As a Web server, WebBase can serve conventional HTML documents in response to Web browser requests. Besides this function, however, the package supports embedded SQL code in special HTML documents that when accessed can contact database applications directly to run queries or data-entry commands. WebBase HTML extensions also include a macro language featuring intelligent decision-making constructs like if-then and case branching, as well as forRow and forIndex looping. A number of other useful functions are also provided, such as string-comparison/matching, math, date-handling, and other logic. These features enable customized responses to Web browser requests based on username, IP address, browser type, and the like.

WebBase enables session state to be maintained throughout a user's session, and has login/password security built in. Databases supported include ODBC platforms like Microsoft Access, Excel, and SQL Server, FoxPro, dBASE III and IV, Paradox, and Btrieve, as well as UNIX database servers running Sybase and Oracle. The package can also search fielded text files as a database. Figure 30.20 shows a WebBase application that provides access to the Dallas-Ft. Worth, TX, Realtors' Multiple List Service. Although WebBase can function as an httpd server, WebBase doesn't provide all the functions of full-featured Web servers, so you can run a traditional Web server for better standard httpd service on the same computer or a different one. WebBase runs on all Intel Windows platforms. For more information about WebBase, including information about no-cost evaluation copies, see http://www.webbase.com/.

FIGURE 30.20.

A sample WebBase query form.

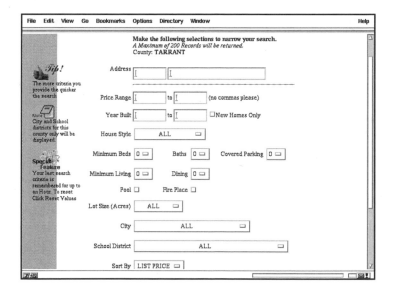

Summary

This chapter has focused on Web interfaces to relational database packages. You've learned about the widespread support of the CGI standards and the frenetic activities of database vendors and database-access vendors as they scramble to bring products to this important market. This chapter has surveyed a fairly representative sample of these vendors' products, some of them in detail, to give you a firm idea of what's possible in this rapidly growing field. Here's a thumbnail summary of the topics you covered in this chapter:

- Important information about the Web's Common Gateway Interface, widely used in database access
- No-cost and commercial gateways to UNIX database packages from a number of sources
- Developing your own Web front ends to these and other UNIX database packages
- Accessing PC database applications using a Web browser front end

Web Groupware: Collaboration on Your Intranet

3

by Tim

IN THIS CHAPTER

Along with the much-discussed Java, group collaboration using World Wide Web technology is one of the Web's most exciting possibilities. This is attested to not only by the fact that IBM's Lotus Notes product has been dragged kicking and screaming into Web integration, but also by the emergence of completely new products built specifically for Web collaboration. After reviewing some simple, and immediately available, means of using your Intranet for group collaboration, this chapter will survey the world of Web groupware and give you some ideas of how you can put it to work on your Intranet.

In this chapter, you'll do the following:

- Learn to distinguish broad categories of Web-based collaboration
- Learn about using personal and group home pages on your Intranet as a means of knowledge and information sharing
- Learn about using hyperindexed Usenet news and e-mail archives as a means of collaboration
- Learn about free-for-all Web resources that allow customers to post their own URLs or other information for all to see
- Learn about Web-based annotation and conferencing systems
- Learn about Web-based training and presentations to do group presentations in real time across your Intranet using Web technologies
- Learn about major commercial groupware packages and how they can integrate into your Intranet
- Learn about miscellaneous Web groupware, including workflow management, collaborative writing and art, and other multiuser activities that may be directly or indirectly useful

The Different Means of Collaboration

It may be useful to begin this discussion by broadly categorizing the means of Web-based collaboration. Several may be defined (although in practice, Web services more often than not cross these neat category boundaries), as follows:

- Simple, one-way information sharing, primarily through the posting of information on Web pages, including individual user home pages
- Free-for-all Web resources, in which anyone is free to add comments and/or hyperlinks
- Multidirectional conferencing systems of various kinds, such as Usenet newsgroups, e-mail distribution lists, bulletin board systems, and the like
- True groupware applications, such as Lotus Notes and the newly important Collabra Share product, in which the preceding categories may be combined into a single monolithic application

Simple One-Way Collaborative Activities on Your Intranet

Leaving aside fancy groupware computer applications for now, remember the most basic means of human collaboration and cooperation is simple, straightforward information sharing. People tell other people what they are doing, what they've learned, and so on. Learning by listening to what other people say about themselves and their activities is one of the most fundamental means by which we are educated and socialized—and by which we grow in our professional lives. Scholars and scientists write books to share information, and information distribution is the *raison d'être* of journalism. Simple information sharing can form the collaborative core of your Intranet, and its value should not be overlooked in the glittery world of groupware. Indeed, online information exchange may be your most important tool. The following sections therefore take a look at some simple but potentially powerful means of Intranet information sharing, beginning with user home pages.

User Home Pages on Your Intranet

Earlier chapters emphasized the need for customer input in the design and content of your Intranet. As you'll recall from Chapter 27, "Designing an Intranet," one criticism of the centralized model of Intranet administration is that a bureaucratic process of Web page approval places obstacles in the way of customers getting their own information out onto your Intranet. Looking at your Intranet from a high-level viewpoint, you've perhaps not focused on how individual users' home pages can contribute significantly to its overall value.

> **NOTE**
>
> Perhaps at this point you're thinking of some of the personal home pages you've seen on the World Wide Web, full of adolescent bravado, bandwidth-eating images of CD covers, song lyrics purporting to state a philosophy of life, self-indulgent posturing, and hyperlinks pointing to similar drivel, and you probably wonder how such things can be a useful part of your Intranet. They can't. But what a 20-year-old college sophomore thinks appropriate for his university home page and what a working scientist, engineer, or other professional might put on a professional page are two completely different matters; this chapter is interested in the latter.

Basic HTML markup can be learned in half an hour. Users' Web pages can be served right out of their home directories on UNIX Web servers, so they don't need to learn anything about Web servers to make their pages available. Figure 31.1 shows a simple yet effective user home page, that of NCSA staff member Briand Sanderson. This author doesn't know Sanderson (though he's given permission to reproduce his home page), but the page shows, in a no-nonsense fashion, basic information about Sanderson's professional activities and academic background. Substantive content is highlighted by hyperlinks, leading to detailed information on Sanderson's work. As you can see, Briand's projects include the Hierarchical Data Format and the development of NCSA Mosaic for Microsoft Windows.

FIGURE 31.1.

A sample user home page.

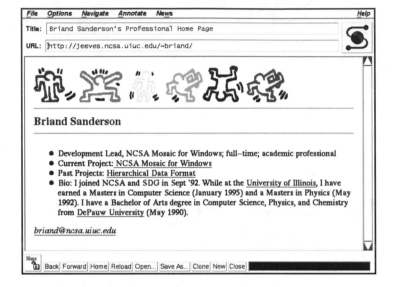

Virtually any computer-literate individual can put together a home page with this sort of information about himself and his work. The HTML document source for the home page shown in Figure 31.1 is only 20 lines long. This source is a great model because it contains just about everything necessary to put together a useful home page:

```
<TITLE>Briand Sanderson's Professional Home Page</TITLE>
<H1><IMG SRC="khbord2.gif"><HR>Briand Sanderson<HR></H1>
<UL><LI>Development Lead, NCSA Mosaic for Windows; full-time; academic
professional
<LI>Current Project:<A HREF="http://www.ncsa.uiuc.edu/SDG/Software/WinMosaic/
HomePage.html">
NCSA Mosaic for Windows</A>
<LI>Past Projects:  <A HREF="http://hdf.ncsa.uiuc.edu:8001/">Hierarchical
Data Format</A>
<LI>Bio:  I joined NCSA and SDG in Sept '92. While at the
<A HREF="http://www.uiuc.edu">University of Illinois</A>, I have
earned a Masters in Computer Science (January 1995) and a Masters in
Physics (May 1992). I have a Bachelor of Arts degree in Computer Science, Physics,
and Chemistry from <A HREF="http://www.depauw.edu">DePauw University</A> (May
1990).
</UL>
<ADDRESS>
<A HREF="mailto:briand@ncsa.uiuc.edu">briand@ncsa.uiuc.edu</A>
</ADDRESS>
```

You can readily see how simple yet effective this home page is. There's little fluff, just a single included image and a bulleted list of substantive hyperlinks. Whether they're office support staff or engineers, paraprofessionals or scientists, your customers can easily create home pages of this sort to share their work with others in your company. Fancy graphics don't usually add much to Web page substance. Here are some possibilities:

- Scientists can share the results of their work with colleagues across the company, placing descriptions of their research on their home pages, together with underlying data in a format accessible with a helper application. Word processing documents containing article or book manuscripts can be made available for viewing, numerical data can be graphed on the fly, and other data can be seen with other helper applications.

- Engineers and draftsmen can place their CAD drawings on your Intranet for organization-wide viewing/sharing.

- Researchers of all kinds can provide links to summaries of their work, or to its details, regardless of its format.

It's hard to overstate the potential value to an organization of this sort of simple information sharing. In a business research environment, for example, the linking of a few important ideas can lead to breakthrough products or services. One researcher, stuck on a project, may find just the thing she needs on some other researcher's home page. Moreover, once the collaborative ball is rolling, customers will add hyperlinks pointing to other customers' home pages on their own pages, making the combined resources of many available to all.

Multidirectional Collaboration and Information Sharing via Usenet News and E-Mail

Usenet news and e-mail are two common Internet services that can be integrated into your Intranet. The following sections look at them in the context of Intranet collaboration.

Usenet News

An organization can set up local Usenet newsgroups for in-house discussions and collaboration. Such free-for-all, online discussion groups can be invaluable as threaded discussions develop consensus on problem resolution or other matters. (Later in this chapter, you'll learn about several other kinds of Web-based conferencing resources.) You can do the same thing with (expensive) commercial groupware software on your Intranet, but netnews, the original groupware dating back to the 1970s, remains both free and viable today. Figure 31.2 shows a portion of the articles in the newsgroup `bionet.immunology` in February 1996; note the indentation, showing the discussion threads.

FIGURE 31.2.

Usenet news.

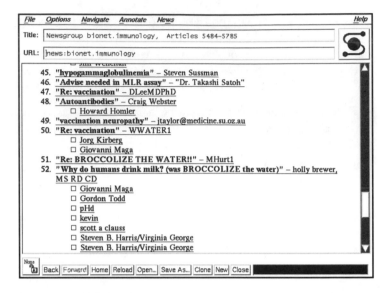

Electronic Mail as a Collaborative Resource

As with Usenet news, there is a potential collaborative value with e-mail in your Intranet. E-mail distribution lists, run manually or with automated list servers, can be an important adjunct to your Intranet by providing another means of group discussions. And since both Mosaic and Netscape now have e-mail interfaces, it's easy to integrate e-mail into your Intranet.

If you expect e-mail to become a major part of your Intranet's collaborative efforts, you'll want to set up a means of retaining and retrieving messages, just as you've done with your Usenet news articles. This will enable your customers to go back to mailing list archives and search for old messages that might have current relevance. There are several ways you can archive e-mail messages:

- Charge someone with the responsibility of manually saving each and every message on your mailing list(s)

- Create a special user account on your system whose only purpose is to receive the mailing list traffic, and then configure that account to automatically save all incoming mail in mailbox folders (a good tool for doing this is the filter utility program that comes as part of the popular freeware UNIX e-mail package called elm, available at `ftp://ftp.virginia.edu/pub/elm`)

- Use an e-mail-to-netnews script that will route all e-mail messages to a local newsgroup for posting as ordinary news articles.

In the latter example, you can use Usenet news-indexing tools to index everything because your e-mail traffic and netnews traffic will be merged into a single database. The elm filter program is a useful one that can be set up to read all incoming mail to a user and automatically dispose of it in some way. In this situation, you'd want filter to automatically save all incoming messages on a mailing list to a file or directory, which can later be indexed.

> **NOTE**
>
> Despite sharing a common name and software ancestor, the version of elm that comes with the HP-UX operating system on Hewlett-Packard UNIX workstations and the freeware version are vastly different. Dave Taylor's original code has developed in substantially different directions under the separate elm development projects. Most importantly in this context, HP's version doesn't include the filter utility. You can build the freeware elm package under HP-UX with little trouble.

However you manage to save your e-mail list traffic, indexing it for future search and retrieval is your next task. Here you have a couple of choices. First, the freeWAIS-sf package has the capability of doing fielded indexing. (You'll find the latest FAQ at ftp://1s6-www.informatik.uni-dortmund.delpub/wais/. There's a mirror site in the United States at ftp://ftp.maxwell.syr.edu/infosystems/wais/FreeWAIS-sf/.) Because all Internet e-mail messages have a standard format, consisting of headers and a body, it'll be easy to generate a freeWAIS-sf format file for e-mail messages so you can do fielded indexing. In fact, the freeWAIS-sf FAQ document includes just such a format file. Here it is, in all its simplicity:

```
record-sep: /^From /
layout:
headline: /^From: / /\J/ 20 /^From: ./
headline: /^Subject: / /\J/ 80 /^Subject: ./
region: /^From: /
from SOUNDEX LOCAL TEXT BOTH
end: /$/
region: /^Subject: /
subject stemming TEXT BOTH
end: /$/
```

Once you've done your e-mail traffic indexing, your customers can use the freeWAIS-sf companion package SFgate to do fielded searches on your mailing list database, using the From and Subject fields of messages for search criteria. Figure 31.3 shows a fielded SFgate search form.

Unless you're already familiar with freeWAIS-sf's fielded-indexing capabilities, you may want try Hypermail instead to index your e-mail list's archives. This package (written by Tom Gruber and Kevin Hughes of Verifone's Enterprise Integration Technologies) converts a standard UNIX mailbox file containing multiple messages into a set of cross-referenced, hyperlinked HTML documents. All the new documents produced by Hypermail contain links to other messages in the archive, so messages in a thread (that is, those which share a Subject line) show up as hyperlinks when you view messages in your Web browser. You can sample a Hypermail archive (which EIT maintains) at `http://www.eit.com/www.lists`, which is an indexed database of e-mail messages from a couple of World Wide Web-related Internet mailing lists.

FIGURE 31.3.

SFgate fielded search form.

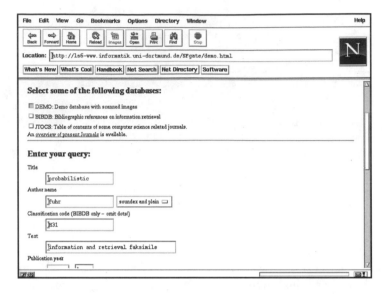

Figure 31.4 shows a partial listing of the Hypermail Subject database of the www-talk mailing list for early 1996. As you can see, the user interface to Hypermail databases is not a fill-in form, but is, rather, in plain, scrollable HTML, with the individual messages shown as clickable hyperlinks. In fact, it looks a lot like the Usenet news article listing in Figure 31.2. (If you scroll all the way to the bottom of the page, however, you'll find a fill-in search form as well for doing keyword searches on the database.) The Hypermail package also indexes and creates hyperlinks based on message authors' e-mail addresses and the creation date of the message, giving you additional search capabilities.

TIP

You can, of course, use both Hypermail and freeWAIS-sf (or any of the other indexing tools, such as glimpseindex) for your archived e-mail, giving your Intranet's customers the capabilities of both kinds of searches. Integrate your e-mail indexes with your Harvest information gathering service and you're well on your way to having a truly useful Intranet.

FIGURE 31.4.

Sample Hypermail index.

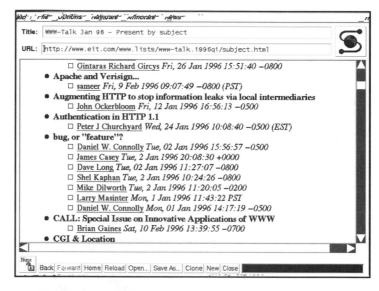

Free-for-All Collaboration

The popularity of the World Wide Web, with thousands of new pages coming on line every day, has generated the need for individual users to share new Web resources they've found or created. Because most Webmasters are busy people, often having job responsibilities over and above their Webmaster duties, ordinary users need a way to post hyperlinks to useful Web resources in a public place for others to see without having to rely on a Webmaster or other system administrator to do it for them. (This is quite a different thing, of course, from users placing new hyperlinks on their own home pages.) However, it doesn't take much thinking to come up with several significant reservations about implementing such a free-for-all Web resource. Leaving questions of appropriate content aside for the moment, the idea of a Web page that allows just anyone to add anything they want should bring shudders to anyone with the faintest sense of network security. Nonetheless, a large number of such services (and the CGI-bin scripts to implement them) have sprung up across the Web. Even the major Web search services (such as Lycos, Yahoo, eXcite, and the others) allow users to fill in forms to have URLs added to the service. Figure 31.5 shows a sample free-for-all page.

Even taking these security concerns into account, though, there are good reasons for implementing a free-for-all page on your Intranet. Not everyone wants to create a home page of their own, but such people may still find useful resources they want to share with other customers. The ability to add URLs to such a page may, in fact, inspire these people to eventually create

Web pages of their own as a contribution to your Intranet; certainly, these people shouldn't be discouraged from doing so. From a collaborative point of view, browsing customers may want to be able to suggest links to those who do have home pages, complementing the information already there. If these folks can add a URL to a free-for-all page easily, they'll do so; if they can't, they may not bother to share their ideas. In any case, giving your customers free rein to add URLs to a free-for-all page can improve overall collaboration and communication on your Intranet. The question of appropriate content on a free-for-all Web page is, in the author's opinion, a management issue, not a technical one, and should be dealt with as such.

FIGURE 31.5.

A Web free-for-all page.

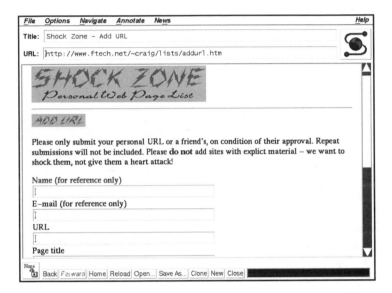

You'll find a long list of Web free-for-all links at `http://union.ncsa.uiuc.edu/HyperNews/get/www.collab/free.html`. This and several other such lists mentioned in later sections of this chapter are maintained by Daniel LaLiberte of NCSA, who may be the Web's foremost collaboration guru; he's also the author of HyperNews.

> **NOTE**
>
> Web pages that collect votes of some kind or take surveys are a special kind of free-for-all page, as are pages that allow you to access some service or enter in a raffle after you've filled in a form with personal information such as your e-mail address or phone number. Many of them are thinly disguised marketing ploys, aimed at generating sales leads.

Web-Based Training and Presentations

Your Intranet is an enormous potential source of training resources for your customers. Moreover, the nature of an Intranet, with all its multimedia capabilities, makes completely new ways of creating and executing training and presentations possible because you can stitch together a wide range of training components. You'll want to give free rein to your imagination in putting together your Intranet's tools for these purposes.

Web-Based Annotation and Conferencing

Almost as soon as the first World Wide Web server and browsers came into use, people wanted some way to use these new tools for interactive conferencing. Being able to post documents is one thing; being able to respond to them in some way is quite another. The following sections look at a couple of the results.

Web Interactive Talk

One of the earliest efforts at developing such a resource was the Ari Luotonen/Tim Berners-Lee project called Web Interactive Talk, or WIT, which was developed when both were at CERN. In WIT, discussions proceed according to traditional dialectic methods, with general topics and subsidiary proposals. The way it works, someone posts a document proposal, and then others are invited to post comments about the proposal in the form of agreements or disagreements. WIT is primarily valuable as a pioneering work in the area of annotation and conferencing (and it's no longer being maintained by the authors, both of whom have left CERN), but you may want to look at it anyway. You can do so at `http://www.w3.org/hypertext/WWW/WIT/User/Overview.html`. Early on, NCSA Mosaic for X Window also had a built-in group annotation feature, which allowed the collection and sharing of group annotations to Web pages. The feature was removed from the package, apparently due to problems with it, and unfortunately it has not yet reappeared.

Stanford's ComMentor

Group annotation has reappeared, however, in a more recent annotation system, Stanford University's ComMentor. The package is described as a generalized form of shared annotations, built on top of the existing Web infrastructure. According to the project's Web page (`http://www-pcd.stanford.edu/COMMENTOR/`), it supports shared comments on Web documents, along with collaborative filtering and seals of approval, guided tours of Web sites, usage indicators, and several other more esoteric features. Figure 31.6 shows a sample ComMentor screen with an annotation in a pop-up box; there's an indication of additional annotations as well. As you can see, the package uses a modified NCSA X Mosaic as its browser, with additional/changed pull-down menus at the top and new navigational buttons at the bottom. You can download the binary versions of the ComMentor server and client software for IBM RS/6000's and Sun UNIX systems, as well as the source code for both, at `ftp://www-pcd.stanford.edu/pub/pcd/brio/`.

FIGURE 31.6.

A sample ComMentor screen.

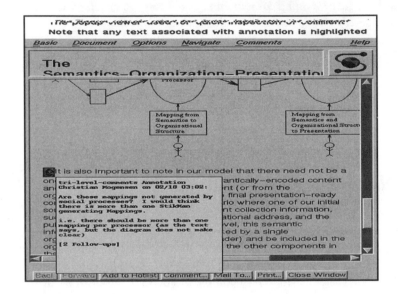

AEX About Server

The commercial About Server product (`http://www.aex.com/`) provides forums for group discussions, much like Usenet news and other commercial groupware packages such as Lotus Notes, but at lower cost and with what AEX calls "tighter integration" with the World Wide Web. About forums have the following characteristics:

- Accessible from Web browsers
- Searchable by keyword, in both document title and text, author name, and date
- Immediately accessible, in that your postings and responses to posting are made right away and are not queued for posting/propagation as in Usenet news
- Subject to quite flexible security, allowing you to restrict access to all or portions of forums by username/password and other means
- User configurable, so each user can customize his view of the available forums, much like traditional Usenet news kill files
- Administered using a Web browser

Demonstration versions of About Server for several UNIX systems are available from the AEX Web site. Figure 31.7 shows a sample About forum. The user interface has individual article hyperlinks and indentations indicating article threads.

FIGURE 31.7.

About discussion forum.

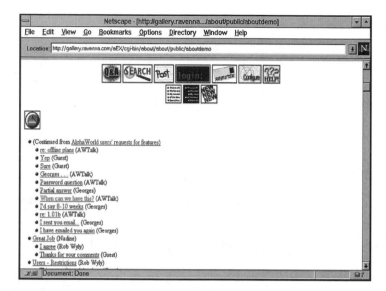

Open Meeting on the National Performance Review

A discussion of Web-based conferencing/annotation systems would not be complete without a brief look at the United States government's Open Meeting on the National Performance Review, reachable on the Web at `http://www4.ai.mit.edu/npr/user/root.html`. Here you can read various findings and recommendations of the NPR, which has been led by Vice President Al Gore, a major influence in the federal government's all-out plunge into the Internet/World Wide Web in the past four years. As shown in Figure 31.8, the service is interactive, and you can add your own comments and questions. It's a bit clumsy, though, requiring you to enter your Internet e-mail address in a fill-in form, after which you're e-mailed a comment form to fill in and send back, also via e-mail. Moderators review submitted comments and questions and not all of them are posted.

You'll find links to Daniel LaLiberte's long list of other Web conferencing/collaboration links at `http://union.ncsa.uiuc.edu/HyperNews/get/www/collab/conferencing.html`.

FIGURE 31.8.

Open meeting on the National Performance Review.

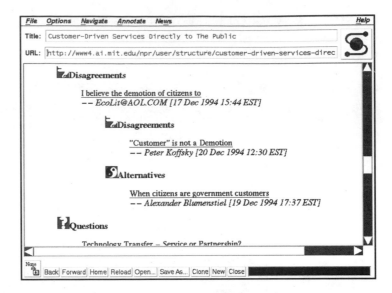

Full-Blown Groupware for Web Collaboration and Communication

The demarcation lines among free-for-alls, conferencing/annotation systems, and the more full-featured Web groupware packages are indistinct. Nonetheless, this section takes a look at the latter. As with the previous sections, this section starts with some very simple ones (and a seemingly not-very-useful one) and works its way up to the more complex, full-featured groupware packages.

Collaborative Art and Games

A large number of collaborative groupware art services exists on the Web. The basic idea of them is that anyone can add Web resources to the picture, the work of fiction, or some other creative work-in-progress. Image collages, for example, can be augmented by adding the URL to your own image on the Web; the next user will see the modified collage with your image added. Figure 31.9 shows the startup page for an interactive literary endeavor; it's interesting in that you can enter the novel at any page, using the clickable HTML image map. Once you're in, you can browse about the work or contribute to it by inserting your own text. Other collaborative groupware on the Web comes in the form of interactive single- or multiuser games or other creative add-a-link pages. The latter are modified free-for-all pages that have a theme of some sort; users are free to add URLs for images, other Web pages, and so on that somehow advance the interactive fiction, enhance the art object, or otherwise contribute to the evolving entity that is that particular Web page. The beauty, if any, is in the eye of the beholder.

FIGURE 31.9.
*An interactive fiction
Web site.*

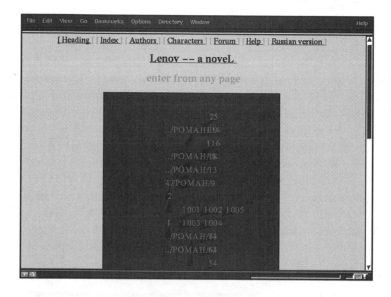

These examples, and others like them (see Danial LaLiberte's long list at `http://union.ncsa.uiuc.edu/HyperNews/get/www/collab/creation.html`) are useful not so much in their substantive content as in the possibilities they represent. After all, the World Wide Web is the world's largest vanity press, where anyone can post anything they want with no evaluation of its actual value (and often no check of the spelling). Although you or your customers might not be interested in these particular endeavors, there is a wide range of possibilities for collaborative groupware for your Intranet, and these may be instructive as examples.

Lotus Notes

Almost from the beginning, the World Wide Web has been called, among many other things, "the Lotus Notes Killer." You can see from the examples given so far in this chapter how this quip derived. After all, many of the Web tools about which you've learned in this book replicate some feature(s) of Notes. Whether it's simple information sharing via home pages, conferencing with Usenet news using a Web browser, Web-based e-mail, or Web-based annotation systems like ComMentor, artful Webmasters can provide their customers with most of Notes' features at a tiny fraction of that package's not inconsiderable cost. The downside of this replication is the lack of Notes' tight integration, but being able to access the wide range of services Web browsers support may be integration enough for many. Making the choice between home-grown collaborative and commercial groupware on your Intranet can boil down to the choice mentioned in Chapter 30, "Web Access to Commercial Database Applications,": Is the 10-15 percent of Notes' capabilities you miss with a homegrown set of applications worth the very substantial cost of the package?

IBM (the new owner of Lotus) thinks not. In early 1996, version 4.0 of Lotus Notes was released, outfitted with a whole raft of new capabilities, including World Wide Web browsing and authoring support, Usenet news access, and a lower (though still pricey) per-seat cost.

Notes R4 (as the latest version of Lotus Notes is called) is, in essence, a document database. Users can search the database according to everyday criteria and can also browse the database. Browsing can be done based on different views of the database, with the ability to step back and see high-level organization or dig in and see the details. Notes R4 databases can be replicated across an organization, over multiple servers, so everyone in a far-flung company, including those on the road, has access to the same consistent information. Integrated e-mail, group document annotations, collaborative functions, workflow management, and group calendaring/scheduling are also featured. Built-in security controls access for authorized users at all levels of the database. Links in documents can be followed to other, related documents with point-and-click. Users can create altogether new Notes applications using a set of graphical tools. Figure 31.10 shows a sample Notes R4 front end, taken from a ScreenCam demonstration on the Lotus Web site, `http://www.lotus.com/`.

FIGURE 31.10.

Lotus Notes R4.

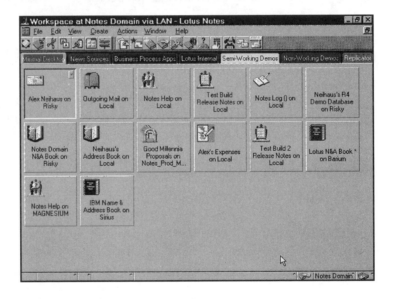

With Notes R4, IBM/Lotus finally jumped into the World Wide Web with what it hopes will be a "Notes-killer killer." Consider these features:

- Notes R4 databases are now browsable using ordinary Web browsers like Mosaic or Netscape because the httpd protocol is now part of the Notes R4 server package.
- IBM plans to add Java support to Notes R4 in the future while maintaining compatibility with its own scripting language, LotusScript.
- Even when viewing Notes R4 databases with a standard Web browser, Notes R4 document links work as Web hyperlinks.

■ Notes R4 forms and database search facilities are also available when viewing Notes R4 databases from a Web browser.

■ Web documents can be created and managed using Lotus InterNotes Web Publisher, and then browsed with both the InterNotes Web Navigator Web browser and a standard Web browser. As shown in Figure 31.11, if you didn't know it had been created with InterNotes Web Publisher, you'd think AT&T's Web page was just an everyday one.

■ The InterNotes Web Navigator client supports the httpd protocol, so it can be used to browse non-Notes Web pages as well as Notes R4 databases.

■ InterNotes News integrates with Usenet news services via the Internet-standard NNTP protocol, but it adds support for Notes R4 database replication, hypertext links, and embedded objects, giving users enhanced news-browsing capabilities.

■ The e-mail capability in Notes R4 supports the Internet-standard SMTP and MIME protocols to provide universal e-mail connectivity for Notes users.

FIGURE 31.11.

AT&T Network Notes Web site.

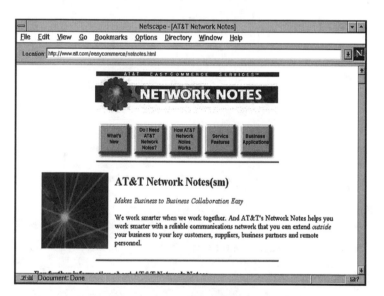

NOTE

You may want to look at Lotus' Web site, http://www.lotus.com/, where you'll find several detailed white papers about Notes R4, as well as some ScreenCam recordings. Interestingly, though, as of late February 1996, none of the available ScreenCam recordings on the site featured any of the Web-related features of Notes R4.

Collabra Share

Among Lotus Notes R4 competitors, Collabra Software Inc's Collabra Share stands out. Despite the fact the package is a direct Notes competitor—providing integrated, collaborative groupware, with document-databases, e-mail, database replication, access to Usenet newsgroups, and even a Notes-compatible client for both Windows PCs and the Macintosh—this isn't the real reason the product has become important in the past year. See Figure 31.12 for a sample Collabra Share screenshot, viewed within Netscape Navigator, from the company's Web site, http://www.collabra.com.

FIGURE 31.12.

Collabra Share.

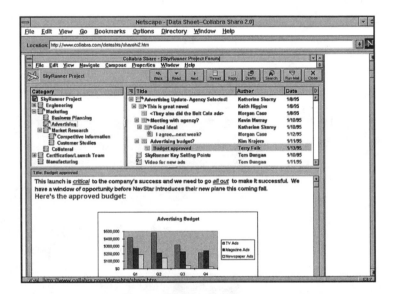

NOTE

From the Collabra Web site, you can download Lotus ScreenCam recordings of Collabra Share in action as well as evaluation copies of the Collabra Share client software itself.

The real reason this upstart company has suddenly become worth mentioning here is not even that Collabra Share won the *PC Magazine* Editor's Choice award in late 1995 (although that must have been a big boost for the product). No, what's really important is Collabra Software, Inc. has been acquired by the Netscape Communications Corporation juggernaut, which has announced plans to integrate all of Collabra Share's features directly into the Netscape Navigator Web browser. Although Netscape says there will continue to be a stand-alone Collabra Share product for Windows PCs and the Macintosh, and a Collabra server, and those products will continue to evolve, the next major release of Netscape Navigator will "incorporate fully the Collabra Share functionality." Given Netscape's dominance of the Web browser market, building in Collabra Share client support will undoubtedly provide a major boost to the Collabra server products, potentially to the detriment of Lotus Notes R4.

The acquisition should also help Netscape itself. Netscape's e-mail and Usenet news-reading interfaces attempt to cram too much information onscreen at once, rendering most of it virtually unreadable. Collabra Share supports integration with both Microsoft Mail (see Figure 31.13, which is a snapshot of a ScreenCam demo of Collabra Share, viewable from Collabra's Web site) and Lotus cc:Mail. The ability to use these popular and mature e-mail products within the Netscape environment should go a long way toward improving these interfaces. It can be hoped Collabra's Usenet news reader will be a similarly major step forward from Netscape's unusable netnews interface.

FIGURE 31.13.

Collabra Share with Microsoft Mail interface.

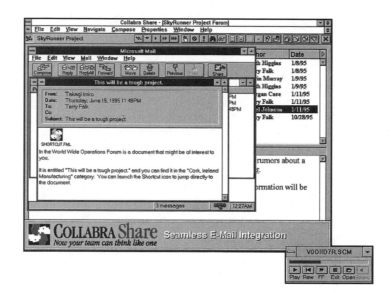

Summary

This chapter has covered the World Wide Web's collaborative waterfront. Along the way, you've seen Web groupware ranging in capability from simple, one-way information sharing on user home pages to elaborate and expensive integrated groupware application suites. Here's a review of the topics that were covered in this chapter:

- A breakdown of broad categories of Web-based collaboration
- The use of personal and group home pages as a means of information sharing
- The use of hyperindexed Usenet news and e-mail archives as a means of collaboration
- Free-for-all Web resources that allow customers to post their own URLs or other information

■ Web-based annotation and conferencing systems

■ Using what you know about Web-based training and presentations in Chapter 21 to do group presentations in real time across your Intranet using Web technologies

■ Major commercial groupware packages and how they can integrate into your Intranet

■ Miscellaneous Web groupware, including workflow management, collaborative writing and art, and other multiuser activities that are potentially instructive

INDEX

R

Visible Analyst Workbench

Integrated Enterprise CASE

Planning - Analysis - Design - Construction - Re-Engineering/BPR

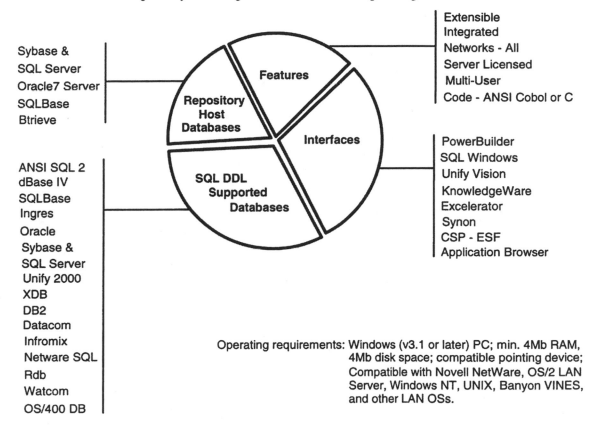

Sybase &
SQL Server
Oracle7 Server
SQLBase
Btrieve

Repository Host Databases

Features

Extensible
Integrated
Networks - All
Server Licensed
Multi-User
Code - ANSI Cobol or C

ANSI SQL 2
dBase IV
SQLBase
Ingres
Oracle
Sybase &
SQL Server
Unify 2000
XDB
DB2
Datacom
Infromix
Netware SQL
Rdb
Watcom
OS/400 DB

SQL DDL Supported Databases

Interfaces

PowerBuilder
SQL Windows
Unify Vision
KnowledgeWare
Excelerator
Synon
CSP - ESF
Application Browser

Operating requirements: Windows (v3.1 or later) PC; min. 4Mb RAM, 4Mb disk space; compatible pointing device; Compatible with Novell NetWare, OS/2 LAN Server, Windows NT, UNIX, Banyon VINES, and other LAN OSs.

The Visible Analyst Workbench® is an object based corporate workgroup CASE tool that combines data, process and objects in an integrated open repository. Powerful modeling support includes Business Modeling, Class Modeling, Entity Relationship Modeling, Data Flow Modeling, State Transition Modeling, and Program Modeling, which is synchronized and cross-balanced, allowing for all development in one singular OO environment. Migration of legacy systems, IEW/ADW and Excelerator data and designs to an OO world make for fast generation of new client/server applications.

Visible Systems Corporation
300 Bear Hill Road
Waltham, MA 02154
Phone: (617) 890-CASE (2273) Fax: (617) 890-8909
Web Page/http://www.visible.com Email: info.visible.com

Free trial copy available on CD-ROM

Developing Client/Server Applications with Oracle Developer/2000

— *Paul Hipsley*

To master the features of Developer/2000, developers need the vital information contained in *Developing Client/Server Systems with Oracle Developer/2000*. This book teaches developers how to rapidly build sophisticated systems that scale from workgroup to enterprise and how to use Oracle Developer/2000's powerful new tools to increase their efficiency and productivity.

CD-ROM includes Oracle Sampler software, third-party tools, source code, and samples of applications developed in the book. This book teaches how to develop forms, reports, and graphics and gives the steps needed to build a database system using Oracle Developer/2000. It also covers client/server.

$49.99 USA, $70.95 CDN
ISBN 0-672-30852-5   640 pp.

Developing Client/Server Applications with Visual Basic 4

— *Dan Rahmel & Ron Rahmel*

This complete guide provides an overview of the client/server system design, with step-by-step examples and ideas on the implementation of cutting-edge technologies, like Winsock, distributed OLE, remote access, and more.

The CD-ROM includes all sample code, relevant third-party custom controls, and additional utilities. *Developing Client/Server Applications with Visual Basic 4* includes coverage of the latest Visual Basic features, including Network Services, Win32, and OCXs. It also provides Visual Basic access to the Information Superhighway—Internet, Mosaic/World Wide Web, FTP, and more.

$49.99 USA, $70.95 CDN
ISBN: 0-672-30789-8   1,072 pp.

Rightsizing Information Systems, Second Edition

— *Steven Guengerich & George Schussel*

Rightsizing Information Systems, Second Edition is an important addition to the library of every corporate information systems strategist. In addition to discussing the present and future status of distributed networks, this book provides:

- Proven methods for streamlining information systems
- An explanation of how downsized information systems will affect a business
- Problem-solving answers and advice
- Suggestions for business opportunities and organizations

$40.00 USA, $56.95 CDN
ISBN: 0-672-30486-4   448 pp.

Understanding Local Area Networks, Fifth Edition

— *Neil Jenkins & Stan Schatt*

This book shows readers how LANs and their various hardware and software components work and helps network administrators decide whether a LAN is a viable option. It provides a comprehensive, easy-to-understand presentation on local area networks and includes discussions about network architecture and transmission methods. This update to the successful *Understanding Local Area Networks, Fourth Edition* covers local area networks.

$29.99 USA, $42.95 CDN
ISBN: 0-672-30840-1   336 pp.

Understanding Data Communications, Fourth Edition

— *Gilbert Held*

This book connects users to the real world by teaching digital communications, the inner workings of data terminals, modems, fiber optics, and satellites. It covers the fundamentals, the functions of data terminals and their components, and the latest network architecture and design techniques. Written by a world-renowned expert, Gil Held, *Understanding Data Communications, Fourth Edition* provides information on the advantages and disadvantages of LAN, packet networks, and network design and management. This book covers communications.

$29.99 USA, $42.95 CDN
ISBN: 0-672-30501-1   432 pp.

Absolute Beginner's Guide to Networking, Second Edition

— *Mark Gibbs*

This book takes readers on a graphic tour of networking. Through illustrations, network maps, and easy-to-follow instructions, users find out how to connect to a network and use Local Area Networks (LANs). *Absolute Beginner's Guide to Networking, Second Edition* leads readers through the historical, planning, and implementing stages of networking. This book covers topics such as remote access, interoperability, and Wide Area Networks (WANs) and outlines the elements of a network, showing how they fit together. This book covers Windows for Workgroups, NetWare, LANtastic, and other various software for IBMs and IBM-compatibles.

$22.00 USA, $30.95 CDN
ISBN: 0-672-30553-4   496 pp.

Add to Your Sams Library Today with the Best Books for Programming, Operating Systems, and New Technologies

The easiest way to order is to pick up the phone and call

1-800-428-5331

between 9:00 a.m. and 5:00 p.m. EST.
For faster service, please have your credit card available.

ISBN	Quantity	Description of Item	Unit Cost	Total Cost
0-672-30852-5		Developing Client/Server Applications with Oracle Developer/2000	$49.99	
0-672-30789-8		Developing Client/Server Applications with Visual Basic 4 (Book/CD-ROM)	$49.99	
0-672-30473-2		Client/Server Computing, Second Edition	$40.00	
0-672-30173-3		Enterprise-Wide Networking	$39.95	
0-672-30486-4		Rightsizing Information Systems, Second Ed.	$40.00	
0-672-30840-1		Understanding Local Area Networks, Fifth Edition	$29.99	
0-672-30501-1		Understanding Data Communications, Fourth Edition	$29.99	
0-672-30553-4		Absolute Beginner's Guide to Networking, Second Edition	$22.00	
❏ 3 ½" Disk		Shipping and Handling: See information below.		
❏ 5 ¼" Disk		TOTAL		

Shipping and Handling: $4.00 for the first book, and $1.75 for each additional book. Floppy disk: add $1.75 for shipping and handling. If you need to have it NOW, we can ship product to you for an additional charge of approximately $18.00, and you will receive your item overnight or in two days. Overseas shipping and handling adds $2.00 per book and $8.00 for up to three disks. Prices subject to change. Call for availability and pricing information on latest editions.

201 W. 103rd Street, Indianapolis, Indiana 46290

1-800-428-5331 — Orders   1-800-835-3202 — FAX   1-800-858-7674 — Customer Service

Book ISBN 0-672-30726-X

What's on the
Disc

The companion CD-ROM contains software developed by the authors, plus an assortment of third-party tools and product demonstrations. The disc is designed to be explored using a CD-ROM Menu program. Using the Menu program, you can view information concerning products and companies and install programs with a single click of the mouse. To run the Menu program, follow the steps in the following sections.

Windows 3.1 Setup Instructions

1. Insert the CD-ROM into your CD-ROM drive.

2. From File Manager or Program Manager, choose Run from the File menu.

3. Type *<drive>*\setup and press Enter, where *<drive>* corresponds to the drive letter of your CD-ROM. For example, if your CD-ROM is drive D, type **D:\setup** and press Enter.

Windows 95 Installation Instructions

1. Insert the CD-ROM into your CD-ROM drive.

2. If Windows 95 is installed on your computer, and you have the AutoPlay feature enabled, the Menu program starts automatically whenever you insert the disc into your CD-ROM drive.

   If Autoplay is not enabled, run SETUP.EXE from the CD drive using Explorer.

Windows NT Installation Instructions

1. Insert the CD-ROM into your CD-ROM drive.

2. From File Manager or Program Manager, choose Run from the File menu.

3. Type *<drive>*\setup and press Enter, where *<drive>* corresponds to the drive letter of your CD-ROM drive. For example, if your CD-ROM is drive D, type **D:\setup** and press Enter.

NOTE

For best results, set your monitor to display between 256 and 64,000 colors. A screen resolution of 640×480 pixels is also recommended. If necessary, adjust your monitor settings before using the CD-ROM.